A Certain Justice

A Certain Justice

TOWARD AN ECOLOGY OF
THE CHINESE LEGAL IMAGINATION

Haiyan Lee

The University of Chicago Press   CHICAGO AND LONDON

The University of Chicago Press, Chicago 60637
The University of Chicago Press, Ltd., London
© 2023 by The University of Chicago
Published 2023
Printed in the United States of America

32 31 30 29 28 27 26 25 24 23   1 2 3 4 5

ISBN-13: 978-0-226-82524-3 (cloth)
ISBN-13: 978-0-226-82525-0 (paper)
ISBN-13: 978-0-226-82526-7 (e-book)
DOI: https://doi.org/10.7208/chicago/9780226825267.001.0001

The University of Chicago Press gratefully acknowledges
the generous support of Stanford University toward the
publication of this book.

Library of Congress Cataloging-in-Publication Data

Names: Lee, Haiyan, author.
Title: A certain justice : toward an ecology of the Chinese
legal imagination / Haiyan Lee.
Description: Chicago : The University of Chicago Press, 2023. |
Includes bibliographical references and index.
Identifiers: LCCN 2022044962 | ISBN 9780226825243 (cloth) |
ISBN 9780226825250 (paperback) | ISBN 9780226825267 (ebook)
Subjects: LCSH: Chinese literature—20th century—History
and criticism. | Justice in literature. | Law in literature. | Motion
pictures—China—20th century—History and criticism. |
Justice, Administration of, in motion pictures. | Law in motion
pictures. | Justice, Administration of—Moral and ethical
aspects—China. | Law and ethics.
Classification: LCC PL2303 .L3763 2023 | DDC 813/.6—dc23
LC record available at https://lccn.loc.gov/2022044962

♾ This paper meets the requirements of ANSI/NISO Z39.48-1992
(Permanence of Paper).

Contents

Figures

Preface and Acknowledgments

I wrote this book first and foremost as a scholar trained in Chinese studies and literary studies. But I also wrote it as an immigrant academic with family roots in the People's Republic of China who has lived in the United States for over three decades as a naturalized citizen. I grew up in a rural market town in Sichuan, spending the first eighteen years of my life living in houses and apartments without any electrical outlets as there weren't any electrical appliances that needed plugging in. The cultural or, if you will, electric shock I experienced when I immigrated to the suburban United States in 1990 was sparked above all by encountering things, or "manufactures," a word I would later pick up in history books on Sino-British relations. Up to that point in my life, the word "button" usually denoted a small piece of plastic or bone affixed to clothing, but now a button was something one pushed to make the world do one's biddings. I was overwhelmed by the cornucopia of "manufactures" in homes and stores, and to this day I still haven't completely made my peace with push-button consumerism.

The second source of cultural shock came from a very different domain. One day while browsing the books-on-tape section in the Ithaca Public Library, I noticed a small box of cassettes titled *May It Please the Court*, a collection of recorded landmark oral arguments made before the US Supreme Court. I checked it out and listened to it several times. It was a revelation to me that there were such cases as *XYZ v. the United States*, featuring an individual or a civil entity taking the federal government to court and sometimes winning the suit. It ignited my enduring fascination with the American culture of law and litigation. I came to appreciate the impersonal majesty of law from these recordings, and I was awed by the kind of reasoned eloquence so unlike what I had thitherto been used to in China. Perforce I became a comparatist of life in my native land versus life in my adoptive country. This frame of mind has never left me.

Parallel to my graduate training in Chinese literature, I kept up an extra-curriculum in American crime fiction, reading practically everything that came into my purview, starting with *An American Tragedy, Native Son, All the King's Men, The Book of Daniel,* and *Libra.* A stint as teaching assistant for an American history course at Cornell helped me situate these engrossing tales and appreciate their larger import. As I grow more observant and knowledgeable about American culture, politics, and society, I become more sensitized to convergences, echoes, and similarities as much as contrasts with China. Parsing these convergences and divergences has become an obsession of mine. Each time I'm struck by a shock of recognition or am poked by a vague sense of déjà vu, I ask myself really? why? how? to what extent? with what implications? I don't always have the space or intellectual wherewithal to pursue these questions, but my scholarship has in one way or another been driven by my desire to understand the different choices people make and the underlying values and dispositions and cultural logics that inform them. Globalization has brought China and the United States much closer now than thirty years ago, and when it comes to consumer capitalism, China seems to have pulled ahead, for good or for ill. But there are also times when the two peoples appear to be living in parallel universes for all the flow of goods, ideas, bodies, and microbes between them. A firmly entrenched exceptionalism on both sides has made it difficult to draw meaningful comparisons and learn from lived experiences.

One can list many recent issues and problems that worry US observers: callout culture and cancel culture, posttruth and fake news, anti-intellectualism and populism, overpolicing and carceral governance, and so forth. All have parallels in Chinese history and politics. This book is my attempt to draw out some of the parallels in the process of charting the patterns and expressions of a nonliberal political-legal culture. It is about how some Chinese think about justice, but a Chinese culture of justice cannot come into focus unless it's set against another, far more hegemonic culture of justice, one that frames the universal discourse of human rights and saturates our global mass culture. It is thus my hope that I have also illuminated something about the American political-legal culture visible only to those whose long process of acculturation is accompanied by an equally long process of relearning their native cultures.

I wrote several chapters during the global coronavirus pandemic. The public health catastrophe, along with the other convulsive events of 2020 (the killing of George Floyd and other Black Americans by police, the historic presidential election, the devastating wildfires), left its imprint on my thinking in both decisive and subtle ways. I'm grateful to those who were willing to listen to me talk about things that were so removed from what was front and center on everyone's mind. Among my interlocutors, I owe a special debt to Stephen Angle, Daniel Bell, Tom Chen, Alexander Cook, Nan Da, Prasenjit Duara, Todd Foley, Anders Hansen, Héctor Hoyos, Heather Inwood, Barak Kushner, Joshua Landy, Li Ying, Elizabeth Perry, Haun Saussy, Simon Stern, Marco Wan, Peter Zarrow, and Lisa Zunshine. In particular, Alexander Cook and Simon Stern kindly corrected some of my misapprehensions in the domains of transitional justice and Anglo-American law, respectively. I would also like to acknowledge the students who took my graduate seminar Chinese Justice: Law, Morality, Literature in 2016 and patiently read Su Li's *Law and Literature* in Chinese with me. Lastly, I want to pay tribute to the individuals who don't know me but whose voices have lived in my ears for the past few years (or longer) and who have taught me so much about so many subjects: they are the podcast hosts of *Hi-Phi Nation, The Last Archive, Very Bad Wizards, Thinking Allowed, New York Times Book Review*, and *New Books in Philosophy*, among many others.

During the lockdown and rumbling post-lockdown, Paul Festa gallantly accepted the office of "social chair" and plotted many a *jiemu*, including several unforgettable getaways. The tiny pod he wove for the two of us was full of warmth and light in a time of fear and gloom. To him I owe everything, not least my sanity.

While working on this book project, I received financial and institutional support from the American Council of Learned Societies (Frederick Burkhardt Fellowship), the Center for Advanced Study in the Behavioral Sciences, the Stanford Humanities Center, and the Dean's Office of the School of Humanities and Sciences at Stanford University. I would like to thank these institutions for their generous support. I also thank the University of Washington Press and Oxford University Press for permitting me to reprint, respectively, in revised form, portions of "The Lives and Troubles of Others" (from Wilt L. Idema, ed., *Mouse vs. Cat in Chinese Literature* [2019], vii–xiv) and "The Silence of Animals: Writing on the Edge of Anthropomorphism in Contemporary Chinese Literature" (*ISLE: Interdisciplinary Studies in Literature and the Environment* 26:1 [2019]: 145–64) in chapter 6; and Taylor and Francis for allowing me to reprint a revised version of "The Importance of Not Being Honest" (forthcoming in *Law and Literature* as this volume goes to press) in chapter 2. In the final manuscript preparation stage, Ting Zheng took on the daunting task, with patience and meticulousness, of managing the illustrations, from checking resolution to securing permission. Kathleen Kageff worked wonders for the prose with her exacting copyeditor's pen. Needless to say, this book would not have seen the light of day without Alan Thomas's willingness to pluck it out of manuscript purgatory. I'm grateful to him and his colleague Randolph Petilos for their stewardship. Last but not least, Haun Saussy and an anonymous reader for the University of Chicago Press read the manuscript closely and critically and lent their expertise and wisdom generously to its improvement.

Thirty years ago I walked into a history class taught by Prasenjit Duara at the University of Chicago. It was the hardest course I ever took in graduate school, but it put me on an intellectual path from which I have not stepped away. I dedicate this book to Prasenjit: scholar, teacher, and dear friend.

INTRODUCTION

This book tackles a three-body problem. The three "bodies" are justice, law, and morality. Unlike in the original physics version of the problem, there is a distinctive and persistent pattern to their triangulating dynamics in Chinese history and culture. Nowhere are these dynamics more visible than in imaginative narratives. In a Yuan dynasty ballad, for example, the legendary Judge Bao valiantly casts aside royal displeasure and brings the emperor's lawless brothers-in-law to justice on behalf of a village woman. On the surface, the story is a celebration of the rule of law in traditional China, a tribute to the ideal that no one is above the law, not even royal kinsmen. The motif of an upright law enforcement official standing up to powerful miscreants is immediately recognizable and highly resonant to modern readers conversant in the idiom of equality before the law. It may well be a Chinese instantiation of the motto "Let justice be done though the world may perish." But I believe this is mistaken. Instead, I maintain that the ballad fits comfortably into the same political-legal culture that has given us more jarring cases such as the following.

(1) In the *Analects*, Confucius condemns a man who testifies against his own father for stealing a sheep. (2) In a Yuan play entitled *Rescriptor-in-Waiting Bao Thrice Investigates the Butterfly Dream*, the wise judge orders the execution of a petty thief in lieu of a murderer whose mother has behaved virtuously during the trial. (3) In a homicide case of the 1930s involving a female avenger who assassinated a warlord responsible for her father's death after a ten-year lag, the defendant won judicial leniency, and eventually a state pardon, and became the subject of media lionization. (4) In the 1992 film *Qiuju Goes to Court*, a peasant wife who wants an apology from the village chief who has kicked her husband in a dispute is forced to resort to formal legal channels, only to be dismayed when at last the judicial machinery catches up and takes him away in handcuffs, long after the two families have reconciled.

These fictional and real-life cases, and many more like them, represent different facets of a political-legal culture that has maintained a high degree of continuity over the course of two millennia of Chinese history and has diverged widely from that of the modern liberal West. I use the concept of "political-legal culture" to foreground law and ideas of legality and justice within the "systems, ideologies, and assumptions that shape power" (Zarrow 2012, 3) in a given political order. At the risk of oversimplification, I contend that the foregoing cases are manifestations of a political-legal culture that mistrusts law's ability to deliver justice and that privileges moral or substantive justice over legal or procedural justice. By the same token, law tracks morality much more closely in China than in the West. Dramatization of their interplay invariably features law's concessions to moral sentiments and the triumph of moral justice via the discretionary agency of a sagacious judge or the defiant agency of a vigilante hero. In other words, justice is associated with either an upright official who operates simultaneously within and above the bureaucratic system or a righteous maverick who, as the saying goes, takes the law into his or her own hands and metes out rough justice. Law, morality, and justice thus form a tension-filled triune, with the distance between law and justice being consistently greater than that between morality and justice. Still, law may have the least gravitational pull, but without it the three-body problem would collapse. Law is both indispensable and inadequate to justice.

In contemporary China, the language of justice pervades public discourse, from high-profile anticorruption campaigns and street-level crime sweeps to social justice movements on behalf of peasants, women, migrants, the disabled, and the environment. *Fazhi*, the closest Chinese equivalent to the rule of law, is officially enshrined as a socialist value, and tales of crime and punishment are avidly consumed in print and on screen. In some of these tales, justice has moved closer to law, but the most memorable ones still situate justice vis-à-vis law in oblique, tenuous, even diagonal ways. As often as not, justice is realized through informal or extralegal channels thanks to the intervention of righteous civilians, rogue cops, or even someone on the run from the law. These justice heroes willy-nilly deliver substantive outcomes while exposing the inadequacy or incompetence of formal government and justice organs. Yet popular faith in the normative order remains strong, and the legitimacy of the ruling Communist regime has not been seriously undermined by exposés of corruption, indifference, and miscarriages of justice. Perhaps what most distinguishes the Chinese legal imagination is the extent to which the Chinese Communist Party (CCP), not the law, has remained the guarantor of the normative order and defender of justice.

A Certain Justice is a study of the Chinese legal imagination that proceeds from the assumption that justice is more than a matter of law and
that law is necessary but not sufficient for justice. It interrogates the idea
of justice in all its iterations: juridical, ethical, poetic, ecological, and cosmological. The legal imagination stretches far beyond imaginings about
law per se, and yet ideas of legality are rarely absent from justice narratives about good and evil, right and wrong, crime and punishment, guilt
and responsibility. Basic questions that drive this inquiry: How has justice been envisioned and pursued in Chinese culture and society, from
dynastic times to the new millennium? Does "liberty and justice for all"
occupy the same exalted place in the Chinese legal imagination that it does
in modern liberal democracies? The book situates the social imaginary
of law, morality, and justice at the intersection of literary studies, critical
legal studies, moral and political philosophy, and cognitive psychology. Its
questions and methodologies are inspired by the interdisciplinary field of
legal humanities, also known as law and the humanities (Sarat, Anderson,
and Frank 2010; Anker and Meyler 2017; Stern, Del Mar, and Meyler 2019).
Its goal is to shed light on the cultural and imaginative dimensions of the
Chinese political-legal culture while pondering larger philosophical questions of freedom, truth, and humanity.

In what follows, I outline my analytical framework ("High Justice and
Low Justice"), situate my book in the existing scholarship ("Law and Chinese Literature"), weave together interdisciplinary theories and questions
("Law and Morality"), explore their relevance in the Chinese context
("Chinese Justice between Law and Morality"), and sketch out the three-
body problem in dynastic times using two Judge Bao tales ("Harmony
above Justice") as a way of laying the groundwork for the subsequent
chapters focusing on mostly modern materials. I end with a chapter-by-
chapter synopsis and a reflection on the etymology of the Chinese character for law.

High Justice and Low Justice

It is commonly observed that vast swaths of Chinese social life remain
largely outside law's purview, given the populace's aversion to litigation
and preference for informal channels of conflict resolution. In premodern
court-case dramas, the magistrate-cum-judge, exemplified by Judge Bao,
is basically a one-man dispenser of justice thanks to his ability to reach
into the penumbra of the orthodox bureaucratic order (including the celestial realm and the nether world) for assistance, revelation, or a *deus ex
machina*. In times of disorder, crime narratives turn to the knight-errant

who defends the righteous way of life that the rotten political center can no longer uphold. Dynastic legal codes, moreover, have built-in concessions to hierarchies of power (rank, age, generation, and gender) and defer to the imperatives of gradated kinship solidarity.

Law's limited role in the maintenance of social order has contributed to the image of China as a realm of Oriental despotism where law is at best window dressing and at worst an instrument of coercion and tyranny. This perception has persisted despite decades of assimilation of Western jurisprudential norms and institutions. It is further strengthened by such conspicuous episodes of law's negation as the Cultural Revolution, in which judicial apparatuses were swept aside as reactionary bourgeois contraptions. In response, scholars within and outside of China are wont to set a great deal in store by the country's transition from "the rule of man" (renzhi) to "the rule of law" (fazhi) (Lubman 1999; Peerenboom 2002; Potter 2003). They account for the fitful progress by pointing to both cultural and sociopolitical factors, above all the quest for national sovereignty in the age of colonialism and imperialism. They observe with wariness the contemporary authoritarian polity's Herculean struggle with the plague of official corruption, its ineffectual petition system, and its suppression of political dissidents, freethinking academics, and human rights lawyers. The rule of law seems an elusive ideal in the face of entrenched obstacles baked as it were into China's cultural and political DNA. At the root of this enduring image of Oriental despotism, I contend, is an ahistorical understanding of both the rise of the legal order in the West and China's political-legal culture, and particularly a failure to distinguish high justice and low justice.

In traditional China, three words make up the basic lingo of justice discourse: qing or renqing (human feelings, moral sentiments), fa or wangfa or guofa (the king's law, law of the land), and li or tianli (heavenly principles, the cosmic order) (Liang Zhiping 2004; Fan Zhongxin et al. 2011; Liang Zhiping 2013; Xu 2020). The trifecta maps roughly onto the three iterations in Roberto Unger's genealogy of Western law (1976, 48–52): customary, bureaucratic, and divine. Customary law is tacit, embedded in the social life of a community and enacted in daily transactions. Bureaucratic law presupposes the separation of state and society and is promulgated publicly in codified form by the state and enforced by its bureaucratic staff. It derives its legitimacy from its claim to instantiate divine law and safeguard customary law. In dynastic China, the state aligns itself with the heavenly will, or Mandate of Heaven (tianming), in order to overcome the taint of instrumentalism, or the very real danger that the ruling elites can manipulate the rules to advance their own interests. The ideology of the

Mandate of Heaven allows the state to deny class divisions or incompatible sectional interests and represent itself as the upholder of the Way (*Dao*) on behalf of Heaven (*titian xingdao*) and "all under heaven" (*tianxia*). For this reason, its rule is inherently legitimate and just (*yi, zhengyi*). It therefore is the very incarnation of "high justice."

I borrow the concept of "high justice," and its companion "low justice," from Delia Lin (2017), though I extend both terms far beyond the context in which she deploys them: ancient Chinese political philosophy. Here is Lin's definition of the paired concepts: "High justice is a moral doctrine that matters to the legitimacy and moral supremacy of the ruler and to the person in a social structure. It is expressed in *yi* and *zhengyi* in the positive and *buyi* (not *yi*) in the negative. However, the demand for fair treatment of people and the idea of society as a fair system, which point to social justice, fall into the realm of low justice; they are at a lower level in the configurations of a just governance concept. Low justice is expressed in *gong, gongzheng* and *gongping* in the positive and *bugong, yuan* and *qu* in the negative, that is, when there is a wrong or miscarriage of justice" (Lin 2017, 68). Contemporary justice discourses, in their preoccupation with fairness, tend to obscure the question of high justice. Yet the question of "Who shall rule?" has always loomed large in Chinese configurations of a just governance concept. The Chinese response to the question, according to Donald Clarke, entails a search not for ways of limiting the ruler's power, but "rather for ways of making sure that the right person holds it so that it will be used well" (1985, 238). The unfair treatment of individuals, being a matter of low justice, can be tolerated if it serves public interests—entrusted to and defended by the ruler. High justice is by definition what the ruler deems justified. Both the penal emphasis of imperial codes and the relative neglect of civil legislation are rooted in the hierarchy of high justice and low justice. The penal emphasis stems from the assumption that any violent crime is an affront and threat to the state's ability to maintain peace and order and its avowed stewardship of the cosmic order. Civil disputes, together with low crimes and misdemeanors, pertain to the problem of fairness (*gongdao, gongzheng, gongping*), or "low justice," and are relegated to the realm of customary law. Most Judge Bao stories operate in the realm of high justice, even when he is adjudicating seemingly ordinary criminal cases of murder, rape, and robbery. So too are twenty-first-century anticorruption dramas as much concerned with how crimes of graft and bribery erode the moral authority of the state as they are with adjudicating private rights and wrongs (Kinkley 2007, 172). Detective fiction as a genre type, with its preoccupation with low justice, did not flourish in traditional China and never really took off in the modern era except for a brief period in the early twentieth century and later in the sinospheres of Taiwan and Hong Kong. Social justice, likewise, did not anchor political movements until the twentieth century with the dawn of rights consciousness.

In the People's Republic of China, high justice has always claimed pride of place in narratives of law and order, though modern ideologies of nationalism and communism have replaced the Mandate of Heaven to serve as the sacred sanction of governmental policies and actions. In the name of serving *zhengyi*, some miscarriage of low justice, even a great deal of it, can be tolerated, if not justified. Policing for this reason has become oriented to low justice only in recent decades. In his study of the evolution of the public security apparatus in CCP history, Michael Dutton identifies its primary mission as defending the Party by policing the fundamental political distinction between friend and enemy. The training materials of the Public Security Bureau (PSB), tellingly, "work to produce a historical imagination that 'claims kin' with both Party and 'people' but not with government and law. Historically, [the PSB's] key task as an organization" was to police the divide not "between crime and its opposite, but between political loyalty and betrayal" (M. Dutton 2005, 8; see also Guo 2012).

In today's China high justice is above all bound up with the question of official corruption. This is due in no small part to the fact that high justice imperatives have been the root cause of injustice at the societal level, as when laws and policies create or deepen social inequities and stymie the hope for redress (*shenyuan*) on the part of the most marginalized and vulnerable. When the Party cracks down on corruption, it may find itself tackling low justice matters, but rarely for their own sake. More often than not, its harsh tactics bespeak high justice motivations having to do with its legitimacy and survival. This is evident, as Jeffrey Kinkley notes, in anticorruption novels, which seldom dwell on questions of law and legal institutions, and in which the professionals of the criminal justice system play second fiddle to "heroic CCP civilian generalists" (2007, 176). Paradoxically, because Party officials' power and privilege are pinned to their higher moral attainment (*suzhi*), they are also subject to a separate system of discipline and punishment that takes priority over the regular juridical process. This is the notorious "dual-track disciplinary regime" or *shuanggui* (Sapio 2010).[1] Due process and procedural justice do have a place in the legal imagination, but mostly in connection to low justice.

As Chinese society grows more affluent, stratified, and mobile, customary law, or whatever is left of it after the ravages of history, is increasingly inadequate in dealing with the frictions of social and commercial life. People readily turn to the courts, and a new body of narratives has emerged to chronicle the trials and tribulations of those who try to navigate the often opaque system to seek redress. There is no shortage of grim depictions of how ordinary citizens are treated cavalierly, contemptuously, even brutally by justice professionals, adding up to a sense of the system being stacked against those at the bottom. In recent decades, a raft of wrongful convictions have been exposed by an energetic and freewheeling media, causing considerable backlash and discontent (Nesossi 2017). Popular protests couched in the language of rights have also become common occurrences across the country, causing fiscal spending on domestic security to exceed external defense (Perry 2008; Guo 2012, 445). Yet the pervasive sense of unfairness does not necessarily impinge on the question of high justice, or the legitimacy and moral supremacy of the ruling Communist Party. This is in large part thanks to the Party's success in circumscribing "rights" to a matter of socioeconomic justice (Perry 2008, 37), its ramping up of the internal watchdog system (Guo 2012, 443), and its willingness to impose harsh sanctions on official malfeasance and sensational crimes (Tsai 2021), as well as its unstinting promotion of narrative scenarios in which humble plaintiffs are able to have wrongful convictions reversed or injuries compensated once they reach, through tenacious efforts, the political center and win a hearing from a wise and kind senior official. Such scenarios cement the belief that Party rule is ultimately compatible with the rule of law, and is indeed its very condition of possibility. The Party and the populace seem to share the conviction that as long as high justice is safeguarded, low justice is only a matter of time, perseverance, courage, and communication.

It has been suggested that *fazhi* is best translated as "rule by law," which comports with the Xi Jinping–era official motto of *yifa zhiguo* or "governing the country in accordance with the law."[2] *Fazhi*'s primary differences from the "rule of law" are the reliance on bureaucratic law, the expedient commitment to generality and uniformity, and the limited latitude permitted to a distinct legal doctrine, methodology, or profession. Under *fazhi*, low justice, or justice as fairness in John Rawls's (1999) formulation and the centerpiece of liberal jurisprudence, is subservient to the high justice of governance and statecraft. Put another way, due process is secondary to the overriding goal of social control and social harmony, a doctrine that has been given a philosophical gloss by Li Zehou as "harmony above justice" (*hexie gaoyu gongzheng*) (2014, 47). One might say that *fazhi* is first and foremost committed to high justice whereas the rule of law is chiefly concerned with low justice.

A Certain Justice seeks to delineate how the two realms of justice stack up in the Chinese legal imagination, how a variety of justice narratives wrestle with righteousness versus fairness, legitimacy versus rights. It makes a case for using high justice and low justice as the organizing concepts to make sense of the political-legal culture of a nonliberal society. This particular binary overlaps a good deal with more familiar conceptual binaries such as politics and law, state and society, substantive and procedural justice, civil and criminal justice, moral and legal justice, retributive and restorative justice, political and ordinary justice, formal and rough justice, and so on. High justice and low justice are not the Chinese equivalents of these supposedly universal dualities but rather mobilize them in different configurations of priority and relevance. In particular, the high-low dichotomy does not map neatly onto the usual opposition between politics and law that preoccupies liberal jurists. Using politics versus law to structure our investigation would limit our horizon to the liberal conception of justice as fairness and incline us to see high justice merely as undue political interference in the judiciary. We would not be able to make sense of many justice narratives that operate in the gray zone of high justice and low justice.

Law and Chinese Literature

Since the 1970s and 1980s, humanistic scholarship has been drawn inexorably toward questions of social justice. Much of this scholarship operates within the liberal framework of justice as fairness, hence the focus on discrimination and oppression structured by differences of gender, sexuality, class, and race and ethnicity. This has also been the case in the Chinese humanities, which has contributed to its disconnect from social science scholarship more cognizant of high justice questions. Previous attention to the problem of justice on the part of literary scholars tends to adopt a genre studies or literary historical approach to crime fiction (Bai 2014; R. Hegel and Carlitz 2007; Kinkley 2000, 2007; Peng 2019; X. Sun 2020; D. Wang 1997; Wei 2020; C. Yeh 2015). These efforts typically do not interrogate the concept of justice itself by subjecting it to genealogical or taxonomical scrutiny. Some of these works have been inspired by the law and literature movement in the Anglo-American academy (Sarat, Frank, and Anderson 2011, 4–5), and partly because of this, none make the crucial distinction between high justice and low justice, or between narratives preoccupied with questions of political legitimacy (exemplified by spy thrillers and anticorruption dramas) and narratives preoccupied with questions of fairness and social justice (exemplified by detective and crime mysteries and social realist novels). Their conclusions are therefore marred by a partial vision that misses all the nonlegal ways in which justice is pursued in modern China, which are often chronicled in narratives not explicitly about crime and punishment.

The existing scholarship also tends to rely on an ahistorical understanding of the rule-of-law ideal, combining "readings of literature with a complacent understanding of law" (Robert Weisberg 1989, 3). Such complacent understanding is derived mostly from popular representations instead of being grounded in the historical circumstances of the rule of law's emergence in postfeudal Europe. The principles of generality and uniformity (equality before the law or "justice is blind"), judicial independence, the right to counsel, the adversarial model, trial by jury, and so on form the general baseline against which Chinese stories are read and found problematic, even infuriating. Moreover, literary scholarship rarely draws on the growing research in history, historical sociology, and critical legal studies on the evolution of Chinese legal thought and judicial institutions. These are among the limitations I hope to overcome in undertaking this project. A Certain Justice, needless to say, is not a nativist defense of the Chinese legal system or a revisionist account of its ability to deliver justice. Rather, it is an effort to make sense of Chinese visions of justice in light of the divergent paths taken by China and the liberal West in pursuit of the universal goal of consolidating the normative order. As China accedes to global superpower status, its vision and practice of justice can no longer be treated as a pale, floundering, and negligible sideshow to the legal drama of defending liberty and upholding human rights in the global north. We need to be ready to recognize the fight for justice outside the familiar arenas of liberal democracy and in terms other than those furnished by the rule of law.

I model this project on Wai-chee Dimock's Residues of Justice: Literature, Law, Philosophy (1996). Literature about crime and punishment, in her view, speaks two languages. First and foremost, it speaks a utopian language that presumes the transcendent universality and ethical primacy of justice, however imperfectly it may be implemented on the ground. Yet it is also powerfully drawn to "the losses as well as the residues occasioned by the exercise of justice" (Dimock 1996, 7), and in so doing it speaks the language of poetic justice. In genre fiction, these losses and residues find expression in the extralegal liberty taken by criminals as well as by agents of the law, though Dimock sees the pattern play out in a far wider range of writings concerned with justice broadly construed. In these texts, "the problem of justice is given a face and a voice, a density of feature that plays havoc with any uniform scale of measurement and brings to every act of judicial weighing the shadow of an unweighable residue. In the persistence of that residue, in the sense of mismatch, the sense of shortfall, that burdens the endings of these texts, we have the most eloquent dissent from that canon of rational adequation so blandly maintained in philosophy and law" (Dimock 1996, 10).

Like Dimock, I value literature's ability to return the question of justice from legal and philosophical fantasies of adequation and commensurability—between crime and punishment, injury and redress, benefit and desert—to the messy realm of human conflict that always leaves behind a trail of residues: the uncompensated, the unresolved, and the unrecovered, as well as the overreach and overkill borne of law's hubris. If law prizes clarity, transparency, and a certain parsimony of meaning, literature casts a shadow over its fantasy of geometric economy and symmetry, or, to shift our metaphor, it illuminates the penumbra of law's edifice by dwelling in the thickets of human entanglements. If justice, as Dimock argues, is an incomplete virtue and a partial answer to human conflict even in the self-styled bastion of the rule of law, then its problematic status vis-à-vis statist and communitarian values in China is little surprising. With the worldwide rise of authoritarianism and populism, it behooves us to take seriously the contestation or sidelining of liberal values and the trajectories of political-legal development in the global south that may well foreshadow what is to come for the global north, as Jean and John Comaroff warn (2012). It is high time that we go beyond the reigning liberal theorizing of justice as fairness, and instead reckon with the visions of justice as righteousness or higher loyalty that seem to be driving much of today's illiberal politics.

In undertaking this project, I hope to accomplish two mutually reinforcing goals: The first is to bring into focus a body of texts—narratives of crime and punishment, subterfuge and exposé, guilt and redemption—that has hitherto remained largely under the scholarly radar and yet has much to tell us about contemporary China and is of much comparative value to scholars of law and literature, history of political thought, and critical legal studies. I intend to set these texts in conversation with the broader scholarship on Chinese law, ethics, and political history in order to demonstrate why the latter cannot afford to ignore the imaginative genres, while also adding a voice from Chinese literature to the expanding field of law, culture, and humanities. My second goal is to hone the interdisciplinary methodology developed in my previous work by making literary texts speak to the big questions that typically concern philosophers and social theorists. Having taken a keen interest in cognitive science, I endeavor to bring recent experimental findings on emotion, cognition, and behavior to bear on cross-cultural materials. In so doing I hope to participate in overarching intellectual debates in which literary scholars have often been

absent or have had a weak voice: Are human rights, democracy, and justice universal and self-evident goods? Can the non-West or global south
offer intellectual resources for overcoming liberal impasses? What are the
implications of China's "rise" for global governance and planetary justice?

Law and Morality

In the three-body problem that we opened the chapter with, law and morality can be seen as two kindred but rivalrous partners for justice. Legal
theorists have long argued that law and morality do not neatly coincide,
and should not do so. While law codifies moral norms, the moral-political
order exceeds legality per se in its preoccupation with legitimacy and its
tolerance of ambiguities, discretions, and hierarchies. In Western jurisprudential thought, law is regarded as a sui generis realm standing above and
apart from common morality. Law's empire governs vast swaths of public
life, while morality is confined to the personal and informal domains. In
Judith Shklar (1986)'s summary, law is concerned with external action,
demanding mere conformity of behavior, while morality is about inner
states of mind, requiring action to follow the dictates of conscience. Thus,
law is more modest in its demands, insisting only on abstention from what
is forbidden, while morality urges that one do the right thing, even if this
involves going beyond the call of duty. "In any case, much of law is morally indifferent, while the truly moral act cannot be legally enforced even
if the content of individual moral and legal rules is the same" (Shklar 1986,
44). This indifference, or moral neutrality, is held as a point of pride and
is jealously guarded by many a legal champion. For Unger (1976, 69–70),
law's neutrality is critical to its ability to stand above the fray of clashing
customs and mores borne of the modern condition of pluralism.

The separation of law and morality finds expression in the proverbial
distinction between the letter and the spirit of the law. This distinction
is also where crime fiction thrives. In his historical-sociological study of
English and French crime fiction, Luc Boltanski (2014) links the genre's
birth and boom to the emergence of a liberal political order that he calls
"the state of law." The state of law presupposes an objectively and empiri-
cally knowable reality that is nonetheless vulnerable to subversion. The
mystery and suspense that lie at the heart of the genre are anchored in an
orderly reality that is guaranteed by the state of law and eventually restored
after being called into question as much by the elites as by petty criminals.
The whole point of crime stories is to dramatize the state of law and the
contradiction that it encounters when it is superimposed on a class-based
society with its morality of hierarchy and deference (2014, 71).

The relationship of law to morality has remained a knotty issue for legal theorists and historians (P. Huang 2015; Posner 1999). Limiting our consideration to the cognitive dimension for the moment, we might say that because law extends our deliberative, reflexive faculty to the regulation, restraint, and even contravening of our moral intuitions and tribal passions (P. Bloom 2013; Churchland 2019; Greene 2013; Haidt 2012; Kahneman 2011; Wilson 2015), we come to regard law with profound ambivalence and remain unconvinced by the imperative to subordinate substantive goals to procedural fairness (Skitka 2002; Skitka and Mullen 2008). While most of us recognize law's necessary and salutatory role, especially in pacifying a world that might otherwise be mired in cycles of violence, we chafe against its many counterintuitive safeguards and measures that appear to side with wrongdoers while turning a cold face toward victims. From the presumption of innocence, the right to remain silent, plea bargaining, and the rules of evidence, to the very adversarial structure of judicial proceedings, where the defendant is placed on an equal footing with the plaintiff, our moral common sense constantly bumps up against a system that seems perversely distrustful of our most deeply held values. Is it any wonder that Western popular culture, which endlessly feeds off the high drama of the courtroom, holds defense lawyers in such low esteem (Rosenbaum 2004, 6; Richard Weisberg 1992, 79–80)? We watch in disbelief, intermingled with fascination, their zealous efforts to get criminal suspects "off the hook" through what appear to be legal casuistry and meaningless technicalities. How can they, in good conscience, defend "those people"? As often as not, we feel that justice has been defeated when the accused, whom the court of public opinion has overwhelmingly found guilty, is acquitted or handed a lenient sentence, or when a sympathetic defendant is unable to win over the judge and jury, even if the trial has been carried out in an exemplary manner.

A harsh indictment of the legal order comes from lawyer-turned-novelist Thane Rosenbaum: "The legal system always seems to ignore that the public has inherent expectations about the law, which conflict with the more circumscribed vision of what the law has in mind for itself" (2004, 16). The residue of legal justice, or what remains when the quest for redress is put through the bloodless procedural wringer of the legal apparatus, is what animates fiction, where moral justice is possible. That is why, Rosenbaum informs us, he abandoned the legal profession and turned to creative writing and education at the intersection of law and literature.

Whereas Rosenbaum speaks from the personal experience of disillusionment, Bruno Latour (2013) offers us a sociological explanation of the paradox of law's augustness and its practitioners' debasement. Modern institutions such as politics, law, and the economy, in his account, are not discrete entities or domains but are, rather, interpenetrating "networks." A person pursuing a legal action must needs pass through a course of action that is full of small interruptions and hiatuses of a nonlegal nature (Latour 2013, 34). Law is thus riven between its "astonishing force" and its "remarkable weakness": "But we feel the weakness every time we despair at seeing that the 'legally justified' decision is not necessarily just, opportune, true, useful, effective; every time the court condemns an accused party but the aggrieved party has still not been able to achieve 'closure'; every time indemnities have been awarded but doubts still remain about the exact responsibilities of the respective parties. With the law, we always go from surprise to surprise: we are surprised by its power, surprised by its impotence" (Latour 2013, 361). He goes on: "What makes law so hard to grasp is that as soon as it has been defined as a separate world, carefully delimited by its own tautologies, we notice how flexible it is, and with what confounding agility it absorbs all sorts of injunctions from other regions: politics, the economy, trends, fashions, prejudices, media. As a result, just when we think we have discovered it as a particular sphere, with its own regulatory modes, we notice that the legal institution is so porous that its decisions look like so many weathervanes, turning with every breeze" (Latour 2013, 362).

There is perhaps no more poignant testimony to law's pliability than the trial scene in *To Kill a Mockingbird* (Mulligan 1962). Here, merely hours after defense lawyer Atticus Finch's rousing speech about the law being a great leveler and a Black defendant standing equal to his fellow men in a court of law, the all-white jury returns a guilty verdict for Tom Robinson. Even so, those sitting in the whites-only part of the courtroom would be the last to own up to the weathervane nature of law, or its hijacking by racism.

Latour is extending a long line of critiques of the modern doctrine of legal positivism stretching from nineteenth-century Marxists and early twentieth-century American realists down to contemporary postcolonial critics, anthropologists, and critical legal studies scholars. According to this doctrine, law is a kingdom unto itself, autonomous, objective, internally coherent, self-sufficient, bounded, and deriving its strength from its principled detachment from politics, religion, morality, ideology, and the market.[3] Embraced by legal theorists and legal professionals alike, it holds up judicial independence as the lynchpin of the rule of law and democracy. Shklar calls this outlook "legalism," identifying its essential ingredients as "the dislike of vague generalities, the preference for case-by-case treatment of all social issues, the structuring of all possible human relations into the form of claims and counterclaims under established rules, and the belief that the rules are 'there'" (1986, 10). She criticizes the single-minded faith in legal rectitude, or what she calls the "policy of justice," which despises arbitration, negotiation, and bargaining as mere "politics." The insistence on law's imperviousness ostensibly protects the diversity of private morals and individual freedom from ideological or religious tyranny, but it also allows legalism to hegemonize the political imagination: "Adjudication of private *lites inter partes* will remain the model for public rectitude, the best way to solve all social conflicts, and 'the law' will remain 'there'" (Shklar 1986, 19). In Lon Fuller's (2001) view, it also conflates the rule of law with what he calls "managerial direction," or effective bureaucracy.

Marxists have long sought to expose this formalistic and ultimately conservative ideology as a tool of class oppression—a critique that was stretched to an extreme in Maoist China. Without quite going along with the Marxist rejection of the rule of law tout court, critical legal studies has jettisoned the aforementioned legalist fictions and interrogated law's imbrication with morals, ideologies, sectional interests, and political goals. In a nutshell, the critique of legalism exposes the fundamentally hollow nature of the liberal definition of law. In excluding goodness and other extralegal desiderata and admitting only morally neutral principles, "such as the fact it is enforced by someone" (Shklar 1986, 52), one is nonetheless confronted with the difficulty of pinning down that "someone" in the age of popular sovereignty and constitutional democracy. However resoundingly "we the people" may be invoked, in the final analysis, we are left with a mere tautology: "the law is what the sovereign says it is, and the sovereign is he who says what the law is" (Shklar 1986, 52–53). This is the crux of what critics commonly speak of as law's fundamental aporia: to wit, its self-image as a disinterested and autonomous universe is predicated on a disavowal (simultaneous recognition and denial) or abjection (simultaneous acceptance and rejection) of the sovereign exception. The explosion of studies of "law and . . ." in recent decades, according to Paul Kahn, has been fueled by the attempt to come to terms with the aporia (2001, 146). Law, in the final analysis, has never been an empire unto itself.

Chinese Justice between Law and Morality

We may trace legalism to a larger trend identified by philosophers and anthropologists as the modern contraction of moral life in advanced industrial societies. Richard Shweder and his collaborators (1997) have shined a light on this process by comparing the world's divergent moral values according to a tripartite model of moral foundations: autonomy, com-

munity, and divinity. Different societies and cultures have built different
moral systems on the basis of these foundations, often privileging one over
the others. Among the WEIRD demographic—Western, educated, and
residing in industrialized, rich, and democratic countries—the autonomy
foundation has largely eclipsed the community and divinity foundations
(see also Asma 2013; Flanagan 2017; Henrich 2020). Elsewhere—both in
more rural and conservative parts of developed countries, and in developing countries—community and divinity still significantly structure moral
discourse and judgment. Jonathan Haidt (2012, 128–54, 170–76) has expanded this model into a sixfold taxonomy to make sense of the deepening
polarization of American politics that goes far beyond ideological difference and policy disagreement. Of the six foundations of morality—care/
harm, liberty/oppression, fairness/cheating, loyalty/betrayal, hierarchy/
subversion, sanctity/degradation—liberals tend to activate only the first
two or three whereas conservatives operate on all six, albeit giving greater
weight to the last three. Conservatives, in his language, have a fuller moral
palate. And the same can be said of many non-Western societies as well,
where hierarchy, for example, carries few of the negative connotations that
it does in the West (Bell 2008; Bell and Wang 2020).

The contraction or thinning out of liberal morality is by and large a
sign of moral progress. It is an openness born of a conscientious effort to
entertain pluralistic, often incompatible values and to tamp down intuitive reactions to perceived violations of the loyalty, hierarchy, and sanctity
foundations. Giving free rein to all six foundations can on the contrary
lead to moral myopia and obtuseness, a failure of reflective reason and
moral imagination. Conservatives may have a fuller moral palate, but that
is not a desideratum by itself if it means an abdication of moral reasoning
or absence of moral growth.[4] Liberal morality's adherence to a single rule
of thumb—does it harm innocent others?—has led to the gradual removal
of stigma from interracial marriage, widow remarriage, premarital sex, extramarital affairs, masturbation, homosexuality, intersexuality, polyamory,
deformity—so that "miscegenation," "chastity," "adultery," "perversion,"
"abomination," and "cripple" have justly dropped out of the modern moral
lexicon. Nonetheless, liberal morality can also be more alienating (Walzer 1994), and insofar as it serves as the moral foundation of the liberal
state of law, the sense of alienation is continuous with our general unease with legal rationality. Haidt likens the liberal moral universe to the
two-dimensional world in Edwin Abbot's *Flatland* ([1884] 2010) in which
lines, squares, polygons, and circles cannot wrap their minds around such
three-dimensional entities as spheres, cones, and cubes.

It is uncontroversial to say that Chinese society, past and present, has leaned toward the conservative end of the moral spectrum and relied heavily on the community and divinity foundations for the elaboration of its moral systems. Loyalty/betrayal, hierarchy/subversion, sanctity/ degradation have on the whole weighed more than care/harm, liberty/ oppression, fairness/cheating. Even during the most revolutionary phase of the socialist era when liberty/oppression and fairness/cheating temporarily gained a stronger foothold, the other foundations remained firmly in place. As I have argued elsewhere, Maoist society was profoundly hierarchical, structured as it was by a caste-like class-designation system (H. Lee 2014, chap. 5). Moreover, in struggle sessions that were designed to denounce class oppression and expose how the exploitative classes cheated the laboring masses out of the fruits of their labor, the target could also be attacked for collaborating with hostile forces such as the Nationalists or the Japanese, hence for violating the loyalty/betrayal foundation. If the target was female, she could be vilified as a "broken shoe" (*poxie*, slang for whore) and subjected to sexist shaming as a way of activating the sanctity/ degradation foundation.

It is also uncontroversial to say that governance in China has always been a moral proposition, or what Susan Shirk (1984) calls "virtuocracy." From the Mandate of Heaven to the dictatorship of the proletariat, the basis of political legitimacy has always been moral-cosmological-ideological rather than contractual. The moral foundations that undergird legitimacy are loyalty/betrayal, hierarchy/subversion, and sanctity/degradation, not care/harm, liberty/oppression, or fairness/cheating. The state to be sure cares about the well-being of its subjects/citizens for any number of reasons, but it has never subscribed to the liberal principle of "putting cruelty first" (Shklar 1984, chap. 1). When cruelty serves the goal of social control, it is visited on the populace without mercy, discreetly or spectacularly. In this it exemplifies a statism that, in Michael Walsh's words, "perpetuates a systemic form of terror" (2020, xv). The Communist Party may have gone through a radical antitraditionalist phase that culminated in the mid-1970s' "Criticize Lin Biao, Criticize Confucius" campaign, but at its core it is still a caesaropapist regime that stakes its claim to rule on moral superiority, albeit couched in the ideological jargon of Sino-Marxism—a case of new forms of legitimacy overlaying old ones (Zarrow 2012, 11). To a degree unrivaled by liberal states of law, it "demands and expects always to be sacrificed to, celebrated, consecrated, worshipped, and sanctified" (Walsh 2020, xv).

As many scholars have observed, the Party never misses an opportunity to trumpet its world-historical feat of freeing China from the crushing weight of feudalism, the sharp claws of capitalism, and the iron boots of imperialism. Although it no longer holds up a communist utopia as the endgame, it nonetheless presents itself as the only thing standing between order and chaos, prosperity and poverty, unity and fragmentation, national autonomy and foreign domination. In abandoning class struggle and discouraging class consciousness, the Party fundamentally denies internal divisions and conflict of interests. A college instructor for a "Political Construction" class that Anders Hansen attended in Beijing, for example, insists that China has no need for a multiparty system or separation of powers because the interests of all Chinese citizens are in fundamental agreement and because "this collective interest is naturally best managed by the institutional arrangement of the single-party state" (Hansen 2012, 54).

Positioning itself at the moral-ideological pinnacle, the Party easily sidesteps the aporia that troubles the liberal rule of law. It simply occupies the space of the sovereign exception and declares itself the moral source of the legal order and perfectly capable of unifying substantive and procedural justice, moral and legal justice. The Party, in other words, decides both what is moral and what is lawful. The distinction between morality and legality becomes moot. If the liberal "political order does not require moral integrity but only law-abiding citizens" (Arendt 2003, 68), the Chinese polity demands far more of its citizens and still more of Party cadres by way of moral integrity. Only then can the Party deny any gap between high justice and low justice, or the possibility that low justice is sacrificed to high justice, or that due process is given short shrift for the sake of "stability maintenance" (*weiwen*). With so much riding on the presumption of the Party's moral supremacy, how, then, does one deal with the problem of "secular theodicy" (Hansen 2012, 51), or the fact that the Party's members routinely succumb to corruption, and that their reckless abuse of power exacerbates social inequities and conflicts?

What Hansen calls the central "problem of evil" in current Chinese politics, however, has been around a lot longer than the People's Republic. The centralized state in imperial China was no stranger to the paradox of grounding legitimacy in virtue while being institutionally vulnerable to power abuse and corruption. The imperial rule was explicitly premised on the emperor's moral supremacy and exclusive access to heaven's will (Thornton 2007; Zarrow 2012, 9–12; Duara 2015, 164; Walsh 2020, 18). The virtuocratic system of selecting officials through a tiered system of examinations, too, was dedicated to the goal of letting the cream of moral excellence rise to the top. The grueling examinations tested not specialized, practical knowledge, but mastery of the classics as the fount of moral wisdom. As Zarrow notes, the virtuocratic logic posed no threat to hereditary monarchy as both were subtended by the currency of virtue (2012, 11). The emperor and his officials stood in relation to the people as their moral betters, or as rulers, parents, teachers, and priests all rolled into one. Corrupt officials, as Joshua Rosenzweig notes, were cast into a separate category and cordoned off from the officialdom as a sanctified institution.

> Generally speaking, individual failures to address injustice did not serve to undermine the ideological foundation of China's state-centered justice paradigm, even when officials were themselves the source of that injustice. In part, this is because it was believed that the imperial state's extensive disciplinary system of oversight and punishment was sufficient to root out isolated cases of bureaucratic wrongdoing. Accordingly, only the quality of individual agents ever came into question, not the fundamental nature of the socio-political order in which they operated. Because the political system itself was the ultimate source of justice, addressing wrongdoing was primarily concerned with preserving the authority of that system, rather than with protecting its subjects from the consequences of any wrongdoing. (Rosenzweig 2017, 30)

The problem of evil was reduced to one of insufficient self-cultivation. The remedy, then, was constant exhortation to be good, supplemented by dire threats and harsh penalties—a form of "costly signaling" (Norenzayan 2013, 101–3) that said the emperor meant business. Su Li (2006, 213–24) believes that the moralist discourse also concealed an economic calculation: Without the kind of fiscal resources and biopower at the command of a modern state, it was more cost-effective to adhere to a strict liability system that harshly punished bureaucrats for wrongful convictions or erroneous rulings, regardless of culpability (fault, negligence, intent). Scapegoating individual officials certainly cost less than establishing empire-wide institutions and rules of accountability to ensure fairness and equal treatment. In other words, procedural justice is a wholesale enterprise that requires extensive and expensive infrastructure, whereas substantive justice can be retailed on an ad hoc basis, within and outside of formal channels. Once a procedurally oriented judicial infrastructure is in place, justice can take on an impersonal character, delinked from the virtue of the ruler. The state can then lose emotionally compelling opportunities to make the deliverance of low justice serve the cause of high justice. Leaving in place an inadequate system focused on substantive justice paradoxically shores up high justice.

Delia Lin gives this assessment of the ineradicable discrepancy between high justice and low justice: "Confucian political philosophy has great difficulty recognising abuse of power, the vulnerability of the powerless, and the powerless of the vulnerable, and hence faces real challenge in addressing unfairness or inequalities in a hierarchically structured collective. Laws, therefore, are not made to prevent abuse of power by the more powerful, or to protect the rights of the less powerful in a social structure. Nor is there a carefully designed judicial procedure to safeguard the legal rights of each individual" (Lin 2017, 88). In a system that prioritizes high justice, there is little incentive to recognize abuse of power or to highlight the vulnerability of the powerless. To the extent that law may promote rights consciousness and be deployed as a weapon of the weak (Rosenzweig 2017, 36–45), the ruling class has no reason to throw its weight behind the law. That it has done so in the European context of interest group pluralism is a historical anomaly in Unger's view: "The decisive event was the success of established aristocracies or of an emergent 'third estate,' composed of merchant and professional groups, in preserving or acquiring a measure of independence from the monarchs and their staffs. Were it not for this success, however limited and transitory, the rule of law ideal might never have won its preeminent place in the modern West" (1976, 70). This explains why property rights became the central pillar of the rule of law, and also why inclusive institutions were the cornerstone of a virtuous circle of prosperity and equity (Acemoglu and Robinson 2012). Elsewhere, few sovereigns warmed to the slogan "Let justice be done though the world may perish" (*Fiat justitia, pereat mundus*) (Arendt 2003, 52). In imperial China, this was unthinkable because high justice and low justice were presumed to be continuous, a harmony grounded in the cosmic order and guaranteed by sovereign power. Indeed, as Elizabeth Perry argues, because the idea of rights in the Chinese moral economy has always been framed socioeconomically as the "right to livelihood," which must be guaranteed by the state, grassroots demand for rights can have the paradoxical effect of affirming state legitimacy (2008, 46–47). The strange idea of rule of law that curtails the power of the ruler from below has had a hard time finding a foothold in the Chinese political-legal culture.

"Harmony above Justice"

Justice in dynastic China is a matter of enacting state laws that manifest heavenly principles (*tianli*) and are cognizant of human feelings (*renqing*) (Xu 2020, 1). In traditional justice narratives, the agent of justice is either an imperial official acting as the emperor's emissary or a righteous avenger in pursuit of vigilante justice. Among the former type, Judge Bao is the most legendary. He is said to be in possession a Golden Sword (*shangfang baojian*) that allows him to "behead first, memorialize afterward" (*xianzhan houzou*). In the Yuan ballad that opens this introduction, he also carries a Golden Tablet inscribed by the emperor with an authorizing couplet: "Irrespective of one's status as an imperial relative, empress, imperial concubine, or prime minister, / Whoever breaks the law, all will be treated equally" (Idema 2010, 227). When the corrupt Cao brothers murder an out-of-town student in order to kidnap his beautiful wife, the cosmic order itself is said to have been upset: "Ever since that student of books had been murdered, / Gods wailed and ghosts wept, leaving no one in peace. / The mill stones whirled around without being pushed, / And the rice mortars kept on stamping all by themselves" (207). The supernatural disturbances betoken the fundamental correspondence between heaven, earth, and human in Chinese cosmology, as well as the presumed continuity between low justice and high justice in Chinese political-legal culture. An act of misprision causes a tear in the social fabric and a breach in the cosmic order of which the emperor is supposed to be the guardian and in which the legitimacy of imperial rule is grounded.

The invariable upward displacement of low justice to high justice underlies the traditional genre convention whereby a crime is committed in full view of the audience and little is in doubt with regard to motive, method, and outcome (Gulik 1976; McIntyre 2013). The suspenseful aspects of crime stories are moral in nature rather than epistemological: Is the judge morally superior enough to surmount the recalcitrance of the culprit and awe him or her into confession? Whereas the Western detective genre posits individuals as mysteries to one another, traditional Chinese crime stories generate tension by pitting the subject population against a state that aspires to be all seeing and all knowing. Confession affirms the fundamental legibility of the former. To achieve this end, judicial torture and trickery, as well as occult methods are all fair game. In fact, a judge that cannot summon supernatural assistance may well be regarded as having been forsaken by gods and spirits and thus not worthy of office. Judge Bao stands out among the legendary judges most notably for his ability to tap into the occult. It is said that during the day he presides over the earthly court, and at night he judges wronged ghosts in purgatory.

Paul Katz (2007) terms the imbrication between the earthly and otherworldly judicial universes "the judicial continuum." People who resort to "indictment rituals" performed in temples have either exhausted their options in the courts or wish to add extra insurance to the lawsuit in which they are involved. While justice is not guaranteed in either the diurnal or the nocturnal court, it is believed that divine justice is more impartial and swift, and gods of the underworld can summon the living as witnesses or defendants and mete out punishments to the living and the dead alike.

Officials in imperial China routinely invoked their invisible counterparts to instill awe and fear in their subjects and were not above staging trials in City God temples. The judicial continuum makes it hard to see such tactics as crassly manipulative. Judge Bao's exploits are shot through with supernatural or paranormal elements, and his superhero status owes as much to his ability to manipulate the occult workings of the cosmos as to his moral incorruptibility and turbo-charged intellect. What he delivers is for all intents and purposes divine justice.

In the Cao brothers case, Judge Bao goes toe-to-toe with the emperor. When the emperor tries to free his brothers-in-law by issuing a limited amnesty, Bao demands a universal one. Their duel in the power of exception, the premodern equivalent of a constitutional crisis, is a rare episode of high jinks of courtroom drama that tacitly acknowledges the peril of sovereign exception: whereas Judge Bao exercises sovereign power for the sake of high justice while also attending to low justice along the way, the emperor uses it for nepotistic goals, which undermine low justice (depriving a village woman's hope for redress) and ultimately vitiate high justice. The outcome could not be more satisfying, both emotionally and cosmologically: the younger brother pays with his life for the forfeited life of the student; the older brother spends the rest of his life atoning for all the moral debts the brothers have incurred throughout their years of debauchery. The cosmic balance sheet is properly restored, the institution of monarchy is saved from the emperor and his kin, and high justice is upheld. In the process, low justice is also delivered: The student's death is avenged, and the abducted wife is restored to freedom and given funds to take her husband's ashes home and provided enough "gold and treasure" to live out her life as a chaste widow. The case is never simply one of solving a murder and abduction, nor is there ever any doubt about Judge Bao's judgment, he being as he is the emissary of heavenly will, dispenser of divine justice, and guardian of imperial legitimacy.

The subsumption of low justice under high justice is even more pronounced in Guan Hanqing's *Rescriptor-in-Waiting Bao Thrice Investigates the Butterfly Dream*. After a local bully murders a farmer surnamed Wang and is in turn killed by the farmer's three adult sons, their mother surrenders them to Judge Bao, who is faced with the challenge of determining which brother should be held legally culpable. To his astonishment, Mother Wang volunteers the youngest brother, her biological son, for death row and pleads him to spare the eldest and middle brothers, both her stepsons. Her righteousness prompts Judge Bao to recall a dream in which he saw a big butterfly rescue two little butterflies from a spider web but leave a third one stuck there. Perplexed, his dream self stepped forward to free the forsaken one. "This was Heaven giving me a sign that foretold what was going to happen and that I should save this little fellow's life" (West and Idema 2010, 62). This he does, ordering the execution of a horse thief in lieu of Third Wang. The play ends with a grand finale in which Judge Bao ventriloquizes the emperor in bestowing high ranks to the three sons and honors to the mother, and the recipients chant their eternal gratitude.

In their pioneering study of law in imperial China, Derk Bodde and Clarence Morris highlight the moral and cosmological orientation of written law as "primarily a legal codification of the ethical norms long dominant in Chinese society" (Bodde and Morris 1967, 3). The contrast with the strenuous separation of law and morals in the liberal tradition cannot be overemphasized. Rather than endeavoring to safeguard individual rights against incursions from other individuals or the state, the law was concerned with acts of moral or ritual impropriety, including criminal violence. Bodde and Morris term this, following Ch'ü T'ung-tsu, "the Confucianization of law" (Bodde and Morris 1967, 29). As a result, customary morality (*li* or *renqing*) and positive law (*fa*) converged to deliver moral or substantive justice. In his decades-long study of Chinese legal history, Philip Huang sees manifestations of moral orientation or what he calls "practical moralism" in every aspect of the hybrid mediatory-adjudicatory system. Indeed, the very privileging of mediation over adjudication points to the centrality of morality (P. Huang 2015, 7). Huang writes: "Chinese law, in fact, has long rejected a proceduralist approach to law and has operated by the principle that the mediator or judge can and should aim to grasp the substantive truth. That point of departure led, in turn, to a host of associated institutional arrangements in the legal system of the imperial period, including allowing judges great latitude in the gathering of evidence, without being bound by procedural rules, and even to employ techniques like discerning the accused's emotional state, even facial expressions, in coming to a decision. [...] Chinese law, therefore, has not evinced anything like the Western distinction between the 'courtroom truth' and the 'real truth'" (P. Huang 2015, 17).[5]

Here Huang also identifies a fundamental epistemological divide between Chinese and Western law. Legal truth or courtroom truth presupposes a faith in the integrity and perfectibility of the process that generates actionable truth (Constable 2019; C. Tang 2019) and an agnosticism toward the truth of "what happened" (the Rashomon effect). Chinese law, however, acknowledges only the latter, the truth of the fact situation that is known to heaven, earth, the perpetrator, and the victim. It must necessarily be brought to light through whatever means possible: *chaqing* (observation, inspection, interrogation), *juzheng* (fact-finding, evidence gathering, forensic examination), *yongjue* (trickery, coercion, occult methods), *xingxun* (torture) (R. Hegel et al. 2009, 14–17; Liang Zhiping 2013, 317–24). The goal is to reach *zhenxiang dabai*, a full revelation of the truth.[6] Hence the plaintiff and the defendant are required to confront each other's testimony in court (*duizhi* or *duibo gongtang*), and a case cannot close until the defendant confesses—all for the sake of arriving at a unitary, substantive truth. Both crime dramas and true crime records are wont to present verbatim renditions of the depositions of the plaintiff and witness and the confession of the defendant "in an effort to eliminate ambiguity about the facts of the case or the guilt of the perpetrator" (R. Hegel et al. 2009, 30).

In his overview of Chinese legal history, Klaus Mühlhahn lists three things that set the imperial system apart from the modern legal order: first, there was a fear that law would make people more contentious and manipulative; second, the degree of concession to social hierarchies was such that one's social standing was directly reflected in one's legal standing and that the law refrained from reaching into the private sphere; third, there were many brakes on enforcement. The last item might come as a surprise considering the notoriety of cruel and unusual punishments that have given rise to the expression "Chinese torture." But as many have emphasized, the imperial penal system was tempered by a persistent strand of humanitarianism comprising a lengthy judicial review process, the postponement of executions until the Autumn Assizes, and the promulgations of amnesty "on a scale unparalleled in other legal systems of the world" (Mühlhahn 2009, 38). The humanitarian tradition was a manifestation of the cosmological foundation of the political-legal order, which had to be in sync with the rhythmic cycle of nature.

The ease with which Judge Bao solves the case in the "butterfly dream" play by substituting a common thief's life for that of a murder suspect is also rooted in the cosmological underpinnings of the criminal justice system. Because the point of punishment is requital and retribution, a dead person can still be subjected to a posthumous thrashing. It follows that in cases in which the outcome cannot be undone, such as homicide, the presence or absence of motive does not affect the sentencing. A son who accidentally kills his father and who voluntarily confesses could still be given the death sentence. In the eyes of the state/emperor/cosmos, the forfeiting of the killer's life is the only way to requite (*di*) the loss of the victim's life (Liang Zhiping 2013, 296–302). This is why Judge Bao has to single out one brother for the death row even though all three brothers confess to the killing, and also why it is good enough to execute the horse thief in lieu of Third Wang. Heaven, being so high up, perhaps couldn't tell who's who, if it even cares. Clearly as far as the thief is concerned, his punishment is unfair and grossly disproportionate to his crime, but the play casts him in a clown role (he is known only by his nickname Zhang Wanlü or Stubborn Donkey Zhang) and essentially treats him as a token. Because punishment does not turn on intent, his identity (being unconnected to the homicide case) ultimately is irrelevant.

Judge Bao's willingness to exercise discretionary power distinguishes him from run-of-the-mill "upright officials" (*qingguan*) who unyieldingly adhere to the letter of the law and lack sufficient wisdom to honor the spirit of the law. Such officials are denounced for their haughty imperviousness to common sense: "After the Han era, any official who steadfastly adhered to the law but was not flexible in observing *renqing* and in adapting to circumstances would have been regarded as a 'harsh official' [*kuli*], even though he might have been an exemplar of honesty and high-mindedness" (D. Jiang and Ma 2020, 296). The unbending upright official comes in for a takedown as late as the twentieth century in *The Travels of Lao Can* (D. Wang 1997, 147–51).

The "butterfly dream" play also showcases the extraordinary pedagogical lengths to which the law goes to reward private virtue. As soon as he sees evidence of loyalty and filial piety among the Wangs, Judge Bao not only makes his adjudication of the case at hand but also showers, on behalf of the emperor, official titles and honors on the family. Legal historians have detailed the many provisions in dynastic penal codes that upheld the moral and legal autonomy of the patriarchal family. The male head of the household enjoyed the greatest leeway and immunity, whereas women and junior members had few protections against abuse. Punishments were calibrated strictly according to a gradated system of ranks and relatedness, a feature most at odds with modern sensibilities (Henrich 2020, 400). Lower-ranked members were practically forbidden from bringing plaints against higher-ranked members. A son who brought a charge against his father, for example, faced stiff penalties even if the charge was proven true.[7] Close relatives were expected and encouraged to shield one another on the authority of a famous anecdote in the *Analects* (mentioned at the top of this introduction) in which Confucius defines uprightness (*zhi*) as a father shielding son, and vice versa, and disapproves of a man for turning his sheep-stealing father in to the authorities (Bell 1998, 558). Similarly, in a dialogue with a student who asks what the sage king Shun would have done had his father committed murder, Mencius opines that Shun would have allowed his minister of justice to do his job and arrest the father, but that he would then abdicate his throne, break into the jail, and abscond with the father to the seacoast to live out their lives in blissful oblivion (*Mencius* 7A:35). Both anecdotes have been at the fulcrum of a sustained debate among Chinese scholars under the rubric of "mutual shielding among kin" (*qinqin xiangyin*) (see Deng Xiaomang 2010).[8] The resolution of the case of the Cao brothers too hinges on the need to honor the principle of "placing filial piety above loyalty" (*xiaoqing dayu zhongjun*) (Fan Zhongxin et al. 2011, 78–79). So is the outcome of the protracted case of the filial assassin Shi Jianqiao, also introduced at the beginning of this introduction (episode number three). As Eugenia Lean (2007) shows, the Republican judicial system, however much it aspired to the rule-of-law ideal, had to accommodate a political-legal culture with its permissive attitude toward private vendettas. That it did so under the pressure of public sentiments, greatly fanned by a burgeoning popular press, bespeaks the strength of that tradition.

The concessions to private morality (*renqing*) or customary law (li_2), however, stopped at treason. In such cases, "the principle of group responsibility was applied with a vengeance, all close relatives of the offender being either executed or permanently exiled" (Bodde and Morris 1967, 41). The exception also applies to the "naturalization of law," or the effort to align bureaucratic law (*guofa*) with the rhythms of nature (*tianli*). The various blackout dates on the executioner's calendar did not apply to rebels.[9] In the end, neither the Confucianization of law nor the naturalization of law fundamentally altered the bureaucratic character of traditional Chinese law, to wit, its top-down application by the state on the subjects. It applied only secondarily between subjects, and rarely in defense of the subjects against state power. The law, Mühlhahn observes, "took notice of human activity only when it affected the state's or the emperor's interests" (2009, 56), that is, only when it threatened high justice. For this reason, traditional China had no private legal profession, and adjudicating court cases was only one of the many bureaucratic functions discharged by county and prefect magistrates, whose paths to officialdom included no formal legal training. This also explains why in popular narratives the judge-investigator can sometimes merge with the knight-avenger, as David Wang notes in his study of turn-of-the-twentieth-century court-case and chivalric story cycles: "the hero of the courtroom emerges from the yamen to play the hero on the road," for ultimately both types of stories occupy "the same moral landscape" (1997, 118) in which high justice must be upheld by whatever means necessary. And the answer to Wang's question of whose justice is being served when state and nonstate agents join forces to fight crime and corruption (120) is none other than high justice—a singular concept that brooks no division or friction.

The limited role played by the formal legal system, however, should not be boiled down to an immutable cultural aversion to litigation. At the institutional level, the imperial state simply did not possess the resources to administer justice in an intensive manner, so that amnesties and sentence commutations were ways of releasing the pressure on the criminal justice system (Mühlhahn 2009, 39). At the ideological level, the state took no pride in prosecuting its subjects, for "the mere occurrence of crime and punishments implied a failure" (41). Allegedly, when Wu You served as governor of Jiaodong, whenever a litigation was brought to his tribunal, he would shut himself in to undergo self-castigation and only then hear the case (A. Chen 2003, 264–65; Liang Zhiping 2013, 331). The state wanted everyone to stay out of the courts and settle their disputes among themselves, so that society could go from *xisong* (abating of litigation) to *wusong* (litigation free). The cultural, institutional, and ideological factors combined to foster a political-legal culture in which the formal criminal justice system played a minimal role in social ordering (A. Chen 2003). Unofficial mediators, on the other hand, "dispensed a wide range of punitive sanctions against offenders that included public censure, fines, ostracism, servitude, and corporal punishment" (Mühlhahn 2009, 51). Bodde and Morris also remark that the clan, the guild, and the council of local gentry were the primary vectors of social order, and it was them that "the Chinese everyman looked to for guidance and sanction, rather than to the formal judicial system per se. Involvement in the formal system was popularly regarded as the road to disaster and therefore to be avoided at all cost" (Bodde and Morris 1967, 6).

In this light, the main plot of the film *Qiuju Goes to Court* (mentioned above) is truly puzzling: why does a peasant woman have so much faith in the formal legal system that she works it indefatigably until she gets more than she has bargained for? We will return to this film and this question in the conclusion, after we have taken a closer look at the evolving ecology of the Chinese legal imagination in the modern century.

Chapter Outline

Because high justice and low justice are central to the overall framing of my investigation of Chinese visions of justice, I start with two chapters that spell out fully the dichotomy with an array of narrative illustrations, from spy thrillers that enchant the state to tales of not playing fair. Subsequently, I extend my inquiry to areas that are not neatly partitioned into high and low justice but rather traverse both: "transitional justice" in the aftermath of the Cultural Revolution as the post-Mao regime attempted to institute a socialist rule of law, "exceptional justice" in the CCP's reformation and piecemeal pardoning of Japanese and Nationalist "war criminals," "poetic justice" as literary and filmic narratives reckon with the challenge of representing systemic injustices, and "multispecies justice" that contemplates the possibility of including nonhuman species in our moral community. Needless to say, the Chinese legal imagination cannot be circumscribed within the realm of law or the narrow confines of crime fiction or even the geobody of the Chinese nation. The verbal and visual narratives surveyed in this study defy genre rubrics, and they are not limited to the modern century or the People's Republic.

I borrowed the main title from P. D. James's 1997 novel *A Certain Justice*. Its double entendre captures well the desire for certain justice, guaranteed not just by human institutions (which can be corrupted) but also by transcendent powers on the one hand, and on the other, the inherently partial nature of justice—the "losses" and "residues" left by exercises of justice that Dimock (1996, 7) speaks of. The through line in the Chinese legal imagination is that for high justice to be certain, low justice has to be curtailed or made partial and uncertain. But this through line and other enduring patterns are crisscrossed by local emergences, hence my metaphorical use of "ecology" to underscore the fact that what I'm delineating here is an evolving political-legal culture as refracted through literature.

Chapter 1 is a political history of the spy thriller, the only genre fiction that can boast a more or less uninterrupted history in the latter half of the twentieth century. Its exceptional status has everything to do with the Maoist ideology of permanent revolution. The romance of the state par excellence, the spy thriller enchants the state as a sovereign power replete with *arcana imperii* and mystifies the reason of state as the locus of high justice. Spy fiction is to high justice what detective fiction is to low justice, hence their contrasting fates in modern China. Focusing on the spy thriller's golden age in the early socialist period and its new millennial boom, I also compare the genre to its Western counterparts (particularly the James Bond franchise) and draw larger points about divergent political-legal cultures. Primary sources include *Blood Monument*, *The Murder Case of Xu Qiuying*, *Undercover*, *In the Dark*, and *Decoded*.

Chapter 2 turns to stories of dissemblance and duplicity, both as a strategy of domination and as a tactic of resistance and subversion. I consider how low justice is attainable when law is largely absent or when laws (and policies that have the force of law) are the very source or instrument of injustice. I suggest that the answer is hypocrisy, whereby the subaltern are forced to resort to subterfuge, deception, and illicit schemes in order to pursue ordinary life goods. In lieu of a survey of detective or crime fiction, I examine narratives of hypocrisy, of not playing fair, of circumventing the law—by both power holders and the powerless. In particular, I focus on what I call "subaltern hypocrisy" as a morally compromised way of achieving low justice and how "communities of complicity" can mitigate the moral injury of power. Primary sources include *The True Story of Ah Q, Gao Yubao, Serve the People!*, and *Dying to Survive*.

Chapter 3 zooms in on two transitional periods in the twentieth century: the 1950s and the 1970s. In the former, the new ruling Communist Party pursued the holy grail of revolutionary justice in mass democracy and ritual politics. Political trials enacted the melodrama of justice by conflating historical causality with legal causality, essentially putting the Old Society on trial. After the end of the Cultural Revolution, the regime inaugurated the socialist rule of law with the historic Gang of Four Trial and selective prosecution of former Red Guards and rebels. Is transitional justice possible when it is a ruling party confronting past crimes and wrongs on its own watch and in the name of its supreme leader? How does the Party-state persuade the populace that its rule is just and that its leadership is the very embodiment of justice in the aftermath of a calamitous decade and amid an ongoing epidemic of official corruption? Primary sources include "The Bloodstained Shirt," "The Second Encounter," *Power versus Law, The Trial*, and *The Case of Huang Kegong*.

In chapter 4, I theorize a Chinese regime of exceptional justice. I begin with how the new regime dealt with Japanese and Nationalist "war criminals" in the 1950s and how it embarked on an experimental program of thought reform that culminated in lenient sentences for the former and special pardons for the latter. In addition to surveying reportage literature and autobiographical and historical accounts to draw a rough picture of the experiment, I read closely two visual narratives that restage the miracle of collective rebirth on the part of a dozen or so prominent Nationalist prisoners. I suggest that it was a program of (half) truth and reconciliation that worked effectively on the ground but was misrepresented in government propaganda with far-reaching implications. To flesh out the implications I construct a translingual history of "brainwashing" that brings together mythmaking and paranoid fantasies across the Cold War divide. Primary sources include *The Final Battle for the Soul, After the Final Battle*, and *Special Pardons 1959*.

Poetic justice, in its usual sense, refers to an unrealistic plot resolution in fiction that satisfies readerly yearnings for justice. Here the term is stretched to include the poetic license taken to accommodate the unnatural and the implausible in realism. I show in chapter 5 that the tendency was present at the inception of realism's career in China and received official sanction and codification during the socialist period. Socialist realism, in its rejection of bourgeois naturalism, became a cryptic form of unnatural narrative that aimed to capture the magic of collective action. By contrast, the postsocialist boom in magical realist literature resorted to very different and overtly unnatural tropes in order to represent structural violence at the low justice level as a direct consequence of high justice pursuits. Moving from a socialist utopian parable to two gritty novels about China's notorious family planning policy, I argue that the swerve from socialist realism to magical realism is one form of unnatural narrative reacting against another form of unnatural narrative for the sake of truth and justice. Primary sources include "The Foolish Man Who Moved the Mountains," *Li Shuangshuang*, *Frog*, and *The Dark Road*.

In the Anthropocene, humans have become a geological force. Environmentalists have long made a case for the integrity, dignity, and rights of the nonhuman—animals, plants, rivers, forests, and the atmosphere—all of which are in peril if we cannot include them in our emotional life and moral deliberation. What do we owe our fellow inhabitants of the planet? Do we need to make animals our equals or grant them legal personhood in order to care for them? What happens when we enlarge our moral circle and run up against the trophic order? Can the high justice of environmentalism be reconciled with the low justice of human and animal rights? In chapter 6, I take up these questions and propose a pragmatist model of multispecies justice that I tease out of close engagements with several works of "multispecies fiction" from the Chinese and Taiwanese literary repertoires. Primary sources include *The Tibetan Mastiff*, *The Stolen Bicycle*, *A Grassland Zoo*, *The Chinese Tiger*, and "The World's Most Desolate Zoo."

In the conclusion I draw some broad observations about the different justice orientations in China and the United States. In contrast to the liberal conception of horizontal justice, the Chinese regime of justice is a vertical structure of high and low justice. Because political legitimacy rests on moral supremacy, the proceduralism of low justice is necessarily curtailed so that the Party-state itself must be called on to deliver substantive, retributive justice. Each time a case or petition ascends the judicial-bureaucratic ladder, the Party-state further consolidates its claim as the ultimate guarantor of justice. I use the most well-known legal drama of modern China, *Qiuju Goes to Court*, to illustrate the vertical orientation of the Chinese legal imagination. Lastly, I briefly consider the curious place of the Tokyo Trial in global popular culture and what it says about divergent regimes of justice.

* * *

In a spirited essay on the history of law in China, Su Li (2007, 131–48) takes issue with the etymology of the character for law (*fa*) that appears in nearly every law textbook in China. In its ancient form, the theory goes, *fa* 灋 consists of three parts: a water radical on the left, a character denoting a mythical beast (*zhi₂*) on the upper right and the character *qu₂* (delete, eject) on the lower right. Water, being inherently level, stands for fairness. The beast is endowed with the uncanny ability to tell the guilty from the innocent and uses its unicorn to expel the culprit. Su Li believes that this is later generations' anachronistic wishful thinking. Modern scholars have carelessly perpetuated this specious etymology because of its appeal to the modern sensibility, further likening the calm, limpid, and all-pervasive quality of water to law's stability, clarity, and generality. Su Li suggests that one can very well follow a contrarian line of deduction. Water, he notes, is not always level or calm or clear. It is just as plausible that it is its propensity to flow from higher to lower ground that makes water an apt metaphor for the top-down application of positive law.

My interest in this book is not etymological, but it may be safe to say that justice as fairness has always had a grassroots appeal, even if it is downplayed in written culture produced by the elites. In folk expression, water does seem to be associated with the leveling effect of law. Consider the scene in the 2014 film *The Case of Huang Kegong* (discussed in greater detail in chapter 3) depicting a peasant couple's divorce case. The husband has found new love and requests a divorce, invoking the new marriage freedom guaranteed by the CCP Border Region government. The judge forthrightly grants the divorce but stipulates an equal division of household property to the consternation of the husband. He protests that he is the sole rightful owner of the property: "Your Honor, you must hold this bowl of water steady and level!" (*Daren, ni kedei yiwanshui yao duanping a*).[10] In any case, even if the ancients may not have valued fairness, later generations have come to regard it as a hypergood, hence motivating the etymological lore. Today, no one can dispute the centrality of fairness as a pillar of low justice in the Chinese legal imagination. My deployment of high justice and low justice is thus an effort to think historically as well as comparatively, and to break the habit of fixing our analytical sight on the flat, even horizons of law.

As I will elaborate throughout the book and more explicitly in the conclusion, my goal is to expand our thinking about justice from a two-dimensional plane to a three-dimensional space, and to entertain possibilities of justice not merely as a good that can be extended horizontally to those on the margins of society through the enlargement of the franchise, moral as well as legal. To reinvoke the three-body metaphor, when justice gravitates upward toward morality, we are in the realm of high justice governed by questions of legitimacy, righteousness, and harmony; when it gravitates downward toward law, we are in the realm of low justice powered by the quest for fairness, rights, and redress. To overcome previous blind spots, A Certain Justice pays greater attention to visions of justice that go beyond equality and fairness among juridical subjects (low justice) and aspire to revolutionary change, common good, and mercy (high justice). Whether high justice and low justice can be reconciled, whether high justice necessarily stymies low justice, whether high justice can come at too high a price—these are questions that no legal doctrines can resolve. One may, however, find intimations of an answer in literature. Or so I hope to show.

1
High Justice

You just have to let this unfairness continue to be unfair.

MAI JIA

Is crime fiction possible only in a liberal democracy? If one has in mind detective fiction, the answer is mostly yes, but spy fiction is truly international. In China, detective fiction is rather like a malnourished stepchild next to the favored and perennially popular genre of spy fiction. The hierarchical logic of high justice and low justice, as I hope to show in this opening chapter, is behind the disparity. What follows is a history of how this pair of concepts play out in modern Chinese literary and film history. It also doubles as a political history of Chinese spy fiction.

Modern detective fiction flowered briefly in China in the first half of the twentieth century (Kinkley 2000; Peng 2019; Wei 2020). Once the Chinese Communist Party (CCP) came to power in 1949, the genre was deemed a misfit and banned. The spy thriller, however, was given a space to thrive. In her brief genealogy tracing the contemporary boom in spy thrillers to their first flowering at the inception of the Cold War, Dai Jinhua (2010) marvels at the genre's exceptional status in the history of art and literature in the People's Republic of China (PRC): Throughout the socialist era the spy thriller was the only genre fiction granted a breathing space under the chokehold of the CCP's strident cultural policy, claiming prominence in the small corpus of "red classics" and even managing to take over two of the eight "revolutionary model works" (*yangbanxi*) during the Cultural Revolution (1966–76). It was also the genre of choice of hand-copied underground novels (Henningsen 2021, chap. 3) and of foreign films imported from the socialist bloc. In the new millennium, the genre has undergone a renaissance and cornered a large share of the entertainment market in the form of best sellers, primetime television dramas, and blockbuster films. Detective fiction, by contrast, has returned but remains a marginal concern. What drives the contrasting fates of the two sister genres?

In Euro-American literary history, the spy novel came of age about half a century later than did detective fiction and, more than any other genre, piggybacked on the geopolitical history of the twentieth century, flourishing alongside the British Empire, the two world wars, and the Cold War. In Luc Boltanski's formulation, whereas detective fiction chronicles crime in a society basically at peace, the espionage story offers glimpses of war, but war under the cover of apparent peace—on the premise that states never cease to be at war, for "it is part of the very essence of a state to be at war" (2014, 127). More specifically, it is the modern nation-state system with underlying imperial ambitions that furnishes the backdrop and impetus for spy thrillers. One might well extend Peter Brooks's (1994) thesis on the tight embrace between melodrama and revolution and regard the spy thriller as the romance of the state. Not surprisingly, twentieth-century China, wracked by wars and revolutions, was awash in melodramas and spy stories, while detective fiction languished.[1]

In this chapter, I advance the thesis that the Chinese spy thriller is the romance of the state par excellence. Moving from the genre's golden age during the Seventeen Years (between the founding of the PRC in 1949 and the outbreak of the Cultural Revolution in 1966) to its new millennial boom, I argue that its enduring salience has everything to do with the centrality of high justice in the People's Republic. More specifically, it is the cultural expression of the Maoist ideology of permanent revolution, the national-security state that emerged out of socialist state building and the geopolitics of the Cold War, and China's recent bid for world power status. Espionage fiction posits a state perpetually at war with shadowy, conspiratorial internal and external enemies and showcases its corps of technocrats and secret agents defending the country through iron discipline, professional brilliance, Machiavellian intelligence, debonair panache, and self-abnegating patriotism. The genre enchants the state as a sovereign power replete with arcana imperii and elevates the reason of state as the locus of august, sublime high justice.

I draw on the sociology of literature, political theory, moral philosophy, and cognitive psychology to reflect on the moral status of secrets and lies, the cognitive challenges of duplicity and suspicion, the relationship between justice and loyalty, and the moral foundations of statism. I also highlight a pragmatic tradition of statecraft that might be traced back to *The Art of War* and that informs the technocratic statist ideology animating contemporary spy thrillers. Moreover, by comparing the Chinese spy thriller to its Western counterpart, particularly the James Bond franchise, I reflect on the problem of freedom vis-à-vis the imperative of national security.

"The Center Cannot Hold"

The military victory of the Chinese Communist Party over its nemesis the Nationalists (a.k.a. Kuomintang/Guomindang or KMT/GMD) in the civil war of 1945–49 and the founding of the People's Republic in 1949 have conventionally been characterized as a communist revolution that installed a radical Marxist regime bent on enforcing the dictatorship of the proletariat by dispossessing and liquidating the propertied classes.[2] The new state saw itself as the institutional expression of the collective will of the newly "turned over" (*fanshen*) laboring classes. Such is the official definition of *guojia* (the state) in the authoritative lexicographical dictionary *Cihai*, citing Lenin,[3] but it is a highly reductive one. Michael Mann (1984) argues that the modern state is an autonomous power, distinct from the power of economic classes, military elites, and ideological movements. The power of the state takes two forms: despotic and infrastructural. In the former sense, governing elites are able to undertake a range of actions without routine negotiation with civil society groups; in the latter sense, state apparatuses are able to penetrate civil society and implement policies logistically throughout the polity. While liberal democratic states are relatively weak in despotic power and strong in infrastructural power, authoritarian states like contemporary China are strong in both. In *longue durée* history, the infrastructural power of the state has grown steadily, culminating in today's welfare, biopolitical, and surveillance state, but despotic power has had a more checkered history.

Mann identifies three sources of the state's autonomous power: its necessity, multiple functions, and territorial centralization. First, all complex societies require a monopolistic center of binding rule-making authority. Secondly, the personnel of a central state are in charge of keeping internal order, providing military defense, maintaining communications infrastructure, and undertaking economic redistribution. They are able to discharge these tasks because, and this is the third source, "only the state is inherently centralized over a delimited territory over which it has authoritative power" (Mann 1984, 198). Because they have a different territorial scope, states cannot simply be the instruments of class interests or ideological movements, nor are they coterminous with military power, despite modern states' monopoly of organized violence. As a distinctive sociospatial organization, the state accrues autonomous power through a two-phase process, from the growth of territorial centralization to civil society's loss of control over it.

Roberto Unger makes a similar point regarding the state's need to project neutrality and impartiality vis-à-vis civil society groups and sectional interests: "Only an entity that somehow stands above the conflicting groups can both limit the powers of all the groups and pretend to the posture of impartiality, impersonality, or providential harmony which sanctions its claim to their allegiance. [...] The state, which is the child of the social hierarchy, must also be its ruler; it must be distinct from any one social group in the system of domination and dependence. Yet it has to draw its staff and its purposes from groups that are part of this system" (Unger 1976, 60–61). He argues that positively formulated and publicly proclaimed rules—what he calls "bureaucratic law"—are the most effective way of asserting the state's autonomy from society. Likewise, Mann acknowledges that states throughout history have represented the interests of dominant groups, but they must not appear to do so or they will lose all claim to distinctiveness and legitimacy. The state justifies and upholds its autonomous power by "a claim to 'universalism' over its territories, a detachment from all particularistic, specialised ties to kin, locality, class, Church, etc." (Mann 1984, 204). Or else it must resort to brute violence, usually the last gasp of a failed state.

This was the fate that befell the Nationalist regime, which had lost its autonomy and legitimacy well before it lost the civil war on the battleground. At least this is how the newly minted CCP state wished to cast the historical verdict—not only in official history, but also in countless literary, dramatic, and filmic representations of the Old Society (*jiu shehui*) or pre-1949 China. Consider the 1965 film *Blood Monument* (*Xuebei*) (Gao Heng 1965) about a peasant's hellish journey through the Republican judicial system under the Nationalists. Lin Youshan, a farmhand who at the beginning of the film has just realized his dream of owning the few acres of cropland that he and his family have reclaimed from wilderness through backbreaking labor. In an early scene we see him bring the land deed home to his family to general rejoicing as they gaze ecstatically at the big red official seal atop the flimsy piece of paper. The young master of a rich landlord family, however, loses no time in claiming the fields as theirs and peremptorily tears up the deed. In the scuffle he also kills Lin's infant. Lin takes the dead infant to the county courthouse and ends up being locked up himself on trumped-up charges. His wife takes their case to the provincial high court in Hangzhou and is given false hope by a careerist judge who is quickly given a promotion and transferred elsewhere through the machination of the landlord family, with its powerful connections in the Nationalist government. The young master brings a posse to the Lin household and burns down the house. The wife is killed in the conflagration. Lin, accompanied by his daughter, treks to the capital city of Nanjing to cry injustice outside the supreme court, only to be forcibly taken to an insane asylum. Ten years later he emerges from the asylum an utterly broken man. He inscribes the words "Never forget the bottomless wrongs!" on a rock before dropping to his death.

Tendentious as it may be, this film came under attack in the leadup to the Cultural Revolution and was never publicly exhibited, possibly owing to its suggestion that the Nationalist judicial system had enough legitimacy, however false, to have misled a man to persist for so long before seeing through it. Nonetheless, watching a film like this, the audiences are to shudder at the ancien régime's ruthless despotism and vow vengeance on behalf of Lin and all who shared his fate. But more importantly they are to recognize the regime's true nature as an instrument by which the three colossal "mountains"—feudalism, crony capitalism, and imperialism— pressed down on the prone bodies of the suffering masses. In becoming beholden to and imbricated with these parasitical interests, the Nationalist regime was incapable of discharging the basic functions of a modern state and barely bothered to maintain a facade of impartiality. The center could not hold, and things fell apart: The country fell prey to warlordism, foreign aggression, economic crises, and infrastructural decay. As the museum docent in the film's frame narrative intones to a group of young visitors while pointing to the rock inscription, or "blood monument": "In the Old Society, people's lives were engulfed by raging floods and fires."

The vast majority of representations about the Old Society depict the misery and suffering of the common people under Nationalist rule in the "speaking bitterness" (suku) mode that frames Blood Monument. These works are unabashedly melodramatic, trafficking in a Manichean worldview and an excess of pathos. Their unremittingly maudlin tone is offset only by the fervor of military combat in the denouement and the dawning of a new age. In this tenebrous world, the state either is absent, leaving the people to the predations of foreign aggressors, or bears down on the people with its own talons and claws in the persons of corrupt officials and local tyrants. Its bureaucratic laws and judicial apparatuses are entirely a sham, the better to subjugate the powerless on behalf of the ruling classes.

A small repertoire of films made in the Seventeen Years (1949–66), however, trains their attention not on the common people, but on CCP underground activists in the "white zone" (baiqu) during the war years. The goal is, as always, to expose the corruption and illegitimacy of the ancien régime. The exiled Nationalist regime headquartered in the inland

city of Chongqing is casually conflated with the Nanjing-based collabo-
rationist regime, and both tend to be lumped together with the Japanese
invaders. The setting is usually urban and the protagonist an educated and
polished Communist agent who is part of a rhizomatic underground network engaged in a range of espionage and subversive activities. *Struggles
in an Ancient City* (*Yehuo chunfeng dou gucheng*) (Yan Jizhou 1963), for example, begins with the Communist agent's arrival in a Japanese-controlled
northern city as Commissar Yang. Once ensconced in a safe house, he
immediately sets about directing the underground activists to infiltrate a
puppet regiment and successfully incite a mutiny to coincide with a Communist guerrilla offensive. In *Everlasting Radio Signals* (*Yong bu xiaoshi
de dianbo*) (Wang Ping, 1958), Commissar Li crosses the war front from
Yan'an to Shanghai, where he adopts the cover of a merchant and becomes
the crucial link, via his telegraphic equipment hidden in the attic, between
Yan'an and a CCP underground cell, to the consternation and fury of the
Japanese and their Chinese toadies.

Films like these perform the ideological work of delegitimizing the
Nationalist state. They show that its despotic power was wholly arbitrary
and oppressive because it was wielded by a venal and feckless cadre bent
on serving private or nepotistic interests rather than the public good. They
also show that its infrastructural power was entirely perverted to serve
extractive purposes and was thus utterly incapable of maintaining a grip
on society and absurdly oblivious to the not-so-surreptitious plotting and
scheming going on right under its nose.[4] By contrast, the Communist underground was staffed by exceptionally steely, upright men and women
(barring the occasional weak-kneed traitor) who were sheltered, succored,
and protected by the salt of the earth, the righteous masses who needed
little persuasion to make common cause with the clandestine fighters. The
message is clear: The Nationalist state was a failed state and deserved to
be toppled.

The CCP regime's self-representation, needless to say, is the diametric
opposite. A much larger portion of espionage films produced in the Seventeen Years concern the foiling of a sabotage or terrorist plot by Nationalist secret agents against the New Society (*xin shehui*). That is to say, the
1949 divide determines whether the spies are Communist or Nationalist.
The Invisible Front (*Wuxing de zhanxian*, 1949), the first film in which the
Nationalists are the spies,[5] begins with a quotation from Mao: "Although
armed enemies have been vanquished, those without guns are still here
and are bound to fight us to the bitter end. We cannot afford to be negli-
gent." Mao made these remarks at a Party central committee meeting in
March 1949, half a year before he stood on Tiananmen Gate to declare the

founding of the new republic on October 1. Thereafter he would sound the alarm about hidden enemies again and again in speeches and writings. About a week prior to the momentous October day, he warned: "The imperialists and domestic reactionaries will certainly not take their defeat lying down and they will struggle to the last ditch. After there is peace and order throughout the country, they will still engage in sabotage and create disturbances in various ways and will try every day and every minute to stage a comeback. This is inevitable, beyond all doubt, and under no circumstances must we relax our vigilance."[6] In a blunt and peremptory manner, Mao's words established the paranoid style of Chinese politics for the next three decades. They also provided the political rationale for the continuous production of spy movies as well as the banning of detective stories.

To understand why detective fiction stood so little chance in Mao's China, let's review the genre's origins in the West. According to Boltanski (2014), detective fiction rose in tandem with the liberal capitalist state of law, which aspired to guarantee a reality more or less rational and rule bound. Crime was a disturbance, a challenge, and a mystery that had to be resolved in order for that reality to be restored. The detective is usually not an agent of the state but a private or ad hoc investigator who takes liberty with the law and is given wide latitude by the police. The greatest challenge confronting the detective is determining the motive behind the crime, the dark continent of the human heart that points to a nebulous, aleatory world beyond the one visible to the state of law. Crime mysteries presuppose the basic social condition of peace, in which human motives ramify like the tangled undergrowth in a jungle, whereas in a state of war, the heart constricts in fear, and motives become simplified, symmetrical, and predictable.

For the most part, detective fiction operates in the low justice register and is fond of sinking its teeth deep into the entanglements of right and wrong among formally equal citizens in a state of law. High justice, on the other hand, is the province of espionage fiction, which goes all out to dramatize the high-wire fight to defend the state against its internal and external enemies. That the two genres remain largely distinct in the West is indicative of a political-legal tradition that tries to wall off the state at war from the state of law and prevent the pursuit of high justice from impinging on the pursuit of low justice. In other words, the rule of law is all about putting a fence around the state so that its imperatives—the so-called reason of state—do not end up abrogating or annulling the rights and liberties of the citizens. For this reason, the detective genre in the West has a longer pedigree, boasts a bigger cast of practitioners, and enjoys a wider readership than the spy thriller, which came on the scene about a century later and thrived primarily during the interwar decades and the ensuing Cold War era.

The Communist state arose from a baptism of fire and had good reasons to keep the embers of war aglow. It is no surprise that the spy thriller became a favored genre alongside melodrama and hagiography. When Mao declared a permanent state of war, he was essentially rendering crimes and criminals transparent to the state so that, as Jeffrey Kinkley puts it, "one knows the motive for the crime without even knowing whodunit" (2000, 250). Kinkley marks the end of the detective genre in China as when "spies, border infiltrators, and enemies gone underground after their defeat in the Civil and Korean Wars" replaced common criminals in films of the Seventeen Years (245–46). Thereafter, no work of fiction revolved around common crimes committed by ordinary citizens, and the press did not report on crime, for "socialism was not supposed to produce it" (2). Also tellingly, the new regime did not promulgate a formal criminal code until 1979, thirty years after coming to power. Until then, the twenty-one articles of the Statute on Punishments for Counterrevolutionary Activity (1951) were "the closest legal text the PRC had to a criminal code" (Mühlhahn 2009, 179). Counterrevolution, the catchall for political crimes of all stripes, was abolished only in 1997 (Hu Jianmiao 2019).

In a spy story, there is no such thing as a random crime. Any crime is inherently political, targeting the body politic rather than individuals, whatever the actual means and tactics. In other words, it pertains to high justice rather than low justice. Spies may maim and kill ordinary citizens, but their objective is never simply life or property. They aim to undermine the legitimacy and moral supremacy of the regime. In Hannah Arendt's terms, they are the "objective enemies" (1968, 424) of the state, which must bear down on them with all its despotic might, without the impediment of legal niceties. Spy fiction is all about the state, about its validity as a centralized sociospatial organization uniquely capable of governance and defense, about its existential struggle for survival. Detective fiction, on the contrary, is almost exclusively about low justice, about whether a social system can guarantee fairness in the adjudication of personal right and wrong, about how the liberal state of law can defend its version of reality against law breakers who are more of a nuisance than an existential threat.

When the Soviet Union tried to compete with the West on the latter's home turf of crime fiction, it developed a formula that was followed closely by writers across the Communist bloc. In Carlos Uxó's summary, the formula includes "the setting of criminal activities in foreign countries, the emphasis on collective work and austerity, the complete absence of investigators outside the organs of state security, the bipolar view of the world, or the conception of any crime as an attack on the state" (Allan et al. 2020, 392). These features are also the bread and butter of Chinese spy fiction, with the exception of the foreign setting. China did not fight the world wars outside its traditional homeland, so the state at war was a state fighting either foreign invasions or internal enemies. Unlike the Soviet agent in Iulian Semyonov's *Seventeen Moments of Spring* (1969) who infiltrates the SS and helps defeat the Nazis, Chinese Communist agents infiltrate the Nationalist high command instead and cause it to implode. Alternatively, foreign agents infiltrate the socialist homeland and are ferreted out in the nick of time. The key is the thorough eclipse of common crime by crime against the state, or low justice by high justice.

In the counterespionage stories of the early socialist period, mystery and suspense are rarely the point though by no means absent. Unlike in detective fiction in which the identity of the culprit is withheld from both the rest of the cast (especially law enforcement agents) and the readers, the enemy agents are usually fully or partially identified at the outset. This is accomplished by any combination of techniques: a label (such as *guote* or Nationalist spy) in the opening credits; a casting choice that signals this identity with unattractive features, rebarbative manners, and skulking comportment; a brief scene in which a sinister plot is hatched before our eyes. The state may not know who these individuals are specifically in a given situation, but their existence is never in doubt. And the general thrust of their plots holds little surprise either, which is to subvert and sabotage the new state by stealing vital supplies and intelligence; by blowing up a factory, a bridge, or a dam on a politically significant date such as May Day or National Day; or, as in *Ten O'Clock on National Day* (*Guoqing shidianzhong*), by setting off chaos and mayhem in Tiananmen Square during National Day celebrations. The only question is how: how will they go about operationalizing their nefarious schemes, and how will the police outfox them through superior intelligence (in all senses of the word) and neutralize them in the final showdown.

The only film made in this period that comes close to a detective story is the exception that proves the rule. Beginning with its title, *The Murder Case of Xu Qiuying* (*Xu Qiuying anjian*) (Yu Yanfu 1956), the film follows the format and stylistic convention of the detective genre fairly closely until the final third of the plotline (figure 1.1). When the eponymous character is found dead on a river islet, all evidence points to her jealous and hotheaded former boyfriend. But as any seasoned reader of whodunits knows well, the most obvious suspect is usually the least likely one, however damning the evidence. The police investigators also know better than

FIGURE 1.1: Posters for *The Murder Case of Xu Qiuying* (Yu Yanfu 1956, Changchun Film Studio).

to swoop down on the hapless fellow. The viewers are kept in the dark about the identity of the real murderer and motive, and they are invited to tag along as the police sedulously follow every lead and brainstorm on the next step. The film even deploys the trick of partially shielding the ratiocinative process of the detective officer so as to heighten the suspense: when examining a footprint left in the ex-boyfriend's room after his apparent suicide, the officer whispers something inaudibly into an assistant's ear. Slowly but surely, what appears to be a romantic triangle case begins to take on a darker hue. Once the least likely character turns out, to our surprise, to be the number one accomplice and key link of a spy ring, the film jettisons all pretense of a murder mystery and shifts gears to the espionage mode: the murderer is revealed to be a Nationalist spy dispatched from Taiwan to prepare the ground for the Nationalist recovery of the mainland during the Korean War.

Introducing the culprit out of the blue so late in the game clearly breaches the contract of the detective genre, but here it serves as a reminder that no crime in the socialist state can be a simple crime of passion and that the true enemy is necessarily exogenous. As a directive from the higher-up warns, never rule out the possibility of a political crime— later this hypervigilance would be condensed in the expression *shanggang shangxian* (politicization or political escalation). The possibility is adumbrated in the detail of the murdered woman's place of employment: the war logistics department of the municipal government of a northeastern city that is at the forefront of the mobilization drive for the Korean War.

We learn that she was being coerced by the enemy to sabotage the war effort and that it was her wavering that sealed her fate. In the end low justice is served in the apprehension of the murderer and the vindication of the wrong done to the victim (and consolation for the victim's mother). But more importantly, high justice is served in the foiling of the enemy's evil plans and the successful prosecution of the war—symbolized by a rapidly moving train carrying China's volunteer troops into the far horizon.

This film is based on a true crime and wrongful conviction case that spanned the entire Mao period and beyond. In 1948 in the northeastern city of Harbin, newly under CCP control, Zhao Jieshan (Xu Qiuying's prototype), a government clerk working in a cultural bureau, was shot dead one evening near the Songhua River. The police investigated several of her suitors but got nowhere as all of them had valid alibis. A few years later at the urgings of Zhao's aggrieved father, the police reopened the case, this time in the midst of the nationwide crackdown on counterrevolution. They homed in on Zhao's girlfriend Shao Yukui and dug up the Shao family's extensive albeit low-level involvement in the former Nationalist regime. They rounded up Shao, her two brothers, and her brother-in-law. Shao was pregnant and near term at the time. Under duress she gave in and confessed to the murder of Zhao, alleging that the murder was to silence Zhao after she tried to pull out of the Nationalist spy ring run by the Shao siblings. The story was widely reported in the press, and the film adaptation was a national sensation. However, Shao immediately began to protest her innocence by writing letters from jail.

In 1956, a new investigation revealed the many discrepancies in the original case, but the exculpatory report was killed by authorities concerned about political blowback. One official allegedly roared: "This case is known all across the country. All the major newspapers have reported it. A book has been written about it. There're even a comic book and a movie. Does it do any good to overturn it?" (Shiwen Lejian 2020). By now the Anti-Rightist campaign was in full swing, and scores of personnel connected with the case were implicated. Although Shao continued her letter-writing campaign, no one was willing to stick their neck out for her. In 1959, one of her brothers and her brother-in-law were executed; the other brother was given a seven-year prison sentence (he later committed suicide); she herself was sentenced to death with a two-year reprieve. Her husband divorced her and disappeared with their son. It was not until 1987 that Shao's wrongful conviction was finally overturned and she was released from prison (Yu Gang 2020). While wrongful conviction cases were all too common in Mao's China, the Shao siblings' victimization was a direct case of politically "objective" enemies being scapegoated for common crime, of high justice taking priority over low justice. Note that the film made two important changes to foist the high justice framework on the case: the timing was pushed forward by two or three years from 1948 to the Korean War, and Zhao/Xu's workplace was changed from a cultural bureau to a war logistics department. I dwell on this film at some length because its generic shape-shifting midcourse from common crime detection to counterespionage exemplifies the near total eclipse of low justice by high justice, so much so that the space for low justice was practically nil.

In the two earliest counterespionage films, *The Invisible Front* (1949) and *The Might of the People* (*Renmin de juzhang*, 1950), the enemy agents actually succeed in their dastardly plots and leave a string of factories in smoldering rubble (as registered in screaming newspaper headlines). In no subsequent films are enemy agents permitted to get that far before they are rounded up and subjected to swift revolutionary justice. In *Hidden Sentry in Canton* (*Yangcheng anshao*) (Lu Jue 1957), a spy ring plots something slightly unusual: to coerce a foreign-trained doctor to defect to Hong Kong and join a US-sponsored delegation to the UN to denounce CCP brutality and repression. The doctor has a private practice because he is reluctant to work in a state hospital for fear of being investigated for his past service in the Nationalist army. A public security officer infiltrates the spy ring, but an element of crime detection is preserved by the withholding of the ringleader's identity. With the cooperation of the doctor's wife and eventually the doctor himself, the police follow the conspirators unto an ocean liner, where they are corralled and subdued. Hand-to-hand combat generates much of the climactic excitement, and a ticking time bomb is thrown in for an extra measure of suspense. To top it all off, and again in a nod to detective conventions, the ringleader turns out to be the least likely suspect, the one hiding in plain sight all along.

In addition to the residual pleasure of mystery and suspense, *Hidden Sentry in Canton* also offers another kind of pleasure rare in socialist cinema: audiovisual displays of sumptuous bourgeois lifestyle. In contrast to the misery fest that is the mainstay of socialist cinema, here the viewers are treated to well-appointed villas and apartments, expensive-looking antiques and bric-a-brac, stylishly dressed women (if verging on vampish), swinging jazz and sentimental ballads, and foreign liquor, cigars, and coffee. Although these things are clearly framed as holdovers from the Old Society, the need to situate the enemies plausibly in their "natural," decadent milieus acknowledges a facet of life that is alluring and yet contravenes the reality as underwritten by the state.

If the spy thriller reassures us with its inevitable ending by which the state substantiates its claim to institute a new reality that is rationalized, regulated, and securitized, it also opens up, through the obsessive return to the conspiracy plot, what Boltanski calls "the gap between lived reality and instituted reality." The nation-state is a political utopian project distinct from previous state forms: It aspires to be more than a higher-order power subject to its own morality, or reason of state. Rather, it "claims to know, control and, to a certain extent, shape the reality within which the populations placed under its authority [lead] their lives" (Boltanski 2014, 17). It thus grounds its legitimacy not only in moral supremacy as did the imperial Chinese state, but also in epistemological supremacy—a dream shared by all high modernist states according to James Scott (1998). It aspires to encompass the entire nation under its purview, with perfect legibility and transparency. The pockets of luxury, vice, and conspiracy depicted in spy films and the idea that these pockets are sustained by exogenous forces seeking to subvert the new regime thus call into question that very aspiration. Boltanski writes: "On the one hand, there is the logic of the *territory*, a unified space bounded by borders enclosing a homogeneous population that the state is expected to protect; on the other hand, there is the logic of *flows* that are unknown to the legitimate inhabitants and that the state is unable to prevent, forces that flow throughout the territory and put it at risk" (2014, 22).

Perhaps the most powerful metonym for these forces of flow is the electrical and radio telegraphy that enables scattered enemy cells to coordinate action with their quartermasters overseas and with one another. Incessantly chirping and pulsating, its nonsensical signals (to the untrained ear) conjure a conspiratorial parallel universe and demand a paranoid state of mind: Appearance may deceive, and nothing is merely what meets the eye or ear. Intercepting a telegram is often the first step in breaking the chain of secret communication and hence the conspiracy itself. The trope of the war of telecommunications would be extensively exploited in the spy thrillers of the new millennium (we will turn to this in the next section). For now, suffice it to point out that at one level the paranoid state of mind works well to bolster the legitimacy of the state because only the state can see through the enemies' camouflage and root them out, but at another level it is also a constant reminder that the society as constituted by a multiplicity of individuals exceeds the state's grasp. Especially at the grassroots level, there are simply too many nooks and crannies that are out of the state's sightline and beyond the tendrils of its security apparatuses. This is exactly what the enemy exploits: Most of the active cells operate at this level, with spies adopting the cover of shop manager, soothsayer, innkeeper, barber, clerk, typist, housewife, maid, and so on. Never are they able to penetrate the Party echelon itself or high-level administrative offices.

Still, the enemy's ability to disappear into the hoi polloi makes it difficult to maintain Mao's distinction between the "two contradictions": nonantagonistic contradictions among the people (*renmin neibu maodun*) and antagonistic ones between the people and their enemies (*diwo maodun*). Casting everyone under suspicion is the stock-in-trade of detective fiction and is evocative of the liberal state of law that presumes a kind of "equality with respect to crime" (Boltanski 2014, 22) as an unacknowledged basis for the hallowed principle of equality before the law. The socialist state, having rejected the bourgeois principle of formal legal justice, cannot avail itself of this trope. Just as the enemies are "objective," the people are a priori beyond suspicion. Yet when enemy aliens can so easily pass as one of "our own," all bets are off. On stage and on screen, the line between the people and the enemy is strenuously drawn if only to disavow the slippage between the two categories in the incessant unveiling of new targets in political campaigns. Gradually, even the idea that a mushy-headed citizen could be bribed or manipulated into doing the bidding of the enemy is intolerable. As noted before, the detective genre was banned early on, and the spy genre tapered off during the most utopian phase of the socialist era—the Cultural Revolution—except in highly attenuated form. The two model operas that bear some resemblance to early socialist spy films are *Taking Tiger Mountain by Strategy* (*Zhiqu Weihushan*) and *On the Lakefront* (*Shajiabang*). Both, however, avoid the risky premises of the counterespionage story centered on enemy infiltration of the socialist homeland and instead set their drama in the Old Society and in enemy territory. Even so, both works feature relatively unglamorous mise-en-scènes and banish the old standby of a coquettish, nubile female in the enemy camp with whom our hero has to tangle.

Yet ironically, in the political domain, the "unlimited extension of suspicion" (Boltanski 2014, 22) to the personnel of the state, who despite the bureaucratic pecking order are truly equal in terms of their potential to err ideologically, ends up rendering the state exposed and vulnerable. Mao's worry that the state's increasing bureaucratization makes it a hotbed of corruption and a prime target of the "sugar-coated bombs" (*tangyi paodan*) of international conspiracy may not be unfounded, but his repeated campaigns to cleanse the cadre ranks by relying on "mass supervision" (*qunzhong jiandu*) (Andreas 2019) rather than on the building of institutions had the effect of delivering the state to fanatical ideological movements and internecine power struggles, thus magnifying the state's despotic power while paralyzing many of its institutions and their infrastructural capacities. The steady stream of startling denunciations and downfalls of top CCP leaders and state officials cemented the belief that the state had been thoroughly corroded by subterranean, conspiratorial forces, and that it was now the duty of politically awakened activists—the rebels (*zaofanpai*)—to save the nation through another revolution. Revolution became its own justification, no longer just a means to communist utopia, but the end in and of itself (Edelstein 2015).

Mao's permanent revolution essentially painted the Communist state in the same light that it did the ancien régime it had overthrown. The upshot is that the state at the height of the Cultural Revolution lost much of its autonomy and mystique. The so-called main-melody (*zhu xuanlü*) culture in the post-Mao era has been devoted to the reparative project of state building, most notably the remakes of "red classics" and new war epics that seek to shore up the moral and epistemological supremacy of the Party-state. But as I will show in the next section, it is spy fiction that does the heavy lifting of reimagining the state as a surprisingly resilient power that was battered and weakened but not fundamentally vitiated. It does so by positing and consecrating a hidden world of arcana imperii at the core of state power, a kind of deep state that operated by its own imperiously pragmatic reason and remained miraculously unruffled by the political tempests of the Mao years.

"Every Country Has Its Secrets"

Boltanski (2014, chap. 4) divides the history of the spy genre in the West into three phases: The first is the genre's golden age (the first three decades of the twentieth century), which boasts such masters as John Buchan, G. K. Chesterton, and Graham Greene. Under their pens, the British state is blind to a grave threat, but an ordinary citizen like Richard Hannay in *The Thirty-Nine Steps* (Buchan [1915] 1993) rises to the occasion with the assistance of an assortment of common folk and against the obstruction of complacent and incompetent officials. In the second phase, which roughly coincides with World War II and the Cold War, a daredevil intelligence officer in the mold of James Bond ventures out into the troubled world to smash Soviet or rogue terrorist plots and to save humanity from the fate of nuclear annihilation, all the while regaining for Britain its lost imperial glory. By the time writers like John le Carré took up the genre, espionage had begun to lose much of the heroic sheen of the Bond era, inaugurating the third phase. In le Carré's novels, a symmetrical structure governs the opposing intelligence bureaucracies: "Their organizations, their norms, the way they function, their brutality, their scorn for the men they use, manipulate and destroy are similar. [...] There are indeed two different conspiracies, but each is justified only with reference to the other" (Boltanski 2014, 162–63). That is to say, the state itself has become a vast conspiracy and a threat to freedom.

George Orwell's *1984* ([1949] 1984), though not a spy thriller per se and written in an earlier time, takes this idea to a different order of magnitude altogether, whereby a state turns on its own citizenry, mobilizing its formidable apparatuses of surveillance and discipline to subjugate all individuals, state cadre included, in the name of national security and collective happiness. Totalitarianism is thus the unholy alliance between the reason of state and the anarchic forces of technology and capitalism. Postmodern spy thrillers have inherited the Orwellian state of mind and directed their suspicion toward the surveillance state that has emerged in the age of "the war on terror." The paradox is that the state is projected as an all-powerful colossus precisely when throughout the liberal West the despotic power of the state has been in a steady decline, in contradistinction to its deepening infrastructural power. Its capacity for secrecy, too, is imagined to have expanded greatly even as it faces mounting pushback from civil society.

Sissela Bok has examined closely the moral unease that secrets of all kinds provoke in modern life. To begin with, conflicts over secrecy are almost always conflicts over power: "the power that comes through controlling the flow of information" (1984, 19). More specifically, control over secrecy and openness is justified on account of the protection of identity, plans, actions, and belongings: It protects a sense of "the sacredness of the self" (21); it guards plans and projects that require deliberation, creativity, and prolonged work and are open to unpredictability and surprise; and it recognizes certain things as properly belonging to someone more than to others. For these reasons, secrecy is always connected to a sense of sacredness and associated with danger—for those who keep secrets as well as for those wishing to uncover secrets. Bok writes:

> Keepers of secrets can experience the powerful, the forbidden, and the sacred with the same awareness that outsiders have of such secrets as both endangered by and dangerous for those who come too near or who expose them. This experience underlies what I shall call the *esoteric rationale* for protecting what is held sacred and the secrets that partake of it. Invoked far beyond the boundaries of the strictly religious, this rationale inheres in the sense of sacredness that people can have with respect to themselves, their families, their professions, their nations. It serves an indispensable function in protecting these, but it can also deflect moral inquiry through the incentives it offers people to remain in a

childish relationship to secrecy and power. They may then see too many secrets as manifestations of some power that must be obeyed, rather than as a matter that requires the assumption of responsibility and the exercise of judgment. (Bok 1984, 39–40)

Government secrecy, in particular, is justified with the "esoteric rationale" that goes beyond the practical necessity of keeping administrative and military secrets. The rationale is best articulated in the principle of arcana imperii, "secrets of rule" or "mysteries of state," which transfers the aura of sacredness from the arcana ecclesiae of the church, ritual, and the clergy to secular institutions and personnel (Bok 1984, 172). Under the halo of sacrality, the state is said to be governed by an exceptional moral code, and its action cannot be subject to ordinary moral deliberation (Walsh 2020, xvi). Here, ends always justify means: "Rulers may be justified when they lie, cheat, break promises, or even torture" (Bok 1984, 173) as long as they do it in the name of defending society against visible and invisible, internal and external threats. And to do so without undue interference or excessive scrutiny on the part of the public is believed to be of the highest importance. Government secrecy thus provokes profound ambivalence in constitutional polities that prize openness and transparency (Geroulanos 2017, 15; see also Fabre 2022). It is widely deemed a necessary evil that all too easily eludes democratic accountability, and in fiction the esoteric rationale has elicited garden-variety antigovernment conspiracy theories.

Chinese spy thrillers, by contrast, have capitalized on the same esoteric rationale to remystify the state not just as the locus of power and authority, but also as the center of moral gravity and epistemological potency. The state is fantasized as a supra-organism with a tightly woven grid of institutions dedicated to the sole purpose of national security and staffed by a professional cadre proudly detached from civil society and scornful of worldly pursuits. As in many contemporary Western espionage thrillers, the state itself has become a vast conspiracy, but the difference is that here the conspiratorial power of the state is celebrated rather than feared. Nonetheless, under an authoritarian regime that jealously guards its secrets, Chinese spy thrillers face the challenge of dramatizing arcana imperii without risking the charge of "leaking state secrets" or "endangering national security," the all-purpose labels routinely wielded by the state to quell political dissent after the crime of "counterrevolution" was abolished in 1997. Their solution is to revive the formula of "infiltrating the enemy camp" deployed in early socialist spy films but with significant departures.

As noted in the previous section, the older stories may feature a Communist agent or a public security officer assuming a fake identity in order to gain access to critical intelligence or to implode an enemy plot. These stints are ad hoc and temporary, and they entail minimal deceit and dissimulation. The undercover agent rarely has to wade deep into the morass where he or she may be placed in a morally and politically compromising situation, such as having to kill, beat, or betray comrades in order to prove his or her bone fides, or having to partake of the vices in which the enemies wallow, such as extortion, gambling, and whoring, or, in the case of a female agent, having to sleep with a superior. On the whole, Chinese spy fiction seldom spotlights the moral dilemmas that might confront an undercover agent who must dally credibly with repellent enemies or the psychic toll of leading a protracted double life—as addressed by Bok in weighing the pros and cons of undercover police operations (1984, chap. 17). In chapter 2, I extend her inquiry to consider the moral injuries inflicted on subalterns in hierarchies of power. In early socialist spy fiction, however, moral dilemmas do not arise not only because communist faith supposedly inoculates against all manner of temptations, but also because these heroes have already renounced their moral freedom and turned themselves into a fearsome instrument of mortal struggle, a "piercing knife" (*jiandao*) thrust into the heart of the enemy camp.

For women, though, there is always the nagging problem of "pollution": A woman cannot simply revert to her former identity if her assignment has been of a sexual nature. The high moral premium of spying while female is what brings special poignancy to Ding Ling's "When I Was in Xia Village" (1941; in Ding Ling 1989) and Eileen Chang's *Lust, Caution* (2007; first published in 1979, Taiwan; see also H. Lee 2010, 2014). Both texts venture into a fraught territory from which socialist spy fiction cautiously draws back for good reasons. Michael Schoenhals relates that although female agents were occasionally recruited, the "honey trap" method was more or less prohibited after 1949 and resolutely denounced after the Sino-Soviet split once the Soviet reliance on sexual entrapment became widely known (2013, 101–9). All this helps explain the rarity of the honey trap plot in socialist spy fiction. When it does appear, it is always deployed by the enemy and invariably proves futile, because communist faith is essentially bulletproof against all base desires. On the other hand, female Communist agents, if fallen into enemy hands, are not subjected to sexual abuse in order to make their return (if they survive) less problematic.

Underwriting the moral clarity and innocence of undercover operations is the image of a youthful brotherhood in robust moral health waging guerrilla warfare against a rotten incumbent regime. The Communist Party headquartered in Yan'an during the war years projects an image of radical egalitarianism, openness, and plain virtue. Party mythology abounds in anecdotes such as Mao sharing a meal with peasants, and Red Army generals yielding horses to wounded soldiers. The fugitive state has yet to become entrenched in bureaucracy or embroiled in turmoil, still imbued with a luster of unsullied nobility. It is this state that is the primary object of reenchantment in post-Mao spy fiction.[7]

Set mostly in the pre-1949 period, the new spy fiction matches up the Communists and the Nationalists in a symmetrical fashion that greatly exaggerates the personnel and logistical strength of the former. We might consider these stories to be China's proxy Cold War espionage thrillers, which restage, in a temporally displaced guise, old-fashioned cloak-and-dagger intrigues and the high jinks of Cold War–style brinksmanship, largely for the delectation of the generation that missed out on such thrills caught as they were in endless political campaigns. Here, the Communist agent is no longer a grunt officer casually plucked from the ranks by a supervisor and put to the unpleasant task of passing temporarily as a crook. Rather, the hero (usually he) is highly educated, professionally trained, and dapperly attired. His assignment takes him to the heart of the enemy camp where he wins the trust of its top brass and lies low for lengthy stretches of time. Utilizing an infinite reservoir of cunning and wiles and an equally infinite network of auxiliary agents, he manages to make short work of every important move by the enemy, and acting on the intelligence supplied by him, the fugitive Communist state is able to inflict shattering losses on the Nationalists. In sum, the genre has moved much closer to its Western model by positing two rival states more or less equal in organizational strength if not in moral rectitude and ideological certitude. Moreover, in recent years it has become acceptable to leave the CCP out of the picture altogether and focus instead on the rivalry between the Chongqing-based Nationalist regime, led by Chiang Kai-shek, and the Nanjing-based puppet regime, backed by the Japanese.

In the thirty-part serial drama *Undercover* (*Qianfu*) (Jiang Wei 2008), we get for the first time a non–Communist Party member in the lead role (figure 1.2). Yu Zecheng starts out in the Nationalist military intelligence service (Juntong) in Chongqing but defects to the CCP side. Immediately after Japan's surrender in 1945, he is transferred to Juntong's Tianjin station. On paper he is supposed to be a married man (though in truth he is a bachelor grieving for the death of his girlfriend who was responsible for converting him to the Communist cause), so the CCP dispatches a female guerrilla fighter from one of its rural bases to live with him as his nominal wife. The serial's comedic charm derives for the most part from the domestic friction between a suave journeyman spy and an uncouth, blustering, and prideful peasant woman. Under Yu's tutelage, the latter

FIGURE 1.2: The protagonists receiving radio signals in *Undercover* (Jiang Wei 2008, Guangdong Southern Television Station).

matures into a self-possessed and resourceful underground agent, and the show's comedic charm morphs into piquancy as we witness the growing affection between the pretend couple, and Yu's adamant refusal to consummate their love without official approval. The show is a genuine thriller for its ample servings of white-knuckle suspense and danger. Yu manages to survive his organization's multiple attempts at flushing out the internal mole (himself) by deflecting suspicion or framing a pugnacious coworker, all the while using elaborate ruses to deliver vital intelligence to his CCP contact without allowing such leaks to be traced back to himself. The mind games played out in the serial clearly aspire to the kind served up in Western spy thrillers. Enemy agents are no longer naive dupes as in early socialist spy films. They too are constantly hatching schemes to give their side an upper hand in the postwar scramble and the run-up to the civil war, and once they suspect the existence of a mole in their midst, they become monomaniacally obsessed with rooting him out.

Other than a few brief action scenes with chases and shootouts, the serial is mostly confined to interior settings—the platonic couple's apartment, the hero's workplace, and the various locations for clandestine rendezvous. As the viewers are perfectly privy to the identity of the major players, viewing pleasure stems from following the recursive game of mind reading played out through dissembling, bluffing, second-guessing, anticipating, probing, testing, cogitating, and so forth. Lisa Zunshine (2006, 2022) has written extensively about how fictional storytelling utilizes what cognitive psychologists call "theory of mind," or our evolved capacity for divining the mental states of others on the basis of linguistic and behavioral cues. Ordinary social life is inconceivable without the constant exercise of theory of mind, and yet it is also inherently frustrating thanks to the stubborn opacity of other minds. Fiction appeals because it gives us a focused opportunity not only to "try on" different mental states but also to peer into other minds and keep track of mental embedment—who doesn't want whom to know what or who wishes to make whom afraid of what and so forth.[8] Also at play is a related cognitive ability called "metarepresentation," or source monitoring, by which we store the sources of information in our head under varying degrees of advisement, and are prepared to reevaluate the truth value of the information based on new evidence. Metarepresentation is the cognitive muscle that gets a strenuous workout in whodunits, wherein we are urged, by the laws of the genre, to suspect everyone except the detective and to take the utterances of every player under advisement—in full preparation for the final reckoning, when we will revisit these utterances and realign their truth or falsehood with newly revealed motives, stakes, and connections (Zunshine 2006).

In Chinese spy thrillers, the audience also get to flex their metarepresentational muscle albeit in a different condition. On the one hand, the characters engage in high-stakes interactions in which they must execute mind reading amid pervasive uncertainty and dread. On the other hand, the viewers who find themselves commanding the enviable God's point of view must constantly shuttle in and out of the minds of characters in order to enjoy the double pleasure of total access and wending the bog of guesswork. That is to say, viewers need to engage in source monitoring at the same time that they partake of theory of mind exercises alongside the characters. In a hypothetical scenario, viewers must keep in mind that what x tells y is a deliberate lie but that y believes it true and acts on it and that though none of this is missed by z, he eggs y on to achieve his (z's) own ends, which somehow short-circuits x's designs. All the while viewers must also keep in mind that y is taking what x tells her with a grain of salt but is feigning otherwise in order to mislead x or that x knows that y is trying to mislead him but goes along in order to entrap her, not knowing that z is waiting in the wing to finish him off. Within the diegetic world of the espionage story, the spy on "our" side is the keeper of secrets pertaining to the identity and mission of himself and his comrades, while also having access to a great deal of secrets kept by the enemy, either openly or covertly. It is his nemesis the enemy spymaster who is placed in the conventional position of the detective who must suspect everybody, who is set up for the shock of discovering (erroneously of course) that one of his most trusted right-hand men is actually a Communist spy, and who is then obliged to recalibrate his assessments of all his men, thus giving our hero a reprieve and another lease on life.

As viewers, we tag along, monitoring informational sources with the spymaster, and we also monitor his monitoring, mindful that his vigilance is merely a piece in the larger confidence game directed by our hero, who by ideological necessity is incomparably superior in brainpower. All the while we are also busy ping-ponging between our hero's inner world (revealed to us through conversations with his "wife" and contact as well as cinematic close-ups)[9] and the web of lies and decoys he spins all around the bureau with no one (but us) being any the wiser. We pull this off effortlessly thanks to the modular nature of our mind, that is, our ability to encapsulate information in different functional brain modules and hold divergent, sometimes contradictory beliefs. This, in Robert Kurzban's (2010) view, is the cognitive key to resolving psychological puzzles such as willful ignorance, hypocrisy, and self-deception (more in chapter 2).

All this is possible because the antagonist is endowed with full interiority and is capable of sparring mentally with the protagonist. Such recursive mental nesting between the good guys and bad guys is largely absent in early socialist spy fiction. It is this cognitive-aesthetic demand that drives the symmetrical pattern of the new crop of spy thrillers of which *Undercover* is arguably the best specimen. The leveling effect is further reinforced in the serial through the incorporation of another set piece: the spy exchange. Yu Zecheng's only direct contact blows his own cover in an effort to shield Yu; at the same time, a Nationalist spy lying low in Yan'an is outed by Yu's girlfriend. Although it is hinted that the Nationalist spy is a sleeper agent and has yet to do any serious damage, the very acknowledgment that the Communist mecca too is vulnerable to enemy penetration is quite unusual. So is the CCP's willingness to let him go—rather than subjecting him to the summary justice dealt to all captured spies in socialist-era stories. Once back in Tianjin, the returned spy becomes a thorn in Yu Zecheng's side, devising ever more devious traps to test his loyalty, and is responsible for causing the death of Yu's girlfriend, hence inviting the feeling that the exchange has been a costly one.

More than any other element, the topos of spy exchange highlights the separate moral plane on which states set their priorities and calculate their interests *and* the radical moral equivalency of such deliberations. Here, states cavalierly disregard moral and ideological scruples and sit down at the negotiating table to hammer out an expedient agreement so as to minimize losses and prolong the game. In the act of exchange, courtesy is extended to the enemy spy, and one's own is given a hero's welcome. Political pragmatism rules the scene. The pragmatic ethos is in fact the dominant ethos of the spy thrillers of the new millennium, accentuating the Chinese discourse of warcraft represented by Sunzi's terse fifth-century BCE treatise *The Art of War* (*Sunzi bingfa*). The Machiavellian philosophy articulated in this classic text is as much about spycraft as about warcraft, with its urgings for deceit, subterfuge, and winning war without firing a shot. In the final chapter on spying, Sunzi counsels: "None in the whole army are more intimate relations to be maintained than with spies. None should be more liberally rewarded. In no other business should greater secrecy be preserved."[10] Citing *The Art of War*, Brett Woods speaks of a "culture" of espionage "wherein the end not only justifies the means, but also serves as a kind of furtive absolution" that neutralizes "the proscribing nature of espionage" (2008, 7). Cécile Fabre considers Sunzi the most forceful defender of espionage in the ancient world to the extent that he makes it morally obligatory for rulers to shorten wars by acquiring knowledge about their enemies (2022, 14).

Spycraft's general disregard for moral scruples sits uneasily alongside the moral preoccupations of Confucianism, though some of its recommendations are as axiomatic in Chinese culture as Confucian precepts. It is the pragmatic supplement to both the Confucian ideal of governance by moral probity (the Kingly Way) and the Legalist ideal of governance by openly promulgated and universally enforced codes. Feng Xiang contends that Sunzi's treatise should be regarded as part of the Legalist tradition that sees the state as an end that justifies all means and sees stratagem and secrecy as its chief modus operandi: "Victory is ever the sole object and morality is for the birds" (2007, 12). This pragmatist streak gets its most celebrated articulation in Mao's dictum that "political power grows out of the barrel of a gun" (Feng Xiang 2007, 13). Wars are acts of state, which, as Arendt points out, "cannot be bound by legal limitations or moral considerations" because they are "sovereign acts over which no court has jurisdiction" (2003, 38). Hence the congenital toothlessness of international tribunals.

Contemporary spy thrillers carry on this pragmatist tradition by re-enchanting the state—both the fugitive state headquartered in Yan'an and the early socialist state—as the magnetic center of fatal attraction and sublime terror. The name that is practically synonymous with the genre is Mai Jia, dubbed China's Dan Brown, an award-winning and best-selling author who has parlayed his short stint in the military intelligence services in the

1980s into fast-paced, suspenseful, and manically exuberant tales of secrets, intrigues, geniuses, incandescent careers, and stymied lives. He enjoys the honor of being the first living Chinese author to be published by
Penguin Books, which put out his award-winning novels *Decoded* (*Jiemi*,
2002) and *In the Dark* (*Ansuan*, 2003).[11] Together with the science fiction
writer Liu Cixin,[12] Mai Jia broke the drought that had long dogged Chinese genre fiction in terms of recognition from the literary establishment
and lay enthusiasm in overseas markets.

For reasons already mentioned, Chinese spy fiction generally avoids
the most typical scenario of the genre: an agent in the "field" (abroad)
gathering intelligence and breaking conspiracies. Schoenhals's history of
espionage in the PRC forewarns its readers not to expect thrilling tales of
"missions abroad": "agent work in the first eighteen years of the PRC [is]
an aspect of domestic politics" (2013, 4). In stories set in the New Society,
"our" spies stay home and occupy themselves with counterintelligence
against an enemy regime that is either named (the Nationalists in Taiwan)
or anonymized (though it is not difficult to slot in the United States).
However, until *Decoded* and *In the Dark*, all counterespionage dramas are
anchored in either a municipal public security bureau or a PLA (People's
Liberation Army) detachment on the frontiers, and the emphasis is always
on the power of everyday vigilance and police-civilian cooperation rather
than on high-wire intelligence warfare. Secrets in these crowd-sourced
counterespionage operations are the preserve of enemy spies. "Our" side
has nothing to hide.

However, to enchant and mystify the state, it has to become the reposi-
tory of secrets. Accordingly, Mai Jia's early novels are the first to depict a
top-secret state intelligence agency as directly as is permissible. Yet given
the precarious status of security and intelligence organs under Mao, especially during the Cultural Revolution, it is difficult to sustain the fiction of a robust apparatus of covert operations when there were so few
in-country foreigners worthy of spying on and when Mao preferred mass
supervision to keep the bureaucracy in check (Guo 2012; Schoenhals
2013). Mai Jia's subsequent novels have thus all reverted to the much safer
terrain of pre-1949 struggles between the Communists, the Nationalists,
and the Japanese; the most successful of these is *The Message* (2009; *Fengsheng* [2007]).

The top-secret intelligence agency in both *Decoded* and *In the Dark* is
called Special Unit 701, modeled on the KGB. The unit comprises three
divisions: Intercepts, Cryptography, and Covert Operations. Accordingly,
In the Dark has a tripartite structure chronicling respectively the exploits
of the "wind-listeners" (those monitoring enemy telecommunications),

the "wind-readers" (those decrypting ciphers), and the "wind-catchers" (field agents). Again for reasons already stated, the last section is quite flimsy, with few adrenaline-pumped covert operations that are the bread and butter of Western spy thrillers. Here I focus on the first two parts of *In the Dark*, which depict the exploits of the Intercepts and Cryptography divisions of Unit 701.

The secluded compound of Unit 701 is a veritable Foucauldian heterotopia, exclusive, exacting, and exemplary. Most significantly, it is a world where professionalism and pragmatism, not ideology, reign supreme. The temporal frame is pushed back to the 1950s, with the Cold War as the backdrop and the Korean War as the catalyst. The new regime, still consolidating power and expending considerable energy eradicating remnant Nationalist forces and roving bandits, has entered the fray on the Korean Peninsula. The specter of an opportunistic Nationalist offensive looms large (also serving as the backdrop of *The Murder Case of Xu Qiuying*). The geopolitical turn of events provides the perfect impetus for counterespionage scenarios. The two stories here are allegedly told to the narrator (a reporter) after the principal players have been retired for more than ten years and the relevant materials have been declassified.

In the first story, the sudden inexplicable disappearance of all enemy chatter from the airwaves plunges the entire unit into a tense limbo. A nationwide talent hunt is launched. Agent Qian is tasked to track down a peasant youth legendary for his extraordinary auditory endowment. Qian succeeds in bringing the autistic Blind Abing to 701, where he is greeted with doubt and disdain by the rank and file. But the leadership has faith in Qian, and the gamble pays off: In a matter of a few days, Abing's magical ears succeed in finding the majority of the enemy stations and their constantly shifting frequencies on the radio spectrum (figure 1.3). Once again, enemy communications are under surveillance control, and Abing is awarded top honors. Soon afterward he is happily married and expecting a child, only to commit suicide upon finding out that the child is not his—he only has to listen to its cries. The wife pleads her case (that Abing is impotent and that she desperately wants to give him a son) to no avail and is banished.

The second story also starts with a talent-scouting trip, this time undertaken by Director An Zaitian. His target is a female math genius with a suggestive name and a flamboyant personality. Dr. Huang Yiyi (Clingy Huang) is a US-trained mathematician who was among the few dozen scientists invited back to China by Premier Zhou Enlai upon the founding of the People's Republic. This special badge of honor shields her from political persecution despite her nonconformist lifestyle that borders on the

FIGURE 1.3: Abing listening for enemy radio signals in *In the Dark* (Liu Yunlong 2005, Guangxi Television Station).

sluttish. She falls head over heels in love with An Zaitian, a dashing widower, and follows him to 701 fully intent on conquering him. An fends off her advances and tries to get her focused on cracking an especially tough Nationalist cipher called RECOVERY. Believing that she can finally win An's heart when RECOVERY is decoded, she pours her heart and soul into it and succeeds at long last, only to be spurned by An again, not knowing that An's wife is still living and working as a field agent abroad (a secret above her pay grade). A shattered Huang shacks up with a married man in another department and before long dies in an ignominious manner— falling to her death in a squat toilet, an accident possibly engineered by the adulterous man's wife.

What is remarkable about these two episodes of *In the Dark* is the fact that the two central characters, Blind Abing and Huang Yiyi, are highly idiosyncratic and ill fit the conventional mold of Communist heroes. Indeed neither is a Communist, and neither professes the desire to join the Party, as is requisite in earlier bildungsromans in which the path to political sainthood must clear the threshold of Party membership. Unit 701 is a heterotopia that seems uniquely freed of political and ideological distractions. The leaders all have professional credentials coupled with practical wisdom gleaned from years of revolutionary praxis in the

FIGURE 1.4: Unrequited love in *In the Dark* (Liu Yunlong 2005, Guangxi Television Station).

underground. No one is clearly identified as a commissar or Party branch secretary—a ubiquitous figure in socialist realist works. Abing is swiftly inducted into the service and granted access to the most restricted part of the compound before a proper background check is completed and before the higher-ups greenlight his appointment. Huang Yiyi's many indiscretions are brushed off and her histrionics stoically endured by An Zaitian, who sees in her only her genius brain. She alone dresses elegantly and is permitted to flirt in a puritanical milieu where moral opprobrium simmers just below the placid surface of professional single-mindedness. There is a sense that because Huang Yiyi has become an instrument of the state, she too is exempted, for the time being, from the standards of ordinary morality (figure 1.4).

However, moral prejudices do catch up with Abing and Huang Yiyi from the authorial angle in that they are cast in a blatantly ableist and sexist mold respectively. Abing's preternatural auditory gift is coupled with intellectual disability and sexual impotence, and Huang lacks sexual inhibition to the point of nymphomania. Her extravagant immodesty seems necessary to undercut her braininess, rendering her a lesser person, more of a child in need of care and protection than a mature woman with rights and dignity. Indeed, on several occasions she has to be rescued from the brink of self-destruction—always by An Zaitian, who is more than happy to be her father, brother, friend, and savior, but not her lover. With his unswerving devotion to service and his unflappable mien, An is the personification of the reason of state. And that, not just the inconvenient fact that An is a married man, is why Huang's love for him can never be requited. The only viable relationship an individual may have with the state is service, sacrifice, and pastoral care, whereas romance requires two private individuals with equal moral status. Whatever the specific causes of their deaths, Abing and Huang Yiyi's fates are more or less sealed the moment they step into 701, the moment they receive the doomed kiss of secrecy. Of states and secrets, Agent Qian offers the following observation:

> Of course, every country has its secrets, its clandestine organizations, classified weaponry, covert agents, secrets . . . there is really no end to the number of secrets kept by a nation. It's hard to imagine a country with no secrets. I wonder what such a nation would be like. But perhaps that's just a fantasy; such a country cannot exist, just like an iceberg would cease to be without its hidden mass lurking beneath the waves. Indeed, how can things exist independently of what is concealed beneath the surface? Sometimes I think that such secrets are terribly unfair, especially to those closest to the person keeping them. But if things weren't like this, quite possibly the country I call home would have long since disappeared, or at least be under threat. You just have to let this unfairness continue to be unfair. (16; 23)

When describing the inner sanctum of 701 into which Abing is being initiated, Qian resorts to tropes of mystery, timelessness, and the simultaneous expansion and diminution of the self, tropes that are typically associated with the experience of the sublime: "To be honest, what really went on in this area was beyond what people could fathom. It couldn't consciously register with them, including those who came regularly to Unit 701, such as the guards, doctors, drivers and cooks. They couldn't grasp what we did in here, even if they tried. Every day was the same. It seemed that even time ceased to exist for this place; it was as though we were outside both time and space. Whosoever entered our division would forever find themselves enshrouded by a web of secrecy. They would become part of the nation, part of the people, but they would cease to exist as individuals" (39; 57). The narrator professes ignorance as to whether 701 is organizationally part of the military or part of the police, but such distinction is immaterial in Mao's China, where the entire society was placed on a war footing (Guo 2012; Schoenhals 2013). Work units in which most of the urban populations were cocooned were run like paramilitary outfits with cradle-to-grave welfare provisions and mandatory communal life. With its dormitories, canteens, and drab office buildings, 701 is a typical socialist workplace. But the high walls, the sentries, and the shroud of secrecy also lift it out of the spatiotemporal grid of everyday life and thrust it at the frontline of an invisible war. Thus 701 is all about discipline and fiat. Anyone who breaks the rules is either banished to the unit's own goat farm (for those who know too much) or sent back home disgraced and jobless (for the rest). There is no appeal, no due process. The director is a de facto one-man military tribunal, an enlightened despot. Here individuals are decidedly expendable, even exceptional ones like Abing and Huang Yiyi.

While at the Chinese Academy of Sciences, where Huang was originally employed, An Zaitian, on his recruiting trip, has a conversation with her supervisor concerning her personal life. The latter demurs at sharing that knowledge on the grounds of respecting her privacy. An gives us the following paraphrase of his brusque reply: "I said that as far as Unit 701 was concerned there is no such thing as a private problem. In fact, it wasn't very clever of him to start talking about something or other being private: it was very disrespectful to us, given that we are ourselves top secret. Besides, who can keep secrets from us? An individual? A country? We investigate other people's private affairs for a living, and they in return try to discover ours. We don't like that feeling, we try to keep it to a minimum, and one of the best ways is to remove the word private from our vocabularies. Excise it. Just like you might excise a disgusting [pimple]" (100; 136).[13] If individuals are defenselessly transparent to the state and to one another in 701 and the usual sort of mind games of social life assume a stunted, elementary form, it is because everyone has been conscripted to play a gargantuan war game on the smokeless battlefield of the airwaves: code breaking. Their eyes and ears, as the hero in *Everlasting Radio Signals* says to his wife-cum-comrade, are the eyes and ears of the Party. In this shadow war, one state strains to read the intentions of another state, via the diabolically esoteric codes devised by the most ingenious minds. In this bleakly amoral world, deviousness and trickery are the means, and torment and despair the goal. Cryptography is a science, but also a demonic weapon. It attracts the best intellects, but is also their graveyard. It is with regard to the Janus-faced nature of cipher war that Mai Jia's novels register a modicum of ambivalence toward state secrets: "Because this was the world of cryptography, and as everyone knows, ciphers are counter-intuitive and inhuman. A counter-intuitive subject is just the same as any other science, and so research and cryptography both require intelligence, knowledge, skill, experience, genius. But at the same time they also need a kind of evil—regardless of whether you are talking about research or cryptography—because both are inhuman. When you get right down to it, ciphers are deceitful, they are concealed, they attack you from the dark. [All's fair in war],[14] and ciphers are a kind of weapon, they are just hidden. They are the biggest trick in the world" (99; 135). No one survives the vertiginous war game of code breaking unscathed, at least not the principal minds caught in the eye of the tornado and trying to peer through the swirling debris of "deceit, danger, wickedness and cruelty" (my translation, 135). Abing and Huang Yiyi are swallowed up whole and obliterated; others go mad and are condemned to a purgatorial existence—too deranged to be of use and too laden with secrets to be let go. If, as is commonly believed, geniuses are often border-line lunatics, secrecy inexorably tilts the scale and seals the fate of these brilliant but brittle individuals.

The same fate is played out at an operatic pitch in the life of Rong Jinzhen, the protagonist of *Decoded*.[15] In college Rong meets a Jewish professor exiled from Nazi-occupied Europe who takes the precocious, fragile youth under his wing. After 1949, Professor Liseiwicz resettles in the United States, and Rong is spirited to 701 to crack PURPLE, which turns out to be Liseiwicz's brainchild. In a letter, the professor warns Rong not to fall for the deathtrap of cryptography:

[Ciphers] are a poison that mankind has developed to destroy science and a conspiracy against the people that work with them. You need intelligence to work in cryptography, but it is a devilish intelligence; every success that you achieve in this field forces other people to become more inventively evil, more fiercely cunning. Ciphers are a kind of concealed warfare, but it's pointless to win this kind of battle, because it achieves nothing. . . . Top-secret work is a form of oppression; it means that you have to abjure the self—do you think you can do that? I am quite sure that you can't, because you are at once too fragile and too stubborn—you are simply not resilient enough. If you are not very careful, this work will break you! . . . From the moment you first take up cryptography, you are straightjacketed and oppressed in the name of national interest and national security. It is crucial to think about what your country is. (153; 162; translation modified)

But Rong Jinzhen never has a choice. If Huang Yiyi at least is able to put up a little resistance, Rong's recruitment to 701 is a virtual abduction: "Once you're wanted by them, you can't refuse" (124, my translation). After cracking PURPLE and becoming a decorated hero, Rong sets to work on decrypting BLACK but comes undone by a trivial accident. On a train jour-ney back from "headquarters," his briefcase is stolen by a common thief. In the briefcase is his notebook containing highly classified information. The frantic, massive search for the notebook involves fifteen government agencies including, besides Unit 701, the police, the military, the railway system, the postal service, and two municipal governments, totaling some thirty-seven hundred personnel. Rong conducts his own wild-goose chase and soon goes off the deep end. By the time his bodyguard finds him digging through a giant heap of scrap paper near a paper mill, he is already in a delirious state of insanity. Having completely lost his mind and memory, he is considered innocuous enough to be discharged from 701 and allowed to spend the rest of his life in a special hospice. When the narrator encounters him there, he is, in his catatonic state, little more than "a heap of clothes, a rag doll" (228; 241).

As does In the Dark, Decoded denounces cryptography as an anti-science and a cruel, inhuman enterprise: Ciphers are "heartless, mysterious things," and the minds of cryptographers are "black holes" that devour one another (165–66; 176). The novel bemoans and accepts the injustice of the state riding roughshod over the individuals who service its secrets and who must surrender mind and body to its imperatives: "It's unfair, but the fact is that it has to be that way" (236; 250). In the end, after chronicling all the heartbreaks, psychic torments, and grotesquely shriveled lives, the novel affirms that this unfairness serves a higher form of justice, or high justice. Just like a genius is often mistaken for a fool, a state that protects lives and guarantees security is liable to be misconstrued as tyrannical. The state, an iceberg kept afloat by a giant mass of arcana imperii, is terrifying because it is beyond the comprehension of ordinary mortals, but it is also sublime—for all those who are talented and unfortunate enough to be its architects, builders, custodians, and chroniclers.

In the precomputer world of 701, analogue technology melds the mental and the physical, the cerebral and the manual: While decrypting is an abstract, unfathomably complex mathematical operation that goes on in the brain vaults of one or two top decoders, the grunt work of running massive amounts of calculation to verify the decoders' hypotheses is carried out by the "calculation team" (yansuan zu) on numerous abacuses. Huang Yiyi, in keeping with her quirky personality, works out her decryption key while hanging out in the woodwork shop of 701's resident carpenter, dreamily contemplating the elegant geometric shapes. The analogue charm arising from the clicking abacuses and gleaming furniture brings the high-wire drama down to human scale, adding a counterweight to the sublime incomprehensibility of cryptography.

Perhaps what is most outrageous about ciphers is the ease with which they go from being the impregnable shield of national defense to worthless rubbish: The moment a cipher is unlocked, countless hours of mental agony are nullified. Moreover, underneath the image of an odorless universe of numbers and symbols, a cipher is said to be shot through with the personality quirks and moral DNA of its creator. The mind of Sivincy, the Russian scientist who defects to the United States and creates RECOVERY in *In the Dark*, is likened to "a dark pit crawling with poisonous snakes and vampire bats," and her cipher is "wicked," "perverse," and "a nasty piece of work" (165; 217). In a pop psychological move tinged with sexism, An Zaitian connects this mean streak to the gang rape by White Russian soldiers Sivincy suffered in her youth. Somehow, a young woman's sexual trauma is able to traverse oceans and continents to torment a group of abstemious Chinese technocrats. Such is the mystery of ciphers.

When an enterprise can elicit so many strong claims and counterclaims about itself, when it is so fiendishly counterintuitive and confounding to ordinary human reason, it has acquired the aura of sacred monstrosity, at once fascinating and terrifying. Is it any wonder that the entity that can subjugate such a monstrosity to its own purposes should become the locus of secular enchantment? When the human calculators' fingers fly across the abacus flicking the beads in a blurry dance, feelings of awe and mystification are channeled toward that which makes all this secular magic happen: the state.

"Society Must Be Defended"

As noted in the previous section, the most striking difference between contemporary Chinese spy thrillers and their Western counterparts is the geographical setting: the former privilege the enclosed, nearly claustrophobic space of the total institution with its disciplined corps of geniuses, technocrats, and functionaries, whereas the latter follow their swashbuckling heroes to far-flung corners of the world traversing metropolises, speedways, bazaars, deserts, mountain peaks, and oceans.[16] The Chinese state as projected in these stories is essentially a defensive Leviathan: powerful, secretive, efficient, and nonaggressive. It is a magnet for China's best and brightest; it takes gifted but defective individuals and makes them scintillate; it transcends ordinary morality and yet commands the moral high ground of international politics—by apparently engaging only in counterintelligence (neither Rong Jinzhen nor Huang Yiyi is made to create ciphers) and by remaining mum about weapons and intelligence programs and offensive operations. If China becomes a world power, it wants to be seen as a benign power, a fundamental departure from previous and current claimants to that status, all of which are known to have engaged in aggressive intelligence operations far beyond their borders. If the spy genre in the West has taken a cynical turn that reflects the growing critique of empire and mistrust of the state, in China it is enjoying a renaissance by riding on the coattails of an increasingly confident and securitized state. It makes perfect sense that the spy thriller should outshine detective fiction to become the new millennium's paean to statism, or the ideology of the state as "the ultimate locus of sovereignty, self-legitimating, and the highest source of good" (Zarrow 2012, 4).

The modifications made in the television adaptation of *In the Dark* (Liu Yunlong 2005) illustrate well the ideological work of the spy thriller. Most significantly, it replaces the novel's feeble part 3 (hobbled by extraliterary constraints), about "wind-catchers" or field agents, with a drawn-out drama about a Nationalist secret service bureau's attempt to ferret out a Communist mole in their midst by sequestering half a dozen prime suspects in a hotel and subjecting them to a harrowing regimen of inquisition, psychological stress test, and backstabbing.[17] The director of this television version, rather self-indulgently, casts himself in the lead role in all three parts—as An Zaitian in parts 1 and 2 and as An's father as a young man in part 3.

In part 1, An goes to Blind Abing's village, establishes a bond of trust and affection with Abing, becomes his mentor and surrogate father in 701, and even arranges a marriage for him. Although not everyone in 701 is a bachelor and several of the minor characters actually live with their families, An lives alone with the ashes of his departed wife and occasionally rues not seeing his two children grow up. His wife's death is now a literal fact rather than deliberate misinformation, making his refusal of Huang Yiyi's love in part 2 all the more a matter of iron will and discipline. Here, Huang falls in the lavatory not to her death but into a vegetative state. Inexplicably, An takes her comatose body to his bachelor quarters and becomes her full-time nurse and guardian. One cannot help but see him as a high priest of the state, tending the sacrificial offerings on its altar. Now that Huang can no longer protest her love for him, she is finally ready for the ritual cleansing and ablution.

In the third part, with the time line pushed back to the 1930s, An Zaitian's martyred father is the mole that the Nationalists try to identify. He pretends to be a devout lay Buddhist who is, incongruently enough, also an avid albeit grim-faced and stiff-limbed tango dancer. When he is not dancing and dazzling his colleagues, he is either meditating with prayer beads or dispensing nuggets of Buddhist wisdom, all the while giving the cold shoulder to a coquettish female coworker, even or especially when tangoing with her. In being imperturbably stoic and asexual, An again merges his self with the reason of state. In doing so, he issues a loud rebuke of the stereotypically womanizing Western spy hero like James Bond.

Scholars have generally regarded James Bond as the distillation of a suite of yearnings and fears specific to the postwar world, ranging from imperialist nostalgia, nuclear anxiety, and capitalist consumerism to neo-

liberal mistrust of state power (C. Bloom 1990; Comentale, Watt, and Willman 2005; Held and South 2006; Lindner 2003; T. Miller 2003; Woods
2008). He is unmistakably a man of appetites, alimentary as well as sexual.
His lusty personality spills forth in his love of fast cars, gourmet food,
artisanal drinks, and voluptuous women—the so-called Bond girls. He
is loyal to the country he serves, has faith in the liberal capitalist world
order he defends, and is deferential to his supervisor, M. But otherwise he
betrays little ideological conviction or organizational mind-set. He seems
to be in it mostly for the heart-pounding thrills of adventure and sexual
conquest. And yet he is trustworthy insofar as he is endowed with basic
human decency, at least toward those on "our" side. He is a state agent, but
his conscience is not entirely swallowed up by the call of duty to lie, cheat,
and kill. Thus, he is vulnerable to exploitation, as in *From Russia with Love*
(Young 1963) where he falls victim to a honey trap laid by the Russians.

This does mean that Bond has not entirely given up his moral freedom
and retains the option of going rogue—as when the state itself becomes
infiltrated by hostile forces or hopelessly saddled with incompetent and
misguided bureaucrats. In such circumstances the rogue hero is the only
one left to save the state from itself. He is thus the moral force that anchors the reason of state and counterbalances the dangerously amoral,
self-aggrandizing, conspiratorial, and despotic tendencies of the state—
especially the post-Snowden surveillance state. He not only defends
democracy against its external enemies—Communists, anarchists, and
terrorists—but is also a bulwark against its own worst impulses and inherent contradictions. In exercising "the license to kill," he is the outward
extension of the detective's power of exception, of sidestepping the law to
defend law and order. Both stand for a transcendent principle of justice
that the state of law strives to approximate but can also pervert and distort.
Bond, in short, is the most approximate defender of high justice one gets
in Western spy thrillers. But high justice here is rarely permitted to eclipse
low justice. Bond's rough and tumble methods are reserved exclusively for
the baddies "out there."

None of this is applicable to or conceivable in An Zaitian. In his self-
abnegating detachment, An levitates above the plane of ordinary existence, with all its moral and emotional entanglements. His refusal of love
is nothing less than a renunciation of moral freedom. Boltanski argues that
in a totalitarian society where the state itself has become a vast conspiracy,
the only possible position of externality is afforded "by chance encounters
between persons, faces, bodies" (2014, 168). Sexual love, such as that between Winston and Julia in George Orwell's *1984*, is envisaged as the only
authentic political resource: "For only in the *immediacy* of a relation that

engages desires and bodies can persons surmount the alienation to which human beings are prey when they give themselves over to a mediation that wrenches them out of themselves" (Boltanski 2014, 168). Here Boltanski is following a long line of philosophers who have theorized love as the sine qua non of human freedom, insofar it is a dyadic, egalitarian, voluntary, aleatory, and inward-looking affair (Kottman 2017). An authoritarian state does not, nor can it, outlaw all such unmediated horizontal encounters, but it frowns on the pockets of chance, opacity, and depth these encounters create and would much prefer a clean, smooth surface purged of all wrinkles. It permits individuals to live in relations of desires and bodies but retains the power to mediate their relations and subsume the latter to its own projects.

If Winston and Julia's illicit affair still fits into the conventional paradigm of rebellious love, the protagonist of John le Carré's *The Spy Who Came In from the Cold* tries to hold on to his love for his girlfriend as the last thread of his humanity. In a poignant moment, the narrator reflects: "He knew then what it was that Liz had given him; the thing that he would have to go back and find if ever he got home to England; it was the caring about little things—the faith in ordinary life; that simplicity that made you break up a bit of bread into a paper bag, walk down to the beach and throw it to the gulls. It was bread for the sea gulls or love, whatever it was he would go back and find it; he would make Liz find it for him" (le Carré 1964, 93). Here love is not an alternative, however dangerous and defiant, but the only thing that can still claim his allegiance, the only spiritual shelter he can return to in a desolate moral landscape. Everything else— family, country, friendship, the free world—have fallen away. In this novel the liberal moral imagination has run its full course and teeters on the precipice of nihilism.

Love as a quintessential expression of human freedom also fascinates Chinese audiences and provides some of the narrative tension and pleasure in stories not primarily about love, but it is invariably subordinated to the claims of larger entities: family, nation, party, state. Consider the status of the love story in *Visitor on the Ice Mountain* (*Bingshan shang de laike*) (Zhao Xinshui 1963). A typical early socialist counterespionage story, the film tells of how a platoon of PLA soldiers stationed at a mountain pass smash an insurrection plot hatched by a cabal of exiled Tajik separatists from Xinjiang. At the beginning of the film, a local family's beautiful bride (a spy, of course) pretends to be the long-lost love of PLA cadet Amir and tries to rekindle his passion. Amir recoils from her out of intuitive doubt ("There seem to be another pair of eyes behind the pair that weep," he murmurs as he tries to put his finger on it) as well as propriety—not aggravating army-civilian relations by being too chummy with a married woman. When his real love appears in the barracks and convinces him of her identity by singing a romantic duet with him, he still hesitates, until his commander (who has already vetted the young woman) barks: "Amir, charge!" (*Amir, chong*). Only then does he take her into his arms. This terse command has become one of the best-known and oft-mimicked movie lines in the socialist era. Allegedly young people were fond of using it to prod a friend in love. It was also an oblique commentary on the total surrender of individual volition in a society that urged everyone to emulate the soldier. It is difficult to imagine a line like this in a James Bond movie. More likely, M would want to holler, "Bond, hold it!"

Also consider Wang Jiazhi, the heroine in *Lust, Caution* (E. Chang 2007; see also H. Lee 2010). As a female spy on a honey trap mission, sex for her is work; seducing and sleeping with Mr. Yi is about serving the mission of the spy ring led by a group of men. But once she falls in love with Mr. Yi, she becomes more than a mere instrument. Love endows her with a measure of autonomy and agency and detaches her morally from the claims of her organization and her cause. When she whispers to Mr. Yi to run, thus allowing him to narrowly escape the assassination plot, she is no longer a secret agent on a mission, but a woman in love who wants to save her lover's life. Before he was just a body to her; now he is a man, a very vulnerable man who cares about her. His swift reprisal—rounding up and marching her and her comrades immediately to the execution ground—makes her act even more a sublime act of free will, with no considerations of consequence whatsoever. Love revives her conscience, and she acts on her conscience before any rational calculation kicks in to stymie it. It is something a Communist hero would never be allowed to do—in fiction or in real life. This is why the story could not have been written in the PRC—Eileen Chang wrote it during her years of sojourning in the United States. The film adaptation by Ang Lee (2007) fared poorly on the mainland, and the bulk of the criticisms were directed at Jiazhi's "betrayal" of her cause.

* * *

Michel Foucault (1990, 1997) coins the term "biopower" to capture the new kind of power that attends on the state's ever-expanding infrastructural reach. A modern authoritarian state, in contrast to a premodern autocracy, very much thrives on the exercise of biopower. But it would be indistinguishable from a liberal state of law if it didn't also rely on a form of despotic power made all the more lethal through its alliance with biopower. For Giorgio Agamben (1998, 2005), this new form of power is sovereign power over bare life: It fosters life not because life is sacred or that people have rights, but because it literally feeds on it. As one reviewer of Agamben puts it facetiously, states don't really mind their citizens dying, as long as "they don't all do it at once" (Bull 2004). The despotic and infrastructural powers can very well be at cross-purposes and risk canceling each other out. In Chinese spy thrillers, however, the tension between the two faces of the modern state is evoked and then suppressed. The Party-state is presented as isomorphic with the common good and the general will. It has no need for the figure of the detective to stand astride society to deliver (low) justice, because it is itself both the fountainhead and the terminus of the highest form of justice.

Interestingly, there is no An Zaitian character in *Decoded*, which was published just before *In the Dark*. Rong Jinzhen's story is told in multiple voices—by his adoptive family, colleagues, and supervisors as well as the narrator—and the mood of melancholy and regret comingles with exuberance, giving it a slightly noirish flavor. The state and its arcana imperii—glimpsed in the cipher war—are still a source of sublime terror, but its status as the terminus of justice comes under question, even if the questioning issues from a disaffected and deracinated Jew. Liseiwicz goes so far as to question the very idea of the state: "Now I have finally come to understand that 'my country' simply means my family, my friends, my language, as well as the bridges, streams, woods, paths, westerly winds, cicadas, and fireflies in my environs—not any particular swath of territory, nor the incarnation of some political party's or personage's will" (154; my translation). Having fled from Europe to China and emigrated from Israel to America, Liseiwicz is able to trust only what can be grasped in the encounters of persons, faces, and bodies. Everything else is a political fiction for him.

The tragic fate of the European Jewry was what gave rise to the reigning political fiction of the postwar era: universal human rights, canonized in UN declarations as an absolute principle that transcends national interests and trumps the reason of state. In his lecture "Society Must Be Defended," Foucault questions the extent to which the juridical-philosophical discourse of universality can truly replace the historical-political discourse that lays claim to truth and right. He contends that human rights are a "perspectival and strategic truth," "stamped with dissymmetry" (1997, 61–62). Richard Rorty, too, contends that justice is merely a larger loyalty by which we try to do right by those who are beyond our face-to-face community where the ties of kinship and familiarity thin out (we will return to this thesis in the conclusion). Liseiwicz, however, rejects any loyalty larger than the face-to-face one, and yet his face-to-face community is mobile and cosmopolitan. This rejection is a discordant note in the corpus of Chinese spy thrillers. In replacing Liseiwicz the stateless subject (and surrogate father of Rong Jinzhen) with An Zaitian the priestly guardian of the state (and surrogate father of Blind Abing and Huang Yiyi), Mai Jia puts the state in the position to intervene in the thick-to-thin process by effectively halting the expansion of loyalty and justice at the national borders.

Statism might well be what Rorty calls "the final vocabulary" of contemporary China, a set of narratives used to justify beliefs, actions, and lives and requiring no prior justification (1989, 73). As the only territorially centralized organization capable of protecting the national community, the state is the locus of both the ethics of community and the ethics of divinity (see the introduction).[18] It is both the means and the end of high justice. It not only commands obedience and loyalty but also elicits such quasi-religious responses as piety, awe, terror, and enchantment. The sense of sacredness, to recall Bok's discussion, undergirds the esoteric rationale behind government secrecy. Independent judgment is deemed not only a threat to security, but also a sacrilege—as when An Zaitian orders the scuttling of privacy as if it were a disgusting pimple. Indeed, "the reason of state" is quite a misnomer: The power of the state, particularly in its despotic register, is vested in mysticism. That is why confoundingly enigmatic ciphers are such a potent way to remystify the state. In that light, the spy thriller is a romance of the state par excellence, the most persistent and ardent defender of its incontestability. But Mai Jia's first two novels (*Decoded* and *In the Dark*), with their unflinching depictions of the ruthless world of cryptography, seem to invite us to "[keep] our ears open for hints about how [the final vocabulary] might be expanded or revised" (Rorty 1989, 197), even if he does not intend to turn us all into Rorty's liberal ironists.

2

Low Justice

Hypocrisy is the homage vice pays to virtue.

LA ROCHEFOUCAULD

In a rambling essay (1926) of reminiscences about his encounters with cats, dogs, and mice, Lu Xun places animal kind in a favorable light: unlike man, no animal is guilty of hypocrisy:

> Although the animal kingdom is by no means as free and easy as the ancients imagined, there is less tiresome shamming there than in the world of men. Animals act according to their nature, and whether right or wrong never try to justify their actions. Maggots may not be clean but neither do they claim to be immaculate. The way vultures and beasts prey on weaker creatures may be dubbed cruel, but they have never hoisted the banners of "justice" and "right" to make their victims admire and praise them right up to the moment they are devoured. When man learned to stand upright, that was of course a great step forward. When he learned to speak, that was another great step forward. When he learned to write, that was yet another great step forward. But then degeneration set in, because that was the beginning of empty talk. (Lu Xun 1973, 90)

In modern Chinese literary history, Lu Xun's short story "Diary of a Madman" (1918) is generally considered the founding text because of its bold adoption of the vernacular language and its searing indictment of Chinese society as cannibalistic. The charge of cannibalism, moreover, is enfolded in another damning charge: hypocrisy. Recall that the madman spends a sleepless night scrutinizing a "history book" with no dates, that is, a time-

A small portion of this chapter will appear in a forthcoming issue of *Law and Literature* under the title "The Importance of Not Being Honest."

less Confucian classic, until finally he is able to discern the word *chiren* or "eat people" in between the lines bejeweled with words like "benevolence," "righteousness," and "morality" (Lu Xun 1990, 32). Cannibalism is horrific, but cannibalism wrapped in the cloak of benevolence is, Lu Xun suggests, far worse, and cruelty compounded by deception is apparently the greatest evil a society can perpetuate. Yet, as he notes, humankind's aptitude for duplicity is a by-product of its greatest evolutionary achievement: language. Without language, there would be no "tiresome shamming" or "empty talk," no hoisting lofty banners while knee-deep in the muck of evil.

More than any other vice, hypocrisy was the abiding target of Lu Xun's formidable rhetoric arsenal, coming in for a side swipe even in a lighthearted essay about cats and mice. In no other text, however, is hypocrisy subjected to more relentless skewering than in *The True Story of Ah Q* (1921). In the fictional world of Weizhuang, hypocrisy is the coin of the realm. The powerful spout benevolence while sitting atop of a ruthlessly oppressive social order; the powerless mime obedience and obsequiousness while swallowing the slings and arrows that punctuate their daily existence. The malcontent, moreover, cope with their humiliation with a false front of complacency while deflecting aggression toward those even worse off. That is, of course, what Ah Q epitomizes, so much so that the hypocrisy of the powerless is forever chiseled into the phrase "Ah Q spirit" (*A Q jingshen*) in the modern Chinese language.

Lu Xun was by no means singular in his utter contempt for hypocrisy. Moral and political philosophers have observed, often with a note of disbelief, the regularity with which hypocrisy ranks among the most detested vices in the eyes of thinkers, writers, and opinion makers in the modern West. What is so execrable about a vice that, as La Rochefoucauld reminds us, pays homage to virtue? Why is pretend virtue so much worse than naked vice? Beginning with Hannah Arendt, a number of liberal thinkers, most notably Judith Shklar, Ruth Grant, and Martin Jay, have tackled the enigma of hypocrisy and proposed a revisionist take that urges a measured acceptance of hypocrisy in social and political life. In this chapter, I intend to synthesize this body of ideas and extend them, with inspirations from the dissident Chinese thinker Hu Ping, toward a reassessment of the place of hypocrisy in Chinese visions and practices of low justice, or rights and wrongs among individuals. My analyses will be anchored in four works of fiction: Lu Xun's *The True Story of Ah Q*; Gao Yubao's autobiographical novel *Gao Yubao* (1955), along with the 1964 animated short *The Rooster Crows at Midnight*, adapted from the novel; Yan Lianke's satirical novel *Serve the People!* ([2005] 2007); and *Dying to Survive* (2018), directed by

Wen Muye. I connect the persistent discourse of antihypocrisy with modern Chinese intellectuals' critique of the Confucian tradition as well as their effort to break with the Maoist past. In doing do I also reflect on the knotty issues in China's socialist legacy surrounding propaganda, organized mendacity, political ritual, and cynicism.

My primary objective in this chapter is to consider how low justice is achievable when law is largely absent or when it itself is the instrument of injustice. Technically, low justice centrally preoccupies the so-called legal system literature (*fazhi$_2$ xitong wenxue*), the subject of Jeffrey Kinkley's pioneering study (2000). I steer clear of this body of writing for two reasons: One, it is cranked out by the trade publications of state justice organs, and its main selling point seems to be luridness and salaciousness. Two, PRC citizens tend to pursue low justice via nonlegal channels, including through quasi-illicit means and nonconformity, which I characterize as "subaltern hypocrisy." If one limits one's sight to stories about the police and the courts where low justice fights do take place, one will miss a great deal of low justice pursuit carried out by individuals who prefer to operate under the state's radar.[1] Hence my decision to pay particular attention to instances of subaltern hypocrisy, or the double existence imposed on those on the lower rungs of a hierarchical social order. Subaltern hypocrisy, insofar as it is a coping mechanism and a defense against the depredations of power, is where low justice finds a niche in a hierarchical society governed by customary law and bureaucratic justice.

Scholarship has customarily celebrated subversion and resistance from below. This chapter departs from this convention. Victimhood, I argue, does not necessarily confer nobility; it can also induce moral compromise, even corruption. I thus take a step back from the tendency to celebrate the subversive logic of noncompliance and ask some uncomfortable questions, uncomfortable because they probe not just the psychological toll of oppression, but also the moral injuries. Moral injury overlaps with but differs from generic immorality in that the former can be directly attributed to structural causes, rather than individual character. In developing this concept, I follow in the footsteps of Richard Sennett and Jonathan Cobb (1972) in their inquiry into the "hidden injuries" of the American class system. Eyal Press (2021) has recently extended this line of inquiry to shine a light on the "hidden toll" endured by those who do America's "dirty work": soldiers, prison guards, slaughterhouse workers, and drone pilots. Similarly, moral injury is a long-term condition that may or may not be associated with trauma. It may manifest in isolated episodes or blend into personality traits, but one must not lose sight of the fact that it is born of power imbalances and of inequality. Those who triumph against such moral adversity become memorable, feted (fictional) heroes. A conspicuous case of failure, in the persona of Ah Q, who wallows in moral corruption, has lived in literary infamy ever since he came to life under Lu Xun's excoriating pen.

Everybody Is a Hypocrite

The political philosopher Judith Shklar is arguably the first to think systematically and level-headedly about hypocrisy in the broader framework of political morality. She begins by asking why it is regarded so universally as an irredeemable sin. Surely it is better to cover up one's moral failings than to be "openly and honestly vicious" (1984, 57)? Liberal democratic societies, she notes, seem to have an especially low threshold of tolerance for hypocrisy, and their politicians are forever panting on a "treadmill of dissimulation and unmasking" (67), and these same societies also pride themselves on their political openness and transparency in comparison with their authoritarian counterparts. To explain the puzzle, she takes us back to the Enlightenment discovery of the inner self, or individual conscience, premised on a radical break with traditional sources of norms and principles. "What happens to a conscience that is uninformed by God or social mores" (58)? Thinkers like Rousseau proffered sincerity. But because a sincerity-based conscience inherently lacks what G. W. F. Hegel calls "objective content" (i.e., naturally or divinely sanctioned rules of conduct), it is peculiarly vulnerable to suspicion of phoniness. To avow one's sincerity then requires a kind of doubling down that can paradoxically provoke further mistrust, thereby giving rise to a modern form of politics dedicated to destroying the credibility of rival factions, with the effect of reducing politics to "an unending game of mutual unmasking" (Shklar 1984, 67).

Hypocrisy and sincerity are thus two sides of the same coin. No amount of antihypocrisy campaigns will eliminate hypocrisy for good as long as values grounded in individual conscience are cherished. Among these are equality and liberty, values that require a leap of faith and a willful negation of what meets the eye. Shklar writes: "If men accept themselves as the sum of their roles, it is said, then they are doomed to inequality. Only if we assume that there is a self apart from all social definition, which is capable of morality and therefore deserves respect, can we justify the claims of equality on which not only social justice but liberty itself depends" (1984, 76–77). Our sensitivity and hostility toward hypocrisy is not a reaction to its proliferation in modern life, but because of its inability to entirely conceal the all-too-visible seams of modern myths. Yuval Harari has argued that nearly all modern institutions require a leap of faith. For example, the modern economy cannot function unless we collectively pretend that the colorful pieces of paper called banknotes are value bearing (2015, 180). Elaine Scarry provides an inventory of these "made-real" things, from nation-states to childhood (1992, 239). Representative democracy surely belongs there as well. It proclaims that the people rule, but they do not—other than playing a limited role in elections. And yet adherence to democratic principles and sentiments, however faith based, is the ideological bedrock of democratic politics. These principles must be invoked on all possible occasions and serve as justification for all policies. This means that elected leaders must learn to present their policies in a shared political language.

A society may share a political language (in the United States, that language is largely derivative of the Constitution) and be held together by a dominant tradition (such as Judeo-Christianity), but insofar as it is a genuinely pluralist society, the gap between collective ideals and policies on the ground—which often answer to sectional interests—can never be fully closed. There is thus a built-in tension, an inescapable discrepancy between what is said and what is done in the political realm: "the better the speaker the larger that distance is likely to be" (Shklar 1984, 69). Michael Herzfeld makes a similar point when he remarks that "although governments speak solemnly of the rule of law, in practice no nation-state can actually function by observing every rule to perfection" (2016, 176). In the gap between "the letter of the law and the raw realities of social life" (177) thrive playful political modalities that he calls irony. He could have easily labeled it hypocrisy. Michael Walzer also recognizes the value of hypocrisy in the more extreme context of war: "The clearest evidence for the stability of our values over time is the unchanging character of the lies soldiers and statesmen tell. They lie in order to justify themselves, and so they describe for us the lineaments of justice. Wherever we find hypocrisy, we also find moral knowledge" (Walzer 2015, 19). Hypocrisy, in other words, is strangely comforting and reassuring and may even be the last line of defense against the Hobbesian state of nature.

We exhibit better behavior as citizens and public officials who are answerable to collective ideals than as private individuals who are free to indulge in private vice within certain bounds. Pretend virtue may serve to shore up idealism as effectively as sincere virtue. Moreover, and this is highly apropos of the current backlash against "political correctness" or "wokism," norms of good behavior in public also serve to curtail all manner of bigotries. Today, no racist or homophobe wants to be publicly called out as such. "Should our public conduct really mirror our private, inner selves," as an antihypocrite might demand, when our public manners are often so much better than our "personal laxities" (Shklar 1984, 78)? The "sugary grin" we put on does more to broadcast our moral aspiration and effort than to cover up our moral failings. "Indeed, one might well argue that liberal democracy cannot afford public sincerity. Honesties that humiliate and a stiff-necked refusal to compromise would ruin democratic civility in a political society in which people have many serious differences of belief and interest" (78). The conservative revolt against political correctness and the rise of a right-wing populism whose members are proud to vote with their middle finger have sadly proven Shklar right.

Ruth Grant reinforces Shklar's defense of hypocrisy by reminding us that politics is much more than just an exercise in reason. Sometimes "doing the right thing" may entail a departure from a purely principled stance. But, she asks, "when is it good to be little bad? And particularly, when and why is it necessary, when being a little bad, to maintain the appearance of goodness?" (Grant 1997, 2). Because political relations are relations of dependence in which people with divergent interests and values have to cooperate with one another, trust is essential. And trust cannot be won through reason alone. "To enlist the support of the other party requires flattery, manipulation, and a pretense of concern for his needs" (13), which amount to appeals to the shared moral sentiments that sustain social life. It is thus important to resist the call to cordon off politics as an autonomous realm governed by the reason of state and recognize that the rhetoric of morality is deeply enmeshed in political discourse. Grant advances the thesis that both Machiavelli and Rousseau, two thinkers often thought to come down on opposite sides of the question of political morality, appreciate the necessity of political hypocrisy: "Hypocrisy requires moral pretense, and that pretense is necessary because politics cannot be conducted solely through bargaining among competing interests. To argue that political hypocrisy is necessary is thus to argue that moral cynicism as a public principle is impossible. *Ironically, the frequency of hypocrisy in politics testifies to the strength of the moral impulse in public life*" (1997, 14, emphasis added). In sum: "Political relations are neither enmities nor friendships but friendly relations sustained among nonfriends. And in order to sustain them, one must cultivate one's reputation and care for the opinion of others. Vanity and pride inevitably are constituents of these relationships. Moreover, it becomes very useful to appear to be other than what you are and to appeal to whatever moral or religious norms constitute the commonly accepted vocabulary of justification for political action. Hypocrisy is generated by the particular sort of dependence that defines political relations" (175–76).

Building on the insights of Shklar and Grant while reaching back to Hannah Arendt's musings on truth and politics, Martin Jay (2010) makes a compelling case for the "virtues of mendacity," which he pits against the utopian dream for transparent politics (see also Geroulanos 2017). The dream of total transparency originated in the French Revolution and put down firm roots in the United States during the Cold War, when American politicians took on the mission to expose the Big Lie of totalitarianism that was made hair-raisingly palpable by George Orwell's *1984* (1949). The quest for perfect legibility and transparency translated into the cult of plain speaking, or "straight talk," which in turn drove the tendency to seek technical, apolitical solutions to political problems, of which the lie detector is a perfect example. This is why "playing politics" is not a job description but a term of abuse in American political culture. In a provocative move, Jay urges us to consider if the prevalence of lying in politics is not precisely what makes politics valuable rather than "merely an unedifying spectacle of human depravity" (2010, 18).

Jay conducts an exhaustive survey of different definitions of politics, from totalitarianism and the aesthetic state to liberal contractualism and republicanism, and finds that mendacity underscores all of them, with varying degrees of latitude and to varying effects. He concludes on a cautionary note: "No matter how much we strive to make [politics] the arena for the triumph of rational argumentation over coercion, manipulation, and mystification, there will always be some resistance to a regime of transparent truth-telling. For even in a democracy, the ultimate fictional quality of the sovereign people is impossible to overcome" (2010, 169–70). Any attempt to overcome the founding fiction of popular sovereignty, to close the gap between the ideal of equality and the reality of distinction, or to upset the delicate balance between "preserving the symbolic myth of unity and refraining from trying to make it fully incarnate in a positive way" (170), can send one down the totalitarian slippery slope.

Elaborating on Arendt's groundbreaking writing on the subject, Jay points to the paradox of truth's incompatibility with politics insofar as truth deals with cold, hard facts and compels acceptance, while politics traffics in the passions and operates by persuasion. Totalitarian politics, however, models itself on science and subsumes everything into the Big Truth—of class struggle, racial purity, and so on. In so doing it simultaneously abolishes politics and institutes a hypertrophic form of politics that is all pervasive and admits of no exterior. It claims to have fully realized such democratic ideals as the sovereignty of the people, equality of gender, and transparency of government, without the charade of democratic proceduralism susceptible to freak outcomes. History has attested to the isomorphism of the Big Truth and the Big Lie. In this perverse union the very possibility of truth is suspended.

The totalitarian destruction of truth cannot be adequately captured in the usual disparagement of the Big Lie as propaganda. In asserting a doctrine of absolute truth while abolishing the political sphere of opinions and hypocritical pretensions, totalitarian regimes in effect render the distinction between truthfulness and falsity moot. Harry Frankfurt's treatise *On Bullshit* points to the heart of this operation. In contrast to an outright lie that presupposes the existence of truth, bullshit is totally indifferent to its own truth status. "The essence of bullshit is not that it is false but that it is phony" (Frankfurt 2005, 47), and it is delivered through bluffing, which can escalate to an art form. Because "it is impossible for someone to lie unless he thinks he knows the truth" (55), the liar in fact enjoys much less freedom, and lying can impose austere and rigorous demands, most notably that of consistency. The bullshitter, on the contrary, is unencumbered by such demands and enjoys "more spacious opportunities for improvisation, color, and imaginative play" (53). In Chinese, the distinction between a lie and bullshit is registered semantically by *jiahua* or *huangyan* for the former, and *dahua*, *konghua*, or *feihua* for the latter. And official discourse in China is so full of the latter that few pay much heed to *guanhua* or "official-speak," and the expression *daguanqiang* ("spouting officialese") is a term of dismissal (Hansen 2017).

Bullshit is what one gets when a modern society tries to reinstate what John Haiman calls "guarantors of sincerity" (1998, 5). In traditional societies, ritual language and aleatory mechanisms such as the throw of the dice enable a speaker to establish "disinterestedness by uttering a script which is attributed to the Culture, the Deity, or some other impartial and superorganic source" (5). In large-scale modern societies, the need to stamp out personal bias is performed by the bureaucratic machinery, particularly the legal system. Here, it is the "whips or spears of the executive authority" (7), not charisma, moral authority, or the threat of ostracism that back up the sincerity of a speaker. But given the limits of political and legal coercion, we moderns can get away with unimaginable amounts of insincerity, or empty talk. "Talk is cheap," and that is a good thing, according to Haiman, because the slippage between the symbolic action of language and events in the actual world is where human freedom resides. In other words, we should rejoice in the fact that language can be insincere and inconsequential, like the hot air in a balloon "anchored to the ground of reality by socially determined guarantees of sincerity and consequentiality" (7). Susan Blum makes a similar point: "in the best of all possible worlds, there should be nothing but the truth. Yet a further glance has shown how much more slippery, complicated, and interesting social life is when we see with open eyes all that people can do with their mastery of language and other kinds of social action" (2007, 163). Modernity has allowed us to arrogate the guarantee of sincerity from the gods to ourselves, to our unanchored consciences. Each of us gets to bounce insouciantly, even recklessly, in a hot air balloon of our own fashioning—we call it freedom. Totalitarianism seeks to puncture the balloons not so much to permanently fasten language to reality as to envelope reality itself in hot air. It leaves both language and human freedom in tatters.

When practiced by totalitarian regimes, bullshit becomes elaborate propaganda that obfuscates, overwhelms, and mystifies more than it deceives. In his ethnography of "authoritative discourse" in China, Anders Hansen observes that the seriousness of "compulsory lectures, political speeches and public anniversaries" (2017, 45) is not detracted from by the fact that few take them seriously. Privately, his student informants regard these *guanhua* rituals as pointless and meaningless, but their compliance is all that matters: "[They] do not have to care what is said, or agree, since they already add to the political ritual by their very presence" (2017, 46). *Guanhua* is thus a form of bad faith monopolized by the ruler and inflicted on the ruled, who are compelled to practice a reciprocal form of bad faith, or what I'm calling "subaltern hypocrisy." "Totalitarianism developed an attitude toward lying that suspended whatever ethical considerations make lying a contested and reviled tactic in virtually all other political contexts, where the vice of hypocrisy still has to pay homage to the virtue of sincerity" (Jay 2010, 136). Hypocrisy is practiced on a colossal scale in totalitarianism, not least in its self-image as the vanguard of truth and its obsessive denunciation of the hypocrisy of the ancien régime. We are now miles and miles away from the mild, salutary variety of hypocrisy given a vigilant pass by Grant, Shklar, and Jay.

If both liberal democracy and totalitarianism rest on the inevitability of hypocrisy, it is only because hypocrisy comes naturally to us. We are evolutionarily equipped for deception and self-deception. Indeed, the social nature of our species requires it. Cognitive psychologists have demonstrated how the modular structure of our mind makes it feasible to hold contradictory beliefs, to be willfully blind to facts that go again our deeply held values, and to lie and cheat with our self-esteem largely intact. We accomplish this through intuition, flexible or motivated reasoning, and post hoc rationalization. Peter Ditto and Brittany Liu describe one common cognitive operation that gives rise to hypocrisy. They begin with the widely accepted view that much of moral life unfolds at the level of intuition or gut feeling: "The essence of moral thinking is deontological intuitions, that some acts are simply right or wrong in and of themselves, no matter their costs or benefits to self or others" (Ditto and Liu 2012, 54). Moral reasoning, that much-prized faculty in Western philosophy, is mostly a matter of post facto justification, especially when there are competing moral intuitions or when one needs to justify one's decision to others—often as a way to manage the cognitive dissonance attendant on any free choice (see also Haidt 2001). Cognitive dissonance is defined by Robert Trivers as "a state of tension or discomfort ranging from minor pangs to deep anguish" that arises from the awareness of self-contradiction (2011, 151). A moral decision grounded in deontological intuition is particularly prone to induce cognitive dissonance because it has to willfully discount the costliness of the consequence.

Ditto and Liu give the example of the trolley problem, a thought experiment in which a subject has to choose between killing one innocent individual versus allowing five individuals to perish as a consequence of inaction. The majority of experimental subjects intuitively choose the latter, refusing to extinguish one life even though doing so would save five others. A common coping strategy for deontological dissonance is confabulation, or "strategically organizing factual beliefs about the costs and benefits of alternate courses of action," an operation that Ditto and Liu tag as "the consequentialist crutch" (2012, 59). This goes a long way to explaining the rise of "alternative facts" in contemporary American politics as well as intractable political conflicts the world over. It also explains why we find the rare individual who disdains confabulation so admirable.[2]

Confabulation can also work the other way. When people are compelled to adopt certain behavior or avow certain creed that is at variance with their private sentiments and beliefs, they cope with the ensuing state of cognitive dissonance by adjusting their sentiments and beliefs accordingly in order to maintain a coherent sense of self. This is because action or speech is public and known and impossible to retract or undo, whereas one's feelings, known only to oneself, are more or less under one's control. This is exactly what Han Shaogong's story "The Leader's Demise" (2001) depicts, as I have discussed at length elsewhere (H. Lee 2007, 290–96). Briefly, the protagonist at first cannot summon any sad feelings upon hearing the news of Mao's death. But he manages to work himself into a fit of sobbing by thinking about a private loss. His tears are so abundant and his grief so infectious that he is paraded around the region as a model mourner. The irony serves to expose the phoniness and hypocrisy of what I have called the socialist grammar of emotion, whereby emotional expressions are untethered from judgments of value not for the sake of aesthetic pleasure, but out of fear or ambition or both. Crucially, Han's story has a further twist: After a few rounds of command performance (and being amply rewarded), our hero begins to tinker with his interior feeling state and slowly convinces himself that he is indeed grieving for Mao. He has thus succeeded at the outside-in form of confabulation. In short, while the first kind of confabulation may be increasingly pervasive in the liberal West, the latter, as Han's story attests, has been a common experience in China, albeit waning in recent decades. The point again is that hypocrisy is common to political life, even if it assumes different guises, valences, and mechanisms.

For Robert Kurzban (2010), everyone is a hypocrite, and politicians stick out only because they are constantly in the spotlight, in which they are required to make their moral stance public while constantly being faced with cost-benefit considerations and tempted to moral corruption. Dan Ariely (2012) disabuses us of the commonsense notion that dishonesty is motivated by material gains and can be deterred by the threat of detection and punishment. Instead, a host of factors conspire to make most of us liars and cheaters some of the time and to some extent: conflict of interests, cognitive depletion, creativity, absence of moral prompts, witnessing others' dishonest acts, and altruistic considerations, among others. Thankfully, our customs and laws and institutions are cognizant enough of these priming factors to have set up defenses against their subtle influences, so that we "don't cheat enough," even when presented with opportunities whereby we can reap the reward of dishonesty without getting caught. In societies fundamentally cleaved by power, freedom from dishonesty is unevenly distributed. Power corrupts the powerless as much as it corrupts the powerful, because domination and oppression make it well-nigh impossible for the powerless to lead an honest existence. Instead, it fosters moral opportunism, or subaltern hypocrisy.

Pseudovirtue and Pseudovice

That lying or dissemblance is not proscribed by the Ten Commandments and other religious canons is indicative of a traditional epistemological order that admitted of what Anthony Giddens calls "formulaic truth." Usually of a religious nature and consisting of incantatory speech, formulaic truth does not depend on the referential property of language; it invites neither agreement nor disagreement. Thus it is a powerful means of preempting dissent. "Truth criteria are applied to events caused, not to the propositional content of statements" (Beck, Giddens, and Lash 1994, 65). Only modern politics is premised on an ideal of transparency and sincerity that turns on the propositional content of statements. Hypocrisy offends the modern sensibility because it calls attention to language's formal, ritual functions. Alasdair MacIntyre (1984, 71–72) correctly observes that the unmasking of hypocrisy is a quintessentially modern preoccupation. Indeed, modern literature is unthinkable without the ubiquitous hypocrite and the indefatigable antihypocrite. Nathaniel Hawthorne's *The Scarlet Letter* (1850), Mark Twain's "Running for Governor" (1870),[3] Oscar Wilde's *The Importance of Being Earnest* (1895), and Charles Dickens's entire oeuvre most readily come to mind. The fact that literature is a privileged arena for the battle of dissembling and unmasking also has to do with the cognitive pleasure it affords in untangling the complicated reasons why an individual's words and actions do not match, and in exercising our mental skills in the recursive game of mind reading. We will return to this shortly.

In her anthropological study of truth and lying in China, Susan Blum highlights the contrast between the way "deception, rusing, lying, exaggeration, and all their cousins" are automatically deplored in the United States, and the absence of such automatic reaction in China, where non-truthful actions may be justified on the basis of "a higher notion of social truth or justice or welfare" (2007, 44). Like Jay, she deplores the cult of transparency and contrasts it unfavorably to more contextual or flexible approaches to truth that she finds in China:

> The notion that words must match inner states comes from a Western model of a self, with its individual, unique, and contextless feelings and thoughts. In speaking, this person must produce words that transparently reveal those thoughts, no matter what the consequences or pressure to others. Anything else would make one untrue to herself. But what of a society where—not to overdraw the contrast—selves are regarded as at least in part nodes in relationships? In that case, the person speaking would be different in different contexts, and therefore the words produced by that person would shift according to the circumstances and situations, without any likelihood that there is something deceptive occurring. (Blum 2007, 162)

This elastic notion of truth is vividly captured in Ted Chiang's novella *The Truth of Fact, the Truth of Feeling*, in which an African teenager explains to a European missionary the plural nature of truth: "Our language has two words for what in your language is called 'true.' There is what's right, *mimi*, and what's precise, *vough*. In a dispute the principals say what they consider right; they speak *mimi*. The witnesses, however, are sworn to say precisely what happened; they speak *vough*. [...] It's not lying if the principals don't speak *vough*, as long as they speak *mimi*" (Chiang 2019, 212).

One might say the same bifurcation obtains in the Chinese conception of truth. Børge Bakken has observed that honesty is not an absolute value in China; rather it can be sacrificed for the sake of conformity and harmony (2000, 419). The lack of a categorical ban on deception in China and most traditional societies bespeaks the many ways in which "the truth of feeling" serves social integration, above and beyond epistemological accuracy.

Deception may also be performative for James Scott (1990), famous for theorizing organized foot-dragging alongside other such tactics of sly noncompliance as righteous acts of resistance on the part of the powerless in a rigidly hierarchical society. Proceeding from a theatrical model of politics, Scott argues that the dominant class imposes a self-flattering, legitimacy-conferring "public transcript" on the subordinate class and compels the latter to pay lip service to it. Both parties, when unobserved by each other, also operate by a respective set of "hidden transcripts" that, if leaked or exposed, would cause at minimum embarrassment and at worst loss of legitimacy for the ruling class and backlash and repression for the ruled. Thus it behooves both sides to hone the art of hypocrisy, of wearing a mask for the sake of self-preservation and self-aggrandizement. "If subordination requires a credible performance of humility and deference, so domination seems to require a credible performance of haughtiness and mastery," a dynamic he demonstrates to great effect with George Orwell's essay "Shooting an Elephant" (see Scott 1990, 11). Scott warns us not to presuppose that the hidden transcripts are necessarily more genuine than the public transcript, or that the private self is necessarily more authentic than the mask, especially in view of the risk of the face growing to fit the mask (as in Han Shaogong's story discussed in the previous section). Politics, he reminds us, rarely amounts to a direct collision of hidden transcripts, or a saturnalia moment of open rebellion and violent confrontation. Rather, it more often than not assumes the form of "infrapolitics" practiced at the interstices of the public transcript, where the powerless put on command performance while engaging in a cat-and-mouse game of symbols, rhetorics, puns, jokes, and rumors. A prominent motif in folktales celebrates precisely such subaltern tactics. "The stories of Rumpelstiltskin, Robin Hood, Br'er Rabbit, and Coyote tell of the underdog using cleverness and deception, knowledge of others' desires, to achieve a greater justice" (Blum 2007, 160–61).

Politics in traditional societies invites analogy to Kabuki theater. In the Confucian tradition, governance was as much about ritual performance as about policy making (Shue 2022). A vast amount of courtly activity in imperial China was devoted to grand ceremonies that enacted the emperor's status as the son of heaven and pivot between heaven and earth (Zito

1997). Ray Huang (1981) gives us a gripping account of how the Ming emperor Wanli chafed under the crushing weight placed on him by the ritual theater of emperorship. James Watson (2007) proposes the well-known thesis that imperial China was governed not by Confucian orthodoxy, but by "orthopraxy," a concept akin to Scott's public transcript. In orthopraxy, what counted was outward behavioral conformity, not inner conviction or sincerity. Throughout human history before the twentieth century, states simply did not have the wherewithal nor the motivation to police the inner lives of their subjects or to stamp out hidden transcripts tout court. Staying in power and maintaining a system of domination and extraction largely defined the goal of governance, but even such a minimalist politics required more than naked force (Fukuyama 2011). The dramaturgy of power serves to convince the subordinate groups of the legitimacy, stability, and longevity of the system of domination, as well as to hypnotize the ruling groups in order to "convince themselves anew of their high moral purpose" (Scott 1990, 67).

The sloganeering and grandstanding of the official story permit some flexibility in interpretation by the subordinates. "What may look from above like the extraction of a required performance can easily look from below like the artful manipulation of deference and flattery to achieve its own ends" (Scott 1990, 34). Scott is attentive to the psychological impact the theater of power has on the powerless—the affront to their dignity, the strain and stress of not being able to let down their guard, and repercussion for any real or perceived noncompliance. However, he is more interested in how such a low-grade simmer can eventually boil over and break the dam of conformity than in the moral tax that command performance levies on subordinates. In other words, he leaves unaddressed the problem of the moral wages of compulsory hypocrisy.

Scott is not alone is overlooking the moral dimension of power relations. In G. W. F. Hegel's master-and-slave parable ([1807] 1997, 143–52), the master, for all his power and dominion, is said to suffer two wants: want of proper recognition, which the slave is not in a position to confer, and want of epistemological accuracy in his grasp of reality because it is buffered for him by the slave. What Hegel does not dwell on is the fact that the slave more than the master has to live a double life: he may have a clearer understanding of how the world really works, but he has to parrot the master's self-flattering version of it and sometimes has to operate under the master's radar in order to get what he wants. Duplicity is the modus operandi of the slave. Domination not only takes away his freedom and dignity but also makes it impossible to lead an honest, spontaneous existence. Moral authenticity and integrity may well be a luxury beyond reach. If the master is unusually cruel and abusive, then anger, resentment, and indignation become the slave's daily bread.

In Agnes Callard's (2020) view, the feeling of being wronged incubates grudges and the thirst for payback. Forgiveness, reconciliation, and recompense may ease the scorching heat of anger, but not its moral complication. In her words, "the morally correct way to respond to immorality is to do things—cling to anger, exact vengeance—that are in some way immoral." She elaborates:

> I believe that, when faced with injustice, we should sometimes get somewhat angry. Such anger is not "pure" and entails submitting oneself to (some degree of) moral corruption, but the alternative, acquiescence, is often even worse. The point I want to emphasize, however, is this: just because the moral corruption of anger is our best option doesn't mean it is not corruption.
>
> The consequences of acknowledging this point are sobering: victims of injustice are not as innocent as we would like to believe. Either these victims are morally compromised by the vengeful and grudge-bearing character of their anger, or they are morally compromised by acquiescence. *Long-term oppression of a group of people amounts to long-term moral damage to that group.* When it comes to racism, sexism, homophobia, anti-Semitism, ableism, classism, religious discrimination, anti-neurodiversity, elitism of any stripe, this argument entails that the oppressors have made the oppressed morally worse people. Of course, oppressing people is also bad for your soul, but we do not need to be reminded of that; we are accustomed to the thought that wronging others makes you a bad person. My point is: so does being wronged, even if to a lesser degree. (Callard 2020, emphasis added)

Here, Callard compresses into a short passage a two-step reversal: First, she echoes the ancient sages who saw past the obvious fact that oppression harms victims and counseled to the powerful moderation and kindness for the good of their own souls. She believes that this has become part of the received wisdom and needs no more reminder. The second reversal, however, may raise a few eyebrows. It is the idea that oppression not only injures the victim's life and limb, but also the victim's soul. In other words, both the oppressed and the oppressor are worse off morally speaking. Michael Walzer concurs in his critique of Jean-Paul Sartre's endorsement of FLN (Front de Libération Nationale) terrorism in Algiers: "Hatred, fear, and the lust for domination are the psychological marks of oppressed and oppressor alike, and their acting out, on either side, can be said to be radically determined" (2015, 205).

The subordinate classes in a rigidly stratified and oppressive society are not only seething with anger and resentment, but also required to hold it all in and put on instead a facade of acquiescence, a sugary grin. The target of subaltern hypocrisy may logically be the powerful, but not infrequently, it could be those on even lower rungs of the social ladder, or outsiders— remember Ah Q. It is this shared state of moral corruption between the oppressor and the oppressed that makes the operation of scapegoating so universal. Again, the crucial if uncomfortable insight from Callard is that oppression does not ennoble; rather, it corrupts—in both directions. Bad faith is its universal outcome. Nowhere is this more true than in authoritarian polities.

In his essay on liberalism and hypocrisy, Hu Ping (2005) agrees with Grant and Shklar that a blanket condemnation of or overzealous campaign to eradicate hypocrisy can backfire and fundamentally undermine democracy. Turning his gaze to China, however, he believes that authoritarianism makes it impossible to sustain a healthy level of hypocrisy. On the contrary, it precipitates a perverse form of hypocrisy that he calls *wei'e* or pseudovice—a play on the Chinese word for hypocrisy *weishan* (pseudovirtue). He argues that a good system brings out the better angels of our nature, whereas a bad one brings out the worst in us:

> Most people want to appear better or more just than they actually are. That is to say, most people have a mixture of good and evil in them. The advantages of liberal democracy reside in its ability to nudge the not-so-good toward good behavior. Bad institutions force even good people to go against their good nature to behave atrociously, whereas good institutions propel even bad people to approximate good behavior, albeit with the consequence of encouraging hypocrisy. This means that hypocrisy is the product of good institutions; and by the same token, bad institutions give birth to a large amount of pseudovice. Many critics have characterized the Chinese as vicious and ugly. In the period when class struggle reigned supreme, sons and daughters struggled against their parents, and wives exposed their husbands. Now the entire population is corrupt and lacking in civic virtue. I say that the Chinese are bad on account of their bad institutions. Chinese vices are "pseudovices." (Hu Ping 2005, 316)

Hu Ping's notion of "pseudovice" is an important contribution to the rethinking of hypocrisy by transposing the revisionist thrust from the liberal context to the authoritarian political culture of modern China. In liberal democracy, hypocrisy, performed to the bitter end, for all intents and purposes redeems itself as virtue. In Grant's words, "every act of hypocrisy involves a pretense of virtue, which necessarily includes public acknowledgments of moral standards for political action, and sometimes, that public statement is the best that can be done" (1997, 189). In contrast, pseudovice in authoritarianism can leave us with pervasive incivility and worse. Here Scott's fear that one's face may grow to fit the mask materializes with a vengeance.

In Mao's China, having to mouth the public transcript of class-based division, domination, and hatred and to daily put it into action may well propel the same individuals to identify with the militant ideology, even if they themselves or their loved ones may be victimized by the same ideology. Thus instead of trying to create, sustain, and spread hidden transcripts that might build coalitions and challenge the dominant order, the oppressed might just be too busy performing and reproducing the dynamics of oppression, even when they slyly disobey. For example, during the Great Leap famine (1959–62), Frank Dikötter finds many instances of nonsubversive disobedience. When survival itself depended simultaneously on compliance and disobedience, people had little choice but "to lie, charm, hide, steal, cheat, pilfer, forage, smuggle, slack, trick, manipulate or otherwise outwit the state" (Dikötter 2010, 197). These tactics of subaltern hypocrisy not only scrambled the moral compass of the practitioners but also became baked into the system as a modus vivendi. Over time, it became difficult to say whether one was justifiably cheating the state or unfairly bilking the public or unscrupulously taking advantage of one's neighbors. In short, "obfuscation was the communist way of life" (Dikötter 2010, xiv).

Lu Xun's savagely biting novella *The True Story of Ah Q* is perhaps the best illustration of how oppression corrupts the oppressed, though written long before the nightmarish extremity of the Great Leap Forward. The protagonist Ah Q's place in the pecking order of Weizhuang's village society is never in doubt in the eyes of everyone but Ah Q himself. A tramp and seasonal laborer who has no proper name or known pedigree and who puts up in the dilapidated village temple, Ah Q indulges in the delusion that he is somehow related to the wealthy, prominent Zhao family. Delusion is indeed Ah Q's modus vivendi. When he is abused by the powerful, he rescues himself from the state of shameful despondence by slapping his own face while muttering something about a father beating a son (figures 2.1, 2.2). By playing simultaneously the abuser and the abused, he manages to neutralize the insults and injuries that make up his lot in life. Even more grotesquely, he exults in his superior ability for self-abuse and vainly claims the title of the world's number one "self-putdown artist" (Lu Xun 1990, 111). In turn he actively seeks out those who are even more marginalized and vulnerable and subjects them to his vindictive reenactment

FIGURES 2.1, 2.2: Ah Q slapping himself; Ah Q rebuked by Mr. Zhao. From Lu Xun's *The True Story of Ah Q*. In *Feng Zikai manhua Lu Xun xiaoshuo ji* (Fujian jiaoyu chubanshe, 1921), 19, 17. Photographs: Courtesy of the Feng family.

of the same ritual of abuse. When he strains hard to be mean toward another ragamuffin named Little D or a nun, we have a classic example of the pseudovice that Hu Ping lays at the door of China's institutional culture.

With Ah Q, Lu Xun presents us with a larger-than-life persona without a moral core, a hollow mask that has swallowed up the face underneath, reducing it to a bundle of indistinct, abhorrent impulses. When the 1911 Revolution is on the horizon, Ah Q aspires to be a revolutionary for the same reason he wants to be a Zhao: to run with the powerful or at least to bask in their reflected glory, and to share in the spoils entitled to the victors. Specifically, he wants to take over the Zhaos' prized possessions—women and property. Had the revolution been truly a grassroots one, it might have recruited just such dispossessed but irrepressibly hopeful peasants like Ah Q—as the Communist Revolution would—and steered them onto a nobler path of collective action, but it did not, and Ah Q is made a scapegoat in the counterrevolution that ensues. Bad institutions and ineffectual social movements turn Ah Q's aspirations for respectability and upward social mobility into mere fodder for folly. In their wake we are left with the most despised fictional character in Chinese literary history, a wretch irredeemably corrupted and crushed by the system, whose unremitting oppression elicits no sympathy, only contempt.

When it comes to the ruling elite, we already have a glimpse of Lu Xun's dim view from his 1926 essay cited at the beginning of this chapter. In another essay called "On Deferring Fair Play" (1925; in Lu Xun 1980, 2:208–18), he goes after the smug self-image of the newly Westernized intelligentsia urging civilized rules ("fair play") on the Chinese while tolerating the double standard of morality still ubiquitous in China. Hypocritical intellectuals, of both the old and the new variety, appear with nauseating frequency in his small corpus of short stories, in which the ringing shibboleths they spout barely conceal baser motives. In "Soap" (1924), for example, a Confucian gentleman is titillated by the suggestion that a beggar girl could be a nice "piece of goods" if someone would "buy a couple of cakes of soap [and] give her a good old rub-a-dub-dub" (Lu Xun 1990, 276). When he meets with his fellow members of the Society for the Improvement of the Social Mores, he repeats this suggestive remark ostensibly to indict the cruel lack of compassion toward the girl from those crowding around her, and then scolds a fellow member for parroting it with lewd delight—exactly what he is doing himself. But far more often, Lu Xun aims his pen at the Ah Q–type subalterns who seem to have been thoroughly evacuated of their moral core and who are eager to play their bit part in deepening the chasms of society. The rottenness of Chinese society in his eyes thus goes beyond its cannibalistic nature and the hypocritical veneer of its ruling class. It rather resides in the dehumanization of the powerless, which turns them into the instrument of their own victimization, and in the evaporation of the spirit of resistance.

Communist Antihypocrisy

The Communist Party would prove Lu Xun's despair unwarranted. It replaced Ah Q with peasant heroes who are full of rebellious spirit and are eminently capable of awakening to their true class standing and acceding to their world-historical mission. They are also for the most part portrayed as *laoshi*—honest, simple, straightforward, on the premise that good people should have nothing to hide. "Blurting out the truth—especially when it corresponded to the truths the Party urged—was seen, suddenly, as desirable. The heroes set up for emulation were all presented as guileless, almost robots programmed to perform moral acts with no concern for self-protection or even anyone's face ('cogs in the machinery of socialism'). All the ordinary concerns about social grace, about politeness, about status and roles, about positions, about reputation—all this was to be overturned by the heroic acts of honesty and bluntness" (Blum 2007, 116). Blum notes that in Liu Shaoqi's *How to Be a Good Communist* (1951), Ah Q–ism comes under pointed attack (116). Under the ultrajust system set up by the Party, Ah Q has become an anomaly, an eyesore. Lu Xun's obsession with the duplicitous character of the Chinese is declared obsolete.

At the same time, the Party also claims Lu Xun's mantle as the uncompromising crusader against an unjust social order, and it weaponizes his antihypocrisy zeal with deadly consequences. In the socialist realistic repertoire, alongside heavy-hitting exposés about the landlord class's ruthless predation of the peasantry in the Old Society (pre-1949 China) are stories about peasant characters not playing fair as a riposte to the ruling class not playing fair. They detail, under the ancien régime, the hypocritical lengths to which landowners would go to squeeze ever more surplus value from the labor of the dispossessed class under the cover of ideological mystification. An episode from the eponymous autobiographical novel (1955) of the PLA soldier Gao Yubao exemplifies this genre. Entitled "The Rooster Crows at Midnight" ("Banye jijiao"), the episode achieved national fame upon its inclusion in primary-school textbooks and its adaptation into an animated short film of the same title by the Shanghai Animation Studio (You Lei 1964) (figure 2.3). With a landlord as the default villain, the story takes a break from the usual litany of heinous crimes committed by class

FIGURE 2.3: Poster for *The Rooster Crows at Midnight* (You Lei 1964, Shanghai Animation Film Studio), adapted from the autobiographical novel *Gao Yubao* (Gao Yubao 1955).

enemies. Instead, we get a zany tale of a practical joke played on Zhou Bapi (Zhou the Skinflint), a villainous buffoon who ends up the laughing stock of his victims and of readers alike.

The story line is evocative of the archetypal folktale about the man who is too clever for his own good. To get the maximum out of his hired hands, Zhou Bapi figures out a way to force them to rise early by sneaking into the chicken coop to stir up the rooster and make it crow in the middle of the night. The hired hands soon catch on and retaliate by laying ambush and beating him up under the cover of darkness, feigning to have mistaken him for a thief. Here hypocrisy is both a strategy of class domination and an artful tactic of resistance. On the surface, the landlord-laborer relationship is a contractual one between employer and employees. The latter hire themselves out to the former for a living wage, and the terms and conditions of employment, such as rising at dawn—announced by cock crow—to commence a day's work are largely a matter of convention to which both sides adhere. Being a ruthless and shiftless employer, Zhou tries to cheat his workers without, however, violating the tacit labor contract, apparently still caring enough about his reputation. So he goes to the trouble of rising in the wee hours and prowling in the barnyard. Though in socialist realism landlords are invariably portrayed as local tyrants who wield unchecked power over their tenant farmers and servants, here Zhou Bapi seems incapable of simply ordering the workers to start working at whatever hour pleases him. Instead, he has to resort to subterfuge and hide his bottomless greed behind a freakish occurrence of nature. In other words, he keeps his hidden transcripts hidden and bends over backward to honor the public transcript that says the work day commences at cock crow. And that veneer of hypocrisy is precisely the leverage needed for the hired hands to turn the tables on him.

The cartoon adaptation, targeted at school-age audiences, stops at the moment of triumph for the workers. The psychological game does not, however, end here. In the original novel (Gao Yubao 1955), the village warden, Zhou's adult son, launches an investigation the next day and prolongs, on behalf of his father, the battle of will and wits with the laborers. As Zhou Bapi lies in bed moaning and groaning, the son tries to break down the united front of the laborers and nail the ringleader. But the laborers, after some effort at internal policing and morale boosting, stick to their public-transcript-compliant story about mistaken identity and misplaced eagerness. How galling it must be for Zhou to listen in on the proceedings. He can probably almost hear the barely suppressed chuckles of the men who let themselves loose on him the night before. It is a classic instance of infrapolitical resistance: in contradistinction to open rebellion, infrapolitics requires feigned homage to the public transcript. In beating up the alleged chicken rustler, the hired hands are ostensibly defending their master's livestock and honoring the sanctity of private property. They have acted under cover of plausible deniability, allowing them to camouflage their retaliation. After all, how can Zhou Bapi have a problem with men who dutifully defended his property and went after a criminal?

The doubling up on duplicity, or class struggle as a battle of wits, is what makes the story so broadly appealing and memorable amid countless shrill, dour works that make up the bulk of socialist propaganda. Humor and irony are enjoyable because, according to Steven Gimbel, who draws on cognitive epistemology, they hone "cognitive virtues" that are useful in real life, such as attention to detail, pattern recognition, open-mindedness, creativity, metaphor creation, and breadth of knowledge (2018, 43–46). Moreover, what makes a humorous act or utterance humorous—intentionality, conspicuousness, playfulness, and cleverness—presupposes the recipient's ability to "read" other minds. In this episode, which grafts the humor effect of a practical joke to an act of sabotage, the audience's theory of mind gets a rigorous workout as they follow along the imbricated scheming and plotting and then join in the good cheer with the hired hands.

We start with Zhou Bapi who *wants* the workers to *think* that it's time to get up and start the day's work when they hear the rooster crow *without suspecting* anything amiss. We move onto the latter's mental state when they discover Zhou to be the agent behind the rooster's unnatural behavior and comprehend his motive: Zhou Bapi *wants* us to start working at midnight and *knows* we can't simply say no to a rooster, but if we *pretend* we *don't know* who it is who steals into the chicken coop and if we *pretend to mistake* him for a common thief, then we will be able to foil his odious scheme. Back to Zhou Bapi, after the thrashing, *realizing* and *fuming* that the workers *have seen through* his trick and *known* very well whom they were beating *to their hearts' content*. To the workers again, *rejoicing* in their minor but gratifying victory over a hated boss because they *know* that Zhou Bapi *knows* that they *knew* whom they had beaten to a pulp. Again back to Zhou Bapi, *knowledge* of the workers *gloating* behind his back because they *know* he *knows* they *knew* make his welts smart even more, and with the escalation of mental embedment the pleasure also heightens. None of this is explicitly spelled out in Gao's novel, but the popularity of this episode can have no other explanation.

If there were no public transcript to uphold, no hypocritical rules of conduct to adhere to, then there would be no incentive to play such a convoluted mental game: Zhou Bapi could lord it over the workers despotically, and the workers would either slavishly submit or openly revolt. This means that every conflict, large or small, would immediately be fought out in the open, which essentially would mean the end of social life, politics, and perhaps human civilization as we know it. Power, as numerous theorists have stressed, requires consent, however coerced, tenuous, or feigned. And consent rides on the upholding of the public transcript by the powerful and powerless alike. When socialist literature permits a vestige of Kabuki theater of class antagonism that grants each side sufficient endowment of cognitive virtues (and by implication agency and freedom), it can generate a measure of aesthetic pleasure and occasional mirth. But when the Old Society is painted as uniformly dark and suffocating, when there is zero overlap between the public transcripts of the antagonistic classes, when the idea of hegemony or government by consent is rejected in toto, socialist narratives of trauma and grievance can be unremittingly grim and unrealistic.

Other than ideological motivations, it is also possible that the more extreme version of socialist realism rejects the dueling game of hypocrisy out of a disinclination to tackle its moral complications. This is connected with the abjuring of the popular genre of spy thriller during the Cultural Revolution (see chapter 1). The persistent challenge is how to portray the proletariat as morally incorruptible when they (or their emissaries) have to tango with the enemy on the enemy's noxious turf and to the enemy's obnoxious tune. The solution, as *The Rooster Crows at Midnight* demonstrates so well, is to provide a political justification for morally problematic actions. Once filtered through a political grid, moral considerations are only for "us"; against "them" all means are justified. This drawing of a firm border around morality is rooted in a long literary tradition that celebrates righteous outlaws who rise up against tyrannical rulers and who fully claim our sympathy and endorsement. Their moral integrity is guaranteed by their punching up instead of punching down—as Ah Q does.

In *The Rooster Crows at Midnight*, no character on "our" side is troubled by the act of violence (of beating an old man to within an inch of his life) or of lying and giving false testimony. The laborers triumph against the moral corruption of oppression because they are able to forge an alternative community in which the politics of class struggle authorizes a hidden transcript to justify their action. Had Ah Q been one of them, he would not have descended so low on the moral ladder. But as a loner and outcast, he is crushed by power instead of contributing to the project of turning the hidden transcript of the oppressed into the public transcript of the New Society. In its turn, the socialist public transcript would require hypocritical compliance from the newly minted masters and servants alike. And who are the masters and servants of the new nation is itself a fraught question to which an honest answer may be a most impolitic, even deadly one.

Performing the Socialist Public Transcript

In the post-Mao zeal to subject the socialist canon to the test of veracity, the beloved story about a rooster bogusly incited to crow at midnight predictably comes up short. It has been reported that the real-life prototype of Zhou Bapi (Zhou Chunfu) was a quiet, nose-to-the-grindstone type. No one in Gao Yubao's native village ever heard anything about midnight prowling and savage beating before the story became a national sensation (Meng Lingqian n.d.). Zhou had already been executed in the Land Reform of the early 1950s, but his descendants became the target of taunts and insults and were ready-made scapegoats in the endless campaigns. Interestingly, the first edition of the book includes an afterword by someone writing under the nom de plume Huang Cao (Wild Grass) entitled "How

I Helped Comrade Gao Yubao Revise His Novel." It is a surprisingly frank and revealing account of how the sausage of the socialist public transcript is made. It relates that when Gao Yubao, a peasant recruit in the PLA, began composing his memoir in 1949 at the tail end of the civil war, he was barely literate: "for every ten characters, he had to ask for help with seven or eight of them" (206). The army sent Huang Cao to assist Gao in wrestling his manuscript into something that could serve the propaganda needs of the new nation. He explains the process: "Because Comrade Gao Yubao's original manuscript was a work of autobiography, to alter it in any way would inevitably compromise the authenticity of Comrade Gao Yubao's personal history. Initially, Comrade Gao Yubao had many reservations about the proposed changes. He worried that the comrades and fellow villagers who knew his past would say that he was making things up and distorting the character of those who were still living. However, without these changes, the work's educational value to its readers would greatly diminish" (Huang Cao 1955, 208).

What Huang Cao articulates here is the paradox that lies at the heart of the socialist public transcript. On the one hand, *Gao Yubao* is meant to be taken as a faithful record of a peasant boy's journey from an illiterate swine herder to a PLA soldier and writer. Indeed, the English edition issued by the Foreign Languages Press promises it to be "a story so truthfully and vividly told" that it is bound to move the reader (Gao Yubao [Kao Yu-pao] 1960, "Editor's Note," n.p.). On the other hand, there is no attempt to hide the deliberate process of hammering empirical facts into socialist truisms, a process that was later codified by Zhou Yang and others as elevating raw life (*shenghua*) and establishing typicality (*dianxing*). Out of the countless instances of elevation and typification would emerge the Big Lie of socialist propaganda. In spite of the outsize influence of this novel and other hagiographical texts, the most impactful and directly transformative process of elevation did not take place on the printed pages, but theatrically in face-to-face settings. This is the so-called *suku* or *fanshen* ritual ubiquitously staged during the land reforms of the 1940s and 1950s and then intermittently throughout the 1960s and 1970s.

The ritual of *suku* is communal festival, street theater, and public tribunal all rolled into one (I will say more about the "tribunal" aspects in the next chapter on transitional justice). In a typical session, the residents of a village or town are gathered together in a communal space by Party cadres. On a raised dais stands the target of "struggle" or *pidou*, a specimen of Maospeak that has disappeared from the contemporary Chinese lexicon. The class enemy is publicly accused, denounced, condemned, sentenced, and sometimes physically assaulted, in front of a mass audience and with mass participation. Select members of the community, identified and vetted and patiently coached in prior investigative processes called *fangpin wenku* (investigating poverty and inquiring about suffering) conducted by work teams, are called up to stand next to the target and to recall "bitterness" by recounting their experiences of suffering in the Old Society. The purpose, according to a handbook, is "to share an oral personal history about being persecuted by class enemies both for the purpose of inspiring class hatred in the listeners, while reaffirming one's own class standing" (quoted in F. Sun 2013, 44). Sometimes material evidence such as a bloodied shirt or a bill of sales is also produced to augment authenticity and emotional impact (for more on these pseudo-forensic props, see chapter 3).

On the basis of his archival research, in particular the contents of a handbook called *Suku and Revenge: Suku Education's Experience and Method* (1947), Feiyu Sun concludes that the "exemplary speakers" were carefully sought out and interviewed by work teams, their stories refined and cultivated, their language modulated and "cleansed." In other words, "the exemplary narrators and the tales they told were not 'discovered'; they were carefully created and crafted" (F. Sun 2013, 57). The handbook acknowledges the hurdle of breaking down peasant reluctance to confront their erstwhile social betters. It took a great deal of perseverance and skill to get peasants to shed what Gordon Wood calls "a down look" (quoted in Sunstein 2016, 136). Liberation or *fanshen* starts with daring to look the landlord in the eye, thus passing the "eyeball test" proposed by Philip Pettit (2014, 98–100) as the true gauge of liberty.

The reluctance likely had multiple sources: fear, timidity, inarticulateness, and, above all, inability to see how their personal grievances against a particular landlord could be connected with the lofty theory of class oppression and exploitation. The primary goal of the ritual was precisely to draw out the variegated tales of woe and meld them into a grand narrative about the abiding struggle between two antagonistic classes.[4] The low justice of past right and wrong, in other words, must be elevated to the high justice of class struggle. The low injustices (beating, defamation, etc.) that individuals ended up inflicting on one another anew in their compulsory performance of pseudovice were also a direct consequence of high justice. The post-Mao regime would have to disavow this causality in its transitional justice project, detailed in the next chapter. In *suku*, all social relationships were to be braided into a single narrative arc, so that the only way individuals related to one another was as comrades or as enemies, not as kinsfolk, neighbors, business associates, and so on. Class antagonism in turn rendered all other social relationships ideologically irrelevant and morally weightless. People of course still related to one another in these capacities informally, but they often had to explicitly repudiate these unofficial attachments in order to be fully answerable to the public transcript. It was in this sense that many felt that they were living a lie, even though the politicized lifeworld had nothing fictional about it. Furthermore, having publicly contributed to the making of the public transcript, one became its coauthor and bound to it by a sense of ownership and allegiance. Hypocrisy, in other words, need not be the antithesis of sincerity and earnestness.

The many political campaigns of the Mao era extended the basic formula of *suku* to a broader arena of political life ranging from criticism-and-self-criticism meetings aiming to reform erring comrades, to public sentencing rallies targeting "enemies of the people." These political theaters shared in common a codified procedure that mandated a public apology or confession from the accused, whether it was censure, demotion, exile, imprisonment, or execution that awaited him or her at the end. Everyone had to fall in line—whether they felt it in their hearts or were merely paying lip service—so that the socialist public transcript could be consolidated. Chen Rong's novella *True or False* (*Zhenzhen jiajia*)[5] is a brilliant portrayal of a series of criticism-and-self-criticism sessions, set in a research institute in the immediate post-Mao years, that turn on the imperative of a public admission of error on the part of the individual caught in the headwind and unanimous avowals of agreement with the Party's verdict. The substance of the offense (publishing a daring academic article) hardly matters, except to one earnest character who breaks rank and tries to speak truth to power. But his outburst is met with stony silence and is swiftly swept under the rug as the leading cadre sums up the meetings with a reconstituted public transcript that papers over all winkles, large and small (Chen Rong 1986; Blum 2007, 128–29).

In his study of labor camps, Jan Kiely also emphasizes the compulsory nature of the Party's favorite mechanism of thought control: small-group discussion, which mixes self-criticism, mutual criticism, denunciation, and "struggle": "Discussion had to follow a particular, repetitive pattern in which each group member had to play his or her assigned role in the manner of coercive voluntarism. The need to be perceived as 'progressive' depended upon a confession that met the formula required and on speaking in the CCP's specific and, for most, strange new vocabulary" (Kiely 2014, 283). In such situations of "coercive voluntarism," the sincerity of the confessor is of little account, since only a public retraction or disavowal can repair the public transcript of apparent compliance (Scott 1990, 57). During the Stalinist purges and show trials of the 1930s, for example, the accused were sometimes coerced and tortured into making public apologies and confessions.[6] That is because, in Scott's view, "doctrinal unanimity was so highly valued [that] it was not enough for the party to crush dissent; the victims had to make a public display of their acceptance of the party's judgment" (1990, 57).

A persistent feature in the Party's Sisyphean struggle against corruption is public shaming, which in the age of mass media has migrated from the street to the television screen, where tearful confessions have replaced abject submission to denunciation and abuse. According to Christian Sorace, these confessions are "intended to separate corrupt cadres from the party, repair the party's image, and shore up the fragile foundation of its moral legitimacy" (Sorace 2019, 148). Insofar as Party cadres are not generic Weberian bureaucrats who go home after work but are rather vessels of "Party spirit" (*dangxing*) and conduits of Party legitimacy, their public disgrace is a way of cauterizing "mutated, necrotic cells" (155), something that cannot be achieved in a court of law, which sees only specific acts and dispenses only low justice. Cadres are the permanent lead actors in the theater of governance. They may have more downtime now than in the past, but they are never supposed to break character. When they do, they may never return to the stage.

It is tempting to go from recognizing the power of the public transcript to the old standby of brainwashing, as if Communist propaganda were diabolically adept at gaslighting its audience (more on brainwashing in chapter 4). It is important to keep in mind that the socialist public transcript sat atop of the vast infrastructure of socialist political economy, without which its "shamanistic incantations" (Snyder 2017, 66) would be mere hot air. What Michael Dutton (2009) calls the gift economy of socialist governmentality yoked real-world advantages to political distinctions. We can never know for sure if people wholeheartedly, unswervingly believed in communism, but when communism was one's entire lifeworld so that it determined everything from whether one could go to college to whether one was entitled to an apartment, the divide between belief and action or between face and mask was largely moot. One learned not to look for propositional content in formulaic truth, for the truth or falsity of a statement mattered little when one's life chances depended on acting as though one believed it (Arendt 1972, 7). When people spouted official cant, it is beside the point to inquire whether they were merely pantomiming the script while keeping an inner distance from it all (Hansen 2017). For Bakken, the demand for behavioral conformity drives "structural 'ways of lying'" (2000, 411), a point echoed by Sonia Ryang (2021) in her study of North Korean regimes of truth.

The ingenuity of *suku* lies in its ability to suture the individual into the socialist scriptural economy regardless of inner feelings. In socialist China, once a person has publicly voiced a half-truth or participated in a violent struggle session out of a desire to conform, please, win recognition, or reap rewards, the most expedient way to reduce cognitive dissonance, as noted earlier, is confabulation or adjusting one's beliefs and feelings to better align with one's public avowals and public actions. It is much easier and less risky than to try to recant what is already seen and heard by others. The awareness of having uttered falsehoods or acted cruelly can be cognitively costly, whereas post hoc rationalization can work wonders in restoring a baseline level of self-coherence and self-respect. This is perhaps the best support of Arendt's contention that the unmasking of the hypocrite does not necessarily lead to the disclosure of "an inside self, an authentic appearance, changeless and reliable in its thereness" and that "the uncovering destroys a deception [but] does not discover anything authentically appearing" (1978, 1:39).

Everybody Is a Cynic

The ultimate legacy of *suku* is not a population of liars and self-deceivers, but a nation of cynics who are as apathetic as they are gullible. "In an ever-changing, incomprehensible world the masses had reached the point where they would, at the same time, believe everything and nothing, think that everything was possible and that nothing was true" (Arendt 1968, 382). Cynicism is the inevitable spawn of what Arendt calls "organized lying" (1993, 232)—exaggerations, simplifications, misattributions, omissions, or outright fabrications. At its worst, the socialist public transcript became completely unmoored from facticity and formed a dome of hot air that smothered everything under it. During the Great Leap Forward (1958–62), for example, a toxic combination of political pressure and incentive structure made it possible for a thousand little falsehoods about agricultural yields to congeal into a gigantic lie at the cost of millions of lives. It was not a matter of how the leadership—which boasted many members with a rural upbringing and who therefore should have known better—could have possibly believed in those wildly inflated harvest figures, but one of having to cleave to the official tenet that revolutionary zeal could wring miracles from nature. Questioning an improbable number would be tantamount to breaching the public transcript—something that even Mao himself could not afford to do.[7] One's only option was to join in the chorus, send in the phony numbers, revel in the sham glory, and let the bureaucratic machinery take over, which meant artificially high procurement quotas that robbed the peasantry of their chance of survival. We now learn, with a shudder, that grain was being aggressively requisitioned for foreign export, aid, and debt service and that excess grain sat rotting in state granaries while millions of peasants starved to death (Dikötter 2010).

Once the struggle sessions ceased, once *suku* memoirs stopped rolling out of printing presses, once career prospects no longer hung on one's political stand, few had any reason to continue to tweak their inner beliefs to better align with the official story. But to the extent that the Party is still in power and still demands a high degree of ideological conformity, and to the extent that the infrastructure of obfuscation is still in place through the state control of media, organized lying goes on, albeit with less urgency and with greater media savvy and technological know-how. Cynicism may be more pronounced today as spaces for voicing doubts and expressing irony open up, but, as Hu Ping suggests, it has always been a tumor eating away at the innards of Communist rule. The hot air of totalitarian propaganda may have receded, and fresh air, even exotic aroma can waft through, but the public transcript is still suffused with formulaic truth that disdains referentiality and "bolsters political compliance by reaffirming the seeming inevitability of the current political order" (Hansen 2017, 48). Qian Gang notes with dismay the resurgence of breathless parallelism (*paibiju*) as a figure of official speech in the Xi Jinping era. For example, a relatively short article in the *Study Times*, published by the Central Party School, contains forty-two parallelisms.[8] Xi's unmistakable fondness for parallelisms is infectious, and everywhere Qian turns, he finds fawning texts that practically choke on their own rhetorical flourishes. "There is a ritual quality to such expressions of loyalty. The parallelism, like the drumbeat, is about the rhythm, music and dance of loyalty" (Qian Gang 2019).

The Party has never ceased to enforce a public transcript that fosters hypocrisy within its own ranks and among the broader populace. And this hypocrisy assumes two faces, as Hu Ping rightly argues: pseudovirtue and pseudovice. Cynicism goes above ground when the public transcript morphs into a collection of open secrets and becomes increasingly divorced from the socialist political economy and its gift economy. Scott defines open secrets as certain facts that are widely known but could never be discussed openly. Examples include forced labor camps, famine, political infighting, and special perks and privileges for high-level Communist officials[9] that blatantly contradict the public transcript built on ideals of progress, equality, unity, and popular sovereignty. "What may develop under such circumstances is virtually a dual culture: the official culture filled with bright euphemisms, silences, and platitudes and an unofficial culture that has its own history, its own literature and poetry, its own biting slang, its own music and poetry, its own humor, its own knowledge of shortages, corruption, and inequalities that may, once again, be widely known but that may not be introduced into public discourse" (Scott 1990, 51).

When both the ruling class and the ruled have a good inkling of each other's hidden transcripts, and yet neither side is willing or dares to poke through the paper screen, cynicism is the only option left. Caring about truth would make one's lifeworld inoperative. This is when the public transcript approximates the epistemological status of bullshit as Frankfurt defines it: the absence of any regard for truth, indifference to how things really stand (2005, 34–35). Margaret Hillenbrand has argued forcefully that the shriveled state of public memory in China is not merely a result of censorship and amnesia, but a societal cultivation of public secrets, a collective endeavor with "many stakeholders, whether willing or otherwise, affiliated with the state or not" (2020, 2). This peculiar state of "knowing not to know" that she scrutinizes describes very well the kind of cynicism that concerns me here. Cynicism is the disavowal of truth, whether historical or in the here and now. The average person might dismiss the official press as full of bullshit, but he or she will not necessarily go out of the way to seek out more accurate reporting, which brings no advantage, only more cognitive dissonance. As Hu Ping notes with evident pain, the cynic has little patience for either the establishment or the opposition (2005, 32–33).

John Osburg characterizes post-Mao China as a postbelief society in which "everyone is presumed to be governed by crude interest" (2016, 50). Cynicism seems to have become the default pose of the rising middle class as well as a large portion of the educated elite. Behind the cynical pose is a realm of infrapolitics woven out of *guanxi* (relationship) networks. Osburg notes that the gap between official representations and informal practices is often vast, yet it can be risky to publicly acknowledge that gap, especially for government officials. This accounts for "the endless hours of ritualized entertaining"—banqueting, drinking, carousing in karaoke clubs, visits to saunas, and so on—that officials and entrepreneurs alike engage in. All of these are "attempts to build the trust and familiarity that might undergird an emergent 'community of complicity,' in which one can safely do away with the necessity to pretend to defer to official representations" (Osburg 2016, 58). Osburg borrows the term "community of complicity" from Hans Steinmüller, who uses it to designate contingent zones of moral obligation and judgment against a backdrop of amoral opportunism and instrumentality (Steinmüller 2016, 8). Within these zones, typically built around family and friendship ties, principles of *renqing* or human feelings, reciprocity, and trust rule provisionally with the aid of a healthy dose of hypocrisy. The upshot of ceding the public arena to cynicism, however, is that the state can easily justify authoritarian rule on the grounds of needing to rein in ruthless instrumentality. Authoritarianism is thus both the cause and the beneficiary of cynicism.

The Community of Complicity

Communities of complicity need not be limited to banquet halls and karaoke clubs. Works of fiction have always constituted mediated communities of complicity with their ludic discourse of irony and satire shared between writers who wield symbols and metaphors and readers who enjoy reading between the lines, much like Lu Xun's madman. Yan Lianke's novel *Serve the People!* (*Wei renmin fuwu*) is an exemplary post-Mao reenactment of the Lu Xun–esque tactic of exposing the hypocrisy of the ruling regime by peering into the yawning gap between "socialist declarations and corrupt practices" (Steinmüller 2016, 1). "Serve the People" is the title of one of a trio of Mao's essays collectively known as the "three constantly read classics" (*lao sanpian*), which formed the core of Maoist liturgy and mandatory reading for the entire nation under high socialism. They were included in school textbooks and excerpted in the Little Red Book, and it was common for people of all ages to be able to recite them from memory.[10] The protagonist of Yan's novel is one such individual. Wu Dawang is an orderly newly assigned to a PLA division commander who is married to a former army nurse nearly twenty years his junior. The wife, Liu Lian, quit her job after marriage and is now whiling away her time in the well-appointed house doing nothing in particular—something unthinkable for socialist realist heroines. During one of the commander's extended absences, Liu seduces Wu, and the adulterous pair indulge in wild and reckless orgies that press into service a plaque bearing the slogan "Serve the People!" and a good number of broken Mao artifacts as sex props.

Officially banned by the Chinese authorities, *Serve the People!* is not among Yan Lianke's best works, relying as it does on crude juxtapositions and contrived gags. It is symptomatic that a writer who wishes to dig into the heap of half-buried truths about the ruling Communist Party dare only go after the Mao cult—the one thing that has been loudly repudiated by the post-Mao regime. Nonetheless, Yan's satire packs a punch insofar as Mao as a political icon continues to anchor the Party's legitimacy and insofar his exhortation to serve the people still adorns government buildings and crops up in official discourse. No reader is so obtuse as not to get the irony of Liu Lian using the wooden plaque emblazoned with "Serve the People!" in Mao's own inimitable handwriting to signal to Wu Dawang her readiness for an assignation, and the two of them wantonly smashing

Mao's plaster busts and ripping up Mao posters and the Little Red Book to aid their sexual arousal. All their lovemaking takes place in the upstairs bedroom of the commander's Soviet-built stand-alone villa, an unimaginable luxury for most Chinese at the time. Even more unimaginable is how the lovers could get away with such blasphemous acts that in the outside world were more than enough to land someone in the direst of troubles, or capital punishment as the blurb for the English edition screams (Yan Lianke [2005] 2007, n.p.). The exposé is quite blunt: in its public transcript, the Party presents itself as the humble servant of the people and casts its rule as a combination of tutelage and service; in its hidden transcript, it makes the people serve the Party in every which way, down to satisfying its most craven desires; and to maximize its pleasure, it would go so far as to trample on its own sacred cows and squeeze the people down to the last drop of vitality.

In other words, the Party is guilty of stupendous hypocrisy. The choice of sex is no accident. Sexual hypocrisy has always been the favorite target of antihypocrisy—recall Lu Xun's "Soap." Feminists have long indicted patriarchy for the sexual double standard. Critics of monastic orders likewise have made good sport of the priesthood's underhanded breach of the celibacy vow. In Mao's China, sex was confined to the marital bed and was supposed to be strictly for procreation. Premarital sex, adultery, and recreational sex (even between a married couple) were considered hooligan behavior, and offenders were often publicly shamed and administratively sanctioned.[11] Just as in Catholicism, lust allegedly turns the individual away from God/the Party. In the novel, the Communist sex code is violated on two levels: First, the commander's marriage to a nubile woman young enough to be his daughter who for the time being remains childless clearly serves more than the purpose of siring the "successors of the revolution." Second, Liu Lian's liaison with Wu Dawang is driven entirely by carnal passion in spite of all the cheeky references to their "great love affair."

It is clearly the second violation that is meant to explode the puritanical facade of the Party. Powerful men acquiring trophy wives or dallying with beautiful young women in extramarital affairs is perhaps the worst-kept secret of all patriarchal societies. Its exposé might raise a few eyebrows but would hardly count as explosive. That it was one of the few open secrets of the socialist period was attested to by revelations in the immediate post-Mao years of sexual predations in the PLA and the Lin Biao family's dissolute lifestyle, followed by rumors and then a tell-all memoir (published overseas) about Mao's habitual philandering (Li Zhisui 1994). In a way, such gender-based sexual oppression has become so ingrained a part of the patriarchal power structure that few writers would consider it fresh enough a subject or jaunty enough an angle for an antihypocrisy exposé.

Jiang Qing, Mao's estranged wife and ringleader of the "Gang of Four"—the officially designated and prosecuted instigators of the Cultural Revolution—was also reported to have wallowed in debauchery while going all out to torment Mao and wreck his revolutionary enterprise. There are unmistakable parallels between the many salacious stories about Jiang Qing and *Serve the People!* In both, the bored wife of a powerful man leverages her status to gratify her unspeakable cravings. In both, the sordid goings-on are carried out in the name of answering the summons to carry on the revolution. When their sexual fervor begins to flag, Liu Lian sets up a trap that causes Wu to break a Mao bust, and she feigns rushing to the telephone to report him. He flies into a rage while trying to stop her and in the tussle finds himself with the biggest erection ever. Inspired by the sight, she rips up a Mao portrait in order to frame herself also as a "counterrevolutionary." Finding the wreckage both terrifying and inexplicably arousing, they run around the house stark naked and destroy every sacred object they can lay their hands on, turning the resulting rubble into an aphrodisiac tonic to their round-the-clock orgy.

In fact the sacrilege starts much earlier, with Liu Lian's deployment of "Serve the People!" as a come-on in their first tryst. Thereafter they routinely mouth Mao quotes to spice things up, turning these sacred words into codes and euphemisms. We are now back to Lu Xun's world of hypocrisy, where characters do not say what they feel, but resort to coded language to camouflage a reality they dare not look in the eye. "Code is both intended and perceived as pretense, as fundamentally dishonest; it is euphemism uttered in the service of hypocrisy" (Haiman 1998, 82). The immediate target of Yan Lianke's satire is Maoist sexual repression, which deprives the couple of a language to express their burning desire for each other, not to mention a medium with which to cultivate romantic feelings. The incongruity between the powdery dry shibboleths and clammy wet passion generates humor, as well as bathos.

When it is all over, Wu is made to take a long leave of absence and is later assigned to a plum job in a factory; his family follow him there and attain the long-dreamed-of status of city residents. It is a reward for his "service," but also a way to buy his silence, which he obliges save for a couple of small gestures of remembrance. In his timid silence Wu is no different from the eunuchs of the inner court or the servants of the colonial officers' club—utterly dependent on the master for their weal and woe and easily sworn into secrecy the better to safeguard the latter's hidden transcript. Wu may have enjoyed the escapade, but that does not change the nature of the encounter or blunt the indictment against a system that allows the ruling class to pleasure itself on the body of the ruled and to get away with parodying its own solemn liturgy for cheap thrills.

The sexist assumption sleeping in the caricature of insatiable female sexuality is that while men who prey on women have no need to go to great hypocritical lengths to justify their behavior, women have to hide their private urges behind a political command ("Serve the people") to get what they want. And for that reason the hypocritical woman seems that much more loathsome than the stereotypical male hypocrite. Another way of looking at this is that because the public transcript of a patriarchal society puts a higher premium on women's compliance, any deviation or violation would provoke that much more outrage at the perpetrator's attempt at pulling the wool over one's eyes—think of the fate of Pan Jinlian, the adulterous archvillain of the sixteenth-century novel *Plum in the Golden Vase* (*Jinpingmei*). Elsewhere I have discussed how women are forced to hone stronger theory of mind abilities because of their greater need to gauge the mental states of their superiors, largely men in power (H. Lee 2020). By the same token, women's greater need to engage in subterfuge makes them especially susceptible to charges of hypocrisy. One need only invoke the image of the sanctimonious Victorian schoolmarm, or Marxist cadre such as Li Guoxiang in *Hibiscus Town*, who is revealed to have a much seamier side (see H. Lee 2014, chap. 3). The gender dimension of hypocrisy and the sexist surcharge of antihypocrisy seem to go hand in hand.

Apart from sexism and plentiful raunchy sex, *Serve the People!* is a bleak tale owing to the absence of a genuine romance, the kind that Winston and Julia in *1984* manage to carry on right under the nose of Big Brother. As noted above, the illicit lovers conspicuously fail to find a language of their own. Instead, they speak a pastiche of official slogans that may be perversely arousing but is in no way conducive to forging a "community of complicity" founded on familiarity and trust and capable of safeguarding a zone of moral obligation and judgment that defies instrumentality. Insofar as romantic love indexes moral freedom (see chapter 1), the lovers remain shackled in the calculations that are obligatory to those for whom a boot in the face is a daily threat. Whatever feelings they may have developed for each other during those two months was too feeble to withstand the exigency of their opposing locations in the power hierarchy. Without love, there is no hidden transcript, no basis for seeking each other out afterward, and no motive for plotting and scheming their way to freedom. Neither sticks his or her neck out for the other, and neither achieves moral redemption. Their lustful congress has brought two bodies together but never succeeds in uniting two souls in a righteous rebellion. Both go on with their separate, subdued existence having reaped much benefit from being the consummate hypocrites. Between Liu Lian and Wu Dawang, we have the unholy union of the hypocrisy of the powerful and the hypocrisy of the powerless literally in the same bed tearing into each other's flesh. The novel succeeds in turning the CCP's tireless critique of the ancien régime as the rule of hypocrisy on the Party itself. However, not only is there no community of complicity at the diegetic level; the novel's banning has also made it impossible for it to engender a community of complicity with readers on the mainland.

In the fourth and fifth decades of the reform period, the necessity for hypocrisy has eased considerably compared with the hyperpoliticized climate in *Serve the People!* Ordinary everyday life no longer has to be laced with citations of the socialist public transcript, which itself has become more slick and hip and more consciously aligned with global, rule-based norms. Political pressure has largely been replaced by ever-ramifying laws and policies that demand compliance on pain of jail or fine. The 2018 film *Dying to Survive* (*Wo bushi yaoshen*) (Wen Muye 2018), based on true events, details how unjust laws drive an ordinary man to illegality and how the community of complicity that coalesces around him sustains and redeems him morally. Cheng Yong is a shopkeeper who imports essential oils from India and markets them as aphrodisiacs to his gullible Chinese customers. However, he is losing market share to Viagra. Reluctantly, he goes into a lucrative business smuggling a generic leukemia drug from India into the Chinese market, where the brand-name drug from a multinational pharmaceutical company is priced way above the average patient's ability to pay. To pull it off, he has to lie, cheat, and dissemble all the way to India and back. He gets rich very quickly. Then he gets cold feet and sells the illicit business to another smuggler. This smuggler recklessly jacks up the price and is ratted out by a customer to the police. The supply of affordable generic medicine dries up, and the patients are desperate. A few years later, our hero learns of the death of the man who first approached him with the business proposition and to whom he had grown close. He decides to resume the operation, except that this time he is not in it for the money: he now retails the drug for only a nominal sum. Finally, he is caught and convicted. On his way to prison, rows of face-masked patients line the street to give him a hero's send-off (figure 2.4).

This film illustrates how the structure of domination—stemming from state policies that bow to the dictates of corporate capitalism—compels the powerless to resort to illicit tactics to get around unjust or unbending laws and regulations. The most conspicuous and well-studied cases in this regard are piracy and other forms of copyright infringement practiced by

你就能保证你这一辈子不生病吗
Can you guarantee you stay healthy as long as you live?

FIGURE 2.4: Cheng Yong surrounded by leukemia patients; an elderly patient speaking truth to power. From *Dying to Survive* (Wen Muye 2018, Dirty Monkey Films Group and others).

denizens of the global south (Pang 2012, 2006; Wong 2013). Drug trafficking, medical tourism, birth tourism, and commercial surrogacy have also emerged as part of the global informal economy, complementing traditional gray markets in recreational drugs and sex work. Few people who traverse these rhizomatic assemblages consider themselves "criminals." Cheng Yong, for example, is an ordinary person with the usual mix of admirable qualities and foibles: a dutiful son to his bedridden father, a caring, indulgent father to his son, a prickly ex-husband to his ex-wife, and a less-than-honest merchant. He is drawn into the smuggling business by both financial incentives and the persistence of one affable leukemia patient. But in the eyes of the law, Cheng Yong is a smuggler and a purveyor of "counterfeit medicine" (*jiayao*). He uses his essential oils business as a front and lies to the police officers who come to investigate. Consequently, he has to constantly and anxiously look over his shoulder. Striking it rich is exhilarating, but the stress of leading a double life wears him down all too soon. He quits after chafing under the moral and psychological burden of subaltern hypocrisy.

In real life, the prototype for Cheng Yong's character is also a leukemia sufferer with limited means. He discovered the Indian alternative on his own before bringing others on board. In the film, however, Cheng's motives are blatantly venal, at least in the beginning. Hence the dramatic impact when he not only returns to smuggling with no intention of making money but is in fact subsidizing the whole operation with funds from his new garment enterprise, which he has launched successfully in the interval. His ability to transcend the profit motive and to achieve moral redemption is critically hinged on the community of complicity that has emerged from the network of accomplices and that has congealed gradually into bonds of friendship and trust. Through these friends he becomes connected with a larger network of leukemia patients who enter into not just a transactional relationship with him, but also a moral relationship of care, assistance, and indebtedness. Among them develops an alternative moral discourse that does not defer to official representations. After a police roundup brings a large group of buyers to a detention center, an old lady looks the police sergeant straight in the eye in a paradigmatic "speaking truth to power" moment: "'Counterfeit medicine'? We are the patients, and we have been taking this Indian drug for years. Don't we know what is genuine and what is fake?" (see again figure 2.4).

The emergence of a community of complicity is indexed touchingly to the surgical mask worn by the patients. In his initial interactions with them, Cheng is put off by the ubiquitous masks, complaining of the weird feeling of doing business with people whose faces he cannot see. In response his inner circle of helpers refrain from wearing masks in his presence (by, in one instance, bunching the mask under the chin), but the others continue to wear them as they congregate to socialize, distribute underground medicine, and provide care and support to one another.[12] It is not until much later in the film that Cheng finally understands the meaning of mask wearing as a gesture of mutual affirmation and solidarity. In the final scene, we follow Cheng Yong's gaze as he looks out of a small window of the police van. As he makes successive eye contact with the tightly arrayed spectators, face masks are being pulled down one by one in hushed silence and back on as he passes, as if saluting him. A continuous, wordless moral community is thus brought into being through this rolling unmasking and remasking: to Cheng Yong the people on the sidewalks are no longer just leukemia patients and customers, but distinct individuals who have been brought together out of their shared debt of gratitude to him. In real life, the patients championed for the smuggler's early release and went on to petition for policy adjustments that eventually made the Swiss drug affordable so that no one has to break the law in order to survive, for now. The happy ending—described in a postscript—is perhaps the key to why the film was greenlighted in the first place. In removing the underlying cause, the state gets to absorb the community of complicity into its own normative order, hence eliminating a small pocket of resistance without having to own up to its policy failure.

*   *   *

Subaltern communities of complicity are typically constructed around *malum prohibitum* violations, or activities that are prohibited by the laws of the state, such as smuggling and counterfeiting. At times such communities also stray into the territory of *malum in se*, or evil in itself, such as murder, rape, and torture. The latter of course are also prohibited by law, but they require a much stronger sense of grievance against authority and righteous insubordination to sustain their community. They also tend to drive life underground, where the modus vivendi goes far beyond the hypocrisy of "policies from above, and countermeasures from below" (*shang you zhengce, xiao you duice*). As countless crime thrillers have shown, the criminal underground is not just a minefield of mortal dangers, but also one of psychological and moral pitfalls. The kind of hypocritical infrapolitics discussed in this chapter does not usually descend to such depths; instead it hovers on the edge of criminality and immorality and derives much of its tenacity from the overreach of the state and from a shared cynical awareness of the gap between the public transcript and the hidden transcript of the ruling elite. When the latter lament the decline of public morality and the low "quality" of the populace, their complaints are not wholly groundless, nor are they wholly honest. In the absence of reliable formal channels of redress, subaltern hypocrisy is the only recourse for low justice. In other words, when the system is not fair, not playing fair may be both necessary and justified. But it comes with a cost: moral injury. Those who succeed in building communities of complicity may mitigate such injury; others merely deflect it by sinking to cynicism.

Cynicism is to hypocrisy what bullshitting is to lying. A lie is a lie only as the negation of truth; as such it must keep truth in sight and can even be said to be respectful of it. But a bullshitter does not have to keep an eye on the facts at all and does not care if what he or she says is tethered to reality. The hypocrite cannot be trusted to play by the rules, but at least a hypocrite recognizes the validity of the rules. A cynic honors no rules, yet with a cynic there is less danger that one will be blindsided because the cynic has not earned our trust in the first place. Hypocrites hide their private vice and act out public virtue, and it is this public/private divide that enables their double dealing. The cynic, by contrast, cannot be bothered to put on an act and does not care enough about virtue to pay homage to it.[13] And yet why does the hypocrite earn our animosity far more than the cynic?

Kurzban argues that hypocrisy violates our fundamental sense of justice—low justice as fairness and impartiality. At its core, he opines, "hypocrisy amounts to favoritism" for practicing a kind of "buffet morality" (2010, 218). Stephen Asma situates the liberal West's peculiar allergy to favoritism in the history of Enlightenment thought. Liberalism, according to him, is all about imposing a "grid of impartiality" on social life to counteract its complex tangle of kinship bonds, tribalism, and nepotism.

In doing so, it activates the moral foundation of fairness narrowly defined as abstract equality, and it does not recognize at all the moral foundations of loyalty, authority, and sanctity that underwrite favoritism. "Well-educated liberal secular Westerners see morality exclusively as the respecting of individual rights. Fairness between autonomous individual agents is the defining feature of our morality (e.g., cheating is perceived more as unfairness to others—disadvantaging competing agents—rather than as a failure of one's own integrity or a disgrace on one's family)" (Asma 2013, 57). The history of Western moral and political philosophy can be characterized as one long battle against favoritism, and its crowning achievement is the rule of law. The corollary of this glorious victory is zero tolerance of lying, cheating, and hypocrisy in the name of rooting out unfairness, in the name of low justice. But as Asma points out, moral life is not a grid, and humans are not variables. Uncompromising intolerance of hypocrisy also drives people to cynicism.

For Ruth Grant, no society can operate on true cynicism, that is, by dispensing with idealism and high-flown principles. By the same token, few, to the extent we are social beings, are thoroughgoing cynics, unless we are willing to become Lu Xun's honest maggots. Even the most hard-bitten of cynics might forge their own protected and fragile communities of complicity. Too often we imagine that the antidote to cynicism is an even deadlier poison—fanaticism borne of the quest for transparency—and therefore resign ourselves to the lesser evil. Let us not forget that there is a middle ground that may be a little slippery and not so elevated but is nonetheless conducive to politics, and it is occupied by hypocrisy. As Shklar succinctly puts it: "hypocrisy is one of the few vices that bolsters liberal democracy" (1984, 248). As the examples discussed in this chapter also show, in an authoritarian context hypocrisy is oftentimes the only means by which low justice can be sought.

3

Transitional Justice

In her reflections on responsibility and judgment in the wake of the Holocaust, Hannah Arendt lends her formidable analytical firepower to the retrospective effort to hold Nazi officers and supporters *individually* accountable. She refutes the so-called cog theory, of which many defendants availed themselves in post–World War II war crimes trials, that is, the plea that they were merely carrying out orders, and that if they had not done it, someone else could and would have (2003, 29). The cog theory, in her view, rests on the specious notion of collective guilt: "There is no such thing as collective guilt or collective innocence; guilt and innocence make sense only if applied to individuals" (29); "where all are guilty, nobody is" (147). Even under the extraordinary conditions of totalitarian rule, a functionary was still a human being. And in a court of law only a human being, not a system, or history, or ism, could stand accused (30). Those who participated and obeyed orders may be no more than "conveyor belt" perpetrators (Arendt 1994, 153). Yet the question they must answer is not "Why did you obey?" but "Why did you support?" (2003, 48).

Arendt's uncompromising position on the question of collective guilt cuts to the core of the theory and practice of transitional justice: how to hold individuals accountable for large-scale atrocities? The concept of transitional justice refers to organized efforts to reckon with the question of responsibility and accountability in the wake of severe social trauma or mass atrocity, such as civil war, genocide, and insurrection. It involves formal, institutionalized steps taken to address past wrongdoings by corporate actors—regimes, parties, mafias, rebels, secret police—in an effort to unearth facts, make amends, and bring about healing, reconciliation, and closure. There is a great deal of variance as to how formalized the steps can be, ranging from political to administrative to legal, as can be seen in paradigmatic cases in South Africa, Argentina, Cambodia, and Taiwan (Elster 2004, 84; Jiang Yihua 2007). At the most formal end, transitional justice is enacted in public trials, which are qualitatively different from ordinary criminal trials. As Jon Elster notes, transitional justice "is characterized not only by its dramatic and traumatic substance but also by numerous deviations from due process" (2004, 118). To begin with, instead of being exclusively concerned with individual guilt, these trials often entertain the validity of collective guilt and go beyond the narrow confines of legal justice in order to perform ideological, pedagogical, and therapeutic functions. They are unmistakably and sometimes unabashedly political trials.

In recent decades, scholars have pushed back against the knee-jerk tendency to equate all political trials with show trials. They point out that this is premised on the untenable supposition of a firewall between law and politics. There is no such firewall not only because, as Arendt notes, insofar as the enforcement of law stands in need of political power, "an element of power politics is always involved in the maintenance of legal order" (2003, 38), but also because in the final analysis politics is never absent from any contentious human affairs, from domestic abuse to genocide. In their comprehensive survey of political trials, Jens Meierhenrich and Devin O. Pendas suggest that we regard these trials as "peculiar legal institutions that embody political dynamics" (2016, 4). Politics here should be understood in both the traditional sense of domination and contestation and the Foucauldian sense of discipline and pastoralism. Show trials are merely the extreme manifestation of the proclivity to use judicial proceedings to achieve political aims, not all of which are to eliminate political enemies. Exogenous factors from regime legitimacy to economic efficiency have always shaped legal reasoning and legal outcomes. Adjudication has always been political in nature, even if it cannot be reduced to the dominant power relations or class struggle. Judith Shklar, one of the earliest theorists of political trials, counters legalistic critics of the Nuremberg Trials with a form of skeptical politics, "which sees trials not as guarded from political life by a fence marked by 'law,' but as part of a continuing process of political development" (1986, 165). Nonetheless, it is possible to single out a subspecies of trials as explicitly political trials enacted to address large-scale traumatic events that cannot be shoehorned into a municipal criminal justice system, for the express purpose of delivering political justice more than ordinary justice, or high justice more than low justice.

To counteract the tendency to discredit political trials as persecutory and as window dressing, Meierhenrich and Pendas advocate a more schematic approach that captures "the diverse universe of political trials" by distinguishing three subtypes: decisive trials, didactic trials, and destructive trials (2016, 51). Decisive trials seek to settle a contentious legal question that has a significant political dimension. Their primary aim is political regulation. The prime example is *Brown v. Board of Education* (1954), which ended racial segregation in the United States. Didactic trials seek to spread a political message and shape collective memory. The most famous case in this rubric is the so-called Scopes Monkey Trial of 1925, which upheld academic freedom. Lastly, destructive trials aim for the elimination of a real or imagined political enemy. Political trials have traditionally been understood in this last sense, most notably by Otto Kirchheimer (1980) and Shklar (1986), because of the preponderance of cases pertaining to the prosecutions of war crime, genocide, and organized crime that fall into this category. However, it is also common for political trials to merge two or three aims. Show trials, in particular, are notoriously aimed at both political communication and destruction. "Indeed, didacticism is at the heart of show trials in the pejorative sense of that term. What are we to make of the 1894 Dreyfus treason trial in France? What of the 1980 'Gang of Four' trial in China that took place before thirty-five judges and 880 'representatives of the masses' . . . ? What are the Moscow 'show trials' of the 1930s if not prime examples of didactic trials?" (Meierhenrich and Pendas 2016, 54).

The inclusion of the Gang of Four Trial is instructive here. Political trials in China have by and large served both didactic and destructive purposes. Thus the narrower definition advanced by Shklar and by Kirchheimer is quite appropriate for our purpose. On the other hand, insofar as political trials are rituals of transitional justice, I extend the latter concept to situations that do not involve regime change. In this connection, I identify two moments of transitional justice in PRC history, each set in motion by a wave of political trials. The first wave took place in the 1950s and 1960s to consolidate the revolutionary regime; the second began with the Gang of Four Trial as the first salvo of rebuilding socialist rule of law. The first sought to establish collective guilt and deliver revolutionary high justice, and the second sought to fix individual guilt and deliver bureaucratic low justice. In Shklar's language, the former put the remote past and remote future, or history itself, on trial, while the latter was concerned mostly with the immediate past and immediate future.

I begin with the political trials of the Land Reform period that staged *fanshen* or the "turning over" of the working class and the overthrow of landlord oppression. These trials often assumed the format of the "people's tribunal" (*renmin fating, gongshen dahui*) that moved through public indictment (*gongsu*), verbal and physical assault (*pidou*), and sentencing (*xuanpan*) (Mühlhahn 2009, 181). In the second half of this chapter, I turn to post-Mao trials of former Red Guards and corrupt officials mounted by reinstated judicial professionals. I read a series of fictional texts alongside pertinent historical events in order to show how the dramaturgy of the trial was utilized creatively and effectively to serve political agendas, both the agenda to dismantle the very idea of legality and the agenda to rebuild socialist rule of law. Whereas Meierhenrich and Pendas seek to expand what is *political* in trials, I intend to enlarge the category of *trials* to include scripted events that may lack formal legal procedures. My goal is to show that political trials have been a fundamental tool of the Chinese Revolution and part and parcel of socialist governmentality. I conclude the chapter by examining a film made in the twenty-first century but depicting an incident in 1930s Yan'an, interpreting it as concluding the post-Mao project of transitional justice by circling back to the most glorious moment of CCP history. The intervening years of judicial paralysis and legal vacuum are to be drowned out by a cinematic encomium to the Party as a pillar of justice from the get-go. The trial of a Red Army captain in the film is unapologetically political, yet one that is tasked to negate all the political trials the Party has ever used to destroy its enemies.

Revolutionary Justice: Trying the Remote Past (and Future)

"What, after all, is a political trial?" asks Shklar. "It is a trial in which the prosecuting party, usually the regime in power aided by a cooperative judiciary, tries to eliminate its political enemies. It pursues a very specific policy—the destruction, or at least the disgrace and disrepute, of a political opponent" (1986, 149). When the CCP swept into power in 1949, it had to decide what to do with its worsted archenemy the Nationalists, at least those who for one reason or another did not or could not follow Chiang Kai-shek to Taiwan. Political trials were not used on this group of men. As noted in chapter 1, the CCP rejected the legitimacy of the Nationalist judicial system and had little interest in rebooting what was left of it after the ravages of war. Mounting war crimes trials in the manner of the Nuremberg and Tokyo Trials demanded a kind of political will, legal expertise, and institutional infrastructure that were simply absent.

Instead the Party resorted to co-optation of high-ranking officers, prominent intellectuals, and wealthy industrialists on the one hand, and swift and decisive pacification of "Nationalist bandits" (*feijun*) on the other. Of the nearly one thousand "civil war criminals," most were made to undergo reeducation in internment camps and were gradually reintegrated into society through a successive series of "special pardons" (*teshe*) that spanned over two decades. The first group, released in 1959, included such bigwigs as Du Yuming and Huang Yaowu, and the story of their collective rebirth is retold, most recently, in a 2019 television series. In the same year, the last Qing emperor, Puyi, was declared fully rehabilitated and permitted to live out the rest of his life as an ordinary citizen. Also noteworthy were the 1956 trials of forty-five Japanese POWs held in Shenyang and Taiyuan. All forty-five pleaded guilty and were convicted and in different waves repatriated to Japan, along with over a thousand POWs who were not indicted. Back in Japan some of these returnees formed a pacifist organization (Chūkiren) and became vocal advocates for the PRC. As Binxin Zhang (2014) notes, the trials were merely a formality to provide closure to an apparently successful reform program these detainees had undergone in custody. She considers it an early example of transitional justice practice. I will consider the policy of leniency for war criminals in greater detail in the next chapter.

As the newly minted Communist state began to pursue socialist economic and political goals in earnest, political trials became a privileged means of enforcing the "dictatorship of the proletariat" and propelling the transition to a communist future. Although the scholarship on transitional justice has generally limited it to democratic transition on the part of formerly authoritarian or totalitarian states, and pointedly excluded merely regime change or reversion to nondemocratic polity, I insist on extending it to the early socialist period. I believe it possible to speak of revolutionary justice, delivered flamboyantly and violently in mass trials, as a form of transitional justice because it was explicitly conceived as an urgent, belated, and collective reckoning with millennia's worth of systemic injustice. It was executed through the curation of evidence and testimonials and the wholesale redistribution of wealth and property, but in the absence of legislation, institution building, or due process. To the extent that mass trials invoked law at all, it was the Marxist law of history, not any positive laws or statutes. On the ground, however, the law of history, like "heavenly principles" (*tianli*) in imperial times, was often given a local, even personal gloss and proved to be highly conducive to a form of transitional justice characterized by "informality, flexibility, and the explicit dominance of political objectives" (Mühlhahn 2009, 149). At its worst, the reliance on mass trials as a technology of justice opened the door to a politics of persecution and the pervasive deployment of the "labor reform" or *laogai* regime, which Klaus Mühlhahn condemns as "one of the major humanitarian catastrophes of the twentieth century" (282). *Laogai* was officially terminated in 2013, though other forms of extrajudicial detention have cropped up as substitutes (Wade 2014; Xu 2020, 265–66).

Unlike in Soviet Russia, where show trials were reserved for disgraced members of the Party elite and where secret arrests and disappearance and exile swallowed up the vast numbers that fell afoul of the regime (Slezkine 2017), in China various genres of public trial were ubiquitous and freely meted out to all manner of malefactors and misfits. In the annals of PRC history, the ritual denunciation of a political enemy at a mass rally was so common that it became an unremarkable fixture of the socialist landscape. Scholars tend to pass over it without much comment, tacitly treating it as the theatrical excess of ideological zealots or simply mob behavior. Or they treat the many variations as discrete, impromptu occurrences, each serving distinct, expedient goals. To be sure, there are considerable differences among a "speaking bitterness" or *suku* meeting, in which peasants recall past sufferings and rejoice in present happiness; a criticism-and-self-criticism session, in which a wayward comrade is put in the hot seat and everyone has to take a stand (*biaotai*); a struggle rally, in which an ideological enemy is subjected to physical and psychological torment; and a public tribunal, in which a criminal is put on trial and made to cower before sloganeering crowds before being paraded in the street on route to prison or the execution ground. Nonetheless, these rituals frequently borrowed from one another, and the overlap grew over time. It is justifiable to treat them as variations on a theme: Maoist political trials. These trials, however distant from the prototypical courtroom trial, fuse the didactic and destructive aims of most political trials, and we can account for their differences along three registers: power, procedure, and performance (Meierhenrich and Pendas 2016, 50).

Mass trials under Mao may appear to be ad hoc or jury-rigged, but it is safe to say that most had the blessings of the Party-state, directly or indirectly, and were therefore state sponsored. It is true that much of the state apparatus was in a shambles during the anarchic years of the Cultural Revolution, yet even as individual leaders and cliques rose and fell and the state lost much of its infrastructural capacity, it never entirely lost its despotic power, or its power to impose terror directly or by proxy. Thus when the so-called rebels (*zaofanpai*) staged mass trials, they invariably invoked the name of Mao and the grand mission of communism. Closely related is the matter of procedure, which often appeared wholly absent. But for all the improvisation, a shared script emerged from popular literary representations and firsthand observations. Where it could, the state issued regulations and dispatched work teams to locales to guide the process. In 1950, for example, the state promulgated the Organic Regulations of People's Tribunals, which sanctioned the use of accusation and sentencing rallies to carry out mass purges (Mühlhahn 2009, 181–82).

The emphasis on performance is probably what truly unites all Maoist mass trials. Mühlhahn calls the PRC state a "theatricalized state" in which "public drama and criminal justice were merged to extend the powers of the regime in its struggle against perceived enemies" (2009, 172).

Mass trials were the mainstay of public drama in which "dramatic devices such as staging, props, working scripts, agitators, and climactic moments were used to efficiently engage the emotions of the audience" (182–83). A former vice president of the Supreme People's Court has likened public trials to "a stage for propaganda" (quoted in McIntyre 2013, 7). What was established in such performance was not factual truth or legal truth but ritual truth or what Anthony Giddens (1994) calls "formulaic truth" (see chapter 2). Formulaic truth is performative in the Austinian sense in that "truth criteria are applied to events caused, not to the propositional content of statements" (1994, 65). It bears some superficial resemblance to legal truth in that both may be at variance with factual truth and yet enjoy greater legitimacy and mobility than the latter. The gap between legal and factual truth has long been acknowledged by legal theorists as a regrettable though inevitable product of the imperative of finality, or the requirement that a trial must come to a conclusion. In the words of one jurist, it is "the price we pay for having a complex multi-purpose system in which actual truth, and what legally follows from it, comprise but one value among a variety of important values competing for legal realization" (quoted in Meierhenrich and Pendas 2016, 37). The most important of these values is the determination of guilt and responsibility. For that reason legal truth and substantive truth may rationally diverge without undermining the legitimacy of a given trial (36). The legitimacy of legal truth is guaranteed by scrupulous adherence to rules of evidence and procedural norms. But to the extent to which truth telling is also storytelling, it also relies on the power of narrative to "frame and persuade, even beyond or against evidence" (Meierhenrich and Pendas 2016, 39). Hence even the strictest proceduralism cannot in the last analysis fully close the gap between legal truth and substantive truth.

If the gap between legal and factual truth is unavoidable in ordinary trials, it can become yawning in political trials in which the reasoning process often flows backward, from a foregone conclusion to faith-based proofs that are beyond disputation. In Denise Ho's study of museum displays of the material evidence of class oppression during the Mao period, torture instruments, tattered garments, photographs of scars, and so on are arrayed as iron proofs of the viciousness of class enemies (2018, 140, 155, 160). The question of *how* these items were gathered and vetted could not be raised, because they were not intended to be forensic evidence presented in a court of law, but were rather tokens of a higher or formulaic truth. In socialist China, Mao's words were the formulaic truth par excellence; so were the pronouncements of Party apparatchiks and the shibboleths of Mao's grassroots defenders. Maoist formulaic truth fixed a priori the guilt of the objective enemies of the state: the capitalists, the landlords, the counterrevolutionaries, the traitors, the Rightists, and so on. Their guilt did not turn on mens rea, or criminal intent. Actual motive or actual conduct was largely irrelevant. What was relevant was the collective guilt of a social class pronounced by Marxist ideology as the counteragent of historical progress, destined to be swept away by the historical tides, or to be buried by their designated gravediggers, the proletariat. In short, Maoist formulaic truth displaced legal truth by peremptorily closing its distance from substantive truth. Legal truth thus no longer had any conceptual purchase.

In Wang Shikuo's famous charcoal sketch *The Bloodstained Shirt* (*Xieyi*, 1959), a peasant woman holds up a bloodied shirt at a paradigmatic *suku* meeting–cum–mass trial (X. Tang 2015, chap. 2; C. Ho 2020, 58). Her figure dominates the center of the composition, and below her a small child clings to her legs. To her left are three men looming over a cloth-covered table. The one in the middle is likely the head of the local peasant association; to his left is a Red Army representative; the third man, also in army uniform, has his head buried in his notebook evidently transcribing the proceedings. On the lower left corner just below the table stands a man with hunched shoulders and wearing the typical rich man's long gown. Unquestionably he is the landlord put on trial for the crimes of class oppression, before all his former victims who have gathered thither, including an old woman with her left hand outstretched as if trying to seize the accused. Some of the brawny peasant youths on the right side of the frame appear barely able to restrain themselves, striking mortal fear into the landlord with their intense dagger stare. As Xiaobing Tang describes the scene, "The central characters, from the reclining man in need of a crutch in the foreground to the woman holding the shirt and standing tall on the raised terrace, form a rising column of humanity, seemingly pulsating with a dynamic rhythm as it leans forward precipitously" (X. Tang 2015, 64).

But none of the angry and anguished faces commands our attention as much as the bloodstained shirt—presumably once worn by the woman's deceased father or husband or son. One could almost hear a plaintive tale pouring forth from her mouth, about how her loved one was hounded to death by the accused. The drawing powerfully captures, in medias res, the expressive body speaking the ritual truth of class injury in the universal (visual) language of blood and tears. The goal of the trial, however, is to transmute anger directed at what an individual *did* to hatred for who the individual *is* and what he or she stands for (Elster 2004, 94).

It is said that the artist spent years in the countryside gathering material for his work, originally intended to be a life-size oil painting. For political reasons he did not return to the project until 1973 but died of exhaustion before he was able to complete the oil painting. Already, the sketch contains all the basic elements of a Maoist mass trial: a judge (flanked by his associate and clerk), a defendant, a plaintiff, and spectators-as-coplaintiffs. Ordinarily, the medium of drawing does not lend itself well to a trial, since a trial necessarily unfolds in time and language. But here, the visual medium, by focusing on the body in pain and material traces of suffering, is more than adequate to the task of accentuating the political and ritual dimensions of the *suku* trial. In Ann Anagnost's words, "speaking bitterness was elevated to the status of 'history speaking itself,' but the body provided the material ground through which this history was made real" (1997, 18). The body in pain does not lie, nor do the "inanimate objects . . . [that] are transformed from silent witnesses of suffering and death to congealed representations of the oppressiveness of the past" (Anagnost 1997, 39).

At a Maoist mass trial, the outcome is a foregone conclusion. The enemy's fate is sealed; what needs to be propagated is the heinous nature of his crime and the ironclad nature of the dictatorship of the proletariat. The bloodied shirt is thus a ritual prop, a token of Maoist formulaic truth, potent and sacrosanct and not subject to any rules of evidence. It is not, as Tang claims, "direct forensic evidence" (X. Tang 2015, 81), yet no one in his or her right mind would question its authenticity, just as no one would permit him- or herself to wonder about the true provenance of the scars in the museum exhibit in Denise Ho's study (2018). Still, a *suku* ritual or a struggle session was practically the only avenue for low justice where ordinary citizens got a chance to air their grievances and seek redress against specific individuals. And yet their grievances were never permitted to remain merely as a matter of low justice, for to do so would deprive mass trials of their didactic function. "This eruption into speech of the peasant subject," observes Anagnost, "must therefore be placed within a whole system of representations in which new conceptions of the social and historical became 'real-ized' through the visceral experience of the speaking subject" (1997, 19). Mühlhahn also emphasizes that little about these trials was left to chance or spontaneity: "The close and direct participation of the masses in this process was carefully rehearsed. Those who served as material witnesses were not only exhaustively instructed as to what to say and when, but they were also carefully chosen for the degree to which they would attract the sympathies of the audience. The organizers liked to involve as witnesses and accusers the very old, the very young, and women" (2009, 184). As revealed in Feiyu Sun's (2013) research cited in chapter 2, once a case was determined to be amenable to a theatrical presentation, a work team would put in extensive preparatory work and closely supervise the proceedings. Facts were culled, physical evidence gathered (bills of sale, IOUs, bloodied shirts, welts and scars), witnesses coached, victim impact statements crafted, confessions extracted, and finally punishments meted out.

The process resembled a legal proceeding insofar as it strove to match facts to codes, except these were not legal codes but political codes: the categories, procedures, and rules prescribed by Marxism-Leninism-Maoism for conducting class struggle. Here as in the legal and other professional arenas, specialists—rabbis, lawyers, bureaucrats, umpires, and medical ethicists—convert cause-effect stories into formulaic codes (Tilly 2006, 119). To Charles Tilly's list of specialists we can add cadres and writers who curated *suku* narratives, both oral and written versions, whereby the ultimate goal was not so much to uncover truth as to establish the ground on which to liquidate an entire social class. The sidelining of factual truth that can happen in legal proceedings was far more flagrant and unapologetic in the construction of socialist codes, or what I have called the socialist public transcript in chapter 2. Low justice was possible, but only for individuals whose grievances were easily transcribed into the codes of class struggle. In the end, righting individual wrongs—the object of low justice—was subordinated to the high justice of consolidating socialism and Party rule.

This point is paradigmatically illustrated in the film *The Red Detachment of Women* (*Hongse niangzijun*) (Xie Jin 1960), which was later adapted for the ballet stage and became one of the eight model works of the Cultural Revolution. Wu Qionghua, a slave girl cruelly abused by her master, Nan Batian, escapes from his dungeon and joins the Red Army. Her zeal for the Communist Revolution, however, is fueled by her burning desire for personal revenge. During a sortie, she tries to capture Nan Batian on her own, thus endangering the mission. The message is of course the absolute imperative of subordinating low justice to high justice. Wu Qionghua fails to understand that revolutionary justice requires seeing Nan as an emblem of the *collective* guilt of the reactionary class as a whole. When the guerrilla fighters at last succeed in capturing Nan, Qionghua leads him through the street on a chain leash and speaks to the crowds of her and her family's suffering in his hands (figure 3.1). But she diligently enumerates his class enemy labels as "an evil gentry, tyrannical landlord, bloodsucker, and commander of his private militia" *before* identifying him as her former master. The masses that have gathered shove and prod him forward through the street, pelt him with objects, and close in on him until the guerrilla fighters

FIGURE 3.1: Parading evil landlord Nan Batian in the street in *The Red Detachment of Women* (Xie Jin 1960, Shanghai Film Studio).

urge them to repair to the site of the public tribunal. Individual anger is thus channeled and coalesced into political hatred and the fuel of collective action, of class struggle.

Common crimes, on the other hand, were rarely dealt with as common crimes. The PRC did not promulgate a comprehensive criminal code until 1979.[1] During the intervening thirty years, the regime relied on a skein of decrees, ordinances, and regulations not so much to maintain order as to defend itself against internal and external enemies. "In this system, the administration of justice was viewed as an eminently political affair. Because crime and deviant behavior had a class character, according to the party, political factors were inevitably involved when a person committed a crime. There was no room for impartiality" (Mühlhahn 2009, 193). As we have seen in the case of Xu Qiuying, discussed in chapter 1, an ostensible crime of passion is inevitably revealed to be the tip of a political iceberg. Tellingly, the acronym that became the catchall for all manner of socialist outcasts, *di-fu-fan-huai-you*, lumped criminals or "bad elements" (*huaifenzi*) together with the political-economic designations of landlord (*dizhu*) and rich peasant (*funong*) and the political-ideological labels of counterrevolutionary (*fandongpai*) and Rightist (*youpai*) (Kraus 1981, 60). Later other baroque labels would be added to enlarge the nomenclature, but they were invariably of a political-ideological nature. "Bad elements" was sufficient to encompass all nonpolitical offenses, and there was little interest in parsing the motives, methods, and degrees of culpability of *malum in se* crimes such as murder, robbery, rape, and theft. *Malum pro-*

hibitum offenses such as graft (*tanwu*) and speculating (*touji daoba*) were always political since the "three antis" and "five antis" campaigns of the early 1950s.

In my previous work, I have borrowed Arendt's notion of "objective enemy" to underscore the logic of revolutionary justice (H. Lee 2014, 204–5). In Mao's China, class enemies were "objective" in that their guilt was not determined on an individual basis, keyed to specific action or identifiable motive. Rather, they were guilty by virtue of membership in a class that had been pronounced reactionary and marked for liquidation according to a political ideology. Their collective guilt was Maoist formulaic truth that could not be subjected to the test of veracity. In a political trial, the goal was not to uncover factual truth according to a legally established grammar, but to coax the fact of the matter to conform to the grammar of the formulaic truth of class struggle. A political trial was miniature warfare waged between "friend" and "enemy." Notwithstanding the superficial legal trappings, the most critical piece of adjudication was discarded: mens rea, or criminal intent. Or rather, mens rea was deduced from class membership and then stretched into a diffuse, impersonal malice.

Once mens rea was presumed as a generalized enmity, the prosecution was freed from the burden of making fine distinctions among the intent to harm, knowledge of the law, recklessness, and negligence. This underlies the paradox of a revolutionary regime's pervasive use of political trials, however informal and ad hoc, to eliminate its enemies. In other words, why the ready recourse to what to outside observers are indubitable kangaroo courts? To the battle-hardened professional revolutionaries who had turned their backs on the ancien régime because it had failed them in the face of foreign domination and invasion, "a legalistic process of punishment seemed arid and false" (Shklar 1986, 159). Maoist mass trials allowed them to put that entire order—not just a few ministers or warlords—on trial and thereby thoroughly erase any lingering legitimacy it might still enjoy. Pace Arendt, it *is* possible to try history, or a system, or an ism. But it requires a conspiracy theory of history to pull it off, a theory that, according to Shklar, conflates historical causal reasoning and legal causal reasoning. "A criminal trial demands a *mens rea*, and there is often no *mens rea* to be found in the development of socially complex events such as war. A criminal trial for waging aggressive war inevitably involves an interpretation of the past which makes it possible to point to specific persons making specific decisions which caused a war. [...] The conspiratorial view of history, in its penchant for unearthing plots and secret machinations, is the very essence of the classical political trial with its simple aim of rooting out all opposition—real, fancied, potential, or improbable" (Shklar 1986, 172).

Socially complex events—wars, organized crime, and uprisings—notoriously defy legal judgments because the relationship between cause and responsibility is exceedingly problematic (Hogan 2009, 169–73). This is where the sine qua non test or "but for X, Y would not have occurred" is inapplicable.[2] Maoist mass trials deliberately conflated these two modes of causality by casting individual players as stand-ins for "abstractions, metaphors, or composites" that historians and philosophers of history "fabricate in order to reduce the past to communicable form" (Shklar 1986, 196), thus reintroducing mens rea through the backdoor, without being burdened by the legalistic requirement to establish the fact and the situation of each individual act. Hence the casual disregard for empirical veracity, the lack of rigorous rules of evidence, and the disavowal of the gap between formulaic truth and factual truth. In essence, mass trials pursued historical thinking in the guise of legal thinking, cutting complex historical events down to size for the trial stage. Instead of being concerned with the immediate past (what did the defendant do to the victim/plaintiff, if anything), the present (what procedures should govern fact-finding and can best guarantee due process), or the immediate future (what punishment and reparation are appropriate), mass trials were propelled by a grand future-directed ideology and looked to "the remote future, to historical necessity, for a justification of decisions" (Shklar 1986, 165). Each time a landlord or a counterrevolutionary was struggled against (*pidou*), it was in fact the age-old system of "feudal oppression" that was the target. The remote feudal past was put on trial for the sake of the remote communist future.

Mass trials could also be explicitly preemptory, in the name of forestalling sabotage of the bright future of the nation. "To revolutionaries true justice has nothing to do with past actions. It holds people responsible for the unintended, as yet unrealized, future consequences of their acts. [. . .] History no longer refers to the past at all; it means the future seen in terms of the predictable course and final end of revolution" (Shklar 1986, 202). Crimes against the future were especially reserved for ideological deviants, branded "sinners against history" (*lishi de zuiren*) and blamed for any and all setbacks. Any error deemed detrimental to the forward march of the revolution became a crime. In the immediate post-Mao reckonings, this equation of error with crime would be turned on its head in order to exculpate Mao, who is said to have made mistakes but committed no crime (see the next section).

Mass trials of counterrevolutionaries turned on the presumption that it was impossible to intend well and still make a wrong political decision. A mistake necessarily pointed to evil intent, to a conspiracy against the revolution. It follows that the so-called line struggle (*luxian douzheng*) in Maoist China was never merely a matter of difference of opinion or insufficient knowledge. The wrong line was necessarily the hostile line, advanced by hidden enemies pursuing subversive or annihilative outcomes. Those who for the moment had the ears of Mao spoke as the very face of political orthodoxy and the harbinger of a limitless future. Achieving that future imposed obligations on the present to strike hard against ideological deviationism. There was little space for routine political give and take, let alone loyal opposition. Nor was there any genuine allowance for epistemological amelioration or ideological improvement, despite all the emphasis on thought reform. A past mistake could be just as useful in tossing a person into the political abyss as any currently held belief. A new conviction could also be linked to a long and deeply buried trail of suspect remarks and actions from the past. An enemy label was not an indictment of a specific criminal act, but an identity badge that broadcast the person as the source of ideological putrefaction, rotten to the core and contaminating those around him or her who failed to "draw a line" (*huaqing jiexian*). Conspiracy, after all, required a clique. And family and friends were the default accessories.

Now consider the not uncommon practice of having a class enemy's descendant take his place should he be too frail to withstand a grueling *pidou* session or recently deceased. There were two kinds of conflation at work. One, mass trials conflated historical causality with legal causality. In history the chain of causality is much longer than in law or common moral reasoning or storytelling. Historians, Shklar notes, settle on a cutoff point according to professional conventions or academic goals, whereas in law, the need to fix criminal responsibility and the purposes of punishment determine the cutoff point (1986, 197). Two, mass trials conflated collective responsibility with individual guilt, a distinction Arendt insists on. A token of an entire social class marked for elimination, the individual landlord was held responsible for the sins of his forebears, a burden also transferable to his descendants (see also Treat 2017, 417). None of them need personally pass the sine qua non test. A landlord's physical absence could be remedied by a kinsman who occupied an equivalent position vis-à-vis the social class. And because the trial was a ritual display of the formulaic truth of class struggle for which the question of premeditation was moot, members of the same class very well became mutually replaceable.

Maoist mass trials could not function without the presumption of collective guilt. There are faint echoes of the *zhulian* and *baojia* systems in traditional China, where a whole community (clan or village) was held responsible for the actions of its members. The logic behind collective responsibility was consistent with the strict liability rule governing official performance (see the introduction), neither of which required the "control condition" (does the agent have any control over an action? does the agent have any evil intent?) requisite in liberal jurisprudence (Sommers 2012, 2, 47–51). Under Mao, class replaced kin filiations and became a hereditary identity in the "class designation" or *chengfen* system (Kraus 1981), in which "one can be praiseworthy or blameworthy for talents and abilities, virtues and vices, that do not trace back to choices made over the course of one's life" (Sommers 2012, 60–61). Relying on a racialist rhetoric, the *chengfen* system went beyond community policing to facilitate a persecutory politics aimed at the wholesale liquidation of social groups. It worked in tandem with the quota system as well as the incessant production of new class enemies and the attendant proliferation of new labels ("hats") of political damnation (H. Lee 2014, 206–10).

It is reported that on different occasions Mao gave estimates of 3 percent to 5 percent of the population as being counterrevolutionaries, thus imposing an enormous burden on local administrations and work units to turn up the requisite numbers in each campaign (Mühlhahn 2009, 203–4). With mens rea taken out of the equation, the population as a whole became equally suspect and equally vulnerable to the constant need for new enemies. Examples of this Maoist regime of strict liability were rife: having once owned a certain quantity of land or other property, having employed a certain number of laborers, having served in the Nationalist government, having a relative overseas, soiling a newspaper bearing Mao's image, breaking a Mao bust, an impolitic slip of the tongue, and so on. Daniel Leese and Puck Engman point out that with the judiciary pushed to the sideline, Party committees and public security organs assumed broad, and mostly unchecked, policing powers, having "a wide repertoire of sanctions at their disposal, including demotion, public shaming, deprivation of political rights, restriction of movement, and re-education through labor. They also had the power to banish people to the countryside, a space that officials treated, in the words of Jeremy Brown, as 'part prison, part garbage dump'" (2018, 11). These ad hoc sanctions were usually preceded by mass trials.

When offenders were hauled before the masses, they were typically subjected to abuses that were meant to inflict as much shame and humiliation as pain. Again, because it was the individual as a token rather than specific action that was the object of persecution, and because mass trials aimed for the destruction of physical bodies as well as personal reputations, public shaming was elevated to an art and freely dispensed. Contrary to guilt, which pertains to the act, shame targets the whole person, the social self. Its damage is quite irreversible. The victims of such public shaming not infrequently ended up committing suicide, as was the case of the writer Lao She, who drowned himself after being "struggled against" by a group of Red Guards in 1966.

The Maoist political was an exemplary instantiation of the Schmittian political of friend and enemy, a Manichean politics of either/or (Dutton 2005; H. Lee 2011). "This is the vision and reality of politics as perpetual total war, of which political trials are but one small battle among many fought to eliminate the enemy" (Shklar 1986, 205). Although Maoist mass trials were ubiquitous, they represented only the front stage of the organized political violence that defined the Mao period as a whole. The intense radicalization of post-1949 politics, driven by the friend/enemy binary, rendered criminal justice irrelevant and invisible. "Mao held that enemies of the people had no rights" (Mühlhahn 2009, 280). And very quickly it turned out that "the people" had no rights either: once the judicial apparatus was swept away, "no agency was left that could have prevented the ruling revolutionary elite from running roughshod over friends and enemies alike" (281). In a poignant scene in the documentary *Morning Sun* (Hinton, Barmé, and Gordon 2005), Liu Shaoqi, then president of the People's Republic, was being hustled out of his residence in Zhongnanhai, the headquarters of central Party leadership, by a posse of Red Guards. Waving at them a copy of the Constitution, he tried to remind the belligerent youths that he, as a citizen of the Republic, had constitutionally guaranteed rights. How deafeningly lame and ridiculous his words must have sounded to the youngsters for whom he had turned into a monster overnight. The treatment he received at the hands of his persecutors was shocking, but not qualitatively different from the fates of countless Chinese who were thrown into the lawless state of exception.

If mass trials were overwhelmingly ad hoc and exhibited little regard for due process, Maoist politics as a whole was prone to excess to such an extent that it nearly cannibalized itself while taking the economy down with it. For all the strident perorations on historical necessity, Maoism was at its core a terroristic politics erected on an utter contempt for rules. "For if necessity is the rule, and necessity is only known to those above, there can be no rules. Necessity does not know them, and those who enforce necessity do not want them" (Shklar 1986, 206). "A theater of catharsis and revenge" (Farquhar and Berry 2004, 131), mass trials were also a theater of ritualized chaos that combined fear and exhilaration to achieve didactic and destructive aims. Understanding the logics and dynamics of these trials goes a long way to teasing out the method of Maoist madness and explaining why undoing that madness required another political trial, one that tried to swing the pendulum of transitional justice from the political end toward the legal end.

Bureaucratic Justice: Trying the Immediate Past (and Future)

When the country, exhausted by the convulsions of the Cultural Revolution, was ready to abandon Maoist politics, the first major public event it staged was the trial of the Gang of Four in a specially convened court in 1980. As noted above, it was a political trial through and through, but shorn of the colorfulness of Maoist mass trials: the rough-hewed informality, the foreshortened process, the tearful accusations, the gratuitous violence, and the public shaming. Although the "scale of the crimes outstripped legal precedent and moral dicta" (Treat 2017, 409) as before, there was little appetite to revivify revolutionary justice. As Mary Farquhar and Chris Berry note, the trial "is underpinned throughout by an insistence on order: a 're-establishment' of the correct Marxist line,' and a re-assertion of order over chaos, of law over violence, and of justice over persecution" (2004, 132). This time, the regime's approach to reckoning with organized political violence of the past was diametrically opposite of mass trials' obsession with collective guilt and trying the "system." Instead, the trial trained its attention scrupulously on a limited set of individuals who could reasonably pass the sine qua non or "but for" test. These individuals were accused of counterrevolutionary conspiracies, but apart from the rhetorical echo of Maoist political trials, the ten-week judicial proceedings marked the beginning of a new era and inaugurated the second major wave of transitional justice in socialist China. It pursued a relatively subdued form of bureaucratic justice that gestured, in a future anterior sense, toward the socialist rule of law premised on positively formulated and publicly proclaimed rules—what Roberto Unger calls "bureaucratic law" (see chapter 1).

In his comprehensive study of this historic trial, Alexander Cook offers the following assessment:

> The trial was expected all at once to model a reformed system of socialist law, determine criminal liability for mass harm, triage open wounds and mend a tattered social fabric, assign meaning to dimly understood historical events, and usher in a new era of sober rationality. The political challenges alone were formidable. It was easy enough to shield Mao from a posthumous legal reckoning, because the late chairman could not be called to testify in court about the events that he had set in motion. But it was impossible to separate the Cultural Revolu-

tion from Mao, or Mao from the larger history of Chinese socialism. [. . .] In the wake of disaster, it was now imperative for Chinese socialism to offer justice. Inevitably, the trial that ensued was inadequate to meet all of these challenges. Nevertheless, the court's orderly legal proceedings posed a stark contrast to both the extensive violence imposed by repressive military and administrative apparatuses and the rough summary justice handed out by unruly mobs during the Cultural Revolution. The trial announced a new political culture and a new way of dealing with the sharpest contradictions in society. Outside the courtroom, this spectacular legal event became the focal point for a larger cultural conversation about history, justice, and the fate of Chinese socialism. (Cook 2016b, 3)

Cook concedes that the trial fits the definition of a show trial to a tee, noting especially the retroactive application of laws, the procedural irregularities, the presumption of guilt, the limited opportunity for defense, and the didactic aim (7). Yet it is still important to ask: "What did it mean for the Chinese to use a legal trial to address the injustices of the Cultural Revolution?" (10).

As Cook notes, despite the enormous publicity it generated both within and outside of China, the trial was only one small part of the state's efforts to confront the legacies of the Cultural Revolution. These efforts included criminal trials of scores of Gang of Four accomplices as part of a comprehensive campaign to reassert legal normalcy under a restored and reformed legal system, to exclude from government office political radicals, and to reverse "unjustly, falsely and wrongly charged, tried and sentenced cases (*yuanjiacuo an*)" (Cook 2016b, 24–25; see also Leese and Engman 2018; Leese 2019; Trevaskes 2002). Nonetheless, the trial was the fulcrum of the post-Mao transition, and its significance turned on the pivot from revolutionary high justice to bureaucratic low justice, on enshrining law as the keystone of governance. Although the state relied on administrative means as much as legal ones in dealing with the staggering number of cases of injustice at lower levels, the Gang of Four Trial, in its approximation of the post–World War II war crimes tribunals, signaled to the world the dawning of a new era of socialist rule of law.

In 1981, six months after the Special Court verdict, the Party released the Resolution on Certain Questions in the History of the Party since the Founding of the People's Republic of China. In Cook's view, the significance of this document can be grasped only next to the verdict of the trial: "The two official accounts were complementary, issuing a binding and authoritative interpretation of the past in separate but related registers: the law, and the laws of history. The verdict provides an account of the Cultural Revolution in terms of crimes at the level of law. Meanwhile, the resolution analyzes the Cultural Revolution at the level of objective historical laws as a series of 'errors' in revolutionary thought and practice" (2016a, 287). The resolution allowed the Party to assume collective political responsibility while drawing a sharp line from moral and legal guilt. It performed the crucial task of bracketing off the Cultural Revolution as an aberration by popularizing such pat phrases as "decade of internal chaos" (*shinian neiluan*) or "decade of catastrophe" (*shinian haojie*), with the aim of exempting the Party from legal and moral blameworthiness. Most critically, Mao was faulted for having made grave errors of judgment and acted rashly, but if there was any hint of mens rea, it was safely contained at the level of recklessness and negligence, not at the level of intent or foreknowledge. His stupendous contributions to the emancipation of the Chinese people more than ensured his immunity and more than eclipsed the mass harm that he didn't intentionally or personally inflict; on top of that he could not have possessed full knowledge of the rippling effects of his schemes and decrees.

At a deeper level, Mao is said to have been led astray by his incorrect grasp of the law of history and to have put too much faith in the power of the general will. However, such epistemological shortcomings need not have translated into a societal tragedy but for the conspiratorial machinations of the "reactionary cliques" (*fangeming jituan*) of Lin Biao and the Gang of Four. It was the latter who must be held legally responsible for the crimes of the Cultural Revolution. In "smashing" (*fensui*) the Gang of Four and decisively reversing national policy, the new leadership has begun to remedy whatever errors could be laid at the feet of Mao and the Party-state. Transitional justice was thus a matter of purging the body politic of cancerous growths and nursing the damaged tissues back to health. But unlike the previous juncture of transitional justice, this time it was pursued in a manner that directly negated the doctrine of collective guilt. Rather, the Gang of Four Trial pointedly disallowed the "cog theory" defense mounted by Jiang Qing on her own behalf. Arendt explains why she finds the "cog theory" defense so reprehensible: "The trouble with the Nazi criminals was precisely that they renounced voluntarily all personal qualities, as if nobody were left to be either punished or forgiven. They protested time and again that they had never done anything out of their own initiative, that they had no intentions whatsoever, good or bad, and that they only obeyed orders. To put it another way, the greatest evil perpetrated is the evil committed by nobodies, that is, by human beings who refused to be persons" (Arendt 2003, 111). When Jiang Qing characterized her role in the Cultural Revolution as Mao's "attack dog" (Cook 2016b, 125), she was literally stripping herself of her humanity and shrinking into a nobody—a grotesque contrast to her profile as a no-holds-barred mover and shaker. The popular animus against her was probably worsened by this attempt to wiggle out of any personal responsibility and shove it all onto a still-beloved supreme leader. On the other hand, she also defended the Cultural Revolution in what Cook calls her "apostrophe to history" by refusing to recognize the authority of the Special Court and instead addressing her words to a transcendent authority (125), thus defusing the court's concerted effort to focus on the present (and immediate past and future) and underscoring the trial's political nature. In response, the court insisted on treating her as an autonomous moral agent in order to affix legal guilt. In so doing it also dignified itself as the somber antithesis of Maoist campaign politics. "It is the grandeur of court proceedings that even a cog can become a person again" (Arendt 2003, 148).

As a historian, Cook chooses, productively in my view, to intersperse a blow-by-blow account of the trial with close readings of literature from the immediate post-Mao years in order to canvas a broader reckoning with the Cultural Revolution, beyond what was possible in the political and legal arenas. This turn to literature may well be informed by the sentiments that originally gave rise to the "law and literature" movement in the 1970s and 1980s. The early proponents of the movement believed in the salutary role of the "voice of passion" one finds in literature in tempering the "cold rationalization of law" (Robert Weisberg 1989, 33; see also Peters 2005). Later practitioners such as Wai-chee Dimock (1996) and Shoshana Felman (2002) have emphasized literature's ability to illuminate the penumbra of law's edifice. Likewise, Cook argues that realist writers went much further than the state and its official pronouncements by pointing to the inadequacy of instrumental rationality represented by the trial. If the malady deep in the marrow of Chinese socialism was "inhumanity," these writers suggested, then anything that was detached from humanistic values could not guarantee a more just society (Cook 2016b, 28).

Forthrightly indicting Mao and his last revolution for violating the law of history, however, was simply impossible then and now. Two of the three texts Cook reads closely—Liu Binyan's *Between Man and Monster* (1979) and Dai Houying's *Humanity, Ah Humanity!* (1980)—do not directly depict the horrors of state-sponsored violence in the preceding decade. Instead they are exposés of graft and embezzlement by regionally powerful Party bosses who took advantage of the loopholes of command economy as well as the new opportunities afforded by the economic liberalization of the late 1970s to enrich themselves and their cronies. Yang Jiang's *Six Chapters of a Cadre School* (1981), too, largely steers clear of the difficult question of culpability and responsibility. Nonetheless, if, as Cook contends, the verdict and the resolution sought to distinguish crimes (violations of statutory laws) and errors (violations of objective laws) with perfect clarity (2016a, 289), it was literature that cast a shadow over this perfect clarity. And the story that most directly takes up this challenge is Jin He's "The Second Encounter" ("Chongfeng"), originally published in *Shanghai Literature* (*Shanghai wenxue*) in April 1979.

The story opens with a pretrial hearing at a provincial public security bureau shortly after the fall of the Gang of Four but before the televised trial in Beijing. The purpose of these hearings, the narrator informs us, is to identify a few cases of the "most serious disorderly elements" (Jin He 1983, 179) for the purpose of a public trial that will be broadcast throughout the district. The "disorderly elements" (*dazaqiang fenzi*) are individuals accused of having engaged in beatings, vandalism, and looting during the Cultural Revolution. The public trial itself is not depicted in the story, but there is every indication that it will not be a Maoist-style mass trial, but a scaled-down precursor of the Gang of Four Trial, with its emphasis on gathering "solid, accurate evidence that would stand the test of time" (179). According to Leese and Engman, hundreds of such trials targeting rebel leaders and Gang of Four followers took place across the country, though "the number of recognized victims greatly exceeded the list of convicted perpetrators" (2018, 16). Most people were allowed to claim victimhood, of being duped by the Gang of Four. But how to usher in a new dawn of law and order without scapegoating a few with blood on their hands?

The official in charge of the hearings is Party secretary Zhu Chunxin, a middle-aged survivor of the Cultural Revolution. The story moves back and forth between his present reencounter with a young man named Ye Hui who had defended him against violent attackers during an armed clash between Red Guard factions and who is now accused of being a "disorderly element," and several flashbacks that recount that first encounter. We learn that Ye Hui went by Ye Weige ("guarding the revolution") during the Cultural Revolution and belonged to the "East Is Red" faction that was locked in a life-and-death struggle with the "Red Alliance" faction. Zhu Chunxin was a local Party cadre who, following Mao's call for Party leaders to "reveal their stand" (i.e., take sides), was made "a revolutionary leading cadre" of the East Is Red faction. When fighting intensified, he took to hiding in an office building to avoid being "dragged out and struggled against" (Jin He 1983, 182). But the other side tracked him down and laid siege to his hideout. He would certainly have been killed or gravely injured had Ye Weige not come to his rescue with a dozen or so crudely armed comrades. During the pitched battle, Zhu had no choice but take part in defending himself and his side by relaying makeshift weapons to the frontline "little generals." In the end, they fought off the attackers, in the process stabbing one to death and crippling another.

In the narrative present, Ye Hui is under investigation for the killing and maiming of the two individuals and, if convicted, is likely to face the death penalty. Ye Hui confesses readily to the killing and maiming, but inexplicably withholds Zhu's name as the object of the fighting. Department Head Li, Zhu's subordinate, does his best to establish mens rea in his questioning:

> "Why did you participate in the fighting? Hm? ... The 'Sixteen Points' have long decreed that one must 'struggle with words, not force.' Then why did you fight? You made your motivation appear so pretty; this is pure sophistry."
>
> The criminal sitting on the square stool smiled calmly and said, "I am relating the facts."
>
> "Facts, facts! You are trying to hide something—otherwise why won't you reveal the name of the leading cadre you were protecting?" Department Head Li retorted.
>
> Hearing Department Head Li's interrogation, Zhu Chunxin's heart gave a start and his ears hummed. Secretly, he resented him for asking such a question. He was worried that the criminal might say "Zhu Chunxin" under pressure and put him in an extremely embarrassing situation. (Jin He 1983, 186)

Leaving aside Ye Hui's reason for remaining mum about Zhu for now, we might ask why Li refuses to accept "protecting a leading cadre" as a legitimate excuse. Clearly, he is fishing for baser motives that would downgrade Ye to a common criminal. Herein lies the crux of all post–Cultural Revolution trials: How to reduce state-sponsored political violence to common criminality? How to exculpate the Party leaders who instigated and sometimes participated in such violence while holding the rank and file to criminal account? That is, how to redress high injustice in a low justice setting?

To do so requires at a minimum a barefaced lie: "no leading cadre would have connived with your fighting!" (Jin He 1983, 186). Thus the population is partitioned into two camps: in the perpetrators' camp are the top-level conspirators and their local lieutenants and opportunistic elements; in the victims' camp are the political and intellectual elites at all levels who were ousted and persecuted, as well as ordinary people from all walks of life who lost life, livelihood, and dignity. As a survivor, Zhu clearly puts himself in the second camp. Revealing his name may bring him embarrassment, although it shouldn't have surprised anyone present given how blurry the line between the two camps actually was. Toward the end of the story, Zhu arranges a private interview with Ye and tries to give him the official line:

> "During the Cultural Revolution, owing to the negative disruptions of the Gang of Four, many people, including myself, committed that kind of mistake. We must learn from experience and raise our political consciousness. We still believe in education . . ."
>
> "The forms of the crime are different; the forms of the 'education' are also different," Ye Hui interrupted Zhu Chunxin smiling. "You committed a mistake, but you can justifiably and forcefully accuse Lin Biao and the Gang of Four of having persecuted you. I committed a mistake, but I have to admit I followed Lin Biao and the Gang of Four in undermining the Cultural Revolution." (197)

Note that the story was written before the Party's "Resolution" that negated the Cultural Revolution in toto, so that ardent participants of Mao's last revolution could have actually been indicted for "undermining" it. Ye reiterates his readiness to shoulder criminal responsibility, but he has no illusions about the scapegoating nature of the campaign against "disorderly elements." Perhaps the reason why he does not rat out Zhu is because Zhu's particular identity is immaterial. Zhu was not Ye's friend—they had never met before the fateful night of the battle. There were plenty of Red Guard clashes that did not turn on the fate of a "leading cadre." Insofar as Zhu was a high-ranking official who had thrown his weight behind Ye's faction, he ceased to be a mere individual and may well have been a local instantiation of Mao. Ye said as much when he came to Zhu's rescue: "Since you stand by our side, you are standing on the side of Chairman Mao's revolutionary line. To defend Chairman Mao's revolutionary line, we revolutionary rebel fighters are prepared to risk our lives and shed our blood!" (Jin He 1983, 185). That is why it is pointless for him to name Zhu specifically in the hearing. He shouldn't have to name anyone. He shouldn't have to supply any personal motive. Mens rea is utterly beside the point here. Putting Ye on trial is tantamount to putting a soldier on trial for killing enemy combatants (see chapter 4).

With Mao as the elephant in the room, the interrogators have to beat around the bush and speak in tautologies. "'Criminal Ye and the deceased Shi Zhihong did not know each other, so we can exclude the element of revenge,' the department head continued. 'But Criminal Ye refused to admit that he was following the Gang of Four and disrupting the Cultural Revolution; nor did he admit the motivation for his crime'" (Jin He 1983, 191). In other words, there is no criminal mens rea to which Ye can credibly own up. If protecting Mao/Zhu/socialism is not a mitigating excuse, nothing is. His only option is to go along with the script and play the docile scapegoat. But his refusal to do so is as confounding as his refusal to name Zhu, with the effect of forcing his interrogators, as well as the readers, to see beyond the foreshortened horizon of legal reasoning and to pursue the long chain of historical causality—something that the actual Gang of Four Trial could not afford to do. Ye does not give his interrogators an easy way out. He forces them, and us, to answer for him the question of why he, a middle-school student with "clean, white teeth" (184), should have taken part in a bloody fight in which he killed someone he didn't know for the sake of protecting someone he barely knew. In other words, why were young people waging war against one another when the country was at peace? Ye does not avail himself of the "cog theory" defense, but is it because Mao never explicitly ordered his "little generals" to fight pitched battles in China's urban streets? If "it was not an order but a law which had turned [Nazis] into criminals" and that law was Hitler's words (Arendt 1994, 149), then weren't Mao's words responsible for turning China's "revolutionary successors" into "disorderly elements"?

It is impossible to answer these questions without reexamining the entire socialist experiment and putting Mao as well as the top CCP leadership (including those who can claim plausible victim status) on trial, as it were. John Treat (2017) points out that at the Tokyo Trial, the opinions of the presiding justices diverged radically around whether individuals could be held responsible for acts of state. Some were troubled by the exclusion of the emperor and the failure to essentially put the Japanese nation and Japanese history on trial, while others objected to aspects of the trial precisely for veering too far in that direction. For decades the CCP readily put Chinese history on trial in pursuit of revolutionary justice, but once history became wholly owned by itself, trying history was no longer thinkable. Yet the short story stages something symbolically close: After Ye Hui's mother unexpectedly pays him a visit to plead leniency for her son, Zhu Chunxin feels that his conscience is on trial. He learns from her how Ye Hui became radicalized: At the start of the Cultural Revolution, he was a sensitive teenager who was terribly shaken up by the public denunciation of his school headmaster. Because of this show of softness he was labeled a "capitalist" and shut out of the early Red Guard groups. "He spent his time reading newspapers and pamphlets, and then he would look dazed and stare at the ceiling" (Jin He 1983, 193). After making a secret trip to Beijing, he returned home a devoted apostle carrying tokens of his conversion: "he took out a packet from his belt and unfolded it layer by layer. At last, he shook out two souvenir badges of Chairman Mao, the size of a fingertip, and carefully put one on my shirt. I asked him to wear one too, but he was reluctant for fear that it would be damaged. Carefully, he wrapped it up and kept it close to his chest" (193). Unmistakably, we are witnessing the behavior of a pious convert, and yet the fingers that tenderly wrapped up the Mao badge would be the same ones that stabbed another student to death.

Who pushed Ye onto the path of radicalization? Who convinced him that throwing bricks and spears at other youngsters was the best or only way to protect Mao and guard the country against a "revisionist" turn (Jin He 1983, 193)? And who drilled into his teenage head the mortal dread of that obscure sin called "revisionism"? In telling his backstory and acting as his character witness, Ye's mother is essentially demanding that the foregoing questions be part of the investigation if true justice is to be done. When she apologizes for her lack of education and eloquence, Zhu consoles her: "'No, you put it very well . . . very well.' A muscle on Zhu Chunxin's pale face kept twitching. He was not annoyed at the old woman worker's long-winded account. On the contrary her wordy account was pounding his heart like a heavy hammer, making him feel that he was being tried on the stand of the accused. He had committed no crime. This was a trial of his conscience!" (194). It is true that he has committed no crime in the technical sense, but he is well aware that he is not free of responsibility. Exactly what responsibility he, and the Party at large, should bear is left unresolved by the end of the story. But at the very least, it succeeds in trailing a moral question after the verboten legal question ("What is a person responsible for?"): "What is it to be responsible?" (Treat 2017, 416–17).

We know from Cook's account that the Party absolved itself of criminal liability by means of the crucial distinction between error and crime. The Gang of Four Trial as well as numerous local trials of "disorderly elements" turned this fiction into reality. But writers like Jin He apparently did not want to let the Party off the hook so easily. Already, as we saw in his retort to Zhu Chunxin, Ye Hui remarks that some mistakes are crimes, while others are the price of an education. At the end of Zhu's private interview with Ye, department head Li comes to the door and booms: "Lead the criminal away!" The story ends with the following lines: "Zhu Chunxin shivered suddenly, and his face turned pale. In his heart, he kept repeating the word: 'criminal?'" (Jin He 1983, 198). Evidently for a split second he has mistaken the command as directed at himself. It is a haunting way to end this profoundly searching story, with its implied indictment of the Party-state not only for the devastations of the Cultural Revolution, but also for its refusal to conduct a full-scale inquiry for the sake of truth and reconciliation.

The Gang of Four Trial was widely applauded by the Chinese public despite its not-so-subtle show trial quality. The dozen or so defendants may have been scapegoats, but certainly not *innocent* ones. Apropos of the post-war trial of Nazi officials, Shklar writes: "Where power is so great the personal impact of the agent is also great. Here the test *sine qua non* [...] can be applied to show that certain individuals were not the indirect or remote cause of the policies but that they, in fact, framed and implemented them" (1986, 192). The Special Court too was able to marshal enough evidence to prove that but for these individuals, the Cultural Revolution would not have become the catastrophe that it did become. However, with regard to everyone else who participated in a struggle session, a factional fight, or a house search, the sine qua non test applies only tenuously. Shklar believes it pointless to go after the small fry: "It is hard to impute conscious criminality to these lesser figures, since all the acts that were subsequently regarded as reprehensible were praised and rewarded by all the authorities and approved by the rest of society at the time of their commission" (193).

Sporting a nom de guerre (Ye Weige), the young man in the story rallied to Mao's call to carry on the revolution, a glorious mission that galvanized a whole generation and then was retroactively pronounced a colossal mistake. Insofar as bodies were killed and maimed, crimes were indeed committed, but only in the post hoc framework of legality. Ye Hui the legally recognized citizen under the new dispensation of socialist rule of law must now answer for the harm inflicted by Ye Weige the revolutionary rebel. Although Mao exhorted the youth of New China to aspire to be the "rustless screws" (*yong bu shengxiu de luosiding*) of socialism, Ye did not see himself as a mere cog but as a heroic fighter who rose to defend Mao and the revolution. But objectively he was a cog in the eye of the state as it conducted politics as total war. Now his personhood is restored to him, but only on condition of holding him legally accountable. He insists on being known as Ye Hui because it is a mark of his newly restored legal personhood and the dignity and price that accompany it. Arendt comments on the momentous transformation a single step across the threshold of a courtroom can effect: "The almost automatic shifting of responsibility that habitually takes place in modern society comes to a sudden halt the moment you enter a courtroom. All justifications of a nonspecific abstract nature—everything from the Zeitgeist down to the Oedipus complex that indicates that you are not a man but a function of something and hence yourself an exchangeable thing rather than a somebody—break down. [...] And the moment you come to the individual person, the question to be raised is no longer, How did this system function? but, Why did the defendant become a functionary in this organization?" (Arendt 2003, 57–58). Neither question was raised in the trial of the Gang of Four, nor are they likely to be raised in Ye Hui's public trial. Ye's last words echo the CCP's resolution on the Cultural Revolution as something to be repudiated tout court (*quanmian fouding*). Whereas the Party need not pay for its errors once it has offloaded them all onto the Gang of Four, Ye Hui does have to pay for his "immaturity and shame" (Jin He 1983, 198) because after all he did choose to join the "organization" and thrust a spear at someone. It is a testament of his character that he fully owns up to the crime, without invoking the "cog theory" that Arendt so detests. One imagines that he is even more inwardly tormented than Zhu trying to answer the question: why did I support it?

In recent years in the United States, legal scholars and advocacy groups have called for mens rea reform so as to make it easier to prosecute white-collar crimes where it is often exceedingly difficult to establish criminal intent. Opponents of the proposed reform, however, have been able to appeal to an almost universal aversion to convicting people in cases that do not meet the control condition. Lurking in the background of this fight is no doubt the specter of political trial that presents the flimsiest mens rea and is all too ready to hand down strict liability penalties. In any case, neither the Gang of Four Trial nor the many local facsimiles delivered transitional justice in one fell swoop. Thanks to the taboos and censorship surrounding the Cultural Revolution, this wave of transitional justice is essentially stalled or aborted. When literary and cinematic works do cast a backward glance at the "decade of upheaval," they tend to lament the helplessness of the common people buffeted by political hurricanes they could not begin to comprehend. The Cultural Revolution in these works rather resembles a giant flood that surged across the country inexplicably, leaving some drowned and the rest dazed and confused. Rarely is the divide between perpetrator and victim troubled to the same extent as in "The Second Encounter."

The Socialist Rule of Law: Trying the Present

"The Second Encounter" declines to give us a true ending: we don't know how Zhu Chunxin will act after his soul-searching. Will outing himself save Ye Hui? At what costs to himself and to the larger political aim of inaugurating a new era? Recall that at the beginning of the story Zhu was trying to prepare "a few typical cases" for a public trial. If he gave Ye an easy pass but went on to prosecute other "disorderly elements," he could undercut his own credibility as well as the legitimacy of the newly restored organs of public security, procuratorate, and courts. Ye has to be sacrificed, it seems, to repair the tattered net of socialist rule of law, if only so that other, larger fish can be caught. Post-Mao literary and cinematic works, like the ones examined by Cook, are overwhelmingly concerned with these big fish, giving rise to the enduring postsocialist genre of anticorruption drama. In this section we read a play and a film that give us gripping accounts of how the fledgling legal system earnestly confronts and manages to rein in arbitrary power. Unlike "The Second Encounter," neither features or even promises a Maoist public trial. Their fictional gazes are intensely trained on the present, on the halting birthing of socialist legality.

Power versus Law (*Quan yu fa*, 1979) is a four-act play by Xing Yixun (1980).[3] It chronicles the downfall of a local Party boss who has embezzled disaster relief funds and attempted to cover it up by incriminating the whistleblower. As one of the earliest anticorruption dramas, it establishes the basic plot pattern: a corrupt official, aided and abetted by toadies, holds the local populace in fearful thralldom, enriches himself and his family, turns a blind eye to the malfeasance of his cronies, and retaliates against his detractors—until a newly appointed leading cadre who outranks him arrives on the scene, wins the trust of the long suffering locals, unearths the truth, and brings the corrupt official to justice in a decisive fashion reminiscent of Judge Bao. Here, the corrupt official is the deputy secretary of the municipal Party committee, Cao Da, and the upright official happens to be his brother-in-law Luo Fang, who at the beginning of the play has just been dispatched by Party central to Cao's district and installed as his immediate superior. Through the diligent investigative work of a journalist and hesitant revelations of Ding Mu the accountant, Cao's misdeeds come to Luo Fang's attention. The play emphatically frames the central conflict as between unchecked power and impartial law, respectively embodied by Cao and Luo. That the two men are affinal kin only accentuates the impartiality of socialist legality that Luo endeavors to inculcate in those around him, from the accountant to the police chief.

The play also conveys a strong sense of the dawning of a new era, marked by a new constitution and rule of law: "Since the fall of the 'gang of four,' everything has changed. Now we're getting back to our Party's fine old tradition. [. . . .] At the Fifth National People's Congress a new constitution was passed" (Xing Yixun 1980, 62). "Now we have a new constitution, how can Cao Da be a law unto himself?" (63). The invocation of the Party's "fine old tradition" is critical here: it implies that but for the disruption of the Gang of Four one-party rule itself is fully compatible with rule of law and is indeed its very foundation—this fundamental article of faith will be thunderously affirmed in *The Case of Huang Kegong* to which we will turn at the end of this chapter. The task of post-Mao transitional justice is thus to dispel the miasma of the Gang of Four in order to restore the Party's honest, clean, and law-abiding tradition. Corruption thus is quarantined from the "Party spirit" (*dangxing*) and pathologized as an alien growth that needs to be lanced (see Sorace 2017, chap. 2). Rhetorically, law is almost always invoked in the same breath as Party discipline, and corruption is thus simultaneously transgression against Party discipline (*dangji*) as well as state law (*guofa*). Luo Fang, for example, is admiringly labeled by his daughter as "an orthodox communist" who has lost none of his "Party spirit" for all his sufferings during the Cultural Revolution (Xing Yixun 1980, 66). His presence reasserts that the center holds firmly and is fully capable of shearing off abscesses like Cao. Like Judge Bao wielding his imperial sword, Luo solemnly invokes the law: addressing his wife, he says, "Chunmei, I know how you feel about your brother. But think of the anarchy stirred up by Lin Biao and the gang. And why for centuries did the people of China think the law not worth the paper it was written on? Because officials always protected each other. You, I and Old Cao are officials. Do Communist officials protect each other? No! Chairman Mao said that blatant cases of bureaucracy and lawlessness should be exposed in the press. And Premier Zhou said they should be taken to court. Chunmei, we mustn't shield him simply because Old Cao is your brother" (76).

When he finally confronts Cao, Luo speaks forcefully in the name of the law and the people: "If anyone breaks the law as you have done, the people have the right to bash him down. Today (*holds up the incriminating materials*) the people are going to bash you! . . . In place of socialist law you've put your personal rule. You take reprisals against those who expose you, accusing them falsely. You should be punished according to the law!" (Xing Yixun 1980, 80–81). Cao fights back by rolling up his trousers to reveal old wounds sustained in the war years, reminding Luo that as a veteran of the Communist Revolution he merits special treatment. Luo retorts: "A veteran Party member? You? You're a disgrace to our Party! You think your past record, your present power, set you above the law! Instead of being a servant of the people you lord it over them. [. . .] You've put power in place of law! Does this socialist country of ours still have feudal rule? 'Nobles are exempt from punishment'—that Confucian maxim still holds, does it? No! The law doesn't just apply to the common people. It doesn't make exceptions for an elite. Neither your past record nor your present power can hide your crime. I warn you, you're going to have the law on you!" (81).

When Cao's case was initially brought to Luo's attention by a newspaper editor, he immediately authorized publication, promising to be "responsible for the consequences" (Xing Yixun 1980, 77). Throughout, Luo is the very image of integrity and decisiveness. The obverse, however, is the very personal nature of the critical lever that sets in motion the process of justice. The press is clearly not an independent watchdog: unfavorable reporting on a high official seems possible only when undertaken by the daughter of another high official and printable only when greenlighted by the same official. Apparently aware of the slide backward into the old pattern of "rule by man," the play ends with Luo reprimanding the police chief for habitually ignoring the law and then assuring a malefactor of his legal rights: "Commissioner Wan, first you came to arrest Comrade Ding Mu on Secretary Cao's orders. Now you're ready to arrest Director Lei [Cao's accomplice] on *my* orders. Do you simply carry out your superiors' instructions? Aren't you even going to look at this material? Is a Party secretary Truth incarnate? Does power equal policy and law? . . . [Turning to Lei] Go back and do some soul-searching, Director Lei. You must have the courage to admit your crime to the Party and the people. Of course you're entitled to put up a defence. The law is no respecter of persons—only of facts" (90–91). In the same breath Luo both pays homage to the impartial rule of law ("entitled to put up a defence") and reinforces the paternalistic model of governance that expects compliance and cooperation and a proper moral attitude of contrition ("admit your crime to the Party and the people"). The tension is papered over by the conflation of the law with the Party (which speaks for the people), hence while the Party secretary may not be "Truth incarnate," he—as either the highest-ranked official or as a special envoy from Party central—is very much justice incarnate. In that sense he is also Judge Bao incarnate. This archetype would consistently appear in postsocialist anticorruption dramas as a way of resolving the basic tension between one-party rule and the rule of law.

Also similarly to familiar Judge Bao plays, the suspense in these anticorruption dramas resides not in whether the culprit will be convicted, but how. The film *The Trial* (*Fating neiwai*) (Cong Lianwen and Lu Xiaoya 1980) stands out for its courtroom denouement, in which the accused, along with audiences on and off screen, await anxiously for the verdict and the sentence. The suspense is genuine: will the judge stand up to power and serve justice, or will she buckle under mounting pressure from all sides and look out for her own career? It's not a matter of exonerating the miscreant—both the judge and the audience are convinced of his crime—but whether the judge will use her power of discretion and hand out a lenient sentence. The death penalty that she actually pronounces thus packs a considerable punch, as attested to by the expression of everyone present. The phrase that sums up the key lesson of the case is "The law is merciless" or more literally "The law cannot be compromised for the sake of feelings" (*fa bu xunqing*). And the thick webs of human relationships glued together by feelings/*renqing* is precisely what the film takes pain to portray.

Judge Shang Qin, played by Tian Hua of *The White-Haired Girl* fame, receives an appeal from the family of the victim of a traffic fatality case. The chauffeur of the Party secretary of the municipal revolutionary committee had run over and killed a gymnast. He turned himself in, confessed to drunk driving, and was acquitted by a lower court on account of his good attitude. Cracks in the case readily surface as soon as Shang Qin and her team begin to scrutinize the evidence and interview the various parties involved. Before long, the ugly truth comes to full light: The son of the Party secretary, Xia Huan, is the real culprit for whom the chauffeur has been bribed to take the fall. When the chauffeur's lie is exposed and Shang's team closes in on the truth, the mother mobilizes her entire network of connections to dissuade, plead, and coerce Shang Qin to desist.

It turns out that the Xias and Shangs go way back in their friendship. Most importantly, Secretary Xia was instrumental in bringing about the posthumous rehabilitation of Shang Qin's late husband, and in bringing her out of political exile and installing her in her present position. The film devotes quite a few scenes to the amicable familiarity between the two families across the generations: in one scene Xia Huan addresses Shang Qin affectionately as "auntie" and engages her in cheerful small talk. Mrs. Xia visits Shang Qin in her home and plays the distraught mother in an attempt to elicit her sympathy. On the heels of this are more personal visits and phone calls by the who's who of the city. Meanwhile, the victim's commoner family is visited by Shang Qin and given a chance to pour out their pent-up grief. The film thus gives us a full taste of how socialist legality unfolds on the ground. As Mühlhahn describes: "The Chinese inquisitorial system was viewed not as a duel between opposing counsels but as a tripartite search for the objective truth, and not merely the legal truth. All the major participants in the process—the judges as well as the prosecution and the people's assessor—were expected to cooperate in the search. Moreover, because of the special situation of the defendant, who usually had no counsel of any sort in a criminal trial in China, the obligation was on the judges and the prosecution to bring out both the incriminating and the exonerating features of the case. The defendant's role was confined to seeking either an acquittal or a mitigation of punishment" (Mühlhahn 2009, 186–87). McIntyre makes a similar point: "[Chinese] courtroom drama does not focus on questions of guilt or innocence, but on whether the accused will face punitive justice. Facts do not emerge

FIGURE 3.2: Judge Shang Qin's own investigation in *The Trial* (Cong Lianwen and Lu Xiaoya 1980, Emei Film Group).

through an adversarial process, but through the instrumentality of a virtuous judge" (2013, 9).

This picture is largely reflected in the film. Shang Qin undertakes her own investigation, including meeting ex parte with the litigants (figure 3.2). Her diligence pays off: Well before the trial, the objective truth, in all its tawdry detail, was already firmly in the hands of Shang Qin's team: no new evidence is expected to emerge in the trial process; no cross-examination is staged; no ungainly legal truth has to be hammered out and swallowed. Shang Qin's mind, it seems, has also been firmly made up before she steps up to the bench. None of this, however, takes away the sense of justice done. Like all such stories, the contest is never simply between perpetrator and victim, but between what each side stands for. The questions driving post-Mao narratives of transitional justice are always the same: Can the Party police itself? Can one-party rule deliver true justice? Can the judiciary really take on powerful Party officials? Is there room for low justice when high justice imperatives loom so large? Can an ordinary family count on having its wrong righted whatever the status of the perpetrator? The film's answer is yes to all, and the answer is anchored not only in Shang Qin's unswerving allegiance to the law, but also in Secretary Xia's willingness to honor the Party's principles (*dang de yuanze*) at the steepest price possible: his son's life.

The final courtroom scene stands out for an unusual detail: the presence of a court-appointed defense counsel who pursues a credible line of defense, that Xia Huan is a victim of parental neglect and bad societal influences during the years when his parents were politically disgraced and he was left to fend for himself. Even after he was reunited with his parents, their sense of guilt made them turn a blind eye to his waywardness and the terrible company he kept. The question for the court and the audience is then whether these circumstances should mitigate Xia's guilt, a question that returns us to the distinction between historical causality and legal causality. In determining guilt and responsibility, how far back in history and away from the individual one goes depends on the goals of punishment. Here retributive and didactic goals clearly outweigh rehabilitative ones, and when Xia Huan is handed the death sentence, it is clear that its import goes far beyond an eye for an eye. Rather, like the Gang of Four Trial, this trial is performative in its enactment of the resumption of legal normalcy, of being the first chapter in a new age of socialist rule of law—a message universally picked up by contemporary commentators.

Xia Huan is a prototype of what would later be called "princelings" (*taizidang, guan erdai, hong erdai*)—children of the Party brass who avail themselves of the protective shield of their parents' status to behave in wanton and reckless manners, often leaving a trail of tears behind them. They have become the bête noire of contemporary Chinese society and a frequent target of public outcry. In 2010, a college freshman ran over two female students on a Hebei university campus, killing one and gravely injuring the other. When he was stopped and questioned by campus security, he taunted them: "Sue me if you dare! My father is Li Gang!" (Belkin 2017, 213). "My father is Li Gang!" became an instant viral meme on the internet, spawning countless commentaries and satirical riffs. Even after the Li Gang in question, a local public security chief, went on national television to express remorse and offer tearful apologies, public outrage remained unabated.

We Have Always Been Just

Xia Huan's conviction in *The Trial* has everything to do with the fact that he is the son of a high official: however certain his guilt, he is also being made an example, a warning, the medium of a political message. The film gives us a glimpse of the seething public outrage that in the internet age could easily boil over and threaten to burst the seam of one-party rule. Keenly aware of the explosive potential of public passion, the Party has espoused a perilous form of judicial populism by carefully monitoring and regulating popular sentiments and harnessing them for the purpose of social control. When official corruption has come to concentrate so much popular anger and vitiated faith in the fundamental fairness of the social order, the Party's self-image as a guarantor of justice is at stake, and every low justice case (drunk driving, rape, murder) has the potential to escalate up to a matter of high justice, that is, to a question of social stability and regime legitimacy. The transitional justice process that was set in motion by the Gang of Four Trial is in fact never completed. One might even say that the entire Reform and Opening Up period is one of perpetual transition as the Party tries to chart a seemingly impossible course between authoritarianism and rule of law. The film that best captures the ongoing nature of this transition—paradoxically in its very denial of any break—is *The Case of Huang Kegong* (*Huang Kegong anjian*, a.k.a. *A Murder Beside Yan River*) (Wang Fangfang 2014), a film based on true events that transpired in Yan'an in 1937, soon after the full-scale outbreak of the second Sino-Japanese war.

On a chilly morning on the bank of Yan River a corpse is discovered. It is the remains of Liu Qian, a young student at Shaanbei College who left her home in coastal China three months earlier to come to Yan'an to join the Communist Revolution. The prime suspect, Huang Kegong, a Red Army captain, is quickly apprehended. He admits to asking Liu out on the previous evening to propose marriage to her. Upon her refusal, they got into a tussle and he fatally shot her in a jealous rage. News of the murder quickly travels beyond Yan'an and the Nationalist media hypes it up as a Communist "crime of passion" (*taose shijian*) and a sign of permissiveness and lawlessness in the CCP-controlled Shaanxi-Gansu-Ningxia border regions. The CCP leadership recognizes the publicity weight of the scandal and orders Lei Jingtian, the chief judicial officer of the brand-new High Court of the Border Region, to adjudicate the case. This is at the very beginning of the second united front between the CCP and the Nationalists. The High Court has been in existence for merely two months and is nominally part of the Republic of China's criminal justice system, though it enjoys de facto independence (X. Cong 2016; Mühlhahn 2009).

Lei decides to hold a public trial. With over two thousand in attendance, the trial is the picture of an orderly court of law in session, with the added feature of a dozen or so "people's assessors" (*qunzhong daibiao*) seated opposite of the procurators' desk. The open court is part of the innovations pioneered by Ma Xiwu, a CCP official who became legendary in the Border Region for his method of resolving disputes through a combination of field investigation, mediation, and democratic adjudication (X. Cong 2016, 187). The Ma Xiwu Method (*Ma Xiwu shenpan fangshi*) was heavily promoted by the Party as a judicial practice uniquely suited to local conditions. A few cases decided by Ma involving rural women's fight for marriage freedom were reported prominently in Party newspapers and adapted as chantefables and musical theater pieces (and later as film and television dramas). The story of Peng'er, for example, endures to this day under the name of Liu Qiao'er (X. Cong 2016). The open court was a critical component of the Ma Xiwu Method noted for its informality and pedagogical ambitions. It would become the core of the "mass line," or the democratic dictatorship of the people, and the hallmark of all subsequent political trials.

After the procurator Hu Yaobang (whose death sparked the 1989 pro-democracy movement) makes his indictment, and after a period of public discussion (we will return to this shortly), it is the defendant's turn to speak. Huang makes a clean breast of his crime but pleads to be sent to the front so that he can die fighting the enemy (*daizui ligong*) (figure 3.3). The court adjourns while the five members of the adjudicating panel deliberate in private and at length (we will also return to this). At last, they agree on capital punishment. Moments after the sentence is pronounced by Lei Jingtian and as Huang is being escorted away, a soldier on horseback rushes in waving a letter. It is from Mao, a joint reply to both Lei and Huang, who have written to him earlier separately. The body of the letter reads:

> Huang Kegong has had a glorious career as a fighter. Today in sentencing him to death, the Party central and I are pained by the loss. But he committed an unpardonable crime. When a Communist Party member and Red Army officer acted in such a despicable, cruel manner, betrayed the Party and the revolution, and lost basic human decency, if we were to pardon him, we would be unable to discipline our Party, our Red Army, and our revolution. Thus we put him to death in accordance with the rules of the Party and the Red Army. Precisely because Huang Kegong is not a commoner, precisely because he is a seasoned Party member, precisely because he is a veteran Red Army officer, we cannot do otherwise. The Communist Party and the Red Army have no choice but enforce harsher discipline on their own members. In the present time of national emergency and revolutionary urgency, Huang Kegong could actually do something so base, shameless, brutal, and selfish—he brought the punishment on himself. Every Party member, every Red Army officer, and every revolutionary must take heart and draw a lesson from the case of Huang Kegong.
>
> At the same time as you proclaim the court's decision, please read this letter aloud to all present, including Huang Kegong. Please provide appropriate condolences and compensation to Liu Qian's comrades and family.

FIGURE 3.3: Huang Kegong pleading for leniency; the trial panel's deliberation. From *The Case of Huang Kegong* (Wang Fangfang 2014, Beijing Film Group).

Lei Jingtian indeed reads aloud Mao's letter in its entirety with appropriate solemnity. The public trial scene takes up a third of screen time and features some rousing speeches by members of the public. Equally gripping is the backroom deliberation among the five all-male members of the adjudicating panel (see again figure 3.3). After four men have affixed their thumb print on the writ, the lone holdout, Li Xingguo, asks on what *legal* grounds they are convicting Huang. The others are caught off guard and admit that they are merely acting on the customary law of "a life for a life" (*sharen changming*), the Chinese expression of *lex talionis*. To underscore the law-based regime of justice, Li pulls out a pamphlet with the title "Chinese Soviet Central Republic's Ordinances on Counterrevolution" (*Zhonghua Suwei'ai Gongheguo chengzhi fangeming tiaoli*, 1934) printed on the cover and reminds his fellow panelists of the stipulation of leniency for individuals of working-class origins as well as those who have rendered meritorious services to the Red Army. Sun Qiguang, an intellectual type in Western attire and Liu Qian's classmate, is incredulous: How can any law be so blatantly discriminatory? Why should a person's birth have anything to do with how one is treated by the law?

Sun seems politically savvy enough not to invoke the criminal code of the Republic of China, which of course has statutes on homicide, though technically it would have been an unimpeachable move given the High Court's nominal status as part of the Republic of China's judicial system. Instead he questions the fairness of the Red Army's own law, and Mao seems to agree with him in his letter. Soon the question of codes falls by the wayside as the human drama takes over, immersing us in the many brooding moments, wrenching conversations, and impossible choices that give the film a great deal of emotional depth. The film also accentuates the thriller elements of the story, for example by making Huang fib about an accidental discharge of his gun, by delaying the discovery of the second gunshot wound on Liu Qian's body, and by pacing the revelation of a succession of other clues that allow the investigators, led by Hu Yaobang, to piece together the truth. The biggest thrill, no doubt, is delivered by the suspenseful trial scene where Huang's fate hangs in the balance until the very end. During the public discussion period, Liu Qian's fellow students hailing from urban China sit on one side, and Huang's fellow soldiers, mostly from the hinterland, sit on the other, forming two opposing camps on whether Huang deserves the death penalty. The student representative's remarks about male CCP cadres' sense of entitlement when it comes to women and sex anticipate Ding Ling's 1942 "Thoughts on March 8" editorial, in which she took to task the persistence of patriarchal values and practices in Yan'an, which resulted in her being targeted during the Rectification Campaign (Ding Ling 1989, 316–21). Here, however, the criticism and the implied disaffection seem to have sunk in with Lei Jingtian, who echoes her during the panel deliberation.

To add some local color, a middle-aged peasant woman, whom Lei Jingtian has granted a divorce early in the film, stands up and in a lilting Shaanbei accent demands the court to "stick up for us women." Most stirring of all is an elderly man who offers to substitute for Huang with his own life so that Huang can go to the front "to kill more Japs." In the old man's reckoning, it is heaven that must ultimately be appeased, and one life is as good as another in restoring cosmic balance—a folksy logic that Judge Bao understands well when he sends a horse thief to the gallows in place of a filial son (see the introduction). A few minutes later during the panel deliberation, Lei Jingtian mobilizes a similar logic to elevate the case to one of high justice. Long before he could have put his thumb on the writ, he explains, he has already given himself a triple death sentence. First, in disregarding the stipulation of preferential treatment for Red Army cadets, he has essentially ended the special privileges granted to the group to which he himself belongs, thus "killing off" his own privileged status. Second, because Huang Kegong saved his life on the Long March, he has to "kill off" his "emotional reasoning" (*ganqing yongshi*) and stymie feelings of gratitude. Third, in not deferring to his superiors, he has "killed off" his lack of courage to judge the case independently and shoulder the consequences. Note that the substance of Lei's speech, beyond the hyperbole, checks the major boxes of the rule-of-law ideal: equality before the law, reason and objectivity, and judicial independence. Yet the speech is couched in a highly personalized and rhetorically circuitous language about personal sacrifices for the sake of a higher cause. It brings Li Xingguo, the last holdout, to the verge of tears and finally we see him slowly lift his thumb.

Lei Jingtian's voice-over then intones slowly in the name of the High

FIGURE 3.4: Judge Lei Jingtian reading the verdict in *The Case of Huang Kegong* (Wang Fangfang 2014, Beijing Film Group).

Court of the Border Region (figure 3.4). Unexpectedly, he cites Article 217 of the Penal Code of the Republic of China that stipulates "death sentence for persons convicted of homicide" (*sharenzhe chu yi sixing*); he then cites the New Provisional Law of the Red Army that prohibits killing comrades. Neither of these codes has been invoked so far, nor do we ever see Lei consult the actual books. Even so, codes are not enough. He moves on to give further rationale as to why Huang Kegong must die. The scene ends with the High Court's imposingly large red seal being pressed on the writ. Thus despite the rhetorical homage paid to the rule of law and the last-minute invocation of statutes, the verdict is justified almost entirely on political grounds: One, the public in Yan'an are watching, the Nationalists are watching, and the world is watching. The CCP cannot afford to have its self-image as the shining city on the hill tarnished. Two, the revolution cannot be accomplished in one generation. It needs to attract new blood and cultivate successors; allowing the killer of a young student to go free would put an end to the pipeline. "Pardoning Huang Kegong," Lei exclaims, "would be tantamount to putting our future to death." On this note Lei pivots the trial from a low justice homicide case to one of high justice implicating the legitimacy, moral supremacy, and future of the Party and the revolution. Moments ago Li Xingguo questioned how Liu Qian's life, belonging to a sixteen-year-old girl student who had never fired a single shot, could be commensurate with Huang's life. Now when Huang's life is stacked against the exigencies of the Party and its enterprise, the choice is stark.

In the face of the incalculable and incommensurate, the minutiae of law seem decidedly trivial and beside the point. During the panel deliberation there is no parsing of the difference between degrees of murder or between murder and manslaughter, no weighing of possible mitigating factors (such as disappointment in love and jealousy), no taking into consideration Huang's confession and contrition. Even one of the three "death sentences" that Lei claims to have inflicted on himself for overcoming his inclination to follow orders is apparently purely rhetorical—or else there is no way to account for the arrival of Mao's letter in the nick of time. The film version is allegedly faithful to the historical events, but the lengthy and contentious meeting in which Huang's fate hangs on one vote is almost certainly a product of poetic license that seriously underestimates audience intelligence.[4] On the surface, Mao has scrupulously stayed away from the case after appointing Lei as the chief justice. Early on, though, he has sent his wife, He Zizhen, to confront Huang and ask him point blank if he did it. Huang's shamefaced admission pains her greatly. We learn that Huang and his brother have followed Mao and He for many years and are as close to them as their own children. Mao never visits Huang; instead we see him, in an interview with a foreign reporter, brush off her hints that the Party won't be able to handle the case impartially. There is no reason to believe that Mao did not discreetly communicate his position on the case to Lei and receive assurance from the latter.

Rather than acting as amicus curiae, Mao in his letter usurps Lei's place and issues a judgment from a sovereign height. The letter cites no law and makes no mention of the investigation. Instead, it condemns Huang Kegong in moral-political and strategic terms. It is the equivalent of the Party's "Resolution" on the Cultural Revolution that overlaid political justifications on the legal verdict of the Special Court convened to try the Gang of Four. Whereas the High Court sentences Huang to death and authorizes the forfeit of his biological being at the low justice level, Mao's letter proclaims the termination of Huang as a moral and political subject for the sake of high justice. Huang was defiant after receiving the verdict, shouting his demand to be sent to the battlefield to die a soldier's death. After listening to the letter, however, he drops his gaze and meekly lets himself be led out of the arena. He now is not only a convicted murderer, but also a scoundrel and traitor who has been excommunicated from the only collectivity that matters to him. His death will not just pay for Liu Qian's death but will also redeem the revolutionary cause and keep the future alive for his fellow Chinese.

Mao's letter speaks in the plural "we," which leaves no room for judicial independence. That Mao was not self-conscious about it could have two explanations: One, he never expected the High Court to render any verdict contrary to his wishes, or else he could have simply court-martialed Huang and subjected him to swift military justice. Two, he seemed aware that his not-so-subtle intervention would not have struck anyone as unwarranted, least of all his political rivals the Nationalists. Scholars have written extensively about the gradual party-fication of law in the Nanjing decade (1927–37) (X. Cong 2016; Mühlhahn 2009; Lean 2007). Indeed, when the news of the murder first reaches the Party leadership, the first thing that is brought up as a cautionary lesson is Chiang Kai-shek's speedy pardon of his wife-killing general and Whampoa alum Zhang Zhonglin (a.k.a. Zhang Lingpu). Yan'an's media at the time was touting the unprecedented liberty and equality women enjoyed in the Border Region. The *Xinhua Daily*, for example, showcased Peng'er's success in winning the freedom to choose her mate "as an example of the CCP's good governance and democratic practices to the outside world" (see X. Cong 2016, 207). How else to claim the moral high ground and quash negative publicity other than for the CCP to execute its feted Red Army captain for a comparable crime? This is pointed out again and again by commentators: "What the Nationalists failed to do, the CCP did" (He Tian 2014, 140).

*   *   *

The Case of Huang Kegong is a late addition to the repertoire of works that have endeavored to performatively enact the transition from a chaotic, lawless past to a present dedicated to "governance in accordance with the law." Unlike *Power versus Law* and *The Trial*, however, *The Case of Huang Kegong* effects this transition by somersaulting backward to the most mythologized moment in CCP history and recasting it as a golden age in which law's rule was the order of the day. Screenwriter Wang Xingdong paraphrases Zhou Qiang, president of the People's High Court: "This film makes a historical argument. As far back as 70 years ago, the Chinese Communist Part was already honoring the rule of law, democracy, equality, fairness, and honesty" (quoted in He Tian 2014, 156).

The resurrection of a rule-of-law Yan'an makes blotting out the "decade of turmoil" as a historical blip that much easier and turns transition into a project of recovery and renaissance. The message is blunt: The Party is a true champion of the rule of law, and has always been. Autocracy, mob rule, and state-sponsored violence are merely an aberration, a result of the Party's core leadership being hijacked by a cabal of conspirators. Just as Mao resolutely executed a man as valuable and dear to him as Huang Kegong—a gesture that is mimicked in Luo Fang's bringing down his brother-in-law Cao Da in *Power versus Law* and Secretary Xia's letting go of his son Xia Huan in *The Trial*—the Party today is fully capable of excising rotten organs from the body politic. It has never stopped performing self-purification since the Yan'an days, which culminated in the decisive ousting of the Gang of Four and continues to this day in the ongoing anticorruption campaigns aiming to catch "tigers" and "flies" alike.

Insofar as the campaigns seem to have broad popular support, they are deemed a success. Neither the Party central nor the populace seems particularly bothered by the abrogation of rights and due process visited on corrupt officials caught in the maelstrom. In cases where popular resentment runs high, the Party seems happy to oblige by meting out harsh punishments in the name of "appeasing public indignation" (*ping minfen*). Ira Belkin calls this practice "judicial populism": "Chinese courts were required to consider the 'people's feelings' and decide cases according to whether their decisions would 'win the broad support of the masses,' 'preserve social stability' and 'reduc[e] social protest'" (2017, 197). Lily Tsai (2021) speaks of "punitive populism" in connection with the same compulsion to dispense retributive justice in order to shore up regime legitimacy.

One can very well trace judicial or punitive populism all the way to the imperial practices of accommodating the customary law of *renqing* and of issuing periodic amnesties (see the introduction). When the source of political legitimacy was heavenly principles (*tianli*), watching the weathervane of popular sentiments was one way to gauge the celestial mood and bolster the regime's claim to the Mandate of Heaven. When the people themselves have become the foundation of political authority, it is all the more imperative to have one's finger on the popular pulse. During the Republican period we have the notorious case of Shi Jianqiao, a filial assassin pardoned by the Nationalist government principally in response to societal pressure (Lean 2007). Huang Kegong's case too, as we have seen, was decided largely out of political and public relations considerations. Under Mao, the term "popular indignation" (*minfen*), together with "blood debts" (*xiezhai*), was used liberally to justify harsh retributive sanctions. Heeding public opinion may seem an admirably democratic thing to do, but high justice concerns are nearly always the driving force. Public opinion is treated as a barometer of regime legitimacy; it matters only in the aggregate and hence is not incompatible with censorship, the trampling of individual rights, and the truncating of low justice. At its worst judicial populism can morph into the routinization of rough justice and mob rule, something that did happen in the Cultural Revolution and persists today in a new media ecosystem. Public sentiments are not just spontaneously expressed or suppressed; as often as not, they are mobilized by the state and other actors.

In the age of the internet and social media, judicial populism risks turning every criminal justice case into a political trial whereby the true contestation takes place in the court of public opinion instead of the court of law. Reacting to the aforementioned "My father is Li Gang" episode, legal scholar Zhou Dawei expresses his discomfort with the virtual public lynching of the Li family, comparing it with the reactions that greeted the Gang of Four Trial. He cites a dialogue between a middle-aged man and his mother-in-law in an episode of the CCTV Spring Festival special program *Year after Year* (*Yinian you yinian*, since 2002):

> MAN: "Mother, let's tune in to the news this evening. The Gang of Four is on trial."
> WOMAN: "Why bother with a trial? Have them shot and be done with it!"
> MAN: "That ain't good enough for them. They should be shot but not fatally. Revive them and shoot them again, and revive and shoot again."
> (Zhou Dawei 2013, 150)

For Zhou, public sentiments can be shockingly lopsided and bloodthirsty and must be set aside if the country wishes to embark on the path of rational governance. He praises the post-Mao leadership for setting up the Special Court to try their erstwhile persecutors and tormentors instead of seeking the immediate gratification of revenge (150–51). Unfortunately, for voicing a dissenting opinion on the Li Gang affair, Zhou became the target of cyber flaming.

When judicial populism rules the day, both the Party and the populace find ways to sideline the law in a dance of petitioning, propagandizing, and "listening to the people's feelings." In Belkin's view, rather than empowering ordinary citizens, judicial populism creates the space for a new business model for enterprising individuals to manipulate public opinion for good or for ill, or simply for profit (2017, 211). But above all it serves high justice by creating opportunities for the Party to dispense substantive justice directly at the expense of strengthening proceduralism (see the introduction). In this state of affairs, postsocialist transitional justice veers even further from the democratic transition model with which most scholars associate the term. In this chapter, I have applied the concept of transitional justice to two unlikely historical junctures: the post-1949 transition to revolutionary justice with its obsession with collective guilt, and the post-Mao transition to bureaucratic justice with its focus on individual responsibility. In both, political trials, broadly defined, were the primary medium of transition, though only the former juncture sat astride a regime change, while only the latter was accompanied by liberalization and institutionalization, but without genuine "truth and reconciliation" capable of mastering the traumas of the Cultural Revolution.

4
Exceptional Justice

In the first half of the twentieth century, the Chinese mainland saw almost continuous warfare. The most devastating were the second Sino-Japanese war of 1937–45 and the civil war of 1945–49. Then soon after the People's Liberation Army (PLA) routed the Nationalist troops and drove the ruling Nationalist regime to Taiwan, the Korean War broke out, and the newly founded People's Republic sent the People's Volunteer Army to the Korean Peninsula to "Resist America and Aid Korea" (*KangMei yuanChao*). While the dust was settling after each conflict, the victorious side invariably had to deal with remnants of the defeated now in its custody: first Japanese POWs and Chinese traitors (*hanjian*) in Nationalist custody; then three groups of captives in CCP custody: Nationalist, Japanese, and Manchukuo collaborators; finally United Nations (mostly American) POWs in CCP custody.[1] The two historic trials of World War II war criminals, in Nuremberg and Tokyo, set precedents and provided a framework of international law for postconflict justice. But with the rapidly evolving postwar geopolitical realignment, the Chinese found themselves in vastly different circumstances when they turned their attention to the many different categories of detainees. As I hope to show in this chapter, the CCP put into practice a very different model of transitional justice that bore more resemblance to the late twentieth-century "truth and reconciliation" processes than to the postwar military tribunals. And this model was almost exclusively reserved for battlefield enemies.

In a nutshell, instead of following legal precedents and systematically putting the different groups of "war criminals" on trial, the CCP resorted to ambitious and expensive programs of thought reform, an experiment that seems to have resulted in at least two success stories according to official accounts. I reexamine the two stories through the lens of a Chinese regime of exceptional justice. In addition to surveying reportage literature and autobiographical and historical accounts to draw a rough picture of the experiment, I home in on two visual narratives that restage the miracle of collective rebirth on the part of a dozen or so prominent Nationalist detainees.

Although the stories of CCP's reformation of POWs were never kept secret, they were not widely known until the 1980s, when a trickle of reportage and memoirs began to emerge in a relatively liberal political climate. These accounts focused almost exclusively on a small cohort of elite Nationalist captives held in the Gongdelin War Criminals Detention Center (Gongdelin zhanfan guanlisuo) in Beijing. The story of the several hundred Japanese war criminals held in the Fushun War Criminals Detention Center (Fushun zhanfan guanlisuo) would not be told until the mid-2000s. At the other extreme is the absence of popular accounts of the Biokdong POW camp, which housed nearly four thousand UN prisoners. This is in stark contrast to the place it occupied in the American imagination during the Cold War. The twenty-one American POWs who refused repatriation directly gave rise to a crisis of cultural confidence and a national preoccupation with "brainwashing."

The purpose of this chapter is not to sort out the historical facts associated with the postwar management of POWs. Instead, it reads popular historical sources and visual representations in an effort to weave together a conceptual account of "exceptional justice," which I define as justice pursued in defense of legal sovereignty but operating outside the confines of positive law, in the domains of morality, diplomacy, and Cold War geopolitics. This chapter is thus a sequel to chapter 3 on transitional justice. Both are concerned with the practice of justice in the interstices of law, morality, and ideology. The previous chapter is primarily concerned with the use of political (show) trials to prosecute, condemn, and eliminate internal ideological enemies of the PRC state, old and new. The current chapter turns its attention to the regime's handling of former military foes who have become dependent wards or "supplicants" (jiexia qiu) of the state. If the previous chapter discloses the merciless, retributive face of transitional justice, then this chapter reckons with its more merciful and pragmatic manifestations, its readiness to forgive, rehabilitate, and co-opt. The point is to understand the moral, legal, ideological, and diplomatic work of exceptional justice both in the volatile milieu of the Cold War and in the current, also highly uncertain geopolitical moment. To underscore the transnational entanglement of exceptional justice, I append a brief translingual history of "brainwashing" that brings to the surface the tissues connecting American legal Orientalist fantasies and Red Menace scares with Chinese utopian drives to reengineer hearts and minds and to win a hostile world to its side.

Devils to Men

The Cold War inaugurated a new geopolitical order that divided the world into two ideological blocs: communist and capitalist, totalitarian and democratic, oppressive and free. It also revived an older colonial discourse of Oriental despotism. Totalitarianism did not just refer to an alien political system but was also an epithet that conjured up the lawlessness of the Oriental other and forever branded the latter as the antithesis of the rule of law. The overheated rhetoric coming out of the Communist bloc occasionally fanned the flame of what Teemu Ruskola calls "legal Orientalism" (2013). As we have seen in earlier chapters, Mao's China did not set much in store by law and legal justice, an attitude that reached a crescendo in the 1967 *People's Daily* editorial "In Praise of Lawlessness" (Wufa wutian zan).[2] Despite its repudiation of fascism, the CCP converged with Carl Schmitt in their shared goal of reversing the exclusion of politics from law and the liberal fireproofing of moral passions with cold, hard rules. Advancing a critique of the liberal state of law from a right-wing standpoint, Schmitt (2005) impugns the liberal disavowal of the sovereign exception. For him, because the rule of law admits only the distinction between the legal and the criminal, it is wholly inadequate to coping with the existential conflict between "us" and "them," between friends and enemies. When Schmitt defines the sovereign as he who decides on the exception, he underscores and celebrates the arbitrary, contingent, and essentially theological foundation of law.

Coming from the left, Hannah Arendt considers the irony of the French Revolution's proclamation of natural rights alongside the assertion of national sovereignty. She writes: "the same nation was at once declared to be subject to laws, which supposedly would flow from the Rights of Man, *and* sovereign, that is, bound by no universal law and acknowledging nothing superior to itself" (1968, 230). The idea of universal human rights, in her view, is dubiously grounded in the human species being (as innate or God-given), when rights can be guaranteed only ever by virtue of membership in a political community. By implication, rights can also be revoked by sovereign decision—a fate that often befalls vulnerable groups. Examples of such groups being cast into what Giorgio Agamben (2005) has called the state of the exception are legion, from enslaved Blacks in the antebellum American South to Jews in World War II Europe and Japanese Americans in internment camps. "National sovereignty, accordingly, lost its original connotation of freedom of the people and was being surrounded by a pseudomystical aura of lawless arbitrariness" (Arendt 1968, 231). It is what the *People's Daily* editorial celebrates. It is also the point of Schmitt's project of political theology: to reenchant secular liberal politics dedicated to low justice by reasserting the transcendental status of the sovereign exception, or exceptional justice.

Intent on carrying out a revolutionary agenda premised on class struggle, the CCP saw no reason to hamstring itself with a legal system that simply could not deliver the kind of redistributive justice possible only through massive mobilization and social engineering. The achievements of the socialist era demonstrated the tremendous potential of exceptional justice, but they also came at tremendous human costs at the low justice level. As Klaus Mühlhahn observes, "the socialist Chinese state operated as a 'state of exception' that vigilantly produced exceptions to its principles and its laws" (2009, 282). POWs, as the vanquished enemies of the state, ironically fared better as tokens of exceptional justice than did internal enemies of the state, whose low justice claims were ruthlessly trampled on. Mao's China pursued exceptional justice that simultaneously was cognizant of international law and politics *and* cleaved to its own moral and ideological vision of restorative and rehabilitative justice. The legal language of rights and redress was largely subordinated to the moral and ideological language of confession, remorse, penance, reform, and rebirth (*chanhui, huiguo zixin, gaizao, gai'e congshan, tuotai huangu, chongxin zuoren,* etc.).

To make sense of the CCP approach to the question of guilt and responsibility with regard to its former adversaries, we need to place it in the immediate context of prior Nationalist and Allied trials of Japanese war criminals of the 1940s and the emerging Cold War ideological polarization of the 1950s. Even before Japan officially surrendered in August 1945, the Nationalist government in exile already began to organize investigations and compile evidence of Japanese war crimes. The International Military Tribunal of the Far East (a.k.a. the Tokyo Trial), spearheaded by the United States, prosecuted some twenty Japanese military and civilian leaders for "crimes against peace," or for violating *jus ad bellum*, that is, for instigating, planning, and implementing aggressive war. Of these infamous A class war criminals, eight were sentenced to death and seven executed. Held at the Sugamo Detention Center, run by the American occupation authority, were also B and C class war criminals convicted of "conventional war crimes," or offenses against *jus in bello*, at trials held in various locations that made up the now defunct Japanese Empire, including China.[3] These other trials have received far less media and scholarly attention owing to the US-centric lens of most postwar historical narratives.

In trials conducted by the Nationalist government, conventional war crimes—mass murder, rape, pillage, and abuse of POWs—were at the fulcrum of postwar restorative justice. The breakdown of negotiation over power sharing and the outbreak of a full-scale civil war between the Nationalists and the Communists, however, injected complications into these trials. Very quickly it became clear to the Nationalists that the Japanese officers in their custody were an asset they could exploit in their struggle with the CCP, hence their leniency toward the nearly nine hundred defendants. One hundred and forty-nine were sentenced to death and executed while the rest were given termed sentences or acquitted. The convicted prisoners were swiftly transferred to the Sugamo Detention Center to serve out their sentences, but they would all be released by 1952, when Japan and Taiwan signed a peace treaty. Most notoriously, the Nationalist government tried Okamura Yasuji, the commander in chief of the China Expeditionary Army, in 1946 and pronounced him "not guilty." In the meantime Okamura had been advising Chiang Kai-shek in his military showdown with the Communists. The instrumental nature of the verdict was all too apparent, provoking vociferous protests from the CCP leadership (Kushner 2015, 178, 256).

In its press communications, the CCP vowed harsh reprisals against Japanese war criminals. Yet its actual policy toward Japanese POWs in its custody followed a path not altogether different from its predecessor, except it did not carry out a single execution. In Barak Kushner's view, the policy toward the Japanese "stood out almost as an aberration of benevolence in the chilly atmosphere of an ensuing Cold War" (2015, 10), a point confirmed by Ian Buruma (2013), who notes that postwar nations from the Netherlands to China all meted out much harsher punishments to traitors than to their former enemies.[4] In July 1950, the Soviet Union transferred about a thousand POWs it had captured during its occupation of Manchuria that concluded World War II in the Far East. Among these was Aisin Gioro Puyi, the last emperor of the Qing dynasty, whose train journey back to China is vividly captured in the atmospheric opening sequences of Bernardo Bertolucci's film *The Last Emperor* (1987). At the Fushun War Criminals Detention Center, a prison facility originally built by the Japanese in the Manchukuo era, the newly arrived POWs joined a small contingent of Japanese soldiers who fought on after Japan's surrender and were captured by the PLA during the civil war, sixty-one former Manchukuo officials, and about three hundred Nationalist officers. Together they underwent fourteen years of reeducation. There were also a smaller number of Japanese POWs held in detention centers in Taiyuan and Xiling. In 1956, forty-five Japanese POWs stood trial as war criminals and were given relatively short sentences while the rest were spared of indictment. By 1964, all of them (minus those who had died of illness) had been repatriated to Japan (Xu Guiying and Ji Min 2000).

Historians have sought explanations for this extraordinary gesture of magnanimity in the broader international circumstances that shaped China's foreign policy agenda. In particular, they emphasize China's desire for rapprochement with Japan for both economic and political reasons. Economically, it urgently needed to establish trade relations with Japan; politically, it feared a remilitarized Japan rising under the wing of the United States. China's political fears were not unfounded: the United States' narrow-focused prosecution of Japanese war crimes—the inadequate attention to the Nanjing Massacre and the omission of the atrocities of Unit 731—was largely driven by its Cold War strategy of turning Japan into a "bulwark against communism" (Kushner 2015, 251). Having Japan as an ally would greatly bolster China's ability to challenge the hegemony of American imperialism. This was clearly laid out in a speech by Zhou Enlai in 1956: "The trials stood for the future. We want to finish with this unfortunate experience and reopen a whole new path of friendship in Sino-Japan relations" (quoted in Kushner 2015, 297). Zhou was confident that the POWs, once fully reformed, would become China's best advocates.

Zhou's calculations panned out at the individual level but failed on the foreign policy front. Normalization of bilateral relations would not happen until 1972. All the while, Japan moved inexorably into the US orbit beginning with the signing of the 1951 Peace Treaty of San Francisco without PRC participation, and culminating in the US-Japan Security Treaty of 1960. But individually, the prisoners apparently did undergo a wrenching spiritual and moral awakening. They spent their days reading, recalling, discussing, and writing about their experiences in China, having been assured that they would not be subject to capital punishment and growing confident that they would not have to endure deprivation or torture. Their diet standard was set above the average Chinese citizen, and their living quarters were clean and sanitary. Moreover, there was no forced labor—something that would become ubiquitous in China's vast carceral system known as laogai (reform through labor) and laojiao (education through labor). Kushner remarks: "It is important to consider how differently the Communists treated the Japanese prisoners, generally speaking, compared with their own internal system of gulags where domestic political prisoners and 'counterrevolutionaries'—not to mention KMT soldiers taken into custody during the civil war—were housed and forced into labor" (2015, 268). Most of the sources attribute the preferential treatment to Zhou Enlai's decisive intervention and fastidious supervision.

Much of what we know about what transpired at the Fushun Detention Center comes from the 1998 memoir of its longtime governor Jin Yuan. An ethnic Korean and veteran CCP member who grew up in Manchuria

and was intimately familiar with the region's history and politics, he steadfastly implemented the Party's program of reform and reeducation. At a
personal level, he is said to have treated the inmates with respect and humaneness, winning much gratitude and affection from them. After China
reopened its gates, Jin was invited to visit Japan twice (1976, 1984) by the
returnees, who soon upon their repatriation organized the Liaison Group
of Returnees from China (Chūgoku kikansha renrakukai, or Chūkiren,
for short) and dedicated themselves to the promotion of Sino-Japanese
friendship and the exposé of Japanese war crimes in China. In 1988, the
group dedicated the "Memorial Stele of Apology" (*xiezui bei*) near the
original Fushun facility (Xu Guiying and Ji Min 2000, 649). While still in
Fushun, the detainees had already begun the work of documenting war
crimes as both perpetrators and witnesses in a variety of genres, from vi-
gnettes to one-act plays that they put onstage themselves. At the 1956 trials,
some of them broke into sobs, knelt down to apologize, or begged for the
death sentence. The trials were reported in PRC media in broad strokes
and with little context, with cautious projection of the events extending
China's political influence over Japan (Kushner 2015, 296).

Perhaps fortunately, as Adam Cathcart and Patricia Nash point out,
the entire episode was largely drowned out by contemporary political developments, particular the Hundred Flowers campaign launched in the
same month (2009, 100). With or without this coincidence, the public
was unlikely to appreciate the political capital these detainees held for the
Party in the diplomatic arena. Nor are the realpolitik calculations obvious to twenty-first-century audiences who have been made to relive the
pain and humiliation of war through endless anti-Japanese war epics. Of
the numerous commemorative works produced in the first decade of the
new millennium to mark the sixtieth and sixty-fifth anniversaries of the
defeat of Japan, very few deal with the subject of the CCP reformation
of Japanese war criminals. The two exceptions I know of are *An Oral and
Documentary History of Reforming War Criminals* (*Gaizao zhanfan jishi*)
by Xu Guiying and Ji Min (2000), which devotes a third of its pages to
reminiscences by those involved in the incarceration and reeducation of
Japanese captives (the other two parts focus on Nationalist prisoners and
former Manchukuo and Mongukuo officials); and *The Complete History of
China's Reformation of Japanese War Criminals* (2005), which was reissued,
in 2010 (Shu Gong and Zhang Jin 2010), in a two-volume expanded edition
under the title *The Final Battle for the Soul: The Complete History of China's
Reformation of Japanese War Criminals* (*Linghun juezhan: Zhongguo gaizao
Riben zhanfan shimo*).[5]

The two-volume compilation, coauthored by Shu Gong and Zhang Jin,

casts the project of reformation entirely in moral terms, scarcely registering the pragmatic considerations that drove the policy of clemency. Written in a florid, breathless style typical of Chinese reportage literature and
popular history, the book borrows and excerpts liberally from Jin Yuan's
memoirs as well as the confessions and autobiographies penned by the
detainees both during and after their stint in Fushun. It adds to the first
edition a great deal more primary documentary snippets pertaining to
Japan's imperialist project in China and its demise and aftermath. In the
preface to the second edition, the publisher provides the following statement of significance:

> Since the book's publication in 2005, the authors have spent five years pains-
> takingly adding about 100,000 words of new content to the expanded edition.
> This is what they present to the world, especially to young people born after
> WWII and under 65 years of age: China not only accomplished the timeless
> political feat of extraditing, detaining, investigating, prosecuting, and reeducat-
> ing warmongers, but also accumulated the timeless spiritual wealth of a whole
> generation loyal to the Communist Party and to the Fatherland. [This is a record
> of] how the young republic overcame great difficulties in order to realize truth,
> justice, humanitarianism, and peace, turning foes into friends, as well as how the
> Japanese war criminals themselves converted to pacifism and fought for peace.
> (Shu Gong and Zhang Jin 2010, 1:1)

The second half of volume 1 gives a detailed account of the intensive prepa-
rations for the 1956 trials in Shenyang and Taiyuan. A directive from Zhou
Enlai set the process in motion: "On the matter of Japanese war criminals,
no death sentence will be handed out, nor life in prison. Only a few will
be given prison terms at all. The indictment documents must clearly state
the crimes, which must be thoroughly investigated and verified. No need
to indict ordinary offenses" (2010, 1:281). Supposedly thousands of investigators fanned out across the country to collect evidence and identify
witnesses. In the meantime, the detention centers organized sessions on
"how to respond to the indictment" to prepare the prisoners to stand for
trial. They were asked to get ready to plead guilty, provide corroboration,
and properly accept government clemency. At a mobilization rally, one
prisoner stated, "Hundreds of thousands of good-natured Chinese victims
can never be brought back to life. We are sinners and deserve to be severely
punished by the Chinese people." Another followed, "China has treated
me more mercifully than my own family could and educated me with great
patience and kindness, returning me from devil to man. When I stand in

the Chinese people's court, I will unconditionally accept the judgment of truth and justice. I will ask the Chinese government to put me to death" (quoted in 2010, 1:286–87).

The cadre instructors then led a discussion under the heading "What proper attitude one should have in response to the China trial." The prisoners were to answer three questions: "What is the goal of the trial?"; "What is the relation between the defendant and the prosecutor?"; and "How should one behave in court?" The answers, of course, were not up for debate. The goal of the trial was to expose the evils of militarism and caution future generations not to repeat the historical tragedy; the defendant and the prosecution were collaborators working toward this common goal, not adversaries; the correct attitude toward the trial was to regard it as an opportunity to apologize to the Chinese people and to denounce militarism to the entire world, and in doing so repay the leniency and teaching of the Chinese government (287). The authors highlight the appearance in court of Puyi as the most high-profile witness. But ordinary Chinese also took to the witness box. A forty-four-year-old peasant man bared his torso to display bayonet wounds and recounted how six of his family of twelve were killed when Japanese troops swept through their village and took everything they owned. The defendant Suzuki Hiraku immediate fell to his knees and bawled: "It's all true! I sincerely apologize! Mercy!" (1:301). (This anecdote is repeated in many sources; see also Xu Guiying and Ji Min 2000, 199.)

The authors reiterate the miracle of the 100 percent confession rate, "an unprecedented feat in the history of international war crime prosecution" (1:301). In contrast, none of the A class war criminals at the Tokyo Trial pleaded guilty and instead did everything they could, including hiring high-powered lawyers, to evade legal sanction (1:294). The authors conclude the first volume by quoting from the outpourings of gratitude and encomia from the returnees about their fourteen years of captivity as a spiritual journey, such as "The detention center turned us devils back into men, militarists into pacifists. Such a tremendous accomplishment is unrivaled in the whole world!" (1:314). The story of their decades of peace activism is not told in this otherwise exhaustive account except briefly in an appendix. Most curiously, after recounting the tale of the POWs' miraculous rebirth in volume 1, the authors devote the bulk of volume 2 to retracing the history of Japanese imperialist adventures in China, beginning with the early incursions in Manchuria and ending with the dedication of the Memorial Stele of Apology. Such stock narratives of the sins of Japanese militarism are abundantly available in today's China across the media landscape, particularly on television. Even if it is for the sake of having both the historical traumas and their resolution between the same covers, why arrange them in this reverse chronological order?

One possible explanation is that it is a symptom of China not having genuinely worked through the trauma of the second Sino-Japanese war, an unmastered past taking on ever more monstrous dimensions. The more gritty aspects of the war experience, alongside some of the worst atrocities committed by the Japanese imperial army, have been revived in popular memory only since the 1990s, after decades of officially enforced oblivion, or what James Reilly calls the period of "China's benevolent amnesia" (quoted in Kushner 2015, 9; see also Mitter 2020). The amnesia was imposed by the state as it pursued rapprochement with Japan. Survivors of the war, including numerous "comfortable women" (military sex slaves), were not permitted to tell their own stories or seek redress outside the narrow confines of state-orchestrated political theater such as the 1956 trials. All their sufferings are supposed to have been vindicated by the CCP at the moment of "liberation"—when all Chinese are said to have thrown off the shackles of foreign domination and taken control of their own fates. Under such circumstances, Kushner suggests, it is difficult to see a Chinese Hannah Arendt emerge to "[raise] our consciousness about the banality of the Japanese wartime bureaucracy and military" (2015, 20) beyond boilerplate denunciations of militarism. An inward focus on wartime traumas has been the predominant way the Chinese remember the war, even after the state relaxed the scope of war experiences that may be remembered at the turn of the new millennium in order to rev up jingoistic nationalism.[6] This forgotten episode of judicial clemency, for example, is now recruited to burnish China's image as a rule-bound and responsible player on the world stage. As for the war itself, its root causes, its articulation with other social dynamics, and its variegated ramifications, the only tool at hand is still the standard Manichaean narrative of Japanese monstrosity and Chinese suffering.

Kushner quotes Yuan Guang, deputy chief judge of the Chinese People's Supreme Military Tribunal, who, when evaluating the CCP trials years later, said, "Justice expanded its reach enough to offer solace to the spirits of those who valiantly fought against the Japanese or were martyred" (2015, 297). Sleeping behind this statement is a belated acknowledgment that low justice may not have been first and foremost on the minds of the decision makers. But this wispy acknowledgment is barely audible next to the operatic ode to the political significance of the trials: "For the first time in modern Chinese history, representatives of the Chinese people in a court of law sat in judgment of imperialist aggressions against our sovereign territory. It bore great significance not only in Chinese, but in world history. It signified that the Chinese people have stood up" (Xu Guiying and Ji Min 2000, 194). Given how little attention the trials received in domestic media, it may be justified to say that they were meant primarily for an international audience, in a bid to win recognition and respect from an increasingly hostile world. After all, it was not until 1943 that the Western powers recognized Chinese legal sovereignty with the abolition of extraterritoriality. The authors of *The Final Battle for the Soul* repurposed the episode for a domestic audience albeit with a half century's time lag, but they broke no new analytical ground. Like Yuan Guang's remarks, the narrative supplement in volume 2 also registers a subtle recognition that low justice has once again been submerged under high justice.

Foes to Friends

In December 1948, the Xinhua News Agency issued a list of forty-three "civil war criminals." Leading the pack was Chiang Kai-shek, followed by a who's who of the Republic of China's ruling political, military, financial, and intelligence elites (among whom were also a few non–Nationalist Party members), "all of whom have committed atrocities and deserve to be executed in the opinion of our countrymen" (Ren Haisheng 1995, 7). Calling it a work in progress, the editorial urged all sectors of society to discuss the matter and nominate more names for an updated list. In January 1949, the agency issued an expanded roster with twenty-four additional names. In the same editorial, the CCP vowed to apprehend every single one of them and turn the whole lot over to the people's courts to be tried without mercy (*gui'an faban, jue bu kuanshu*). By the time the country was firmly under CCP rule, the regime had nearly one million former enemy troops in its custody. Contrary to its wartime rhetoric, the CCP adopted more nuanced approaches to the problem of what to do with these men. To begin with, they were classified according to the manner in which they fell into CCP hands: defection (*qiyi*), surrender (*toucheng*), or capture (*fulu*). Rank-and-file soldiers were mostly absorbed into the PLA, whereas officers and cadres were corralled into special camps for reeducation (D. Chang 2020, chap. 2).

By the early 1950s, some of those named in the expanded "civil war criminals" list, plus many more not on the list, had been rounded up and interned in detention centers across the country. The most prominent individuals found themselves transferred in two or three waves to Beijing's Gongdelin War Criminals Detention Center, located at the eponymous prison facility built during the warlord period. Here they would undergo a rigorous regime of thought reform akin to that implemented in Fushun and Taiyuan detention centers for Japanese war criminals. Then starting in 1959, on the tenth anniversary of the founding of the People's Republic, they were granted special pardons by the government in quick succession, though the last and largest group were released as late as 1975 owing to the disruption of the Cultural Revolution. Other than deaths from infirmity, illness, or persecutions (during the Cultural Revolution), most of these men lived to reclaim their freedom. They were all granted citizenship and assigned jobs (for those who could still work) and housing, unless they chose to leave China. Ten chose to go to Taiwan, but when they were in Hong Kong awaiting entry permit, they were told by the Nationalist regime that their admission was contingent on their willingness to denounce the CCP. They refused and were stuck in limbo; one committed suicide (Ren Haisheng 1995; 204–21; Xu Guiying and Ji Min 2000, 697–707).

As noted earlier, accounts about what these men went through began to emerge in the 1980s and have continued unabated into the new millennium. As a result, the story of the civil war POWs is far better known to the Chinese public than that of the Japanese POWs, though both have been relatively neglected by academic historians. Few of these accounts fail to cite a passage concerning counterrevolution in Mao's well-known 1956 politburo speech entitled "On Ten Relations" ("Lun shida guanxi"). In this speech, Mao affirmed the correctness of the 1951–52 campaigns to suppress counterrevolution in a rebuke of skeptics who likened these to Stalin's purges. Those who were executed, he averred, entirely deserved the fate as they were the most hated by the people and had the most blood on their hands. But execution need not be the only method of quelling the reactionaries; one could also resort to incarceration (*guan*), supervised release (*guan₂*), and outright release (*fang*). So who should be spared of the firing squad?

> Who are the ones we do not execute? We don't execute people like Hu Feng, Pan Hannian, and Rao Shushi, or people like Puyi and Kang Ze. This is not because they don't deserve the death sentence, but because there's no advantage to be had in killing them. If we killed these people, it would be difficult to know where to stop, and many more heads would roll. This is the first reason. The second reason is the possibility of wrongful execution. Once a head is chopped off, history has proven that it cannot be reattached to the body, unlike garlic chives, which reliably grow back. With a human head, a wrong cut cannot be undone. Thirdly, it's about the destruction of evidence. When suppressing counterrevolution, we can use one reactionary as a material witness against an-

other. In litigation, he can be called on to testify. If you have killed him, you've destroyed the evidence. This can help only the counterrevolution, not the revolution. Lastly, killing these people does nothing to boost productivity, advance science, eradicate the four pests, strengthen national defense, or recover Taiwan. If you executed them, you would get a bad rap for killing POWs. [. . .] If they can be reformed through labor, put them to work; those who are not amenable, we'll keep them alive nonetheless. Reactionaries are like refuse and pests, but once in our grip, they can be made to do a few useful things for the people. [. . .]

However, do we need to pass a law stipulating that reactionaries found within our ranks will not be executed? This is our internal policy, so no need to broadcast it, as long as we do our best to stick to it.[7]

There is perhaps no better articulation of the idea of exceptional justice than the second paragraph quoted here, in which Mao counsels keeping the tools of justice pliable by avoiding the legal and institutional route. This speech very much defined the informal approach the Party adopted toward their erstwhile civil war enemy. Unlike the Japanese war criminals, none of the Nationalist generals and high-ranking personnel were put on trial before they were pardoned and released. The lack of a legal basis to try these individuals was both a fact and a choice, a choice based on an intuitive understanding that the civil war presented a different case from the one presented by the war of resistance against the Japanese. In a fratricidal conflict, war crime can be a slippery proposition.

Judith Shklar makes the following observation in her effort to show that conventional war crimes are in fact far more difficult to prosecute than crimes against humanity despite the latter's novelty and lack of legal precedents, because war as such has never been regarded as inherently criminal: "War has for most of history been regarded as a normal part of social life. It is not regarded as an ignoble activity. Even those who object to aggressive wars admire the qualities of the soldiers engaged in them, if not the ends to which their valor is put. Given the impossibility of distinguishing between aggressive and defensive wars there only remains war, hallowed by tradition, for ages regarded as a natural part of social life. A mere legal pronouncement that some wars are criminal is not likely to alter the general view that war, as such, is not a crime, or the belief that any war in which one's nation-state is involved must be supported" (Shklar 1986, 191). Charges of war crimes can very quickly get bogged down in *tu quoque* ("you also") arguments (Shklar 1986, 161). No side emerges from a war with clean hands. The moral equivalency that subtends war also extends to individual combatants. In war, what matters is objective membership in the opposing camps, not ill will borne by one individual against another. A hilarious dialogue in Joseph Heller's satirical antiwar novel *Catch-22* captures this irrelevance of intention:

> "They're trying to kill me," Yossarian told him calmly.
> "No one's trying to kill you," Clevinger cried.
> "Then why are they shooting at me?" Yossarian asked.
> "They're shooting at *everyone*," Clevinger answered. "They're trying to kill everyone."
> "And what difference does that make?" (Heller 1955, 17)

The absurdity of this dialogue derives chiefly from Yossarian's mistaking a confrontation between hostile forces in a combat situation as a moral encounter between intentional individuals (Walzer 2015, 36). In combat soldiers are little more than functional parts programmed to achieve the goal of winning a war (Taylor 2017). In a war zone what obtains is the most brutal form of strict liability: One lives and dies simply by virtue of the uniform one wears and the trenches in which one moves—the most superficial registers of who one is. The belligerents must presume that their counterparts are determined to kill them, whatever their private reasons for joining the fight. Putting combatants on trial for war crimes is thus inherently problematic because it seeks to affix personal responsibility and guilt in situations that are designed to diffuse and suspend mens rea. The CCP understood this well, absorbing most Nationalist troops into its own ranks without much ado. The question of guilt, therefore, settled on the choices made by civilian and military leaders.

Had the CCP captured Chiang Kai-shek and his inner circle, it would still have hesitated to put them on trial for crimes against peace, or hold them to account for the breakdown of the peace negotiation and for the lives lost and livelihoods destroyed, or charge them with conventional war crimes such as the torture and summary executions of imprisoned CCP members. War guilt, as Walzer notes, is quintessentially a matter of moral blameworthiness. The Nuremberg and Tokyo Trials were both defensible and necessary only because "the law must provide some recourse when our deepest moral values are savagely attacked. But such trials by no means exhaust the field of judgment" (2015, 288). That law is the last resort is the crux of the CCP's decision to try the Japanese POWs but not the Nationalists *and* to subject both to prolonged thought reform.

Only one individual from the original group of forty-three "civil war criminals" fell into the Communists' hands: Du Yuming, a lieutenant general who commanded and lost the decisive battles in eastern China. He and a few dozen high-ranking officers all ended up in Gongdelin. In most accounts, these men are said to have rejected the "war criminal" label and been slow to bow to their captors. For example, Shen Zui, spymaster and protégé of the Nationalist chief of intelligence Dai Li, confesses in his memoirs that at first he was loath to accept the guilt of killing Communists, though he freely admitted to having arrested, kidnapped, and assassinated scores of them during his stint as the southwest chief of the Nationalist internal security bureau. He believed it justified for a regime to suppress insurgency and that had the Nationalists won the civil war, he would have been decorated for his service. He was of course voicing the basic critique of victor's justice, which he says he learned to repudiate later through reeducation (Shen Zui 1990, 304). The adage that constantly hung on the inmates' lips, "Victors are crowned kings; losers become bandits" (*chengze wei wang, baize wei kou*), served to voice their sense that losing a war was a matter of strategic failure, not a moral one, and that holding them responsible for the war went against the tradition of honoring those who remained loyal to their leaders and fought valiantly to the last man.

It was in view of this general sentiment that the CCP needed to figure out what to do with the individuals that it insistently labeled "war criminals." With a few exceptions, these men were neither monsters nor cowards who could be charged with conventional war crimes or treason (*hanjian zui*). Indeed, some of them were known for their valor and heroism in fighting the Japanese imperial army. What then was the exact nature of their guilt? In the end, the CCP settled on "counterrevolution," a political label. Instead of pursuing their legal guilt, the Party decided to go after something far deeper: the ideological error that drove them to board the sinking ship of Chiang Kai-shek. It was not their personal fault that the ship sank and brought countless lives down with it, but the moral-political bankruptcy of the Nationalist Party, which chose to defend the interests of the ruling class and ally with the imperialists, turning its back against the Chinese people. For such a gigantic political-historical mistake, no court of law could render any meaningful judgment. Guilt calls for punishment, but mistake requires correction. This distinction would decades later underscore the Party's verdict on itself regarding the Cultural Revolution, as we have seen in chapter 3. It also framed the all-out program of thought reform that was carried out in Gongdelin and elsewhere throughout the 1950s and beyond. These proud if dejected men must be made to realize that their defeat was not a matter of poor strategy or bad luck, but one of aiding and abetting evil and sinning against righteousness. Their flesh would be spared of pain, but they had to submit their souls to a process akin to religious conversion.

The earliest documentary account of what these men went through was

FIGURE 4.1: POWs receiving regulation garb; POWs chasing after a pig. From *After the Final Battle* (Li Qiankuan and Xiao Guiyun 1991, Western Movie Group Co. Ltd., 1991).

The Battlefield Is Not the Only Arena to Test the Mettle of Generals (*Jiangjun juezhan qi zai zhanchang shang*) by Huang Jiren (1982). It was made into a film called *After the Final Battle* (*Juezhan zhihou*) in 1991 (figure 4.1). Throughout the 1980s and 1990s, similar books appeared on the mainland intermittently, attesting to sustained audience interests. (In Taiwan, in contrast, the one title I have found on this topic strikes a completely different note—I will return to this later.) Most noteworthy is the Historical Series on the People's Republic's Reformation of War Criminals (Gongheguo gaizao zhanfan jishi congshu) put out by the publishing wing of the PLA. The series include the memoirs of Jin Yuan, an account of Puyi's life before and after his release, and a compilation of the lives and activism of Chūkiren members. Bringing this steady trickle to a climax is the 2019 thirty-nine-part television serial *Special Pardons 1959* (*Teshe 1959*), a tribute to the seventieth anniversary of the founding of the People's Republic (Dong Yachun 2019).

Directed by the husband-and-wife team Li Qiankuan and Xiao Guiyun (1991), *After the Final Battle* adopts an austere documentary style in place of the intimate, third-person point of view (tied mostly to Qiu Xingxiang) preferred by Huang Jiren. The historical figures are identified by their real names, and the events depicted are by and large truthful—with the notable exception of the episode concerning the death and funeral of the former Nationalist spymaster Xu Yuanju (who actually died in 1973, but in the film his death occurs nearly two decades early). Remarkably, this is a rare film set in the 1950s in which Communist Party members do not occupy the center stage. The chief warden is not even given a full name. Known only as Director Li, he maintains a compassionate but reserved demeanor toward the prisoners. The rest of the prison staff are not individualized and remain detached and mostly offscreen. Screen time is instead shared by an ensemble cast, with Du Yuming leading the contingent of "progressive" inmates and Huang Wei standing in for the recalcitrant type. Du is given several flashbacks to flesh out his character as a patriotic general during the anti-Japanese war and a misguided and mistreated follower of Chiang Kai-shek during the civil war. When the prisoners duly turn in their confessional autobiographies (*fanxing zizhuan*), Du Yuming is kindly reminded by Director Li that he has left out the heroic battle of Kunlunguan, in which Du's troops beat back the Japanese. Du is profoundly moved. On another occasion, the prisoners excitedly chew over a speech given by Mao in which he extolled the two united fronts between the Communists and the Nationalists and spoke of the two sides "fighting shoulder to shoulder." Clearly, the film is registering its own moment in history when the mainland was actively seeking to co-opt the Nationalist Party in post–martial law Taiwan against a common foe—the pro-independence Democratic Progressive Party.[8] For the first time, it was permissible to acknowledge the Nationalist contribution to the war of resistance (Mitter 2020, 167–68).

At the time of the film's release, it probably struck the audiences as daring to depict Nationalist officers in a sympathetic light. Jettisoning their cartoonish image in socialist-era cinema, the film uses pathos and humor to humanize these erstwhile movers and shakers as they come to terms with their status as "groveling prisoners." The prisoners take active control of their transformation by, in one instance, interpellating one of their own as belonging to the "people." When Xu Yuanju dies, the prisoners petition for a proper funeral by quoting from Mao's "Serve the People" essay: "From now on, when anyone in our ranks who has done some useful work dies, be he soldier or cook, we should have a funeral ceremony and a memorial meeting in his honor. This should become the rule. And it should be introduced among the people as well."[9] At the funeral, a carefully crafted and approved eulogy is read aloud and wins a warm applause. The boldness of this scene cannot be lost on Chinese audiences reared on the so-called Red Classics. Xu is immortalized in the novel *Red Crag* (*Hongyan*, 1961) as Xu Pengfei, the spy chief who orchestrated the sweep-up of the CCP underground in Chongqing, and who imprisoned, tortured, or executed over 130 of them in the infamous Baigongguan Prison. Among these was Jiang Zhujun or Jiangjie (Sister Jiang), arguably the most storied female martyr in CCP hagiography (Luo Guangbin and Yang Yiyan 1961). Indeed a torture scene with Jiangjie in it briefly flashes across the screen. Still, Xu gets a memorial service and a eulogy in which his interrupted progress toward becoming a socialist new man is the biggest regret of his life. In real life, Xu was passed over in several rounds of pardons and died in the Qingcheng Prison in 1973.

Judging from online audience comments, one would have to credit the use of low-key humor in rendering the inmates sympathetic and the film memorable. Two episodes stand out: In one, the crew in charge of kitchen duty find themselves giving desperate chase to a squealing pig running for dear life in the courtyard. Observing the posse wielding butcher's knives, sticks, and sackcloth and trying to coordinate their chase, an inmate on the sideline makes a snide comment that at long last the Nationalists are fighting for a common purpose (see again figure 4.1). In the second comedic episode, dubbed by viewers as the "Battle of Little Coal Mountain" (Xiao meishan zhi zhan), several inmates shoveling coal on camp ground are surprised to espy three Japanese prisoners playing tennis nearby and provoke a brawl with them. More inmates soon join the melee, tumbling up and down a mound of coal. The camera then cuts to Du Yuming being informed by two inmates about the skirmish. He assumes a solemn air and asks in formal diction: "How did our side fare?" (Wojun zhanji ruhe?), then relaxes into a broad grin when told that "our side" has achieved a decisive victory.

In most scenes, the prison staff are absent, and the inmates seem to have the run of the place. Director Li does preside over a couple of study sessions in which the men criticize themselves and denounce one another in a fashion familiar to all who have lived through the Maoist era—see chapter 3. The brevity of these scenes is not surprising: too many Chinese have participated in such rituals to take them too seriously. They are accustomed to claims of successful reform while knowing very well the pro forma nature of the process. At the denouement of the film, the first cohort of thirty-three men are called to the auditorium stage one by one to receive their writ of pardon. Du Yuming is the first on the list. He and a few others are then summoned before Zhou Enlai for an audience and photo ops. They are assigned jobs as editors-cum-archivists (wenshi zhuanyuan) at research centers attached to the People's Political Consultative Conference or Zhengxie for short. By now, Du's profile has grown considerably following the award of a Nobel Prize in Physics to his son-in-law Yang Chen-ning in 1957. The film shows him attending state functions hosted by Zhou Enlai, who refers to him jovially as General Du. His value to the state clearly went beyond whatever service he was able to render at the research center. For this he received special protection from Zhou during the Cultural Revolution.

In most accounts, Du Yuming's remarkable metamorphosis from Nationalist general to war criminal to citizen and Zhengxie representative is always the marquee story. Yet one could argue that as the poster boy of the CCP's model of exceptional justice, his success story occludes the many more who were deemed not exceptional enough to merit justice. These include the Nationalist "bandits" executed during the Quelling Counterrevolution (Zhenya fangeming, or Zhenfan) campaigns of 1951–52 and the prisoners who languished in detention centers until the final pardons of 1975. It is said that when Mao heard that there were still Nationalist officers in captivity, he was taken aback and said: "Let them all go. They've put down weapons for 25 years!" (Ren Haisheng 1999, 4–5). In the last analysis, the fates of these men depended little on what they actually did or didn't do, but overwhelmingly on their value to the state.[10] No one articulates this utilitarian philosophy more forcefully, even lyrically, than Mao. In focusing on the story of the rebirth of Du Yuming and others, the film subsumes realpolitik considerations to the grand project of rebuilding the socialist fatherland, to which the detainees, being true patriots at heart, gladly sign on. Converting to communism may be a tall order, but revitalizing China is a matter of honor and duty.

This is the theme most heavily hit on in the 2019 teledrama about the same group of men, *Special Pardons 1959*. After a hiatus of thirty years, nationalism is still the only thing that can do the heavy lifting of reconciling sworn enemies. Accordingly, the serial repackages shopworn Maoist-style thought reform, which is already short-changed in *After the Final Battle*, as a Chinese-style truth and reconciliation process driven by patriotically inspired humanitarianism. *Rendao zhuyi* (humanitarianism), resting on "three guarantees" (of dignity, health care, and decent living standards), becomes the keyword and leitmotif of the show. The story is then no longer predominantly that of the prisoners, as in *After the Final Battle*, but is evenly split between jailors and jailed. For this purpose, the show invents a charismatic chief warden named Wang Yingguang and endows him with a biography studded with educational, military, political, and romantic credentials.[11] According to commentators, Wang's character is a composite of at least two prototypes: Jin Yuan, director of the Fushun Detention Center, and Wang Yanggong, who ran the Biokdong Camp for UN POWs during the Korean War. The latter evidently did not leave any writings behind, but there is much to draw on from Jin Yuan's memoirs (which postdate *After the Final Battle*) as well as an anecdotes-rich eyewitness account of daily life in Gongdelin by Shen Zui. Historical fidelity, however, is not the show's priority. This is also evident in the decision to insert four fictional prisoners loosely modeled on real personages. These invented characters permit greater space to embellish or flesh out history and greatly enhance the emotional appeal of the show.

Young, handsome, energetic, and witty, Wang Yingguang is occasionally given to melancholy (over memories of his martyred wife) and excruciating bouts of headache (caused by shrapnel in his head). In other words, he is everything that the staid Director Li is not. We learn that he comes from a cultured background with a good education, and that he is a veteran Communist fighter specializing in inciting uprising in the enemy camp (*cefan*). His widower status takes him off the marriage market until very close to the end, in a way similar to the situation of Yu Zecheng (who loses his girlfriend early on) in *Undercover* and An Zaitian (who loses his wife early on) in *In the Dark* (chapter 1). Though impervious to the flirtatious attentions of a vivacious nurse and ingenue working by his side, he nonetheless comes off as exquisitely vulnerable and endearing. He is also given a family in Beijing, which he occasionally visits, and these visits give us a chance to witness the happiness in which the hutong residents now bathe in the New Society. The other prison staff are cast in types: The commissar is a wiser, calmer older man whose role is usually to give the Party's stamp of approval to Wang's decisions (and to catch him during his one and only lapse) and in general to personify the Party. The deputy director is a straight shooter who himself needs a lot of "thought work" to come around to the idea of treating the prisoners as potential comrades.

Among the prisoners three groups soon coalesce: the "progressives" (*jiji fenzi*) with Wang Yaowu and Du Yuming at the core; the "vacillators" (*dongyao pai*), including Kang Ze and Shen Zui; and the "intransigents" (*wangu fenzi*) with Huang Wei as the star attraction. Before long, a few vacillators successfully advance to the progressive circle. But the intransigents have to remain more or less incorrigible to fulfill their role as the show's villains. In real life, all the *jiji fenzi* (excluding the fictional Chen Ruizhang) were among the first to be pardoned; Huang Wei was among the last three hundred or so to be pardoned twenty-five years later.

Two overarching questions frame the entire narrative of *Special Pardons 1959*: Given the vast disparity in weaponry and other resources, why did the CCP win the civil war, and why did the Nationalists lose? In the first half of the show, the prisoners press Wang Yingguang for an answer to the first part of the question and are told to wait patiently for it; in the second half, they shift their attention to themselves but still have a hard time pinpointing the decisive factor (figure 4.2). Scientific Marxism of course holds the key to all historical puzzles, but the idea is for these men to meet the Party halfway, as old-style indoctrination is at the outset deemed ineffective on

FIGURE 4.2: A political study session; a heated debate in the library. From *Special Pardons 1959* (Dong Yachun 2019, Xingfu Lanhai and others).

these proud, well-educated, and battle-hardened men. The answer, gradually revealed, is none too profound: those who win the hearts and minds of the people win all under heaven (*De minxin zhe de tianxia*). It is a truism rooted in Confucianism and would have struck any educated Chinese as self-evident. But the challenge for the POWs is to figure out how the CCP managed to win hearts and minds, and this they would learn firsthand in Gongdelin. What could have been a punishing regime of disciplining and indoctrination is thus tempered by a political courtship. The official policy of three "no's"—"no trials, no sentences, no executions" (*bushen bupan yige busha*), attributed to Mao—is supplemented by another three "no's": "no beating, no scolding, no insults" (*buda buma buwuru*). The Party may be courting the prisoners, but it is the latter that have to learn to serenade. The Party relishes hearing fulsome praise of itself from its former nemeses and loses no opportunity to encourage it. The vicarious self-apotheosis harps on a few supreme virtues: true faith, unswerving constancy, superhuman courage, wholehearted dedication, indomitable will, unbreakable solidarity, iron discipline, adherence to truth, evenhandedness, indifference to worldly perks, willingness to eat bitterness, compassion for the weak, forbearance with the misguided, magnanimity for the repentant, and so forth. Does anyone have a chance against such a Party and its army? The Party has always asserted, quoting Stalin, that the Communists are made of "special stuff" (*teshu cailiao*, or *partinost* in Russian) (Sorace 2017, 42), but coming from the mouth of one's former enemy, the boast acquires the ring of truth universally acknowledged.

Beyond the ideological work of turning foes into friends, the serial also devotes considerable screen time to the exhilarating project of socialist modernization—as befits a tribute project to the founding of the People's Republic. Wang Yingguang's brother is the head of a lightbulb factory that is badly in need of electrical engineers. Wang volunteers the expertise of

Ye Lisan (a fictional character), the bespectacled scholar-officer with a prewar stint in Germany as an engineering student. Through this collaboration we learn about the pace and ambition of socialist industrialization. Wang's best friend is a reporter who is also courting his adopted sister. Through the reporter we learn about the infrastructural transformation of Beijing, such as the cleaning up of a slum area called Dragon Whisker Ditch, which Lao She chronicles in an eponymous play. In one scene, the prisoners watch with rapt attention a newsreel of the first National Day parade in Tiananmen Square, their faces beaming with pride. The 1950s is the CCP's honeymoon with the Chinese people, and in this show it is rosier than ever, so much so that even those temporarily excluded from it yearn to partake of it. But nothing serves to galvanize the prisoners as much as the Korean War.

Although in reality several of the prominent prisoners were transferred to Gongdelin at later dates, for the sake of drama all of them are already gathered at the facility at the outbreak of the Korean War. Every day they huddle together poring over the newspapers and keeping track of every development on the front; they draw maps on the ground and argue about tactics. At first, all of them are convinced that the Chinese and North Koreans would collapse quickly. The more reactionary among them begin to fantasize about a Nationalist recovery of the mainland. As the tide of war turns, these men are profoundly shaken. When the People's Volunteer Army push past the thirty-eighth parallel, Ye Lisan makes a presentation on the war and concludes with three words: "Wo fu le!" (I'm bowled over or I concede defeat). Thereafter they resume their quest to find the secret to the CCP/PLA's greatness and invincibility.

As Wang Yingguang understands very well, for the purpose of reeducation, the best answer is not a conventional one (because the Party is morally superior and has the people on its side, de minxin), a codified one (because it is armed with Marxism–Mao Zedong Thought), or a technical one (as might be given by historians and social scientists mindful of the overdetermined nature of all large-scale conflicts), but a narrative one. He wants the prisoners to incorporate the above explanations into stories they tell themselves and in so doing integrate themselves into the "exegetical community" that David Apter and Tony Saich (1994) argue is key to the CCP's success. In these stories, they are protagonists whose choices and actions partly determine how the stories end, thus suturing themselves into the socialist scriptural economy that gives meaning and purpose to their lives. In Michel Foucault's language, they have to become subjected in order to become subjects. Beneath the hype about Communist indoctrination perpetuated by both the CCP and its detractors, the program of reeducation operates on an astute grasp of human psychology. As has been demonstrated in many studies, total institutions such as monasteries, armies, asylums, cults, and prisons are the ideal environment to effect profound ideological and identity transformations. Individuals in these institutions are usually stripped of all the prior social ties that define and anchor their sense of self. Their social and psychic nakedness renders them susceptible to new frameworks of meaning by which to orient themselves and make sense of the world. But the salience of new worldviews and new values can overshadow the importance of communal bond, ritual reinforcement, peer pressure, material inducements, and institutional guardrails, without which a spiritual conversion can be short-lived.

This is very much the case with the men in Gongdelin, and there is nothing miraculous about their transformation. Yet nearly every account deems it nothing short of a miracle, which paradoxically feeds into the anti-Communist paranoia about "brainwashing" (more on this question in the next section). For example, Huang Jiren writes in the concluding chapter of *The Battlefield Is Not the Only Arena to Test the Mettle of Generals*: "In this ancient country of ours, no one knows how many miracles have transpired. But no miracle can measure up to the one created by the Chinese Communist Party in successfully transforming the Nationalist war criminals" (1982, 408). The first group to receive special pardons comprises mainly the Nationalist Party's top military brass, who held their comrades in the political and intelligence departments in contempt and blamed the latter's corruption and incompetence for their defeat on the battleground. In the serial, these men are also most forthright in expressing admiration for the Volunteer Army's performance in Korea and repeatedly implore Wang Yingguang to send them to the front to atone for their past sin of killing Communists. Short of that, they ardently take part in cooking military MREs (meals ready to eat) and eagerly draft reports summarizing what they know about American military equipment, capabilities, and maneuvers in hopes of aiding the volunteers. When they hear that their reports have reached Mao and Zhou, who commended their efforts, the expression of elation on their faces is such that we are to surmise that some sort of inner transformation has genuinely taken place.

Beatific moments like this would recur to drive home the message that the CCP not only defeated these men militarily, but also conquered them spiritually. Their lives were spared, their wounds healed, their health restored, their dignity honored, and their souls saved and renewed (figure 4.3). A party that can accomplish all this is destined for greater enterprises, "gan dashi de," in the words of one inmate. For the sole individual who refused to be reformed, Huang Jiren points out, the Party furnished

FIGURE 4.3: POWs engaging in gardening; the POWs' banquet party on New Year's Eve. From *Special Pardons 1959* (Dong Yachun 2019, Xingfu Lanhai and others).

him a "battlefield" all to himself so that he could carry on the futile fight. This was Huang Wei, who pleaded for and received a well-stocked lab in which to build his cockamamie "perpetual motion machine." "Huang Wei's battlefield was a 24-square-meter lab, his troops were his lab assistants, and his war chest held nearly a thousand yuan disbursed from the Party-state's coffers" (Huang 1982, 409).

The Battlefield Is Not the Only Arena to Test the Mettle of Generals and *Special Pardons 1959* bookend the four momentous decades of Reform and Opening Up. Compared with the 1980s and early 1990s, the broader geopolitical context has shifted significantly in the second decade of the new millennium. As an economic powerhouse with a growing presence on the global stage, China is particularly keen to burnish its image as a champion of humanitarianism and to parry accusations of human rights abuse. What better evidence than this story of clemency? This explains why the teledrama is as much about the Party as it is about the prisoners. Whereas in the earlier text (and its film adaptation) the Party is little more than a facilitator, in the serial it is an octopoid being: warden, teacher, doctor, caretaker, pastor, guardian, liberator, and savior all at once.

We don't know how many domestic viewers could appreciate the irony of sitting through thirty-nine episodes of a self-congratulatory depiction of CCP benevolence and mercy when hundreds of thousands of Turkic-speaking ethnic minorities in Xinjiang are sitting in detention centers undergoing involuntary reeducation and labor reform.[12] As I have argued elsewhere (H. Lee 2017), television programs like this one are rarely directed at non-Chinese audiences, and yet they are often made with international politics in mind. We can view them as part of China's domestic soft power agenda meant to counter various centrifugal forces pulling the populace away from the Party and to refute constant international criticisms. They serve an eminently high justice goal. Such high justice narratives are the primary lens through which the nation sees itself. As China begins to exert more influence in global politics, it will want to be seen by the rest of the world through the same lens and may also be inclined to see the world in like fashion.

Excursus: A Translingual History of Brainwashing

As noted above, Wang Yingguang's character is partly inspired by Wang Yanggong, the onetime director of the Biokdong POW camp on the banks of Yalu River. Wang did not leave behind any memoirs, and relatively little has been written about life in the camp from the Chinese perspective. Yet its place in world history is sealed as the putative birthplace of Chinese brainwashing. Infamously, at the conclusion of the war, twenty-one American POWs refused to be repatriated and chose to make the PRC their new home. They would come to be known as the Turncoats, though almost all of them returned to the United States on their own by 1966 (B. D. McKnight 2014; S. Wang 2005). Their choice flummoxed the American public, who could not wrap their minds around the idea that these good American boys preferred life in impoverished and repressive Communist China to free and comfortable American life. "Americans began to ask whether there was something wrong with their supposedly superior way of life that US soldiers would choose the enemy" (Kushner 2015, 280). Incomprehension and hurt fed into fantasies of diabolical Communist plots: the Chinese must have figured out how to manipulate the minds of these men in their clutches by, say, wiping clean their brains and dousing them with communist dogma and all manner of false ideas. If this was true, then those who did return could be human trojan horses or sleeper agents that could be activated telepathically anytime to do the biddings of their masters. Thus was born a cottage industry of conspiracy theories that culminated in *The Manchurian Candidate* (novel 1959, film adaptation 1962) in the realm of popular culture and, at the governmental level, secret CIA psychological and biological warfare research programs.

The etymology of "brainwashing" can be traced to the Chinese expression *xixin gemian*, which Geremie Barmé translates as "washing the heart and changing the skin on one's face" (1999, 391n7). The idiom, originating in the *Book of Change*, treats face and heart as body parts that are easily soiled and should be periodically cleansed. The idea may have been reinforced by the Buddhist injunction to keep the mirror of the soul free of dust. The word *xinao*, however, has a modern origin connected with

Chinese absorption of modern Western science. The heart in Chinese folk psychology is the seat of emotion and thought, much as it is in Western folk psychology. With the introduction of modern biology and biomedicine at the turn of the twentieth century, the Chinese embraced the notion that consciousness resides in the brain. The age-old idea of moral self-improvement and self-renewal through internal cleansing became grafted onto this newer understanding of human physiology, so instead of washing the heart, one now washes the brain. The earliest instance of this translingual hybridization is an 1899 magazine essay that called for the need "to wash away the millennia of dregs and filth from the brain matter of our countrymen, and project upon it the model of the modern world" (quoted in Mitchell 2019). A few years later it was echoed by Yan Fu, who hoped that the study of sociology would serve to "wash our brains and purify our hearts" (*xinao dixin*) (quoted in Mitchell 2019). Another few years later a science fiction story imagined a series of "brain-washing institutes" (*xinaoyuan*) that will finally awaken the Chinese and catapult them to the modern world (Mitchell 2019).

Ryan Mitchell points out that these early references to brainwashing were "envisioned as a form of enlightening pedagogy, not violation or control," and that in the modern Chinese lexicon, *xinao* was almost never used to describe any particular reeducation or indoctrination practice. "Rather it continued to convey a very general sense of political awakening. Indeed, it was a sufficiently generic term that at times it lost its political character entirely, appearing for example as a way to express feelings of mental rejuvenation brought on by a trip abroad" (Mitchell 2019). Kathleen Taylor (2017) also notes that scrubbing out the poison of imperialist and reactionary thoughts is the desired and stated goal of Chinese socialism—that is, there is nothing underhanded about the program of thought reform. The idea of keeping the body and mind free of dust and germs appears frequently in Mao's writings, mostly in reference to the quintessential Communist technique of self-discipline: "We must not become complacent over any success. We should check our complacency and constantly criticize our shortcomings, just as we should wash our faces or sweep the floor every day to remove the dirt and keep them clean."[13] The injunction of self-purification, when applied to the body politic, can lend spurious justification to a politics of purges and witch hunts. But the sinister freight carried by the English word "brainwashing" is the single-handed creation of the journalist and CIA aide Edward Hunter, who in his 1951 book *Brainwashing in Red China* conjured up the bugaboo of "terrifying methods that have put an entire nation under hypnotic control" (Mitchell 2019; see also Seed 2004; Taylor 2017; Lovell 2019).

When the American hysteria over brainwashing reached China in the 1960s, the Chinese were amused but also grew cautious. The official media explicitly associated the term with Americans and their quest for mind control. In *Special Pardons 1959*, Chiang Kai-shek, firmly entrenched on the other side of the Bamboo Curtain, is the only one to utter the word, after he sits through in sheer disbelief a PRC propaganda film about the good life in Gongdelin featuring cheery testimonials by his own former generals and captains: "They must have all been brainwashed by the Communists!" None of the cadres describes what they are doing in Gongdelin as brainwashing. A quintessential "supersign" as Lydia Liu (2004) defines the term, today the word *xinao* is most commonly used in the Sinophone world in its pejorative American valence. The United States' linguistic and ideological hegemony has thoroughly dislodged the earlier positive meaning of enlightenment and self-renewal from the supersign.

In contemporary parlance, invoking brainwashing discredits one's opponents by insinuating that the latter have ceased to think for themselves and have outsourced thinking to an alien entity. In other words, those who disagree with us do so because their brains have been hijacked. "Where 'washing the brain' once seemed a perfect way to express casting aside unexamined prejudices to let in the light of scientific rationality, we now use it to embody the tainting of consciousness by insidious political doctrines that prevent it from perceiving the self-evident truths of nature—whatever our tribe may consider those to be" (Mitchell 2019). In my view, the reason why brainwashing can take on such sinister dimensions has to be sought in deeper cultural assumptions about personhood and subjectivity. That the Chinese could shift so readily from "washing the heart" to "washing the brain" has to do with a holistic cosmology that accords no special ontological status to the heart-mind. In *Special Pardons 1959*, the favored metaphor for what the prisoners are undergoing is *tuotai huangu* (severing ties with the womb and replacing old bones with new ones), which locates rebirth in the body, not in the heart or soul.

In the Judeo-Christian West, Cartesianism locates a person's autonomy and subjectivity in his or her conscience or soul. Manipulating a person's mind brings one dangerously close to meddling in the domain of the spiritual, hence the hysterias over witchcraft and demonic possession in Church history. The soul should be accessible only to God and the person him- or herself. Tampering with the soul is tantamount to playing God—something that violates the moral foundation of divinity and evokes shuddering horror in a culture that deems individual autonomy sacrosanct. A Manchurian candidate is no ordinary spy, for a spy still has a soul whatever woeful state it might be in, but a Manchurian candidate is soulless, having traded in the soul for a machine. He or she "has been hypnotized to the extent that he/she is willing to perform atrocious crimes, such as assassinations, without fail, and against the 'candidate's' own will" (quoted in Seed 2004, 106–7).

The myth of brainwashing focuses almost exclusively on the dark intentions of the handlers, and much less on the methods. In the 1962 Frankenheimer film *The Manchurian Candidate*, for example, the brainwashing sessions are recalled in sweaty bouts of nightmare, and the dream sequence is evocatively portrayed not so much to explain how it works as to provoke horror—at a form of "mental rape" (Taylor 2017, 5). In his pioneering study of the CCP program of rehabilitating POWs, J. A. Fyfield points out that the Party's explicitly stated goal of turning these individuals into "socialist new men" is reprehensible only when viewed in the liberal democratic framework that values individual rights, privacy, and freedom of thought (1982, 87, 93). But if one can put aside the cultural aversion, it is difficult to find fault with the fundamentally humane means deployed to reach that goal: the self-criticisms, study sessions, tours, work programs, and so on. On the basis of his interviews with former wardens and prisoners as well as archival research at the Fushun Detention Center, Fyfield concludes that "there was no hint of harshness or brutality, no use of solitary confinement, no punitive restriction of diet, no use of labour as punishment and no administration of drugs. Indeed, the Fushun staff seem to have been possessed of extraordinary patience coupled with an impressive insight into human motivation and behaviour and a nice subtlety of approach" (88).

Fyfield concedes that in the end it is impossible to gauge the degree to which these men have been intellectually and emotionally liberated, or to answer the question as to "the nature of their commitment to the ruling ideology, policy and practice" (1982, 95). But he is convinced that they have never been stripped of their humanity and personality, never passed through the state that Robert Lifton believes is critical to thought control, that is, a state in between human and animal, adult and child (Fyfield 1982, 97). At the very least, the men Fyfield interviewed did not invite comparison with the Manchurian candidate. We can safely say that both brainwashing and Manchurian candidates are American inventions. And the American determination to win the psychological and ideological contest with the Communists had real consequences that played out in the Korean War.

Although China's "victory" in the Korean War was decisive in turning the Gongdelin inmates' mind-set around, in fact it was Taiwan that scored a genuine victory in a war with no clear winners, according to

David Chang (2020). He documents the lengthy negotiations over the fates of the prisoners held in United Nations Command camps. Because the United States unexpectedly introduced a policy of "voluntary repatriation," the question of who was willing to go where became the sticking issue. As a result, the war was prolonged for two more years, resulting in additional casualties on all sides. In exchange, about fourteen thousand of the twenty-one thousand Chinese POWs got their wishes and were "repatriated" to Taiwan (D. Chang 2020, 4–5). These prisoners' choice seems to be connected with the American psywar program, which set out, with personnel assistance from Taipei, to reindoctrinate the Communist soldiers for the goal of their "future use as a nucleus for democratization" (129), a fraught process painstakingly captured in Ha Jin's novel *War Trash* (2004). Immediately, it was obvious that the voluntary repatriation policy was working at cross-purposes with the reindoctrination program. Instead of returning to the PRC as the Chinese version of Manchurian candidates, these men demanded to go to Taiwan instead, thus handing Chiang Kai-shek a victory that helped turn the tide in his bitter rivalry with the CCP. "Chiang's once bankrupt and moribund regime was revitalized and renewed. The 'defection' of 14,000 Communist prisoners to Taiwan provided a much-needed shot in the arm, boosting morale among the population and adding legitimacy to Chiang's claim that the ROC [Republic of China] was the only lawful government of China" (D. Chang 2020, 7).

Chang argues that the Korean War has become the "forgotten war" largely because of American leaders' belated realization of the human cost of their contradictory policies stemming from poor planning, arrogance, and inattentiveness, and their subsequent effort to bury this embarrassing episode. Essentially, for every Communist soldier to exercise his "freedom" not to return home, one American GI lost his life; so did six Chinese soldiers and ten North Korean civilians. "These unsettling equations have apparently never entered the collective memories of Americans, Chinese, Taiwanese, or Koreans in the past six decades" (D. Chang 2020, 5). Americans never celebrated their propaganda coup against communism, and the Chinese deemed it a humiliation too profound to be salvaged for any mobilizational use. After prominent coverage in the official media, the entire POW question was dropped for good.[14] But it is impossible not to see a connection between this diplomatic debacle in Korea and the special attention given to the rehabilitation of the Nationalist "war criminals" in Communist custody. For all the talk of humanitarianism, the television serial makes no bones about the fact that the prisoners are chess pieces in an ideological and diplomatic game. Every small detail, every policy move in Gongdelin is put in place with a lot more than the prisoners themselves in mind. There is always a distant, skeptical, even hostile audience who is the real target of all the painstaking work: the paternalistic bounty, the pastoral care, the infinite patience bordering on indulgence (as with Huang Wei's "perpetual motion machine" project).

For example, when the Gongdelin leadership is alerted to overseas smear campaigns about alleged abuse and torture of POWs in Communist prisons, they decide to fight back with a propaganda blitz that includes the aforementioned documentary featuring the most high-profiled *jiji fenzi*. However, they decide to exclude Du Yuming so as not to throw a monkey wrench into his wife's effort to leave Taiwan and return to the mainland via a third country (Fyfield 1982, 13). As soon as he finishes watching the film, Chiang Kai-shek, fuming with rage, orders his son Chiang Ching-kuo to suspend stipend payments to the dependents of these feckless men and forbid them from leaving Taiwan. The repercussions for these men's family members are not dwelled on, since the point is merely to show Chiang's ruthlessness, which culminated in 1975 when he denied entry permits to the ten newly pardoned and released Nationalist officers. Permission to go to Taiwan after the final pardons of 1975 can be seen as a citation of the "return to Taiwan" of the fourteen thousand soldiers who, like the ten officers, had never been to the island. This time the CCP was able to make a dent retroactively in the Nationalists' propaganda win two decades earlier.

Exaggerated claims about the miracle of conversion made by propaganda films like the one viewed by Chiang paradoxically fed into the fear and paranoia about the Communist menace, when in fact thought reform fell far short of its much-touted goals and was rarely effective without coercion and violence. Aminda Smith notes that initially those sympathetic to the new regime were moved by boastful accounts by the CCP about its efforts to transform, rather than punish, its adversaries as well as *elements déclassés*. They were inspired by "the promise that schools could replace prisons" (Smith 2013, 5). By the 1960s, however, attitudes outside China took a southward turn as more damaging reports began to trickle out. A consensus gradually coalesced that regarded the rhetoric of thought reform as "little more than window dressing for a much more cynical program of suppressing dissent and punishing resisters, while increasing labor resources in the process" (Smith 2013, 5). But again, the POWs did seem to have received a more favorable treatment than what was meted out to dissenters and resisters.

Jan Kiely provides a fuller account of this controversial PRC institution by tracing it to the age-old discourse of *ganhua*, or reformation through moral suasion, and connecting it to the fitful process of penal reform and prison modernization in the early twentieth century. In his view, the CCP far surpassed its predecessor regimes in its ability to link "long-standing utopian dreams of morally cultivating people to secure earthly order, justice, and harmony to modern institutional techniques of governance" (Kiely 2014, 306). The Party spelled out its vision early on in a 1950 documentary film about organizing the lumpenproletariat of Shanghai into production collectives dedicated to reclaiming wasteland and founding "New People Villages." As typical total institutions, these collectives yoked together welfare, livelihood, and education, all to ensure "an emotional awakening to the realization that the Communist Party cared for them like no one else" (Kiely 2014, 267).

Kiely shows that this model was widely replicated and became the core mechanism of social control throughout the Mao era. The dual emphasis on thought work and manual labor, the utilization of group dynamics, and the demand for discursive and behavioral conformity were common features in all reformatory settings, penal or nonpenal. The Party presented this model to the Chinese people as well as the outside world as a uniquely humane and effective way to restore social order, heal the traumas of war and upheaval, and remake a people and a nation. In the course of a few years, it rounded up all manner of "undesirables"—urban underclasses, Nationalist officers and troops, bandits, vagrants, reactionaries, and the like—and placed them in an ever-expanding gulag archipelago. In doing so it inaugurated "a form of a state authority unleashed and unrestrained in its diffusion yet concentrated and disciplined in its pursuit of the grand imperative to reconstruct, as it was seen, a society rent asunder by war and rotted by an array of corrupt, repressive historical forces" (Kiely 2014, 271).

The 1950s, commonly depicted as a honeymoon period for the new regime and the populace, was also a time of mass detentions, mass trials, and mass executions. For those who lived through that period, the image of open-back trucks carrying condemned criminals, with placards thrust behind their necks, being paraded through the streets was graven in their memory. There is evidence that the majority of labor camps had substandard living conditions with widespread illness and death. Indeed, during the Great Leap famine of 1959–62, labor camp inmates accounted for a large portion of the staggering death toll (Yang Jisheng 2012). None of these grim facts is reflected in the representations of Communist humanitarianism discussed in the previous sections. In *Special Pardons 1959*, the captives initially consider themselves POWs and are pessimistic about the CCP's willingness to abide by the Geneva Conventions. When they learn that they are actually "war criminals," fear morphs into terror on the assumption that they will be summarily tried for "war crimes" and shot. Instead, they are treated to an air-brushed rendition of the thought reform regime, over the objections of many of the cadres assigned to the task. This is basically true to history: none of the men was ever put on trial, thus the label of "war criminal" clearly was meant to serve not a legal purpose of seeking justice but a political one of winning a propaganda war.

On the basis of memoirs by ex-prisoners published outside of China, Kiely believes that thought reform excelled in compelling superficial compliance that was rarely accompanied by inner transformation. And behind all the exemplary cases was a great deal of compromise and adjustment on the part of the state. After all, the Party had no way of definitively ascertaining the state of the soul of those it pronounced "reformed." And it didn't need to (see chapter 2). In fact, its ability to reorient individual conduct around its formulaic truth rests on a repertoire of practical wisdom poorly captured in its reductive phraseology. By combining its experience of mobilizing grassroots uprisings, waging guerrilla warfare, and binding supporters from all walks of life to its idealistic vision, the Party has accumulated a rich fount of practical know-how that meshes surprisingly well with the findings of modern psychology and behavioral science. Most notable was the method of incentivizing "activists" or "progressives" through material and status privileges as well as prospects for early release, and empowering them to enforce discipline, thus undermining the "communal inmate bond of the *nanyou* [prison comrades]" (Kiely 2014, 304). We see in *Special Pardons 1959* how these activists or *jiji fenzi* make it impossible for any hidden transcript or community of complicity (chapter 2) to emerge among the inmates despite the rather optimal conditions of communal living and minimum surveillance.

As noted in the previous section, the Party was a victim of its own success. The psychological soundness of many of its policies contrasted sharply with the philosophical poverty of its theory, compounded by the tendency to credit Marxism-Leninism and Mao Zedong Thought for every accomplishment on the ground. Overtime, the power of ideology became reified, misrecognized, and mystified, so much so that Mao Zedong Thought became the Chinese people's "spiritual atom bomb" (*jingshen yuanzidan*). Completely missing in this hyperbolic, delirious discourse was an acknowledgment of the intractability of the material and social world. When it turned out that Mao's words were not enough to iron out all the kinks of human plurality, literature and art were commissioned to represent the People-as-One.

Fyfield notes that the abundant pride exuded by the official media on the occasions of the successive pardons was not limited to the reform process itself but included also how it redounded to the greatness of the Party: "In these statements there was no hint of concern for the individual, no recognition of the mental turmoil he must have suffered in the course of his conversion, no reference to the doubts he may still have had. Some nods in the direction of the individual would have softened the conclusion that the overriding concern of the authorities was to squeeze out of the amnesties the last ounce of political capital to be exploited both at home and abroad" (Fyfield 1982, 94). One could argue that such "nods" would be quite out of place in platitudinous official statements. Concern for the individual would come later, in the narrative representations discussed in this chapter. In these we do see a fair amount of mental turmoil and doubt, at least in the beginning. The self-mythologizing is still unabashed, but as we can see in the literary, historical, and scholarly sources surveyed here, the CCP was not nearly as aggressive in pursuing mind control as feared owing to cultural, economic, and technological constraints. The key ingredients contributing to the success of the thought reform model are mostly low tech and improvisational, albeit labor intensive. For instance, the perceptive memoirist Shen Zui credits the unusual number of tours organized for the POWs as decisive in turning hearts and minds. Expensive and logistically cumbersome, these tours, he recalls, were the brightest moments in his long years of captivity and had the most profound impact on all inmates, including the recalcitrant ones (1990, 359–61).

Psychological warfare, it is safe to say, was a veritable American obsession and a far more costly endeavor with dubious results. The case of John David Provoo, an American GI tried for treason in World War II, convinced the American leadership of the critical importance of mind control. The rise of behaviorism in the mid-twentieth century boosted confidence in the scientific community in the possibility of remolding the human mind through induced conditioning. With massive funding from the CIA and other agencies, adventurous scientists conducted invasive psychological experiments on unwitting patients under the cover of psychotherapy. Programs like MK-Ultra, David Seed notes, "included pharmacological trials of LSD and other substances, the use of hypnosis, sensory deprivation, electroshocks, the application of radioactive elements, and even ESP. In short, every conceivable means of mind control was investigated during the 1950s and 1960s" (2004, xiii; see also Lemov 2011; Morris 2017; Taylor 2017; Kinzer 2019). Countless experimental subjects were damaged and traumatized beyond repair, and lawsuits against individual scientists and institutions are still ongoing to this day. One might say that the specter of Communist brainwashing was introjected in the body politic of the "free world" both literally and figuratively. In the labs, bodies and minds were manipulated and tortured; in fictional narratives, incarnations of the Manchurian candidate walk in our midst, ready to wreak havoc at the snap of a handler's finger. Postwar American fiction, in the words of Tony Tanner, is haunted by "an abiding dread that someone else is patterning your life, that there are all sorts of invisible plots afoot to rob you of your autonomy of thought and action, that conditioning is ubiquitous" (quoted in Seed 2004, xvii).

At bottom this dread had little to do with what governments were doing, openly or in total secrecy, on either side of the Bamboo Curtain. Rather, it responded to the all-too-legal culture of media and advertising that was growing by leaps and bounds and with astounding ingenuity in the capitalist world. Seed writes: "In effect a double displacement of the original meaning of brainwashing occurs here. First, it is transposed on to the home scene, thereby apparently losing its original demonized sense of an alien process. Second, it takes place through the most familiar day-to-day social activities" (2004, xviii). Brainwashing has truly come home, after an imaginary tour abroad. What ensued was a crisis of cultural confidence and a sustained interrogation of the values and assumptions that undergirded liberal democracy and market capitalism—against the backdrop of the civil rights movement, antiwar protests, and women's liberation. This would then merge with newer questions engendered by the rise of computing technology and artificial intelligence in the 1970s and onward (Taylor 2017).

*　　*　　*

In the early 1990s, a Taiwanese journalist interviewed half a dozen former Nationalist POWs (along with the relatives of some of them) and, in ornate prose and addressing his interviewees in the second person, chronicled their tales of woe, particularly during the Cultural Revolution (Chen Zongshun 1993). Some of these men saw their fellow inmates die during this period—a fact omitted in the celebratory accounts surveyed in this chapter. Even Jin Yuan, governor of the Fushun Detection Center, was "sent down" to the countryside twice and publicly denounced numerous times. He was reinstated only after Zhou Enlai intervened (Kushner 2015, 265). Zhou's protective wings shielded scores of individuals from the violent excesses of the Cultural Revolution. Among them were Du Yuming and Puyi, as well as James Veneris, the sole American POW of the Korean War who elected to stay in China and never left. But Zhou's protective umbrella was limited in size, and he could do very little for those caught in the crosshairs of Mao's last revolution, including Liu Shaoqi, who issued the special state pardons before he disappeared into the political abyss.

At the Korean War POW camps controlled by the CCP, initially twenty-three men opted to go to China. They were placed in a holding camp briefly to allow for second thoughts, which two of them did have (and upon their return to the United States they were immediately court-martialed and imprisoned). Those who, after a stint in China, returned quietly to the States found themselves shunned by their fellow country-men and had trouble finding housing and jobs. They couldn't shake off the label of "turncoats." Their fates contrasted starkly with the so-called draft dodgers and pacifists who opposed the Vietnam War and went to prison for it. All of them were set free in a general amnesty at the end of the war. Commenting on the CCP pardons of Nationalist POWs, the US amnesty of war resisters, and the "Millennial Amnesty" issued by then South Korean president Kim Daejung in 2000, Liu Renwen affirms the value of such exercises of the sovereign exception and their compatibil-ity with the rule of law: "Deployed judiciously, amnesty can ameliorate the inflexibility of law, win hearts and minds, and conserve judicial re-sources" (2015, 340). Unfortunately, he notes, the PRC has not issued a single special pardon, let alone general amnesty, since the last contingent of Nationalist POWs were released in 1975, even though the power to do so is stipulated in the Constitution.

Instead, a "strike hard" mentality has dominated criminal justice throughout the reform period. If anything, it has fed into the persistent Orientalist disparagement of China's legal institutions and practices. One need only think of a film like *Red Corner* (Avnet 1997) to appreciate the staying power of the image of Chinese justice as a travesty. In this over-the-top caricature of the Chinese judicial process, an American corporate lawyer (played by Richard Gere) is framed by Chinese mafia in cahoots with law enforcement officials during a business trip to Beijing. After a har-rowing ordeal, he narrowly regains his freedom thanks to a female lawyer who fearlessly throws herself between him and the careening penal ma-chinery dead set to crush him. *Red Corner* is merely the tip of the iceberg. In her survey of English-language crime fiction wholly or partially set in China, Isabel Santaulària i Capdevila finds that the country is invariably painted as a legal backwater, "ridden with corruption, oppression, poverty, eco-deterioration and mass migration" (2016, 67). Law enforcement boils down to "wily bad cops, frame-ups, extorted confessions, death sentences delivered with rapid dispatch, tight control over information" (76). *The Case of Huang Kegong*, discussed in chapter 3, can be read as a rejoinder to this damning chorus. Tellingly, the film's resounding panegyrics to the rule of law barely conceal an act of sovereign decision in the form of a let-ter of judgment by Mao.

Exceptional justice is practiced on both sides of the Pacific with different ramifications. Pardons and amnesties are built into the US legal system in such a way that their exercise by presidents and state governors are routine (Moore 1989). From the annual Thanksgiving turkey pardon to the pardoning of convicted felons, the American public may debate the merit of a particular case, but the legitimacy of the institution, however peculiar, is rarely questioned. In many ways, it resembles the imperial Chinese practice of amnesty studied by Brian E. McKnight (1981) in that both are unconditional and both are rooted in the recognition of the imperfection of legal justice.[15] The more disturbing expressions of the sovereign exception are found elsewhere in American legal history and the American legal imagination. The internment of Americans of Japanese descent is perhaps the most egregious one. The Charlie Chan franchise is another example. Here, the sovereign exception took the form of a symbolic pardon, as it were, granted to a fictional "Oriental" detective tasked to defend the state of law when actual Orientals were under a legal ban. American audiences loved Charlie Chan but feared and loathed his compatriots. Aesthetic pleasure served as an alibi to occlude the racist underpinnings of legal justice; laughing at Chan while rooting for him amounted to an underhanded celebration of the sovereign exception's pseudomystical aura of lawless arbitrariness.[16]

In the Chinese context, the sovereign exception finds expression less in routine gestures such as pardon or amnesty than in judicial populism (chapter 3). Bernadette Meyler characterizes early modern English plays centered on pardoning and sovereignty as a genre that invites audiences to "safely rethink the foundations of the state" (2019, 4). In contrast, the "theaters of pardoning" in the Mao era were spectacular displays of the capaciousness and self-confidence of the socialist polity. Pardons were explicitly framed as a reward for good behavior and a substitute for legal justice, as summed up in the policy of three "no's"—"no trials, no sentences, no executions"—recited again and again in *Special Pardons 1959*. Behind the three no's was the Janus face of the sovereign exception: clemency and cruelty, which for Aminda Smith were two sides of the same coin of Maoist social experiments (2013, 8).

5

Poetic Justice

Take care of freedom and truth will take care of itself.

RICHARD RORTY

If we could use only one word to sum up the literary history of twentieth-century China, that word would be *realism*. The reformers and revolutionaries at the turn of the last century sought to appropriate useful things from world-conquering Europe in order to strengthen a declining China and to forestall the seemingly inevitable fate of colonization and annihilation. Among these useful things was a particular way of telling stories, in the mode of social realist fiction as practiced and perfected by nineteenth-century masters such as Charles Dickens, Émile Zola, and Leo Tolstoy. The story of modern Chinese literature is thus a story of the indigenization of realism, of its zigzagging career starting with critical realism as pioneered by the May Fourth generation, to socialist realism under the aegis of the Chinese Communist Party (CCP), and culminating in magical realism embraced by the postsocialist generation.

Already, in this barebones account, the path of realism traverses terrains marked by contrapuntal narratives that sometimes depart from reality in the very name of reality. The irrealist impulse is most apparent in the experimental styles of writing that flourished in the last decades of the twentieth century and continue to thrive in the twenty-first century. But I hope to show that the attraction for the unreal and unnatural, driven largely by a desire to capture what lies beyond the perceptual, was present at the inception of realism's career in China and received official sanction and codification during the socialist period. Socialist realism, in its rejection of bourgeois naturalism, was a cryptic form of unnatural narrative that aimed to capture the magic of collective action. By contrast, the postsocialist boom in magical realist literature, driven by a profound disillusionment with the stultifying code of socialist realism, resorted to very different and overtly unnatural tropes in order to capture the magic of multiple worlds, be they ontological, epistemological, or psychological.

For the generation that came of age in the 1970s, the reacquaintance with Republican-era literature beyond the May Fourth canon and the re-importation of Western literature (especially modernist and avant-garde works) were exciting, but not nearly as electrifying as the belated discovery of Latin American magical realism. Almost overnight, writers like Mo Yan and Han Shaogong seem to have made a quantum leap from the uninspired, bombastic form of prose that was the standard fare of socialist realist fiction to a postmodernist carnival of letters whereby magic jostles reality as a force of liberty and play, as well as critique. The style can thus be characterized as China's own signature postmodernist literature. However, unlike in Latin America, where magical realism was a postcolonial reworking of a hegemonic literary style that was bound up with European colonialism, the critical dimension of Chinese magical realism has to be grasped in its relationship to socialist realism as a defense against the perversion of realism. As I intend to argue in this chapter, the swerve from socialist realism to magical realism is one form of unnatural narrative reacting and rebelling against another form of unnatural narrative for the sake of the true and just.

The genealogy from bourgeois realism to socialist realism to magical realism that I trace below emphasizes literary or formal manifestations of the high-low justice hierarchy. The central argument here is that despite their divergent ideological and aesthetic commitments, both socialist realism and magical realism aim to represent structural injustices caused by social and historical forces that cannot be reduced to individual agents. This chapter thus deals with two forms of compensatory justice—the people's justice and poetic justice—that the law cannot deliver. More than the previous chapters, it cements the book's central claim that justice is not law's sole preserve and that literature furnishes the best lens to peer into the residues of justice. To the degree that state policies in China have the force of law, stories that chronicle the wrenching ramifications of the enforcement of state policies—always in the name of high justice—must be brought within the purview of any project that interrogates the triangulating dynamics of law, morality, and justice.

The Magic of Collective Action

Unnatural narrative is the rubric narratologists use to designate a broad array of storytelling strategies premised on physically or logically impossible events and scenarios. It is a form of storytelling that deliberately—for aesthetic or ideological reasons, or both—violates the laws of physics or the rules of logic. In such narratives, an animal or an inanimate object or a dead person may speak, a person may levitate or even ascend heavenward, time may flow backward, and so on. These elements are the hallmarks of magical realism, though unnatural narratives encompass a much wider spectrum ranging from fairy tale and gothic tale to speculative fiction. In terms of narrative voice, one might even consider, as Jan Alber does, the most familiar form of realist fiction as unnatural. The omniscient narrator, for example, appears natural only because it has become so conventionalized that we no longer question how a person can have such unimpeded access to other minds or be at many places at the same time. Genre, Alber argues, evolves precisely through a process of conventionalizing unnatural styles and techniques and spurring new experiments in the unfamiliar and unnatural (2011, 43). The eighteenth-century rise of the psychological realist novel, Monika Fludernik reminds us, required a mental leap of its readers: "What is realistically impossible, the presentation of a fictional protagonist's consciousness from his/her own perspective, begins to constitute an ever larger portion of fiction narratives" (Fludernik 2003, 252–53). Likewise, the by-now-familiar modernist technique of free indirect discourse also presents an unrealistic scenario in which the teller or narrator's consciousness merges with that of the protagonist. Readers have to combine the "telling" schema with the "experiencing" schema to get past the unnatural erasure of the separation between teller and told.

A key element that is sometimes sidelined in unnatural narratology is the stipulation that the impossible is only that which a culture deems so. What is possible or impossible, or what constitutes fictional truth, hinges on what Kendall Walton calls the "mutual belief principle" (1990, 150–61). In premodern storytelling, for example, it is common to have supernatural characters, magical occurrences, plots hinged on metamorphosis, disparate temporalities, and so on. Nineteenth-century European realism, however, instituted the "reality principle" and defined itself by declaring the foregoing elements as unnatural and the antithesis of Enlightenment rationality. And in turn these unnatural tropes were recuperated and renovated in modernist and postmodernist narratives in an effort to break through the hegemony of reason and attendant strictures of realism. In this light, mimetic realism, with its insistence on physical and logical plausibility, is the exception rather than the rule in literary histories across the globe.

Unnatural narratives are ubiquitous even in places and cultures where verisimilitude is accorded unprecedented prestige. Cognitive scientists tell us that unnatural narratives are rooted in categorization through analogy making, to wit, our ability to grasp the abstract and the unknown via analogs from experience-based source domains. Time, for example, is almost always understood as a spatial concept that is directional and continuous, as in the expression "life is a journey" (Lakoff and Johnson 1999, 138). Once time is analogized to a physical path or journey, other possibilities of thinking about it open up: if one can travel in any direction on a path, one should also be able to travel in any direction in time—time travel thus becomes thinkable. Time travel also presupposes that the past and future exist in the present just like the point of departure and the destination already exist before one embarks on a journey (Lakoff and Johnson 1999, 159; Boroditsky and Prinz 2008, 111). In this fashion we generate novel ideas and ascend the ladder of abstraction by blending words, images, ideas, and frames from different mental spaces (Fauconnier and Turner 2002; Hofstadter and Sander 2013). Take Franz Kafka's novella *The Metamorphosis*, for example. Two input mental spaces that are mutually incompatible, one with the image of a bug, the other with the idea of thinking, are combined to engender an emergent concept: a thinking bug, which is then able to give us a previously inconceivable perspective on the world. Nearly all unnatural tropes are created effortlessly in this manner. They become suspect or illegitimate only under specific historical conditions. The dialectic of natural/unnatural narratives can thus be used to frame the history of narrative fiction in the West and elsewhere.

As already noted, social or critical realism rose to prominence in eighteenth- and nineteenth-century Europe by disdaining romance, gothic, and all manner of fanciful storytelling that contravened the new Enlightenment faith in reason and empiricism. In Amitav Ghosh's account, probability and the modern novel are twins, and their twinned birth has steered fiction away from "the unheard-of and the unlikely" (2016, 16). Art is to imitate life, and the artist is to think of him- or herself as holding up a mirror along the bustling highway of social life according to realism's best spokesman, Émile Zola. Banished are the vampires, witches, werewolves, and revenants as the hobgoblins of a benighted mentality or the hallucinations of an unhinged psyche. Representation is now governed by the "mimetic ambition" (19), employing textual details or "fillers" to convey the "new regularities of bourgeois life" and to rationalize the novelistic universe by "turning it into a world of few surprises, fewer adventures, and no miracles at all" (19). The most privileged novelistic technique is omniscient narration, which has been so thoroughly conventionalized that its replacement by limited third-person narration initially struck some readers as paradoxically unnatural. Similarly, in the hands of May Fourth writers, realism adhered to the same mimetic contract, abjuring anything that might carry a whiff of "feudal superstitions" and expelling beloved figures that had long populated the Chinese literary landscape: gods, ghosts, spirits, and were-animals. Some commercially oriented writers went on weaving these mythic creatures into their popular yarns until such creatures were officially banned in the People's Republic.

The new socialist state mandated an atheist worldview and proscribed the supernatural across the board in cultural production. Ghosts and spirits were permitted a limited scope if they were properly wrapped up in the preservationist discourse of folklore or cultural heritage undergirded by the mutual belief principle. But such tolerance for pluralism faded as Maoist politics radicalized. Socialist realism, the official style of Communist literature, was to be the final stage of realism in its long evolutionary ascent to Truth, overcoming along the way the shortcomings of bourgeois naturalism. While socialist writers were expected to gather empirical materials by going down to the grassroots and living among the masses in a manner similar to their bourgeois counterparts, they were not permitted to think of writing as merely transposing what they saw and heard and felt onto the page. Fidelity to lived reality, or verisimilitude, was condemned as a pernicious bourgeois conceit that was incapable of capturing a higher truth—the truth of class struggle.

One of the founding fictions of socialist China, *The White-Haired Girl* (He Jingzhi et al. 1946), powerfully showcases the imperative of going beyond what meets the eye. The story is said to be derived from a folk legend about a white-haired goddess whose occasional sightings by villagers fueled a thriving local cult. When the Eighth-Route Army led by the CCP tries to implement its reformist agendas in the region, it is met with an unresponsive populace who would rather go and pray to the goddess. Two brave cadres lay ambush in the temple and chase the goddess, who has come thither to retrieve the ritual offerings, to her hideout in a mountain cave. Under interrogation, she confesses to being the long-lost daughter of a poor peasant who had sold her to an evil landlord in lieu of rent arears. She fled to the mountains to escape from the landlord's cruelty, and her hair turned white from lack of salt and sunlight. Her only source of nourishment, beside what she can find in the wild, is the food offerings provided by the faithful in the village temple. Bringing her out of the cave and restoring her to the bosom of the community, the Party is able to teach a powerful lesson: the landed and propertied classes are the real author of peasant suffering (figure 5.1). Yet with their incense smoke and prayers, the peasants unwittingly partake of the spectralization of one of their most

FIGURE 5.1: *The White-Haired Girl*: a peasant beaten to death (opera version) (adapted from He Jingzhi et al. 1946; China National Peking Opera Company and Jingju Theater Company of Beijing); the White-Haired Girl brought back to the village (ballet version) (Shanghai Ballet Company, 1972).

vulnerable members; only the Party, armed with Marxist theory, understands the true nature of religion and can bring to light the hidden truth of class oppression (H. Lee 1999; 2014, chap. 1).

The basic plot device employed in the story, that of debunking a superstition through rational, empirical exposition, is borrowed from the Enlightenment project. It denies ontological status to the supernatural by laying bare the epistemological and sociological paths to the mirage. In this way, the device is qualitatively different from a minor genre in traditional Chinese literature in which a brave heart, when menaced by a ghost, mocks its hideous countenance and ridiculous antics, thereby cowing the apparition into a shamefaced retreat. In the latter case, we are firmly in the domain of the mutual belief principle: the ghost's ontological reality is never questioned by the author (and the implied reader), merely its spookiness quotient. *The White-Haired Girl*, by contrast, brings the reality principle to bear on the supernatural beliefs of fictional characters as well as audience members. It exposes such beliefs as a form of alienation rooted in the epistemic limitations of the individual point of view, or the difficulty of going beyond the superficial or epiphenomenal to penetrate hidden power relations grounded in property relations, or people's unequal relations to the means of production. When confronted with the overwhelming reality of class inequality and class exploitation, the uncomprehending peasantry attribute it to divine arrangements. By hypostatizing and apotheosizing the invisible forces of their oppression, they legitimize and help perpetuate the unjust social order as preordained.

A writer tasked to write about village life, therefore, must not merely recreate the daily comings and goings, the emotional ebbs and flows, and the interpersonal gives and takes. Doing so would be to commit the grave error of naturalism. In rejecting naturalism, socialist realism becomes a cryptic form of unnatural narrative caught in a bind. On the one hand, it resolutely repudiates all things "superstitious," that is, the physically, logically, or epistemologically impossible in an empirical world. On the other hand, it is not content with representing only what is physically, logically, or epistemologically possible. It wishes to be allied with neither fantasy nor reality, hence the all-purpose modifier "socialist." The poetic license authorized by "socialist" allows literature to overcome the limitations of bourgeois realism without an overt recourse to magic. Realism as practiced in the West is believed to be blindly committed to the individual as the fundamental unit of representation. Even when the omniscient voice is adopted, individual characters still remain the focal point of narrative interest, and the truth of class antagonism rarely emerges from the myriad ways in which social relations are diced and sliced in the service of verisimilitude. Narrative techniques that privilege the first-person point of view or limited third-person point of view are even more incapable of rising above the morass of details, piled on merely for the aesthetic goal of achieving "reality effect." Socialist realism would overcome this fatal flaw by adhering to protocols designed precisely to render visible the invisible, without making it strange.

Socialist realism's twin goals are to unmask class enemies as the true author of the misery and suffering of the laboring masses, and to reveal the latter, as a collective subject, as the true agent of history and civilizational achievements. *The White-Haired Girl* served well the first purpose and was canonized as a model work that appeared in many iterations across multiple media. Another story, "The Foolish Man Who Moved the Mountains," plucked from an ancient source by Mao Zedong in 1945, served well the second goal. In Mao's retelling, Yugong, "a foolish old man," decides to remove the two mountains sitting outside his doorway obstructing the way. With his sons in tow, he begins the removal project with a shovel. Zhisou, "a wise old man" and neighbor, scoffs at his foolhardiness. Yugong replies confidently that after he dies his sons will carry on digging, and that after they die his grandsons will carry on, and then their sons and grandsons will go on to infinity: "High as they are, the mountains cannot grow any higher, and with every bit we dig, they will be that much lower. Why can't we clear them away?" (quoted in Mittler 2012, 196). When Shangdi, or "lord on high," hears this exchange, he is so moved by the old man's grit that he sends two minions to carry off the mountains (figure 5.2).

FIGURE 5.2: Xu Beihong, *The Foolish Man Who Moved the Mountains* (1945). Photograph: Courtesy of Xu Beihong Museum, Beijing.

So far Mao's narrative hews closely to the source. He too does not ask how Yugong's house ended up there in the first place or why moving house was not an option. He seems to be operating by the mutual belief principle whereby one does not poke around basic story parameters. But he would have failed his role as the Party's storyteller in chief if he had not appended an epiphany that demystifies the deus ex machina ending by revealing the true source of the miracle: "Today, two big mountains lie like a dead weight on the Chinese people. One is imperialism, the other is feudalism. The Chinese Communist Party has long made up its mind to dig them up. We must persevere and work unceasingly, and we, too, will touch God's heart. Our God is none other than the masses of the Chinese people. If they stand up and dig together with us, why can't these two mountains be cleared away?" (quoted in Mittler 2012, 197). In the premodern version of the story, the people misrecognize their own agency and project it onto the deities. By retelling the myth of Yugong as an allegory of collective action, Mao restores agency to the people qua collective historical subject. For him, "a ruler's inspiration is no longer caught on the winds of a divine cosmos, but found immanent, instead, in the ideas of the masses" (Shue 2022, 689).

If religion, as Émile Durkheim contends, is ultimately communal self-sanctification, then Mao wants the Party to officiate the celebration of the power of solidarity, collective action, and transformation. It is a power that no individual can actualize, and yet is accessible to anyone who is willing to become part of the collective enterprise. What confronts an individual as a sheer impossibility, as the stuff of pipe dream and fantasy—something as monumental as removing a mountain or throwing off the yoke of oppression—turns into reality when individuals act in concert. To be sure, the experience of merging into a superorganism, of transcendence and elevation, has always been known to humankind and has subtended the universality of religion. The Party taps into this universal yearning by presenting itself as the catalyst by means of which the people recognize and realize their own superhuman greatness: the Party as the superglue so to speak. Although here Mao casts the people as the divinity that assists the Party in bringing about a miracle, it is really the Party, or rather Mao himself, that delivers the magic of collective action.

That is indeed what came to pass in the Cult of Mao during high socialism. Just as Yugong's descendants might worship him as a euhemerized god who made the mountains vanish, Mao, sitting at the apex of an ascending political party, achieved something similarly miraculous: he had galvanized the Chinese people, long disparaged as a sheet of loose sand by frustrated political leaders, into an iron-willed superorganism capable of carrying off mountains, literal and metaphorical. He too would be apotheosized as a godhead directing the general will of the People-as-One. Realism, with its preoccupation with individuals in all their splendid "roundedness" or jagged heterogeneity, is deemed not adequate to the task of communicating what it is like for the people to come together to form a gargantuan, unstoppable body politic. Enter *socialist* realism.

In socialist realism, individuals are flattened into types and reduced to functional parts (screws and bolts), so as to fit more snugly into the machinery of society. What is lost in colorful individuality is made up for in the superhuman strength and power of the collectivity. Because the latter eludes ordinary perception, special literary techniques are required to render it palpable. It is in response to this imperative that socialist realism acquires the hue of unnatural narrative. What is unnatural, however, has little to do with violations of ordinary ontological and epistemological expectations but is what happens when individuals shed their disparate intentions and desires and meld into a corporate entity. Consider *Li Shuangshuang* (see R. King 2010), a novella published at the height of the Great Leap Forward, Mao's disastrous utopian project that resulted in the death by starvation and malnutrition of approximately thirty million. The titular heroine is a vivacious peasant housewife who finds her voice and agency in rural collectivization and who takes the lead in setting up a communal canteen so that the commune members can devote even more time to the various public works projects as part of the rural modernization push. The story culminates in her miraculous invention of Great Leap noodles, which she and her comrades churn out in great quantities and feed to the sweaty and grateful builders of communist utopia. The entire story is told in a down-to-earth realist mode enlivened with a dash of local color and comedic interludes. The episode of the invention and produc- tion of Great Leap noodles, too, is related in a matter-of-fact manner, for all the heightened emotion and frenetic energy that permeate the communal kitchen. There is no self-conscious stylization, or any authorial wink of the eye, as if such an amazing event is a mere everyday occurrence.

In the 1958 film *Ballad of the Ming Tombs Reservoir* (*Shisanling shuiku changxiangqu*), a commissar promises to send a skeptical foreign reporter a telegraph on the projected date of the reservoir's completion, merely 160 days after breaking ground. The reporter rolls his eyes and mutters, "God willing." The commissar corrects him, "Here God is not in charge. The people are" (Jin Shan 1958). Even more than *Li Shuangshuang*, the film is an exuberant ode to the magic of collective action, with its montage of massed bodies in frenzied physical exertion, interrupted only by brief in- terludes highlighting labor heroes and newsreel footage of Mao and other Party leaders hoeing the earth. Twenty years into the future, on the precise spot where Mao shoveled dirt is a giant fruit tree laden with ripe apples, pears, bananas, grapes, pomegranates, and whatnot—a miracle presented as reality as the camera lovingly circles the lush canopy. The commune di- rector then explains the science behind this amazing specimen to a group of awestruck visitors (see Van Fleit Hang 2013, 154).

Instances like these bring socialist realism closer to science fiction than to magical realism. Classical science fiction, according to Brian Richard- son, constructs entirely realistic scenarios that could occur in the future (2011, 31), and in that sense it is not unnatural on the same order as a ma- gician waving a wand while muttering hocus-pocus. *Li Shuangshuang*'s Great Leap noodles and the miracle fruit tree are embedded in a recog- nizable recreation of the phenomenal world. And by dispensing with the "aura of surprising craziness" (Faris 1995, 171) that usually hovers around an extraordinary event, socialist realism encourages us to think that the invention is not beyond the realm of possibility, and that it is technologi- cally feasible, if not at present, then very probably in the future (and not- so-distant future considering the abundance of mass-produced foods that overflow our supermarket shelves nowadays). Unlike a typical magical realist narrative that leaves room for hesitation or doubt as to whether a strange event is a genuine miracle or an instance of hallucination, socialist realism invites investment in the believability of the miracle in the canteen or in the garden.

On the surface, it is Li Shuangshuang and her fellow canteen workers who invent the Great Leap noodles, but it is reasonable to assume that credit is due the entire commune and, by extension, the Great Leap Forward campaign itself. Li, a peasant wife hitherto cooped up in the home, cannot achieve what she has achieved without the mass mobilization and coordination of labor. The miracle in the kitchen redounds not to the genius of an individual, but to the might of the collectivity. That the magic of collective action is fused with the magic of technology is no coincidence. Both are beyond our sensory perception and schema-based intuition, and both require considerable cognitive effort and embodied practice to grasp. Given this shared quality, it is no surprise that Mao was able to convince so many Chinese that they could make up for the country's lacunae in science and technology with an overabundance of muscle power and communist zeal. Collective action, it was further believed, could outstrip the most advanced technology. Before the six hundred million Chinese people armed with "the spiritual atom bomb" (*jingshen yuanzidan*) of Mao Zedong Thought, the imperialist powers, in the favorite metaphor of the era, were pathetic "paper tigers" (*zhi laohu*). If Chinese socialism is a quasi-religious quest crossed with techno-utopia, then socialist realist fiction is its official scripture replete with saints and sinners in the persons of labor heroes and backsliders, and manna and miracles in the form of production sputniks and spiritual atom bombs.

It is not a stretch to say that socialist realism in its heyday is realism in name only. What it exploits is the human thirst for greater meaning and transcendent reality (what and why), and our relative unconcern and incompetence with epistemological questions (how). As Jerome Bruner puts it: "We are natural ontologists but reluctant epistemologists. The intellectual news in any generation is not that there *are* meaning and reality, but that it is extraordinarily difficult to figure out how they are achieved. The ontology [. . .] looks after itself. It is epistemology that needs cultivating" (Bruner 1986, 155). For this reason, the Party discouraged, even prohibited, the cultivation of epistemology, or the critical interrogation of how factual truths are arrived at, resulting in the decimation of the social sciences. In the realm of artistic creation, it dictated meaning and reality through dogmatism. In interpretation and criticism, it monopolized the interpretative community in which critics and readers were goaded to come up with the most politically correct interpretation in an "ever-renewed auction" (157). Verisimilitude, coherence, accuracy, reasonableness, and proceduralism all fell by the wayside.

Yet it is important to remember that socialist realism's de facto repudiation of realism stems from the same discontent with the latter's epistemological, moral, and ideological limits that motivated magical realism and other experimental genres that flourished globally in the twentieth century. In China as early as the 1920s, writers were already troubled by what Marston Anderson (1990) calls the "moral impediments" and "political impediments" of realism. Anderson shows how Lu Xun, the forefather of modern Chinese literature, resorted to "deliberate distortions" (*qubi*) in order to overcome realism's dispiriting and debilitating inadequacies vis-à-vis the project of national awakening. Thus at the moment of its birth in modern China, realism was already joined with modernism at the hip (X. Tang 2000). This is hardly surprising considering that realism, in Peter Lamarque and Stein Olsen's view, is less about a text's relation of fidelity to an extratextual reality than it is a literary convention mobilized for specific social goals: "The realistic novel, contrary to the claims of its early French proponents, is now widely regarded by literary theorists as having no privileged status in representing the world 'as it really is.' The whole modernist movement in art amounted to a challenge at a fundamental level to the idea of 'representing reality.' The point of modernism, at its best, was to exhibit the plurality of worlds, private and public, in contrast to some single 'objective' world given in experience. Once representation itself had been exposed as a kind of artifice it was natural for artists to highlight the artifice of their own media" (Lamarque and Olsen 1994, 170).

When the goal of the literary revolution was revolution itself—not merely representing but changing China—realism took a dramatic swerve. Left-leaning writers such as Ding Ling experimented with depicting crowd scenes untethered to any individual point of view in order to capture that extra dimension of human experience possible only in collective action. For these politically committed writers, if literature was to live up to its lofty ambition of revealing the truth about society and ushering in real change, it could not be contented with merely representing what was knowable and thinkable to the individual, since so much of social life unfolded in what Charles Tilly describes as the "incremental, interactive, indirect, unintended, collective, and environmentally mediated causal processes" (1999, 259). Insofar as realism abides by the basic format of storytelling that features a limited set of self-propelled characters acting within a bounded temporal and spatial range in a causal chain of events, it "provides an execrable guide to social explanation" (264). Of course literature is never in the business of providing social explanation in the first place and can never be boiled down to the kind of "standard stories" that Tilly has in mind. And yet his complaint does overlap with the discontent on the part of countless writers who have sought ways to circumvent the limitations of conventional storytelling in order precisely to capture, on the one hand, the culturally and psychologically alternative dimensions of experience, and on the other hand, the emergent property of social life in the aggregate.

Tilly's critique of narrative is echoed by Ghosh in his treatise taking the modern novel to task for failing to respond to the planetary crisis of climate change. Once upon a time, he argues, literature regarded as its proper subject calamities such as war and natural disasters (Ghosh 2016, 10). But ever since the modern novel took an inward turn to plumb the depth of individual interiority, freakish weather events have been deemed too improbable and contrived to fit comfortably into the realist frame. He calls out John Updike, who, in a review of the Jordanian novel *Cities of Salt*, complains that it does not measure up to his idea of the novel because it depicts "men in the aggregate" rather than "individual moral adventure" (77). Ghosh writes: "It is a fact that the contemporary novel has become ever more radically centered on the individual psyche while the collective—'men in the aggregate'—has receded, both in the cultural and fictional imagination. Where I differ from Updike is that I do not think that this turn in contemporary fiction has anything to do with the novel as a form: it is a matter of record that historically many novelists from Tolstoy and Dickens to Steinbeck and Chinua Achebe have written very effectively about 'men in the aggregate.' In many parts of the world, they continue to do so even now" (2016, 78–79). Decades earlier, Fredric Jameson bemoaned the same trend toward psychologism and the absorption with private subjectivity in his controversial essay on third-world literature. Like Updike, he confesses a sense of alienation when confronted with third-world novels, which tend to return obsessively to "the national situation itself" and which do "not offer the satisfactions of Proust or Joyce" (Jameson 1986, 65). The reason, he conjectures, is because postcolonial nations' life-and-death struggle with imperialism has blocked "a radical split between the private and the public, between the poetic and the political, between what we have come to think of as the domain of sexuality and the unconscious and that of the public world of classes, of the economic, and of secular political power" (69). The upshot is that "third-world texts, even those which are seemingly private and invested with a properly libidinal dynamic—necessarily project a political dimension in the form of national allegory: *the story of the private individual destiny is always an allegory of the embattled situation of the public third-world culture and society.* Need I add that it is precisely this very different ratio of the political to the personal which makes such texts alien to us at first approach, and consequently, resistant to our conventional western habits of reading?" (69). Jameson undertakes a lacerating self-critique and concludes by berating his fellow Western critics for being stuck in their un-Marxian conviction that "the lived experience of our private existences is somehow incommensurable with the abstractions of economic science and political dynamics" (Jameson 1986, 69). Reading third-world texts, therefore, is a salutary antidote that exposes the epistemologically crippling relationship between the master and the slave, whereby the slave knows what reality really is, whereas the master—"we Americans, we masters of the world"—is condemned to "the luxury of a placeless freedom" (85). The inescapably allegorical mode of third-world texts can therefore rescue Western culture from "the poverty of the individual experience of isolated monads [and the fate of] dying individual bodies without collective pasts or futures bereft of any possibility of grasping the social totality" (85).

Ghosh denies that there has ever been a divergence between the novelistic practices of the first and third worlds of which Jameson speaks so ruefully. Of the four writers who he believes have written effectively about "men in the aggregate," three (Tolstoy, Dickens, Steinbeck) are from the first world. However, I would argue that these novelists still train their primary narrative attention on individual characters and their subjective experiences and moral adventures, although there is also a conscious effort to enlarge the cast and to embed them within, rather than pitting them against, a world of circumstance, or the public world of economic domination and political power. Invariably, a few central figures "develop enough reality to attract our sympathetic interests" and become fixed in our minds "by a face or a manner or a developed motivation" (Updike, quoted in Ghosh 2016, 76).

As Lamarque and Olsen maintain, the appeal literature has for us consists in its "humanly interesting content": "individual objects, places, characters, situations, events, actions, and the interaction between them" (1994, 265, 266). Strictly speaking, no novel can be about "men in the aggregate" without turning into a social science treatise. As I will further argue in the next section, there is a cognitive limit to the extent to which the collective and the structural can be represented in literary language better suited to describe, mimic, and narrate than to explain. Writers who take up large-scale events like natural or man-made disasters have found a way to reduce to human scale that which eludes sensory perception and emotional engagement. They are able to do so because these crises, however large and overdetermined, still impact individuals in an immediate, visceral manner and are liable to place them in wrenching moral quandaries—the very definition of humanly interesting content. Climate change, insofar as it cannot be equated with day-to-day weather, poses a special challenge because it does not lend itself to such downscaling. Few of us could answer questions like "Where were you at 400 ppm [parts per million]?" or "Where were you when the Larsen B ice shelf broke up?" (Ghosh 2016, 129). Ghosh faults the modern novel's preoccupation with individual minds, bodies, and desires to the exclusion of humanity's shared fate. But I believe at least part of the blame should be placed on our inherent cognitive limitations. (I will return to this question in the next section.)

In claiming that the modern novel's failure to respond to climate change has little to do with the novel as a form, Ghosh may also have in mind writers who have tackled the abstractions of "secular political power" in the form of racial and gender domination. After all, feminism's originary fighting words—"the personal is political"—deny precisely the radical split between the private and the public. For writers motivated by identity-based social justice, the holy grail is none other than to disclose the tangled threads between private existences and "the abstractions of economic science and political dynamics." For them, "the telling of the individual story and the individual experience cannot but ultimately involve the whole laborious telling of the experience of the collectivity itself" (Jameson 1986, 85–86). In *Native Son*, after the Black protagonist Bigger Thomas kills the daughter of his white employer, a passage of free indirect discourse makes the same leap: "He knew as he stood there that he could never tell why he had killed. It was not that he did not really want to tell, but the telling of it would have involved an explanation of his entire life" (Wright 1940, 285–86)—a life, in the words of Martha Nussbaum, "deformed by racial hatred and its institutional expression" (2003, 94).

The reason that these writers seem to fall outside of Jameson's purview is later spelled out by Arif Dirlik (1999), who contends that identity politics has stolen the revolution by sidelining class in favor of race and gender. There is some truth to his claim insofar as class domination is less experientially and emotionally salient than racial and gender oppression. The class ladder, when not overtly reinforced by social stratification and ossifying into caste, can be scaled. At the very least, it is easier for a member of the underclass to cross the class line (which can be fluid in a market economy) than to cross the boundaries of race and gender. Indeed, an entire subgenre of narrative fiction, from "Cinderella" to *Pretty Woman*, is singularly preoccupied with the miraculous ascent of a beautiful commoner woman marrying a prince, a nobleman, or a tycoon, vaulting up the class hierarchy with as little as a kiss or a fetching smile. Against such a powerful and enduring cultural myth, the structure of domination based on the relations of production is that much harder to translate into phenomenological experience. Mobilizing on the basis of class has always been difficult for the same reason that mobilizing on the basis of climate is today.

Ghosh, Jameson, and Dirlik all shy away from socialist realism, although arguably it is the most aggressive program to depict "men in the aggregate," to grasp "the social totality," and to advance a radical politics of class struggle. Yet as I have shown elsewhere (2014), socialist realism succeeds in making class struggle viscerally palpable only by recourse to a racialist repertoire of metaphors and emotions. Even so, it ends up pushing literary representation to its uppermost limit of plausibility. Characters that are "typified" do not undertake "an interior journey guided by the conscience" (Ghosh 2016, 127), because moral conscience has been resolutely replaced by class consciousness. Just as socialist politics is not about identity—not a search for personal authenticity or a journey of self-discovery—socialist realist fiction must not revolve around identity issues such as religion, ethnicity, language, gender, and so on. Instead, it is only about class struggle. What socialist realism exploits is legitimate discontent with the myopia of the novel form, but its solution essentially negates "the great, irreplaceable potentiality of fiction," which is "the imagining of possibilities" (Ghosh 2016, 128). When class struggle exhausts all collective action, any possibility of alternative politics, including ones that extend moral consideration to the enemy and the nonhuman, becomes nil. Thus even someone as manifestly disillusioned with the apolitical irrelevance of Western writers as Jameson cannot bring himself to warm to socialist realism.

The Magic of Multiple Worlds

By the early 1970s, socialist realism had pretty much spent whatever artistic capital it had ever possessed. Narrative fiction weathered the process of calcification the worst and withered the fastest—the total output of fiction was negligible during the Cultural Revolution, and only a handful of titles are remembered today for their historical value. Mao's wife, Jiang Qing, who emerged in the 1960s as the culture tsar, had little love for narrative fiction and instead lavished her attention and state resources on the visual and performing arts, especially Peking opera and ballet. On the stage and on screen, art seemed most liberated from the dull constraints of verisimilitude and could at last take wings. Lip service was still paid to the imperatives of "penetrating life" (*shenru shenghuo*) and "experiencing life" (*tiyan shenghuo*) so as better to "reflect life" (*fanying shenghuo*), but ideology trumped everything else. Writers, when not subject to persecutions, were pressed into service as members of writing teams tasked to crank out propaganda pieces or scenarios for the next revolutionary model play (Clark 2008; Pang 2017). Everyone had to be prepared for shrill denunciations when some invisible line was inadvertently or retroactively crossed. It was in the wake of this political pressure cooker that the postsocialist generation found a breath of fresh air when translations of Latin American literature, alongside other experimental works from Europe and elsewhere, became widely available on the Chinese market. A burgeoning crop of experimental fiction emerged in the 1980s, and writers like Mo Yan, Han Shaogong, Gao Xingjian, Yu Hua, Su Tong, Can Xue, and Ma Jian went on to craft their own distinct brands of magical realism to great acclaim.

Mo Yan, for one, openly credited Gabriel García Márquez for opening his eyes and dislodging the entrenched notions he had about what it meant to write fiction. Mo Yan's exuberant style, which the Nobel Literature Prize committee labels "hallucinatory realism," bears unmistakable marks of Latin American influence. The five essential characteristics that Wendy Faris distills from a global canon of magical realism can all be found in Mo Yan's oeuvre: (1) the presence of "an irreducible element" of magic, something that nonchalantly violates common sense and is accepted after the initial reaction of wonder instead of being explained away; (2) the copresence of the phenomenal world, rich in mimetic detail, that anchors the story in history and distinguishes it from out-and-out fantasy or allegory, though the version of history that emerges can be idiosyncratic, messy, and fragmentary compared with official or grand narratives; (3) the reader's experience of hesitation between the uncanny, which can have a psychological explanation, and the marvelous, which requires an alternative ontology; (4) the merging of antinomic worlds: that of ordinary people and that of the witches, the living and the dead, the human and nonhuman, the animate and inanimate, and so on; (5) the upending of received ideas about time, space, and identity (Faris 1995, 167–74). In sum, instead of merely resurrecting premodern mythologies filled with "the unheard-of and the improbable" (Ghosh 2016, 27), magical realism seeks to embed wondrous elements seamlessly within the rationalized and observable world of "everyday details, traits of character, [and] nuances of emotion" (27). It shows and tells with equal gusto.

Frog (Wa), Mo Yan's 2009 novel about China's draconian three-decades-long population control policy (1979–2015), operationalizes nearly all the above techniques. The central figure, Gugu (Auntie), starts out her career as an energetic and beloved rural obstetrician. Midway through the novel, when the state policy shifts from pronatalism to one-couple-one-child, she is forced to assume the role of birth-control-enforcer-in-chief and forced-abortion-provider-in-chief. In Andrea Riemenschnitter's words, she goes from a transmitter of "local, sedimented knowledge" to a mediator of "alien epistemes," from "a savior [to] an annihilator of life" (2014, 10, 13). In her second career, she is universally reviled and shunned by the same community. Shortly after she retires from active service as a confirmed old maid, she suddenly marries a local artisan famous for his folksy clay dolls. Together they bring back all the "illegal" fetuses lost to Gugu's cold surgical instruments as finely and lovingly wrought figurines on the strength of Gugu's infallible recall. Their workshop becomes a temple that houses the souls of the unborn children in the rows and rows of dolls on display (and never for sale).

Gugu's abrupt marriage decision comes on the heels of a harrowing scene described in high magical realist mode. It is relayed to us by the first-person narrator and Gugu's nephew. On a moonlit evening while making her way home after leaving her retirement banquet somewhat inebriated, she finds herself chased and attacked by a horde of frogs:

> It was at that moment, she said, when an incalculable number of frogs hopped out of the dense curtain of reeds and from lily pads that shimmered in the moonlight. Some were jade green, others were golden yellow, some were as big as an electric iron, others as small as date pits. The eyes of some were like nuggets of gold, those of others, red beans. They came upon her like ocean waves, enshrouding her with their angry croaks, and it felt as if all those mouths were pecking at her skin, that they had grown nails to scrape it. When they hopped onto her back, her neck and her head, their weight sent her sprawling onto the muddy path. [...] She shrieked each time she caught one of the frogs, which she flung away. The two attached to her ears like suckling infants nearly took some of the skin with them when she pulled them off.
>
> Gugu screamed and ran, but could not break free of the amphibian horde. And when she turned to look, the sight nearly drove the soul out of her body. Thousands, tens of thousands of frogs had formed a mighty army behind her, croaking, hopping, colliding, crowding together, like a murky torrent rushing madly towards her. As she ran, roadside frogs hopped into the path, forming barriers to block her progress, while others leaped out of the reedy curtain in individual assaults. (Mo Yan [2009] 2015, 250–51)

The passage screams out for allegorical reading. More than once, the novel makes it abundantly clear that frogs are homophonic stand-ins for infants, as both are pronounced *wa* (frog is *wa* and infant is *wa₂*) (Riemenschnitter 2014, 17). At the start of Gugu's horrific night walk, the frogs' croaks are said to be "infused with a sense of resentment and of grievance, as if the souls of countless murdered infants were hurling accusations" (Mo Yan [2009] 2015, 250). Finally, nearing collapse, Gugu stumbles into the arms of the doll maker and promptly asks him to marry her.

Despite the allegorical cues, the hyperrealistically rendered frog attack merges two antinomic worlds, that of humans and that of animals, that of the mundane and that of the marvelous. It thus presents the reader with a difficult choice: either reading the episode allegorically as Gugu's troubled conscience tormenting her under the influence of alcohol, or accepting the possibility of ferocious frogs assaulting a hapless wayfarer who has disturbed their peace. If the reader leans toward the former, the vivid and vividly revolting description of the frog attack makes the latter rather hard to dismiss, thereby creating an aesthetically pleasurable sensation of hesitation. For Jan Alber and colleagues this sensation of hesitation ensues from a "Zen way of reading" practiced by readers who "accept both the strangeness of unnatural scenarios and the feelings of discomfort, fear, worry, and panic that they might evoke in them" (2018, 462). They liken it to John Keats's "negative capability" of entertaining "uncertainties, mysteries, doubts without any irritable reaching after fact or reason" (quoted in Alber et al. 2018, 462). In Walton's terminology, the Zen way of reading shuttles back and forth between the reality principle and the mutual belief principle.

Mo Yan prods his readers to exercise their negative capability by resorting to a magical realist technique he has made his signature style: juxtaposing the world of folk beliefs and practices (requiring the mutual belief principle) with that of modern rationality (requiring the reality principle), and presenting the former with a sense of wonder that is "fresh, childlike, even primitive" (Faris 1995, 177). We have come a long way from the anti-superstition (*pochu mixin*) crusade of *The White-Haired Girl*. To the extent to which Mo Yan's readers are familiar with these beliefs even if they don't profess them explicitly, the Zen way of reading holds its attraction. Magical realism appeals precisely because it disinclines us against impatiently reaching after fact or reason, and reminds us of other worlds in which what we deem "unnatural" may well be unremarkable, a point made by Andrea Moll (2011) in regard to Australian aboriginal storytelling. One might also say that magical realism trains readers to be armchair anthropologists who must navigate between the emic (insider) and etic (outsider) ways of knowing.

Indeed, the idea of frogs exacting revenge on behalf of "murdered infants" may not be so outlandish in light of the folk belief in the infant spirit (*taishen*). The infant spirit is said to hover about the birth chamber, not becoming fully attached to the infant body until the child reaches seven or eight, past the critical phase marked by high infant mortality rates in premodern times (Ahern 1978, 272–73; Snyder-Reinke 2019). Hence the caution against knives and scissors in the birth chamber for fear of accidentally injuring the infant spirit. Spirits in traditional Chinese cosmology are disembodied beings that are perpetually seeking to attach themselves to physical entities and, if wronged, perpetually seeking vengeance through haunting and other tactics. Thus, it is not inconceivable that the spirits of aborted fetuses might find temporary host bodies in frogs, having confused frogs for babies (perhaps not only people but spirits too are prone to mix up homophones). And it is also not inconceivable that they might turn frogs into fleshly weapons against the person who deprived them of a human host body, Gugu.[1]

The frogs thus act out our tendency to assign blame to discrete persons for injustices that stem from complex social enterprises driven by divergent intentions, interests, and goals. By placing Gugu between multiple and clashing worlds—with population science, central planning, government regulations, and public health on the one side, and kinship ties and neighborly obligations, individual conscience and moral debt, folk cosmology and folk art on the other—the novel celebrates the magic of a pluralistic universe in which no single truth reigns supreme. In contrast to socialist realism that extols the cryptomagic of collective action, Mo Yan's magical realism revels in the alternative, peripheral, and shadowy worlds thought to have been lost to decades of political repression and ideological homogenization. If women like Li Shuangshuang are eventually reduced to "typical" characters valued only for their functions in the socialist machinery, the female characters in Mo Yan's novel are scattered all across the experiential terrain as agents and victims and agents-cum-victims, each standing in complicated relation to the state and to family, which define the antipodes of their worlds. How indeed to capture these multiple worlds, each encompassing myriad individual interiorities and circumstances other than through the trope of magic?

Ma Jian, a coeval of Mo Yan but now a dissident writer living in exile, also finds himself resorting to magical realism when chronicling the trials of a peasant woman whose body is caught between a Malthusian state and a despotic patriliny. In *The Dark Road* (*Ying zhi dao*) (Ma 2013), published in Taiwan in 2012 and banned in the PRC, Ma Jian goes a step further by giving voice to an infant spirit, who narrates a significant portion of the story about its struggle to be born. This struggle is the obverse of "Mother" or Meili's subjection to an unending stream of abuses by her husband, who demands a male heir and who sells off their second baby girl to human traffickers; by state family planning personnel who administer abortions and

kill off her near-term fetus by lethal injection; by predatory brothel opera-
tors; and by callous and unscrupulous entrepreneurs of e-waste. Each of
Meili's pregnancies, abortions, and (failed) births is told in part by the
infant spirit, giving the reader a glimpse of a world entirely outside of ordinary perception and prompting reflection on the many imponderables of a
state policy peremptorily justified on demographic and developmentalist,
or high justice, grounds.

During her second unauthorized pregnancy, Meili and her husband,
with their firstborn daughter in tow, are forced to flee their hometown
and join China's guerilla army of "family planning fugitives." During their
furtive wanderings across the waterways of South China, Meili meets an
assortment of people and begins to see herself as more than a wife and
mother. And yet despite her desire to further her education, learn new
skills (English, computer, etc.), and start a business, she is repeatedly
saddled with unwanted pregnancy by her husband Kongzi (rendered in
the same characters as those for "Confucius"). With her third, protracted
pregnancy, the novel shifts fitfully into the surreal. When contractions
finally come after twenty months of pregnancy, Kongzi takes Meili to
an unlicensed doctor. The fetus, however, fends off the doctor's forceps.
"Fighting for its life, the fetus grips Mother's pelvic bone and propels itself
back into the womb" (Ma 2013, 271). The rest of the scene is told from the
limited third-person point of view of the infant spirit: "The infant spirit
watches the fetus curl up with fright. When it was expelled from Mother's
ovary and rolled down the fallopian tube at the beginning of this third
incarnation, it was aware of the two previous times it had made this journey. It remembered Mother's screaming: 'Don't come out into this world,
my child! Return to me in another incarnation. Murderers! Animals! ...'
[...] It realized it would have to choose between the poisons of the womb
and the hostility of the outside world. [...] It decides that it must stay
inside Mother's womb" (272–73). Five years later, the fetus, whom Meili
names Heaven, is still in the womb, a fact that scarcely elicits wonder or
concern from any of the characters, least of all Meili. By now, the family
of three and a half have settled in the Heaven Township of Guangdong,
which specializes in recycling imported e-waste using primitive methods
and with zero protection against health hazards. Many of the recyclers are
migrant women who have eagerly sought out this toxic wasteland on the
conviction that the place is so polluted that their menfolk quickly go sterile
and thus can no longer impregnate their wives against their will. Moreover,
no family planning cadres care to come hither to check up on the women.
Meili insists on coming here for the same reason and goes so far as naming
her unborn child after the township. At the end of the novel, her daughter

has gone missing, and the distraught couple find the boat that brought them to Heaven Township five years ago and decide to make their way back home. As soon as they board the dilapidated vessel, Meili goes into labor. With no one but her panicked husband next to her, she acts as her own midwife. The next three pages deliver a high-pitched medley of reality and hallucination, hope and desperation, memories and tears.

> Tears stream down Meili's face. As another wave of pain comes over her, she tugs at her hair with her right hand and shoves her maimed left hand into the vagina. Immediately, the stump of her index finger sends images to her brain, giving her an interior view of the mysterious dark channel that she has never visited before. She moves her hand deeper inside and sees on the wet and creased walls the marks left by male intrusions. [...]
>
> A rancid, yeasty smell starts to escape from her. After another intense push, blood drips out from her vagina onto the damp deck, forming blossom-like stains, then gushes out with greater force. "Little Heaven, come down to earth now," Meili cries. "Mummy's waiting for you ...". She thrusts her left hand inside again, grabs hold of a leg and, with one final tug, rips the child from her womb and lets it flop down onto the deck. Desperate for a first glimpse of her child, she cranes her neck down between her legs and sees it lying in a pool of blood, its body as green and shiny as an apple, its eyes and mouth wide open. Kongzi steps aboard again and hurriedly opens its legs. He hears another plank crack underfoot. "My God, you shook this boat about so much, it's falling apart," he says. [...]
>
> Water begins to lap over Meili's legs. Her white toes rise above the surface like lotuses on a green lake. "He still hasn't cried yet," she says. "Carry him up onto the field so that the sun can shine on his face." Meili isn't smiling any more. (374–75)

The closing paragraphs tell us that the infant spirit begins to travel upstream toward "its final place of rest," while Kongzi, clutching the green-hued stillborn baby tightly to his chest, stumbles across "a grey expanse of waste": "his legs shaking from exhaustion, he struggles up a hill of stripped scanner motherboards and lifts the motionless child up to the first light of dawn" (375).

Like the frog attack scene in Mo Yan's novel, the ending of *The Dark Road* also cries out for allegorical reading. The five-year pregnancy can be read as Meili's resistance and protest against the double bind in which patriarchy and the state place all women. On the one hand, carrying a fetus appeases the husband forever hopeful for a son (they don't have a way of finding out the gender of the fetus on their own); on the other hand, deferring childbirth allows her to evade state reprisal (a squawking infant is harder to hide than a pregnancy). Kongzi's apocalyptic trek across a quagmire of e-waste can be read as a pilgrimage that offers up his stillborn son as a sacrificial lamb to the twin gods of patriarchy and capitalism. On the final page, Kongzi is no longer recognizably human, showing no concern for his waterlogged and dying wife and allowing his joy over the birth of a long-yearned-for son blot out the reality of stillbirth. Thus not only are women objectified as biological birth machines whose wombs are fought over by the family and the state; men too are little more than mindless puppets whose strings are pulled by oppressive ideologies and developmentalist agendas. The low justice of individual life, liberty, and happiness has been thoroughly smothered by the high justice of the national quest for wealth and power.

The Magic of Fiction

Magical realism is widely recognized as the literary style of choice of the postcolonial world. Its global appeal bespeaks the heterogenous, multivalent, and unruly nature of lived reality beyond the Enlightenment cult of reason. In its bold strivings to capture that heterogeneity, magical realism may be said to be a genuine and sincere mode of realism, and in that sense it is a kindred spirit with modernist and postmodernist efforts, emanating mostly from the metropolitan West, to approximate the subjective and the experiential. In China, magical realism is the preferred literary language of postsocialism, mobilized by writers, many of whom are former rusticated youths, to articulate the absurdities and devastations of the Mao years in the so-called Root-Searching movement, and to reckon with the new absurdities and devastations resulting from the frictions between state capitalism and a population newly authorized to get rich and pursue happiness on their own.

As I have showed in this chapter using Mo Yan's *Frog* and Ma Jian's *The Dark Road* as examples, there is hardly another style that is more adequate to the challenge of representing the enormity of China's One-Child policy: the sheer scale of the program, the multitudinous actors and interests, the complicated and colliding motives and stakes, the misalignment between intentions and outcomes, the misplaced fears and erroneous projections, the miscalculations and duplicities, the myriad ways in which power is abused and illicit gains made, the countless hearts and lives broken, the marriages and families torn part, the careers derailed or destroyed, the reputations ruined, the children born out of quota and unreported, the abandoned female infants, the loneliness of older couples who lose their only child to illnesses or accidents, and so on and on. And if these are still conceivable within the critical realist framework (although in trying to cover as much empirical ground as they can, both novels strain credibility and border on being sensationalist, just as Ghosh fears), what about the untold number of fetuses lost to forced abortion? What about the so-called missing girls lost to selective abortion and infanticide? And even more inconceivably, what has the program done to a cosmology that recognizes the unbroken bond between the living, the dead, and the unborn, and that sees childbirth not just as a biological event to be managed by reproductive and population science, but as a cosmic event jointly undertaken by humans, ancestors, guardian spirits, infant spirits, reincarnating souls, and other numinous forces? If realism excels in depicting the violent clashes between the agents of the state and their victims, magical realism, I contend, excels in rendering palpable the slow violence, the far-reaching ramifications, and the existential imponderables.

Unnatural narrative's unique advantage in representing the unrepresentable is best explained through the cognitive psychological lens. As noted in the introduction, the cognitive mechanism underlying most unnatural narratives is conceptual blending, to wit, our ability to combine two real-world scenarios into a third, impossible one. Alber and colleagues suggest that when confronted with a physically or logically impossible scenario, readers will likely adopt a double vision, foregrounding and savoring the unnaturalness of the represented phenomenon while searching for interpretative strategies to make sense of it. This echoes Joshua Landy's (2015) thesis that fiction affords us an opportunity to exercise our capacity for entertaining incompatible ideas—a state akin to lucid dreaming. Self-reflexive fiction, in his view, ratchets up this game of double consciousness by repeatedly breaking the fourth wall, by alternately plunging us into a world of illusion and then yanking us out of it, by making us believe and disbelieve in something almost at the same time. This exercise in oscillation of belief and disbelief takes advantage of the modular structure of our mind, or the functionally specialized systems that can hold divergent information and run parallel operations. Optical illusions such as the seemingly bent straw in a glass of water—of *seeing* a bent straw (believing our eyes) while *knowing* it is not (believing the result of rational inference)— are the best illustrations of this mental phenomenon (Landy 2015, 567–68). Magic shows' whole business model is built on optical illusions. This is also the fundamental state of split consciousness we are all in when we enter a story world; otherwise we would be running out of the theater when a fire erupts on the screen. Conceptually the split consciousness is also captured by the simultaneous mobilization of the reality principle and the mutual belief principle: when we read a ghost story, we make allow-ances for the mutually shared belief in the supernatural within the story world in which we partially enter and are thus perfectly capable of being spooked. At the same time we hold no expectations of seeing a ghost when we turn away from the book. The pleasure of horror movies capitalizes on the same cognitive makeup (Carroll 1990; P. Bloom 2010). Tamar Gendler (2008) calls the state of mind "alief."

Magical realism may or may not deploy the kind of formal devices com-mon in the experimental works Landy discusses to achieve the double effects of engagement and detachment. But in embedding the impossible within a phenomenal world and in suspending the magical between the uncanny and the marvelous, magical realist fiction also gives us a chance to practice "believing what we don't believe" (Landy 2015, 566), or, more familiarly, suspending our disbelief. It is cognitively more demanding than old-school realist fiction or out-and-out fantasy fiction, both of which cre-ate immersive story worlds that induce absorption without the periodic prod toward detachment. Like self-reflexive fiction, magical realism brings to the foreground the generalized double consciousness that underlies all fiction-reading experience and compels us to step back from the thicket of action and reach for more global or deeper insight.

Alber and coauthors spell out this readerly double consciousness in their reading of D. M. Thomas's *The White Hotel* (1981). In the novel, Sig-mund Freud is unable to correctly diagnose, let alone heal, his patient Lisa's inexplicable pains in her chest and pelvic region. We learn toward the end of the novel that these pains are actually caused by future events, when Lisa is brutally murdered and mutilated in the Babi Yar Massacre of 1941. Lisa's pains thus fuse two folk biological and psychological under-standings: that physical harm causes physical pain and that some people are clairvoyant. The result for Lisa is that clairvoyance is transposed into the realm of bodily experience and hence her anticipatory pains: "Freud is incapable of healing Lisa because he fundamentally misconstrues the causes of her pain from the perspective of his theory, which is based on the belief that the essential truths about our personalities are to be discovered in traumata of the past. [. . .] Freud is so obsessed with the ideas of past traumata and repressed memories that he fails to take into account his patient's Jewishness and the potential dangers related to the rise of anti-Semitism" (Alber et al. 2018, 465). The novel's inversed causal-ity thus prompts a critical examination of psychoanalysis's blind spots, and perhaps also a willingness to entertain the possibility of nonlinear causal relationships.

The White Hotel is a complex specimen of what Mark Turner calls "double-scope stories," rooted ultimately in the ways in which we make sense of our world through conceptual metaphors. According George Lakoff and Mark Johnson (2003), we make sense of new, abstract ideas in the target domain by drawing on a source domain of familiar embodied experiences. This metaphorical operation takes place in the literary imagination in far greater complexity and with far greater artistry (Turner and Fauconnier 1999; Fauconnier and Turner 2002). Take the Passion of Christ, for example. It blends one man's crucifixion with the sinning of humanity to arrive at the startling idea of universal redemption. Whereas collective sin is abstract, diffuse, and difficult to process, the death of one man is "human scale" (Turner 2003, 129). Likewise, Lisa's clairvoyant pains compress the liquidation of an entire ethnos to human scale and prompt us to reach for global insight about evil. Nancy Easterlin, while critiquing a reductive evolutionary reading of "The Little Mermaid," opines that the mixed ontology of the mermaid (half fish and half human) indexes the underlying recognition that humans and animals are fundamentally joined at the hip: "In folklore, merfolk and seal-folk are frequently endowed with powers of transformation, and in this such stories bear witness to the psychic *recognition* that human and animal are part of a larger whole and, paradoxically but not illogically, the psychic *need* to knit the two into a more cohesive whole than the evidence of our senses indicates" (Easterlin 2001, 261). The mermaid may defy the evidence of our senses, but she captures deeper truths about human existence, including our ambivalence toward female sexuality, large bodies of water, and outsiders, all compressed in the petite figure of a fairy maiden.

Moreover, Easterlin points out that "The Little Mermaid" is an original tale authored by Hans Christian Andersen, not a retelling, and that it registers modern romantic themes such as the loneliness of an alienated individual—themes that are decidedly absent in conventional fairy tales. Easterlin (2005) extends this insight to consider why modern experimental fiction tends to militate against our evolved cognitive predispositions for pattern and linear narration. In contrast to traditional storytelling, which is highly constrained by the cognitive limitations of memory and the social demands of oral performance (transmission of knowledge and integration of the group), written literature is at greater liberty to give free play to our propensity for novelty. As a result, "works that go against the grain of forms based on rudimentary cognitive predispositions will not only be written but, if written well, be valued highly" (Easterlin 2005, 30). If rudimentary cognitive predispositions once served our ancestors well on the savannah, they have become epistemologically limiting in our own world, a world characterized by social complexity. Modern literature, therefore, has become ever so restless, both formalistically and thematically. Concomitantly, modern readers, at least the more experienced set, have come to value works of fiction that attempt to overcome the epistemic limitations.

Recall Ghosh's complaint about the paucity of climate-themed fiction. For better or for worse, as climate change–related weather events have become more frequent and widespread and as more people's lives are directly impacted by them, it has become possible for the modern novel to anchor climate change in "individual moral adventures," thereby giving rise to so-called climate fiction or "cli-fi." What distinguishes this new genre from familiar postapocalypse dystopian fiction is its courage to place the climate crisis in the present and permit it to ramify across our moral and social landscape. Kim Stanley Robinson's *The Ministry for the Future* (2020), for example, refuses to wipe out civilization in a Big Bang version of climate catastrophe only to clear the stage for a few survivors to act out bare-knuckle moral dramas against a social void. Still, there are constellations of complex social or natural phenomena that are well-nigh unnarratable, such as evolution by natural selection. As Porter Abbott shows, our cognitive bias for the clarity of linear narration makes Darwinism truly a hard sell. Evolution is a slow creep without a driving force or agent: "The patterns of change are not the direct product of the combined cause-and-effect actions of the myriad parts, but rather an emergence that exceeds all real or imagined narratable models" (Abbott 2003, 158). Without entities or events, there is no story, and according primacy to chance as Darwin does "makes for a very bad story" (148). Species, pace popular misconceptions, are not self-directed agents. Rather, they "ooze" in no particular direction, and speciation is "a silent, hidden event that takes place unheralded within the still ongoing ooze of species" (151).

Abbott provides a powerful explanation as to why evolution by natural selection is no match for rival theories such as creationism, social Darwinism, and Lamarckianism (evolution by acquired traits) when it comes to the ease with which the latter can emplot a satisfying story and gain narrative portability. Lamarckianism, for example, replaces the role of chance variation with the agency of the will, essentially blending the idea of human motivation with the impersonal process of evolution to generate an appealing story, in which evolution becomes "a team effort, with all of us pulling together in the same direction, acting as joint agents of the species to which we belong" (Abbott 2003, 156). Scientists, of course, have valiantly resisted the pull of such narrativization even if they occasionally have to resort to the "sloppy language" (144) of metaphors to communicate with the general public. For the latter, however, the kind of vigilance against what Tilly calls "standard stories" necessary in science is especially difficult in the face of many attractive alternatives that smuggle in human interest hooks to help us wrap our minds around literally mind-boggling phenomena.

To return to the subject of this chapter, we might say that both socialist realism and magical realism are narrative strategies that seek to overcome the cognitive-based epistemic limits of realism. Both compress what is monumental and diffuse down to human scale to capture nonintuitive truths. But one can go too far in pursuing this goal. The heroes and heroines of socialist realism often come off as robotic because they are subjected to an additional operation: typification. Translated into the language of cognitive science, typification transposes human characters from the category of natural kinds (discrete individuals with souls or essences) to that of artifacts (things defined by their functions). In science fiction, this is done overtly to create novel effects. Thus when we meet a pensive android or a rebellious robot in a sci-fi story, we need to oscillate between what we know of and expect from entities that breathe and have putative essences and what we know of and expect from things that don't breathe and have man-made functions. The pleasure generated from this exercise can be immense and addictive in large part because it is a heightened version of what we engage in routinely in daily life, to wit, our tendency to make "domain-crossing attributions, imputing essences to artifacts (for example, to works of art) and viewing various natural kinds in terms of their functions," a tendency amply registered in our language: "objectification," "commodification," and "fetishization" (Zunshine 2008, 15). Typification is an ideologically motivated form of domain crossing or stereotyping and, like all stereotypes, is dehumanizing precisely because it reduces individuals to tokens and replaces intentions with functions.

I noted earlier that socialist realism, in celebrating the cryptomagic of collective action, shares science fiction's investment in the magic of technology. It also mimics the latter's penchant for making domain-crossing attributions, except that it does so cryptically, casting characters according to ideological stereotypes and essentially reducing human beings to the functions they are assigned to play in the socialist machinery as "rustless screws." If the essence of being human, according to Hannah Arendt, is to begin something anew, then the socialist realist heroes are stripped of their essential humanity by being made to act in profoundly predictable, almost preprogrammed ways. Without "the properties of novelty, unpredictability, ambiguity, and surprise to increase arousal potential for a species that prefers moderate to low or high arousal" (Easterlin 2015, 619), readers habituate. Overtime, the tedium of "clichés and trite language [that] rely on conventional meanings and ideological positions outside the text" (619) offsets whatever pleasure that the folksy art forms in which socialist realism often dresses itself can still impart. In leaving the readers' cognitive gears idle, particularly those for making projections and drawing inferences, socialist realism is unable to deliver an elementary aesthetic pleasure—the pleasure of surprise (Tobin 2018). It is owing to this starvation diet that socialist realism fails as an artistic venture and is swiftly jettisoned by practitioners and readers alike once the state mandate is withdrawn in the post-Mao era. The one genre that still claims a cult following is the spy thriller (see chapter 1).

The two magical realist novels discussed in the second half of this chapter accomplish a great deal of compression without, however, squeezing out the element of surprise, at the level of either plot or character. In *Frog*, infant spirits, themselves already conceptual blends, are further blended with frogs (activating the sensation of coming into contact with a frog's clammy skin) and swarming insects (activating the horror of being defenseless against mindless organisms), and then blended with the idea of retribution or karma. In *The Dark Road*, pregnancy is blended with the urge to protect, the necessity of appeasement, the fear of persecution, and the resolve to resist. More specifically, the five-year pregnancy blends the biological phenomenon of a human female carrying a fetus in her womb for nine months, a mother's instinct to shield her infant from harm, a wife's need to appease her husband (as long as she is still carrying the fetus, the husband can remain hopeful that it may be a boy), the imperative to evade state surveillance and penalty (again, an unauthorized pregnancy is easier to conceal than an illegal birth), and a woman's desire to take charge of her own body and turn a biological event into an act of free will. In both novels, the gap between the human-scale story of one woman's tribulations and the diffuse story of a ruthless national policy that touched millions of lives is so vast that magic seems to be the unavoidable emergent property of the double-scope narration. Magic, moreover, introduces friction to the familiar operation of poetic justice, or the convention of providing imaginary correctives to real-world injustices (D. Wang 1997, 121), which William Flesch traces to our "innate capacity for and tendency toward altruistic punishment," which in turn gives rise to "our desire to see the good rewarded and evil punished, whether they exist or not" (2007, 4). Here, reward, punishment, and redemption are enacted in a diffuse and convoluted and fantastical manner, so that low justice is essentially deferred to another realm, beyond human morals and bureaucratic laws. Under the dome of high justice, low justice could only be glimpsed in literary soap bubbles that refract possible alternative worlds.

*   *   *

I have argued in this chapter that both socialist realism and magical realism resort to unnatural tropes and techniques to represent that which escapes individual sensory perception and emotional engagement. In passing off fantasy for lived reality and ostentatiously rejecting the figurative and the supernatural, socialist realism becomes a duplicitous enterprise. Its glorification of the magic of collective action, then, comes at the expense of erasing the multiple worlds attendant on the plurality of "human intentions and human plights" (Bruner 1986, 50). It is yet another mechanism by which high justice stymies low justice. As we will see in the next chapter, when low justice is brought even lower, to the kingdom of the nonhuman, realism becomes inoperative without magic. Magical realism not only rescues realism from the fate of mummification but also revivifies literature at large and makes it a powerful tool, no less so than systematic social science analyses, in making sense of our social world, animated by the infinity, indeed magic, of the human imagination.

Although he mentions only in passing magical realism in his meditation on the modern novel's woefully inadequate response to the unthinkable crisis of our time, Ghosh himself deploys it to great effect in his own literary practices (e.g., *Calcutta Chromosome* [1995]). In the end, no one, not even the most hardnosed realist, believes that the project of fiction is to "reproduce the world as it exists" (Ghosh 2016, 128) or appears to exist, either to the senses or to the introspective consciousness. Ghosh's worry that a politics of sincerity will inevitably demean fiction as the expression manqué of authentic experience is perhaps unwarranted. Fiction's value has never been vested in truth, but in freedom, not so much the freedom to transcend our material condition, as the freedom to "approach the world in a subjunctive mode, to conceive of it *as if* it were other than it is" (128). Or in Bruner's words, literature that opens us "to dilemmas, to the hypothetical, to the range of possible worlds" is "an instrument of freedom, lightness, imagination, and yes, reason. It is our only hope against the long gray night" (1986, 159).

6

Multispecies Justice

*Nothing is either just or unjust in the eyes of those animals that have been unable
to make agreements not to harm each other or be harmed.*

EPICURUS

*All of Nature is
Indifferent, alas, to the good and the evil.
Quite a problem for us, I am afraid.*

CZESŁAW MIŁOSZ

The Trophic Order and the Moral Order

In Edward Hicks's 1846 portrayal of Noah's Ark, wild and domesticated
animals, carnivores and herbivores, predators and prey follow one another
in an orderly procession toward the titular ark. Amazingly, two top predators, a lion and a tiger, turn a calm gaze toward the viewer while the other
animals' attention seems randomly directed (figure 6.1). Neither predators
nor prey seem interested in one another. One imagines that once they
are safely ensconced on the ark, this mutual indifference will continue to
obtain and Noah won't have to do much to keep peace and order among
his charges—certainly no need to resort to cages and chains to prevent
his water-borne sanctuary from devolving into a jungle. Apparently divine
power has intervened to alter the nature of things, and the new dispensation presages the Christian prophecy of a heavenly kingdom in which the
wolf shall dwell with the lamb and the leopard shall lie down with the
kid—which Hicks also depicted in multiple iterations. The prophecy, perhaps the first multispecies fiction, is meant to resolve finally the problem
of theodicy: if God is all powerful and just, why should there be preda-

FIGURE 6.1: Edward Hicks, *Noah's Ark* (1846). Photograph: Courtesy of Philadelphia Museum of Art (Bequest of Lisa Norris Elkins, 1950, 1950-92-7).

tion and suffering? Or as Czesław Miłosz puts it in his famous cat poem, "Nature devouring, nature devoured, / Butchery day and night smoking with blood. / And who created it? Was it the good Lord?" (Bast 1995, 30).

In an early nineteenth-century Chinese folk ballad, a mouse, freshly killed by a cat, files a lawsuit against its murderer in the underworld court presided over by King Yama. The mouse explains that, as a puny creature, it is incapable of "pushing a cart or carrying loads" (Idema 2019, 109), and that it lives in a hole and steals food for no other purpose than "to make a living" (110). In this capacity it has been blessed by both divine and secular authorities—so much so that it was once decreed that "From each stone of grain / First we rodents / Would receive full three cups" (110). Moreover, the mouse has never courted trouble with the cat, who, without provocation and without "any clear writ or sagely edict," carried off the mouse's flesh and bones (110). The cat is then duly brought down to Hades by Yama's runners to defend itself. And its counteraccusations run the gamut of rodent offenses: stealing grain, chewing government documents and Buddhist scriptures, "messing up" embroidering needle and threads, and so on. Unable to adjudicate right and wrong, the judge orders both to return to the world of light to "act as they did before" (113).

The court case of the mouse versus the cat is an enduring, if minor, motif in Chinese folk literature. In the majority of these tales, the judge is affirmative of the natural order of things, so that the mouse is usually condemned to eternal punishment in hell while the cat is praised and rewarded. Short of that, the cat is permitted to go on with its predacious way, as in the above example. These tales, however, are an exception, according to Wilt Idema (2019, 6), to the general reluctance in traditional Chinese literature to accord speaking roles to nonhuman animals, in contrast to the prevalence of talking animals in other literary traditions. Perhaps the underworld court case of the cat and the mouse offers a clue: if creatures like mice and rats could speak, wouldn't they protest their lot in life, of having to hole up in crevices and steal food and live in mortal fear of redoubtable nemeses, from cats and dogs to humans? Where is justice when a prey species has no hope of liberation or revenge? As much as we desire to hear animals speak, we might not like what they might have to say.

Consider a sixteenth-century animal fable that features a rare talking beast, the Wolf of Zhongshan. A Mohist scholar who believes in universal love encounters a wolf on the run from hunters and agrees to hide it in his book bag. After the danger has passed and the wolf is let out, it begs to eat the scholar to assuage its hunger. When the scholar accuses the wolf of ingratitude, it counters that "ingratitude is the way of the world" (Idema 2019, 11). If reciprocity is the bedrock of human morality, what does it mean, then, to extend such moral sentiments as pity and compassion to animals that cannot acknowledge or return them? When animals talk, they may not only reveal to us the amoral trophic order in which they are stuck, but also justify looping us back into the food chain from which we have strenuously extricated ourselves. The scholar is saved only when a tutelary god tricks the wolf back into its hiding place and instructs the scholar to make a swift end of it. The point is made loud and clear: in dealing with an amoral being, only Machiavellian manipulation is called for.

If the biblical story of Noah's Ark strikes us as hubristic, the Chinese tales of the mouse, cat, and wolf communicate a lesson that is stark and uncomfortable. Both point to the fundamental gulf between the human moral order and nonhuman trophic order, and both suggest that the price of admission into the human moral sphere is that the nonhuman submit to the human will to order and tame the world. Such a lesson can grate on the contemporary sensibility, especially in an age that is grappling with the devastating impacts of human terraforming, from climate change, ocean acidification, and the melting of glaciers to mass extinction and loss of biodiversity. Environmentalists have long been making a case for the integrity, dignity, and rights of the nonhuman—animals, plants, rivers, soils, forests, and the atmosphere—none of which can be taken seriously if we cannot include them in our emotional life and moral deliberation. They have also been accused of sentimentalism, of romanticizing Nature as a zone of peace, kindness, and harmony, and of reducing the nonhuman to the status of pure victim, utterly helpless before the most rapacious predators on earth: *homo sapiens*. A more radical brand of environmentalism, often associated with posthumanism and theories of assemblage, goes so far as to advocate a "flat ontology" whereby all living things are entitled to equal rights of surviving and thriving. Toward that end, humanity would have to curb its appetites and cede habitats and resources it has robbed from its fellow inhabitants of the planet. It is believed that such a radical retrenchment is the only way to ensure planetary justice and ultimately the survival of the biosphere as a whole, humanity included.

With these debates in mind, I propose in this chapter a pragmatist model of multispecies justice, which I tease out of close engagements with several works of "multispecies fiction" from the Sinophone literary repertoire. Multispecies fiction is the literary equivalent of the multispecies ethnography increasingly practiced by anthropologists as a way of acknowledging "the entanglement of non-human species in what have normally been considered simply human societies and cultures" (Heise 2016, 166). Such fiction drives home the point that no human story can be told in its full ecological sense without embedding humans within a multispecies community, "a single, continuous field of relationships" (Ingold 2000, 87). I exclude from this survey the conventional genre of animal fable (except in the first two sections) and consider only stories in which animals are agents and victims in their own right and do not communicate with humans in human language. In this chapter, the framing concepts of this book, high justice and low justice, are brought to bear on situations furthest from the original context in which Delia Lin (2017) used them. Not only is low justice taken out of its anthropocentric circle of concern; high justice too is no longer merely a matter of political legitimacy and social order, but a question of ecological balance and planetary sustainability. The driving question nonetheless echoes those that have recurred throughout the book: can low justice be extended to where law does not reach without jeopardizing or clashing with high justice? In acknowledgment of the unboundness of ecological crises, I include a text from Taiwan, a geopolitical formation whose own story of high and low justice exceeds the scope of this study.

The primary lesson I draw from Sinophone multispecies fiction is that the posthumanist flat ontology is an inoperable response to the ecological crises of our age because it denies the moral gradations and entanglements of multispecies communities. Ultimately, as Ursula Heise maintains, the ecological question is never simply a question of science or philosophy, but also one of culture, history, and politics. Our knowledge of and engagement with the nonhuman can "gain sociocultural traction to the extent that they become part of the stories that human communities tell about themselves: stories about their origins, their development, their identity, and their future" (Heise 2016, 5). The multispecies novels examined in this chapter all tell powerful stories of mixed or entwined human and nonhuman communities and the moral complexity that ensues when the moral order intersects the trophic order.

A Wrinkle in the Universe

In the same meandering 1926 essay cited at the beginning of chapter 2, Lu Xun reminisces about a thumb-sized mouse he once rescued from a snake and kept as a pet when he was a young boy. The cute little rodent, known as *yinshu* (literally a "shadow mouse," or a mole rat), enjoyed his tender affection in part because of his fascination with a New Year print near his bed called "The Wedding of the Mouse." In the picture, "from the groom and the bride to the bridesmaid, guests, and officiant, each sported a pointy chin and slender legs, looking rather refined like scholars; nonetheless all were decked out in garish clothes. I thought, who can mount such a grand ceremony but my favorite shadow mice?" (1973, 8–9). The young Lu Xun longed to witness an actual mouse wedding believed to take place annually on the eve of the Lantern Festival, the fourteenth day of the first lunar month. He would stave off sleep to wait for a procession to emerge from under his bed, but all that greeted his bleary eyes were a few unclothed mice scurrying about and giving off hardly any festive vibes. Invariably he would drift into sleep and wake up the next morning to these musings: "Perhaps mouse weddings do not entail sending out invitations to solicit presents and have no use for spectators. This may well be a rodent tradition, and it's not for us to object" (9).

In many parts of China well into the twentieth century, a minor ritual observance during the monthlong New Year celebration consisted of retiring to bed early on a given evening (the date varies according to the locale) owing to the folk belief that on such a day mice conducted their matrimonial affairs and that it was prudent not to disturb them, or else there would be endless mice trouble in the year to come. An environmentally minded modern scholar may well consider this custom indicative of a bygone way of life that embedded humans in what Tim Ingold (2000) calls "an ecology of life," which included the divine as well as the nonhuman and fostered an attitude of proper respect for the teeming lifeworld. Although in some quarters there is a tendency to simplify this attitude as the Eastern way of living harmoniously with Nature, one cannot deny that a tradition that extended consideration to as lowly and universally detested creatures as mice and rats at least one day a year was animated by a cosmology radically different from the one that fueled the mass campaigns launched by Mao to exterminate the "four pests" in the 1950s. In the latter case, it was all about giving no quarter. Most notoriously, people banged loudly on pots and pans to prevent sparrows—labeled as pests for "stealing" grains—from landing, until the hapless birds dropped from the sky from exhaustion and fright.

Surely the status of mice and rats as vermin is less in doubt than is that of sparrows, and since ancient times these rodents have been the object of contempt, resentment, and disgust. Most memorably, they appear in the *Book of Songs* as symbols of the rich and powerful who plunder the common folk to fatten themselves. Yet during the New Year festivities they are given a wide berth, and their arguably parasitical way of life is granted a measure of legitimacy and even dignity. It certainly helps that, in an anthropomorphic light, they are good at mimicking human sociability and organizing their society through the orderly, patriarchal exchange of females. Apparently they too lead a civilized life, even if it cuts across that of humans in pesky ways. The ambivalence is unmistakable, enough to give wings to the fantasy life of a young boy growing up in the twilight years of imperial China.[1]

For readers reared on a diet of Disney cartoons, there is perhaps nothing novel about anthropomorphizing mice into adorable icons of human desires and foibles. But there are interesting differences, and they become clear when we examine the folktales centered on the clash between the cat and the mouse. Some of these weave an elaborate sequence of events to explain why the mouse has an enormous grudge against the cat, and it usually has to do with the cat's raid of the mouse's wedding party. Others dispense with these complications and rest the case simply on the predator-prey relation. Disney cartoons are far less diffident to the ruthless logic of the trophic order: a Disney rodent wedding party would never include a cat devouring merrymakers in full view of the bride. More often than not, it is the prey that triumphs over the predator, or they make common cause against a greater peril—think of *Tom and Jerry*.

A more realistic mode of animal narratives, somewhat similar to the Chinese cat-and-mouse tales, emerged in a modern Europe in which animals are driven by species-specific instincts and needs and anthropomorphism is kept to a minimum. This convention has given us many memorable animal stories in the Western canon, notably *Black Beauty* (1877), *White Fang* (1906), *Flush* (1933), *Lassie Come Home* (1938), and *The Incredible Journey* (1961). To be sure, a good deal of human thoughts and feelings are still projected onto the animal characters, and their lives invariably revolve around human activities and projects; moreover, they communicate with each other effortlessly in sophisticated language, but they do not speak to humans. The conceit, of course, is that the narrator has special access to the animal world and can transcribe or translate their thoughts and conversations for our sake.[2]

Nonetheless, these furred, feathered, and finned characters hold our interest because they are almost always cast in moral molds, as intentional beings that are implicated in human moral conflicts, or have to navigate their own moral dilemmas, or both. As pointed out in chapter 5, unnatural narratives win readerly buy-in through Kendall Walton's "mutual belief principle"—here the mutually shared belief is that animals of whatever species can and do communicate with one another. Walton adds that readers are willing to go along provided that what is unnatural is of a factual, not moral, nature (1990, 154–55). Not surprisingly, it is the dog and the horse that are the darlings of this genre, given the ease with which they are incorporated into morality tales about loyalty, betrayal, and sacrifice. In sum, we are willing to drop the reality principle with regard to loquacious creatures as long as they are capable of reciprocity. But amoral creatures, whose action can be explained simply at the biological and functional level, belong to nature documentaries. In the same way that natural selection is antinarrative (see chapter 5), no narrative is possible that strictly abides by the reality principle of the trophic order, whereby cats hunt mice, without malice, without rhyme or reason. One can give a low-level, blow-by-blow description of a hunt in the style of a *National Geographic* piece, but to tell a story, one needs to scaffold it with higher-level explanatory beams: purpose, intention, emotion, and goal. The imperfect alignment of thought and action, as Daniel Wegner and others have shown with their "action identification" theory (Wegner 2017, 149–51), is greatly compounded in nonhuman animals. A given action of a person can have multiple levels of description or explanation, and the person typically is aware of just one, but introspection and analysis can disclose more. When it comes to identifying the action of an animal, somewhere between object (which requires mechanistic explanations) and conscious person (which requires intentional explanations), we tend to vacillate between the mechanistic and the intentional, settling sometimes on cautious anthropomorphism.

Traditional Chinese literature has largely refrained from availing itself of the animal trope in either the parabolic or the quasi-realist mode (the most well-known exception is the sixteenth-century religious allegory *Journey to the West*, starring a highly anthropomorphic monkey and a pig—see my discussion of this novel in H. Lee 2014). The holistic cosmology in which it operates mitigates against a sharp ontological line that makes it possible for René Descartes to regard animals as automatons. In other words, animal tales can create a wrinkle in the canvas of a holistic worldview that encompasses all living things and assigns each to a proper place in the cosmic hierarchy. Telling stories from an animal's point of view entails foregrounding low justice issues that may break the spell of perfect harmony. In theory, what is natural is necessarily fair, and it is the nature of things to be unequal. But how can the "continuous massacre" (McMahan 2016, 268) that goes on in the animal kingdom be called fair? If the stalked, chased, and pounced on can speak, might they not protest their lot? In allowing animals to stay silent, traditional Chinese literature prioritizes high justice over low justice.

The human-animal traffic in traditional Chinese literature typically runs one way and involves either fox or snake (Huntington 2003). These creatures are believed to aspire to human civilization and values, but they must undergo an assiduous regime of cultivation and transformation and then insinuate themselves into human society in disguise. And when things go wrong and they are expelled from society, they invariably revert to their beastly shape. This way they merely circumvent or burrow beneath the cosmic hierarchy but do not overtly challenge it. Humans and were-animals may mate and produce progeny, but there are few genuine friendships. There are no Chinese tales of human-animal bonding resembling that between Lassie, Rin Tin Tin, Ed the talking horse, Seabiscuit, and Charlotte the spider on one side and their human sidekicks on the other. When it comes to thinking with animals, Chinese tales tend to see them as either food and resources (livestock), or servants (draft animals), or dangerous strangers (wild beasts). It is only in modern times that the newer metaphors of family (pets of all kinds), friends (dogs, horses, birds), and neighbors (endangered species, charismatic megafauna) have acquired currency under the impact of globalization. These newer metaphors necessitate the imputation of intention, thus going beyond the identification of animal action (e.g., hunting) as mechanistic à la Descartes (wired at the level of genes and instincts) or merely functional (to satiate hunger). Now their behavior is driven by desires, goals, and emotions (they hunt to show off or to win our approval, they trek to be reunited with their true friend, they pounce to avenge their master). Lassie and other animal stars are so memorable because they are fully intentional moral subjects.

The story of the Wolf of Zhongshan, recounted in the previous section, warns of the danger of incorporating an amoral creature into the human moral circle. And yet the point can be made, it seems, only by ceding a measure of moral quality—or intentionality—to the wolf: instead of pouncing on the scholar, it politely requests permission to eat him and is willing to submit to third-party arbitration. This twist attests again to the point that the trophic order pure and simple cannot be narrativized. In any event, the allegorical thrust serves to score a Confucian point against the Mohist doctrine of universal love—a doctrine that anticipates today's radical call for animal liberation. Confucianism prides itself on moral discrimination, propounding a granular scheme of moral franchise that thins out as one moves from close kin to distant strangers. Animals, as either servants or strangers, ought to be treated humanely but must not disrupt the cosmic hierarchy that, as Wang Yangming spells it out rather schematically, authorizes us to feed plants to animals and animals to our parents, guests, gods, and ancestors (Blakeley 2003, 152). In China, past and present, there are no dystopic fantasies along the lines of *The Planet of the Apes* (1968) and *Open Season* (2006) in which animals turn the tables and teach us a lesson about the brutalizing effect of inequality and oppression. An eccentric genius like Dr. Doolittle (*Doctor Doolittle*, 1967), who prefers animal to human company and who goes to great lengths to free a circus seal, would be equally inconceivable. The low justice of animal rights and welfare must be subordinated to the high justice of cosmic harmony.

The moral hierarchy, however holistic, admits of an enormous amount of violence: in harvesting and slaughtering, living things are killed, and blood is shed, and the pain and agony of death are difficult to behold. Mencius thus counsels prudent distance so that one does not lose sight of the larger purposes of life for the sake of momentary emotional relief. In an oft-quoted passage, he queries King Xuan of Qi if it is true that during a religious ceremony he spared an ox from being sacrificed at the altar because he couldn't bear to see it tremble in fear. Mencius then praises the king for his humaneness (*ren*) but also endorses his decision to substitute a lamb for the ox. Mencius offers the following bon mot: "The gentleman keeps his distance from the kitchen" (quoted in Slingerland 2014, 124). By averting his eyes from the scene of brutal instrumentality and low injustice, the gentleman effectively prevents raw emotions and instinctual reactions from overwhelming what is right and what is necessary, or high justice. Mencius's psychological insight here is remarkable in light of modern neuroscience and the countless testimonials of vegetarians that point to some primal moment of witnessing animal suffering. However, Mencius's explicit goal in this episode is to help the king reconnect with the "moral sprouts" that he didn't know were ingrown in his breast—given his reputation as a ruthless tyrant. He just needs to redirect his innate goodness toward the proper object: his subject people (Slingerland 2014, 122–25).

It is all very well for philosophers and kings to cultivate their moral sprouts by shuttering their mental blinds. The plebeians, however, have far fewer ways of skirting the dirty work of ministering to the omnivorous appetites of our species. And the literary imagination, unlike philosophy, is perversely drawn to the emotional and moral complications that arise in the low justice arenas where cruelty, gore, and necessity comingle. Out of this penchant grows a small stream of colorful, feisty, and often poignant tales about humble rodents daring to question the natural order of things. These tales pointedly adopt the perspective of the mouse, thereby shaking loose at the outset its automatic equation with vermin, pest, and plague— things to be eradicated rather than creatures whose fear and pain one can identify with and whose cosmic fate one is invited to contemplate.

None of these cat-and-mouse tales seek to subvert the high-low justice hierarchy, but together they crease the otherwise smooth canvas of a holistic cosmology into a wrinkle of doubt: Just because a creature is miniscule or its mode of survival is a nuisance to others, does it mean it deserves to be quashed forthwith? Rodents become pests only in relation to humans in the context of sedentary agrarian civilization. Behind all the vilification and extermination efforts, there lurks a recognition that these creatures too are only trying to survive and when possible to thrive. And if they betake themselves to carry off grain from the granary or to chew through fineries and treasured books, who exactly is to blame? By the same logic, when cats hunt mice, that too is part of the ongoing affairs of the universe, and the felines too are at no fault. That their predaceous instinct benefits humans is convenient and well exploited by the latter, but humans are not the author of the trophic order. Having taken themselves partially out of the food chain, homo sapiens are able to live by the values and ideals of their own making. They have achieved "a two-tier existence, half-in nature and half-out, both as organisms with bodies and as persons with minds" (Ingold 2000, 63). When it comes to nonhuman animals, some of these tales adopt a cautious mode of anthropomorphism, the kind that keeps the three-dimensional animal intact instead of allowing us to see right past it. They prod us to ask: Is what is natural necessarily just? What separates predation from murder? If a mouse could think and feel, where could it turn for redress?

The folktales about the war between the cat and the mouse and their underworld lawsuit clearly invite allegorical reading and fit comfortably into folkloric traditions from around the world that analogize the wretched of the earth to feeble, defenseless prey. The implied social commentary also extends to the institutions of law and order that invariably side with the strong and turn a blind eye to the plight of the weak. Social and political hierarchies are affirmed and justified in the name of the natural order of things. But the subaltern can still complain, and in complaining they make waves, or at least a few ripples. As one of the few nonhuman species in Chinese folk literature that have major speaking parts *as animals*, neither in human guise nor in human company, mice are accorded remarkable dignity and moral gravitas. Their burning sense of injustice is the impetus behind the underworld court cases. Although King Yama invariably affirms the righteousness of the predator-prey arrangement, the reader cannot fail to notice the unease with the way the whole system is stacked against the mice in favor of humans and their feline retainers. Sleeping in the mouse's despair is the Laozian aperçu that heaven and earth are hard-hearted and treat the myriad things as straw dogs.

The point can be made quite bluntly: Justice is a human construct. Take the human out of the equation, and the moral ballast vanishes, and the mouse's grievances become imponderable. Justice for all is a noble aspiration, but in the final analysis, the human ledger of right and wrong cannot fully register the workings of the universe. We are a long way from the moral Manicheanism of commonplace bestiaries and animal fables. Interestingly, the impulse to assign good and evil blossoms into full-blown protest in the modern retellings whereby predators and prey are to make peace with one another, and "if a cat kills a mouse, he'll be hung from a tree" (Idema 2019, 158), feline instinct be damned. This is no mere pipe dream of some naive utopian; nowadays there are philosophers seriously pondering the advisability of eradicating predation once technology makes it possible and not overly costly, effortful, or disruptive (McMahan 2016; Johannsen 2021).

Such aspirations of universal peace and harmony return us to the biblical vision of a fully pacified heavenly kingdom. Lu Xun probably would have scoffed at such dreams. In the aforementioned essay, he recounts his brief bout of skirmishes with cats after learning from a servant that a cat had gobbled up his pet mouse. In the end, however, he resigns to the fact that cats will be cats, neither good nor bad, just annoying. At least, he concedes, when they make mincemeat of their prey, they do not hoist the banners of "right" or "justice" or make the victim sing their praises till the doomed hour (1973, 5). Thereafter he merely shoos them away when they get on his nerves. The challenge we face today, once we become cognizant that the human quest for universal justice and perpetual peace has hidden boundaries, is how to negotiate these boundaries so that more and more of the earth's inhabitants can be included in our moral community.

In the new millennium, a spate of literary fiction has raised the curtain on a cast of four-legged creatures from wolves and tigers to dogs and cows, ushering in a veritable animal turn on the mainland.[3] In Taiwan, animal-themed writings have a longer lineage, as showcased in recent critical surveys (Huang Zongjie 2017; C. Chang and Slovic 2016; C. Chang 2018). In contrast to premodern tales of the strange or modern children's stories in which animal characters converse glibly with human and nonhuman species, these furry stars neither speak the human language nor assume the human shape. They are flesh-and-blood creatures that share habitats with humans and whose alien species being prompts introspection on human values, practices, and institutions. They belong to a new genre of multispecies fiction that strives to reinvent anthropomorphism in order to confront the biological and existential alterity of animal kind while grappling with the implications of incorporating them into our moral life—as both agents and victims.

When these writers thrust animals onto center stage and yet refrain from making them communicate in human language, they are implicitly asking: If animals can think and feel as we do, is it justified to use them as stage props to act out our desires and fantasies? In animal fables, their species being is all but lost behind the anthropomorphic mirage that barely conceals our anthropocentric preoccupations. In the words of Lorraine Daston and Gregg Mitman, we exhibit "species provincialism" when we "assimilate the behavior of a herd of elephants to, say, that of a large, middle-class, American family or . . . dress up a pet terrier in a tutu" (2005, 4). In such instances, the elephant or the terrier has become, "like that of the taxidermist's craft, little more than a human-sculpted object in which the animal's glass eye merely reflects our own projection" (5). Striving to capture the subjectivity of another being that cannot speak human language is, in my view, what sets the new crop of multispecies fiction apart from not only the allegorical genres featuring talking animals but also earlier practices of magnifying the pathos of human suffering by juxtaposing it with the suffering of dumb beasts, as in Xiao Hong's *The Field of Life and Death* (*Shengsi chang*, 1935).

To meet the challenge of letting animals carry the emotional gravitas of a story without falling back on anthropomorphism, these new works have resorted to either outright ventriloquism or a style unique to modern storytelling: free indirect discourse. In Western literature, ventriloquism was used to startling effect by the first generation of animal-fiction writers such as Ann Sewell, author of *Black Beauty: The Autobiography of a Horse*. In such texts, animals narrate their own life stories to human readers using human language, but they do not cross the species divide by communicating directly with humans or mimicking human mannerisms. The storytelling animal is thus an expedient conceit employed to force us to confront the pain and suffering of our animal servants. Free indirect discourse, on the other hand, is more common in the genre of pet biography, where the narrative interest lies chiefly in the human-animal bond against a realistic or historical backdrop.

In literary history, free indirect discourse, also known as stream of consciousness, is typically associated with early twentieth-century modernism. For Peter Goldie (2012), the modern novel excels in moving among diverging perspectives: those of the author, narrator, character, and reader. Free indirect style simultaneously opens up and closes the gap between diverging perspectives and in the process generates much of the pleasure and attraction of narrative fiction. When a character is a nonverbal animal, free indirect style is especially effective in holding the narration suspended in the space between verisimilitude and anthropomorphism, or between the reality principle and the mutual belief principle. The textbook example is Virginia Woolf's *Flush: A Biography*, about a cocker spaniel whose life coincided with the celebrated courtship and marriage of Elizabeth Barrett and Robert Browning. Most of the Sinophone multispecies novels surveyed below also revolve around human-animal bonding, but they are rarely about just one human master and his or her companion animal. The bonding usually takes place at the communal level, with wild, feral, or zoo animals acting as ties that bind, or "public things."

Public Things

Bonnie Honig develops the concept of "public things" by drawing on D. W. Winnicott's object relations theory. Winnicott is best known for paying serious attention to the special status of certain things in an infant's world: a blanket, a teddy bear, or a pacifier. These are what he calls "transitional objects," which help the infant cope with the mother's absences and renounce infantile omnipotence in recognition of a world that is "not-me." Their powers to soothe, enchant, and stabilize are invested by infants, and these objects are their "first possessions." For that reason, not any object will do. "Winnicottian objects are resilient, possessed of permanence, and not prone to obsolescence, though they are not immune, either, to wear and tear" (Honig 2017, 43). They must be able to survive the child's destructive love: soiling, disfigurement, and battering. The opposite of transitional objects, according to Honig, are commodities, things that are manufactured and marketed as desirable because they are new and whose obsolescence is preprogrammed. What is lost in a commodity economy is "the thingness of things," or their capacity to hold us while we hold on to them through care (53). While a commodity could be repurposed by an individual for idiosyncratic uses, a society that has only private commodities and few public things cannot sustain a healthy democracy.

Honig characterizes public goods and institutions such as parks, schools, armies, hydropower plants, electrical grids, public telephones, and so on as "public things" that nurture the democratic citizenry in an in-between "holding environment." While some of these public things do have practical functions, their significance goes beyond their specific utility. In occupying the in-between space, these worldly things have the magical power to enchant, alter, interpellate, join, equalize, and mobilize us, but they also need tending. Neoliberal capitalism, however, has been on the offensive to privatize and marketize everything, while at the same time substituting consumer products and planned obsolescence for the shared enjoyment of public things and mutual disclosure of subjectivity. Honig relates conservative politicians' effort to defund PBS and their disdain for the public's puerile attachment to cartoon characters like Big Bird. Big Bird, she writes, "represent[s] democracy's rootedness in common love for shared objects, or even in contestation of them, for such contestation betrays a common love, more than sentimental claims of devotion do" (Honig 2017, 61).

In this light, wildlife, particularly endangered species, activate a democratic holding environment for play and action in ways that livestock, pets, and zoo animals do not. The critical point to keep in mind here is that a public thing, as a transitional object for the citizenry, must be something of which we lack direct ownership or total mastery but which nonetheless is inescapably ours in a collective, default sense. Livestock are easy to exclude on account of their instrumental status and inability to survive purposeful destruction—the harvesting of meat, hide, and fur. Pets, on the other hand, do not usually serve any utilitarian purposes and often play the role of transitional objects for children and private individuals. But as privately owned and well-domesticated beings, they are the ultimate "private things" and are not conducive to constellating a public or cultivating affinities and attachments across social divisions.[4]

Are zoo animals not obvious ready-made public things? Do they not daily draw large mixed crowds to the playground-like milieu of the zoo to ooh and ah in wonderment and sometimes even in unison, and do zoo-goers not come away with renewed love for our animal "friends"? Under typical circumstances, zoo animals are under total human management and are little more than taxidermic museum pieces put on display for the amusement and, allegedly, edification of fee-paying customers. Zoogoers may throng boisterously in front of popular attractions such as the monkey cage, the bear pit, and the panda house, but they are discrete consumers unconnected by any common goals or projects that require them to disclose themselves in speech and action. The fences and cages place the animals out of reach, making them utterly harmless and paradoxically also lifeless. When we go to the zoo, in Randy Malamud's view, "we are not seeing a creature who acts or feeds or sleeps or eats or mates or nurtures or fights in the way a real animal would" (2012, 121).

Like commodities that have lost their thingness, zoo animals have lost their animal freedom and vitality and are unable to enchant the world and animate what Hannah Arendt calls "a life of action" (1958). Under special circumstances, however, they may regain this capacity, as when cohorts of zookeepers and visitors form special bonds with a couple of charismatic animals in *The Stolen Bicycle* (*Danche shiqie ji*), or as in *A Grassland Zoo* (*Caoyuan dongwuyuan*), when a gaggle of zoo animals are transplanted to the frontier, where they become denizens whose status resembles that of migrants rather than captives or commodities. These displaced zoo animals are better candidates for public things than are the vast majority of rodents, insects, reptiles, birds, and fish, which rarely enter the orbit of our social and fantasy life. The prototypical public things, however, are communal guardian animals like the Tibetan mastiffs and a few dozen critically endangered species that have intermittently become flashpoints in the media sphere and have given rise to organizations, projects, and legislation devoted to their protection and preservation and involving both state and nonstate actors. Endangered wildlife reminds us that while nature is resilient and possessed of permanence, it is also fragile and vulnerable. The recognition of the destructive aspect of our love of nature—the ecological equivalent of the soiling, disfigurement, and battering that infants inflict on their transitional objects—can enable and mediate public action in ways not very different from the public outcry provoked by the threat to Big Bird. Both cases involve something whose value is difficult to reckon in dollars and cents and which instead points to the realm of the intangible, be it moral, ecological, or existential.

One might ask if viewing wildlife as "public things" vital to democracy still casts animals in an instrumental and therefore anthropocentric light. It is to a certain extent, yet it enables a guarded perspective that is attuned to animal alterity without pretending to be able to speak from beyond the species divide. The idea that once anthropocentrism is replaced by biocentrism then animals can be left to be themselves and do their own things is naive in the Anthropocene, when "nature" as such is almost entirely a cultural construct and a humanitarian project (Heise 2016). Biodiversity is an ecological good, but the value of biodiversity is not a purely scientific question that can be objectively settled. As the authors of Sinophone multispecies fiction well recognize, it is difficult for people to care about such an abstract good without seeing any connection to what they cherish: their values, institutions, and ways of life. Each work in its own way shows that it is possible to tell riveting multispecies tales from a "weak anthropocentric" (Norton 1984) perspective.

The Tibetan Mastiff

Yang Zhijun's 2005 novel *The Tibetan Mastiff*[5] is widely admired among Chinese readers for its grandiloquent depiction of the famed Himalayan canine species as a supreme paragon of courage and loyalty and a stalwart guardian of humanity. A Han writer, Yang spent over four decades of his life on the Tibetan plateau and is intimately familiar with Tibetan Buddhism and Tibetan culture. The novel also fed a growing hunger among China's white-collar urbanites for the spiritual fullness of being that Tibetan culture seems to exemplify. But more than anything else, it rode on a high tide of interest generated by Jiang Rong's best-selling novel *Wolf Totem*, which for all intents and purposes ushered in the animal turn in mainland Chinese literature. As I have argued elsewhere (H. Lee 2014), *Wolf Totem* is a backhanded rehash of the century-old discourse of social Darwinism under the banner of panegyrics to central Asian grasslands. Both the steppe wolves and the Mongols are conscripted into a scriptural economy emblazoned with the Han Chinese obsession with "wealth and power." The novel laments the environmental destruction and the ensuing disappearance of the wolf packs and the nomadic way of life, but for reasons beyond ecology, biodiversity, or indigeneity. Rather, the grassland is seen as a new springboard—an alternative to China's spiritually desiccated hinterland—that could launch China to the acme of world power—if only the Han Chinese could figure out how to reanimate the dormant wolf spirit in themselves and pump enough lupine blood into their veins. The author professes to have been steeped in "wolfology" for the better part of his youth, but the zoological and ethological interests are edged out by the allegorical impulse and geopolitical ambitions. As a result, the wolves are little more than apotheosized sledge dogs that will pull China down the fast lane to the Darwinian contest's finish line.

Yang Zhijun's novel bears some resemblances to *Wolf Totem*. It too is obsessed with a pack animal species that is emblematic of a frontier region populated by an ethnic minority group with a distinctive culture and history. It too lavishes as much narrative attention on the animal inhabitants as on the human inhabitants, treating both as mutually dependent denizens of a holistic ecosystem. The mastiffs, or mountain dogs, roaming the snowy landscapes of Tibet in feral packs are said to be invincible warriors and loyal-unto-death guardians of territory, people, and chattel. They can preternaturally divine human speech and intention and fully participate in human emotional, moral, and spiritual life. For this reason, they are revered by Tibetans as divine incarnations and messengers. But above all, they are portrayed as animal prostheses, or animated and hypertrophied extensions of the nomadic tribes, forever vigilantly guarding tribal members of all species. They are intensely and jealously territorial, constituting a peculiar kind of transitional objects, at once shared and exclusive. The Tibetans, for their part, act out their social and political alliances and rivalries by proxy, offloading some of the bloodiest conflict onto the mastiffs so that human lives and limbs can be spared. Canine politics then becomes a shadow puppet theater whereby provisionary selves and tentative truce can be performed, tried, and tested. The novel thus diverges from *Wolf Totem* in its deep immersion in several overlapping mixed-species communities, in contrast to the latter's claustrophobic obsession, on the part of a Han youth, with elusive wolves.

Beginning its action in the early 1950s, the novel presents a political landscape in which the Han presence is minimum and government representatives tread lightly when handling ethnic affairs. It avoids the politically sensitive topic of the Tibetan Uprising of 1959 and touches only cursorily on the scourge of the Cultural Revolution in the final pages. The Tibetan way of life, however, has been thrown off balance by the intrusions of warlord and Nationalist troops in previous decades. The protagonist, a Han journalist known only as "my father," manages to tap into the special human-canine bond that obtains on the plateau and thereby helps put an end to the cycle of violence stemming from an age-old tribal feud but aggravated by entanglements with Han forces. In place of ritual maiming and killing, Father introduces education and economic development, enacting the dual "gifts" of civilization and development bestowed on the Tibetan people by the PRC state (E. Yeh 2013). This he does single-handedly by exhibiting devotional love for every mastiff that comes his way and by risking his own life to save a couple of extraordinary but battle-injured warrior dogs from enemies, human as well as canine. Essentially, he converts the dogs to the universalist ethics of the Han regime through the sheer nobility of his action, rallying them to the cause of pacification and assimilation of the Tibetans into the multiethnic nation. Once the dogs stop doing their masters' vengeful bidding—and once a wounded mastiff from the enemy tribe, now nursed back to health by Father, defeats the alpha of the host tribe's guardian pack and is enthroned as its new king—the Tibetans have no choice but to get with the program of reconciliation.

Despite this Han-centric ideological overlay, the novel's primary attraction, I suspect, lies in its thick, lyrical depictions of the mastiffs, both as individuals and in packs. Indeed, other than Father, humans largely play supporting roles and oftentimes are on the sidelines looking on with awe, fascination, and helpless despair. While making his way to his new job assignment in the heart of Tibet, Father comes across seven disheveled Tibetan waifs and their guardian dog Gangri Senggé or Snow Lion. Later he will learn that the children are orphans from a neighboring tribe and are trying to make their way to a mythological site beyond the snow peaks. Unfortunately, the tribe from which the kids hail owes blood debts to the tribe whose territory they are passing through. What ensues is a convoluted tale of pursuit, clash, revenge, bloodshed, kindness, and mercy. Snow Lion becomes mortally injured and would have lost his life were it not for Father. Nak Ril, a female mastiff from the host pack, becomes attracted to Snow Lion and, caught between love and loyalty, crashes against a wall in a ferocious act of suicide. She too is brought back to life by Father, with the assistance of a Tibetan medicine man. The headsmen of the local tribe insist on, per some ancient rules, chopping off the hands of the seven children in repayment of the blood debts. The Han officials in the regional office, citing the perils of getting embroiled in tribal feuds, prefer to stay uninvolved. But Father refuses to stand by. Time and again he puts himself in harm's way and successfully exploits the Tibetans' veneration of the mastiffs to save the children from ritual mutilation.

What does the trick is Father's proposal, which hinges on the time-honored rule that the king of the mastiffs be chosen through a contest of strength and bravery. If Snow Lion can dethrone the current king, Tiger Head, then he shall be the new king, and because the seven kids are his masters, then they too shall be honored as divinely protected. In the epic combat that follows, Snow Lion, whose superiority resides equally in his brute ferocity and tactical wisdom, does indeed worst Tiger Head, only to confront an even more fierce opponent. This is a mastiff named Blood Sucker, who has been raised in a dungeon and nourished on a diet of starvation, insult, torment, and furious beatings by a lonely, twisted man whose life's purpose is to exact revenge on the enemy tribe to which the seven kids belong. A canine Frankenstein, Blood Sucker rains a lifetime's worth of unappeasable rage and hatred on Snow Lion. And yet he too loses the joust, to the utter incredulity of all who have beheld the titanic clash of jaws and talons and the thunderous throttling of limbs and torsos.

With the exception of Blood Sucker, all mastiffs are cast as noble warriors in sharp contrast to the wolves. There are many takedowns in *The Tibetan Mastiff* of the wolf worship hyperbolically promoted in *Wolf Totem*. Wolves, Yang's novel claims, are shiftless and care solely about their own survival. The spirit of loyalty and self-sacrifice that Jiang Rong eulogizes is unknown here. In one instance, a she-wolf actually pushes her mate into the maw of Snow Lion in order to secure her own escape. Everything noble belongs to the mastiffs, if only because, unlike the wolves, who keep their distance from humans but also prey on humans and livestock, the mastiffs live for the singular purpose of defending their human masters and their livestock from all threats, wolves included. The difference between the mastiffs and the wolves is then the difference between soldiers and enemies.

There are many passages that swath the mastiffs in soldierly virtues. Early on, we are informed that mastiffs are no mere sheep dogs or guard dogs, not to mention pets. The majority of them belong to feral packs attached to specific tribes and never voluntarily venture beyond their own turf. They defend the tribe and the turf but do not have to answer to any individual tribesperson. In other words, they defend the common good, not private will or interests. "The meaning and purpose of life for the mastiffs go far beyond the utilitarian goal of survival. When they fight to death with wolves, human outsiders, and other beasts, they are not looking to devour the latter; their action has nothing to do with themselves being alive or dead or getting enough to eat. Rather, everything they do is driven by loyalty and devotion to their masters and the imperative to safeguard yurts and pastures—not unlike a nation's army" (Yang Zhijun 2005, 64). Like soldiers, mastiffs are maintained by the entire community with regular food offerings by the clergy of the lamaist temple, who themselves subsist on the offerings of the faithful. Also like soldiers, they abide by established rules of engagement but are also capable of moral deliberation and conscientious objection. Indeed, it is this space of moral autonomy that makes them true historical agents capable of shaping human destiny. They will charge ruthlessly at enemies at the incitement of their human masters, but they also obey a higher spiritual authority so that when a special incantation is chanted, they will desist from all violence. They are not Cartesian automata that can be programmed to blindly follow orders and commit atrocities. Like humans, they too have transcended the trophic order: "Wolves live to eat; mastiffs follow the Way" (160).

On the other hand, the mastiffs are also endowed with a species being that is distinct from that of humans, and some of the dramatic tension stems from this small wedge deep within the tight bond between man and dog. This comes through on a heightened note when a male mastiff gobbles down his own cub when he is unable to prevent it from being claimed by Snow Lion and Nak Ril, who have acted as its surrogate parents. This heart-stopping act of filial cannibalism is described as "a dark shadow that flashes across the azure sky that nearly blinds Father and sends him into a swoon: What I love cannot be loved by others . . . Because to love is to possess, and to possess exclusively" (Yang Zhijun 2005, 229). Who is speaking here? The mastiff? Father? The narrator? A quintessential instance of free indirect discourse, it could be any of the three. An unconscionable act is thus given a moral gloss: love, after all, is an eminently moral emotion, however crazed.

Moments like this are rare. In most cases, dogs and humans are on the same wave length, so much so that they appear to share the same nervous system. In the scene in which Father puts himself between the seven children and the butcher appointed to chop off their hands, he wrests the knife away from the latter and mimes to kill Snow Lion. And when the knife actually falls on his left hand that is holding down Snow Lion, the dog shudders: "It hurt. Being an exceptional mastiff that had a special bond with humans, it immediately felt pain throughout its body, as if Father's body were its own and Father's nerves were connected to its nerves. When the wound on Father's hand began to throb, it was the dog that truly experienced the torment" (Yang Zhijun 2005, 102). This typifies the seamless nonverbal communication between the two species. It is as if humans and dogs are different embodiments of the same cosmic will, except that humans are slightly favored and given greater freedom of choice. But the same freedom also lures humans off the righteous path, or the Way.

Take, for example, the contrast between the only two sex scenes in the novel: the rape of a beautiful Han cadre by her colleague, also a Han, while they are on the prairie looking for a missing cub, on the one hand, and the mating scene between Snow Lion and his consort Nak Ril, a consensual union and the culmination of an extended period of companionship and mutual assistance, on the other. Both are observed by a third party: the former by a tramp and the latter by Father. Father's adult eyes appreciate the poetry and potency of the canine congress, whereas the rape scene is made even more brutal and senseless when the child spectator's perspective is taken into consideration. If animal sex typically provokes disgust in humans for its lack of inhibition, here it is depicted in an operatic register.

Father later learns that this epic mating bout is actually two seasons ahead of schedule: apparently owing to the extraordinary intensity of her love, Nak Ril has gone into heat even though it is not the mastiffs' typical mating season. This is one of several instances in which the mastiffs are said to transcend their biological nature and act willfully like humans. The canine sex scene is also a manifestation of the uncorrupt way of the mastiffs that would rectify the crooked way of the humans. The rapist, having also killed a mastiff in panicked self-defense, would eventually be run out of the grassland; his victim would stay and marry the tramp once he reaches adulthood. Most importantly, the mastiffs are able to navigate the treacherous waters in which human wishes and the canine law of succession are at odds: their masters are against accepting Snow Lion even after he has vanquished Tiger Head. After considerable confusion and moral anguish engendered by the conflict between obeying their human masters and obeying their primal instincts, the mastiffs accept Snow Lion as their new king. Faced with this new reality, the headsmen find it hard to cling to vengeance and become amenable to the peacemaking efforts of the Han cadres. Peace and harmony soon reign on the grassland until the terrible chaos of the Cultural Revolution, during which time the canine packs are decimated and Father, with a broken heart, returns to the hinterland with two orphaned mastiffs (one descended from Snow Lion and the other from Blood Sucker) who fail to procreate, thus spelling the end of two heroic lines. The elegiac ending, however, does little to detract from the exuberant tone of the novel as a whole. In the same way that *Wolf Totem* stirred up a "wolf fever" and spawned many spin-offs, *The Tibetan Mastiff* allegedly opened the floodgate of consumer demand for mastiffs as pets as well as sequels and all things Tibetan. Nonetheless, commercialization is clearly deemed the antithesis of the proper way of living with animals, as Father resolutely refuses to surrender his two mastiffs to stratospheric bids from would-be buyers. What then is wrong with the Han Chinese way of putting dogs either in cages or in luxury apartments that are no less confining? The novel shows that only by being free—freely roaming the grassland in feral packs and attaching themselves voluntarily to human tribes but at no individual's beck and call—are the dogs truly "public things" serving to protect and unite humans. In this regard, they are a force of good, as one of the headsmen puts it when he challenges Snow Lion to contest Tiger Head's supremacy:

> Let your Snow Lion come up here and fight. A truly great mastiff does not cower in the protective arms of its human master. [...] Mastiffs live on the grassland, and at the same time they live in our hearts. We respect them profoundly, but

we don't get chummy with them or whisper tender words into their ears. They are neither children nor women that one can hold in one's arms all day. They are wild beasts that gallop in dark nights, they are ice cliffs that glint in howling gales, they are majestic rivers that crest against giant boulders, they are forest trees that brave thunder claps, they are wide meadows, they are wintry storms, and they are sculpted by the grassland after its own image. They are not your pet dogs that coyly and limply submit to cuddling and petting. (Yang Zhijun 2005, 262)

In other words, the mastiffs are the transitional object of the Tibetan people, the prosthetic extension of their communal self. They are not private possessions. Han outsiders like Father who recognize and reinforce this principle essentially join force with the mastiffs in helping the Tibetans make the transition from parochial feudalism to cosmopolitan modernity, from hierarchical caste to egalitarian citizenship, from ignorance to enlightenment. Thus despite a degree of paternalism and ethnocentric fantasy, ultimately, it is the mastiffs, as public things extraordinaire, that give birth to a new society.

The Stolen Bicycle and *A Grassland Zoo*

Another Han character in *The Tibetan Mastiff* begins the story with a canine phobia and ends as a martyr, taking a bullet for a mastiff. This too serves to code the Han presence in Tibet as benign and beneficent, reinforcing a larger narrative that seeks to brand Sino-Tibetan relations as noncolonial and nonimperialist. The implicit foil is necessarily the three centuries of global conquest by European powers (as well as latecomers like Japan and the United States) that proceeded by gunboats, unequal treaties, settlements, resource extraction, enslavement, missionary activities, and so on. For too long, however, the story of colonialism has been told with minimal attention to the role played by nonhuman inhabitants of conquered territories. And yet capitalism and settler colonialism have been the primary driver behind the large-scale movements of flora and fauna across oceans and continents and the resulting ecological topsy-turvy. To be sure, the trading and transportation of goods like spices, fur, pelts, minerals, timber, and so on have been an integral part of the history of global capitalism, and yet these goods are treated mostly as inert substances. Newer kinds of multispecies histories, however, have begun to reckon with the ways in which nonhuman animals are vital players in the colonial encounter, not least in their prosthetic roles as warhorses, pack animals, game, trophies, and objects of humane society activism (Brecher

2022; Chee 2021; Hevia 2018; Lander et al. 2020; I. Miller 2013; Sen 2022; Sterckx et al. 2019; Swislocki 2012). The two novels examined in this section, Wu Mingyi's[6] *The Stolen Bicycle* (2015) and Ma Boyong's *A Grassland Zoo* (2017), are pioneers of multispecies fiction set against the background of colonial war and encroachment.

The Stolen Bicycle is a complex novel with multiple threads and intertwining episodes spanning many decades and geographical locations, all held together by the narrator's obsession with vintage bicycles and his search for his lost father and the family bicycle. It places three categories of subjects—human, animal, and bicycle—in crisscrossing actor networks in which agency is by no means the exclusive preserve of the first category. Three animal species figure prominently in the novel: butterfly, ape, and elephant. The story of butterflies crosses the story of A-hun, who learns to make a living by catching butterflies and turning them into ornaments for domestic and export markets. The incorporation of handicrafts into the consumer economy is part of the larger story of Taiwan's economic take-off of the 1960s and 1970s, which relied on the exploitation of cheap labor as well as of the island's rich natural resources. While her earnings allow A-hun to move to Taipei in search of a better life, the butterfly population dwindles.

As members of a swarm species, the butterflies are not given individual names or granted particularized biographies. Three mammalian characters, in contrast, stand out with proper names and extended story lines, and their lives also intersect those of their human associates at a deeper emotional and social level. The stories of Ichiro the ape and Miss Ma the elephant are told in a series of reminiscences by Shizuko, an elderly Taiwanese woman, in conversation with the narrator while he pushes her wheelchair around the Mu-cha Zoo in Taipei. A second elephant, Lin Wang (a.k.a. Ah Mei), also a resident in the same zoo, comes into Shizuko's orbit via Squad Leader Mu (*Mu banzhang*), a World War II veteran and solitary zoogoer. The fates of all three animals are bound up with Japan's colonial adventures in East and Southeast Asia, particularly Taiwan. All three are removed from their native habitats, transported across war-torn territories, and resettled in Taipei. In the process they are alternately captives, servants, companions, and star attractions, becoming part of the lived experiences and enduring memories of the city's human residents and bringing settlers and natives into tangled relationships. Their presence in Taipei, and the demands, obligations, and attachments it engenders, greatly blur the line between colonizer and colonized, thus sustaining a "mixed" community in all senses of the word.

Shizuko's reminiscences are interwoven with casual descriptions of an array of zoo animals as she and the narrator meander through the park in the narrative present (sometime in the 2000s). Having grown up nearby and spent much of her childhood and youth in and around the zoo in the 1930s and 1940s, she has become an amateur zoologist with deep affections for its heterogeneous denizens and an irrepressible urge to tell stories about them. Her first story concerns Ichiro, a baby ape brought back from Borneo by a Japanese technician and added to her elementary school's menagerie. Ichiro quickly endears himself to the schoolchildren until one day he escapes from his cage, precipitating the decision to hand him over to the municipal zoo. "Afternoon classes were canceled. Along the boulevard beneath the heart of the sun and the cool of the trees, the students watched Orii-sensei lead Ichiro by the hand, like father and son, on the way to the zoo. Ichiro's soft red fur was amazingly lustrous. Standing up, his hind legs bent slightly into an oblong O. For the first time, the students, who didn't yet understand what leaving meant, realized what sorrow was" (Wu Mingyi 2017, 260). If Ichiro's story fits rather comfortably into the familiar family romance about how children learn the basic lessons of life through beloved pets, then the story of Miss Ma is a veritable romance of colonial entanglements. Not long after Ichiro is transferred to the zoo, where his despondent countenance greatly disturbs Shizuko, an elephant arrives to cheer everyone up. Miss Ma, as she is affectionately called, is the most enchanting animal Shizuko and most Taipei residents have ever seen. Thanks to her father's friendship with the zoo manager, Mr. Katsunuma, Shizuko gets to ride Miss Ma a few times and develops a special bond with her. Miss Ma's exalted status is further augmented when she is chosen to preside at a special ceremony held in a Buddhist temple to appease the souls of animals that have died in the zoo, a ritual apparently carried over from similar practices in slaughterhouses in Japan. The last time Shizuko attended one of these ceremonies, the object of pacification also included the souls of dead military animals, or "animal martyrs" (268). The ceremony doubles as a communal festival, keeping alive a sense of human-animal coexistence and codependence, a state of affairs that nonetheless spells dislocation, pain, and doom for animals when humans turn against one another in armed conflict.

A particularly wrenching episode took place after the first American bombs were dropped on Taipei. Following precedents in the Japanese homeland, municipal officials organized a systematic slaughtering of the animals in the Taipei Zoo—both to prevent harm to humans in the event of enclosures being damaged by aerial bombing, and to concentrate scarce resources on the war effort. The killings are described in graphic detail, down to how the remains are carved up and consumed by city officials. But

Miss Ma has been spared because Katsunuma, Shizuko's father, and a few friends took it upon themselves to hide her in a secret underground pass and kept her alive against all odds. Divided between those who hide and care for the animals and those who shoot and eat them, different mixed communities coalesce.

As I have argued elsewhere (H. Lee 2014), animals are quintessential bare life in a zone of indistinction wherein they are alternately a spirit medium, a source of enchantment, a fount of nourishment, an inconvenient burden, and an unaccountable threat. Both morally and legally, they exist in the state of exception, and the emotional bonds some of them form with humans can do little to shield them from the fate of being disposed of as mere matter. The parallel with the fate of civilians in war zones is unmistakable—something poignantly captured in Picasso's *Guernica*, in which the heads of a bull and a horse are part of the jumble of anguished faces and lifeless limbs. In the novel, the massacre of zoo animals is explicitly juxtaposed with the massacre of civilians in the 2/28 Incident of 1947. Soon after Shizuko's return from a stint of medical service on the front, she loses her father to the mass arrests and executions carried out by the Nationalist regime newly installed in Taiwan. The bodies that float down Tamsui River are initially mistaken by locals as sharks because of the way their arms are all bound behind their backs. The Taipei Zoo massacre is a mere prelude to the island-wide human massacre. The inability to care for shared public things presages the breakdown of community and solidarity.

An incipient romance develops between Shizuko and Squad Leader Mu, and their mutual attraction has everything to do with their unusual closeness to animals. It turns out that Mu frequents the zoo only to be with his wartime comrade Lin Wang the elephant, who used to be known to him as Ah Mei. They first met fifty years ago in Burma, when Ah Mei and twelve other elephants were seized by the Nationalists after routing a Japanese contingent that had employed the parade of elephants and their handlers, or mahouts, to transport war supplies. Mu was put in charge of driving the elephants overland to South China to join the war effort there, but along the way half of the elephants were lost to exhaustion and injury. Having reconnected with Ah Mei / Lin Wang, Squad Leader Mu has taken to volunteering at the zoo in order to be close to him, "to be with him wordlessly, one outside the fence, the other inside, both reminiscing about the time they had spent together in the jungle" (Wu Mingyi 2017, 282). When Lin Wang behaves erratically or violently, only Mu understands what is going on, knowing something about the "corrosive effect" of war memories (286). Lin Wang's war trauma is then retold, in greater detail and to a fuller extent, from his own perspective in a separate chapter titled "Limbo." It is a bold stylistic move that, without slipping into anthropomorphism, lifts the elephants out of the zone of indistinction and restores them as intentional subjects with thoughts, feelings, memories, and perceptions that make up the qualia of war as a violent event collectively endured by all living things. In Dingru Huang's words, the chapter is "inscribed with the subaltern heterotemporality of suffering and endurance shared by the elephants and the soldiers" (2019, 67).

The chapter begins with "the elephant" being awakened from his dreams by the sound of firefight. Thereafter the sights, sounds, and smells of jungle warfare are meticulously taken in by him, as presented in the third-person limited point of view. The narrative voice is calm and restrained; even in the face of death and destruction, it is never shrill or hysterical, as if trying to approximate the unhurried dignity of these hulking beasts. Their appearances are described with exactitude, and their inner lives are laid out with subtlety through the use of free indirect style. The effect is eerily powerful and chastening: How easy it is to forget that when humans wage warfare in the jungle, a myriad of life-forms are disturbed, disrupted, uprooted, and destroyed. Trees are burned down, shrubs are flattened, creatures are blown to smithereens; those who survive temporarily are put through all manner of ordeals. The magnitude of the trauma is simply unimaginable, and made so much worse by its utter senselessness to the denizens of the jungle. "The elephant didn't understand why it had been caught up in all this. Its mind, body and past had not prepared it for such a world" (Wu Mingyi 2017, 295). "The elephants had adapted to the jungle, and were now perforce adapting to the fireballs raining down from above, to lead bullets that penetrated their skin and lodged in their guts, and to ubiquitous forest fires. They wordlessly followed the orders of the mahouts, who followed the orders of another group of people who spoke a strange language. Maybe those people were following the orders of another master the elephants could hardly comprehend. Bond after invisible bond bound them. That nobody knew how to break" (297).

But the elephants are never mere dumb tools or passive victims. They have a hyperactive sensorium, and their trunks are able to infiltrate the nocturnal dreams of the soldiers by merely hovering a couple of inches above their slumbering bodies. They can anticipate a parade member's imminent death and mourn the loss with powerful wails. Years later, when Shizuko puts her cheek against Mu's back while riding on the rack of his bicycle, she "heard a kind of voice, non-linguistic, low, muffled, and invested with bodily warmth" (Wu Mingyi 2017, 286). One is tempted to draw a line between the two scenes and see the lovers' feelings for each other as having coursed through these warm pachyderm bodies and comingled with their vast reservoirs of feelings. As they move across jungles, villages, fields, cities, and finally oceans, traveling on foot and by truck, train, and boat, the elephants become worldly creatures. They still retain their pre-ternatural ability to see and smell things humans cannot, but they also learn new roles, such as doing circus tricks to entertain war-weary crowds: "Seeing these giant creatures performing such antics, [the spectators] felt like they had recovered a scrap of dignity" (305).

In this chapter, Mu is not singled out from the generic categories of mahouts, soldiers, and crowds; all humans fade into the background even as they continue to orchestrate the march. Other human markers of time, space, and the material and social world are also blurred, unidentified, or rendered strange. At some point, the elephants are made to carry stones, move lumber, and pack gravel to build a mausoleum in a southern Chinese city, but no details are given as to for whom the mausoleum is meant. Tai-wan, their final destination, is simply referred to as "a torrid island whose rainforest smelled a bit like the jungles of home" (Wu Mingyi 2017, 310). What is described in abundant detail is the elephant's sensory and psychic experiences of the harrowing journey. Back in the present, after endur-ing the torment of posttraumatic stress disorder, the elephant decides to end it all:

So strong was its will to forsake life, it started to force the spirits and souls from its body, one by one. [. . .] The elephant felt everything relaxing—eyebrows, eyelids, pupils, scalp, tongue, ears, cheeks, mouth, throat, land, air and legs. Its legs had carried it countless miles, and now brought it to its final destination in this life. It knelt down on its right foreknee, like an old, collapsing house, and then on its left. Its anus loosened, its legs lost strength and, like boulders roll-ing down a slope, its long lashes closed up upon its small and once bright eyes.

It would never hear another elephant mourning it, in a low rumble of sorrow like silent thunder that carried from the faraway edge of a grassy plain. No, it would pace forever in limbo, in a reflection of a reflection of the jungles, moun-tains and torrents of home. (311)

The death of an elephant, a mere biological event in the eyes of humans, is here rendered in all its somatic, emotional, and spiritual dimensions. Souls are released, body parts are returned to the land, and the sheer loneliness and desolation of the dying elephant recall earlier descriptions of collec-tive mourning and remembrance of other members of the parade. This elephant, being the last of the parade and stranded on a strange island thousands of miles from home, must "pace forever in limbo." Still, in the bond that is growing between Shizuko and Mu, some part of Lin Wang the elephant seems to live on. Just as the elephants are able to read the soldiers' dreams, humans too carry the pain of the elephants as a way of atoning for the trauma and destruction wantonly inflicted on them and their habitats. War is truly a multispecies cataclysm, and victimhood goes far beyond what casualty figures and war crimes trials can possibly disclose.

The death of the elephant is particularly poignant because it is unmourned by its own kind. Humans may assuage their consciences by honoring the interspecies contract that imposes a certain restraint on animal exploitation and brutalization. For example, when the zookeepers executed the big cats, they "bowed deeply at the bodies, not as a gesture of respect, but rather out of an ineffable guilt" (270). Guilt because they have broken the implicit, if also involuntary, agreement that the animals surrender their freedom for the sake of entertaining humans in exchange for food, shelter, and security. Overnight, humans have gone from custodians to executioners. Likewise, when A-hun's father is found dead in the mountains, he is believed to have violated a contract with nature. "The butterfly catchers all said that he'd been lured by the devil, disguised as a rare butterfly, deep in the mountains. Unable to find his way out before night fell, he had stepped off a cliff. Butterfly catchers all believed in a devil of the hills who set quotas for the catchers. Her father had already caught all the butterflies he'd been allotted in his lifetime. He'd carried on catching them anyway—and caught the eye of the devil, too" (Wu Mingyi 2017, 122). In both cases, the feeling of guilt and the symbolic atonement seem a residue of the tradition of acknowledging the claims of the nonhuman on us and our shared habitat.

Ma Boyong's novel *A Grassland Zoo* gets at the other side of the coin with a magical realist tale in which animals rewrite the interspecies contract. Known for his inventive historical novels, Ma merges two historical facts—the decline of the Royal Menagerie and the spread of missionary activity to frontier regions in the final decade of the Qing empire—to create a story of outlandish adventures and incredible encounters. The Menagerie, or Wanshengyuan, the first public zoo in China, opened in 1907, shortly before the fall of Qing. It was created at the recommendation of a reformist minister as part of the New Policy initiatives alongside the establishment of libraries, museums, and parks. A few dozen animals were acquired and shipped from Germany, accompanied by German zookeepers. More animals were subsequently added to the collection as gifts and tributes from provincial officials and foreign visitors. Empress Dowager Cixi took a particular fancy to the Menagerie and visited it multiple times. But after her death in 1908, the Qing state, at its last gasp, no longer paid it any attention. When our protagonist comes for his first visit, the place is a shambles reluctantly tended by three German zookeepers who are eager to raise funds off the remaining creatures for their passage home.

The protagonist of the novel, Morgan Callaway, is an American missionary affiliated with the Congregationalist Church. While browsing a local newspaper, he alights on the idea of purchasing a few of the zoo animals being advertised and using them to attract converts. In the teeth of the mission headquarters' objections, he procures an elephant, a lion, two zebras, five baboons, a parakeet, and a python. It just so happens that he is independently wealthy and is perfectly ready to finance the quixotic trek, with his animal cargo, to his self-chosen destination of Chifeng, a frontier city over four hundred kilometers northeast of Beijing. After much trouble and with a great deal of tenacity, he secures the service of a horse caravan headed by veteran coachman Lao Bi. The animals, all in terrible condition after long neglect, need to be first nursed back to health before setting off on such a long, assiduous journey. Lao Bi's mute son, Xiaoman, turns out to be a great help, for he is an animal whisperer of sorts who befriends the animals effortlessly. Callaway himself is particularly drawn to Wanfu the elephant, their bond to withstand the test of time during their adventure on the grassland.

When the caravan comes across a river, Wanfu discovers the joy of bathing for the first time in her life, having been born and raised in captivity. She douses herself again and again with fresh cool water, and after the encrusted gunk is washed away, she is revealed to be a beautiful white elephant to everyone's amazement. Much of the first half of the novel is similarly taken up with the animals trying to adjust to the new dispensation of becoming mobile and traversing strange terrains and being assailed by unknown stimuli. All along the way, Lao Bi chastises Callaway for his foolhardiness and speaks apprehensively of the perils that lie in wait for them, topmost among which are attacks by a ferocious Mongolian band of outlaws called Jindandao. And sure enough, when they are within shouting distance to Chifeng, the band ambush the caravan, killing all the drivers and seizing the valuables before Huben the lion scares them away and devours one of their horses.

Callaway luckily escapes the assault, but his wits have now completely fled him. At this point, the novel's prose shifts to a magical realist mode, as if trying to capture the preacher's posttraumatic delirium. Guided by an ethereal song drifting over from the edge of the moonlit grassland, he opens all the cages and then stumbles into the darkness in a catatonic state. "In that moment, the moonlight stirred up a nocturnal breeze that blew a mixture of grass seeds and dust into the nostrils of every living being. Each animal seemed a little different. Their gazes grew contemplative, and in their pupils danced fire and moonlight" (Ma Boyong 2017, 132–33). As if entranced, the animals trail Callaway, forming an orderly file reminiscent of Edward Hicks's Noah's Ark (see again figure 6.1):

> Huben's green eyes had turned a shade lighter. He exhibited no interest in the delectable food walking in front of him, only occasionally casting a glance at the backside of the preacher and shaking his mane. The tiger-striped parakeet had at some point returned and landed on Huben's hind quarters, looking about smugly.
>
> As for Wanfu, she had never left the preacher's side, moving quietly, her gaze calm and gentle, and her pale hulk blending into the moonlight.
>
> The song never stopped. Like a nimble snow hare, it vanished when you pricked up your ears, but arose again as soon as you relaxed.
>
> Thus, on the grassland on a silvery night, a black-clad missionary was trudging slowly forward, followed by a file of exotic animals: an elephant, a lion, zebras, baboons, a parakeet, and a python. They did not fight, they did not break order; instead they stayed in a neat formation like soldiers, treading closely on the heels of Callaway. Under the moonlight, man and animals had merged into a solemn dark silhouette moving across the horizon, past the enormous disc of the moon, and toward the far end of the grassland.
>
> This indescribable, fantastic scene repeatedly appeared in the dreams of many residents of Chifeng, though no one could explain why.
>
> This was how everything fell into place. (133–34)

The mysterious song, it turns out, is sung by a Mongolian shamaness who rescues the multispecies band of refugees and conducts them safely to Chifeng. Chifeng, the narrator tells us, sits astride the crossroads of Manchuria and China proper and has flourished as a gathering place for people of different religions, languages, trades, and customs. As the animals approach the city, the narration subtly shifts its reliance on vision to olfaction, presenting them with a hodgepodge of unfamiliar odors. In time, a zoo would be built, and the city would fall in love with it, and in time the city would turn against it, and the animals would be scattered, and the preacher would disappear into the void. Emerging out of this convoluted story is a multispecies allegory in which zoo animals, serving as transitional objects under improbable circumstances, enable the residents of Chifeng to dream a very bold dream. It is as if the residents are taken on a ride on Noah's Ark at the invitation of the animals, only to capsize it in the end.

On the day of their arrival, the animals break free from their temporary shelter in the dead of the night and fan out across the city, trotting, flying, bounding, slithering. "These exotic creatures were filled with a desire to explore this unfamiliar city on the grassland, to walk in every alley and sniff in every corner. The entire city was sound asleep, unaware of these strange intruders in its midst. This was a ritual: before they were to satisfy the curiosity of the city, the city had to first satisfy their curiosity" (Ma Boyong 2017, 176). It is a benign ritual in which no one is harmed. After they are rounded up, the spiritually devout residents, once recovered from their stupefaction, "recognize" Wanfu and Huben as incarnations of the sacred animal icons in Buddhist iconography. This absorption into indigenous cosmology greatly eases the way for Callaway to get the zoo approved by the local magistrate and recruit voluntary labor for its construction, while thwarting the obstruction of the abbots of a local lamaist temple. Callaway then arranges for Xiaoman, now an orphan, to be brought to Chifeng to be his helper. Eventually, the ringleader of Jindandao, the one who killed Lao Bi, comes to hide in the zoo to avoid capture by the government. With the odd trio of zookeepers, the zoo becomes the center of attraction in town and miraculously manages to survive the harsh grassland winter.

Much to Callaway's dismay, however, the visitors are here not so much to "appreciate wild animals" as to pay homage to what they believe to be Buddha's special envoys. He tries to intercept those prostrating before Wanfu and Huben with Christian teachings but is met only with polite, mild interest. He gradually notices that the locals are shockingly promiscuous religiously speaking: "When they discussed business, prayed for health, embarked on a journey, or cursed enemies, they became devotees of completely different deities, even though these deities belonged to different belief systems that were mutually incompatible. It didn't seem to bother these people at all. [. . .] As the preacher saw it, inside each person's head was a zoo. In it an assortment of animals lived peacefully in their own enclosures and occasionally paid one another a visit. But no one animal had dominion over the zoo. It seemed that for the residents of Chifeng this was how the world should operate" (Ma Boyong 2017, 199). Religious syncretism and ecumenicalism are of course in keeping with the city's demographic heterogeneity and cosmopolitan spirit. Indeed, no one bats an eye when a shamaness, a lama, and a few unkempt Buddhist monks come to the assistance of a Protestant missionary. And yet this does not mean that Chifeng is a city on the hill, uniquely free of conflict and violence. The monks, it turns out, are ex-bandits in disguise who are thrilled to find their former chieftain hiding in the zoo. In the end, the abbots of the lamaist temple succeed in turning the city against Callaway and his animals.

Noah's Zoo, as Callaway christens it, rises and falls on the same basis:

as a novel public thing for Chifeng. First of all, unlike a typical commercial zoo, the grassland zoo houses animals that have trekked hither peacefully and stayed more or less voluntarily, having foregone multiple opportunities to escape. They have checked out the city upon their arrival and adopted it as their new home. They quickly become the most honored guests and the pride and joy of the inhabitants. "Everyone was head over heels about the zoo. Inside it, everyone became a kid. [...] Whenever folks from elsewhere came to see the animals, the prideful locals would thrust out their chests and launch into a speech while guiding the newcomers to the zoo. Everyone's eyes sparkled and all felt elated as if the zoo was the city's new totem" (Ma Boyong 2017, 223). Insofar as they are venerated as divine envoys, the animals stand above the residents and exercise a spell over them, uniting them into a new kind of pious community that can overcome their myriad differences and petty disputes. In this capacity the animals transcend their superficial function as objects of mass amusement and tools of religious conversion. They are the transitional objects that are loved and treasured and yet vulnerable and fragile. "It must be acknowledged that by conventional standards, Rev. Callaway's mission was not a success. However, he was well aware of the special place the zoo now occupied in the heart of every Chifeng resident. This wondrous grassland zoo had taken root in everyone's memory, causing the entire city to dream" (265). And more: "Whether a rich man or a poor man, whether a nobleman, a merchant, a peddler, or a foot soldier, whether a Mongol, a Han, a Hui, or a Manchu, for every Chifeng resident, this was a marvelous escape, a pureland that permitted all to take leave of the petty concerns of the mundane world. It was pristine. Having been built here out of sheer curiosity, the zoo was like the grassland sky after a rain, azure from end to end" (266).

True to their status as public things, no one, not even the preacher, is really in control of the animals. The shamaness does a special hypnotic dance that seems to send everyone, human and animal, into a trance, but she does not abuse this power and takes no possession of any of the creatures. The only role she plays in this story is to keep the animals in the "holding environment" of the zoo so that they belong to everyone and no one in particular. It is only when the abbots demand that Wanfu and Huben be brought to their temple in a move to monopolize the animals' prestige and boost their own standing in the community that the zoo comes apart and ceases to be a public thing. The normal wear and tear inflicted on transitional objects then escalates to wanton destruction. Callaway fails to convert a single person to Christianity, and Chifeng is not reborn as a heavenly kingdom in which a lion would lie down with a kid. The Noah's

Ark imagery quoted above, of the animals trailing Callaway in a solemn and peaceful queue, is repeated at the end of the novel, but it is even more evidently a hallucination, the faint trace of an earlier, more vivid dream.

When a mob set fire to the zoo, Huben the lion is shot to death by police while the other animals vanish amid the chaos. The brigand chieftain is believed to have run off with a wolf pack, sowing the seeds for future mischief. The preacher is nowhere to be seen. Only an inconsolable Xiaoman is left behind. Just before the conflagration, the mutual dependency between Callaway, Xiaoman, and the animals is such that they stand together against the rumor-mad mob. Xiaoman is injured trying to defend the animals, Callaway refuses to surrender any of the animals to the vengeful mob, and when he opens all the cages to free them, the animals, once again, refuse to leave: "The animals, including the python, surrounded the makeshift pulpit in the zoo and enclosed the preacher therein, their gazes exuding calm serenity. When he saw this, the preacher was awash in tears. He knew that this had nothing to do with God's will, nor the protective powers of any other divinities. It was the doing of the animals themselves, the animals of Noah's Zoo" (Ma Boyong 2017, 209).

In moments like this, the novel is quite deep in the waters of anthropomorphism. Animals have completely transcended the trophic order and become full participants in human dramas. But the magical realist trope serves to capture a larger truth: the tenuous artificiality of human dominion over wild animals. Xiaoman the animal whisperer's survival is akin to Squad Leader Mu's surviving the war and connecting with Shizuko romantically. All three characters are posthuman avatars whose bodies, sensoria, memories, feelings, and dreams are bound up with those of the animals who have entered their physical, emotional, and moral obits. As survivors, they augur a different future for humanity, one that is premised on what Wu Mingyi calls "weak anthropocentrism" (quoted in D. Huang 2019), en route to truly "becoming animals."

The Chinese Tiger

In the same way that Wu Mingyi's novel balloons out of an obsession with bicycles, Li Kewei's *The Chinese Tiger* bears witness to the obsessive compulsion of a self-professed tiger lover. In high-stepping liveliness, the novel serves up action, suspense, romance, comedy, lyrical rhapsody, and plenty of wonkish disquisition. We learn that the South China tiger has been classified as critically endangered by the International Union for Conservation of Nature since 1996, and is very possibly extinct in the wild given that the major factors contributing to its diminishment—low prey density and habitat degradation and fragmentation—have not changed, even if hunting and poaching have been brought under control. No tigers have been directly observed since the 1980s, and the few dozen specimens in zoos across the country are showing signs of inbreeding.

The situation is so bleak that it takes evidence of three separate incidents to convince the authorities that an outlying tiger may still be prowling the wilderness of Baishanzu: a disemboweled brown bear, a fear-paralyzed farmer, and an indistinct but suggestive snapshot by Gong Ji, a local photographer. Gong shoots to national fame overnight and is added as an honorary member to the team of experts tasked to verify the tiger's existence. The team consists of Captain Zhao, a forest ranger; Professor Lin, a renowned zoologist from the Chinese Academy of Science; Cui Jia'er, a fetching female scientist from the State Forestry Administration; and, much to Gong Ji's chagrin, a tall, fastidious, and Chinese-speaking American wildlife conservation specialist named Quentin Stevens. Also setting out for Baishanzu, albeit stealthily, are a pair of professional poachers, the Peng brothers. On the sidelines are international organizations, Chinese government officials, nature lovers, wide-eyed volunteers, the police, and local residents. A largely forgotten corner of the country suddenly finds itself ground zero of a blockbuster reality show. All of China and a good part of the world are transfixed by the elusive comings and goings of a tiger that seems to have survived in the wild against impossible odds. A nervous and agonistic fellowship emerges in the collective holding of the breath.

After much anticipation and frustration, a solitary female tiger, newly christened Zuzu, is introduced to the reader in a hair-raising close encounter. Midway into the novel, a male tiger named Kuikui also appears on the scene, and from their union issue three cubs, one of which survives at the end of the story to keep hope alive. The novel moves at a brisk pace following the three groups of actors: the investigation team, the poachers, and the tiger family as they act out an imbricated drama of care and injury, love and vengeance, gaiety and anxiety, psychic warfare and physical jousting, ethical heroism and execrable brutality, sublime tragedy and riotous farce. Woven in between are kinetically rendered Technicolor primal scenes of survival up and down the jungle's food chain starring large predators such as jackals, wild boars, bears, leopards, vultures, and of course tigers, as well as a panoply of small but crafty and feisty critters. The breathtaking biodiversity and pulsating vitality of the primeval forest are all too real because half the narrative space is given to nonhuman players and some of the most lyrical and heart-pounding moments occur in the jungle theater. None of the animals speak, yet they communicate and interact through a rich spectrum of sensory languages. Li Kewei captures this otherworldly dimension of the forest biota through frequent shifts of rhetorical registers, from the lyrical to the scientific, the dreamy to the expository, the heavyhearted to the hilarious. A combination of the third-person limited point of view, free indirect discourse, and ventriloquism does much of the heavy lifting in portraying the preternaturally intelligent Zuzu, who not only knows how to see through a trap but also can tell the vicious poachers apart from the well-intentioned investigators-cum-rescuers.

From the very outset, the team has been a contentious bunch, with Gong Ji playing the hotheaded patriot and vainglorious ham who is constantly sniping at Stevens, whom he regards as a romantic rival. Stevens, on his part, is unflappable and has a way of aggravating Gong with his mulish adherence to science and imperviousness to emotional appeals. Caught in the crossfire, Jia'er makes an ineffective peacemaker. And from time to time the wise old Professor Lin has to step in to negotiate a temporary truce. But when a true crisis like Zuzu's going into heat confronts them, they are instantly sucked into even bigger contestations involving many more players, domestic as well as international. After much debate and hand-wringing, a plan is drawn up to mate Zuzu with a zoo tiger. Three rigorously vetted "bridegrooms" are flown to Baishanzu, each with his retinue of keepers and minders. One by one, the zoo tigers make fools of themselves when thrust in the vicinity of Zuzu's lair. The humans observing the farcical spectacles share a hearty laugh at the expense of the pathetic trio, but not without a tinge of regret and soul-searching about what human civilization has done to the erstwhile king of the jungle: "Just think of all those men who are counting on tigers to help boost their virility!" (Li Kewei 2007, 142)—a reference to the tradition of sympathetic magic in Chinese medicine, whereby ingesting animal parts is believed to replenish the corresponding parts in the human body; many a tiger has perished thanks to the demand for their penises and bone marrow; and here, the emasculation of tigers, in a burlesque rendition, is but the tip of the iceberg of the colossal-scale and largely irreversible human depredation of the natural environment.

Throughout the novel, Gong Ji ventriloquize the tigers' motivations and intentions only to be questioned, contradicted, and even ridiculed by the team's scientists. Essentially, Gong plays the role of the artist, striking an unabashedly anthropomorphic stance in order, at a couple of critical junctures, to stop the scientists from seeing the tigers only as broken objects in need of repair. He wants them to think *with* as well as to think *about* the tigers, connecting with the latter as fellow moral beings, with blood that can boil and hearts that can break. For example, in a flashback recounting of Zuzu's lone survival in Baishanzu, the scene in which she witnesses her mother's murder in the hands of hunters is depicted in free indirect style:

> The first things she saw were torches brightly illuminating the mountainside. She crawled forward through clumps of azalea and saw her mother splayed out bloodily on the grass, her skin having already been peeled off. Her familiar motherly scent permeated the surroundings.
>
> Feline animals are semi-color-blind. In their visual world, there are only a few shades of black, white, purple, and gray. So perhaps the color of freshly spilled blood may not be so joltingly frightful.
>
> Yet at this moment, what Zuzu saw was her mother's corpse, her mother's flesh and blood.
>
> She also saw several men remove her mother's head, tail, and limbs with axes, hack her torso into several chunks, and load everything into their shoulder baskets. Lastly, they rolled up the pelt and stuffed it into a basket as well.
>
> . . .
>
> Zuzu fought back rage with all her might. She did not act on her thirst for revenge not because she was scared of the men's weapons, but because her mother, while still living, had drilled it into her that these erect bipeds were so much stronger, crueler, craftier, and more vengeful than tigers. (103–4)

Here the limited point of view apparently belongs to that of the tiger cub; so do the sensory impressions of sight and smell. But the narrator's perspective is also present, busily speculating about the emotional impact of the grisly sight on the young Zuzu. Only in the last paragraph does the narrator infer from Zuzu's nonaction humanlike mental attributes and processes, such as emotion, memory, intelligence, and the capacity for forbearance and future-oriented action.

In due course, Zuzu passes on this vital wisdom to her partner Kuikui. Upon learning of Kuikui's measured attack on the younger brother Peng, Gong Ji connects the dots for his baffled colleagues in the following manner: Having remembered the poachers' scent, the tiger couple patiently lie in wait for the Pengs. When one of them stumbles into the tigers' ambush, however, Zuzu permits Kuikui only to teach him a lesson, as it were, instead of killing him outright. With sincere conviction, "Gong Ji makes a whole bunch of conjectures by treating Kuikui as a person and tells a tall tale about his behavioral psychology and trajectory of action" (253). At the end of his animated speech, even the coolheaded Professor Lin turns agnostic: "Your story is not entirely implausible. But there's no way to prove it, never ever" (254).

The many extravagantly rendered moments of emotional upheaval are more comfortably reserved for the human world, where nervous systems seem synchronized with the biorhythm of the forest. The point, it seems, is that the fates of the animals and humans are irrevocably bound up together, not just emotionally but physiologically. There are several episodes in which animals and humans come to each other's aid at critical moments and often at great peril to themselves. In between, the novel downshifts to lower registers of affective and aesthetic pleasure, particularly humor, irony, and burlesque. In these lighthearted moments, humans voluntarily give up their high and mighty position as the masters of the universe and gladly act clownish if only to accentuate a new ecological equation: the tigers, being the last of their species, are more precious at this moment than many things human. Since their rediscovery, they have seriously disrupted the lives of the locals, what with the banning of foraging, the sealing off of the mountains, and the repeated police combings of the area in search of the poachers.

The novel tacks gingerly between including wildlife in the ever-widening human moral circle as objects of care and compassion on the one hand, and according animals moral agency and subjectivity on the other. Both have affinity with the Lévinasian ethics of responding to the summons of the weak, the vulnerable, and the needy, without regard for whether the object of our moral concern can speak, think, use tools, remember the past, plan the future, or contemplate its own mortality. Our obligation toward others is unconditional, contingent on neither considerations of worth nor anticipation of gratitude or reward (Lévinas 2003). Admittedly, it is an exacting ethic even when applied only to humans. Not all of us can find comfort in an asymmetrical relationship in which our moral sentiments and acts go unacknowledged and unreciprocated, hence the many lurches toward anthropomorphism in a novel that has largely renounced the allegorical mode. It seems impossible to resist the idea that the beneficiaries of our moral largesse will repay us profusely, especially when these are self-locomotive beings who resemble us so vividly.

Although *The Chinese Tiger* strains the reality principle and veers into anthropomorphism to underscore the tigers' moral integrity, remarkably it refrains from reaching for a kumbaya moment, nor does it turn animals into a whip with which to castigate humanity on the conviction that animals can teach us a thing or two about good and evil. Perhaps the author is well aware that there is a thin line separating condemning humanity for its myriad atrocities on the one hand, and on the other justifying human aggression by appealing to our "animal nature." Either way, animals are robbed of their species being in a moral taxidermic operation. Equally remarkably, the novel resists the temptation to point to nature "red in tooth and claw" and trot out the old saw that might makes right, as does Jiang Rong in *Wolf Totem*. In a way reminiscent of *A Grassland Zoo*, it nudges our reading experience toward the aesthetic realm of enchantment in place of an exclusive focus on the moral questions of right and wrong, innocence and guilt, blame and forgiveness. The live theater of the jungle always leaves the human peeping toms shaken, humbled, and profoundly grateful for the lesson that nature is not just something to be exploited and made useful, but also something to be held in awe and at a respectful distance.

To the extent that the tigers are treasured not for their own sake or for the sake of biodiversity, but as China's ecological patrimony and humanity's "public things," the novel is unable to evade the charge of anthropocentrism, nor does it need to. In the final analysis, this is a human story, but one written with the awareness that it is no longer possible to tell any human story in the Anthropocene without animals and the question of biodiversity figuring prominently in it. Zuzu and company are the transitional objects of the research team as well as all who train their attention on the fate of the tiger family in Baishanzu, including the readers. The beleaguered South China tigers give birth to a transnational civil society (as well as its shadowy twin, the criminal underworld) peopled by a host of nonstate actors—scientists, conservation activists, photographers, journalists, forest rangers, farmers, and volunteers—with the state playing an auxiliary role. Together they constitute a global eco-commons. It is a fractious coalition, but also robust and resilient, with Chinese citizens working alongside foreigners as comrades and partners instead of as victims or disciples (as in older narratives featuring foreigners). The former's love of the South China tiger may be rooted in nationalist pride, but it is a capacious love with a cosmopolitan bent. Not once do they question Stevens's membership in the team on the basis of his nationality. What brings the team together is their shared enchantment with and abiding sense of obligation toward something that is precious and yet heartachingly fragile. In the course of the rescue saga, all of them are bruised, scraped, stung, gored, lacerated, frightened out of their wits, or flung about wildly on an emotional roller-coaster ride, but they have relished every moment of it and emerged morally and spiritually reborn, all without a word passed between them and the tigers.

Ecological High and Low Justice

The four animal-themed novels examined in depth in this chapter, *The Tibetan Mastiff, The Stolen Bicycle, A Grassland Zoo*, and *The Chinese Tiger*, are multispecies novels because they treat animal characters as subjects in their own right. And like all multispecies novels, they manifest what Karen Thornber (2012) calls "ecoambiguity," an awareness of the impediments, confusions, and discrepancies that pervade the human engagement with the environment. They skirt cartoonish anthropomorphism while negotiating with the predicament of having to use human language to conjure animal subjectivity. Without pretending to put humans and animals on an equal footing, the novels invite us to imagine human solidarity and redemption through the mediation of animals who are not reduced to a mere prop. The mastiffs, the elephants, and the tigers get to live their own animal lives even as these inevitably and tragically intersect with human lives. All four novels stop short of championing animal liberation, nor do they push the Golden Rule (do as you would be done to) to its logical conclusion to advocate a radical realignment of the interspecies hierarchy. For example, Stevens is teased by his Chinese colleagues as a namby-pamby animal rights "fundamentalist" (*yuanjiaozhi zhuyizhe*) for refusing to swat mosquitos (Li Kewei 2007, 313). All four novels implicitly abide by the "weak anthropocentrism" that Wu Mingyi borrowed from Western ecocriticism.

Species egalitarianism, whether inspired by Lockean liberalism, Latourian flat ontology, Mohist universal love, or Buddhism, seeks to apply the principle of equality to all living beings. But it is fundamentally incompatible with the hierarchy of the trophic order, the long history of human terraforming and animal breeding, and the asymmetrical relations of care between humans and other species. The Darwinian principle is not, as Mark Sagoff quips, a humanitarian principle (2001, 89). Ecosystems are pyramidal and premised on the trophic relations between producers and consumers, predators and prey. This is what Aldo Leopold's "land ethic" unblinkingly recognizes and also why it often clashes with animal rights (see H. Lee 2018). We might say that the land ethic honors environmental high justice, with its concern for populations, species, and ecosystems, whereas animal rights is chiefly focused on low justice, or the fair treatment of nonhuman individuals. Between the two is a pragmatist approach to multispecies justice that stops short of asserting that all things exist equally.

This pragmatist ethics is propounded by Sue Donaldson and Will Kymlicka. They fault animal rights theory for failing to recognize the "relational duties" we owe nonhuman animals on the basis of our historically conditioned differential relationships to various categories of animal species. In its place, they propose a three-pronged model that treats (1) wild animals as strangers forming sovereign communities on their own territories, (2) liminal opportunistic animals as migrants or denizens who live in the interstitial spaces of human habitation, and (3) domesticated animals who have been bred and groomed to cohabit with humans and serve human purposes (Donaldson and Kymlicka 2011, 14). Just as our relationships to strangers, denizens, neighbors, and dependents engender different duties—"duties of care, hospitality, accommodation, reciprocity, or remedial justice" (6)—there cannot be a one-size-fits-all ethic governing our duties to all animals. Zoo animals, moreover, cut across all three categories, making our relationship to them even more contingent and improvisational.

Donaldson and Kymlicka further point out that animal rights theory is largely indifferent to the perils of slow violence, which does not involve the direct killing or capturing of individual animals. Conversely, if an animal's right to live and thrive required a safe and healthy environment, humans would be obligated to intervene, on a massive scale, "in the wilderness in order to protect animals from predators, food shortages, and natural disasters" (2011, 11). Baird Callicott likewise points to the questionable logic of species egalitarianism, which when pushed to an extreme would outlaw all trophic processes beyond photosynthesis (2001, 149). Indeed, anything short of the death of human civilization is only a compromised effort to restore to animals their right to live and flourish without human interference and obstruction. With the exception of parasites, certain insects, rodents, and domestic animals, most animals do not benefit from our presence on this planet. On the contrary, they are faced with mass extinctions in an anthropogenic biodiversity collapse.

In full cognizance of this fundamental asymmetry, Wai-chee Dimock sketches a new ethics for the Anthropocene that stands the myth of Noah's Ark on its head: Instead of proceeding from a position of strength and dominion, humanity needs to touch base with its existential condition of weakness, vulnerability, and susceptibility to harm. Only then can we hope to bounce back from the ecological catastrophes of our time, in the long haul, through resilience and "the steadfast presence of a mediating network" (Dimock 2020, 7). Our survival is and will always be "assisted survival": "Hanging on perilously and not by its effort alone, it needs an infrastructure, a support team on permanent standby, making up for imperfect outcomes with incessant labor" (7). For Dimock, an essential part of this support network is literature, with its persistence, its continual crowdsourcing, and its inclination to imagine the world as other than it is. We can also circle back to Honig's idea of "public things" (2017) as transitional objects, on "permanent standby" (Dimock 2020, 7) and seeing us through the crises of our own making. We tend to them so that they can assist our survival, and deliver us from perdition.

The pragmatist approach insists on keeping both high justice and low justice in sight. It proceeds from the recognition that nonhuman species have long been incorporated into humanity's support network through terraforming and domestication. What we call "nature" is not a separate domain that can be fenced off and declared off-limits, but a vast reservoir of hospitality that supplies us with nourishment, warmth, tools, labor power, entertainment, companionship, protection, playmates, and transitional objects. In our hubris and in our eagerness to overcorrect our ecological impact, we have underappreciated animals in their prosthetic role. We career from crass instrumentalism to naive romanticism, sentimentalizing wildlife as wholly autonomous. We forget that even exotic animals straddle the boundaries between nature and culture because, in enchanting us, they help us realize our human potential for play and collective action.

As "a newly constituted endangered species," humans have to learn to make weaker claims on the planet and take their place among other endangered life-forms (Dimock 2020, 4). This lesson is given flesh in Yann Martel's *Life of Pi* (2001). In a rebuke to *Robinson Crusoe* and *The Old Man and the Sea*, *Life of Pi* recounts, in the retrospective voice of the protagonist Pi, the 277 days that he spent in a lifeboat with an adult Bengal tiger adrift the Pacific Ocean after a shipwreck killed his entire family and their stock of zoo animals. Pi makes utmost use of the lifeboat's sundry provisions as well as his human ingenuity to keep "Richard Parker" the tiger at bay. The greatest challenge is of course feeding the tiger with enough meat so that it does not feed on him, and meeting that challenge consumes all his attention and energy, leaving little room for despair or boredom. His adult narrative voice tells us that he fully credits the tiger's urgent appetite for his improbable survival. Yet unlike the relationships between human and nonhuman characters in the multispecies novels discussed in this chapter, the relationship between boy and tiger is not a moral one of mutual care and devotion, but a trophic one held in abeyance. The tiger is kept in its end of the lifeboat only through the combined tactics of threat, torment, manipulation, and clever evasion, not tenderness or trust. In return, the tiger shows no gratitude. After they are finally washed ashore on a Mexican beach, the tiger jumps off the boat and waddles into the jungle without so much as casting a single glance at Pi, his companion, caretaker, and savior for many months, leaving Pi weeping desolately in the sand.

Pi does not bond with the tiger in the sentimental mode of popular animal stories that simply erase the trophic logic that governs animal existence. But the close proximity of an animal "at large," one that does not renounce its animality, has done much more to call out his humanity and cast it in sharp relief. *Life of Pi* returns us full circle to the cat-and-mouse tales with which we began this chapter. In both cases, multispecies justice is not about achieving or imposing species egalitarianism. Pi's position is analogous to the mouse's: before the big cat, he cannot demand friendship or beg for mercy on egalitarian or right-to-life grounds. Instead of seeking redress in the underworld, an outlet no longer available in the modern world, Pi treats the cat with a combination of affection, respect, fear, loathing, and Machiavellian trickery, and out of this vortex arise peace, purpose, and wholeness. Multispecies justice is not about restoring nature to its prelapsarian tranquility. By way of concluding this chapter, let us see how Su Tong's (2004) short story "The World's Most Desolate Zoo" ("Shijie shang zui huangliang de dongwuyuan") exemplifies this pragmatist ethos.

The "I" narrator in this story is a young student who is sent to an abandoned zoo by his art teacher to practice life drawing. There he finds a few sickly animals that were left behind after the zoo moved to a new location. His favorite models are a pair of monkeys. On one of his visits there, he runs into his biology teacher, who seems to have some private, shady dealings with the old zookeeper. The biology teacher, the student learns, is looking to acquire the abandoned animals for his taxidermic collection and is making steady inroads through bribery and quid pro quo. On a stormy day the two men kill the older monkey, and a few days later the student discovers his stuffed shell in the teacher's lab. The older monkey used to have a blind eye, having lost it to a drunk zoogoer wielding an iron rod. The student was having trouble drawing that lifeless eye. He doesn't understand why his art teacher insists that the only way to capture "the spirit of the animal" (Su Tong 2013, 49) is to get the blind eye right. Now the biology teacher has in a way done the work for him: He has restored the eye taxidermically and made it "bright and faultless" (57).

The student is caught between two conflicting approaches to the nonhuman. Although both teachers profess love for animals, the upshots of their loves cannot be more divergent. Whereas the biology teacher desires perfection and is willing to go to great lengths to create the "miracle" (Su Tong 2013, 57) of a perfect specimen, the art teacher accepts nature as imperfect and animals as leading a curtailed and damaged existence courtesy of humans (represented here by the cages and the drunkard). In urging his student to attend to the scars of injury and tears of sorrow, the art teacher is saying that we must face the ugly, broken reality and acknowledge the consequences of our action. It is only when the student feels the monkey's anguish that he understands his teacher's words: "It seemed to me that I was seeing the actual moment that the monkey had lost its eye, and an intense, piercing pain suddenly coursed through my entire body.

I felt like I had captured the spirit my drawing teacher had talked about, and this spirit was anguish" (51). After this he can no longer stomach the sight of the stuffed animals in the biology teacher's lab.

The biology teacher's love of animals takes the form of control and perfection: living animals are not nearly as lovable as his taxidermic recreations. His lab is essentially a modern Noah's Ark with a collection of "clean and tranquil" (Su Tong 2013, 57) specimens elevated to a utopian moral plane by their human shepherd: no struggle for existence, no nature red in tooth and claw, no blind eyes. When the student questions the zookeeper about the killing, the old man defends his action: "Is there anything people don't kill easily? [...] The relationship between me and Mr. Xu runs very deep. He did me a great favor, and I had no choice but to agree to his request. People aren't like animals. People have to listen to their consciences" (56). Self-contradictory as he may sound, he is merely practicing a relational ethic whereby he owes a greater obligation to his grandson (whom the teacher helped place in a good school) than to the unwanted zoo animals.

The sad irony is that when humans try to act ethically, animals are readily sacrificed, as bargaining chips or tokens of exchange. Animal lives and freedom are abrogated as the price of human morality and progress. After all, the biology teacher's lab is a pedagogical instrument, meant for the enlightenment and edification of pupils like the narrator. The fact that the narrator practically flees from the lab tells us that something is wrong with the way humans have come to relate to the nonhuman world. It is the art teacher's urgings we should heed: Instead of trying to make nature whole and perfect, instead of expecting gratitude and reciprocity, we need to attend to the wounds and anguish that pervade animal existence and come to terms with our complicated entanglements with it. We should and must care for animals without having to make them our equals. In turn they will help us help them. This is what a pragmatist model of multispecies justice enjoins.

CONCLUSION

To end a dispute in justice, one always has to seek out something other than justice.

LUC BOLTANSKI

A Larger Loyalty, a Higher Loyalty

To a large extent, this book was inspired by the final, resounding phrase of the Pledge of Allegiance: "and liberty and justice for all." It proceeded from the suspicion that justice may not be a self-evident, universal good. In China, as I have argued, justice is split into high and low justice, and this vertical nexus has structured the Chinese legal imagination in ways that render it opaque to those acculturated in a liberal state of law. The justice narratives that I have surveyed in this book thus reveal an ecosystem with very different terrains, climes, flora and fauna, and atmospheric disturbances. And yet it is not wholly unrecognizable. I will use the following space to draw some broad observations about the different justice orientations in China and the United States. For the sake of simplicity, let me say that, for the most part, justice in China is a vertical concept, whereas in the United States it is a horizontal one.

In the liberal tradition, justice has always been regarded as an inherent good in the deontological sense, a transcendent principle standing apart from loyalty to family, tribe, and nation. It is the principle of fairness as guaranteed by due process and inextricably bound up with the rule of law. Taking exception to this legalist view, Richard Rorty (1997) proposes that we instead regard justice as a larger loyalty, an allegiance to ever-larger communities that may ultimately embrace all humanity. In this light it does not merely belong to law's empire but tracks morality closely. He builds on Michael Walzer's (1994) model of morality that goes from "thick" to "thin," from the circles of family and neighbors to distant strangers, from primordial affection and reciprocal trust to moral obligation and respect for human dignity. As our loyalty expands, it grows increasingly weak and has to rely on institutional scaffolds and legal guard rails. This thinning-out process is what we commonly, but mistakenly in Rorty's view, refer to as the triumph of reason. Moral dilemmas do not arise from the incompatibility between parochial loyalty and universal justice, supposedly underwritten by the opposition between emotion and reason, but rather from the conflict of different scales of loyalty, or conflict between "alternative selves, alternative self-descriptions, alternative ways of giving a meaning to one's life" (Rorty 1997, 12).

Although Rorty urges his readers to strive for ever-larger loyalty, his reformulation creates an opening to the idea that loyalty to one's own clan or country and the favoritism and parochialism it subtends are not inherently unjust. This is precisely how Stephen Asma finds ground to reject fairness as the essence of justice, contending that favoritism or nepotism, within bounds, should not be categorically spurned as the enemy of justice. He cites the example of Confucius affirming the supremacy of familial loyalty when hearing of a son who turned his sheep-stealing father in to the authorities, a case we also encountered in the introduction of this book. Confucius's advice that the son shield the father and vice versa would probably grate on the ears of those reared on an ethical education dead set against according moral privilege to kith and kin: "From children's stories to religious parables to technical philosophies, we are encouraged to eliminate our personal connections from considerations of justice. The idea of fairness that many of us are raised on requires us to assign all parties equal weight. Lady Justice herself is often represented as blindfolded when she balances her scales. She cannot factor in people's money, status, or power, and she cannot play favorites" (Asma 2013, 15). Asma traces this hostility to favoritism to the Enlightenment project to render society into a grid, with each unit perfectly commensurate and value neutral. Ethics would then become a branch of mathematics or physics, and society would be governed entirely by impersonal and impartial rules.

Asma points out that most people outside the liberal West do not see their societies as defined by this "grid of impartiality." And he believes that it can be salutary for Westerners to "get off the grid" and entertain an ethics that goes beyond defending individual rights and adjudicating competing interests (2013, 57). In making this point he references Jonathan Haidt's work, which builds on the moral foundations theory advanced by Richard Shweder and colleagues (1997), previewed in the introduction. To review, the ethics of autonomy predominates in affluent liberal democratic societies and emphasizes individual rights, liberty, equality, harm reduction, and justice as fairness. In much of the rest of the world, the ethics of community and divinity are the keystones of the moral edifice. Communitarian values such as duty, authority, respect, honor, and loyalty are exalted, and individualist ones are regarded with ambivalence and circumspection. Communal solidarity, moreover, is strengthened through codes of conduct based on the distinction between purity and pollution, sacrifice and sin, the sacred and the profane.

Haidt (2012) has fine-tuned and expanded this tripartite schema to account for the polarization of the American political and moral landscape. For my purpose here, I find most compelling his analogy of liberal morality to the fictional Flatland under the pen of Edwin Abbot (see the introduction). In the Flatland the squares and circles simply cannot comprehend what it is like to be a sphere. In a way, Rorty's reformulation of justice as a larger loyalty is still bound by the Flatland thinking of liberalism, as it envisions justice on a horizontal plane, rippling further and further out to cover the entire ocean of humanity and beyond. Justice as a larger loyalty is reckoned in terms of closeness and distance, thickness and thinness, but not high and low, sacred and profane. It reaches for ever-greater fairness, pitting what we owe to our loved ones against what we owe to distant strangers without a road map that is "politically realistic, historically grounded, and psychologically compelling" (Bell 1998, 577–78).

Like Asma, other contemporary moral philosophers have tried to bound out of the liberal Flatland and grant greater recognition to the vertical dimensions of the moral experience still palpable in the liberal West, albeit under a kind of theoretical embargo. They have found a rich fount of inspirations in non-Western philosophy that helps them stretch their theorization beyond rights and fairness to include such virtues as patriotism and piety. Daniel Bell and Pei Wang argue that hierarchies—among intimates, citizens, and states, and between humans and animals—can be morally justified if they are not founded on violence or fixed for eternity (2020, 18). Roger Scruton turns to both Hegel and Confucius for greater attention to the virtue of piety in the spheres of family and state. In Confucianism, he writes, "the ability to recognize and act upon unchosen obligations indicates a character more deeply imbued with trustworthy feeling than the ability to make deals and bide by them" (Scruton 2017, 126). Hegel sees the state as offering a bond of allegiance that rescues people who struggle to break away from the ties of the family but flounder in civil society's sphere of free choice and contract (Scruton 2017, 127).

Patriotism is more "abstract" (imaginary) and "rational" (thin) than kinship bonds—recall Michael Mann's (1984) point about states' claim to universality vis-à-vis particularistic ties—but it is still rooted in emo-

tion and powerfully so thanks to the workings of ideological state apparatuses. It can inspire such passionate devotion that, to use one of Rorty's
examples, one is willing to leave one's parents in the lurch by going off to
fight in wars (1997, 12). Patriotic loyalty thus anchors a higher justice, beyond what the liberal state of law can deliver. But when one unflinchingly
chooses the chambermaid or valet who happens to be one's mother or
father over the archbishop to rescue first from a burning building, one is
also honoring a higher loyalty, not a narrower loyalty (Asma 2013, 170; Bell
1998, 559). When Albert Camus withheld his support for Algerian nationalists' resorting to terrorist bombings, he simply had to imagine his own
mother riding in the tramways.[1] Much of modern moral philosophy, from
Kant to John Rawls, can be summed up as a relay effort to remove this situational element from the grid of impartiality. Following Rawls, Paul Kahn
(2001, 169) locates freedom in our ability to inhabit the "original position"
in which we bracket all our particularistic commitments and voluntarily
work from behind a veil of ignorance to legislate a just society. Once such
a society is in place, we would all be bound by its rules, come what may.

In her critique of legalism, Judith Shklar quotes H. L. A. Hart in naming
justice as "the most legal of virtues." The virtue of justice, she elaborates,
is "the commitment to obeying rules, to respecting rights, to accepting
obligations under a system of principles" (Shklar 1986, 113). The morality
of rule following, however, has to compete and compromise with other
values such as love, service, charity, even aesthetic enhancement. Love
and service return us to our vertical relationships with family and state,
piety and patriotism. From the latter perspective, rule following may well
be regarded as "an inferior attribute and an unworthy end" (Shklar 1986,
113). Plato's solution is to redefine justice to align it better with the higher
morality of love and service. "Here the educative polity in pursuit of harmony was termed just, in opposition to the legalistic politics of 'dueness'
which was rejected as inferior. To do this, justice must be identified with
insight into moral truth in the individual and with social harmony in collective life" (113).

This comes close to the Confucian conception of high justice, whereby
rule following at whatever cost has never been elevated as a virtue. As noted
in the introduction, because political legitimacy rests on a cosmic-moral
foundation and is embodied in the ruler's virtue, the state has no incentive
to delegate the ministration of justice to an impersonal, procedure-bound
system, that is, an independent judiciary. Low justice cannot become an
autonomous domain that does not redound to the cause of high justice.
Leaving low justice in a weak, inadequate, and informal state paradoxically
strengthens high justice by compelling the aggrieved to ascend the ladder

of litigation and petition and viscerally experience the vertically growing potency of the state. Instead of building a judicial infrastructure dedicated to procedural justice, the state prefers to retail substantive justice and accrue moral and political capital from each transaction. This vertical orientation of justice would be pushed to an extreme in Mao's China, where the morality of rule following was labeled "formalism" (*xingshi zhuyi*) and legal justice a bourgeois conceit and a tool of oppression. Maoism is thus one of the "grand ideologies of the present century [that] have no use for justice" (Shklar 1986, 114). In the era of socialist rule of law, the Party does have use for rule-based justice, but informality, opacity, and discretion are still at the heart of one-party rule. As Christian Sorace observes, "the legitimacy of Communist Party rule depends less on its institutionalization and more on the 'cultivation' (*xiuyang*) and work style of its cadres" (2017, 40–41).

The liberal West, on the contrary, has mostly followed Aristotle rather than Plato on whether rule following is a moral good, and redirected its attention to the source and content of just rules. Joseph Henrich (2020) attributes the rise of "impersonal prosociality," as opposed to "interpersonal prosociality" (i.e., nepotism), to the Christian Church, among other forces, which broke up kin-based institutions in the Middle Ages and shifted Europe's course of cultural evolution toward WEIRD (*W*estern, *e*ducated, *i*ndustrialized, *r*ich, and *d*emocratic) preferences for abstract thinking, impersonal markets, and impartial law. For Shklar the truly WEIRD religion is legalism:

> To see the deep roots that legalism and trials have in Western culture one need think only of the part which legal imagery plays in literature, in metaphor, and in religious discourse of every kind. The court of love, the court of conscience, the trial of wits, the court of honor, Judgment Day—how much these phrases tell us about ourselves! How many trial scenes appear in dramas and novels! How central to our everyday speech and to our imagination is the picture of a contest between diametrically opposed wills, judged according to some general rule! Even fate as we think of it behaves legalistically. The trial, the supreme legalistic act, has served us with an image around which we have structured a vast variety of experiences—ethical, religious, and aesthetic. (Shklar 1986, 181)

In his advocacy of the cultural study of law, Kahn also comments on the degree to which the rhetoric of rule of law has shaped the American identity. "The deepest criticism that one can make of political behavior is that it is in violation of a legal norm. Who in this country does not believe that 'not even the President is above the law'? And who does not understand the deep resonance of the assertion, in the face of injustice, that the injured party is going to take the case 'all the way to the Supreme Court'?" (Kahn 2001, 152). The Supreme Court, though not immune to political controversy, is venerated as "the literal embodiment that ours is 'a government of laws, and not of men'" (141–42). Jerold Auerbach likens American legal pietism to that of medieval religious zeal, noting that "law is our national religion; lawyers constitute our priesthood; the courtroom is our cathedral, where contemporary passion plays are enacted" (1983, 9). This may well be how Americans come off to outsiders: "To peoples of certain non-Western cultures, often less confident in or hopeful for their legal institutions, this faith in law's extraordinary restorative potency seems nearly indistinguishable from their belief in magic, as they are quick to observe" (Osiel 2019, 147).

Unlike priests or shamans, however, lawyers enjoy a scurrilous reputation grossly incongruous to the augustness of law. For every Arthur Kirkland (*And Justice for All*, 1979), there are a dozen Saul Goodmans (*Breaking Bad*, 2008–13). As we noted in the introduction, this incongruence in part has to do with law's alignment with a narrow strip of the moral landscape, concerning itself chiefly with, to use Haidt's typology, care/harm, fairness/cheating, and (minimally) liberty/oppression, while leaving loyalty/betrayal, hierarchy/subversion, sanctity/degradation to religion. This is more familiarly known as the doctrine of the separation of church and state. Nonetheless, to a greater and greater degree American political contests, not excluding presidential elections, are fought in the courts, as legal claims and counterclaims. In the same way that the market has gobbled up large swaths of social and cultural life under neoliberalism (Satz 2010), law has become a master metaphor that has effectively pushed out alternative ways of conducting politics (Sumption 2019). In Luc Boltanski's language (2012), the regime of justice has eclipsed the regime of love so that people's repertoire of action has been reduced to either denunciation or violence. Consequently, the questions that dominate the national conversation have been narrowed to two: What should and should not be for sale? And what should and should not be criminalized? And the two are also increasingly being braided into one in the carceral state where "justice is sold for a fee" (Auerbach 1983, 9).

Kahn maintains that the discourse of law's rule should not be reduced to a discourse of rights, as both liberal and communitarian thinkers tend to do. Rather, it is a language of both legitimacy (high justice) and rights (low justice). "The American discourse of legitimation through law's rule is a discourse of popular sovereignty. We only get to the discourse of rights when we ask what it is that the popular sovereign 'says'" (2001, 156). This is where high justice has a small toehold in the American legal imagination. Its absence from much political theory is a feature, not a bug, of the Flatland of American political and moral life. Kahn acknowledges that popular sovereignty is remote from most people's day-to-day reality and does not frame how they define themselves, especially among disadvantaged groups who see themselves "as victimized by the majority's actions and beliefs, which they perceive to be embodied in the law" (156). And yet these groups still have to frame their fight for recognition and rights within the discourse of law's rule. This is indeed the case when one considers the prolonged battle over hate crime legislation, which is fundamentally an effort to prosecute systemic inequities at the level of low justice. Consider also how the earth justice movement has centered on "earth jurisprudence" and the securing of legal rights for the nonhuman: rivers, forests, wetlands, animals, or nature as such.[2]

However, law's rule has no shortage of detractors, from both the left and the right. Kahn wants his fellow scholars of jurisprudence to keep in mind "that people have lives of meaning outside of law's rule, [and] that many of our richest and deepest experiences must be protected from the imperialism of law's rule" (quoted in Osiel 2019, 133). Conservatives have long chafed against the separation of church and state and rallied behind high justice crusades against terrorism and illegal immigration. On the left, the Black Power movement of the 1970s and today's Black Lives Matter protests also grew out of a profound frustration with law's limitations and complicity. The injustices that Black citizens experience on a daily basis reveal high justice as a source of oppression—as both motivation and justification for "tough on crime" legislation and mass incarceration (Alexander 2010). This instrumentalization of law as a tool of governance, whether one calls it "governing through crime" (Simon 2007) or "rule by law" (*fazhi*), is where the United States and China are converging.

Black Lives Matter activists are not necessarily agitating for revolution in spite of the calls to defund the police and occasional confrontational tactics in the streets. Many harken back to the nonviolent tradition of Martin Luther King Jr. and invoke the ideal of mercy, "a state of grace that is beyond, not below, law" (Kahn 2001, 161). Mercy is also the note on which Bryan Stevenson (2014) concludes his harrowing account of his decades-long fight for the rights of death-row inmates and other voiceless victims caught in the relentless, vengeful, and racist machinery of criminal justice in the American South. The rule of law in the view of the dominant society is a triumph over the state of nature, but for Stevenson and his clients, it is a tragedy of our fallen condition.

As a practicing lawyer, Stevenson also observes a contrapuntal trend:

the attenuation of high justice in the American judiciary. Before the era of governing through crime, he notes, a violent crime was a crime against an entire community, and the district attorney prosecuted the case on behalf of the community in pursuit of vertically imposed justice. Today, with the rise of victim advocacy (most notably the inclusion of victim impact statements in trials), violent crimes have been privatized. The kind of communal demand for retributive justice that Lily Tsai (2021) argues is the key to regime support in China has quieted down owing to its association with carceral governance and retrograde politics. Instead, the prosecutor increasingly acts like a lawyer for the victim's party, a trend that pits the defendant and the victim against one another as individuals. The justice sought is thus horizontal low justice, while high justice in the name of the community drops out of the picture altogether. A by-product of the stripping bare of low justice—of pitting individuals against one another and framing all political and social conflicts as legal contests—is the growing loss of trust in governmental authority and disinvestment in the common good. When the principles of general equivalence are themselves in dispute, the regime of justice becomes inoperable for lack of second-order metrics for measuring and comparing the claims of the disputants (Boltanski 2012, 91). The bungled response to the Covid-19 pandemic in the United States is only the latest and most grievous manifestation of this fraying of the American social fabric that scholars and observers have been lamenting for several decades (Putnam and Garrett 2020). Blinkered by a tunnel vision of liberty and justice, many Americans are not willing to make the kind of sacrifices that impinge on their rights and liberties. Lawsuits challenging shelter-in-place and face-covering orders are merely the tip of the iceberg of a political-legal culture that recognizes only horizontal low justice.

Horizontal Justice, Vertical Justice

It may surprise Stevenson that the American adversarial model of jurisprudence, visible in the very layout of the typical courtroom in session, has long served as a beacon for legal reformers in China. When Liu Renwen (2015, 234) sat in on several jury trials in the United States in the 2000s, he was amazed to find defendants, in suit and tie, sitting next to their similarly attired counsels, making it hard to tell the former apart from the latter. He also notes that the defense team and the prosecution team are seated at identical tables facing the bench, a spatial arrangement that grants the two sides moral equality. The trial rather resembles a sports competition between two evenly matched teams with the judge and jury acting as referees. It is a temporal process unfolding in an orderly way in the space of horizontal justice.

China's inquisitorial system, in contrast, uses the courtroom configuration to visualize vertical justice. The accused, usually in prison garb and handcuffed and shackled, stands alone in a box in the center of the courtroom facing the bench on a raised dais. The prosecution and the defense are arrayed on the two sides of the chamber, away from the defendant. In Liu's view, this arrangement places the defendant at an undue disadvantage (Liu Renwen 2015, 347–49). The cage-like box and the sartorial rules invite the presumption of guilt and the sentiment of contempt before any formal verdict has been rendered. Moreover, the inability of the defendant to communicate with his or her attorney (or anyone else, including family members present) unnecessarily accentuates the inquisitorial nature of the proceedings by symbolically pushing the defense team toward the state. And yet as we have noted in the introduction, that is precisely the design: When individuals commit a crime (or are accused of doing so), they have disrupted peace and harmony in the community and turned their backs on their fellow citizens. They have taken themselves out of the community's embrace and are now confronting it as estranged, hostile entities. The defense and the prosecution are *both* duty bound to assist the judge, acting on behalf of the community, to bring the accused to justice. The rights and dignity of the accused must be subordinated to the overriding imperative to restore order and repair the social fabric they have breached.

The Chinese courtroom layout and sartorial convention thus communicate very effectively the hierarchy of high and low justice and preserve what Stevenson believes is lost in American criminal justice. The elevation of high justice above low justice is the bedrock of Chinese political-legal culture and a leitmotif that runs throughout the justice narratives surveyed in this book. The philosopher Li Zehou has distilled the hierarchy of high and low justice into a maxim: "Harmony above justice" (*hexie gaoyu gongzheng*). In his response to Michael Sandel, he uses *gongzheng* or *gongping* to translate Sandel's communitarian notion of justice. Drawing on ancient Chinese philosophy, he proposes three harmonies as the basic structures of feeling that should underwrite the commonweal and the good life: interpersonal harmony (*renji hexie*), body-soul harmony (*shenxin hexie*), and ecological harmony (*tianren hexie*). On the one hand, a society must place all three harmonies above justice defined as the fair and rational adjudication of right and wrong. On the other hand, harmony cannot replace justice. It can only guide and structure justice when appropriate but cannot determine justice. Harmony is an ethical and pedagogical project (*yi de hua min*) whereas justice is a tool of governance (*yifa zhiguo*) (Li Zehou 2014, 47).[3]

Translated into practice on the ground, Li's ideas have their counterpart in the renewed interest among legal scholars in the tradition of mediation and other informal methods of settling disputes. Philip Huang, for example, regards mediation as an undervalued pillar of the Chinese legal system: "Mediation . . . is about virtue, even more than justice. It is about 'harmony,' not rights and their violations" (2015, 7). Likewise, Su Li (2006) has forcefully argued against the wholesale implementation of the adversarial model of legal justice in China, citing its potential to displace indigenous methods of dispute resolution. He discusses two films to illustrate the dangers of an unrelenting commitment to the rule of law. In *Defendant Uncle Shangang* (*Beigao Shangangye*) (Fan Yuan 1994), a local official (the eponymous Uncle Shangang) who resorts to old-school methods such as public shaming to enforce social norms is arrested for driving an abusive daughter-in-law to suicide. When he is taken away in handcuffs, the whole village comes out to give him a tearful send-off on their knees. How is it that when the state brings the might of law to defend the people against abuse of power, it wins not their gratitude but befuddlement and resentment?

Su Li believes the problem lies in the state's double failures: one, it does not allocate the requisite resources for bona fide legal services in remote regions except in serious criminal cases; two, it fails to recognize the legitimacy of the informal rules and customs that locals have employed to settle disputes from time immemorial. Stuck in a dualist mind-set, the state regards any practice that deviates from the ideal of rule of law as the "tyrannical rule of man" (2006, 379), which must be rooted out. Thus the state presents a quandary to Uncle Shangang and his fellow villagers: "When a mother-in-law is mistreated, the formal judicial apparatus can't do anything about it, yet it won't allow the villagers to take the matter into their own hands. We blame Uncle Shangang for being illiterate about the law, but why should he bother with any law that has so little to do with village life?" (379). However unsavory the means, Su Li seems to suggest, if it serves the goal of harmony and if it is acquiesced to by the community at large, then it has the force and legitimacy of law and should be tolerated.[4]

On the face of it, the case for informal, moralistic, and substantive justice made by Li, Huang, and Su is fairly solid. But that is only because they make their case in the abstract, divorced from the specific course that twentieth-century Chinese political-legal history has taken. They posit a more or less intact, prototypical organic rural society fully capable of governing itself before the arrival of an intrusive state bent on imposing its modernizing agenda. What they skip over is the far-reaching impact of "state involution" that, according to Prasenjit Duara (1988), has upended the balance of power between center and locality and hollowed out local self-governance. In their overzealous drives to modernize China, early twentieth-century states sought to bureaucratize informal power structures, which had traditionally remained beyond the reach of the imperial state. The result was the destruction of local autonomy and the penetration of despotic, extractive state power down to the village level. Local elites morphed into opportunistic "local tyrants and evil gentry" (*tuhao lieshen*) whose foremost allegiance was owed to the state rather than the community. Once the state has liquidated these local strongmen in its many political campaigns, the power vacuum is sooner or later filled by Party or Party-backed officials, a fact that the state is often reluctant to acknowledge. The film *Courthouse on Horseback* (*Mabei shang de fating*) (Liu Jie 2006), an ode to the socialist service ethic, posits an anomic state of affairs in a remote mountain village whose members are unable to resolve even the most trifling of domestic squabbles, hence the need for the county judiciary to dispatch a horse-powered mobile courthouse to do the job for them. It's a job that entails trekking across miles and miles of treacherous mountain paths, transfiguring an imposition of state power as paternalistic self-sacrifice.

In some ways, the state has been thinking along lines similar to those pursued by Su Li and others. For example, it promoted the "village compacts" (*xiangyue*) movement in the 1980s in the name of stemming the tide of moral decline and social decay. Ann Anagnost asks us to attend to the degree to which these compacts, which are "supposed to operate entirely through the force of moral persuasion and public opinion" (1997, 145), are propped up by coercion, such as fines and physical punishment and detention. When the Party denounces the "crude methods" (*tu banfa*) deployed by local officials like Uncle Shangang, it in effect obfuscates the question of responsibility: "Indeed, the routinization of this disavowal suggests yet another example of the 'euphemization' of the violence of the state, in which the local party officials operate as 'loose cannons' to deliver results desired by the center in exchange for the local concentration of power in their hands. In other words, the supplementarity of the compacts gives special license to local officials to abuse the power limits of their authority, and this ability to exceed the limits is something that the center is absolutely dependent on in order to function at all" (145). Her example is *Qiuju Goes to Court* (*Qiuju da guansi*, a.k.a. *The Story of Qiu Ju*) (Zhang Yimou 1992), which ironically is also cited by Su Li (2006, 371–83) as another, even better known film that cautions against blind faith in the Western model of rule of law via the persona of an insupportably litigious farm wife.

What Does Qiuju Want?

Qiuju Goes to Court begins with a scuffle in the fields in which the village chief kicks a farmer in the groin. The farmer's wife Qiuju is indignant, perceiving the kick as physically inappropriate (it might render the husband impotent or infertile) and symbolically demeaning.[5] She visits the chief's home to seek an apology, but to no avail (figure 7.1). As the chief is the highest authority in the village, she is left with no choice but to go to the nearby township's public security office to lodge a complaint (see again figure 7.1). Officer Li tries to mollify Qiuju by imposing a fine on the chief, but when she goes to collect the money, the chief insults her by scattering the bills on the ground. Proud and headstrong as she is, she walks right out and wastes no time in venturing to the provincial capital to seek intervention from higher authorities. Eventually, with the help of a lawyer, she gets a hearing in the basic court, where, to her astonishment, the defendant is not the village chief, but the director of the provincial public security bureau who has been unusually kind to her. She loses the case and goes home more confused and dejected than ever. Meanwhile, life intervenes. During the entire saga, with each trip out of the village, her pregnancy is more visible and her movement more encumbered. She goes into difficult labor during a snow storm that practically seals off the village. Fortunately, the chief mobilizes a posse of men and manages to get her to the county hospital where she delivers a healthy baby boy. At the baby's one-month

FIGURE 7.1: Qiuju seeking an apology from the village chief; Qiuju filing a complaint. From *Qiuju Goes to Court* (Zhang Yimou 1992, Sil-Metropole Organization Ltd. and others).

celebration party, at which the chief is the guest of honor for having saved mother and child, he is taken away in handcuffs by police.

As it turns out, thanks to Qiuju's mulish persistence, a medical exam has been ordered and the result shows that her husband had also sustained injuries to the rib cage during his scuffle with the headman, enough to warrant a charge of battery and a sentence of administrative detention. As the police van drives away, Qiuju chases it until it disappears beyond the horizon, and the camera lingers on her sweaty, stunned, and crestfallen face. Clearly this is not what she wants, yet it is the logical conclusion to her lengthy, ever-escalating quest for a *shuofa*, which Zhang Yimou glosses as "an answer, an explanation, a clarification" (quoted in Anagnost 1997, 138). *Shuofa* can also be translated as justice, albeit not in a legal sense. Even the most casual viewer can see that Qiuju is after moral justice, something that can be delivered by an apology with no legal overheads. The fine is welcomed and can almost substitute for an apology (parting with money carries its own hurt), but without accompanying contrition the sting remains. Why won't the chief apologize?

In addition to Su Li, a number of other scholars have commented on the film from a range of disciplinary perspectives, including law, literature, and anthropology. Ann Anagnost believes that the *shuofa* Qiuju wants is "a public avowal of where the limits of power lie" (1997, 138); Jerome and Joan Cohen (2007) fault the film's overly rosy portrayal of the socialist rule of law, noting the many distortions for the sake of drama. Jeffrey Kinkley focuses on the novella from which the film is adapted and sees it as a critique of state paternalism. He also points out that the novella's title, *The Wan Family Sues* (*Wanjia susong*), has a secondary meaning.[6] Wan is a common Chinese surname, but literally it means "ten thousand" or "numerous." The title can alternatively be rendered as "Ten Thousand Families Sue" or "Everyperson Sues" (Kinkley 2000, 348), evoking the prevalence of litigations and growing fractiousness of Chinese society (this layer of meaning is removed when the film changes the husband's surname to Wang). Building on these insights, I would like to advance a more historically grounded interpretation of this intriguing film that speaks to some of the central questions of this book: Is law coterminous with justice? Is low justice possible in a system that prioritizes high justice? To begin with, we need to attend to a couple of details that are often overlooked.

First, the clash between the village chief and Qiuju's husband has a political subtext. On the surface it is a dispute over land use: the chief won't allow the Wangs to build a chili-drying shed on land slated for wheat growing (chili is a cash crop that enriches the Wang family alone whereas wheat is needed to meet state grain quotas). Wang hurls an insult at the chief that hits a soft spot: the chief and his wife have had several daughters in a row in violation of the family planning policy and no son to carry on the family line. And the chief retaliates with force. At the heart of the matter, however, is the problematic status of the chief's authority: if he himself is in violation of state policies, he cannot claim moral superiority on which to rest his authority; moreover, if the policy of household responsibility (*baochan daohu*) gives farmers land-use rights, to what extent can the state still impose its priorities on them? Anagnost is thus correct in identifying the central question of the film as one about the limits of power. What Qiuju wants to know is the extent to which the state can exercise power over private individuals with impunity, or to what extent high justice trumps low justice.

That the chief has to resort to force already partially answers this question, for under high socialism the chief would have had almost total control over the allocation of goods and resources and could have easily brought an insubordinate peasant to heel. Kicking Wang is in fact a sign of frayed authority under conditions of market economy, amounting almost to an admission of defeat. To be sure, as Su Li observes, Qiuju does not object to the chief throwing a few punches or kicks (2006, 373). She accepts the hierarchical relationship between the chief and the villagers as just in the sense defined by Bell and Wang. But where those kicks land indicates that it is not a simple case of a social superior acting impulsively but excusably toward an inferior. She is convinced that the kick in the groin is a symbolic assertion of unchecked power, and therefore unjust. Hence she wants a *shuofa*/apology that walks back that assertion, that acknowledges that the chief does not have the right to jeopardize a man's reproductive health and deprive him of his manhood and dignity in the community.

If "how people dispute is, after all, a function of how (and whether) they relate" (Auerbach 1983, 7), then the fact that, after the spat, Qiuju goes directly to the headman's home, where she socializes with his wife and daughters, shows that she fully intends to operate within the customary order and give him a chance to make amends in a low-key manner that does not threaten his reputation. His stonewalling is the only reason that she turns to the formal channel and escalates the case all the way to the provincial capital. That she does not hesitate to do so signals an awareness of the larger world of bureaucratic and legal apparatuses. Apparently the 1980s' state-sponsored "legal knowledge education" (*pufa jiaoyu*) has paid off (Altehenger 2018). That she does not get what she actually wants, however, has both formal-institutional and political-historical causes. The formal legal system is centered on procedural justice and deals with guilt and liability that can be proven with proper evidence (such as medical examination results); psychological and moral injuries are not excluded but require a much higher threshold. It delivers a formal resolution according to procedural rules but cannot guarantee substantive justice, or compel attitudinal change, or repair breaches of the social fabric. It is also liable to bring about a worse outcome by destroying the preexisting social bonds in the village: The chief will be stigmatized by having been taken away in handcuffs and "done time"; the Wangs will be ostracized for making the chief lose face and for undermining hierarchy and solidarity (Su Li 2006, 377). As Auerbach puts it, "law begins where community ends" (1983, 5).

Who is to blame for the outcome that is sought by no one and that makes everyone worse off? The answer, I contend, has to do with the second detail that few critics have noticed, to wit, the total absence of an alternative center of moral authority in the village. Given that what Qiuju wants is moral, not legal, redress, there is never any need for her to go outside the village and set in motion the legal machinery in the first place. In traditional China, as we have observed in the introduction, civil disputes were commonly handled at the local level by unofficial mediators. They were the key players in what Duara (1988) calls "the cultural nexus of power." Local gentry and elders played the role of protective brokers of local interests. Their power and authority flowed from below but were also bolstered by recognition from the imperial center. Twentieth-century state building, which reached its feverish apogee in the socialist era, thoroughly dismantled the cultural nexus of power, leaving in its wake a dysfunctional local society defenseless against the designs and whims of the Party-state. As we have noted above, an immediate ramification is the inability on the part of villagers to resolve minor conflicts among themselves, and rural society seems to exist in a "moral vacuum" (P. Huang 2015, 24) with no respected clan elders or local gentry that can step into the void and play the role of peacemaker. This is also what is conspicuously absent in Qiuju's village.

Technically the headman, invariably a Party member, is expected to play the role of peacemaker, since the Party has installed itself in the position of monopolistic authority in place of the traditional power-sharing arrangement in the cultural nexus of power (P. Huang 2015, 8). But when a Party cadre himself has a dog in the fight, the villagers are left with no neutral arbiter and no communal recourse. The chief can stonewall because the source of his power stems from above, not below. It is therefore surprising that so few critics have asked why *he* persists in not apologizing while they universally fault *Qiuju* for her pigheadedness, apparently chalking his behavior up to humdrum male pride. In my view, each of Qiuju's painstaking and foolhardy treks out of the village toward an uncertain goal is an indictment not of the fledgling legal system but rather of one-party rule that has further evacuated an already attenuated nexus of self-governance. To be sure, the Party also believes in the advantages of informal mediation over the formal legal system in resolving civil disputes, knowing well that "law is not about the repair of relationships" (Rosenbaum 2004, 192). Hence its first line of defense is to send a police officer down to the village to mediate and persuade. Officer Li understands very well what Qiuju wants—a moral resolution—and tries to satisfy her with his double-pronged proposal: the chief should "say a few nice words" and also pay a fine.

But autocratic rule stands in the way of implementing this proposal: No one but the chief's immediate political superior can compel him to do something he is loath to do. Officer Li is not in that position of authority, nor are the other officials in the judicial system even if they nominally outrank the chief. This concentration of power in the hands of a single individual is in fact by design—it is the local instantiation of one-party rule and sovereign exception. As Donald Clarke points out, to discipline the chief for violating Party policy is almost a contradiction in terms: "It would thus in a sense be beside the point to object that a cadre acted against Party policy: his ability to do so was inherent in the system deliberately adopted by the Party. The power of the Party backed up the local cadre as a whole individual, not just to the extent of his legal powers however defined" (1985, 244).

The chief, in the lingo of Maoism, is a veritable local tyrant whose power, for the most part, stands uncontested, and not every farmer has the gumption and stamina of a Qiuju to ensnare him in the "ponderous gears of the legal system" (Anagnost 1997, 139) at her own expense, in more senses than one. The film steers our attention to the iterative lesson that Qiuju is too thickheaded to learn: at each stop up the judicial ladder, she is handed more or less the same decision, with a slight increase of the fine at some point and the all-too-quick disappearance of the stipulation of apology. It's all too easy to make us disidentify with Qiuju the "pregnant hysteric" (Anagnost 1997, 144). Having largely tolerated the village head's obstinacy, the state suddenly makes an about-face and bears down on him with the ponderous weight of its legal apparatus. That is because, in Anagnost's view, "the state's culpable reliance on the personalized power of its local officials cannot be exposed. The village head must be sacrificed to leave the larger question of power and its limits unaddressed" (144). Individual bureaucrats in an authoritarian system are after all eminently disposable, all the more to preserve the arrogance of power.

In a way quite inconceivable in a Judge Bao play, a slow-forming avalanche of procedural justice suddenly catches up with Qiuju to overwhelm the modest substantive justice she seeks. By now, as we know, Qiuju is no longer even seeking a verbal apology, the chief's storm night action having more than righted the wrong and restored neighborly amity. In Kinkley's words, "moral debts have sorted themselves out without the law, much less the ridiculous pursuit of the letter of the law in stuffy courtrooms far away and high above" (2000, 357). The film also breaks the mold of old-style courtroom drama by giving us an anti–Judge Bao hero, namely, the director of the provincial public security bureau. Although Qiuju waylays him like a plaintiff in traditional China throwing him- or herself in front of an official's palanquin to cry wrong (*lanjiao hanyuan*), he does not activate his discretionary power on her behalf, as Judge Bao might. Judge Bao would understand that what was needed was not a legal win, but "a readjustment of human relations" (Kinkley 2000, 357). Instead, the director insists that she operate within the formal system and maintain her faith in its ability to give her final satisfaction. What's more, he subjects himself to procedural protocols and invites her (or rather her lawyer) to sue him under the newly promulgated Administrative Litigation Law. When she hesitates to step into the role prescribed for her in this bizarre legal drama, her bafflement comes off as comic relief, stemming from the incongruence between a peasant's quest for moral justice and the impersonal and impertinent technicality of the law. Litigation, which produces clear winners and losers in a zero-sum fashion, may give her a momentary winner's high, but sooner or later she has to return to the muddy waters of village life comprising "human associations which depend on spontaneous and informal collaboration" (A. Chen 2003, 284). Qiuju evidently understands this very well, hence her readiness to forgive the chief after his action has effected "a readjustment of human relations."

Kinkley argues that Zhang Yimou pits what is legally proper against what is morally right so as to elevate the film from the ho-hum genre of "legal system cinema" preoccupied with lurid crimes to one concerning "higher, more abstract questions of justice beyond the law" (Kinkley 2000, 357). In so doing Zhang is able to mount a critique of government paternalism. But this results in a highly improbable scenario. The Cohens point out how odd it is that none of the kindhearted and solicitous people that Qiuju encounters in her quest suggest that she and her husband file a civil suit against the headman, civil suits being quite common in 1980s China. The administrative suit that pits Qiuju against the director with the goal of revising the bureau's decision was, by contrast, extremely novel. In a civil suit, "the headman himself would have been summoned to court, [and] the worst that could have happened to him would have been a judgment demanding that he pay damages and apologize, precisely the justice that Qiuju wanted" (Cohen and Cohen 2007, 172). "Pursuing that course, however," they concede, "would have robbed the film of its dramatic denouement, the shocking detention of the headman," whereas the actual ending "gives the movie an exquisite twist and an ambivalence that makes *Qiuju* a film to remember" (173).

This unexpected tip of the hat to the power of fiction by two legal scholars circles us back to the point with which I began the book: that justice narratives are valuable because they call our attention to the lack of adequation and commensurability between law and justice. In the Chinese context, the key to grasping the gap is the distinction between high justice and low justice. If Qiuju and her husband had sensibly filed a civil lawsuit, the story would have been a low justice affair. As such it would not have acquired its wide resonance and would not have fascinated a broad spectrum of scholars for so long. It would not have brought to the fore "the losses as well as the residues occasioned by the exercise of justice" (Dimock 1996, 7). It would have remained a case of village kerfuffle without "an exquisite twist." What is exquisite about Qiuju's quest is that it reveals the teeth marks of high justice on low justice. While she is awaiting trial in the provincial capital, an innkeeper confidently predicts that she will win the case (figure 7.2) because the Party needs a show case to convince the populace that it is possible and okay to bring lawsuits against officials (*min gao guan*)—something that goes so deeply against the cultural grain that it is unthinkable to Qiuju: "Surely the state will not find itself guilty?" as Kinkley ventriloquizes (2000, 348). Such a lawsuit places an ordinary citizen in an adversarial relation with an agent of the state, effectively bringing the latter down from the pedestal of moral supremacy.

FIGURE 7.2: A very determined Qiuju; an innkeeper offers legal counsel to Qiuju. From *Qiuju Goes to Court* (Zhang Yimou 1992, Sil-Metropole Organization Ltd. and others).

That Qiuju even gets this far testifies to the Party's commitment to "governing in accordance with the law" and the greater latitude granted to low justice to the extent that a trifling case can end up putting a government official in the defendant's seat. The state has become confident enough not to elevate every low justice case to the realm of high justice as it was wont to do under high socialism (chapter 1). Rather, it invites citizens to project the logic of low justice upward and frame governance as a matter of fairness. To be a socialist citizen, it is no longer enough to be loyal and obedient; one must also be trustful of the Party and see it not as an anxious ruler but as an indulgent partner. The Cohens find the director's "cheery patience" at odds with the generally "nasty and brutish" manners with which the police force deals with commoners (2007, 168). They may well be correct, but the false note serves an ideological purpose. The cheery patience that the legal system exhibits in dealing with a case of low justice is recruited to serve the overarching goal of solidifying the Party's image as isomorphic with justice as such. That it backfires for Qiuju is none of the Party's concern, as long as her mulishness has allowed the Party to ostentatiously demonstrate its commitment to the rule of law. The film thus serves as an allegory for the larger story I tell in this book: the fraught relationship between high justice and low justice as refracted through storytelling.

Another source of appeal of *Qiuju Goes to Court* is its image of rural China as composed of close-knit moral communities, the signature chronotope of Zhang Yimou's early oeuvre. It would have come off as exotic not only to foreign viewers, but also to contemporary domestic audiences in a country where more than half of the population now reside in cities. The conditions that have conduced to the development of a legal culture in the West are also framing urban Chinese residents' relations to justice. Su Li and others' qualms about legal reforms' impact on a primordial way of life would be quite misplaced in metropolitan centers, where lawsuits have become all too familiar a feature of urban living. Not surprisingly, Hollywood-style legal thrillers have emerged to capture this newly litigious landscape. For the first time, suave and urbane lawyers are cast in lead roles in Chinese cinema, and twisted plots are spun out of legal intrigues as much as political machinations. *Silent Witness* (*Quanmin muji*) (Fei Xing 2013), for example, revolves around an elaborate deception engineered by a key witness to extricate his daughter from a murder charge. When the high-powered lawyer discovers the scheme, she is faced with the moral and professional dilemma of exposing the father and ruining the daughter, or colluding with him in a brazen act of perjury.

The plot echoes that of *Witness for the Prosecution* (Wilder 1957), though in the latter film the perjury is committed by a woman in a crazed attempt to exculpate her lover. In both cases, love and personal loyalty drive individuals to burrow deep beneath legal justice, and their subversion of procedural fairness wins them sympathy and endorsement from audiences. Law's rule may not be identified with the fallen condition of mankind as Kahn rues, but it is shorn of the majestic inviolability that Western jurists are fond of attributing to it. Martin Luther King Jr. (1968) famously said that "the arc of the moral universe is long but it bends toward justice." When fiction invites us to root for love over law, it is also reminding us that the arc of the moral universe vaults high above the dome of the courthouse.

A Certain Justice

This discussion returns us to the question of adequation between law and justice that launched this book. In her comparative study of the prosecutions of war criminals at the Nuremberg and Tokyo Military Tribunals, Shklar offers a dim assessment of the latter as a specimen of political trial. On top of echoing some of the widely known dissenting opinions by Indian justice Radhabinod Pal, Dutch justice Bert Röling, and French justice Henri Bernard, she delivers a far blunter verdict, pronouncing the Tokyo Trial "a complete dud" (1986, 181). As a political trial, its shaky legal basis may have been excusable, but it also had little didactic impact in a country lacking a legalistic tradition. To ordinary Japanese, it was "a bit of a bore," not because they had any great sympathy for the defeated leaders, but because there was little interest in the "legalistic gymnastics" of the victors (181).

Shklar goes on to contrast the Japanese "situational ethics" with the American tradition of legalism. The former rests not on universally applicable rules but requires specific ethical responses to specific situations. "Until the war personal conflicts were rarely resolved by a resort to courts; they were handled informally by local worthies, who made communal cohesion, rather than what is due to the individual claimant, the main object of conciliation" (Shklar 1986, 180). One immediately hears echoes of what scholars have identified as the preferred Chinese way of conflict resolution past and present. The Tokyo Trial did not ignite the Chinese imagination either until very recently, when a feature film (Gao Qunshu 2006) centered on Chinese justice Mei Ru'ao was released amid rising anti-Japanese nationalism. *The Tokyo Trial* (*Dongjing shenpan*) has little patience for the legal wrangling that made the trial such a protracted affair. It manages to turn a "dud" into a rousing morality play between a crusad-

FIGURE 7.3: Justice Mei Ru'ao in *The Tokyo Trial* (Gao Qunshu 2006, Shanghai Film Group).

ing justice (Mei) and his allies on the side of good, and the twenty-eight military and political leaders of the defeated Japanese Empire on the side of evil (figure 7.3). It reverts full throttle to the Judge Bao mold by casting Mei as the personification of truth and righteousness, going so far as to superimpose his narrating voice over documentary footage (McIntyre 2013, 15). The main obstacle that Mei has to sweep away is not so much the shiftless Japanese defense lawyer (only one lawyer is given screen time) as Mei's wishy-washy fellow jurists. In the sentencing phase, Pal is given his sole chance to speak, and all he seems capable of is invoking some vaguely Buddhist principle of universal mercy. Clearly, the filmmakers are banking on the lack of audience appetite for the intricacies of international law while lowballing the intelligence of those who do not see the world in black and white.

It seems that the only way the Tokyo Trial can be made meaningful in Chinese political-legal culture is through a filter of moralistic melodrama. Hence the disproportionate attention to the sentencing debate and the tagline that brags about Mei's pivotal role in sending the seven condemned men to the gallows—a requisite ending in all traditional justice narratives. As Stephen McIntyre elaborates, "the Chinese tradition reflects a highly punitive sense of justice, which is not achieved through presumptions of innocence, guarantees of due process, adversarial litigation, or jury verdicts, but through the swift punishment of criminals at the hands of authoritarian judges. This orientation eschews any acknowledgement of conflicting narratives, instead favoring the moral clarity that comes with a single story—that of guilt" (2013, 2). One could also see the film as an enactment of poetic justice, a supplementary trial that recognizes the necessary but limited role of law to "provide some recourse when our deepest moral values are savagely attacked," but sees the "field of judgment" extend far beyond the courtroom (Walzer 2015, 288). Like Dimock, John Treat maintains that when juridical accounting proves inadequate, literature can provide powerful tools of judgment (2017, 410). It does so not by stipulating rules, but by affording us "thinking company" from which consensus may emerge (431). *The Tokyo Trial* represents the consensus that is currently keyed to the thinking company the Chinese are permitted to keep. On the other hand, that China's own trials of Japanese war criminals remain uncelebrated in popular culture until very recently may have something to do with their uncathartic denouement, with not a single capital punishment and a preponderance of lenient sentences and pardons (see chapter 4).[7] If these were ever to be dramatized, it would likely be along the lines of *Special Pardons 1959*, with the trial proceedings serving merely as an epilogue to the wrenching journey of reeducation and repentance.

Interestingly, the most memorable and commented on legal drama from contemporary China, *Qiuju Goes to Court*, includes only a blip of a courtroom scene. When Qiuju goes to court, she is not being litigious, for she has no basis for associating the judicial system with *shuofa* or moral justice. She is merely enacting the time-honored tradition of "lodging a plaint" (*gaozhuang*) or "petitioning" (*shangfang*) by scaling the bureaucratic edifice. She intuitively follows the vertical path that countless petitioners have trod before her. The trouble for her is that beyond the village the bureaucratic hierarchy has undergone a legal makeover. Hoping that someone "up there" with power and authority over the village chief, a modern Judge Bao perhaps, would give her justice, she is sucked into the maw of an alien beast that spits out something altogether unrecognizable and undesirable to her. *Qiuju Goes to Court* is not a prototypical legal drama as the genre has been practiced in the West in that it does not climax in a stirring courtroom showdown in the manner of *And Justice for All* (Jewison 1979). Indeed, few Chinese justice narratives can be called legal thrillers or crime mysteries given how peripheral detectives, lawyers, and trial scenes usually are. As Kinkley (2000) has shown, crime fiction is meant to celebrate law enforcement's ability, under Party leadership, to guarantee the social order, and the mission of "legal system literature" is to lionize the crime fighters, never the criminals.

Certainly, the thrill of a courtroom showdown is not alien to the Chinese legal imagination, but it pales in salience in comparison to the moral drama of a victim seeking justice by hook or by crook. In general, justice narratives celebrating the offended as they fight to defend their honor and exact revenge enjoy more popular and critical acclaim than do those chronicling how offenders are caught and punished by law officers. In this preference we see traces of an honor culture that emphasizes personal retaliation rather than third-person (including state) punishment (Sommers 2012, 42–46). And yet clearly discernible is the reverse tendency of appealing to the state to enact retributive justice (Tsai 2021), hence the peculiar phenomenon of judicial populism, which may be characterized as a form of institutionalized vigilante justice whereby the state and the populace converge in sidelining procedural justice (chapter 3). Justice narratives thus follow two seemingly divergent pathways that nonetheless intersect or even merge in unexpected ways thanks to the vertical orientation of the Chinese culture of justice.

The vertical orientation also makes the Chinese culture of justice surprisingly inclusive, obviating questions of legal standing that trip up advocates of rights of nature. All manner of agents, regardless of ontological status, may ply the highways and byways of justice. Recall that even lowly mice do not hesitate to bring a case against their feline nemesis to the netherworld judge in an impossible pursuit of cross-species justice (chapter 6). Here the rodents are acting out the quintessential Chinese understanding of vertical justice: the higher (or lower in the inverted hierarchy of hell) one goes, the more certain the hope for justice. For animals, the bureaucratic hierarchy extends beyond the human sphere into the netherworld, where demon judges have jurisdiction over all souls, human and nonhuman. For higher beings such as gods and spirits, there is the celestial court of the Jade Emperor. When Monkey King in *Journey to the West* (*Xiyouji*) stirs up trouble in the aquatic world, for example, the incensed dragon kings make a beeline to the Jade Emperor's court to lodge a complaint against the simian trickster. If Beijing today is the end point of the road to justice for most petitioners, before the twentieth century the cosmic terminus of the "judicial continuum" (Katz 2007) is the lowest level of hell or the highest reach of heaven. It is a *certain* justice in both senses of the word: only a higher authority, or heaven itself, can guarantee the kind of justice yearned for in the Chinese legal imagination.

To conclude, we might say that the ecology of the Chinese legal imagination is the sum total of multiple assemblages. The most imposing and impactful of these is the arboreal structure of the political-legal system formed around one-party rule and with deep roots in the soil of tradition. We might call it the tree of justice. But it would be a mistake to look for justice only in the ripe (and perhaps worm-eaten) fruit hanging from the thick, majestic boughs of the state tended by professional gardeners, or regard the tree of justice as the only entity holding the ecosystem in balance. Justice also courses through the rhizomatic undergrowth (grassroots activism), mountain brooks (intellectual dissent), and ocean currents (global circulation of the ideal of rule of law), where writers and artists sing odes to justice, and to love and mercy and all the light we cannot see.

Glossary

Abing 阿炳
A-hun 阿雲
Amir, chong 阿米爾，沖
An Zaitian 安在天
A Q jingshen 阿Q精神
baiqu 白區
baochan daohu 包產到戶
baojia 保甲
biaotai 表態
bilu 筆錄
bing bu yan zha 兵不厭詐
buda buma buwuru 不打不罵不侮辱
bugong 不公
bushen bupan yige busha 不審不判
　　一個不殺
buyi 不義
Cao Da 曹达
cefan 策反
chanhui 懺悔
chaqing 察情
chengfen 成分
Cheng Yong 程勇
chengze wei wang, baize wei kou 成則
　　為王，敗則為寇
chiren 吃人
chongxin zuoren 重新做人
Chūgoku kikansha renrakukai
　　(Chūkiren) 中国帰還者連絡会
　　(中帰連)
daguanqiang 打官腔
dahua 大話

daizui ligong 戴罪立功
dang bagu 黨八股
dang de yuanze 黨的原則
dangxing 黨性
Daren, ni kedei yiwanshui yao duan-
　　ping a 大人，你可得一碗水要
　　端平啊
dazaqiang fenzi 打砸搶份子
de minxin zhe de tianxia 得民心者得
　　天下
di 抵
dianxing 典型
di-fu-fan-huai-you 地富反壞右
Ding Mu 丁牧
diwo maodun 敵我矛盾
dizhu 地主
dongyao pai 動搖派
duibo gongtang 對薄公堂
duizhi 對質
Du Yuming 杜聿明
fa 法、灋
fa bu xunqing 法不殉情
fandongpai 反動派
fang 放
fangeming jituan 反革命集團
fangpin wenku 訪貧問苦
fanshen 翻身
fanxing zizhuan 反省自傳
fanying shenghuo 反映生活
fazhi 法治
fazhi$_2$ 法制

fazhi$_2$ xitong wenxue 法制系統文學

feihua 廢話

fensui 粉碎

fulu 俘虜

funong 富農

Fushun zhanfan guanlisuo 撫順戰犯管理所

fuzeren 負責人

gai'e congshan 改惡從善

gaizao 改造

gan dashi de 干大事的

ganhua 感化

ganqing yongshi 感情用事

gaozhuang 告狀

geming he fangeming de guanxi 革命和反革命的關係

geming jiebanren 革命接班人

gongdao 公道

Gongdelin zhanfan guanlisuo 功德林戰犯管理所

Gong Ji 龔吉

gongping 公平

gongshen dahui 公審大會

gongsu 公訴

gongzheng 公正

guan 關

guan$_2$ 管

guan erdai 官二代

guanhua 官話

guanliyuan 管理員

guanxi 關係

Gugu 姑姑

gui'an faban, jue bu kuanshu 歸案法辦，絕不寬恕

guofa 國法

guofen 國粉

guojia 國家

guote 國特

hanjian zui 漢奸罪

hexie gaoyu gongzheng 和諧高於公正

He Zizhen 賀子珍

hong erdai 紅二代

huaifenzi 壞份子

Huang Kegong 黃克功

Huang Wei 黃維

huangyan 謊言

Huang Yiyi 黃依依

huaqing jiexian 劃清界線

Huben 虎賁

huiguo zixin 悔過自新

Ichiro 一郎

Jia'er 嘉兒

jiahua 假話

jiandao 尖刀

Jiang Zhujun (Jiangjie) 江竹筠（江姐）

jiexia qiu 階下囚

jiji fenzi 積極份子

Jindandao 金丹道

jingshen yuanzidan 精神原子彈

Jin Yuan 金源

jiu shehui 舊社會

juntong 軍統

juzheng 舉證

KangMei yuanChao 抗美援朝

Katsunuma 勝沼

konghua 空話

Kongzi 孔子

Kuikui 奎奎

kuli 酷吏

lanjiao hanyuan 攔轎喊冤

Lao Bi 老畢

laogai 勞改

laojiao 勞教

lao sanpian 老三篇

Lei Jingtian 雷經天

li 理

li$_2$ 禮

Li Guoxiang 李國香

Lin Wang (Ah Mei) 林旺（阿妹）

Lin Youshan 林有山

lishi de zuiren 歷史的罪人

Li Shuangshuang 李雙雙

Liu Lian 劉蓮

Liu Qian 劉倩

Liu Qiao'er 劉巧兒

Li Xingguo 李興國

Luo Fang 羅放
luxian douzheng 路線鬥爭
Ma Xiwu shenpan fangshi 馬錫五審
　判方式
Meili 美麗
min gao guan 民告官
Minguo re 民國熱
Mu banzhang 穆班長
nanyou 難友
paibiju 排比句
Pan Jinlian 潘金蓮
pidou 批鬥
ping minfen 平民憤
poxie 破鞋
pufa jiaoyu 普法教育
Puyi 溥儀
qing 情
qingguan 清官
qinqin xiangyin 親親相隱
qiyi 起義
qu 屈
qu₂ 去
quanmian fouding 全面否定
qubi 曲筆
qunzhong daibiao 群眾代表
qunzhong jiandu 群眾監督
ren 仁
rendao zhuyi 人道主義
renji hexie 人際和諧
renmin fating 人民法庭
renmin neibu maodun 人民內部矛盾
renqing 人情
renzhi 人治
Rong Jinzhen 容金珍
shangfang 上訪
shangfang baojian 尚方寶劍
shanggang shangxian 上綱上線
Shang Qin 尚勤
shang you zhengce, xiao you duice 上
　有政策，下有對策
Shao Yukui 邵玉魁
sharen changming 殺人償命
sharenzhe chu yi sixing 殺人者處以
　死刑

shehui xieshi 社會寫實
shenghua 昇華
shenru shenghuo 深入生活
shenxin hexie 身心和諧
shenyuan 申冤
Shen Zui (Yan Zui) 瀋醉（嚴醉）
shinian haojie 十年浩劫
shinian neiluan 十年內亂
Shizuko 靜子
shuanggui 雙規
shuofa 說法
suiri shōsetsu (tuili xiaoshuo) 推理
　小說
suku 訴苦
Sun Qiguang 孫啟光
suzhi 素質
Suzuki Hiraku 铃木启久
taishen 胎神
taizidang 太子黨
tangyi paodan 糖衣爆彈
tanwu 貪污
taose shijian 桃色事件
teshe 特赦
teshu cailiao 特殊材料
tianli 天理
tianming 天命
tianren hexie 天人和諧
tianxia 天下
tiaojian bugou 條件不夠
titian xingdao 替天行道
tiyan shenghuo 體驗生活
toucheng 投誠
touji daoba 投機倒把
tu banfa 土辦法
tuhao lieshen 土豪劣紳
tuotai huangu 脫胎換骨
wa 蛙
wa₂ 娃
Wanfu 萬福
wangfa 王法
Wang Jiazhi 王佳芝
wangu fenzi 頑固分子
Wang Yanggong 王央公
Wang Yingguang 王英光

Wanshengyuan 萬牲園
wei'e 偽惡
weishan 偽善
weiwen 維穩
Weizhuang 未莊
wenshi zhuanyuan 文史專員
Wojun zhanji ruhe 我軍戰績如何
Wu Dawang 吳大旺
Wufa wutian zan 無法無天讚
wusong 無訟
Xia Huan 夏歡
xiangyue 鄉約
xianzhan houzou 先斬後奏
Xiaoman 小滿
Xiaomeishan zhi zhan 小煤山之戰
xiaoqin dayu zhongjun 孝親大於忠君
xiezhai 血債
xiezui bei 謝罪碑
xinao dixin 洗腦滌心
xinao yuan 洗腦院
xingshi zhuyi 形式主義
xingxun 刑訊
xin shehui 新社會
xisong 息訟
xixin gemian 洗心革面
xuanpan 宣判
Xu Yuanju (Xu Pengfei) 徐遠舉（徐鵬飛）
yangbanxi 樣板戲
yansuan zu 演算組
Ye Hui (Ye Weige) 葉輝（葉衛革）
Ye Lisan 葉立三
yi 義
yi de hua min 以德化民

yifa zhiguo 依法治國
yinshu 隱鼠
yong bu shengxiu de luosiding 永不生鏽的螺絲釘
yongjue 用訣
youpai 右派
yuan 冤
yuanjiaozhi zhuyizhe 原教旨主義者
Yugong 愚公
Yu Zecheng 余則成
zaofanpai 造反派
zhanfan 戰犯
Zhang Zhonglin (Zhang Lingpu) 張鐘麟（張靈甫）
Zhao Jieshan 趙潔珊
zhengli 整理
Zhengxie 政協
zhengyi 正義
zhenxiang dabai 真相大白
zhenya fangeming (zhenfan) 鎮壓反革命（鎮反）
zhi 直
zhi$_2$ 鷙
zhidaoyuan 指導員
zhi laohu 紙老虎
Zhisou 智叟
Zhonghua Suwei'ai Gongheguo cheng-zhi fangeming tiaoli 中華蘇維埃共和國懲治反革命條例
Zhou Bapi (Zhou Chunfu) 周扒皮（周春富）
Zhu Chunxin 朱春信
zhulian 株連
zhu xuanlü 主旋律
Zuzu 祖祖

Notes

Introduction

1. In a recent speech, Xi Jinping hinted at the imminent abolition of *shuanggui* (Wade 2017). I thank Alexander Cook for bringing this report to my attention.

2. Another term used to translate "the rule of law," *fazhi₂* has the same pronunciation but uses the character for system or institution instead of the character for governance. It seems that this term might be a better fit for "rule by law" (personal communication from Elizabeth Perry).

3. The principled separation of law and morality is mostly limited to legal positivism, whereas recognition of their imbrication informs much of Western jurisprudential thought. The debate between H. L. A. Hart (2001) and Lon Fuller (2001) is a case in point. I thank Marco Wan for helping me make this distinction.

4. Haidt (2012) deploys the moral foundations theory very effectively to account for the strength and endurance of the conservative movement in the contemporary United States. His book predates the rise of Donald Trump, but many of its insights apply to the latter's populist appeal very well. Take one small example: One of Trump's favorite adjectives is "beautiful." A 2017 article in *Quartz* lists "21 unexpected things that Donald Trump thinks are beautiful," including coal, Confederate statues, the border wall, the Dakota Access Pipeline, and a baby about to be vaccinated (https://qz.com/1086942/21-unexpected-things-that-donald-trump-thinks-are-beautiful/). Apropos of the last, according to a 2019 ABC News report, he notoriously recounted the story that after an outsize syringe "meant for a horse" was used on a "beautiful" two-year-old, she developed a fever and ended up autistic (https://abcnews.go.com/Politics/trump-shifts-position-vaccinations-urges-parents-shot/story?id=62665258). Clearly, Trump's indiscriminate use of "beautiful" tells us little about his aesthetic sensibility. Rather, it is one of the many dog whistles by which he activates the sanctity foundation (insofar as beauty is linked to the sacred and inviolable) and evokes the moral emotions connected with elevation and degradation in his audiences.

5. Brackets have been used around ellipses that indicate omissions from quoted matter; ellipses in quoted matter that appear without brackets are reproduced from the original.

6. Parallel to the absence of legal truth in the Chinese legal imagination is the absence of legal fictions, such as corporate personhood, coverture, attractive nuisance, and civil death. On legal fiction as a form of metafiction, see Stern 2017 and 2020.

7. This rule was enforced as late as the end of the nineteenth century, when Li Hongzhang punished a man for denouncing his father for fabricating an official seal (in addition to putting the father to death). Li justified his decision by quoting the passage in the *Analects* about the obligation of concealment (D. Jiang and Ma 2020, 283–84).

8. Defenders of this practice often point to the similar practice of not compelling close kin to testify against each other in Western law. Still, the concessions seem more limited than in the Chinese tradition.

9. Scholars have often invoked the Greek tragedy *Antigone* to posit a radical break between positive law and private morality or natural law in the Western legal tradition. Note that the tension between the two comes to a destructive end only because Antigone's brother is guilty of treason. In other contexts, positive law also makes concessions to private morality (such as not compelling family members to testify against one another), albeit less extensively than in the Chinese tradition.

10. The judge's response, like other aspects of the film, is a logical poseur: "We're not talking about one bowl of water. I have to hold both bowls steady and level!"

Chapter 1

1. In Taiwan, detective fiction flourished thanks to the influence of Japanese *suiri shōsetsu* (*tuili xiaoshuo*). In the late 1970s and early 1980s, a sensationalist "social realist" (*shehui xieshi*) genre of crime film took domestic and overseas markets by storm before giving way to New Taiwan Cinema (Hou Chi-jan 2005). The genre bears some resemblance to the "legal system literature" on the mainland in steering clear of political subjects and relying heavily on sex and violence as box office hooks.

2. The heading for this section is taken from W. B. Yeats's poem "The Second Coming" (1920), with Americanized spelling.

3. *Cihai* 2002, 605.

4. In his memoir about life as a "war criminal" in CCP detention, Shen Zui, a former Nationalist internal security chief in charge of operations in the Southwest relates his and his fellow inmates' reactions to these caricatures of Nationalist officers in PRC counter-espionage films. They were offended by the uniformly good-for-nothing images of themselves, commenting that if victory had been that easy, then the victors had nothing to be proud of, and asking rhetorically how it was that the lives of tens of thousands of martyrs could have been lost to such inept enemies (Shen Zui 1990, 302).

5. Dai Jinhua (2010) points out that China's first spy film, *Code Name Heaven No. 1* (*Tianzi diyihao*) was made in 1947. It set the pattern for later productions on both sides of the Taiwan Strait.

6. *Quotations from Mao Tse Tung* (Foreign Languages Press, 1966), Mao Tse Tung Internet Archive, http://large.stanford.edu/history/kaist/references/marx/mao/c2/ (accessed August 11, 2022).

7. Because of space constraints, I pass over the spate of spy films produced in the late 1970s and early 1980s, soon after the end of the Cultural Revolution. These films are precursors of the slicker productions of the new millennium, sharing the latter's preference for the pre-1949 time frame but continuing the tendency from the Seventeen Years to caricaturize Nationalist characters as gullible dupes who have a welcome habit of showing exasperated admiration for the bravery, mental agility, and indestructibility of their Communist antagonists. An exception to this pattern is the 1995 television serial *Relentless Chase* (*Wuhui zhuizong*) (Yin Li 1995). Here a Nationalist sleeper agent undergoes a soulful transformation in the New Society, becoming a model citizen but eventually turning himself in after a lifetime of exemplary living.

8. I qualify this observation in my essay (H. Lee 2020a) that seeks to historicize the affinity between theory of mind and the modern novel. In brief, I argue that theory of mind is

mostly prized in contexts in which strangers are thrown together and cannot rely on folk psychological heuristics such as stereotypes and behavioral schemata. The spy thriller deploys theory of mind so extensively precisely because of the radical isolation and pervasive mutual suspicion that constitute the espionage status quo. Erik Hoel (2019, 2020) further speculates that fictions, like dreams, prevent our brain from becoming "overfitted" to the training data set of real life and thus rigid and incapable of labile generalization and adaptability.

9. These close-ups of fleeting and barely perceptible facial or bodily expression give the impression that the hero's interior thoughts and feelings are inadvertently captured on camera and hence invisible to his enemies. Lisa Zunshine (2012) calls these moments "embodied transparency" and argues that it is a universal trope in the performing arts. I critique this claim in the context of traditional Chinese theater in H. Lee 2016a. But in the ultramodern genre of spy thriller, embodied transparency is utilized without apology.

10. Sunzi, *The Art of War*, translated by Lionel Giles. See MIT's classics website: http://classics.mit.edu/Tzu/artwar.html (accessed August 11, 2022).

11. For both novels, in-text citations give page number from the Chinese original followed by page number from the English translation. *In the Dark*: Mai Jia 麦家 2014a and Mai Jia 2015; *Decoded*: Mai Jia 麦家 2014b and Mai Jia 2014.

12. Liu Cixin's (2014) Hugo Award–winning novel *The Three-Body Problem* (*Santi*, 2006) makes an oblique contribution to the retroactive enchantment of the socialist state. Part of the novel is set during the Cultural Revolution, when an astrophysicist and daughter of a persecuted scientist is exiled to the hinterland. By some bizarre accidents, she finds herself in a mysterious research station equipped with state-of-the-art scientific instruments and ensconced deeply in the mountains. Its mission, to her astonishment, is to search for and make contact with possible intelligent life in outer space. However implausibly, the state is projected, even in the midst of chaos and destruction, to have the will and wherewithal to mount such a quixotic project, and to be capable of not only staying in the space race with the superpowers, but actually surpassing them thanks to the unauthorized action of this brilliant but disillusioned female scientist.

13. The translator erroneously renders *fenci* (pimple, cyst) as "tumor."

14. The English translation of the idiom *bing bu yan zha* as "soldiers do not despise tricks" is too literal, hence my modification.

15. Although *Decoded* was the first title in Mai Jia's espionage trilogy, it was the last to be adapted for the screen, big and small (the forty-four-episode television serial was first aired on Hunan Satellite Television in 2016). The commonly cited reason for multiple aborted attempts is that the novel is too literary. In my close reading of Mai's major works, I have gone against the chronological order because *Decoded* is indeed least recognizable as a spy thriller.

16. The title of this section is also the title of a lecture by Michel Foucault (1997, 59–66), in which he traces how and since when war has become the permanent basis of institutions, laws, and the social order.

17. Mai Jia cowrote the screenplay of *In the Dark*. The experience might have seeded his next novel, *The Message* (*Fengsheng*, 2007), which again revolves around a Communist spy defeating the enemy's effort to smoke him out through physical sequestration and psychological tactics. It was promptly adapted into a highly successful film by the same title with a star-studded cast in 2009. See Yang (2019).

18. Elaine Scarry (Scarry et al. 2003) questions the claim that the state is the only entity capable of defending the nation, a claim that gives rise to militarism and undermines democracy. Her example is the September 11 terrorist attacks, against which the only success-

ful defense was mounted by civilians—the passengers on United Flight 93 who charged the cockpit after an informal vote.

Chapter 2

1. A newer body of literary and cinematic works have emerged in the new millennium that stare unflinchingly at the makeshift life of those falling under China's ruthless motor of progress. This noirish genre has attained considerable critical acclaim and international recognition. Its proper study, however, awaits a future monograph. Suffice it to observe that these works offer an increasingly nuanced mapping of criminality that overlaps with the patterns of causal knowledge identified by Stephen Kern (2004) in modern crime fiction: specificity, multiplicity, complexity, probability, and uncertainty. See H. Lee (forthcoming a) for a reading of Xu Yigua's *Sunspots* (2010) as an example of this new genre of crime fiction.

2. Consider the real-life hero depicted in *A Hidden Life* (Malick 2019). Franz Jägerstätter, an Austrian farmer and army recruit, refused to salute Hitler, not to mention fighting his war of aggression. He was dragged through a scarifying process of communal and institutional sanctions, which also made life excruciatingly painful for his wife and children in their native village. Most of their neighbors, like the vast majority of the civilian populations in Germany and German-controlled territories, either simply went with their moral realist calculations, and acted in the best interest of themselves and their kinfolk, or subtly adjusted their factual beliefs (say, about what was happening to the Jews or the degree of pain and suffering the war was inflicting on enemy nations) to fit with their intuitive aversion toward killing and maiming. They were therefore able to prop up their moral convictions and hold on to their self-image as decent folks with the aid of a well-hewed consequentialist crutch. Amid these consummate hypocrites, Jägerstätter was truly awe inspiring. Small wonder that Terence Malik devotes three hours to trying to make sense of what makes him tick.

3. See Amy Qin's 2014 *New York Times* article for an account of how this story achieved canonical status in China after a forty-year run as a required middle-school text (https://sinosphere.blogs.nytimes.com/2014/01/06/the-curious-and-continuing-appeal-of-mark-twain-in-china/?_r=0) (accessed October 15, 2018). It explains why I myself, not a Twain scholar but someone who received her primary, secondary, and college education in China in the 1970s and 1980s, am familiar with this story unknown to most American readers.

4. The paired German concepts *Erlibnis* and *Erfarhung* capture well the process of narrative sublimation from the individual and experiential to the collective and universal (see Jay 2005, 162).

5. Translated as *Snakes and Ladders—or Three Days in the Life of a Chinese Intellectual* (Chen Rong 1987).

6. In anticipation of their public disgrace, moreover, some of these victims, most notoriously Nikolai Bukharin, wrote plaintive letters to Stalin protesting their innocence, all the while affirming their deepest love for him and the Soviet Union and their undying devotion to the Communist Revolution (Slezkine 2017, 720–24). A few of these persecuted individuals who were lucky enough to dodge the executioner's bullet returned to the political fold as ideologically gung ho as their persecutors, testifying to the strength of the public transcript in enforcing command performance whether or not it is able to genuinely colonize individual consciousness. This pattern was also very much visible in the cycle of persecutions in the Mao and immediate post-Mao era.

7. Mao did try to extricate himself from the hot air that entrapped everyone else. In a 1942 essay called "Oppose the Party 'Eight-Legged Essay,'" Mao blasts the spread of bu-

reaucratic boilerplates (*dang bagu*) in the Communist Party (Mao Zedong 1956). Yet as subsequent history shows, no one except Mao himself could afford not to hide behind the shield of the loathsome style. As the sovereign who placed the country under a permanent state of emergency, he alone was exempt from slavishly toeing the official line. But even so, some of his saltier utterances were kept "offline" and hence remained part of the regime's hidden transcripts until they were leaked or later dug up by researchers.

8. For example, loyalty to and faith in the Party "are concrete, not abstract; are felt in the heart, not skin deep; are steadfast and resolute, not whimsical and fleeting" (Qian Gang 2019; translation modified).

9. Frank Dikötter points to the many ways in which the Communist Party's ideological commitment to egalitarianism was belied by an elaborate and rigid system of hierarchy in the PRC. At the apex of the hierarchy was the central Party leadership, "who had special residences ensconced behind high walls, security guards round the clock and chauffeured cars. Special shops with scarce goods at discounted prices were reserved for them and their families. Dedicated farms produced high-quality vegetables, meat, chicken and eggs" (2010, 192). See also Ying Zhu (2022) on the Party leadership's fondness for "internal reference films" (mostly Hollywood classics) forbidden to the hoi polloi.

10. The illiterate Tibetan shepherd in the film *Tharlo* (Pema Tseden 2015), for example, can still recite "Serve the People" from beginning to end in monotone Mandarin Chinese without a hitch, decades after he was made to memorize it as a little boy, even though he otherwise cannot speak a word of Chinese. Other characters in the film regard it as a wondrous gift and often crowd around to watch him perform—or reenact what could not have been anything other than a traumatic childhood experience.

11. On Wu Dawang's wedding night, his peasant bride shows zero interest in sex and accuses him of behaving like a "hooligan." A standoff ensues. Before she relents, she makes him promise to work hard, get promoted, and have her transferred to the city. Thereafter they would have intercourse, but always sans sensuality. This cringe-inducing scene sets the stage for sex as pleasure to become an act of resistance. It strains credibility that a farm girl would be thinking about her household registration status on her wedding night. True, it is satire, but it's condescending to imagine that the pleasures of the flesh are unknown to peasant couples even after they get over their initial shyness and inhibition.

12. For historical contexts of the practice of mask wearing in East Asia, see Sand (2020) and Jing Zhu (2020).

13. In both academic and lay discourse, there is a tendency to conflate hypocrisy and cynicism. Kevin Latham, for example, writes about journalists in post-Mao China who practice a deft but cynical form of self-censorship. In my view, the kind of "conformist, cynical practices" (2009, 207) that he witnesses among his journalist informants is really an instance of subaltern hypocrisy, of going along with the official mandate for the sake of professional survival. Neither the state nor the journalists care about sincerity or honesty. As I have argued in this chapter, hypocrisy is fundamental to politics. In an authoritarian state, it is practiced in a more brazen manner, thus teetering on cynicism. In liberal politics, hypocrisy is denounced more often and thus held somewhat in check.

Chapter 3

1. The first comprehensive civil code took effect only at the beginning of 2021, though stand-alone laws governing specific areas have been around since the early 1980s, and a marriage law was promulgated as early as 1950.

2. Mens rea is not always required in Anglo-American law. In some cases, a formula is used to assign intention so that a person "may be assumed to intend the natural and probable effects of their actions" (personal communication from Simon Stern). One may argue that the House managers of the second impeachment trial of Donald Trump were trying do something similar—by suggesting that intent could be posited because Trump should have foreseen the "probable effects" of his words. His defenders, in response, cite his "peaceful protest" injunction as exonerating evidence, which incidentally calls to mind Mao's "Sixteen Points," urging the Red Guards to fight with words, not force. Conventional reasoning about mens rea doesn't work for either side because this is not a low justice case. The impeachment trial should have been conducted unapologetically as a political trial with political objectives of the "decisive" kind: to remove and disqualify; to shore up democratic norms that are often tacit and for that reason difficult to apply legal braces to. The trial failed not because Trump didn't commit any crime (he may not have technically speaking) but because political consensus could not be achieved in the polarized climate of American politics. The only recourse left is litigation in the realm of low justice, but individuals suing Trump for death or injury will have to meet the high bar of proving mens rea, or clearing the even higher hurdle of First Amendment protection. The "Sixteen Points" refers to Mao's 1966 directive "Guidelines for the Great Proletarian Cultural Revolution," in which he laid out the goals of the Cultural Revolution. It had the force of law and is invoked as such in "The Second Encounter."

3. The play was put on stage in September 1979 by the China Youth Theater Company to critical and popular acclaim. It is said that the queue outside the theater's box office was so long that it reached the bazaar of Dongdan, giving rise to the saying: "In Xidan there's a Democracy Wall; in Dongdan there's *Power versus Law*." After the script was published in *Theater* (*Juben*), the Youth Theater took it on the road, and local theaters across the country also put on their own productions. Altogether the play logged in over five hundred performances and received enthusiastic media coverage nationwide. Xi'an Film Studio began to adapt it for the big screen, but the project was called off in 1983 with the launching of the "Anti-bourgeois Spiritual Pollution" campaign (Shi Ming 2012).

4. Amazingly, no commentators, including those with legal credentials, have paid (or been allowed to pay) any heed to this glaring glitch of logic and credibility. Screenwriter Wang Xingdong explicitly rejects the criticism that because Mao actually called the shots, the case was not about the rule of law, but rule of man. Calling this question a "minefield," he defends Mao's decision not to exercise his power of pardon and asserts that the letter, because it was a reply to Lei Jingtian's plea for leniency on behalf of Huang, is "in accordance with legal procedures" (quoted in He Tian 2014, 149).

Chapter 4

1. In the majority of the historical and literary sources I survey in this chapter, these captives are almost always labeled "war criminals" (*zhanfan*). For the most part, I follow this convention and use the label without quotation marks. When appropriate, however, I use the more neutral term POW or detainee.

2. *Remin ribao*, January 31, 1967, 6; see Leese (2019, n14).

3. Technically, C class stands for "crimes against humanity," a category invented at the Nuremberg Trials to prosecute the masterminds of the Holocaust, but it was not deployed in the East Asian context, where B and C classes were lumped together (Kushner 2015, 7). For the distinction between *jus ad bellum* and *jus in bello*, see Walzer (2015, 21–22).

4. See Xia (2017) and Zanasi (2008) for accounts of postwar prosecutions of and campaigns against *hanjian*.

5. The historical accuracy of the accounts found in these sources is difficult to gauge. For one thing, there is a great deal of repetitiveness and mutual echoing and little attempt to provide documentation. For another, some of the reminiscences have been "recorded" (*bilu*) and "edited" (*zhengli*) by others. One reporter who was present at the trials and was charged, together with a colleague, with the news write-up recalls sitting down with Liao Chengzhi, China's number one "Japan hand" and chief consultant at the trials. Liao ordered him to strike out words describing the distraught emotional state of some witnesses and audience members, and to insert a line after a sentence stating that a defense counsel has made his statement—to the effect that the counsel also asked the court to show leniency on account of his client's contrition. Apparently sensing the reporter's reluctance to put words in people's mouths, Liao intones: "You think lawyers are only here to speak on behalf of the Japanese war criminals, don't you? This is incorrect. When lawyers ask for leniency in accordance with international law and humanitarian principles and with in view the Japanese war criminals' actual repentance, they are not behaving inappropriately. On the contrary, they are bringing out the fairness of our nation's court trials" (Xu Guiying and Ji Min 2000, 216). Liao's harangue completely elides the question of accuracy and fixates instead on whether the made-up quotation would be permissible or not. In any event, my purpose here is to read these sources symptomatically, not historically.

6. Since the turn of the twenty-first century, China has begun to reframe the second Sino-Japanese war as China's own "good war" and part of the worldwide fight against fascism (H. Lee 2020b; Mitter 2020). The inward orientation is increasingly being supplemented by outward glances, such as Fang Jun's *The "Devil Soldiers" I Knew* (*Wo renshi de guizibing*, 1997), a compilation of interviews with Japanese World War II veterans (Mitter 2020, 130–36).

7. Mao Zedong, "On Ten Relations" (*Lun shi da guanxi*). Marxist Archive in Chinese 马克思主义文库, https://www.marxists.org/chinese/maozedong/marxist.org-chinese-mao-19560425.htm (accessed August 11, 2022). My translation.

8. The CCP-Nationalist rapprochement has deepened in the new millennium and taken root in popular culture. See Rana Mitter's fascinating account of the *Minguo re* (Republican craze) and *Guofen* (Guomindang/Nationalist fans) phenomena (2020, 159–65).

9. Mao Zedong, "Serve the People," *Selected Works of Mao Tse Tung* (Foreign Languages Press, 1966), Marxist Internet Archive, https://www.marxists.org/reference/archive/mao/selected-works/volume-3/mswv3_19.htm (accessed August 11, 2022).

10. This is keenly realized by Shen Zui, another former Nationalist spymaster featured in *Red Crag* (as Yan Zui). In his lighthearted memoirs, he includes the few years he spent in a special "training academy" (*xunlian ban*) in Chongqing before he was transferred to Gongdelin in 1956. He documents the high living standards set for POWs like himself. Rank-and-file POWs complained: "The higher one's rank, the greater one's crimes, the better the treatment" (Shen Zui 1990, 3). Envious of the comfortable lifestyle they witnessed, unwitting locals searched for ways to be accepted into the "academy" only to be told that they weren't "qualified" (*tiaojian bugou*). One day when Shen Zui was taking a stroll in a nearby martyrs' park, he was recognized and accosted by angry mourners, an incident that precipitated his northward transfer.

11. There doesn't seem to have been any single warden who stood out and left a lasting impression on the inmates. In most accounts, the prison staff are referred to collectively as the "wardens" (*guanliyuan*), "supervisors" (*fuzeren*), or "cadre-instructors" (*zhidaoyuan*).

Shen Zui, for example, never identifies any prison staff by name in his memoirs, which document, among other things, many close interactions between the authorities and the prisoners. In one instance, after he got into a heated argument with fellow inmates upon claiming to have become a proletarian—"Nowadays with my villa, my car, my gold, and my entire family all gone, I'm but a bare branch holding a pair of chopsticks; why don't I count as a proletarian?"—he was summoned by an unnamed warden for a lengthy talking-to (Shen Zui 1990, 306). Huang Jiren (1982) too identifies only two or three wardens by family name and position.

12. Such irony is not confined to China. In a memoir chronicling his struggle to defend poor Black and indigent citizens in the South against a predatory criminal justice system, Bryan Stevenson (2014) contrasts the reverence with which the residents of Monroeville regard Harper Lee and the frequency with which her masterpiece *To Kill a Mockingbird* is staged as part of the local tourist attractions on the one hand, with the regularity with which justice is miscarried in cases involving Black defendants and white victims on the other. This is poetic justice at its worst, a veritable Plato's cave where the dancing shadows on the wall become the soothing alibi for allowing injustices to fester and ramify.

13. *Quotations from Mao Tse Tung* (Foreign Languages Press, 1966), Mao Tse Tung Internet Archive, https://www.marxists.org/reference/archive/mao/works/red-book/ch27.htm (accessed August 11, 2022).

14. In the television serial *Relentless Chase* (Yin Li 1995), a Korean War veteran returns home under hushed circumstances. We learn that he has spent time in a POW camp. No one asks him, nor does he utter a word, about life in the camp. A decade later he is denounced by the Red Guards as a cowardly traitor. Still, it is a rare acknowledgment of a buried historical episode. As a rule, official representations of the Korean War, including the latest blockbuster film *The Battle at Lake Chosin* (*Changjinhu*, 2021), recognize only heroes and martyrs who fight to the last breath.

15. I treat the topic of pardons in the context of law and world literature in the forthcoming essay "Pardon and Forgiveness" (H. Lee, forthcoming b).

16. See H. Lee (2016b) for an extended analysis of the paradox of Charlie Chan. To summarize, I situate the Charlie Chan franchise against the backdrop of American racism and legal Orientalism (Ruskola 2013) in order to make the case that in a liberal state of law, the sovereign exception can be paradoxically displaced onto marginal or eccentric figures. The "Chinaman's chance" that excluded Chinese immigrants from legal protection and cast them into a zone of exception was what made it possible for Chan to deliver low justice without unsettling high justice, or raising the question of popular sovereignty. I propose to see Chan as an auratic figure that feeds on the anxiety engendered by law's inevitable intercourse with the extralegal (including racist discrimination) and its inadequacy in relation to justice. Exceptional justice here is not a matter of sovereign decrees or special pardons, but one of displacement and disavowal.

Chapter 5

1. Decades of antisuperstition campaigns apparently have not succeeded in eliminating beliefs in infant and other spirits as well as in the traffic between the living and the dead. But the destruction of the folk religious infrastructure that has done away with temples, shrines, and ritual accoutrements and decimated the ranks of religious specialists does make it much harder to revive certain practices that used to be integral to the balance of the cosmic order. Such things as "baby towers" are no longer possible in mainland China

(Snyder-Reinke 2019). In Taiwan, where folk religion has thrived more or less unmolested by the state, women who have had abortions would file petitions in a Dizang temple to placate the wronged infant spirits (Katz 2007, 175).

Chapter 6

1. The leeway granted to mice is strong, albeit residual, evidence of an older cosmology governing the relationship between humans and nonhumans, apart from the Buddhist-inspired respect for all sentient beings. Another practice of similar origins is the avoidance of eating beef on account of oxen's contribution to agriculture (Goossaert 2005).

2. For a survey of literary animals in Western literature in the context of comparing welfarist and rights-based approaches to animal advocacy, see A. Miller (2011).

3. Notable titles from the mainland include Jiang Rong's *Wolf Totem* (*Lang tuteng*, 2004), Yang Zhijun's *The Tibetan Mastiff* (*Zang'ao*, 2005), Mo Yan's *Life and Death Are Wearing Me Out* (*Shengsi pilao*, 2006), Li Kewei's *The Chinese Tiger* (*Zhongguo hu*, 2007), Jiang Zidan's *Animal Files* (*Dongwu dang'an*, 2008), and Ma Boyong's *A Grassland Zoo* (*Caoyuan dongwuyuan*, 2017).

4. Memorable pet stories usually feature a pet that goes on some kind of adventure that takes it outside the confines of the home. In that capacity, it can bring people together across social chasms and forge a community of care and purpose. Examples include *Lassie Come Home* (1943) and *Because of Winn-Dixie* (2005).

5. I thank Christopher Peacock for transliterating the Tibetan names in this novel.

6. Although the hyphenated spelling Wu Ming-Yi appears in some works, I will use the closed spelling Wu Mingyi throughout.

Conclusion

1. Camus's impromptu response at a conference when queried by an Algerian student reportedly was: "Je crois à la Justice, mais je défendrai ma mère avant la Justice" (I believe in justice, but I will defend my mother before I defend justice). There is also a slightly different version of this remark. Dicocitations: le dictionnaire des citations. https://dicocitations.lemonde.fr/citations/citation-148142.php.

2. Even an influential Buddhist thinker like Shi Chao-hwei, who rejects the Christian theological underpinnings of liberal rights discourse, supports the drive to win legal protection of the environment (Nicolaisen 2020).

3. The Confucian philosophy of harmony largely elides the perennial problem of deontology versus consequentialism, as posed in Fyodor Dostoevsky's *The Brothers Karamazov* ([1880] 1992) and Ursula Le Guin's "The Ones Who Walked Away from Omelas" (in Le Guin 2004). In both, low injustice (the abuse of children) is deemed unacceptable as the price of the high justice of universal harmony and happiness.

4. In a later work Su Li (2018) walks back some of the claims he makes in *Law and Literature*.

5. Qiuju is about six months pregnant at the beginning of the film. But if she gives birth to a girl, per the state's birth control policy's special stipulations for rural couples, she and her husband are permitted to have a second child. And patriarchal inertia still very much hitches a woman's worth to her ability to provide male heir(s) to the patriline. Hence the special hurt felt by Qiuju in the chief's targeting of the "family jewels" during the altercation.

6. Haun Saussy wondered in personal correspondence whether Chen Yuanbin's novella (1995) may have been inspired by Heinrich von Kleist's "Michael Kohlhaas" (Kleist
1962), about a horse trader whose fanatical pursuit of justice comes to a ruinous end.
Chen, however, makes no mention of the German story in his reminiscence of the origin
and afterlife of *Wanjia susong*. Kleist's story also bears some resemblance to the 1965 film
Blood Monument (see chapter 1). Insofar as the film serves as a justification for the Communist Revolution, its message is remarkably similar to the one given by Kohlhaas in his
meeting with Martin Luther (117): that since he has been denied the protection of the
laws, he has essentially been cast out of society, and that an outcast's action is not a crime,
but a revolution.

7. An eight-part documentary series called *Asia-Pacific War Crimes Trials* (*Ya-Tai zhanzheng shenpan*, Shanghai Jiaotong University 2020), focusing on B- and C-class war crimes
trials throughout the Asia-Pacific region, was aired in mainland China in 2020. It was sponsored by the Ministry of Propaganda and produced by Shanghai Broadcast and Television
Station. I thank Barak Kushner for bringing this series to my attention.

Bibliography

Abbott, Edwin. (1884) 2010. *Flatland*. Edited by William F. Lindgren and Thomas Banchoff. Cambridge: Cambridge University Press; Mathematical Association of America.

Abbott, H. Porter. 2003. "Unnarratable Knowledge: The Difficulty of Understanding Evolution B Natural Selection." In *Narrative Theory and the Cognitive Sciences*, edited by David Herman, 143–62. Stanford, CA: CSLI.

Acemoglu, Daron, and James A. Robinson. 2012. *Why Nations Fail: The Origins of Power, Prosperity and Poverty*. New York: Crown.

Agamben, Giorgio. 1998. Homo sacer: *Sovereign Power and Bare Life*. Translated by Daniel Heller-Roazen. Stanford, CA: Stanford University Press.

———. 2005. *State of Exception*. Chicago: University of Chicago Press.

Ahern, Emily M. 1978. "The Power and Pollution of Chinese Women." In *Studies in Chinese Society*, edited by Arthur P. Wolf, 269–90. Stanford, CA: Stanford University Press.

Alber, Jan. 2011. "The Diachronic Development of Unnaturalness: A New View on Genre." In *Unnatural Narratives—Unnatural Narratology*, edited by Jan Alber and Rüdigger Heinze, 41–67. Berlin: De Gruyter.

Alber, Jan, Marco Caracciolo, and Irina Marchesini. 2018. "Mimesis: The Unnatural between Situation Models and Interpretive Strategies." *Poetics Today* 39 (3): 447–71.

Alexander, Michelle. 2010. *The New Jim Crow: Mass Incarceration in the Age of Colorblindness*. New York: New Press.

Allan, Janice M., Jesper Gulddal, Stewart King, and Andrew Pepper. 2020. *The Routledge Companion to Crime Fiction*. Abingdon, Oxon: Routledge.

Altehenger, Jennifer E. 2018. *Legal Lessons: Popularizing Laws in the People's Republic of China, 1949–1989*. Cambridge, MA: Harvard University Asia Center.

Anagnost, Ann. 1997. *National Past-Times: Narrative, Representation, and Power in Modern China*. Durham, NC: Duke University Press.

Anderson, Marston. 1990. *The Limits of Realism: Chinese Fiction in the Revolutionary Period*. Berkeley: University of California Press.

Andreas, Joel. 2019. "Mass Supervision." In *Afterlives of Chinese Communism: Political Concepts from Mao to Xi*, edited by Christian P. Sorace, Ivan Franceschini, and Nicholas Loubere, 127–34. Canberra, Australia: ANU; New York: Verso.

Anker, Elizabeth, and Bernadette Meyler, eds. 2017. *New Directions in Law and Literature*. Oxford: Oxford University Press.

Apter, David Ernest, and Tony Saich. 1994. *Revolutionary Discourse in Mao's Republic.* Cambridge, MA: Harvard University Press.

Arendt, Hannah. 1958. *The Human Condition.* Chicago: University of Chicago Press.

———. 1968. *The Origins of Totalitarianism.* New York: Harcourt Brace and World.

———. 1972. *Crises of the Republic: Lying in Politics, Civil Disobedience on Violence, Thoughts on Politics, and Revolution.* New York: Harcourt Brace Jovanovich.

———. 1978. *The Life of the Mind.* 2 vols. New York: Harcourt Brace Jovanovich.

———. 1993. *Between Past and Future.* New York: Penguin Books.

———. 1994. *Eichmann in Jerusalem: A Report on the Banality of Evil.* New York: Penguin Books.

———. 2003. *Responsibility and Judgment.* Edited by Jerome Kohn. New York: Schocken Books.

Ariely, Dan. 2012. *The (Honest) Truth about Dishonesty: How We Lie to Everyone—Especially Ourselves.* New York: Harper.

Asma, Stephen T. 2013. *Against Fairness.* Chicago: University of Chicago Press.

Auerbach, Jerold S. 1983. *Justice without Law?* New York: Oxford University Press.

Avnet, Jon. 1997. *Red Corner.* United States: MGM.

Bai, Ruoyun. 2014. *Staging Corruption: Chinese Television and Politics.* Vancouver: UBC.

Bakken, Børge. 2000. *The Exemplary Society: Human Improvement, Social Control, and the Dangers of Modernity in China.* Oxford: Oxford University Press.

Barmé, Geremie. 1999. *In the Red: On Contemporary Chinese Culture.* New York: Columbia University Press.

Bast, Felicity. 1995. *The Poetical Cat: An Anthology.* New York: Farrar, Straus Giroux.

Beck, Ulrich, Anthony Giddens, and Scott Lash. 1994. *Reflexive Modernization: Politics, Tradition and Aesthetics in the Modern Social Order.* Stanford, CA: Stanford University Press.

Belkin, Ira. 2017. "Justice in the PRC: How the Chinese Communist Party Has Struggled with Managing Public Opinion and the Administration of Criminal Justice in the Internet Age." In *Justice: The China Experience,* edited by Flora Sapio, Susan Trevaskes, Sarah Biddulph, and Elisa Nesossi, 195–228. Cambridge: Cambridge University Press.

Bell, Daniel. 2008. *China's New Confucianism: Politics and Everyday Life in a Changing Society.* Princeton, NJ: Princeton University Press.

———. 1998. "The Limits of Liberal Justice." *Political Theory* 26 (4): 557–82.

Bell, Daniel A., and Pei Wang. 2020. *Just Hierarchy: Why Social Hierarchies Matter in China and the Rest of the World.* Princeton, NJ: Princeton University Press.

Bennett, Jane. 2001. *The Enchantment of Modern Life: Attachments, Crossings, and Ethics.* Princeton, NJ: Princeton University Press.

Blakeley, Donald N. 2003. "Listening to the Animals: The Confucian View of Animal Welfare." *Journal of Chinese Philosophy* 30 (2): 137–57.

Bloom, Clive, ed. 1990. *Spy Thrillers: From Buchan to le Carré.* New York: St. Martin's.

Bloom, Paul. 2010. *How Pleasure Works: The New Science of Why We Like What We Like.* New York: W. W. Norton.

———. 2013. *Just Babies: The Origins of Good and Evil.* New York: Crown.

Blum, Susan D. 2007. *Lies That Bind: Chinese Truth, Other Truths.* Lanham: Rowman and Littlefield.

Bodde, Derk, and Clarence Morris. 1967. *Law in Imperial China: Exemplified by 190 Ch'ing Dynasty Cases.* Cambridge, MA: Harvard University Press.

Bok, Sissela. 1984. *Secrets: On the Ethics of Concealment and Revelation*. New York: Vintage Books.

Boltanski, Luc. 2012. *Love and Justice as Competences: Three Essays on the Sociology of Action*. Cambridge, UK: Polity.

———. 2014. *Mysteries and Conspiracies: Detective Stories, Spy Novels and the Making of Modern Societies*. Cambridge, UK: Polity.

Boroditsky, Lera, and Jesse Prinz. 2008. "What Thoughts Are Made Of." In *Embodied Grounding: Social, Cognitive, Affective, and Neuroscientific Approaches*, edited by Gun R. Semin and Eliot R. Smith, 98–115. Cambridge: Cambridge University Press.

Brecher, W. Puck. 2022. *Animal Care in Japanese Tradition: A Short History*. Asia Shorts 13. Ann Arbor, MI: Association for Asian Studies.

Brooks, Peter. 1994. "Melodrama, Body, Revolution." In *Melodrama: Stage, Picture, Screen*, edited by J. S. Bratton et al., 11–24. London: British Film Institute.

Bruner, Jerome S. 1986. *Actual Minds, Possible Worlds*. Cambridge, MA: Harvard University Press.

Buchan, John. (1915) 1993. *The Thirty-Nine Steps*. Edited by Christopher Harvie. The World's Classics. Oxford: Oxford University Press.

Bull, Malcolm. 2004. "States Don't Really Mind Their Citizens Dying (Provided They Don't All Do It at Once): They Just Don't Like Anyone Else to Kill Them." *London Review of Books* 26 (24): 3–6.

Buruma, Ian. 2013. *Year Zero: A History of 1945*. New York: Penguin.

Callard, Agnes. 2020. "The Philosophy of Anger." *Boston Review: A Political and Literary Forum*, January 21. https://bostonreview.net/philosophy-religion/agnes-callard-angry-forever.

Callicott, J. Baird. 2001. "Animal Liberation and Environmental Ethics: Back Together Again." In *Environmental Philosophy: From Animal Rights to Radical Ecology*, edited by Michael E. Zimmerman, 147–56. Upper Saddle River, NJ: Prentice Hall.

Carroll, Noël. 1990. *The Philosophy of Horror, or, Paradoxes of the Heart*. New York: Routledge.

Cathcart, Adam, and Patricia Nash. 2009. "War Criminals and the Road to Sino-Japanese Normalization: Zhou Enlai and the Shenyang Trials, 1954–1956." *Twentieth-Century China* 34 (2): 89–111.

Chang, Chia-ju, ed. 2018. *Animal Writing in Taiwan Literature*. Vol. 41, *A Special Issue of Taiwan Literature: English Translation Series*. Santa Barbara: Center for Taiwan Studies, University of California.

Chang, Chia-ju, and Scott Slovic, eds. 2016. *Ecocriticism in Taiwan: Identity, Environment, and the Arts*. Lanham, MD: Lexington Books.

Chang, David Cheng. 2020. *The Hijacked War: The Story of Chinese POWs in the Korean War*. Stanford, CA: Stanford University Press.

Chang, Eileen. 2007. *Lust, Caution*. Translated by Julia Lovell. New York: Anchor Books.

Chee, Liz P. Y. 2021. *Mao's Bestiary: Medicinal Animals and Modern China*. Durham, NC: Duke University Press.

Chen, Albert H. Y. 2003. "Mediation, Litigation, and Justice: Confucian Reflections in a Modern Liberal Society." In *Confucianism for the Modern World*, edited by Daniel A. Bell and Hahm Chaibong, 257–87. Cambridge: Cambridge University Press.

Chen Rong 谌容. 1986. *Chen Rong ji* 谌容集 [Collected works of Chen Rong]. Fuzhou: Haixia wenyi chubanshe.

Chen Rong. 1987. *Snakes and Ladders—or Three Days in the Life of a Chinese Intellectual*

[Zhenzhen jiajia]. Translated by Geremie Barmé and Linda Jaivan. In Chen Rong, *At Middle Age*, 119–236. Beijing: Panda Books.

Chen Yuanbin 陈源斌. 1995. *Wanjia susong* 万家诉讼 [The Wan family sues]. Beijing: Zhongguo qingnian chubanshe.

Chen Yuanbin 陈源斌. n.d. "Guanyu *Wanjia susong* 关于《万家诉讼》 [About 'The Wan family sues']." https://www.kanunu8.com/book4/9253/208397.html.

Chen Zongshun 陳宗舜. 1993. *Zaohun: Guomindang zhanfan milu* 造魂：國民黨戰犯秘錄 [Engineering the soul: Untold stories of Nationalist war criminals]. Taipei: Kening chubanshe.

Chiang, Ted. 2019. *Exhalation*. New York: Alfred A. Knopf.

Churchland, Patricia Smith. 2019. *Conscience: The Origins of Moral Intuition*. New York: W. W. Norton.

Cihai. 2002. Shanghai: Shanghai cishu chubanshe.

Clark, Paul. 2008. *The Chinese Cultural Revolution: A History*. Cambridge: Cambridge University Press.

Clarke, Donald C. 1985. "Political Power and Authority in Recent Chinese Literature." *China Quarterly* (102): 234–52.

Cohen, Jerome A., and Joan Lebold Cohen. 2007. "Did Qiuju Get Good Legal Advice?" In *Cinema, Law, and the State in Asia*, edited by Corey K. Creekmur and Mark Sidel, 161–74. New York: Palgrave Macmillan.

Comaroff, Jean, and John L. Comaroff. 2012. "Theory from the South: Or, How Euro-America Is Evolving toward Africa." *Anthropological Forum* 22 (2): 113–31.

Comentale, Edward P., Stephen Watt, and Skip Willman, eds. 2005. *Ian Fleming and James Bond: The Cultural Politics of 007*. Bloomington: Indiana University Press.

Cong Lianwen 从连文 and Lu Xiaoya 陆小雅. 1980. *Fating neiwai* 法庭内外 [The trial]. Emei Film Studio.

Cong, Xiaoping. 2016. *Marriage, Law and Gender in Revolutionary China, 1940–1960*. Cambridge: Cambridge University Press.

Constable, Marianne. 2019. "The Facts of Law." *PMLA* 134 (5): 1121–28.

Cook, Alexander C. 2016a. "China's Gang of Four Trial." In *Political Trials in Theory and History*, edited by Jens Meierhenrich and Devin O. Pendas, 263–94. Cambridge: Cambridge University Press.

———. 2016b. *The Cultural Revolution on Trial: Mao and the Gang of Four*. Cambridge: Cambridge University Press.

Dai Jinhua 戴锦华. 2010. "Dieying chongchong—Jiandiepian de wenhua chuxi 谍影重重—间谍片的文化初析 [Spies galore: A preliminary cultural analysis of espionage films]." *Dianying yishu* [Film art] 1. http://www.guancha.cn/DaiJinHua/2015_04_07_315014_s.shtml.

Daston, Lorraine, and Gregg Mitman, eds. 2005. *Thinking with Animals: New Perspectives on Anthropomorphism*. New York: Columbia University Press.

Deng Xiaomang 邓晓芒. 2010. *Rujia lunli xin pipan* 儒家伦理新批判 [New critiques of Confucian ethics]. Chongqing: Chongqing daxue chubanshe.

Dikötter, Frank. 2010. *Mao's Great Famine: The History of China's Most Devastating Catastrophe, 1958–1962*. New York: Walker.

Dimock, Wai-chee. 1996. *Residues of Justice: Literature, Law, Philosophy*. Berkeley: University of California Press.

———. 2020. *Weak Planet: Literature and Assisted Survival*. Chicago: University of Chicago Press.

Ding Ling. 1989. *I Myself Am a Woman: Selected Writings of Ding Ling*. Edited by Tani E. Barlow and Gary J. Bjorge. Boston: Beacon.

Dirlik, Arif. 1999. "How the Grinch Hijacked Radicalism: Further Thoughts on the Postcolonial." *Postcolonial Studies* 2 (2): 149–63.

Ditto, Peter H., and Brittany Liu. 2012. "Deontological Dissonance and the Consequentialist Crutch." In *The Social Psychology of Morality: Exploring the Causes of Good and Evil*, edited by Mario Mikulincer and Phillip R. Shaver, 51–70. Washington, DC: American Psychological Association.

Donaldson, Sue, and Will Kymlicka. 2011. *Zoopolis: A Political Theory of Animal Rights*. Oxford: Oxford University Press.

Dong Yachun 董亚春. 2019. *Teshe 1959* 特赦 1959 [Special Pardons 1959]. Xingfu lanhai and others.

Dostoevsky, Fyodor. (1880) 1992. *The Brothers Karamazov*. New York: Everyman's Library.

Duara, Prasenjit. 1988. *Culture, Power, and the State: Rural North China, 1900–1942*. Stanford, CA: Stanford University Press.

———. 2015. *The Crisis of Global Modernity: Asian Traditions and a Sustainable Future*. Cambridge: Cambridge University Press.

Dutton, Michael. 2005. *Policing Chinese Politics: A History*. Durham, NC: Duke University Press.

———. 2009. "Passionately Governmental: Maoism and the Structured Intensities of Revolutionary Governmentality." In *China's Governmentalities: Governing Change, Changing Government*, edited by Elaine Jeffreys, 24–37. London: Routledge.

Easterlin, Nancy. 2001. "Hans Christian Andersen's Fish Out of Water." *Philosophy and Literature* 25 (2): 251–77.

———. 2005. "How to Write the Great Darwinian Novel: Cognitive Predispositions, Cultural Complexity, and Aesthetic Evaluation." *Journal of Cultural and Evolutionary Psychology* 3 (1): 23–38.

———. 2015. "Thick Context: Novelty in Cognition and Literature." In *The Oxford Handbook of Cognitive Literary Studies*, edited by Lisa Zunshine, 613–32. New York: Oxford University Press.

Edelstein, Dan. 2015. "From Constitutional to Permanent Revolution, 1649 and 1793." In *Scripting Revolution: A Historical Approach to the Comparative Study of Revolutions*, edited by Keith Michael Baker and Dan Edelstein, 118–30. Stanford, CA: Stanford University Press.

Elster, Jon. 2004. *Closing the Books: Transitional Justice in Historical Perspective*. Cambridge: Cambridge University Press.

Fabre, Cécile. 2022. *Spying through a Glass Darkly: The Ethics of Espionage and Counter-Intelligence*. Oxford: Oxford University Press.

Fan Yuan 范元. 1994. *Beigao Shangangye* 被告山杠爷 [Defendant Uncle Shangang]. China: Emei Film Studio.

Fan Zhongxin 范忠信, Zheng Ding 郑定, and Zhan Xuenong 詹学农. 2011. *Qing li fa yu Zhongguo ren* 情理法与中国人 [Sentiment, principle, law, and the Chinese]. Beijing: Beijing daxue chubanshe.

Faris, Wendy B. 1995. "Scheherazade's Children: Magical Realism and Postmodern Fiction." In *Magical Realism: Theory, History, Community*, edited by Lois Parkinson Zamora and Wendy B. Faris, 163–90. Durham, NC: Duke University Press.

Farquhar, Mary, and Chris Berry. 2004. "Speaking Bitterness: History, Media and Nation in Twentieth Century China." *Historiography East and West* 2 (1): 116–43.

Fauconnier, Gilles, and Mark Turner. 2002. *The Way We Think: Conceptual Blending and the Mind's Hidden Complexities*. New York: Basic Books.

Fei Xing 非行. 2013. *Quanmin muji* 全民目击 [Silent witness]. China: Anhui Huaxing Media Investment Co.

Felman, Shoshana. 2002. *The Juridical Unconscious: Trials and Traumas in the Twentieth Century*. Cambridge, MA: Harvard University Press.

Feng Xiang 冯象. 2007. *Mutui zhengyi* 木腿正义 [Wooden-legged justice]. Beijing: Beijing daxue chubanshe.

Flanagan, Owen J. 2017. *The Geography of Morals: Varieties of Moral Possibility*. New York: Oxford University Press.

Flesch, William. 2007. *Comeuppance: Costly Signaling, Altruistic Punishment, and Other Biological Components of Fiction*. Cambridge, MA: Harvard University Press.

Fludernik, Monika. 2003. "Natural Narratology and Cognitive Parameters." In *Narrative Theory and the Cognitive Sciences*, edited by David Herman, 243–67. Stanford, CA: CSLI.

Foucault, Michel. 1990. *The History of Sexuality: An Introduction*. Translated by Robert Hurley. New York: Vintage Books.

———. 1997. *Ethics: Subjectivity and Truth*. Edited by Paul Rabinow. Essential Works of Foucault: 1954–84. New York: New Press.

Frankfurt, Harry G. 2005. *On Bullshit*. Princeton, NJ: Princeton University Press.

Fukuyama, Francis. 2011. *The Origins of Political Order: From Prehuman Times to the French Revolution*. New York: Farrar, Straus and Giroux.

Fuller, Lon. 2001. "The Morality That Makes Law Possible." In *Law and Morality: Readings in Legal Philosophy*, edited by David Dyzenhaus and Arthur Ripstein, 83–105. Toronto: University of Toronto Press.

Fyfield, J. A. 1982. *Re-educating Chinese Anti-Communists*. London: Croom Helm; New York: St. Martin's.

Gao Heng 高珩. 1965. *Xuebei* 血碑 [Blood monument]. China: Shanghai Film Studio.

Gao Qunshu 高群书. 2006. *Dongjing shenpan* 东京审判 [The Tokyo Trial]. China: Shanghai Film Group.

Gao Yubao 高玉寶. 1955. *Gao Yubao* 高玉寶. Beijing: Zhongguo qingnian chubanshe.

Gao Yubao (Kao Yu-pao). 1960. *My Childhood*. Beijing: Foreign Languages Press.

Gendler, Tamar Szabó. 2008. "Alief and Belief." *Journal of Philosophy* 105 (10): 634–63.

Geroulanos, Stefanos. 2017. *Transparency in Postwar France: A Critical History of the Present*. Stanford, CA: Stanford University Press.

Ghosh, Amitav. 2016. *The Great Derangement: Climate Change and the Unthinkable*. Chicago: University of Chicago Press.

Giddens, Anthony. 1994. "Living in a Post-traditional Society." In *Reflexive Modernization: Politics, Tradition and Aesthetics in the Modern Social Order*, edited by Ulrich Beck, Anthony Giddens, and Scott Lash, 56–109. Stanford, CA: Stanford University Press.

Gimbel, Steven. 2018. *Isn't That Clever: A Philosophical Account of Humor*. New York: Routledge.

Goldie, Peter. 2012. *The Mess Inside: Narrative, Emotion, and the Mind*. Oxford: Oxford University Press.

Goossaert, Vincent. 2005. "The Beef Taboo and the Sacrificial Structure of Late Imperial

Chinese Society." In *Of Tripod and Palate: Food, Politics, and Religion in Traditional China*, edited by Roel Sterckx, 237–48. New York: Palgrave.

Grant, Ruth Weissbourd. 1997. *Hypocrisy and Integrity: Machiavelli, Rousseau, and the Ethics of Politics*. Chicago: University of Chicago Press.

Greene, Joshua David. 2013. *Moral Tribes: Emotion, Reason, and the Gap between Us and Them*. New York: Penguin.

Gulik, Robert Hans van. 1976. *Celebrated Cases of Judge Dee: Dee goong an; An Authentic Eighteenth-Century Chinese Detective Novel*. Unabridged, slightly corr. ed. New York: Dover.

Guo, Xuezhi. 2012. *China's Security State: Philosophy, Evolution, and Politics*. Cambridge: Cambridge University Press.

Ha Jin. 2004. *War Trash*. New York: Pantheon Books.

Haidt, Jonathan. 2001. "The Emotional Dog and Its Rational Tail: A Social Intuitionist Approach to Moral Judgment." *Psychological Review* 108 (4): 814–34.

———. 2012. *The Righteous Mind: Why Good People Are Divided by Politics and Religion*. New York: Pantheon Books.

Haiman, John. 1998. *Talk Is Cheap: Sarcasm, Alienation, and the Evolution of Language*. Oxford: Oxford University Press.

Hansen, Anders Sybrandt. 2012. "Purity and Corruption: Chinese Communist Party Applicants and the Problem of Evil." *Ethnos: Journal of Anthropology* 78 (1): 47–74.

———. 2017. "Guanhua! Beijing Students, Authoritative Discourse and the Ritual Production of Political Compliance." In *Emptiness and Fullness: Ethnographies of Lack and Desire in Contemporary China*, edited by Susanne Bregnbæk and Mikkel Bunkenborg, 35–51. New York: Berghahn Books.

Harari, Yuval N. 2015. *Sapiens: A Brief History of Humankind*. New York: Harper.

Hart, H. L. A. 2001. "Positivism and the Separation of Law and Morals." In *Law and Morality: Readings in Legal Philosophy*, edited by David Dyzenhaus and Arthur Ripstein, 43–68. Toronto: University of Toronto Press.

He Jingzhi 賀敬之, Ding Yi 丁毅, and Ma Ke 馬可. 1946. *Baimaonü: Liu mu ge ju* 白毛女：六幕歌劇 [The white-haired girl: An opera in six acts]. Yan'an: Xinhua shudian.

He Tian 禾田, ed. 2014. *Huang Kegong anjian* 黃克功案件 [The case of Huang Kegong]. Xi'an: Xibei daxue chubanshe.

Hegel, Georg Wilhelm Friedrich. (1807) 1997. *Phenomenology of Spirit*. Edited Arnold V. Miller. Oxford: Oxford University Press.

Hegel, Robert E., and Katherine Carlitz. 2007. *Writing and Law in Late Imperial China: Crime, Conflict, and Judgment*. Seattle: University of Washington Press.

Hegel, Robert E., Maram Epstein, Mark McNicholas, and Joanna Waley-Cohen, eds. 2009. *True Crimes in Eighteenth-Century China: Twenty Case Histories*. Seattle: University of Washington Press.

Heise, Ursula K. 2016. *Imagining Extinction: The Cultural Meanings of Endangered Species*. Chicago: University of Chicago Press.

Held, Jacob M., and James B. South, eds. 2006. *James Bond and Philosophy: Questions Are Forever*. Chicago: Open Court.

Heller, Joseph. 1955. *Catch-22*. New York: Dell.

Henningsen, Lena. 2021. *Cultural Revolution Manuscripts: Unofficial Entertainment Fiction from 1970s China*. New York: Palgrave Macmillan.

Henrich, Joseph Patrick. 2020. *The WEIRDest People in the World: How the West Became Psychologically Peculiar and Particularly Prosperous*. New York: Farrar, Straus and Giroux.

Herzfeld, Michael. 2016. "Afterword: Ironic Reflections in a Cynical Age." In *Irony, Cynicism, and the Chinese State*, edited by Hans Steinmüller and Susanne Brandtstädter, 174–85. London: Routledge.

Hevia, James Louis. 2018. *Animal Labor and Colonial Warfare*. Chicago: University of Chicago Press.

Hillenbrand, Margaret. 2020. *Negative Exposures: Knowing What Not to Know in Contemporary China*. Durham, NC: Duke University Press.

Hinton, Carma, Geremie R. Barmé, and Richard Gordon. 2005. *Morning Sun* [Bajiu dianzhong de taiyang 八九点钟的太阳]. Independent Television Service (ITVS) and the National Asian American Telecommunications Association (NAATA), the BBC, and ARTE.

Ho, Christine I. 2020. *Drawing from Life: Sketching and Socialist Realism in the People's Republic of China*. Oakland: University of California Press.

Ho, Denise Y. 2018. *Curating Revolution: Politics on Display in Mao's China*. Cambridge: Cambridge University Press.

Hoel, Erik. 2019. "The Neuroscientific Case for Art in the Age of Netflix." *Baffler* 45. https://thebaffler.com/salvos/enter-the-supersensorium-hoel.

———. 2021. "The Overfitted Brain: Dreams Evolved to Assist Generalization." *Patterns* 2 (5): 100244.

Hofstadter, Douglas R., and Emmanuel Sander. 2013. *Surfaces and Essences: Analogy as the Fuel and Fire of Thinking*. New York: Basic Books.

Hogan, Patrick Colm. 2009. *Understanding Nationalism: On Narrative, Cognitive Science, and Identity*. Columbus: Ohio State University Press.

Honig, Bonnie. 2017. *Public Things: Democracy in Disrepair*. New York: Fordham University Press.

Hou Chi-jan 侯季然. 2005. *Taiwan heidianying* 台灣黑電影 [Taiwan black movies]. Taiwan: Guojia dianying ji shiting wenhua zhongxin; Shiguang caomei dianying gongsi.

Hu Jianmiao 胡建淼. 2019. Fangeming zui de cunfei: Cong zhengzhi xingfa dao falü xingfa 反革命罪的存废—从政治刑罚到法律刑罚 [The fate of the counterrevolutionary crime: From a political penal code to a legal penal code]. *JCRB.com*. http://www.jcrb.com/xueshupd/mt/201903/t20190320_1978711.html.

Hu Ping 胡平. 2005. *Quanru bing: Dangdai Zhongguo jingshen weiji* 犬儒病：當代中國精神危機 [Disease of cynicism: Contemporary China's moral crisis]. Mountain View, CA: Broad.

Huang Cao 荒草. 1955. "Wo zenyang bangzhu Gao Yubao tongzhi xiugai xiaoshuo 我怎樣幫助高玉寶同志修改小說 [How I helped comrade Gao Yubao revise his novel]." In Gao Yubao, *Gao Yubao* 高玉寶, 206–15. Beijing: Zhongguo qingnian chubanshe.

Huang, Dingru. 2019. "Compound Eyes and Limited Visions: Wu Ming-Yi's 'Weak Anthropocentric' Gaze for World Literature." *Ex-position* 41:53–70.

Huang Jiren 黄济人. 1982. *Jiangjun juezhan qizhi zai zhanchang* 将军决战岂止在战场 [The battlefield is not the only arena to test the mettle of generals]. Beijing: Jiefangjun wenyishe.

Huang, Philip. 2015. "Morality and Law in China, Past and Present." *Modern China* 41 (1): 3–39.

Huang, Ray. 1981. *1587, a Year of No Significance: The Ming Dynasty in Decline*. New Haven, CT: Yale University Press.

Huang Zongjie 黃宗潔. 2017. *Taxiang hechu? Chengshi, dongwu yu wenxue* 牠鄉何處？城市 ‧ 動物與文學 [What has become of their habitats? Cities, animals and literature]. Taipei: Xinxuelin chuban gufen youxian gongsi.

Huntington, Rania. 2003. *Alien Kind: Foxes and Late Imperial Chinese Narrative*. Cambridge, MA: Harvard University Asia Center.

Idema, Wilt L., ed. 2010. *Judge Bao and the Rule of Law: Eight Ballad-Stories from the Period 1250–1450*. Singapore: World Scientific.

———, ed. 2019. *Mouse vs. Cat in Chinese Literature: Tales and Commentary*. Seattle: University of Washington Press.

Ingold, Tim. 2000. *The Perception of the Environment: Essays on Livelihood, Dwelling and Skill*. London: Routledge.

Jameson, Fredric. 1986. "Third-World Literature in the Era of Multinational Capital." *Social Text* 15:65–88.

Jay, Martin. 2005. *Songs of Experience: Modern American and European Variations on a Universal Theme*. Berkeley: University of California Press.

———. 2010. *The Virtues of Mendacity: On Lying in Politics*. Charlottesville: University of Virginia Press.

Jewison, Norman. 1979. *And Justice for All*. United States: Columbia Pictures.

Jiang, Dong, and Xiaohong Ma. 2020. "The Analects and Sense of Justice: The Spirit of Law and Historical Practice." *Modern China* 46 (3): 281–306.

Jiang Wei 姜伟. 2008. *Qianfu* 潜伏 [Undercover]. China: Guangdong Southern Television Station.

Jiang Yihua 江宜樺. 2007. "Taiwan de zhuanxing zhengyi ji qi shengsi 台灣的轉型正義及其省思 [Reflections on transitional justice in Taiwan]." *Sixiang* 思想 [Scholars] (5): 65–81.

Jin He. 1983. "The Second Encounter." In *Mao's Harvest: Voices from China's New Generation*, edited by Helen F. Siu and Zelda Stern, 179–98. New York: Oxford University Press.

Jin Shan 金山. 1958. *Shisanling shuiku changxiangqu* 十三陵水庫暢想曲 [Ballad of the Ming Tombs Reservoir]. Beijing Film Studio.

Johannsen, Kyle. 2021. *Wild Animal Ethics: The Moral and Political Problem of Wild Animal Suffering*. New York: Routledge.

Kahn, Paul W. 2001. "Freedom, Autonomy, and the Cultural Study of Law." *Yale Journal of Law and the Humanities* 13:141–71.

Kahneman, Daniel. 2011. *Thinking, Fast and Slow*. New York: Farrar, Straus and Giroux.

Katz, Paul. 2007. "Indictment Rituals and the Judicial Continuum in Late Imperial China." In *Writing and Law in Late Imperial China: Crime, Conflict, and Judgment*, edited by Robert E. Hegel and Katherine Carlitz, 161–85. Seattle: University of Washington Press.

Kern, Stephen. 2004. *A Cultural History of Causality: Science, Murder Novels, and Systems of Thought*. Princeton, NJ: Princeton University Press.

Kiely, Jan. 2014. *The Compelling Ideal: Thought Reform and the Prison in China, 1901–1956*. New Haven, CT: Yale University Press.

King, Martin Luther, Jr. 1968. "Remaining Awake through a Great Revolution." Speech given at the National Cathedral, March 31, 1968. https://www.si.edu/spotlight/mlk?page=4&iframe=true.

King, Richard. 2010. *Heroes of China's Great Leap Forward: Two Stories*. Honolulu: University of Hawai'i Press.

Kinkley, Jeffrey C. 2000. *Chinese Justice, the Fiction: Law and Literature in Modern China*. Stanford, CA: Stanford University Press.

———. 2007. *Corruption and Realism in Late Socialist China: The Return of the Political Novel*. Stanford, CA: Stanford University Press.

Kinzer, Stephen. 2019. *Poisoner in Chief: Sidney Gottlieb and the CIA Search for Mind Control*. New York: Henry Holt.

Kirchheimer, Otto. 1980. *Political Justice: The Use of Legal Procedure for Political Ends*. Westport, CT: Greenwood.

Kleist, Heinrich von. 1962. *The Marquise of O——, and Other Stories*. New York: New American Library.

Kottman, Paul A. 2017. *Love as Human Freedom*. Stanford, CA: Stanford University Press.

Kraus, Richard Curt. 1981. *Class Conflict in Chinese Socialism*. New York: Columbia University Press.

Kurzban, Robert. 2010. *Why Everyone (Else) Is a Hypocrite: Evolution and the Modular Mind*. Princeton, NJ: Princeton University Press.

Kushner, Barak. 2015. *Men to Devils, Devils to Men: Japanese War Crimes and Chinese Justice*. Cambridge, MA: Harvard University Press.

Lakoff, George, and Mark Johnson. 1999. *Philosophy in the Flesh: The Embodied Mind and Its Challenge to Western Thought*. New York: Basic Books.

———. 2003. *Metaphors We Live By*. Chicago: University of Chicago Press.

Lamarque, Peter, and Stein Haugom Olsen. 1994. *Truth, Fiction, and Literature: A Philosophical Perspective*. Oxford, UK: Clarendon.

Lander, Brian, Mindi Schneider, and Katherine Brunson. 2020. "A History of Pigs in China: From Curious Omnivores to Industrial Pork." *Journal of Asian Studies* 79 (4): 865–89.

Landy, Joshua. 2015. "Mental Calisthenics and Self-Reflexive Fiction." In *The Oxford Handbook of Cognitive Literary Studies*, edited by Lisa Zunshine, 559–80. New York: Oxford University Press.

Latham, Kevin. 2009. "Media and the Limits of Cynicism in Postsocialist China." In *Enduring Socialism: Explorations of Revolution and Transformation, Restoration and Continuation*, edited by Harry G. West and Parvathi Raman, 190–213. New York: Berghahn Books.

Latour, Bruno. 2013. *An Inquiry into Modes of Existence: An Anthropology of the Moderns*. Cambridge, MA: Harvard University Press.

Lean, Eugenia. 2007. *Public Passions: The Trial of Shi Jianqiao and the Rise of Popular Sympathy in Republican China*. Berkeley: University of California Press.

le Carré, John. 1964. *The Spy Who Came In from the Cold*. New York: Coward-McCann.

Lee, Ang. 2007. *Lust, Caution* [Se, jie]. United States, Hong Kong, Taiwan: Focus Features.

Lee, Haiyan. 1999. "Huashuo Baimaonü: Minzu xushi zhong de jieji yu xingbie zhengzhi [The white-haired girl: Class and gender politics in a national narrative]." *Ershiyi shiji* [Twenty-first century] (52): 110–18.

———. 2007. *Revolution of the Heart: A Genealogy of Love in China, 1900–1950*. Stanford, CA: Stanford University Press.

———. 2010. "Enemy under My Skin: Eileen Chang's 'Lust, Caution' and the Politics of Transcendence." *PMLA* 125 (3): 640–56.

———. 2011. "'Nowhere in the World Does There Exist Love or Hatred without Reason.'" In *Words and Their Stories: Essays on the Language of the Chinese Revolution*, edited by Ban Wang, 149–70. Leiden: Brill.

———. 2014. *The Stranger and the Chinese Moral Imagination.* Stanford, CA: Stanford University Press.

———. 2016a. "Chinese Feelings: Notes on a Ritual Theory of Emotion." *Wenshan Review of Literature and Culture* 9 (2): 1–37.

———. 2016b. "'Two Wongs Can Make It White': Charlie Chan and the Orientalist Exception." *Transnational Asia: An Online Interdisciplinary Journal* 1 (1). http://transnationalasia.rice.edu/Content.aspx?id=101.

———. 2017. "The Soft Power of the Constant Soldier; or, Why We Should Stop Worrying and Learn to Love the PLA." In *Chinese Visions of World Order: Tianxia, Culture, and World Politics*, edited by Ban Wang, 237–66. Durham, NC: Duke University Press.

———. 2018. "Through Thick and Thin: The Romance of the Species in the Anthropocene." *International Communication in Chinese Culture* 5 (1–2): 145–72.

———. 2019. "When Nothing Is True, Everything Is Possible: On Truth and Power by Way of Socialist Realism." *PMLA* 134 (5): 1157–64.

———. 2020a. "'Measuring the Stomach of a Gentleman with the Heart-Mind of a Pipsqueak': On the Ubiquity and Utility of Theory of Mind in Literature, Mostly." *Poetics Today* 41 (2): 205–22.

———. 2020b. "A Sino-Jewish Encounter, a Humanitarian Fantasy." *Verge: Studies in Global Asias* 6 (1): 142–67.

———. Forthcoming a. "In Praise of the Criminal Imagination." In *Cambridge Companion to Philosophy and Literature*, edited by Karen Zumhagen-Yekple and R. Lanier Anderson. Cambridge University Press.

———. Forthcoming b. "Pardon and Forgiveness." In *Elgar Concise Encyclopedia of Law and Literature*, edited by Simon Stern and Robert Spoo. Edward Elgar.

Leese, Daniel. 2019. "General Introduction: The Politics of Historical Justice after the Cultural Revolution." Freiburg: University of Freiburg. https://www.maoistlegacy.de/db/politics-of-historical-justice-after-the-cultural-revolution.

Leese, Daniel, and Puck Engman, eds. 2018. *Victims, Perpetrators, and the Role of Law in Maoist China: A Case-Study Approach.* Berlin: De Gruyter.

Le Guin, Ursula K. 2004. *The Wind's Twelve Quarters: Stories.* New York: Perennial.

Lemov, Rebecca. 2011. "Brainwashing's Avatar: The Curious Career of Dr. Ewen Cameron." *Grey Room* 45:60–87. https://scholar.harvard.edu/files/rlemov/files/lemov-cameron-greyroom2011.pdf.

Lévinas, Emmanuel. 2003. *Humanism of the Other.* Translated by Nidra Poller. Urbana: University of Illinois Press.

Li Kewei 李克威. 2007. *Zhongguo hu* 中国虎 [The Chinese tiger]. Beijing: Renmin wenxue chubanshe.

Li Qiankuan 李前宽 and Xiao Guiyun 肖桂云. 1991. *Juezhan zhihou* 决战之后 [After the final battle]. Xi'an Film Studio.

Li Zehou 李澤厚. 2014. *Huiying Sangde'er ji qita* 回應桑德爾及其他 [A response to Michael Sandel and other matters]. Hong Kong: Oxford University Press.

Li Zhisui. 1994. *The Private Life of Chairman Mao: The Memoirs of Mao's Personal Physician*. New York: Random House.

Liang Zhiping 梁治平. 2004. *Fayi yu renqing* 法意与人情 [The spirit of the law and human sentiment]. Beijing: Zhongguo fazhi chubanshe.

———. 2013. *Falüshi de shijie: Liang Zhiping zixuanji* 法律史的视界：梁治平自选集 [The view from legal history: Selected works of Liang Zhiping]. Guilin: Guangxi shifan daxue chubanshe.

Lin, Delia. 2017. "High Justice versus Low Justice: The Legacy of Confucian and Legalist Notions of Justice." In *Justice: The China Experience*, edited by Flora Sapio, Susan Trevaskes, Sarah Biddulph, and Elisa Nesossi, 67–91. Cambridge: Cambridge University Press.

Lindner, Christoph, ed. 2003. *The James Bond Phenomenon: A Critical Reader*. Manchester: Manchester University Press.

Liu Cixin. 2014. *The Three-Body Problem*. Translated by Ken Liu. New York: Tor Books.

Liu Jie 刘杰. 2006. *Mabei shang de fating* 马背上的法庭 [Courthouse on horseback]. China: IC Films.

Liu, Lydia H. 2004. *The Clash of Empires: The Invention of China in Modern World Making*. Cambridge, MA: Harvard University Press.

Liu Renwen 刘仁文. 2015. *Yuanyou yu shensi* 远游与慎思 [Wandering far and thinking deeply]. Beijing: Shangwu yinshuguan.

Liu Yunlong 柳云龙. 2005. *Ansuan* 暗算 [In the dark]. China: Guangxi Television Station.

Lovell, Julia. 2019. *Maoism: A Global History*. New York: Alfred A. Knopf.

Lu Jue 卢珏. 1957. *Yangcheng Anshao* 羊城暗哨 [Hidden sentry in Canton]. China: Haiyan Film Studio.

Lu Xun. 1973. *Silent China: Selected Writings of Lu Xun*. Translated by Gladys Yang. London: Oxford University Press.

———. 1980. *Lu Xun: Selected Works*. Translated by Yang Xianyi. 4 vols. Beijing: Foreign Languages Press.

———. 1990. *Diary of a Madman, and Other Stories*. Edited and translated by William A. Lyell. Honolulu: University of Hawaii Press.

Lu Xun 鲁迅. 1973. "Gou, mao, shu 狗猫鼠 [Dogs, cats, and mice]." In *Zhaohua xishi* 朝花夕拾 [Dawn blossoms plucked at dusk], 3–12. Beijing: Remin wenxue chubanshe.

Lubman, Stanley B. 1999. *Bird in a Cage: Legal Reform in China after Mao*. Stanford, CA: Stanford University Press.

Luo Guangbin 罗广斌 and Yang Yiyan 杨益言. 1961. *Hongyan* 红岩 [Red Crag]. Beijing: Zhongguo qingnian chubanshe.

Ma Boyong 马伯庸. 2017. *Caoyuan dongwuyuan* 草原动物园 [A grassland zoo]. Beijing: Zhongxin chuban jituan.

Ma Jian. 2013. *The Dark Road: A Novel*. New York: Penguin Books.

MacIntyre, Alasdair. 1984. *After Virtue*. 2nd ed. Notre Dame, IN: University of Notre Dame Press.

Mai Jia. 2014. *Decoded*. Translated by Olivia Milburn and Christopher Payne. New York: Farrar, Straus and Giroux.

———. 2015. *In the Dark*. Translated by Christopher Payne. London: Penguin Books.

Mai Jia 麦家. 2014a. *Ansuan* 暗算 [In the dark]. Beijing: Beijing shiyue wenyi chubanshe.

———. 2014b. *Jiemi* 解密 [Decoded]. Beijing: Beijing shiyue wenyi chubanshe.

Malamud, Randy. 2012. *An Introduction to Animals and Visual Culture*. Houndmills, Basingstoke, Hampshire: Palgrave Macmillan.

Malick, Terrence. 2019. *A Hidden Life*. United States: Fox Searchlight.

Mao Zedong. 1956. "Oppose the Party 'Eight-Legged Essay.'" In *Selected Works of Mao Tse-tung*, 4:46–62. London: Lawrence and Wishart.

Mann, Michael. 1984. "The Autonomous Power of the State: Its Origins, Mechanisms and Results." *European Journal of Sociology* 25 (2): 185–213.

Martel, Yann. 2001. *Life of Pi: A Novel*. New York: Harcourt.

McKnight, Brian Dallas. 2014. *We Fight for Peace: Twenty-Three American Soldiers, Prisoners of War, and "Turncoats" in the Korean War*. Kent, OH: Kent State University Press.

McKnight, Brian E. 1981. *The Quality of Mercy: Amnesties and Traditional Chinese Justice*. Honolulu: University Press of Hawaii.

McIntyre, Stephen. 2013. "Courtroom Drama with Chinese Characteristics: A Comparative Approach to Legal Process in Chinese Cinema." *East Asian Law Review* 8 (1): 1–20.

McMahan, Jeff. 2016. "The Moral Problem of Predation." In *Philosophy Comes to Dinner: Arguments on the Ethics of Eating*, edited by Andrew Chignell, Terence Cuneo, and Matthew C. Halteman, 268–93. New York: Routledge–Taylor and Francis.

Meierhenrich, Jens, and Devin O. Pendas, eds. 2016. *Political Trials in Theory and History*. Cambridge: Cambridge University Press.

Meng Lingqian 孟令骞. n.d. "Wo de zengwaizufu Zhou Bapi 我的曾外祖父周扒皮 [My great maternal grandfather Zhou Bapi]." *Minjian lishi* 民間歷史（香港中文大学中国研究服务中心）. http://mjlsh.usc.cuhk.edu.hk/Book.aspx?cid=4&tid=2458.

Meyler, Bernadette. 2019. *Theaters of Pardoning*. Ithaca, NY: Cornell University Press.

Miller, Alyce. 2011. "The Legal and Literary Animal." In *Teaching Law and Literature*, edited by Austin Sarat, Cathrine O. Frank, and Matthew Daniel Anderson, 206–16. New York: Modern Language Association of America.

Miller, Ian Jared. 2013. *The Nature of the Beasts: Empire and Exhibition at the Tokyo Imperial Zoo*. Berkeley: University of California Press.

Miller, Toby. 2003. *Spyscreen: Espionage on Film and TV from the 1930s to the 1960s*. Oxford: Oxford University Press.

Mitchell, Ryan. 2019. "China and the Political Myth of 'Brainwashing.'" *Made in China*. https://madeinchinajournal.com/2019/10/08/china-and-the-political-myth-of-brainwashing/.

Mitter, Rana. 2020. *China's Good War: How World War II Is Shaping a New Nationalism*. Cambridge, MA: Belknap Press of Harvard University Press.

Mittler, Barbara. 2012. *A Continuous Revolution: Making Sense of Cultural Revolution Culture*. Cambridge, MA: Harvard University Press.

Mo Yan. (2009) 2015. *Frog*. Translated by Howard Goldblatt. New York: Viking.

Mo Yan 莫言. (2009) 2012. *Wa* 蛙 [Frog]. Beijing: Zuojia chubanshe.

Moll, Andrea. 2011. "Natural or Unnatural? Linguistic Deep Level Structures in AbE: A Case Study of *New South Wales Aboriginal English*." In *Unnatural Narratives— Unnatural Narratology*, edited by Jan Alber and Rüdigger Heinze, 246–68. Berlin: De Gruyter.

Moore, Kathleen Dean. 1989. *Pardons: Justice, Mercy, and the Public Interest*. New York: Oxford University Press.

Morris, Errol. 2017. *Wormwood*. United States: Netflix.

Mühlhahn, Klaus. 2009. *Criminal Justice in China: A History*. Cambridge, MA: Harvard University Press.

Mulligan, Robert. 1962. *To Kill a Mockingbird*. United States: Brentwood Productions.

Nesossi, Elisa. 2017. "Wrongful Convictions: The Useful Injustice?" In *Justice: The China Experience*, edited by Flora Sapio, Susan Trevaskes, Sarah Biddulph, and Elisa Nesossi, 141–67. Cambridge: Cambridge University Press.

Nicolaisen, Jeffrey. 2020. "Protecting Life in Taiwan: Can the Rights of Nature Protect All Sentient Beings?" *ISLE: Interdisciplinary Studies in Literature and Environment* 27 (3): 613–32.

Norenzayan, Ara. 2013. *Big Gods: How Religion Transformed Cooperation and Conflict*. Princeton, NJ: Princeton University Press.

Norton, Bryan G. 1984. "Environmental Ethics and Weak Anthropocentrism." *Environmental Ethics* 6 (2): 131–48.

Nussbaum, Martha C. 2003. *Poetic Justice: The Literary Imagination and Public Life*. Boston: Beacon.

Orwell, George. (1949) 1984. *1984*. San Diego: Harcourt Brace Jovanovich.

Osburg, John. 2016. "Morality and Cynicism in a 'Grey' World." In *Irony, Cynicism, and the Chinese State*, edited by Hans Steinmüller and Susanne Brandtstädter, 47–62. London: Routledge.

Osiel, Mark. 2019. *The Right to Do Wrong: Morality and the Limits of Law*. Cambridge, MA: Harvard University Press.

Pang, Laikwan. 2006. *Cultural Control and Globalization in Asia: Copyright, Piracy, and Cinema*. London: Routledge.

———. 2012. *Creativity and Its Discontents: China's Creative Industries and Intellectual Property Rights Offenses*. Durham, NC: Duke University Press.

———. 2017. *The Art of Cloning: Creative Production during China's Cultural Revolution*. London: Verso.

Peerenboom, R. P. 2002. *China's Long March toward Rule of Law*. Cambridge: Cambridge University Press.

Pema Tseden. 2015. *Tharlo*. China: Beijing Fenghua Times Culture Communication.

Peng, Wei. 2019. "'The Scientific Devices of Truth': Crime, Detection, and Policing in Modern China (1890–1949)." PhD diss., Stanford University.

Perry, Elizabeth J. 2008. "Chinese Conceptions of 'Rights': From Mencius to Mao—and Now." *Perspectives on Politics* 6 (1): 37–50.

Peters, Julie Stone. 2005. "Law, Literature, and the Vanishing Real: On the Future of an Interdisciplinary Illusion." *PMLA* 120 (2): 442–53.

Pettit, Philip. 2014. *Just Freedom: A Moral Compass for a Complex World*. New York: W. W. Norton.

Posner, Richard A. 1999. *The Problematics of Moral and Legal Theory*. Cambridge, MA: Belknap Press of Harvard University Press.

Potter, Pitman B. 2003. *From Leninist Discipline to Socialist Legalism: Peng Zhen on Law and Political Authority in the PRC*. Stanford, CA: Stanford University Press.

Press, Eyal. 2021. *Dirty Work: Essential Jobs and the Hidden Toll of Inequality in America*. New York: Farrar, Straus and Giroux.

Putnam, Robert D., and Shaylyn Romney Garrett. 2020. *The Upswing: How America Came Together a Century Ago and How We Can Do It Again*. New York: Simon and Schuster.

Qian Gang. 2019. "Parallelisms for the Future." *China Media Project*. http:// chinamediaproject.org/2019/03/12/parallelisms-for-the-future/.

Rawls, John. 1999. *A Theory of Justice*. Rev. ed. Cambridge, MA: Belknap Press of Harvard University Press.

Ren Haisheng 任海生. 1995. *Gongheguo teshe zhanfan shimo* 共和国特赦战犯始末 [The complete history of pardoning war criminals in the People's Republic]. Beijing: Huawen chubanshe.

———. 1999. *Bubi shashen chengren: Guomindang zhongyao jiangling gaizao jishi* 不必 杀身成仁：国民党重要将领改造纪实 [Martyrdom is uncalled for: A history of reforming elite Nationalist officers]. Beijing: Jiefangjun chubanshe.

Richardson, Brian. 2011. "What Is Unnatural Narrative Theory?" In *Unnatural Narratives—Unnatural Narratology*, edited by Jan Alber and Rüdigger Heinze, 23–40. Berlin: De Gruyter.

Riemenschnitter, Andrea. 2014. "Another Modest Proposal? Science and Seriality in Mo Yan's Novel *Wa* (Frogs)." *International Communication in Chinese Culture* 1 (1–2): 5–19.

Robinson, Kim Stanley. 2020. *The Ministry for the Future*. New York: Orbit.

Rorty, Richard. 1989. *Contingency, Irony, and Solidarity*. Cambridge: Cambridge University Press.

———. 1997. "Justice as a Larger Loyalty." In *Justice and Democracy: Cross-Cultural Perspectives*, edited by Ron Bontekoe and Marietta Stepaniants, 9–22. Honolulu: University of Hawai'i Press.

Rosenbaum, Thane. 2004. *The Myth of Moral Justice: Why Our Legal System Fails to Do What's Right*. New York: HarperCollins.

Rosenzweig, Joshua. 2017. "State, Society and the Justice Debate in Contemporary China." In *Justice: The China Experience*, edited by Flora Sapio, Susan Trevaskes, Sarah Biddulph, and Elisa Nesossi, 26–66. Cambridge: Cambridge University Press.

Ruskola, Teemu. 2013. *Legal Orientalism: China, the United States, and Modern Law*. Cambridge, MA: Harvard University Press.

Ryang, Sonia. 2021. *Language and Truth in North Korea*. Honolulu: University of Hawai'i Press.

Sagoff, Mark. 2001. "Animal Liberation and Environmental Ethics: Bad Marriage, Quick Divorce." In *Environmental Philosophy: From Animal Rights to Radical Ecology*, edited by Michael E. Zimmerman, 87–96. Upper Saddle River, NJ: Prentice Hall.

Sand, Jordan. 2020. "We Share What We Exhale: A Short Cultural History of Mask-Wearing." *Times Literary Supplement*, May 1. https://www.the-tls.co.uk/articles/a -short-cultural-history-of-mask-wearing-essay-jordan-sand/.

Santaulària i Capdevila, Isabel 2016. "'This Is Getting a Little Too Chinese for Me': The Representation of China in Crime Fiction Written in English." *Coolabah* (20): 67–82.

Sapio, Flora. 2010. *Sovereign Power and the Law in China*. Leiden: Brill.

Sarat, Austin, Matthew Anderson, and Cathrine O. Frank, eds. 2010. *Law and the Humanities: An Introduction*. Cambridge: Cambridge University Press.

Sarat, Austin, Cathrine O. Frank, and Matthew Daniel Anderson. 2011. *Teaching Law and Literature*. New York: Modern Language Association of America.

Satz, Debra. 2010. *Why Some Things Should Not Be for Sale: The Moral Limits of Markets*. New York: Oxford University Press.

Scarry, Elaine. 1992. "The Made-Up and the Made-Real." *Yale Journal of Criticism* 5 (2): 239–49.

Scarry, Elaine, Joshua Cohen, and Joel Rogers. 2003. *Who Defended the Country?* Boston: Beacon.

Schmitt, Carl. 2005. *Political Theology: Four Chapters on the Concept of Sovereignty.* Chicago: University of Chicago Press.

Schoenhals, Michael. 2013. *Spying for the People: Mao's Secret Agents, 1949–1967.* Cambridge: Cambridge University Press.

Scott, James C. 1990. *Domination and the Arts of Resistance.* New Haven, CT: Yale University Press.

———. 1998. *Seeing Like a State: How Certain Schemes to Improve the Human Condition Have Failed.* New Haven, CT: Yale University Press.

Scruton, Roger. 2017. *On Human Nature.* Princeton, NJ: Princeton University Press.

Seed, David. 2004. *Brainwashing: The Fictions of Mind Control: A Study of Novels and Films since World War II.* Kent, OH: Kent State University Press.

Sen, Tansen. 2022. "Giraffes and Elephants: Circulation of Exotic Animals in the *Longue Durée* History of the Indian Ocean World." In *Cargoes in Motion: Materiality and Connectivity in the Indian Ocean,* edited by Burkhard Schnepel and Julia Verne, 113–44. Leiden: Brill.

Sennett, Richard, and Jonathan Cobb. 1972. *The Hidden Injuries of Class.* New York: Knopf.

Shanghai Jiaotong University. 2020. "Ya-Tai zhanzheng shenpan 亚太战争审判 [Asia-Pacific war crimes trials]." Baidu Baike, 2020. https://baike.baidu.com/item/%E4%BA%9A%E5%A4%AA%E6%88%98%E4%BA%89%E5%AE%A1%E5%88%A4/53487617.

Shen Zui 沈醉. 1990. *Zhanfan gaizaosuo jianwen* 战犯改造所见闻 [An eyewitness account of the rehabilitation of war criminals]. Beijing: Qunzhong chubanshe.

Shi Ming 石鸣. 2012. "'Quan yu fa': Yichu wei guoshi de shidaiju 《权与法》：一出未过时的时代剧 ['Power and law': A play that transcends time]." In *Sanlian shenghuo zhoukan* 三联生活周刊, 31. http://www.lifeweek.com.cn/2012/0807/38163.shtml.

Shirk, Susan. 1984. "The Decline of Virtuocracy in China." In *Class and Social Stratification in Post-revolution China,* edited by James L. Watson, 56–83. Cambridge: Cambridge University Press.

Shiwen Lejian 史文乐见. 2020. "Shui shi xiongshou, fante yingpian *Xu Qiuying anjian* li de shiji xuan'an 谁是凶手，反特影片《徐秋影案件》里的世纪悬案 [Whodunit, the half-a-century-old mystery behind the counterespionage film The murder case of Xu Qiuying]." Sina 新浪网. https://k.sina.com.cn/article_6512490685_1842cb8bd00100ndkg.html#/.

Shklar, Judith N. 1984. *Ordinary Vices.* Cambridge, MA: Belknap Press of Harvard University Press.

———. 1986. *Legalism: Law, Morals, and Political Trials.* Cambridge, MA: Harvard University Press.

Shu Gong 叔弓 and Zhang Jin 张巾. 2010. *Linghun juezhan: Zhongguo gaizao Riben zhanfan shimo* 灵魂决战：中国改造日本战犯始末 [The final battle for the soul: The complete history of China's reformation of Japanese war criminals]. 2 vols. Beijing: Renmin chubanshe.

Shue, Vivienne. 2022. "Regimes of Resonance: Cosmos, Empire, and Changing Technologies of CCP Rule." *Modern China* 48 (4): 679–720.

Shweder, Richard A., Nancy C. Much, Manamohan Mahapatra, and Lawrence Park.

1997. "The 'Big Three' of Morality (Autonomy, Community, Divinity) and the 'Big Three' Explanation of Suffering." In *Morality and Health*, edited by Allan M. Brandt and Paul Rozin, 119–69. New York: Routledge.

Simon, Jonathan. 2007. *Governing through Crime: How the War on Crime Transformed American Democracy and Created a Culture of Fear*. Oxford: Oxford University Press.

Skitka, Linda. J. 2002. "Do the Means Always Justify the Ends or Do the Ends Sometimes Justify the Means? A Value Protection Model of Justice Reasoning." *Personality and Social Psychology Bulletin* 28:588–97.

Skitka, Linda J., and E. Mullen. 2008. "Moral Convictions Often Override Concerns about Procedural Fairness: A Reply to Napier and Tyler." *Social Justice Research* 21:529–46.

Slezkine, Yuri. 2017. *The House of Government: A Saga of the Russian Revolution*. Princeton, NJ: Princeton University Press.

Slingerland, Edward. 2014. *Trying Not to Try: The Art and Science of Spontaneity*. New York: Crown.

Smith, Aminda M. 2013. *Thought Reform and China's Dangerous Classes: Reeducation, Resistance, and the People*. Lanham, MD: Rowman and Littlefield.

Snyder, Timothy. 2017. *On Tyranny: Twenty Lessons from the Twentieth Century*. New York: Tim Duggan Books.

Snyder-Reinke, Jeffrey. 2019. "Cradle to Grave: Baby Towers and the Politics of Infant Burial in Qing China." In *The Chinese Deathscape: Grave Reform in Modern China*, edited by Thomas S. Mullaney, n.p. Stanford, CA: Stanford University Press.

Sommers, Tamler. 2012. *Relative Justice: Cultural Diversity, Free Will, and Moral Responsibility*. Princeton, NJ: Princeton University Press.

Sorace, Christian P. 2017. *Shaken Authority: China's Communist Party and the 2008 Sichuan Earthquake*. Ithaca, NY: Cornell University Press.

———. 2019. "Extracting Affect: Televised Cadre Confessions in China." *Public Culture* 31 (1): 145–71.

Steinmüller, Hans. 2016. "Introduction." In *Irony, Cynicism, and the Chinese State*, edited by Hans Steinmüller and Susanne Brandtstädter, 1–13. London: Routledge.

Sterckx, Roel, Martina Siebert, and Dagmar Schäfer, eds. 2019. *Animals through Chinese History: Earliest Times to 1911*. Cambridge: Cambridge University Press.

Stern, Simon. 2017. "Legal and Literary Fictions." In *New Directions in Law and Literature*, edited by Elizabeth Anker and Bernadette Meyler, 313–26. Oxford: Oxford University Press.

———. 2020. "Legal Fictions and Legal Fabrication." In *Fictional Discourse and the Law*, edited by Hans J. Lind, 191–99. New York: Routledge.

Stern, Simon, Maksymilian Del Mar, and Bernadette Meyler. 2019. *The Oxford Handbook of Law and Humanities*. New York: Oxford University Press.

Stevenson, Bryan. 2014. *Just Mercy: A Story of Justice and Redemption*. New York: Spiegel and Grau.

Su Li. 2018. *The Constitution of Ancient China*. Edited by Yongle Zhang and Daniel Bell. Translated by Edmund Ryden. Princeton, NJ: Princeton University Press.

Su Li 苏力. 2006. *Falü yu wenxue: Yi Zhongguo chuantong xiju wei cailiao* 法律与文学：以中国传统戏剧为材料 [Law and literature: From the perspective of traditional Chinese drama]. Beijing: Shenghuo, dushu, xinzhi sanlian shudian.

———. 2007. *Zhidu shi zenyang xingcheng de* 制度是怎样形成的 [How institutions are formed]. Beijing: Beijing daxue chubanshe.

Su Tong. 2013. "The World's Most Desolate Zoo." In *Irina's Hat: New Short Stories from China*, edited by Josh Stenberg, 45–57. Portland, ME: Merwin Asia.

Su Tong 苏童. 2004. "Shijie shang zui huangliang de dongwuyuan 世界上最荒凉的动物园 [The world's most desolate zoo]." In *Xiangrikui* 向日葵 [Sunflower]. Shanghai: Shanghai wenyi chubanshe.

Sumption, Jonathan. 2019. "Law's Expanding Empire (Part I of Law and the Decline of Politics)." *The Reith Lectures.* BBC Radio 4. https://www.bbc.co.uk/programmes/m00057m8.

Sun, Feiyu. 2013. *Social Suffering and Political Confession: Suku in Modern China.* Singapore: World Scientific.

Sun, Xiaozhong. 2020. "Before the Law: Literary and Art Works and People's Sovereignty around Land Reform." *Frontiers of Literary Studies in China* 14:357–405.

Sunstein, Cass R. 2016. *The World According to Star Wars.* New York: Dey St., an imprint of William Morrow.

Swislocki, Mark. 2012. "Imagining Irreconcilability: Cultural Differentiation through Human-Animal Relations in Late Qing Shanghai." *Positions: East Asia Cultures Critique* 20 (4): 1159–89.

Tang, Chenxi. 2019. "Making Facts, Using Facts: Two Poetics of the Factual and One Theory of the Political." *PMLA* 134 (5): 1165–72.

Tang, Xiaobing. 2015. *Visual Culture in Contemporary China: Paradigms and Shifts.* Cambridge: Cambridge University Press.

———. 2000. *Chinese Modern: The Heroic and the Quotidian.* Durham, NC: Duke University Press.

Taylor, Kathleen E. 2017. *Brainwashing: The Science of Thought Control.* 2nd ed. Oxford: Oxford University Press.

Thomas, D. M. 1981. *The White Hotel.* London: Gollancz.

Thornber, Karen Laura. 2012. *Ecoambiguity: Environmental Crises and East Asian Literatures.* Ann Arbor: University of Michigan Press.

Thornton, Patricia M. 2007. *Disciplining the State: Virtue, Violence, and State-Making in Modern China.* Cambridge, MA: Harvard University Asia Center / Distributed by Harvard University Press.

Tilly, Charles. 1999. "The Trouble with Stories." In *The Social Worlds of Higher Education: Handbook for Teaching in a New Century*, edited by Bernice Pescosolido and Ronald Aminzade, 256–70. Thousand Oaks, CA: Pine Forge.

———. 2006. *Why?* Princeton, NJ: Princeton University Press.

Tobin, Vera. 2018. *Elements of Surprise: Our Mental Limits and the Satisfactions of Plot.* Cambridge, MA: Harvard University Press.

Treat, John Whittier. 2017. "Arendt in Asia: Responsibility and Judgment in Nanjing and Hiroshima." *Harvard Journal of Asiatic Studies* 77 (2): 407–35.

Trevaskes, Sue. 2002. "People's Justice and Injustice: Courts and the Redressing of Cultural Revolution Cases." *China Information* 16:1–26.

Trivers, Robert. 2011. *The Folly of Fools: The Logic of Deceit and Self-Deception in Human Life.* New York: Basic Books.

Tsai, Lily L. 2021. *When People Want Punishment: Retributive Justice and the Puzzle of Authoritarian Popularity.* New York: Cambridge University Press.

Turner, Mark. 2003. "Double-Scope Stories." In *Narrative Theory and the Cognitive Sciences*, edited by David Herman, 117–42. Stanford, CA: CSLI.

Turner, Mark, and Gilles Fauconnier. 1999. "A Mechanism of Creativity." *Poetics Today* 20 (3): 397–418.

Unger, Roberto Mangabeira. 1976. *Law in Modern Society: Toward a Criticism of Social Theory*. New York: Free Press.

Van Fleit Hang, Krista. 2013. *Literature the People Love: Reading Chinese Texts from the Early Maoist Period (1949–1966)*. New York: Palgrave Macmillan.

Wade, Samuel. 2014. "Criminal Detention Replacing Re-education through Labor." *China Digital Times*. https://chinadigitaltimes.net/2014/04/criminal-detention -replacing-re-education-labor/.

———. 2017. "Doubts Surround End of Abusive *Shuanggui* Detention." *China Digital Times*. https://chinadigitaltimes.net/2017/10/doubts-surround-end-abusive -shuanggui-detention/.

Walsh, Michael J. 2020. *Stating the Sacred: Religion, China, and the Formation of the Nation-State*. New York: Columbia University Press.

Walton, Kendall L. 1990. *Mimesis as Make-Believe: On the Foundations of the Representational Arts*. Cambridge, MA: Harvard University Press.

Walzer, Michael. 1994. *Thick and Thin: Moral Argument at Home and Abroad*. Notre Dame, IN: University of Notre Dame Press.

———. 2015. *Just and Unjust Wars: A Moral Argument with Historical Illustrations*. 5th ed. New York: Basic Books.

Wang, David Der-wei. 1997. *Fin-de-Siècle Splendor: Repressed Modernities of Late Qing Fiction, 1849–1911*. Stanford, CA: Stanford University Press.

Wang Fangfang 王放放. 2014. *Huang Kegong anjian* 黄克功案件 [The case of Huang Kegong]. China: Beijing Film Group.

Wang Ping 王苹. 1958. *Yong bu xiaoshi de dianbo* 永不消逝的电波 [Everlasting radio signals]. China: August First Film Studio.

Wang, Shui-bo. 2005. *They Chose China*. Canada: National Film Board.

Watson, James L. 2007. "Orthopraxy Revisited." *Modern China* 33 (1): 154–58.

Wegner, Daniel M. 2017. *The Illusion of Conscious Will*. New ed. Cambridge, MA: MIT Press.

Wei, Yan. 2020. *Detecting Chinese Modernities: Rupture and Continuity in Modern Chinese Detective Fiction (1896–1949)*. Leiden: Brill.

Weisberg, Richard H. 1992. *Poethics, and Other Strategies of Law and Literature*. New York: Columbia University Press.

Weisberg, Robert. 1989. "The Law-Literature Enterprise." *Yale Journal of Law and the Humanities* 1 (1): 1–67.

Wen Muye 文牧野. 2018. *Wo bushi yaoshen* 我不是药神 [Dying to survive]. China: Huaihouzi yingye.

West, Stephen H., and Wilt L. Idema. 2010. *Monks, Bandits, Lovers, and Immortals: Eleven Early Chinese Plays*. Indianapolis: Hackett.

Wilder, Billy. 1957. *Witness for the Prosecution*. United States: Edward Small Productions.

Wilson, David Sloan. 2015. *Does Altruism Exist? Culture, Genes, and the Welfare of Others*. New Haven, CT: Yale University Press.

Wong, Winnie Won Yin. 2013. *Van Gogh on Demand: China and the Readymade*. Chicago: University of Chicago Press.

Woods, Brett F. 2008. *Neutral Ground: A Political History of Espionage Fiction*. New York: Algora.

Wright, Richard. 1940. *Native Son*. New York: Harper and Row.

Wu Mingyi 吳明益. 2015. *Danche shiqie ji* 單車失竊記 [The stolen bicycle]. Taipei: Maitian chubanshe.

Wu Mingyi. 2017. *The Stolen Bicycle*. Translated by Darryl Sterk. Melbourne: Text Publishing Melbourne Australia.

Xia, Yun. 2017. *Down with Traitors: Justice and Nationalism in Wartime China*. Seattle: University of Washington Press.

Xie Jin 谢晋. 1960. *Hongse niangzijun* 红色娘子军 [The red detachment of women]. China: Shanghai Film Studio.

Xing Yixun. 1980. "Power versus Law." *Chinese Literature* 6:31–91.

Xu Guiying 徐桂英 and Ji Min 纪敏, eds. 2000. *Gaizao zhanfan jishi* 改造战犯纪实 [An oral and documentary history of reforming war criminals]. Beijing: Zhongguo wenshi chubanshe.

Xu, Xiaoqun. 2020. *Heaven Has Eyes: A History of Chinese Law*. New York: Oxford University Press.

Yan Jizhou 严寄洲. 1963. *Yehuo chunfeng dou gucheng* 野火春风斗古城 [Struggles in an ancient city]. China: August First Film Studio.

Yan Lianke. (2005) 2007. *Serve the People!* Translated by Julia Lovell. London: Constable.

Yang Jisheng. 2012. *Tombstone: The Great Chinese Famine, 1958–1962*. Edited by Edward Friedman, Jian Guo and Stacy Mosher. Translated by Stacy Mosher and Jian Guo. Introduction by Edward Friedman and Roderick MacFarquhar. New York: Farrar, Straus and Giroux.

Yang, Min. 2019. "Spy, Abjection, and Post-socialist Identity: Chinese Neo–Spy Films since 2009." *Studies in the Humanities* (44): 92–112.

Yang Zhijun 杨志军. 2005. *Zang'ao* 藏獒 [The Tibetan mastiff]. Beijing: Renmin wenxue chubanshe.

Yeh, Catherine Vance. 2015. *The Chinese Political Novel: Migration of a World Genre*. Cambridge, MA: Harvard University Asia Center / Distributed by Harvard University Press.

Yeh, Emily T. 2013. *Taming Tibet: Landscape Transformation and the Gift of Chinese Development*. Ithaca, NY: Cornell University Press.

Yin Li 尹力. 1995. *Wuhui zhuizong* 无悔追踪 [Relentless chase]. China: Beijing dianshi yishu zhongxin yinxiang chubanshe.

You Lei 尤磊. 1964. *Banye jijiao* 半夜鸡叫 [The rooster crows at midnight]. China: Shanghai Animation Studio.

Young, Terence. 1963. *From Russia with Love*. United Artists.

Yu Gang 余刚. 2020. "Xu Qiuying anjian zhenxiang 徐秋影案件真相 [The truth behind the Xu Qiuying case]." *Yanhuang chunqiu* 炎黄春秋. http://www.yhcqw.com/30/4945.html.

Yu Yanfu 于彦夫. 1956. *Xu Qiuying anjian* 徐秋影案件 [The murder case of Xu Qiuying]. China: Changchun Film Studio.

Zanasi, Margherita. 2008. "Globalizing *Hanjian*: The Suzhou Trials and the Post–World War II Discourse on Collaboration." *American Historical Review* 113 (3): 731–51.

Zarrow, Peter Gue. 2012. *After Empire: The Conceptual Transformation of the Chinese State, 1885–1924*. Stanford, CA: Stanford University Press.

Zhang, Binxin. 2014. "Criminal Justice for World War II Atrocities in China." FICHL
    Policy Brief Series. Torkel Opsahl Academic EPublisher. https://www.toaep.org/pbs
    -pdf/29-zhang.
Zhang Yimou 张艺谋. 1992. *Qiuju da guansi* 秋菊打官司 [Qiuju goes to court]. China:
    Yindu jigou.
Zhou Dawei 周大伟. 2013. *Fazhi de xijie* 法治的细节 [The fine grain of the rule of law].
    Beijing: Beijing daxue chubanshe.
Zhao Xinshui 赵心水. 1963. *Bingshan shang de laike* 冰山上的來客 [Visitor on the ice
    mountain]. China: Changchun Film Studio.
Zhu, Jing. 2020. "Who Wears a Mask? The Global Pandemic and a Brief History of
    Masks in Republican China." University of Warwick Global History and Culture
    Center. June 20. https://warwick.ac.uk/fac/arts/history/ghcc/blog/who_wears_a/.
Zhu, Ying. 2022. "How Madame Mao Remade Hollywood for Chinese Audiences." *Liter-
    ary Hub* (blog). 2022. https://lithub.com/how-madame-mao-remade-hollywood-for
    -chinese-audiences/.
Zito, Angela. 1997. *Of Body and Brush: Grand Sacrifice as Text/Performance in Eighteenth-
    Century China.* Chicago: University of Chicago Press.
Zunshine, Lisa. 2006. *Why We Read Fiction: Theory of Mind and the Novel.* Columbus:
    Ohio State University Press.
———. 2008. *Strange Concepts and the Stories They Make Possible: Cognition, Culture,
    Narrative.* Baltimore: Johns Hopkins University Press.
———. 2012. *Getting Inside Your Head: What Cognitive Science Can Tell Us about Popular
    Culture.* Baltimore: Johns Hopkins University Press.
———. 2022. *The Secret Life of Literature.* Cambridge, MA: MIT Press.

Index

Note: page numbers set in italics refer to figures.

How I

MW01253182

How Do We Help?

The Free Market in Development Aid

Patrick Develtere

in collaboration with
Huib Huyse and Jan Van Ongevalle

LEUVEN UNIVERSITY PRESS

© 2012 Leuven University Press / Universitaire Pers Leuven /
Presses Universitaires de Louvain
Minderbroedersstraat 4
B-3000 Leuven (Belgium)

ISBN 978 90 5867 902 4
D/2012/1869/5
NUR: 740

Design: Het vlakke land
Cover photo: "Mzungu, mzungu!" © Lisa Develtere

It is not the man who has too little,
but the man who craves more, that is poor
(Seneca)

Wealth is not what you own, but what you give away
(Ibo saying)

Many small things done in many small places by many small people
can change the face of the world
(Chinese saying)

Content

Preface

Development cooperation has existed for around fifty years. In 1958, a great many countries were on the eve of independence, and the high-profile Treaty of Rome was coming into force, mapping out a new course towards a more unified Europe. The Treaty also laid the basis for continuing work with the ex-colonies over many decades.

Over these fifty years, the West has spent more than $3,000 billion on development aid. It is reasonable to ask whether this has been a good investment. Development cooperation specialists are asking themselves the same question – more than ever, in fact. In recent years, donor countries, non-governmental development organisations, academics and recipient countries have been taking a highly critical look at the instruments and workings of the development sector. There has even been talk of a new 'aid architecture'. In good architecture, the form follows the function, not vice versa. We may ask whether the proposed new aid architecture satisfies this principle. In other words, is the reconstruction of the aid apparatus about rescuing the Third World or rescuing the apparatus? Why is there a desire to rescue development cooperation? No doubt because it can boast a fairly strong track record: development aid has helped many countries and many people. But there is another reason too: it is currently facing challenges from a host of new players – official, international and private – who have brought with them radically new ideas and ways of working.

Of course, this is not the first time that development aid has been the subject of examination and soul-searching. The first studies of it appeared back in the 1970s. People wondered then, as they still do, whether development aid is not a veiled form of neo-colonialism or imperialism; how great a gap there is between the rhetoric and reality in this area; to what extent aid generates unwelcome side-effects such as bureaucratisation and irresponsible policy-making behaviour; and whether emergency aid does not exacerbate emergencies. Since the 1990s, various new themes have been added to this list. People want to know about the effectiveness and impact of aid, how the participation of local people can play a role, and what effects new forms of aid such as fair trade and budget support are having.

This book continues this research tradition and introduces a number of new questions. It is a study *of* development cooperation: we want to know how it works. It is also a study *for* development cooperation, and more specifically for what we later refer to as 'the development cooperation community'. We attempt in particular to identify a number of significant aspects and principles of development cooperation, so as to gain a better understanding of them, but also so as to enable a strategic approach to be taken to them.

In 2005, I brought out a book about Belgian development cooperation. In it, I presented development cooperation as a *community* of thousands of development workers, as an *arena* with much competition and many antagonisms, and as a *market* in which large sums of money circulate. I pointed out that the sector was subject to two trends. Firstly, development cooperation was becoming increasingly internationalised in terms of both dialogue and coordination. Secondly, we were seeing its localisation or mainstreaming. In addition to the development cooperation specialists, we were seeing the rise of what we have called the 'fourth pillar' of development cooperation. These new actors, such as foundations, trade unions, businesses, schools and large numbers of small clubs, took very little notice of the specialists, but they were creating turmoil in the sector.

In this book, we attempt to understand what is currently going on. We seem to have reached a pivotal moment. The internationalisation of development cooperation may well have reached its peak. In principle, virtually everyone supports the Millennium Development Goals, *the* major development agenda the purpose of which since 2000 has been to guide all donors and beneficiaries towards 2015. Hundreds of development actors have signed up to the Paris Declaration on Aid Effectiveness. Everyone is singing from the same hymn-sheet. Yet at the same time the sector's fragmentation seems to be increasing. We are seeing competition everywhere. The arena and market dimensions of the development sector seem to be overtaking the community dimension. Anyone can call themselves a development worker and claim to have a wonder cure.

I am very conscious that this book, like all studies, is marked by what is known as 'researcher bias'. With a subject like this in particular, neither our personal values and standards nor our emotions are ever very far away. It is true that *ethos* and *pathos* determine to a large extent what we see and how we see it. Our involvement with various organisations and institutions which are examined here makes us privileged witnesses, but also undoubtedly influences our perception of them.

In any case, I wish to take this opportunity to thank the people who have contributed to this book in various ways with their suggestions and their critical reflections. Above all, I am thinking of my two colleagues who worked so closely with me to finish this project as well as Kaat Torfs and Steffie Neyens, who performed thorough fact-finding work for this book over several months. I also wish to thank all our colleagues at HIVA KULeuven, and in particular the development cooperation research group: Ignace Pollet, Bénédicte Fonteneau, Zhao Li, Tom De Bruyn, Mame Khady Ba, Raf Peels, Sonja Wuyts, Katleen Postelmans and also Sandra Volders. The collaboration and discussions that took place in the context of the Living Stone Competence Centre on Intercultural Entrepreneurship were unusually fruitful. My thanks go to Bob Elsen and Lut Dusart. Thanks too to our colleagues at the Leuven Centre for Global Governance Studies: Jan Wouters, Jo Swinnen, Hans Bruyninckx, Stefaan Keukeleire and Axel Marx. We have also gathered a plethora of data, experiences and viewpoints during the debate sessions and seminars which we have held in recent years with staff members at the Belgian Directorate-General for Development Cooperation (DGD), the Belgian Technical Cooperation (BTC), the Antwerp Institute for Development Policy (IOB), the Centre for International Development Issues Nijmegen (CIDIN), Context Masterclass, NGOs and countless fourth-pillar initiatives. In addition, we have gained many insights through our own cooperation with the Chair of Social Dynamics at the University of Kinshasa (DR Congo). Thanks go to Professors S. Shomba, F. Mukoka, D. Olela, J. Mulamba and their dynamic team, including I. Feza and S. Badibanga. Finally, many thanks to the home base: Kaat, Lisa, Hanna and Eline.

Patrick Develtere

Introduction

Sarro looked at the mini-screen in front of her: 'Swiss and Edelweiss Air: Flying to Paradise.' She had just sat down next to me, on the flight from Nairobi to Zurich. Sarro was wearing the same colourful Somalian shawl as the other twenty or thirty women who had boarded the flight along with her. The men and children had shaven heads and wore sweaters clearly marked with the letters 'USRP'. United States Refugee Program, I guessed. Each of them was also carrying a single plastic bag, marked 'IOM', International Organisation for Migration. Around sixty to eighty dishevelled-looking people, on a plane for the first time in their lives, headed for the United States. Sarro herself reckoned she was 22 years old. In 1992, at the age of five, she had fled the civil war in Somalia together with her mother. She lost her mother on the way to Mombasa, Kenya, where she found shelter in a camp. In 1997 she was taken several thousand kilometres to the northwest in the back of a truck. Ethnic tensions with the local population had been making life at the camp in Mombasa impossible. Since then, Sarro had been at the Kakuma refugee camp, one of the biggest camps in the world. Its more than 80,000 inhabitants are refugees from Somalia, Ethiopia, Sudan, Burundi and Angola. Ironically, they are somewhat better off (in material terms) than the surrounding Turkana people, who do jobs in the camp for payment, or raid it now and then to plunder and steal. Sarro was familiar with the humanitarian work of the WFP (World Food Programme) there. She did not know what the abbreviation stood for – just that they handed out food bearing the stamp 'USA' on every bag. Twice a month, they were given some flour, oil, salt and meat. The IRC (International Red Cross) had an infirmary in Kakuma, she said. GTZ (the German technical cooperation organisation) distributed firewood. There was also a project to heat food using solar power. You could get building materials from UNHCR (United Nations High Commissioner for Refugees), Sarro told me. The LWF (Lutheran World Federation) and Act (Action by Churches Together) were everywhere, doing lots of things... The Windl Trust gave English lessons and the JRS (Jesuit Refugee Service) provided social support in the event of problems in families and between ethnic groups. Sarro had been working for the

JRS for two years. She had earned about 1 euro per day giving advice and help to battered mothers, quarrelling neighbours and children who had got lost, and thus felt like one of the more prosperous residents in the camp. She had a lamp in her tent and a mobile phone. There were some people there who were even better off: quite a few camp-dwellers received money from their families in the US or the UK. There were always long queues outside the Western Union office in the camp.

Clearly, then, a refugee camp is a market – one with many players. These players stake out their territory, make deals, perform all kinds of transactions, compete with one another. There is supply and demand. Sarro had a clear sense of this, but she could not understand it at all. Why were all these organisations doing this? How did they stand to gain? One thing was clear to her: she had been able to survive because of them. She had even been given the chance to go to the USA, which she was thrilled about. She would work and become rich, and one day she would see her friends again, *inshallah*.

Many people in the Third World come into direct or indirect contact with development aid or cooperation in the course of their lives, just like Sarro. For most of them, however, that contact is far more fleeting, limited and less crucial to the opportunities they receive in their lives. There is a good chance that at the time of their birth their mother was assisted by a midwife who was trained by a non-governmental development organisation (NGDO), that the village well was originally dug with the support of the Americans, the French or the New Zealanders, or that the school was built with aid from Unicef. The road from the village to the city may be repaired every ten years with money from the European Commission, and the three churches and two mosques, each of which has a medical aid station, were probably also constructed with foreign money. For most of the more than 5 billion people in Africa, Asia and Latin America, development cooperation does not impinge on their daily lives. However, they are aware that there are 'projects' in the local area, and that a number of four-wheel-drive vehicles travel round, conveying 'gringos' or 'mzungu'. It is said that you can get certain things from them. Most know that if you are seriously ill, it is best to go to a distant hospital which receives outside support. They also see how white people regularly come to the village or the district together with officials, to look at the local population, the huts, the market and the fields. Sometimes these foreigners ask very difficult questions about what is most needed, or what people would like most in the village or district. And many of them make big promises.

I have rarely heard critical views about development cooperation in the Third World itself: not in the villages, and seldom or never in the media; to a limited degree among local politicians, and occasionally with slightly more openness in academic circles. But even then the critics adopt a fairly passive position on the demand side. They are interested in the resources, goods and services of development cooperation if it is provided there. They know that that provision is limited and hard to gain access to.

Likewise, in most Western countries, development cooperation is only rarely the subject of heated debate in living-rooms, in the pub, in the media or in parliament. Oddly, the one time when we do have debate is when development cooperation becomes linked in a negative way with diplomatic relations with an important country. We had good examples of this in the 1980s, when Belgium, France and the USA continued to give significant support to the rotten Mobutu regime in Zaire. There was also a considerable outcry in the Netherlands during the same period because of the messy relationship with the Suharto regime in the former Dutch colony of Indonesia. In both cases, it was the dictator who put a stop to the flow of aid, in 1991 and 1992 respectively. In the USA, critical voices were heard in the media when the American development agency USAID had to be brought in to clear away rubble after the fall of the Iraqi dictator Saddam Hussein in April 2003, and it became apparent that plans had already been made for this before war had even been declared. The sector also sometimes becomes the subject of public reflection for a while when development cooperation ends up being negatively linked with commercial interests. Thus in the mid-1990s, official aid became a topic of debate in various donor countries due to the 'white elephants' or megalomaniac projects which were being funded in Africa, Latin America and Asia. More recent examples constitute the poorly coordinated humanitarian aid after the Haiti earthquake in 2009 and the food aid that came too little and too late to rescue the starving people in East Africa in 2011. Suddenly, everyone had an opinion about whether this kind of aid was right, whether other priorities needed to be set or whether development aid was to blame for the disasters.

The lack of public discussion may have more to do with the fact that development cooperation is not among those domestic themes of contention that have the capacity really to stir up public opinion, the press and politicians in a country, rather than reflecting a general lack of interest in the topic. In fact there are reasons to believe that there is growing support for development aid. Nor am I referring here solely to the wave of solidarity in late 2004 and early

17

2005 that followed the tsunami which ravaged Thailand, Myanmar, Sri Lanka, the Maldives and the eastern coast of India. In the rich countries we also have a high density of organisations (NGDOs and others) which have specialised in development cooperation. Studies have even shown that interest in development aid is on the increase everywhere. But those same studies also show that people are particularly ignorant about the aid sector and that the support is not very deep-rooted.

We want to use this book to do something about that lack of knowledge and debate. Development cooperation is a maze. It is a very unusual community of many thousands of institutions and organisations which specialise in it and are engaged in it on a daily basis. Some of them are government institutions; they are to be found above all in the 24 members of the Development Assistance Committee (DAC) of the OECD. Other institutions belong to the United Nations and specialise in various forms of development aid. There are also international organisations outside the UN which play an important role in the development community. The International Organisation for Migration, which brought Sarro to the USA, is one example. Yet other organisations are 'non-governmental' in nature. These NGOs are private initiatives by people looking for a solution to the North-South problem. There are thought to be more than ten thousand NGDOs which are recognised by their respective governments for their expertise in the field of development work.

These official, international and non-governmental aid organisations all make their own choices. Some specialise in emergency aid operations, while others work more in the long term. There are institutions and organisations which provide technical aid, and others which just give money. Some provide loans; others only make donations. Over a hundred institutions and organisations are mentioned in this book.

Do not be deterred. The institutions and organisations are discussed according to the category to which they belong. Thus we examine official 'bilateral' development cooperation (the 'first pillar') separately from the international institutions (the 'second pillar') and from the NGDOs (the 'third pillar'). Text boxes provide information about specific projects, initiatives and points of interest.

We will describe the development sector not just as a community but also as an arena, a place where quite a number of opposing interests meet. It is the scene for sometimes fierce discussions and even conflicts. And it is also a market. Goods, services and a great deal of money circulate in the sector, and ever

greater quantities of these are sought and promised. Thus this sector, just like any other, is full of opportunists, marketers, dealers and canny accountants.

The field of development cooperation is now also populated by new EU member states and by developing nations such as China, India and Brazil. One important factor is the ambition of cities and municipalities, provincial authorities and other governmental levels such as the communities and regions in Belgium, the *Länder* in Germany and the regions in Spain to gain more powers with regard to development cooperation. What is less widely known is that in most donor countries other ministries are now also becoming involved in development cooperation. Thus we are seeing a kind of mainstreaming of development cooperation. Non-specialists are starting to offer aid in all kinds of forms.

The field of international players is also expanding. Both the United Nations and Europe are themselves giving a boost to new forms of development work and eagerly creating additional development institutions. There are already over two hundred intergovernmental organisations positioned in different ways on the development cooperation market.

By now, we all know that Bill and Melinda Gates have set aside a huge amount of money for Africa. And we all also know a local business leader, trade unionist, schoolteacher or hospital director who has set up an initiative from within their business, union, school or hospital to provide aid to acquaintances in the Third World.

Because most of these new 'players' are not development cooperation specialists and take an approach which is different from that of the first, second and third pillars referred to earlier, we have suggested using the term 'fourth pillar' for them. They have not been established within the context of post-war 'North-South relations', but in response to the more recent globalisation trend.

The traditional development cooperation community has never defined what constitutes good or bad aid. Hitherto, it has seemed obvious that trying to do good *is* good, or is better than nothing. After all, 'every little helps' as the often-used expression has it. In recent years, though, doubts have been growing. We know that not all help is (equally) helpful. We know that there is an art to giving. We also know that there are certain shortcomings in the aid apparatus. Work is therefore being done in some quarters on a 'new aid architecture'. But there is not yet any sign of a collective set of standards that clearly defines what constitutes good aid, let alone an arbitration system that defines who is *allowed* to engage in development cooperation, or that includes

correction or sanction mechanisms to filter out faulty or counterproductive work. In other words, anyone can carry out development work, or claim to do so, in their own way. Anyone can offer any kind of supply. The market is free and highly competitive. This is the thesis of this book. What dynamics can we discern on the supply side? What reactions do we find on the demand side? And what can we learn from this about one of the most difficult tasks that mankind has ever set itself: the eradication of the poverty for which it itself bears the responsibility. These are the questions of this book.

Development cooperation:
community, arena and, increasingly, market

Most Western countries have been formally involved in development cooperation for over fifty years now. During this period, specialist organisations and
institutions have been created, projects and programmes have been launched,
there has been debate about ideas and strategies – the good and the not so good
– for achieving efficient development cooperation, regulatory frameworks have
been devised, and then further new specialist organisations and institutions
created, further new projects and programmes launched, and so on. In other
words, a typical cycle has occurred through which a social sector has taken
shape, a process in which institutional innovations, a permanent war of ideas,
new action models and policy have influenced one another, giving rise to a
particular 'system'. Such a system ends up with an established pattern which
is rather stubborn and hard to move away from. In the case of development
cooperation, for instance, you can count the number of specialist organisations
which have emerged since the early 1960s and been shut down since that time
on the fingers of one hand. Organisations remain and adapt their goals. They
rarely admit that their task has been accomplished or (even worse) that they
have failed and should therefore simply shut up shop.

Even new regulations and new agreements hardly ever lead to deficient parts
of the system being dismantled. Regulations usually define new institutions
and methods which are grafted onto the previous ones. Thus the reforms in
different European countries of their development apparatus in the 1990s led
to the creation of a number of new institutions, such as technical and executing
agencies. But 'the sector' was prepared to accept those reforms only if they also
produced a win-win situation for the existing players (Ministries, NGDOs etc.).
The UN is another example: whenever new agreements are made on combating
poverty, the approach to certain diseases or the linking of environmental and
development issues, everyone invariably wants to jump onto the bandwagon
and a series of new specialist institutions are created as leading agencies.

Nor is it just certain distinctive patterns – ingrained and complex – that
are acquired over time: a particular subculture also emerges. The sector gains
typical characteristics, its own 'house style' and 'house culture'. Exactly what

that style or culture is is particularly hard to grasp. Throughout this book we shall repeatedly come upon this cultural component, without really being able to explain it scientifically (i.e. after examining it in a methodologically correct fashion). Foreign colleagues and development workers now and then venture an informal character sketch of one another's style. American development cooperation is messianic and patronising and bears imperialistic traits. The French and British approach is said to be characterised by a constant struggle for leadership, by the conviction of the universality of their socio-economic and political model and the dominance of their language. In the case of Belgium, reference is usually made, we are afraid to say, to the country's colonial past to justify labelling Belgian development cooperation as paternalistic and idiosyncratic. Dutch development cooperation is renowned for its generosity and its pedantic character, the Scandinavian version for its progressive approach and high level of trust in the local partners, and so on.

No definition of development cooperation?

Readers will notice that we provide no definition of development cooperation. There are good reasons for this. There is no available scientific definition of the concept, nor is there any definition that is accepted by all the key players, such as the international institutions or the non-governmental development organisations. It is thus a wide-ranging term. Anybody can claim – on his own behalf – to be engaging in development cooperation. Not everything, however, is 'official development assistance': the Development Assistance Committee (DAC) of the OECD has devised a number of criteria for this.

'Official development assistance' (ODA) consists, according to the DAC, of grants and loans to developing countries. These countries appear on the DAC List of Aid Recipients (developing countries)[1].

These grants and (low-interest) loans must also originate from the government sector and must primarily be intended to promote economic development and welfare. In financial terms, the aid must be concessional, meaning that it has a grant element of at least 25%. Technical cooperation – sending out specialist personnel and training managers in developing countries – can also be regarded as aid. Grants, loans and credits for military purposes are excluded. Payments to individuals, for example for pensions, repatriation or insurance payouts for donor country personnel, are likewise excluded from the definition.

Reference is usually made to 'net ODA' because the repayment of the capital element of concessional loans is deducted from the aid total.

At present, more than 150 countries and regions are receiving official development assistance. The income level of the recipient countries has nothing to do with this.

When a Western country makes a grant to relatively prosperous Venezuela, this is regarded as development aid just as when it makes a donation to poverty-stricken Malawi. The country's growth rate is also irrelevant. Aid to China or India is also counted. It is significant that the definition of development aid is based on the actions of the givers, not the value of the 'aid' to the recipient. The official aid figures which are presented in this manner give no indication whatsoever of what the developing countries receive, but only what is declared as given. It is estimated that the governments of the developing countries receive less than half of what the rich countries report as aid. This is because these figures include both liquid funds and goods and services. A proportion of these amounts never even leaves the donor country (development workers' pay, resources for the reception of refugees, operational funds for the ministry of development cooperation, government money used by NGDOs for development education or for training Africans at Western universities for example). And who determines the value of the goods and services that are purchased in the donor country? Could they not have been purchased more cheaply elsewhere? In recent years, it has also become clear that debt cancellation is inflating the aid figures. In reality, debt cancellation is a transfer from one government department (ministry of development cooperation) to another (the official 'export credit agency'). Many of these debts were no longer expected to be repaid. Some people ask whether emergency aid can be counted as development aid. It usually consists of Western goods which are supposed to solve short-term problems and do not bring about structural changes. The lack of any definition of development cooperation is harmful to the sector. The lack of any definition of what constitutes 'good' development cooperation is even more problematic, as it means that anyone can label their own initiatives as development aid, and even as 'good', 'better' or 'the best' development aid.

In what follows, we will find out more about 'the development cooperation system'. We will do so by characterising it in three different ways. By viewing the system at times as a community, at times as an arena and at times as a market, we can detect different dimensions and different frames of reference. In sociological terms, these characterisations are therefore 'ideal types' which do not directly represent the reality, but which do make it easier to understand.

Our position is that development cooperation is never exclusively and fully a community or an arena or a market. Which characteristic is dominant depends on the moment of observation. Thus we seek to demonstrate that at present the market dimension has gained the upper hand at the expense of the arena, and especially at the expense of the community.

An expanding community

A survey commissioned by the European Commission in 2009 showed that 74% of Europeans had never heard of the Millennium Development Goals (European Commission, 2009). Moreover, people generally do not know who the minister for development cooperation is in their country, greatly overestimate the extent of official aid, can name only a few non-governmental development organisations and have little or no knowledge of recent trends in the development world.

The 'popularity' of development cooperation, on the other hand, was evidenced by a special Eurobarometer study, which revealed that – despite the economic turmoil – nine out of ten Europeans consider development aid to be fairly to very important (European Commission, 2010).

The development cooperation community can be seen as a rather closed community. This does not in itself mean that the sector lacks transparency or does not communicate sufficiently. Many people will even agree that the development organisations bombard them with leaflets, begging letters, emails and TV and radio ads. What our findings do indicate, though, is that a development cooperation system has evolved which comes across as a specialised and separate entity. It has become a fairly closed world, with its own organisations, elite, personnel, procedures, jargon, symbols, public events and subculture. As a community, the sector also likes to present itself as a set of organisations and people who are driven by a values-based frame of reference, as promoters of values such as equality, solidarity and justice.

A community of this kind gains cohesion through four unifying processes: by developing a collective consciousness, by insisting on the coherent character and the consistent behaviour of those participating in it, by the establishment of a collective agenda, and, finally, coordinated lobbying. Firstly, a collective consciousness arises within the community. In the case of development cooperation, there is a very strong collective awareness that without this community the rich West would decline into an introverted condition, driven by national egoism and materialism. The community is needed to watch over it and ensure that the rich countries and their citizens behave properly towards people in developing countries. If contact with the developing countries were left exclusively to those outside the community (such as companies or private individuals), this would have a negative impact on the developing countries.

Overview of the community of development actors (examples)

	Non-profit-making Public					For Profit Private
	Bilateral donors	Multilateral donors	Global programmes	NGDOs	Fourth pillar	Private sector
	Min. for development cooperation (USAID in USA, DFID in the UK, DGIS (Minbuza) in the Netherlands, JICA in Japan)	UN	Specialist agencies of the UN (ILO, FAO, UNESCO, WHO, UNIDO)	International NGDOs from traditional donor countries (e.g. Oxfam International, Plan International)	Social movements (trade unions, farmers' organisations)	Companies
	Bilateral development banks – and agencies (GTZ in Germany, BIO and BTC in Belgium)	Bretton Woods Institutions (World Bank, IMF)	Global Fund to Fight Aids, TB and Malaria, Global Alliance for Vaccines and Immunisation, etc.	International NGDOs from non-traditional donor countries	Associations (migrants' associations, sports clubs, musical groups, etc.)	Commercial banks
	New donors (China, India, Brazil, Thailand, Dubai, etc.)	Regional development banks and –agencies	Global Environmental Facility	National NGDOs in traditional donor countries: World Vision, Save the Children, Care (U.S.)	Social institutions (schools, hospitals, etc.)	Private investors
	Other ministries (agriculture, health, labour, etc.) and government institutions (national banks, etc.)	European Commission	Fast Track Initiative/ Education for All; Forest Carbon Partnership Facility; Emerging Africa Infrastructure Fund	National NGDOs from non-traditional donor countries: BRAC and Grameen from Bangladesh	Foundations	
	Other governmental levels (Länder in Germany, regions in France, communities and regions in Belgium, provinces in Canada, cities and municipalities)	Other international institutions			Company funds	
					Individuals and groups of friends	

A second means by which the community is bound together is coherence and consistency. It issues its own marching orders and social control. Thus tabs are kept on the non-profit-making character of development actors' initiatives. Whether on the part of government institutions or private actors, the community does not allow the principal or subsidiary purpose of development cooperation to be commercial. However, there is no set of standards or recipe book defining what the ideal form of development cooperation would be like. What we have had in recent years is talk of 'a new aid architecture'. Reference is made to a number of generally accepted principles in the sector, such as the right of initiative of governments in developing countries ('ownership' in the jargon of the sector), equal partnership between donor and recipient, joint efforts to reduce poverty and sector-wide initiatives instead of project-based work. At the same time, according to this 'aid architecture' the donors need to adapt to national administrative and procedural systems and coordinate their input more effectively. The fact that terminology from the construction sector is used indicates that the sector believes that this is a complete, coherent, consistent and integrated set of principles.

The next unifying factor is the collective agenda. The community – and more specifically its elite – does all it can to defend its collective interests and extend its influence. For obvious reasons, it suffers from a structural handicap in this respect. Development cooperation is not one of the traditional political and social issues. In a society that tends to pay most attention to the most contentious issues, this represents a serious handicap. In addition, the community is not directly driven by a conventional social movement or special interest group that represents private interests and is capable of mobilising its supporters. We will also see how the NGDO movement is more of a network movement than a social one. This enables it to form numerous connections and take countless initiatives, but it also prevents it from acting as a visible actor on behalf of the sector's interests. The most contentious issues within the community of development actors include increasing the development cooperation budget, scrapping tied aid and making the foreign policy (indeed, all policy) of rich countries 'Third World-friendly'. To what extent the development community has succeeded in securing increased funding for development aid can be seen from the next chart.

Net official development assistance over 50 year, 1960-2010

Source: OECD-DAC, *DAC Statistics*, 2010

The graph shows clearly that we are supplying a larger combined volume of aid nowadays, but that when we look at our wealth (GNI), we have become far stingier. All the rich countries combined invest around USD 120 billion in official development cooperation every year, but that has to be compared with the USD 40,000 billion or so of wealth that these countries created in 2009.

Some countries budget larger sums of money for development work than others. As the following tables makes clear, countries such as the USA and Japan are significant players in the development sector because they have large budgets, but they dig less deeply into their pockets than countries such as Norway or the Netherlands.

Total ODA (USD millions) in 2010

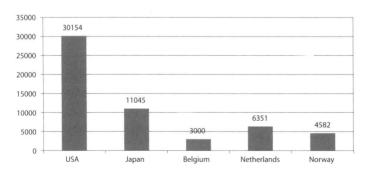

Source: OECD-DAC, Aid at a glance, 2010

27

ODA/GNI (%) in 2010

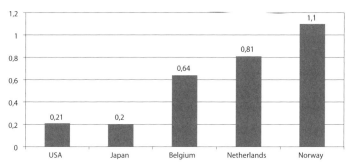

Source: OECD-DAC, *Aid at a glance,* 2010

It is around these issues that the elite of the community also coordinates most of its lobbying. For years indeed, most of their lobbying efforts have been expended on getting the rich countries to commit to spending 0.7% of their wealth on official development assistance. As the table below shows, only a handful of countries have reached that target: Sweden, Luxembourg, Norway, the Netherlands and Denmark. Luxembourg joined this club in 2000, proving that promises are kept at least sometimes. These countries were referred to as the 'G 0.7' by Eveline Herfkens, former Dutch Minister of Development Cooperation.

Net ODA in 2009 – as a percentage of GNI

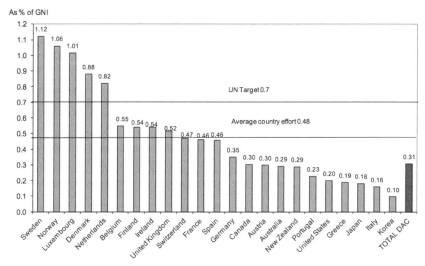

Source: OECD-DAC, *Net Official Development Assistance in 2009*, 2010.

28

How relevant is the 0.7% target?

The 0.7% target has become a political mantra, if not a fetish, within the development cooperation community. The idea arose within the World Council of Churches. In 1955, this Protestant institution asked the Dutch agronomist Egbert de Vries, who worked at the World Bank and was a devout Christian, for advice on its own aid initiatives. De Vries stated that donations from the churches would never be enough to raise the standard of living in the poor countries. So the World Council resolved to ask the rich countries to invest 1% of their national income in grants and soft loans. This was exactly twice the amount of all public and private flows of capital into the poor countries at that time. The request from the World Council of Churches soon reached the United Nations.

In 1960, the United Nations General Assembly passed a resolution, with the agreement of the rich countries, calling for 1% of the national wealth of the rich countries to be spent on international aid and capital for the poor countries[2]. Academics backed the idea. Econometric studies showed that the developing countries at that time and in the years ahead needed around USD 10 billion to compensate for their savings and investment handicaps and leave the starting blocks. As it happened, at the start of the 1960s this turned out to be precisely 1% of the rich countries' income.

The first session of the UN Conference on Trade and Development (UNCTAD) urged the economically developed countries to make an effort to make funds available of 'a minimum net amount approaching as nearly as possible to 1 per cent of [their] national income…' It was assumed that around three-quarters of this would be official bilateral aid. There was no mention as yet of an aid target – not until the Commission on International Development. This influential commission, chaired by the former Canadian Prime Minister Pearson, chose 0.7% as a target because it seemed simple, attainable and sufficient. The UN adopted the idea.

At the launch of the Second Development Decade in 1970, it was declared that 'Each economically advanced country will progressively increase its official development assistance to the developing countries and will exert its best efforts to reach a minimum net amount of 0.7 per cent of its gross national product … by the middle of the Decade'. The undertaking was thus confined to a 'best effort commitment', with no engagement regarding outcomes, either then or later. At the launch of the Third Development Decade (1980-1989) and the Fourth Development Decade (1990-1999), as well as at the UN Conference on Financing for Development in Monterrey, Mexico (2002), the stress was invariably on effort, and none of these international declarations contains a promise to reach 0.7%. The 0.7% thus sounds like what the political philosopher Thomas Hobbes once called 'senseless speech'. However, a number of European countries, including the United Kingdom, France, Finland, Ireland, Belgium and Spain, have unilaterally undertaken to reach 0.7% by 2015.

In the mean time, scientists have been calling the idea of 0.7% into question. The model that was used in the 1960s assumed a mechanistic relationship between capital

and growth. If we apply it to present-day financial and economic figures we end up with completely different (and lower) figures. According to development economist Jeffrey Sachs, USD 124 billion is needed to finance the basic needs of the 1.1 billion people living in extreme poverty. That is just under 0.7%. But the question is whether this is enough to set poor countries on the road to development.

The development community is also searching diligently for innovative mechanisms to generate more funds for development cooperation.

In 2006, France, Brazil, Chile, Norway and the United Kingdom decided to create an international instrument for purchasing drugs for developing countries, called UNITAID. By the end of 2008, the number of UNITAID members had grown from five to 29 countries – of which the majority are African – and one foundation. They looked for additional sources of income for it, which needed to be long-term, predictable and economically neutral. They opted for a solidarity tax on flight tickets. The tax is levied on all flights which depart from the countries in question, and the airlines have to collect it. It is already levied by France, Chile, the Ivory Coast, Congo-Brazzaville, Korea, Madagascar and Niger, and many more countries are examining the proposal. 80% of UNITAID's funds (more than USD 300 million) come from this innovative system of financing.

The International Finance Facility for Immunisation Company is another new mechanism for raising additional funds for development cooperation. The company, which was created on the initiative of the United Kingdom, receives donations from traditional donors, but also issues bonds. The funds that it raises in this way are being invested in a new programme for vaccination and immunisation in poor countries (the GAVI Alliance).

A recent mechanism is the auctioning and sale of emissions permits (2009), in which EU Allowances (EUA) are sold for carbon dioxide emissions in order to provide funds to temper climate change. This can be counted as ODA when proceeds are spend on development cooperation.

The development cooperation community is also trying out numerous other possibilities for raising additional funds. Consideration is being given to a tax on arms and financial speculation.

Some campaigns launched by the development sector have failed so far really to get off the ground. For instance the so-called Tobin-Spahn Tax Act was approved in 2004 by the plenary session of the Belgian Senate, under pressure from the non-governmental development organisations. The law creates

ODA of new bilateral donors

	Country	ODA 2007 (USD million)	ODA 2009
New OECD member which recently joined the DAC	Korea	**672**	**816**
OECD members which do not belong to the DAC	Turkey	602	718
	Poland	356	343
	Czech Republic	179	224
	Hungary	103	116
	Slovakia	67	74
	Iceland	48	34
	Total	**1355**	**1509**
New EU member states	Bulgaria	24	24 (n.a.)
	Cyprus	35	37
	Estonia	16	22
	Latvia	16	22
	Romania	118	123
	Slovenia	54	68
	Malta	10	10 (n.a.)
	Total	**273**	**306**
Arab donors	Saudi Arabia	2079	5564
	Kuwait	110	283
	United Arab Emirates	429	2430
	Total	**2618**	**8277**
Other donors	China	1467	1800
	India*	369	517
	Taiwan**	513	n.a.
	Israel	111	138
	Venezuela	n.a.	n.a.
	Chile	n.a.	n.a.
	Brazil	437	1200
	South Africa	n.a.	109
	Russia	n.a.	200
	Malaysia	n.a.	n.a.
	Thailand	67	178
	Total (estimated)	**5000**	**5400**
Total (estimated)		**10000**	**15000**

Source: OECD-DAC, *Net ODA of 2009*, 2010; OECD-DCD, *Beyond the DAC*, 2010.
* Source: globalhumanitarianassistance.org; ** 2006, Source: UN ECOSOC

the possibility of a tax on international financial transactions, but comes into operation only when such a law is passed in the other eurozone countries. In 2010, the European Commission was requested by the European Parliament to assess and make efforts to implement a plan of financial transaction taxes and to compare it with other sources of revenue. This is an important piece of legislation for the development community, not just because it is intended to prevent or limit the negative effects of financial speculation on weaker economies, but also because it is hoped that the tax will generate extra funds for development cooperation.

It is a sociological fact that a community like the development cooperation community is driven by the urge for self-determination. Outside interference is not welcomed: the community responds by closing ranks and becoming more or less impenetrable. New would-be participants are regarded with suspicion.

However, the community of development actors has come under pressure in recent years.

Firstly, a process of mainstreaming of development cooperation has been taking place. Numerous new players are coming forward. They are rarely organisations, institutions or individuals claiming to specialise in development work. (we will take a closer look at the most important newcomers later). Each of them is contesting the existing community's monopoly. They are introducing new ideas, new values and standards, and new working methods. So far, the reaction of the existing community to their request to join the club has been lukewarm.

Nevertheless, we can already talk in terms of a pluralistic aid community with four main pillars. The first is formed by official bilateral development cooperation, in other words the development cooperation organised by specialist government departments. The second pillar is multilateral development cooperation: projects and programmes which are financed by bilateral donors, but executed by international institutions. The third pillar consists of the private and specialised development cooperation actors, who obtain funds from the government to carry out specific projects and programmes; the most important of these are the NGDOs, the non-governmental development organisations. The fourth and most recent pillar is formed by the motley collection of organisations, institutions and companies which have begun to take an interest in development cooperation in recent years. We will devote a separate chapter to these.

As the table given earlier also suggests, pluralisation and fragmentation of the development community are also continuing because the traditional actors are themselves channelling aid from an increasing array of sources. In every country, the specialist ministry of development cooperation has been joined by numerous other government departments which – untrammelled by the rules applied in the sector – are taking steps of their own in the development world. But perhaps even more challenging is the arrival of new donor countries: the new EU member states, new middle-income countries (Brazil, Venezuela, Thailand, South Africa) and new emerging markets (China, India).

The international institutions also form a fragmented community. There are currently estimated to be more than 260 international organisations. Before, the United Nations Development Programme (UNDP), Unicef and the World Bank group were regarded as the main development specialists. Some years ago, Reisen counted 47 UN agencies, funds and commissions; as well as 97 specialist multilateral institutions and programmes, 12 regional development banks and funds, 2 IMF trusts, 5 World Bank institutions, 4 development institutes of the European Commission and at least 5 major public-private partnerships (Reisen, 2008).

An arena with plenty to fight over

So far, we have sketched out a picture of a development sector driven by a values-based rationale. This also happens to be the most familiar image of the sector: development cooperation is widely seen as the ultimate 'good cause'. But the sector cannot be exclusively regarded as a collective movement the professed principles of which are also put into practice. Development cooperation is also subject to a power-based rationale.

Both directly and indirectly, the sector brings together actors belonging to a huge variety of different categories: civil servants, ministerial staff, NGDO employees, field workers, consultants, researchers, local employees, target groups, recipient governments and all kinds of local institutions. Each of these actors has a battery of action strategies which he/she uses to obtain or gain control of the largest possible share of the resources and opportunities provided by the sector.

Following the French social anthropologist Olivier de Sardan (1997), we can see development cooperation as a plurality of arenas. These are located in the donor country, in the recipient country, in the villages where the projects and programmes are run. But arenas can also be formed which involve donor countries, recipient countries or local beneficiary groups. In an arena, we see heterogeneous strategic groups encountering one another. These groups of actors are driven by material and symbolic interests which are not always made explicit. Relational power is unevenly distributed among the different groups because the system assigns more power to one than to another, and because some actors and groups are able to accumulate more economic and social capital than others.

Although there are sometimes storms over the development cooperation arena, the climate is usually tempered because of an unwritten agreement that the community must be able to continue to exist as a single community and must be able to move forward collectively. People are therefore prepared to negotiate, forgive mistakes and cut one another some slack.

The objects of conflict in the arena are a useful guide to identifying power relations within the sector. They also help us to discern contradictions and inconsistencies. As it is not possible to deal with every object of conflict here, we have selected what we believe to be the most characteristic and perhaps the most relevant themes that give rise to clashes between strategic groups.

Firstly, ever since the beginnings of development cooperation there has been an ideological rift which partly informs all other debate. The central question that 'the sector' grapples with is whether the best way to resolve the acute but also structural problems of the Third World countries is through the redistribution of the global wealth pie or through its growth and development. The sustainable development concept – widely used in the sector for a number of years now – is also interpreted differently by groups opting for redistribution from the way in which it is interpreted by those advocating a growth model. Those in favour of redistribution point out that sustainable development can come about only through greater international solidarity and through a radical rearrangement of the available wealth. The defenders of the growth model emphasise that only the joint growth of the economies of the North and the South can help. The latter position is constantly criticised, but has had the upper hand in the development world for years now. Even in the poverty alleviation programmes which are now so popular, considerable

emphasis is placed on economic growth, which is supposed to provide fertile soil for social development.

A classic debate then relates to the type of intervention that donors should undertake. Should long-term strategies and more structural measures take precedence over short-term and emergency aid operations? The emergency aid agenda has definitely had the wind in its sails for the last ten years. The advocates of structural strategies point out that emergency aid can actually reinforce poverty by making people dependent.

But more structural strategies abound, and all have their advocates and their opponents. Is sending technical experts out to other countries a good thing, or does it force local people out of the labour market? Are short-term projects better than long-term programmes or not? Does debt cancellation reward and encourage bad policy, or is it necessary for a new start?

Another arena is formed by the opposition between public and private actors. The terms 'governmental' and 'non-governmental' actors are used in the sector when referring to donors, and 'public' and 'civil society/private sector' when referring to recipients. The questions of which type of actor has the best credentials in terms of its contribution to development and how the roles should be divided between public and private are ever-present. Over the last decade, the NGO/civil society group has been particularly successful in consolidating its position and turning it to good account financially.

The relations between 'donors' and 'recipients' are constantly tense, too, with clashes taking place over concepts and principles such as accountability, national ownership and sovereignty. Donors should be accountable to the taxpayer. Recipient countries should also be accountable for what they do and should map out their own development strategies. Although a great deal of lip-service is paid to the idea of a more back-seat role for donors, the balance of power is still tipped in favour of the donors: *la main qui reçoit se trouve en bas*, as the French saying goes: 'the receiver's hand is lower than the giver's'. And in any case, many donors are not convinced that all governments in the Third World can be entrusted with a free hand in the administration of development budgets.

Those involved in development cooperation also disagree on the right local levers for development. On the one hand there are those who firmly believe in local strengths: in their view, development cooperation is merely a window of opportunity or catalyst the purpose of which is to help local dynamism to unfold (for example by giving local institutions financial means). On the other

hand, a gloomier position stresses the weaknesses of local actors and institutions. In this view, the purpose of development cooperation is to address local shortcomings and deficiencies (for example by sending in experts).

Different strategic groups can also disagree on the question whether development work should be 'generalised' or 'concentrated'. Some argue in favour of broad measures which have a general effect on North-South relations. Examples include improving access to Western markets for products from the developing countries and the general cancellation of debts. Others believe that concentrated, focused work in specific countries and areas with a high development potential does more good. They refer to the Least Developed Countries and particularly those which show signs of good governance.

One theme of contention which has become very prominent again in recent years relates to the purity of both the motives for and approach to aid provision. Many hardliners from the idealistic school in the sector are unwilling to compromise on this point. Developed donor countries must not seek any advantage for themselves (of any kind at all). Financial gain and profit-based approaches are anathema. Others argue that it makes no difference why and how cooperation takes place, provided it delivers the right results. Remarkably, a realistic school of thinking is also becoming prominent in the South. At the height of the oil crisis in July 2008, the left-wing populist President Chavez of Venezuela very proudly announced that he would sell oil to Madrid at just over USD 100 per barrel (25 per cent less than the price at that time). With the income he would buy Spanish goods, and in exchange the Spanish oil company Repsol would invest in new oil fields in the Orinoco Basin. A clear win-win situation for both countries. Not long afterwards, the now despised and dead Guide of the Libyan Revolution, Muammar al-Gaddafi, signed a cooperation agreement with his Italian counterpart Berlusconi. Italy promised USD 200 million of support for 25 years in compensation for the colonial occupation of Libya (1911-1934). In exchange, Gaddafi was supposed to help prevent illegal migration from Africa. Another win-win situation, it was argued. The advent of new donors, such as China, who explicitly seek advantages (e.g. market access and proximity to much needed raw materials) when giving aid to African countries puzzles traditional donors. Should they condemn the Chinese or should they rather accept this approach as the only realistic one?

It is clear that strategic groups form round each of these contentious issues, developing a more or less coherent set of arguments to defend their case. Win-

ning such a debate has important symbolic value. But there are also other interests at stake in each case – including financial ones. This brings us to the third rationale that strongly influences development cooperation: the market dimension

A market with many transactions

We have by now abandoned the illusion that development cooperation is a system or sector which is exclusively driven by a values-based rationale. Power relations also play an important role. Furthermore, the field of development cooperation can be regarded as a market, too. Thus a more calculative rationale, that of the market, is also present. Just as they do in a marketplace, the various players treat one another as vendors and customers, as competitors, as hard-headed opportunists who are out to increase their turnover, as marketeers who are angling for a good position on the market, as investors seeking the maximum return on investment and as business managers who want to win out and make a profit. At first sight, this seems strange, as most of the actors claim to be working towards a public goal (improving the lot of others and general global welfare) rather than a private one.

Whether the actors are government departments which are involved in development work or non-governmental development organisations, they do not strive for financial gain. Profit is defined, in line with practice in the public and non-profit sector, as 'non-distributable social gain' (number of people employed, social reserves accumulated, etc.). In addition, the means of production which are available in or deployed by the sector are not privately owned, but jointly owned by various stakeholders. For that matter, it is hard to say who has legal ownership of the output. Who owns the well that was purchased with support from a Western NGDO and with additional funding from a Western government, but which was built through the combined efforts of the population of the Burkinese village of Mané? The Western NGDO will assure its supporters that 'its' well has raised the quality of life of the Burkinese. The Western government (which probably paid 85% of the bill) claims co-ownership of the well in several ways. It asks for the original purchase receipts, reports and impact evaluations. The Burkinese government also feels itself to be the owner of the pump, which lies in its territory and must meet the standards that the government has set for water pumps. The pump is counted as part of

the national effort to combat poverty, and features handsomely in the reports submitted by the Ministry of Planning to the World Bank and the United Nations. The provincial authorities and politicians also boast about this achievement. Their department for water supply had performed the soil surveys and correctly indicated where a large aquifer was present at a depth of 170 metres. And anyway, was it not they who were asked to cut the ribbon at the inauguration of this local project? Finally, they were the ones who succeeded in bringing the Western NGDO to the area. The local king reasons along similar lines. The drought has never been so bad as during his reign, but he has managed to attract many *toubabs* (whites) to his area. The local non-governmental organisation is equally proud of 'its' pump. A yellowing map hangs in its local headquarters with 120 drawing pins in it, and the pump at Mané is neatly marked as one of the achievements of its project. And the local people? The members of the well committee who are responsible for hygiene and maintenance regard themselves as co-owners of the pump. They are scarcely able to cope with the limited financial contributions from local users. The rest of the population sees the pump as a gift of the *prozè* (project), a gift from the white man who came past a few harvests ago.

Without this being explicitly intended by the development actors, the risks (failure, theft, loss, natural disaster, etc.) which are necessarily associated with any form of financial interaction are depersonalised in the development sector. Rarely or never does a development agreement specify who should bear such risks. The water pump in Mané comes from Europe. Replacement parts are hard to obtain and expensive. While the project is running, the partnership between the local and European NGDO ensures that the necessary transactions take place if the pump plays up. But both the co-financing government and the NGDO's supporters quietly believe that a ten-year investment in the area has been enough. Was it not promised that the project would make the local population more self-reliant? More often than not development work is practised as a risk-free venture. None of those involved take full responsibility and engage to pay the bill when things go wrong. But also: it is rarely if ever made clear who can lay claim to any gains or benefits resulting from the investments.

Projects and programmes are also often managed via an interactive process in which several parties are associated. In recent years, as we will see, the development community has placed enormous stress on ownership, meaning that the recipient government or population group is supposed to 'be in the driver's seat' determining which goals should be worked towards, how this should be

done and how the results should be evaluated. The donors must 'bring down their flag', take a more behind-the-scenes role and act like a partner. In other words, the idea is to replace 'donorship' with 'ownership'.

These examples hopefully make it clear that the development cooperation market – like any market – is a social construct. The players in the market behave to a significant degree according to the social, cultural, symbolic and power patterns characterising the domain. Yet the market rationality sometimes has a considerable influence on relationships between the players. Even the most fervent advocates of the non-profit-making character of development cooperation cannot escape this fact.

Firstly, there is competition between the players (and groups of players) on the market. The public funds available in the donor countries for development cooperation have in most cases decreased or only marginally increased during the last decade, but the number of programmes and the number of actors have significantly increased. In all donor countries, ministries for development cooperation, other ministries, public institutions, multilateral 'partners' and non-governmental development organisations are embroiled in a permanent struggle over the distribution of these scarce resources.

Components of DAC donors ODA

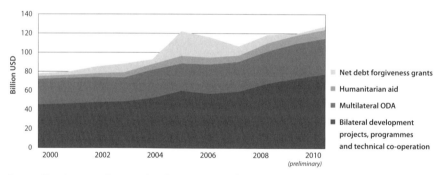

Source: Development Co-operation Report 2011: 50th Anniversary Edition – OECD 2011

Also the so-called charity market lacks elasticity. The amounts donated by private individuals and businesses towards development cooperation are not significantly increasing. Moreover, there has been a proliferation of fund-raisers. Competition between organisations is particularly fierce, and they are increasingly resorting to modern marketing techniques in order to increase

and activate the generosity of the general public, and to channel it (towards themselves).

Between USD 80 and 100 billion has to be converted into goods and services on the international development cooperation market every year. (Debt cancellation is obviously excluded from this calculation.) This market can be seen as a segmented one (Taupiac, 2001). Firstly, there are the emergency aid operations. Where purchasing is concerned, speed and accessibility are paramount for such operations. To save lives, the goods (food, medicines, tents, logistical equipment) need to reach their destination as quickly as possible. They are often simple in design. Although they are increasingly subject to competitive bidding, they are usually also more expensive because of the short delivery period. The other segment – that of the so-called structural and support programmes – works on a somewhat different basis. Goods and services which need to be supplied must above all be suitable for the achievement of the long-term objectives of the project or programme in question. The range of goods and services is far wider than on the emergency aid market. A significant proportion of the budget is spent on industrial machinery, vehicles, engineering services, basic chemicals, fertilisers, seed, audiovisual equipment, contraceptives, medical equipment, medicines, school equipment and construction resources. In recent years, there has been a growing awareness that more local input can and should be provided: in other words, goods and services should be purchased locally if possible. Despite this, most goods and services are still supplied by multinational, Western concerns: UN figures indicate that the proportion of purchases made by international aid institutions in transitional and developing countries is still only 51%. The largest suppliers of goods and services to the UN, the total annual purchases of which are worth around USD 13.6 billion, are, in descending order, the USA (7.7%), India (4.6%), Switzerland (4.2%), France (3.7%), Italy (3.4%), Russia (3.2%), Afghanistan (3.1%), Peru (3%), Sudan (2.8), Denmark (2.4) (UNDP, 2008). The developing countries in this list are either suppliers of coveted goods (for instance India supplies numerous generic medicines), large markets due to an emergency aid situation (Afghanistan) or provide construction services (Afghanistan and Peru) and fuel oils (Sudan).

Again, the larger trends that we identified earlier in the case of community and arena aspects of development cooperation also apply to the development cooperation marketplace. To start with, it is subject to mainstreaming and

localisation. There has been a proliferation of new national and sub-national government actors. Kharas (2007), a senior expert at the Brookings Institute, estimated the contribution made by 29 so-called new or emerging bilateral donors for 2005 at more than USD 8 billion. We found that this increased to an estimated USD 10 billion by 2007 and 15 billion by 2009. However, we agree with Kharas who argues that an exact calculation of the amount of official development aid provided by new bilateral donors is highly problematic, because 'the hybrid nature of some of their transactions disguises whether the purpose is developmental or commercial.' (Kharas, 2009)

As the example of China shows, these new donors are not so new at all. But they have a different conceptualisation of development aid and are introducing new intervention methods. Not only are the combined donation and exchange operations of the Chinese based on looking for an explicit win-win situation, China also takes pride in the fact that it arranges turnkey projects. Chinese projects are delivered in comprehensive packages including the planning, financing, manpower and training that are necessary to carry out the project (including Chinese language lessons to facilitate contacts). China draws on its strong tradition of implementing and managing large-scale infrastructure projects in order greatly to shorten the project cycle (from planning to execution). By doing so, it has become a formidable competitor for traditional donors.

Chinese money sounds different in Africa!

Contrary to popular belief, China is not a new development player. China's foreign aid began in 1950, when it provided material assistance to the Democratic People's Republic of Korea and Vietnam. As early as the Mao era, many African leaders were attracted by the Chinese alternative. In exchange for their sympathy, China would construct their national parliaments, give them a national football stadium to be proud of or install a railway[3]. Chinese experts, such as doctors and engineers, were sent out. Between 1954 and 1971, this young, poor nation gave more than USD 2 billion in development aid, more than half of it to Africa. In 1964, Prime Minister Zhou Enlai set out the principles of Chinese aid:

- Chinese aid must benefit both donor and recipient;
- China respects the sovereignty of the recipient country and does not impose any conditions[4];
- Few if any interest charges;
- The goal is self-reliance;
- Priority for projects which require little investment but yield rapid results;

- China supplies its own equipment at competitive prices;
- Local technical personnel are trained to manage suitable technology;
- Chinese experts live like their colleagues in the host country.

Strikingly, all these principles apart from the first and the last could have come straight out of a DAC manual, and Chinese aid today still seems to be inspired by the same principles. So why the current controversy about Chinese aid in Africa?

In the last ten years, Chinese-African cooperation has progressed in leaps and bounds in terms of both quality and quantity. Paradoxically, this originates from the anti-African movement of students, who protested in 1988-1989 against the higher grants for African students, a protest which eventually led to the violent suppression of the demonstrations in Tiananmen Square. This was promptly followed by a series of visits by high-ranking Chinese officials to Africa and the beginning of friendly diplomatic relations between China and Africa. But the relationship acquired a more functional economic basis when the Chinese economy started to boom in the 1990s (Chung-lian Jiang, 2006).

Midway through that decade, President Jiang Zemin defined Chinese relations with Africa as being based on five principles: true friendship, fair treatment, true reciprocity, dynamic cooperation and common goals for the future.

African leaders were in no doubt why they were keen to receive Chinese officials or drink tea with them during the summit meetings at the Forum on Chinese-African Cooperation (Beijing Forum or FOCAC).

During the first Forum in 2000, China unilaterally cancelled 1 billion euro of African debt and afterwards signed debt cancellation agreements with more than 20 countries (Jian-Ye Wang, 2007). Chinese cooperation is consistently based on the principle of non-interference in domestic affairs. Exports from China to Africa are growing faster than those in the other direction, but China has given the purchase of African goods an enormous boost by exempting certain of them from import duty thanks to its massive appetite for African oil, metal and timber.

For over a decade now, exports from Africa to China – although still very limited in relative terms – have grown many times more than its exports to the USA and the EU. During the first half of 2009, when the global economic crisis reached rock bottom, Chinese investment in Africa increased dramatically (OECD, 2010).

The fundamental differences between Africa and China in terms of natural resources, available manpower and the capital structure of the economy make them complementary commercial partners, and this relationship is set to continue for a long time (Broadman, 2008). The Chinese government is also encouraging its businesses to invest in Africa by giving them all kinds of facilities such as loans and insurance. Chinese companies have a particularly high profile throughout Africa in the construction sector, road-building, the ports, agriculture and the fishing industry, but the processing industry is also seeing more and more Chinese initiatives. In addition – or as a consequence – China is inputting large amounts of money in development aid. Chinese aid is estimated at USD 1.8 billion.

At the 2010 FOCAC Ministerial Conference China pledged to assist African countries

with 100 clean energy projects in the fields of solar energy, bio-gas and small hydro-power stations. China also proposed a China-Africa Science and Technology Partnership Plan and promised to cancel debts in the form of interest-free government loans which had matured by the end of 2009 and were owed by all HIPCs and the LDCs in Africa having diplomatic relations with China. China also wants to increase to 20 the total number of agro-technology demonstration centres built for African countries and proposes to train an additional 2,000 African agro-technicians, 3,000 doctors and nurses and 20,000 professionals in various sectors.

Because Chinese aid is not coordinated, is not transparent, is linked to political and economic issues and often gives the impression of being an exchange operation, it has received fierce criticism in traditional, Western, development cooperation circles. Traditional donors insist on good governance, while the Chinese do not meddle with local politics, do business with bandits as well as with democrats, and by means of their projects reinforce the status of those in power. In any case, traditional economic and aid actors are conscious of the Chinese presence. Chinese companies outbid other foreign firms by also promising substantial aid in the form of new dams, deep-sea ports or social infrastructure. Aid Traditional donors' aid projects are dwarfed by the big, fast and highly visible Chinese projects. Everybody becomes more and more impressed by Chinese assertiveness in the development sector. China's financial resources for foreign aid have increased rapidly, by almost 30% from 2004 to 2009. It gives grants to build hospitals, schools and other medium-sized and small projects for social welfare; interest-free loans for public facilities and concessional loans for productive projects. 'Complete' projects account for 40% of China's foreign aid expenditure. In those projects the Chinese side is responsible for the whole or part of the process, from study, survey, to design and construction; provides all or part of the equipment and building materials; and sends engineers and technical personnel to organise and guide the construction, installation and trial production of these projects. After a project is completed, China hands it over to the recipient country.

The Ministry of Commerce of China is the administrative department authorised by the State Council to oversee foreign aid. In order to strengthen the coordination of all the departments concerned, the ministry of commerce, foreign affairs and finance officially established the country's foreign aid inter-agency liaison mechanism. In February 2011, this liaison mechanism was upgraded into an inter-agency coordination mechanism.

In any case, the increase in trade, investment and aid initiatives on the part of China on the African continent is ensuring less dependence on the West. In 2006 there were 600 Chinese infrastructure projects in Africa. China's Eximbank provided around USD 13 billion of funding for these, far more than what the traditional donors invested in African infrastructure. In a 2007 deal with DR Congo, China promised around USD 6.5 billion of loans to lay 3,200 km of roads and the same length of rail track and build 31 hospitals, 145 health centres and 2 universities within 36 months. A further USD 2 billion loan for the modernisation of the existing mining infrastructure was also involved in the deal. As a guarantee of repayment a Sino-Congolese joint venture has been

set up to exploit Congolese copper, gold and cobalt. Compare that with the USD 1.5 to 2 billion that the development community gives to Congo every year. However, the contracts had to be reviewed on the instructions of the IMF which judged that Congo should not venture into new and colossal debts which could compromise future generations. In 2009 amendments were made to the agreement reducing the cost of the infrastructure by half (Marysse & Geenen, 2009).

The number of Chinese working in Africa is estimated to be in the hundreds of thousands. Contact with China and the Chinese is opening African eyes to an alternative model. The Beijing Consensus is at odds with the Western liberal Washington Consensus, but results in high growth figures and a considerable reduction in poverty. So what do the Africans think about this? 'The West has had 50 years or even far longer to bring us development. It's time to let the Chinese show what they can do.' 'The Chinese seek their own interests, you say? But don't the Westerners do that too?' 'What is the USA doing in Angola, Chad and Equatorial Guinea?' 'Chinese products are of poor quality, you say? I can finally afford a mobile phone.' 'They brought a container of nail clippers with them. Everyone in the village got one!' Opposing voices, such as that of the African trade unionist who complains about working conditions in Chinese businesses and projects, or of the intellectual who says that the 'colonisability' of Africa is not a Chinese but an African problem (Mana, 2008), seem quiet by contrast.

The fourth-pillar initiatives which are sprouting up everywhere in both Europe and North America are also posing a challenge to the development specialists. They bring in large amounts of new money, engage in the charity market in ways that are often innovative, introduce know-how from the sectors from which they derive (such as banking or sport), look for win-win situations and conduct their projects and programmes along lines which differ from those followed in the mainstream development sector. As we are continuing to see, they are replacing the planning logic by something more 'anthropo-logical'. They are not even averse to co-ownership, or even donorship provided there is a good return on investment.

The number of international development agencies is growing steadily: there are currently estimated to be 263! They vie for funds from the national donors for their specialist interventions. Many of them also appeal to the private sector or even to the general public for funds. International 'development NGOs' raise funds more or less anywhere. New web-based fund-raising techniques mean that you can choose the projects or people whom you wish to support directly, and in the United States in particular e-philanthropy has increased hugely. More than USD 1 billion per year is raised by the large American chari-

ties via this new medium. The 'causes' application in Facebook enables you to introduce your online friends to your own favourite NGO or project. But it is not just about giving. For example KIVA is an online platform on which you can select entrepreneurs from Southern countries who are affiliated to a microfinance institution and to whom you can then give a loan. More than 540,000 people have funded loans via this system, and every week USD 1 million is provided to poor entrepreneurs via the KIVA platform. Chequebook activism, promoted by NGDOs which want to secure the loyalty of their supporters by means of standing orders, is facing stiff competition from online activism, which ensures more freedom, initiative and transparency to the donor.

Such forms of decentralised, almost personalised interactions between donors and beneficiaries create the impression that the development system – driven by a market logic – is subject to lower transaction costs than when a community logic is dominant. However, where an increased number of players compete fiercely with one another, many latent costs become prominent: profiling, communication, fund-raising, target group screening, contractualisation of the relationship and evaluation. Every party has to demonstrate that it is whiter than white, has to get this message across to generous donors, has to bring in a share of the scarce resources, has to find a target group and make a contract with it, has to be able to turn the relationship into development output, has to be able to provide evidence that it has done so and has to give feedback to its supporters.

Key aid agencies in 'emerging' donor countries

Ministry of Commerce of China
India International Development Agency
Saudi Development Fund
Office for the Coordination of Foreign Aid (United Arab Emirates)
Brazilian Cooperation Agency
African Renaissance Fund/Ministry of Foreign Affairs (South Africa)

There are indications that, relatively speaking, those who have benefited least from the multiplication of the number of official donors are the recipient countries and populations. Kharas (2007) calculated that in 1975 59% of all aid (the total ODA at that time was USD 41 billion) arrived in the recipient

countries as money that could be spent freely on projects and programmes such as building and maintaining schools and clinics, building roads or install ing power stations. By 2005, this had fallen to 37% of a total ODA of USD 107 billion. The difference was creamed off by stakeholders in the donor countries. Experts' salaries, the administration of donor agencies, the purchase of goods and services and debt cancellation do not give financial levers to the recipi- ent countries, although they do to the donors. On the other hand, it seems that new private development players (foundations, businesses, social organi- sations of various kinds) are bringing in additional funds for the recipient partners. The costs that they incur in the home country (salaries, advertising costs, etc.) are often not reported as 'development aid'. Kharas (2009) calcu- lated that up to USD 60 billion of the USD 170 billion aid industry comes from private sources.

Furthermore, this proliferation of donors in developing countries also has a great many consequences locally. In a typical developing country, there are now several dozen bilateral donors, often as many multilateral institutions and hundreds of international NGOs. There are also interventions from dozens of international vertical programmes to combat certain diseases, introduce new technologies (such as the Internet) or tackle global problems such as defor- estation. In 2002, Vietnam, for example, had 25 official bilateral donors active in its territory, 19 multilateral donors and 350 international NGOs. They were running more than 8,000 projects, representing a ratio of 1 project per 9,000 people (Acharya, et al., 2007). Studies have shown, incidentally, that the pro- liferation of donors and the fragmentation of their investment channels have been substantially increasing (Kharas, 2007, 2009), and that poor and African countries are the main victims of this. The word 'victims' is chosen advisedly, since donor proliferation and fragmentation do not automatically mean more funds and are associated with numerous difficulties for the local government and population. The accompanying transaction costs can be considerable. In the 1960s, the average developing country dealt with 12 donors. That has now risen to 33. Tanzania received 541 official visits from donors in 2005 (IDA, 2007). Thus the local government has to deal with numerous different ideas, strategies, regulations, procedures, languages, financial calendars, rules of eti- quette and attitudes on the part of foreigners. Projects reduplicate one another or even counteract one another, neutralising individual positive effects… Due to scarcity on the local market, the prices of goods and the wages of the limited group of competent personnel are pushed up by fierce competition between

the donors. They encroach on one another's territory, poach one another's ideas and personnel and so on (Knack S. & Rahman, 2007).

On the other hand, the untying of aid, a process promoted by the OECD Development Assistance Committee, especially on behalf of the Least Developed Countries (LDCs), is making it easier for foreign companies to supply goods and services which used to be obtained exclusively on the national market. More and more donor countries are allowing businesses from other countries to compete for contracts. The proportion of untied aid rose from 46 to 82% between 2000 and 2008 (OECD DAC, 2010). The Development Committee has also created a web platform on which donor countries are able to advertise their projects and invite companies to submit tenders. However, in 2005 60% of these contracts were still secured by Western businesses and only 22% by businesses from developing countries. The European Commission also took an initiative in 2005 to untie its external aid to the LDCs completely and to grant access to this market for developing countries and for those Western countries which would also open up their aid markets to European businesses in return (DAC, 2007). Whether this increased international competition also had positive effects on the price and quality of the goods and services supplied and increased the aid's impact is not yet known. A recent report of the ODI, *Untying Aid: Is it working?* (2009), reveals that many formally untied development initiatives remain *de facto* tied, at least partially. The donors continue to prefer project support to programme or budget support and try to influence project regulations and implementation. However, one of the key findings of the study is that the untying of aid not only improves the cost-effectiveness of development cooperation, but also constitutes a major contributing factor to capacity building and knowledge transfer in the receiving partner country. Moreover, the use of untied funds is likely to promote ownership and facilitates alignment with the priorities of the recipient country, leading to greater aid-effectiveness.

From colonialism to the
Millennium Development Goals

The complex history of cooperation with the countries in the South has been and continues to be determined by numerous different factors. These can broadly be divided into three categories. Firstly, the international climate and framework always play a role. National development actors (policymakers, non-governmental development organisations, consultants and so on) are heavily influenced by what is said about North-South cooperation in other countries and in international forums. Secondly, power relations in the home country play a decisive role. To a very significant extent, they determine how cooperation is put into concrete practice in policy frameworks, laws, structures, control mechanisms and so on… Finally, and probably only in third place, the 'recipient' region or institution also plays a role. Local structures and actors filter the cooperation and determine what effect it can have on local social, economic, political and cultural conditions. But, as we will see, their influence on the donor countries' development policy, cooperation instruments and development practice is only very limited.

Thus in order to gain an understanding of the complex fabric of North-South cooperation, we will undertake a chronological analysis which takes all these factors into account. In this way we will see how large guiding concepts or ideas, such as trusteeship, technical cooperation, development aid, development cooperation and international cooperation, have successively arisen.

Colonial warm-up exercises

Some commentators reach back all the way to the Enlightenment to explain current ideas and practices to do with international cooperation. The Enlightenment is thought to have provided the ideological superstructure or legitimisation for the large-scale colonial project of the European powers. Although colonialism was initially a mercantile venture in which the colonisers' own political and economic interests were paramount, it was justified on the basis of a certain 'duty to civilise'. The English called the colonial mission 'the White

Man's burden', the accursed duty of the white man to spread his civilisation. This was coupled with claims that the peoples concerned lacked the capacity to determine their own course of development. In this way, what Edward Said termed 'the incapable other' was created.

But colonialism was not the same at all times and in all places. Belgium, Italy and Germany, for example, were latecomers to the colonisers' club. They joined Spain, Portugal, the Netherlands, France and Great Britain only during the second half of the 19th century. Until then, the focus had lain on the colonisation of Latin America and Asia. The 'scramble for Africa' began when Britain attempted to gain control of the Cairo (Egypt) – Cape Town (South Africa) axis and France took territory from the East (Djibouti) to the West (Senegal). Germany squeezed in between them in present-day Togo, Cameroon, Namibia and Tanzania. Belgium established a position in the centre in Congo, and Italy sought to gain a foothold in Libya and Eritrea.

Until then, imperialistic and colonial circles had been convinced that an overseas colony could be justified on the basis of a 'doctrine of complementarity'. It was taken for granted that the exploitation of the available natural, material and human resources in the colony was beneficial to both the mother country and the colony. The economies of home country and colony would gradually become more interdependent, and each would specialise in areas in which it had a comparative advantage. France, Spain and Portugal operated in this way in a closed, protectionist framework. They allowed their own goods into their colonies freely, but imposed high import duties on goods from other states. For a long time, Great Britain, the Netherlands and Belgium observed the principles of free trade.

In the face of some of the worst excesses of colonial exploitation, the idea arose at the start of the 20th century that the motherland must also make additional efforts for 'colonial development'. Or, as Lord Lugard, the ideologue of the trusteeship doctrine, put it in his famous pronouncement of 1922, 'Our present task is clear. It is to promote the commercial and industrial progress of Africa, without too careful a scrutiny of the material gains to ourselves' (quoted by Fieldhouse, 1999). But due to the international recession, nothing came of a dynamic policy of public investment in the case of any of the colonial powers before 1939. Instead, efforts were confined to reformist social programmes, in which somewhat greater efforts were put into healthcare, education and basic infrastructure and in which trade unions and cooperatives were permitted, albeit under the strict control and supervision of colonial officials.[5]

Such a palliative could not solve the social and development problems in the colonies, however. Riots and uprisings, a burgeoning racial, political and social emancipation movement in the colonies and an anti-colonial intellectual climate in the United States ensured that 'the colonial question' could no longer be ignored. The consequence was a kind of 'welfare doctrine'. The British set up their Colonial Welfare and Development Scheme in 1940, and the French their Investment Fund for the Economic and Social Development of the Overseas Territories (FIDES). Faced with pressure from the community of black évolués, Belgium set up a Native Welfare Fund in July 1947. The core idea in each case was twofold. The colonial government had the task of promoting development in overseas territories on behalf of the 'natives', and the local population needed to be more involved in the modernisation process. From this point onwards, substantial investments were made in social development programmes, healthcare, education and so on.

The colonial governments remained faithful to their general principles of colonial administration in all this. The British were outspoken advocates of 'indirect rule' for maintaining law and order in their colonies. This meant that the colonies were administered via existing local power structures such as kings, maharajas or tribal chiefs. The government and administration system of the British colonial authorities was also fairly decentralised and allowed plenty of room for local, voluntary participation. The French, true to the Jacobin tradition, opted for a more centralised system and introduced 'modern' government and administration systems. In the name of the great republican principles, they thus wanted to assimilate the *indigènes* so that they became citizens of a single French empire. The distinction between indirect and direct rule is not always clear. Often, the English intervened heavily, while the French gave local power-holders a free rein. The Dutch inclined more towards indirect rule in Indonesia, but towards direct rule in Suriname and the Antilles. Belgium gave the existing power structures a place in its colonial strategy.

The division of roles between the protagonists (state, army, private sector, missionaries, etc.) was different in each colonising country. For example, the Belgian colonial process was driven by the so-called trinity. On the basis of a kind of colonial corporatism, the state, large companies and missionaries worked on the same project. Everyone knew its specific role.

The large companies, the majority of which were controlled by the Société Générale[6], controlled the production of cotton, rubber, palm oil, coffee and

cocoa and the exploitation of the mines (zinc, copper, tin, gold, diamond and uranium). Social development was the joint responsibility of the government and the private sector. The large companies established their own schools and health services. From 1906, healthcare was coordinated by the Prince Leopold Institute for Tropical Medicine (the ITG), while education was largely run by the missions. By contrast, the British Empire did not give any role to missionaries. In its most important overseas territory, India, the activities of the churches were deliberately and actively discouraged.

Colonialists, colonisers, colonists and colonials

Of course, the way in which a country practises development cooperation today cannot be derived directly from the way in which it was involved in a colonial venture. But there are still interesting links. One only has to look at the countries which receive most support from a donor to find that former colonies invariably have a prominent place in the list of those most favoured.

But perhaps the nature of the colonial presence also plays an important role. Colonialists – in other words, people who were sent out by the coloniser (usually their home country) in order to defend its interests there and put ideas into practice – always remained just that. They believed in their mission. But the nature of the superiority concept varied. The British were convinced of their racial superiority. The French felt their culture to be of greater value. The Belgians acted as strict tutors. The Americans were always there 'to clear up the mess', for instance in the Philippines between 1899 and 1946.

Colonists were sent from some countries to settle permanently in the colony, for example the numerous Portuguese who settled in Latin America, Angola, Mozambique and Cape Verde, the Spanish in Latin America and the French in Algeria and West Africa. Other countries, such as the UK, the Netherlands and Belgium, did not have such a tradition. They confined themselves to colonials who assumed temporary (and usually official) functions in order to rule the colony. Thus there were never more than 10,000 British citizens among the 400 million inhabitants of the Indian subcontinent. For most of the colonised peoples, the relationship with 'the white man' was thus a fairly remote and paternalistic one which had to be conducted in the cultural and linguistic language of the coloniser. The patterns forged in this way have persisted, as is shown by the fact that many Congolese still address and regard the Belgians as their 'noko' or uncles.

The colonial approach towards the local population was usually highly pater-nalistic. Everyone concerned – colonial officials, entrepreneurs and mission-aries – was supposed to help the native population take the difficult step from tradition to modernity. That population had the potential, but as yet lacked the capacity, to act autonomously. A phase of acculturation still needed to be passed through. Modernity needed to be spoon-fed to them so that modern Western values, norms and practices could be adopted.

Colonial thinking was not static, however. As we have seen, it evolved from a rather *laissez-faire* approach into a more interventionist one. There was con-stant debate about objectives and means. However, the moral concept of supe-riority was a firm and important basis for thinking about the colonial mission and duties. Attention was increasingly focused on the interests of the colonised in terms of welfare and well-being, but the asymmetrical, hierarchical, unequal relationship between those concerned was not discussed – even in the 'devel-opment projects' of the time.

Technical cooperation and knowledge transfer

After the First World War, the League of Nations was created by the Treaty of Versailles in 1919 'to promote international co-operation and to achieve in-ternational peace and security'. The International Labour Organization (ILO) was established at the same time as an affiliated body.

Although the League of Nations was primarily intended as a means of pre-venting disputes between 'developed' countries or keeping them to a minimum, it established a number of important tenets.

Thus the Versailles Treaty stated that the best way to guarantee the well-be-ing and development of peoples who were not yet able to stand by themselves was that 'the tutelage of such peoples should be entrusted to advanced nations who by reason of their resources, their experience or their geographical posi-tion can best undertake this responsibility...'[7] (Article 22).

The same treaty also stipulated that the members of the League (1) should endeavour to ensure fair and humane conditions of labour for men, women and children both in their own countries and in all countries to which their commercial and industrial relations extended; (2) should undertake to secure just treatment of the native inhabitants of territories under their control; (3) would entrust the League with the general supervision of agreements with re-

gard to the traffic in women and children; (4) should endeavour to take steps in the prevention and control of disease (Article 23).

Inspired by this multilateral vision of international development and interdependence, the League and its specialised agencies, such as the International Labour Office, began to offer technical assistance to governments responsible for colonies or mandated territories. The method of technical assistance was based (as it still is) on the idea of common progress and the underlying principles of linearity, convergence, predictability and manageability. Technical assistance could be used literally to bring about development 'in the image and likeness of the developed West'. More specifically, technical assistance was provided in the field of social policy, which in accordance with the 'welfare doctrine' was to be pursued in every field. The ILO gave technical advice on the introduction of trade unions, social dialogue and labour legislation and inspection. The League's Health Organisation arranged contacts between epidemiologists from different countries and exchanges of health personnel and encouraged public health as a separate discipline and distinct policy field.

Many African, Asian and Latin American countries, colonies and regions were involved. China's approach was exceptional and promising. As a member of the League, China wanted technical cooperation to contribute to its own modernisation through the transfer of knowhow and capital. In 1933, a technical expert visited at the request of the Chinese government to act as a liaison figure between the National Economic Council of China and the technical organisations of the League. His task was to inform the Chinese about the functioning of the League's organisations, convey cooperation requests from China to the League and coordinate League experts' activities locally. Significantly, the Chinese themselves stated that 'the duration of his mandate shall be one year and his travel and accommodation costs shall be defrayed by the Chinese government' (letter from W. Koo to the General Secretary, 14 July 1933, quoted in Rist, 1996).

When the League of Nations proved unable to prevent the Second World War, its activities were discontinued. But the League's successor, the United Nations, pursued the path of technical assistance further in order to address the knowledge and skills deficits of the developing countries. In 1949, the UN established the Expanded Programme of Technical Assistance (EPTA). The following year, it organised the very first aid-pledging conference, at which it was able to raise USD 20 million (approximately USD 175 million at today's rates), mainly in order to finance technical assistance.

**From technical assistance to poverty alleviation:
CDI-Bwamanda in Congo**

Very few projects and programmes have had a very long life. One noteworthy exception is the Centre for Integrated Development (CDI), a Congolese non-profit-making
organisation set up in 1967 by the Capuchin monk Leonard van Baelen and Dr Jan
van Mullem. Started as a small initiative in the village of Bwamanda in the northern province of Equateur, in the space of a few years the CDI developed into a large
organisation covering a surface area three times the size of Belgium. The CDI has
participated in all stages of development cooperation (from technical assistance to
combating poverty). It has often also taken new paths of its own, but the Belgian,
Dutch, German and European sponsors of the project have repeatedly imposed new
development cooperation approaches on it.
The CDI followed a multisectoral strategy and created structures in agriculture, healthcare, education, water supply, road construction and rural project management. The
CDI's strength lies in its organisational model, which provides for the phased participation of the local population. More than half a million people have been involved in the
CDI in one way or another. In the mid-1980s more than 1,500 people were working
for the project, as well as 65 foreign technical experts (mainly Belgian and Dutch). But
perhaps even more important are the CDI's economic underpinnings. The project buys
soya, coffee and other agricultural produce from local farmers and sells them in Kinshasa and on the international market. Coffee is a particularly important product in the
area: thousands of tonnes are purchased every year. When the coffee price collapsed
in 1987, the Max Havelaar fair trade organisation came to the rescue. In the 1995-2003
period, when the crisis reached its peak and the area was cut off from the rest of the
world, sales of coffee via this circuit yielded a surplus of 3 million euro for local farmers.
The income from coffee and other products is also used to 'subsidise' the CDI's other
services, although these also endeavour to work on a partly self-funded basis. Thus
110,000 people are affiliated to the CDI's health insurance fund, as a result of which
they are eligible for lower charges at hospital; at the same time, the hospital is able
to cover a significant proportion of its expenses.
Since the war ended and the region's isolation came to an end in 2005, the 600 local
CDI employees, as the only development actors in the region, have started to rebuild
the economy and the social fabric. According to the new development philosophy
promoted by the international community, the CDI should now be entering into partnerships with other actors to combat poverty. Yet the government in this region, or
what passes for it, is dysfunctional, and there are few if any other economic actors
such as traders and no other NGOs. The CDI has therefore resolved to work with the
numerous local self-help groups which arose during the crisis. A recent study in the
region shows that nearly 90% of all local people belong to one or more associations
(Shomba, et al., 2008).

Faith in development aid

It was only at the end of the Second World War that the idea finally took shape that all countries would benefit from the participation of all nations in a world-wide development project. As the United Nations Charter of 1945 puts it: 'We the peoples of the United Nations determined to save succeeding generations from the scourge of war … agree to employ international machinery for the promotion of the economic and social advancement of all people.' The idea of development was invented.

But right after the war, attention was not focused on the problems of the southern hemisphere.[8] Just before the creation of the United Nations, in the summer of 1944, international monetary and financial agreements were made in Bretton Woods (New Hampshire) which were intended to prevent economic nationalism and waywardness from again leading to political nationalism and major wars. The International Bank for Reconstruction and Development (IBRD, better known as the World Bank) and the International Monetary Fund (IMF) were established[9] in an attempt to define a new international order.

Furthermore, Europe, which had been thrown into turmoil by the war, needed to be reconstructed. The United States and the Soviet Union manoeuvred to establish their positions. The Marshall Plan[10], also known as the European Recovery Plan, was launched in 1948 in order to give the USA's European allies financial breathing space; USD 17 billion was earmarked for it.[11] The funds were not made available unconditionally. The participating countries had to make arrangements together to coordinate the use of the aid, and the money had to be repaid.[12] To this end, the Organisation for European Economic Co-operation (OEEC) was set up. The OEEC assumed a transatlantic dimension when it was transformed into the Organisation for Economic Cooperation and Development (OECD) in the early 1960s. This also represented the first move to institutionalise development aid. Even today, the OECD's Development Assistance Committee (DAC) remains one of the most important coordinating bodies for the Western donor community.

But the USA was not just concerned about better economic and financial links between its own economy and those of its European allies. The USA also had outspoken anti-colonial views and regarded development aid as having a role to play in a new relationship between developed and less developed nations. In his State of the Union address of 20 January 1949, President Harry Truman declared that 'Fourth, we must embark on a bold new program for

making the benefits of our scientific advances and industrial progress available for the improvement and growth of underdeveloped areas'. The other rich countries were called upon to carry out this grandiose plan together with the USA within the framework of the United Nations. The old imperialism, said Truman, was based on exploitation and profiteering and must be replaced by a development programme based on a democratic concept and on fair relations between peoples.

Sure enough, the USA took the lead in development aid. In June 1950 the US Congress approved a law making it possible for the administration to conclude bilateral development agreements.

Interest in development aid also began to be shown in academic circles. Aid was scientifically legitimated in two ways in the 1960s. Firstly, there was the sociological and functionalist argument that modernisation of the young nations or transition from traditional to modern societies could be facilitated or accelerated through the transfer of cultural and institutional elements that were necessary in any modern society. The Western, industrialised and modern societies could thus offer their tried and tested patterns to countries in the South, which in this way could speed up their modernisation artificially. Secondly, there was economic rationalisation, which mainly revolved around the so-called two-gap model. This assumed that development in many developing countries was being held back by a lack of local savings and hard currency. Because of this, they were unable to set up investments and attract foreign capital. Aid could and should address these two gaps. Both the sociological and the economic arguments regarded aid as a win-win situation for developed and developing countries.

Faith in the benefits and effectiveness of aid and in the altruism of the donor countries was particularly strong, among both donors and recipient countries. Resolution 1522 of the United Nations General Assembly named the 1960s the 'Development Decade' and stated that the developed countries must endeavour to devote 1% of their wealth to aid and investments in developing countries.

Despite the fine-sounding declarations and theoretical support, it quickly became clear that development aid was to a great extent focused on the international and national interests of those providing it. In 1954 the USA was already spending around USD 6 billion on 'development aid'; 86% consisted of military aid.

Local interests also managed to obtain their place in aid provision. In 1954 the US Congress approved Public Law 480 on the Food for Peace Program, in

which allies in the southern hemisphere were offered free or cheap American crops. At the same time, however, the American farming lobby acquired a new destination for its food surpluses which had arisen as a result of the recovery of European food production.

In this way, development aid in practice became a unilateral initiative on the part of a donor country by which it sought to contribute to the recipient country's development, but also wished to safeguard its own interests. The self-interest and opportunism of 'aid' were never more clearly formulated than by US President Richard Nixon, when he stated in 1968 that 'the main purpose of American aid is not to help the other nations but to help ourselves'.

During this period, development aid therefore could not be credibly associated with altruism. Aid served to give support to allies and friends or to check the progress of other countries' allies and friends. Most British aid went to the Commonwealth countries, most French aid to French-speaking countries, and most Portuguese, Spanish, Dutch and Belgian aid to their former colonies. The majority of US aid was intended for states and regimes which were held to be located on the front line in the struggle against communism. The bulk of the Soviet Union's aid went to its allies and to socialist regimes. In fact, development aid thus became an instrument in the bitter struggle of the Cold War.

The official line was that development aid was a duty of the rich countries, which had to transfer the necessary technical and financial resources to under-developed countries without damaging their own interests. To put it another way, it was assumed that protecting and promoting one's own geopolitical and economic interests was compatible with the development objective of the aid system. It was with this aim in mind that virtually all Western countries set up their own aid bodies and ministries from the 1960s onwards. Canada was the first country with such an institution: the Office for Foreign Aid, established in 1960 and replaced in 1968 by the Canadian International Development Agency (CIDA). In 1961 the US set up the United States Agency for International Development (USAID). Belgium initially had a Ministry for African Affairs (1960-1961) and then a Ministry of Foreign Trade and Technical Assistance. In the Netherlands, the cabinet had a Secretary of State for Development Cooperation by 1963. In 1964 the Directorate-General for International Cooperation was set up within the Ministry for Foreign Affairs.

What effect development aid had was not yet clear to anyone. The OECD was still taking a downbeat line in 1969: 'We have only a vague idea of what we are doing'.

Development cooperation: aid in a global setting

In the 1960s, the economy of the developing countries as a whole grew at a rate of 5% per year – faster than ever before. Yet there was no immediate sign of any euphoria. The report by the Pearson Commission (*Partners in Development*, 1969) stated that the gap between developed and developing countries was growing ever wider. The United Nations introduced the Second Development Decade with a call to devote more resources to development and make every effort to ensure that the developing countries' economies grew by 6% per year. The decade thus started with a good resolution. At the UN General Assembly, it was declared that the industrialised countries should work to give away 0.7% of their GNI per year to Third World countries.

The 1970s were to be characterised by four significant developments. The first oil crisis pushed oil prices up by 350% in 1973-1974. Suddenly, there was a strong sense of global interdependence, in both the northern and southern hemispheres. The crisis also lent force to calls for a New International Economic Order (NIEO) to sort out the structural inequalities between developed and underdeveloped economies. The developing countries, which had been cooperating ever more closely within the Group of 77 since the early 1960s and were gradually gaining more of a voice in the UN, stated that they – despite all the development aid – were not receiving any development opportunities. Their call was for 'Trade – Not Aid'. There was growing political support for international agreements to bring stability to the prices of primary goods sold by developing countries on the international markets. The World Bank spoke of the need for 'redistribution with growth' (Chenery, 1974). The ILO presented its basic needs approach, and launched the World Employment Programme, with which it sought to encourage developing countries to focus their national development policies on employment, income distribution and basic needs. Finally, a pro-Third-World movement emerged – in both NGDO circles and certain Third World regimes – which argued in favour of self-reliance and popular participation as a double springboard towards national development.

Each of these four developments represented a challenge for development aid.

For the first time, the flow of aid from North to South was considered in a global context. Donor countries realised that the problems went deeper than just a lack of resources for developing countries. International trading relations also needed to be adapted in their favour. The donors proved willing to

discuss these matters with the developing countries within the framework of UNCTAD, but the discussions and impressive declarations about a New International Economic Order (UNCTAD, 1974) did not usher in any noteworthy structural measures. However, development aid did grow. Many donors substantially increased their budgets. They gradually changed their discourse. 'Development aid' became 'development cooperation'. The terminological change was supposed to reflect the fact that a more horizontal relationship had arisen between the donors and the more self-confident recipient countries. People argued in favour of 'partnership' and 'cooperation on an equal footing'. The Lomé Convention, which the nine member states of the European Community in 1975 concluded with former colonies in Africa, the Caribbean and the Pacific Region, made provision for favourable commercial measures for these so-called ACP countries, as well as for additional aid. The donors' preference, but also that of many developing countries, remained large-scale, capital-intensive projects with a high degree of technical assistance.

Many donors also promised to invest more funds in basic facilities. In reality, little came of this. The share of ODA that was spent on basic needs fell from 38% in 1971 to 22% ten years later. The official development bodies were not great advocates of the nationalist-populist path that many countries – led by Tanzania and Chile – sought to take. Support for it came instead from the NGDOs which were emerging in all donor countries and rapidly increasing in scope.

The Washington Consensus and structural adjustments

The years between 1980 and 1990 are described in the development sector as 'the lost decade'. Everything seemed to go wrong. The developing countries' debt burden became intolerable. Those debts were pushed up by the higher costs associated with importing oil and by generous economic policies that were made possible only by a surfeit of petrodollars combined with low interest rates. The loans in question were not granted because of any expected favourable return on the investment, but because of a need in the recipient country and the pressure to promote exports from the donor countries (Dijkstra, 2008). Debt repayment, falling prices on the goods markets and the recession in the industrialised countries brought the Third World regimes to their knees.

The Bretton Woods institutions – the IMF and the World Bank – set strict conditions for the issue of additional international loans. Developing countries received concessional loans only if they devised and followed a policy of 'structural adjustment'. Most bilateral and multilateral donors derived their own aid policies from that of the World Bank and the IMF.

As a result, the international aid community collectively aligned itself with the neoliberal economic orthodoxy generally known as the Washington Consensus. Among many politicians in developing countries too, the conviction was growing that their wayward, virtually self-sufficient economic and social model had no future. The idea gained ground that developing countries needed to tune in – otherwise they would be left out.

John Williamson, the intellectual father of the term 'Washington Consensus', himself describes the term as a by-product of that change. In order to convince a sceptical Bush Senior administration in Washington that changes really could be seen in the economic policy of Latin American countries in particular, his Institute for International Economics organised a conference on the subject in 1989. During the conference, Williamson emphasised ten points that he thought could meet with a general consensus among the Bush administration (Williamson, 2003). He mentioned fiscal discipline, selectivity in government spending (for example no more general subsidisation of healthcare and education), tax reforms, liberalisation of interest rates, competitive exchange rates, liberalisation of trade, liberalisation of foreign direct investments, privatisation, deregulation and property rights. Points that he himself regarded as important, but which he did not believe could count on general support, were disregarded. The most striking of these was a focus on income redistribution and rapid growth. The unintended side-effect of this academic and intellectual exercise was far-reaching. The Washington Consensus became a trademark. It was not a consensus, but it became a political manifesto – according to Williamson a 'myth driven by a powerful elite'[13] – which put forward a kind of universal one-size-fits-all solution for developing countries.

Donor institutions increasingly focused their attention on growth rather than on redistribution. So-called 'safety nets' were the solution for those who failed to find their place in 'the market'. Foreign aid was used to push through the 'right' macro-economic measures. The project aid that had previously financed large-scale projects such as infrastructure works, power stations or ports was

replaced by programme aid. The structural adjustment programmes (SAPs) and adjustment loans were intended to finance the deficits in the balance of payments, while the recipient country made structural alterations to its policy so that it could export more. In the 1980s, the first generation of reforms was pushed through in this way. The World Bank and the IMF closely followed the progress of the SAPs. Devaluation and trade liberalisation were standard ingredients and conditions, but far more conditions were usually imposed on the recipient countries. The average SAP contained between ten and twenty conditions, and in some cases as many as a hundred (Boas and McNiell, 2003).

The total volume of 'aid' stagnated in the 1980s. The proportion of aid given to the Least Developed Countries (LDCs) fell. Because the developing countries had to repay ever-increasing debts, net financial transfers fell to an historic low. In 1985, the poor countries transferred approximately USD 15 billion more to the rich donor countries, their banks and businesses than they themselves received in the form of aid, loans or investments.

By the start of the 1990s, a hundred developing and transitional countries – together representing one-third of the world's population – were poorer in terms of per capita income than they had been ten, twenty or sometimes even thirty years earlier (Jolly, 2002).

International cooperation and the Millennium Development Goals

The structural adjustment programmes came in for fierce criticism from all sides: NGOs, social movements, international coalitions[14], academics and even insiders in the Bretton Woods institutions frankly stated that the SAPs were being forced to an excessive degree as ready-made, one-size-fits-all solutions on all developing countries, with little or no regard for the differing starting conditions in those countries. There was also criticism of the sometimes disastrous social consequences that they had. Social services such as healthcare and education – which many Third World states had previously provided for free – were made subject to market mechanisms by the SAPs ('customers' should pay). The consequence in many cases was serious inroads into the social sector in terms of both quantity and quality. The economic results of the SAPs were also a matter of fierce controversy.

The World Bank answered the criticism by introducing the notion of 'the social dimensions of adjustment'. Special programmes were financed to com-

pensate for the negative social consequences of the SAPs. In the meantime, however, the Bretton Woods institutions pressed ahead with the 'second-generation reforms'. Countries could obtain concessional loans if they privatised state corporations and carried out financial reforms (including liberalising financial controls). New 'output conditions' continued to be imposed. The implementation of the second-generation reforms proved highly problematic, especially because such changes required even more institutional capacity than the first-generation adjustments (Addison, 2002).

The governments in developing countries implemented the imposed measures with great reluctance, and often resisted them. The application of the conditions was particularly difficult and led to violent popular protests on more than one occasion. The Bretton Woods institutions and the bilateral donors did not succeed in pushing all the measures through in every country, even when they temporarily halted the flow of aid, as they did in Mozambique, Nicaragua, Tanzania, Vietnam, Zambia and Zimbabwe (Riddell, 2007).

Criticism of the SAPs and a sense of aid fatigue laid the basis for a tough debate on the role of development cooperation and the effectiveness of the conditions associated with it (Thorbecke, 2000). Towards the end of the decade, in 1989, the World Bank started to refer to a governance crisis in Africa. It was concluded that the African crisis and the scant effectiveness of the aid were due to imperfect commitment to the reforms on the part of the local governments and endemic corruption in developing countries.

With the end of the Cold War, the bureaucratic and authoritarian states in the Third World also lost much of their external legitimacy. The fall of the Berlin Wall (1989) marked the symbolic end of the bipolar power relations which had been integral to the aid system. The speech given by the French President, François Mitterrand (during the Summit of the Francophone Countries at the fashionable Breton resort of La Baule in 1990), made it clear that the donor community was looking for a new legitimisation and a new goal for its development cooperation. Mitterrand bluntly said that although France wished to remain loyal to its French-speaking allies in the South, it wanted to do so only if those countries made swift and definite progress towards more democracy and freedom.

In the 1990s, the United Nations and their specialised institutions organised large-scale summit meetings in the search for new legitimisations and goals for development cooperation.

The conferences made it clear that a joint effort – and one on an enormous scale – was needed in order to tackle the many problems in the world: the degradation of the natural environment; the demographic developments which provoked Malthusian fears; unsustainable and explosive social conditions in many countries; the exponential growth in the number of city-dwellers living in poverty; systematic and structural underdevelopment in the Least Developed Countries; and the lack of sufficient financial levers to fund development efforts. These problems provided the new legitimisation for future collective efforts and international cooperation among the donor countries and between donors and recipient countries.

The international conferences of the '90s

1990 UN World Summit for Children, New York
1992 UN Conference on Environment and Development (Earth Summit), Rio de Janeiro
1994 International Conference on Population and Development, Cairo
1995 UN World Conference on Women, Beijing
1995 World Summit for Social Development (Social Summit), Copenhagen
1996 Habitat II, Istanbul
1997 Earth Summit + 5, New York
1999 International Conference on Population and Development + 5, New York
2000 Millennium Summit on the Role of the United Nations in the 21st Century, New York
2000 Social Summit + 5, Geneva
2001 Third UN Conference on the Least Developed Countries, Brussels
2002 International Conference on Financing for Development, Monterrey
2002 World Summit on Sustainable Development, Johannesburg

The Post-Washington Consensus which arose in this way, like the Washington Consensus itself, is not a coherent political manifesto, but rather a form of convergence of ideas, insights and paradigms. Firstly, the consensus is founded to a great extent on new insights regarding human development (also known as the New York Consensus). The *Human Development Reports*, which have been published by the United Nations Development Programme (UNDP, based in New York) since 1990, define development as a process that increases people's choices and reinforces human capabilities. The reports have been heavily in-

fluenced by the work of Nobel Prize winner Amartya Sen and UNDP leading light Mahbub ul Haq. Human development is both an analytical framework and a strategy. It relies on four indicators to assess development: the HDI (Human Development Index), the GDI (Gender Development Index), the GEM (Gender Empowerment Index) and the HPI (Human Poverty Index). The human development strategy is also called a 'rights-based approach' because it assumes that people who are given no development opportunities are treated unfairly in political, civil and socio-economic terms.

This did not mean that everyone radically moved away from the adjustment policies of the 1980s and 1990. In World Bank and IMF circles, some argued in favour of pursuing the second-generation reforms, but paying far more attention to the institutional aspects of development (Williamson, 2003; Easterly, 2002). In their opinion the state must safeguard the institutional infrastructure of the market economy by providing public goods and even by correcting the distribution of income. The World Bank report of 2004, *Making Services Work for Poor People*, for example was an explicit plea for a holistic approach to 'pro-poor growth'.

The Post-Washington Consensus is also founded on a renewed faith in development aid, this time in the form of international cooperation. The many studies that were conducted in the 1990s into the efficiency, effectiveness and impact of international aid all came to the same conclusions. Firstly it was found that aid had not contributed to the speeding up of growth in developing countries – contrary to the original expectations. Secondly, aid can also have undesirable negative effects, for example by interfering with local prices and interest rates. Thirdly, aid turns out to be highly 'fungible' or 'mutually interchangeable'. Governments that receive aid do not always use it for the agreed purposes, but to finance initiatives which are not immediately relevant to development (senior officials' salaries, the apparatus of repression, etc.). Finally, apart from a few anecdotes, no evidence was found that aid programmes succeeded in reaching the poor population.

The World Bank concluded that financial aid works only if there is a good policy environment. That means sound macro-economic policies (low inflation, budget surpluses and an open trading regime) and sound institutions (legal security, good government services and the absence of corruption). But aid can also serve as the midwife for good policy (Dollar and Pritchett, 1998).

At the end of the last century, the World Bank put forward the Comprehensive Development Framework (CDF) as an institutional vehicle or cooperation

platform for all donors and recipient countries. With the CDF, the World Bank explicitly came out in favour of poverty reduction, reducing inequalities and improving opportunities for the poor.

The key elements of this holistic framework are as follows:

- poverty reduction must occupy a central position in a policy that is overseen by the recipient country itself. To this end, the national government must enter into dialogue with other actors in society, such as the private sector and civil society. This should lead to greater 'national ownership' of the decisions taken. The poorest countries must put forward this national strategy for poverty reduction in a 'poverty reduction strategy paper' (PRSP);
- the poverty reduction policy should be result- and outcome-oriented and should start with an analysis of the national poverty problem and its causes;
- a comprehensive look should be taken at the processes which help to reduce poverty, taking macro-, sectoral and intersectoral issues into account;
- international support must be based on partnership, and all sources of aid should be deployed in a coordinated fashion, under the leadership of the recipient government;
- all of this can be visualised as a process over the medium to long term. Medium-term commitments are therefore necessary, and the timing should be agreed, as should the performance criteria and the monitoring system (Booth, 2003).

The Millennium Development Goals were adopted by the 189 member states of the United Nations in New York in September 2000. This took place during the so-called Millennium Summit. The Millennium Development Goals are a compilation of the various goals and commitments formulated and adopted during the numerous international conferences in the course of the 1990s. As such, it is the definitive international reference and road map for international cooperation. The strength of this blueprint lies in the fairly concrete, verifiable and controllable indicators that are defined. For each goal, it is clearly stipulated when it should be attained and how progress will be checked.

The United Nations Millennium Development Goals

All 189 United Nations member states have solemnly pledged that by 2015 they will meet the following eight goals:

1. **Eradicate extreme poverty and hunger**
* Halve the proportion of people whose income is less than one dollar a day.
* Halve the proportion of people who suffer from hunger.

2. **Achieve universal primary education**
* Ensure that children everywhere, boys and girls alike, will be able to complete a full course of primary schooling.

3. **Promote gender equality**
* Eliminate gender disparity in primary and secondary education by 2005, and in all levels of education no later than 2015.

4. **Reduce child mortality**
* Reduce by two thirds the under-five mortality rate.

5. **Improve maternal health**
* Reduce by three quarters the maternal mortality ratio.

6. **Combat HIV/AIDS, malaria and other diseases**
* Halt and begin to reverse the spread of HIV/AIDS.
* Halt and begin to reverse the incidence of new cases of malaria and other major diseases.

7. **Ensure environmental sustainability**
* Integrate the principles of sustainable development into countries' policies and programmes.
* Reduce biodiversity loss.
* Halve the proportion of the population without sustainable access to safe drinking water.
* By 2020, have achieved a significant improvement in the lives of at least 100 million slum dwellers.

8. **Develop a global partnership for development**
* Develop further an open, rule-based, predictable, non-discriminatory trading and financial system. Linked to this system are promises concerning good governance, striving for development and eradicating poverty – at national and international level.
* Address the special needs of least developed countries. This includes removing tariff barriers and quotas for their export goods; extra debt relief for countries with the most acute financial problems; discontinuing official bilateral debts; and more official development support for countries which seriously address the eradication of poverty.
* Address the special needs of developing landlocked countries and poor small island states.

* Deal comprehensively with developing countries' debt, by taking measures at national and international level which reduce the problem to reasonable proportions.
* In cooperation with the developing countries: create proper and productive employment for young people.
* In cooperation with pharmaceutical companies: provide access to affordable essential drugs in developing countries.
* In cooperation with the private sector: make available the benefits of new technologies – especially information and communications.

Addressing poverty in exchange for debt relief

The new development paradigm under construction has a number of cornerstones. First of all, far more extensive and better organised dialogue and cooperation are sought between the stakeholders. 'Multistakeholdership' and 'multilevel governance' are the terms that are widely used for this.

'Multistakeholdership' refers to the need to achieve the broad participation of all kinds of stakeholders. Governments must listen to the private sector and civil society, for example chambers of commerce, employers' and workers' organisations, non-governmental organisations, and associations of farmers, fishermen, women or slum dwellers. Ideally, they should all be involved in policy. They should help define it and implement it.

'Multilevel governance' means that such interaction between all kinds of state and non-state actors must be possible at numerous different levels: firstly at national level, of course, but also in sub-states, provinces and at local level. The private sector and civil society organisations also need a say in regional interstate organisations such as the African Union or at international conferences. For the donor community, these are not just fine-sounding new words. They are new 'process conditionalities'. Where specific policy outcomes used to be imposed (such as fewer rules for investors), an open relationship of cooperation between government and private actors is now a condition for (continuing) support.

A second cornerstone consists of the ideas of country ownership, accountability and partnership. These express the wish – it is generally acknowledged that it is more a wish than a reality! – that the recipient countries should define their own policies and be accountable for them to their own populations. Donors are then 'partners' who help make that policy possible. But there is also a desire for the policies of national governments receiving support to be

consistent with the internationally agreed development goals, and more specifically with the agenda for poverty reduction. Techniques such as 'rolling programming' and 'performance-based aid allocation' ensure that donors can increase their volume of aid to a specific country at any time (if 'good' work is being done there) or reduce it (if 'good' performances are not recorded).

A third cornerstone relates to the working methods of the donors themselves. More than in the past – and above all under pressure from the international NGO community – attention is being paid to the coherence of donors' foreign policy. It is expected of donors that not only their development cooperation but also their policy on trade, migration, the environment or agriculture will be 'Third World-friendly'. Moreover, there is also a desire to use the new agenda to achieve more coordination and streamlining of donors' efforts.

Two development instruments are fine examples or embodiments of the new paradigm: the poverty reduction strategy papers (PRSPs) and budget support. Both show that the innovations of the new paradigm are more than trivial or rhetorical.

The PRSPs were introduced in 1999. Their initial goal was to ensure that the debt cancellation that countries could obtain via the Enhanced Highly Indebted Poor Countries programme of the World Bank and the IMF was used properly.

The Highly Indebted Poor Countries Initiative and the Multilateral Debt Relief Initiative

The HIPC initiative was set up in 1996 by the World Bank and the IMF and has two objectives. Firstly, the aim is to relieve a number of low-income countries of their intolerable burden of debt to donors; debt is regarded as intolerable when its net discounted value is more than 150% of the country's export income. Secondly, the aim is to support reforms and sound macro-economic and social policy.

As a result of the Enhanced Highly Indebted Poor Countries programme, which was started in 1999, more countries are becoming eligible and there is also a higher level of debt relief. Debt cancellation takes place in two phases. When a country has demonstrated that it will follow an IMF reform programme and has a poverty reduction strategy paper (PRSP) or is in the process of preparing one, and when it signs a plan to pay off debt arrears, the 'decision point' comes. The multilateral and bilateral creditors[15] then embark on debt reduction, although they reserve the right to go back on it if the country's policy is no longer consistent with the agreements. When the IMF programme and the poverty reduction policy work properly, a country reaches the 'completion point'. It can then count on cancellation of at least 90% of the debts that it has with bilateral and multilateral creditors.

At the turbulent G8 summit in Gleneagles in 2005, it was decided to go a step further. In 2006, the World Bank, the IMF and the African Development Bank launched the Multilateral Debt Relief Initiative (MDRI). Through this, countries which have reached the completion point obtain the cancellation of 100% of their debts to these multilateral institutions[16]. The Inter-American Development Bank joined the initiative a year later. How do things look after more than ten years?

Thirty HIPCs have reached the completion point. Six countries are still at the decision point. Four countries which also have an intolerable burden of debt but are embroiled in serious conflicts have not yet got even that far. The stock of debt and the amount of interest paid by the participating countries have fallen as a result of the HIPC and the MDRI initiative, but the IDA and the IMF themselves admit that several implementation concerns continue to demand attention. The principal challenges are an increased focus on the remaining countries that have not yet started or completed the HIPC process and the assurance of full creditor participation. As a third challenge, IDA and IMF staff aim to address litigation against HIPCs, warning about the vulture funds, which buy up debt on the cheap but then go through the courts in the developing countries to demand repayment of the full amount plus late payment penalties (IDA & IMF, 2010).

The Jubilee 2000 campaigners have been fierce in their criticisms. Jubilee is a coalition of civil organisations which in 2000 obtained a record number of signatures (24 million) from people calling for a radical clearance of debts. The Jubilee Debt Campaign (JDC) believes that the total debt mountain of USD 3,700 billion (including around USD 500 billion of so-called 'dictator debt') is being dismantled too slowly. Just USD 110 billion has been cancelled so far, while USD 400 billion of debt cancellation is the estimated minimum to meet basic needs. Moreover, too few countries are able to participate in the programmes referred to (Williams, 2008).

Criticism has also come from academic circles. Some argue that these measures merely free up money to pay off debts to other creditors, but do not provide the economy with enough oxygen to grow or to reduce poverty. Others point out that the HIPC countries are usually countries with inadequate policies and are being rewarded twice over: with debt reduction and with extra grants. Researcher Geske Dijkstra (2008) finds it reprehensible that the World Bank and the IMF are continuing to issue loans and are not opting for grants often enough. The bilateral donors are footing the bill. First they give money to these international institutions so that they can issue loans, then they have to come to the institutions' rescue again in order to finance the cancellation or repayment of the same loans. Thus the international institutions themselves are not bearing the consequences of their own incorrect choices: a clear problem of 'moral hazard'. Although the World Bank has since 2005 given part of its funds in the form of grants, this has been exclusively to poor countries which are more likely to be unable to repay their loans. The result is a form of adverse selection: countries with less effective policies and governance receive more grants and are thus rewarded.

In order to obtain substantial debt cancellation, the national governments of countries with an intolerable debt burden must first compile an interim PRSP and later a PRSP. They are required to involve other national stakeholders (such as the private sector and civil society) in the latter. PRSPs have by now become easily the most important policy documents in recipient countries (they are sometimes referred to as 'the real constitutions'). It is not just poor countries with extremely high debts that compile them: others do too. Nor are they nowadays just a ticket giving access to debt relief: they also open the way to IMF adjustment loans or concessional credits from the World Bank. Both institutions have also developed new credit instruments (such as the World Bank's Poverty Reduction Support Credit and the IMF's Poverty Reduction and Growth Facility) to make the achievement of developing countries' poverty reduction policies possible. Virtually all major donors are reorganising their own national strategies in the light of the PRSPs. But because donors often attach great weight to defining and elaborating PRSPs and countries can feel trapped by this approach, they are sometimes also cynically referred to as 'Property Reduction Strategy Papers'. The participation process that accompanies the definition and implementation of such a PRSP is undermined through government manipulation. As a result, barely ten years after the introduction of the participation condition, there is already talk of participation fatigue (Molenaers & Renard, 2007). Another innovation relates to the way in which aid is given. Development projects and programmes have been criticised for their rigidity. They establish goals, working methods and budgets for several years and lack flexibility. Moreover, they tend to disregard national strategies and processes. The high proportion of technical assistance in projects and programmes is typical: they are largely 'donor-driven'. The same goes for programmes, although these are often more flexible and leave room for adjustments en route. Inherent weaknesses in programmes relate to the fact that they are often inconsistent with local policy, that donors rarely or never harmonise or coordinate their programmes with one another, that they are 'fungible' and fail to give national governments the right stimuli for good governance, and finally that they are hard to manage.

Because of this, donors in some countries are switching to 'budget support', in which development money is put directly into the government budget of the country in question. The World Bank assumes that budget support can make aid flows even more predictable. Some donors are not yet willing to go that far, because the recipient governments are unable to offer sufficient guarantees that

the budget will be managed properly. They therefore prefer to restrict budget support on a sectoral basis. Funds are given to the government for a specific sector, such as healthcare or education. At present, the decision is often made to link this with the functioning of a Sector Wide Approach (SWAp). This is a kind of collective working programme – for the relevant local ministry, the donors, the NGOs and the private sector – which is supported by a pre-agreed management and financing system.

Some countries are rewarded with more budget support than others. In Cambodia, less than 5% of all aid comes in the form of budgetary support to the government (OECD, 2008). In Mozambique, nearly half of the aid consisted of budget support in 2008 (AfDB/OECD, 2008). Moreover, this country is merging its bank accounts into a Single Treasury Account, through which at least 60% of the aid was disbursed in 2009. This difference may be related to the difference in governance capacity, but this explanation turns out not to be completely accurate. The World Bank (IDA) has devised a tool for evaluating government administration, the so-called Country Performance Rating. It is true that Cambodia scores very poorly, but the best score is obtained not by Mozambique but by Chad: yet budget support in that country constitutes just 7% of total development aid.

Knowledge for development

The world is changing rapidly. One of the reasons for this is that knowledge is increasingly replacing physical capital as a source of welfare. Knowledge and its creation and acquisition are becoming ever more important levers for developing countries. Naturally this includes research and higher education.

For a very long time, the development community assumed that the emphasis should lie on primary or secondary education. But research by David Bloom (2005) has shown that higher education can deliver both private and public benefits. Individuals who have received higher education have better access to (better paid) jobs, can save and invest more, and have a better quality of life. But with more highly educated people, countries can also place more emphasis on new, advanced technologies and introduce knowledge that has been amassed in other countries.

One development organisation that has put the role of knowledge uppermost in its strategy is the UK's Department for International Development (DFID). Between 2008 and 2012, the DFID planned to invest no less than 800 million euro in knowledge that is relevant to development. Its new International Growth Centre aims to conduct research into developing countries' growth strategies. Extensive research will also be conducted into sustainable agriculture, fisheries and forestry. Climate

change, good governance, migration, conflict management and social exclusion are also on the research agenda. In addition, money will be invested in the search for drugs and vaccines for the treatment and control of diseases such as HIV/AIDS, TB and malaria.

These are positive signs. Even so, it has to be concluded that in most donor countries academic and non-academic research into development remains doubly marginalised: it is not valued by the academic world, and its results and findings are rarely if ever taken up by those designing and executing policies, programmes and projects in developing countries.

Is Paris introducing order to the market?

Meanwhile, the clock is ticking. Many in the aid community began to fear very soon after they had been announced that the Millennium Development Goals would not be achieved. The UN's annual reports show that many countries – particularly African ones – are behind schedule, and are very likely not to achieve most of the goals by 2015. The UN Millennium Project, led by the economist Jeffrey Sachs, has become one of the driving forces bringing together the 'believers', quantifying needs in individual countries, opening up new avenues of reflection and even setting up very concrete initiatives (www.unmillenniumproject.org). It will and must succeed! More than 250 experts provided their input in a large-scale, practical plan which was published in 2005: *Investing in Development: A practical plan to achieve the Millennium Development Goals*. One of the new ideas is to link the PRSPs much more closely with the Millennium Development Goals and to arrive at what is called the 'MDG-based PRSP'. This is surely no straightforward matter, since the Millennium Development Goals were established on an international, uniform basis, whereas the PRSPs are primarily supposed to reflect countries' own national choices and thus differ greatly from one another. However, the idea is helping to move the discussion forward. The World Bank and the IMF have conceded that the poverty reduction plans still resemble one another too closely, for the simple reason that they themselves have too much of an influence on them. The plans also have too short a time horizon – usually three years. In addition, Sachs and his colleagues have called for bolder, more expansionistic economic plans. They should be based not on the current aid budgets, but on actual needs. USD 100 per African is needed

in order for him to escape the poverty trap, they have calculated. Development aid currently provides about USD 10 per African! Additional funds are thus needed – from the development community, but also from within the countries themselves. In other words, they must work to acquire more tax income, especially from the elite[17]. In the meantime, concrete projects in poor villages can already eradicate a great deal of poverty, which is why Sachs and his colleagues are promoting Millennium Villages with relatively large investments in healthcare, food production, education, drinking water and basic infrastructure.

Donors also seemed to move up a gear during the first few years of the new millennium. Many promised additional funds, and several did actually increase their development budgets. But there was also a desire to do things better. The Paris Declaration on the effectiveness of development aid set the seal on the new aid paradigm, as it were. It was signed in 2005 by over 100 countries and multilateral institutions. The donors regard the Declaration as an unprecedented consensus on a global scale about increasing the effectiveness of development cooperation via reforms to the delivery and management of aid (CCIC, 2006). Essentially, the Declaration is about replacing the traditional donor-recipient relationship with a partnership. It promotes five principles: ownership, alignment, harmonisation, managing for results and mutual accountability. Visually, this new edifice is presented as follows.

A visual representation of the Paris Declaration

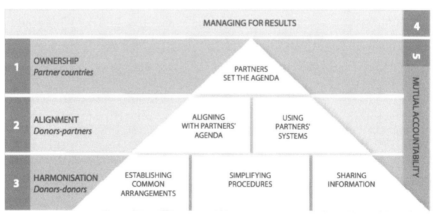

Source: OECD, *Aid Effectivenes, A survey on Monitoring the Paris Declaration*, 2007.

First of all, developing countries have the right, but also the responsibility, to exercise leadership: they are the owners of the development process. It is often also said that governments in the developing countries need to be behind the steering-wheel. They need to take the lead in the development and implementation of their development strategies and to coordinate the different donors.

In the driver's seat?

The development cooperation community is particularly fond of using metaphors. This has its advantages: it brings intercultural differences to the surface. The expression 'the local government needs to sit in the driver's seat' elicited the observation from many Africans that a leader or important person never sits behind the wheel himself. That lowly task is reserved for uneducated but discreet drivers. Americans tend to respond that they don't want to be in a car which is driven by incompetent drivers. Others say that it is not sitting in the driver's seat that is the most important thing, but obtaining (getting or buying) a good car and constructing decent roads.

With the second principle, 'alignment', attention is turned to the donors. They must respect ownership, and they must use the partner country's institutions and systems. Why come along with their own procurement procedures and accounting systems if others already exist in the country? Why create parallel institutions to carry out projects when there are governments, businesses and NGOs in the country that can do it themselves? Moreover, the donors need to make their aid more predictable. They need to inform the partner countries accurately and in time about future aid, and also deliver it on time ('in-year predictability'). Less emphasis is placed on the need for long-term predictability, although developing countries find it hard to plan if they do not know what resources they can count on in subsequent years. Alignment also means that the aid must be largely untied. Partner countries can use the funds they have acquired to purchase goods and services from whoever they want.

According to the OECD's Development Assistance Committee, harmonisation would not be an important point in the Paris Declaration if the principles of ownership and alignment were applied properly. But as donors do place such an administrative burden on the recipient countries, they are asked to devise joint sets of rules, send joint missions, and conduct evaluations together.

The importance of the first three principles – ownership, alignment and harmonisation – has been acknowledged for quite a long time. Managing for results and mutual accountability are relatively new options. The idea is that everyone (recipient government and donors) should continue to focus on poverty reduction, ensure that it is not surreptitiously deviated from, actually evaluate it quantitatively and report on it transparently. Finally, it is no longer just the recipient countries which should account for their actions: donors must justify their decisions too. Donors have for years sought to penalise poor project and programme implementation by recipient countries, but there has been little mention of penalising broken promises or malpractice by the donors themselves.

Does this amount to anything more than fine intentions and declarations? In any case, the OECD Development Assistance Committee has developed a monitoring tool that enables dialogue between the governments of developing countries and the relevant donors on the basis of concrete data about progress or obstacles in the realisation of the Paris agenda. DAC reports conclude that there is some progress in certain areas. The proportion of untied aid that is reported by DAC members has risen significantly, up to 82%. The recipient governments' financial management has already improved significantly. Despite this progress, there is still a long way to go. Donors are tending not to use the recipient countries' financial management systems. Donors are also still failing to comply with the harmonisation goal. Just 20% of their numerous missions are organised jointly, and significant progress is made in just a few countries (OECD, 2009). Governments are increasingly making use of a variety of modalities to harmonize their aid, including SWAps, harmonized basket funding and budget support, but nevertheless they stubbornly continue to carry out their own studies, analyses and plans. In some cases, it is still the 'chicken or egg' question: as yet, less than a quarter of the recipient countries have a proper and operational national development strategy that the donors can take as their starting-point.

Some developing countries regard this new paradigm as a great opportunity. For example, Tanzania launched a Joint Assistance Strategy several years ago and brought the traditional donors to the table for far-reaching agreements about the elaboration and implementation of its own plans. We have already seen that this poor, badly organised country receives more than two official foreign delegations every day which wish to make arrangements concerning

their aid. Every year, the government also has to compile some 2,400 reports for the thousands of projects that are carried out there. The government and a group of donors are therefore trying to achieve greater alignment, harmonisation and coordination. An ever-increasing proportion of aid money is being paid into the national treasury. Tanzania is also experiencing a high level of participation by civil society in the dialogue between the Tanzanian government and development partners. The support given to Tanzanian non-governmental organisations has been identified and a document has been drawn up that regulates and harmonises relations with the civil organisations. For the Tanzanian government, the unpredictability of (mainly project-related) aid remains a major source of concern, as does the difficulty of also bringing the vertical funds (such as the Global Fund to Fight Aids, TB and Malaria) on board. An independent group of experts is responsible for the monitoring and evaluation of both the government and the donors. South Africa has been asked to conduct an analysis of the whole system. Particularly significant is the advice from the South Africans not to ask new donors, such as China, to comply with the Paris Declaration. If Tanzania plays its cards right it can take advantage of both models, suggest the South Africans: the 'Paris Declaration version of traditional aid' and the 'China version of new aid'!

HLF-4 in Busan: a stepping stone to what?

In November 2011, South-Korea, a country that rose from aid recipient half a decade ago to a leading G20 economy and a major aid donor at present, hosted the Fourth High-Level Forum on Aid Effectiveness (HLF-4). With 2010 as the deadline for the commitments made in the Paris Declaration, HLF-4 needed to be both an end and a new beginning. The forum assessed the progress made during the years in which common principles and targets agreed on in Paris (2005) and Accra (2008) guided development cooperation. On the other hand, it attempted to outline the future agenda for aid effectiveness that reflects the changing context in which development occurs today. In recent years a wide range of agreements on development cooperation have used the Paris principles as their foundations and the implementation of the Paris declaration has led to a better overview of the development cooperation environment. Yet the results of the final 2011 Survey on Monitoring the Paris Declaration were sobering. While progress has been made towards many of the 13 targets established for 2010, at the global level only one of these targets has been met. The survey also showed that of the five principles at the core of the Paris Declaration, "country ownership" has advanced farthest. "Alignment" and "harmonization" progressed more unevenly. "Managing for development results" and "mutual accountability" advanced least.

The discussion in Busan needed not only to look back, but also to look forward to the fast approaching MDG deadline of 2015 and beyond. The need to revitalize the international commitment to the MDGs is pressing. In the meantime, the development landscape has grown even more complex, with significantly more actors in development assistance, quickly changing needs and capacities in partner countries, an increasing number of instruments to promote development, and the rise of global challenges such as food insecurity and climate change. A global consensus on what the framework for development cooperation should look like through 2015 and beyond needed to be reached. Different stakeholders came to the fore with different expectations. For developing countries predictability, the use of country systems, the removal of policy conditionality, country-driven capacity development, mutual accountability and reduction of transaction costs were major priorities. Donor countries placed issues such as Value for Money (VfM), managing for results, accountability and impact high on the agenda, but also pushed for a more central role for the private sector. Civil society organisations (CSO's) – for the first time in the history of high level OECD events represented and recognized as official participants – emphasised the need for a thorough evaluation and analysis of current progress. Introducing a rights based perspective towards development effectiveness, the recognition of CSOs as independent development actors and the creation of an equitable and just development cooperation architecture were also considered central.

At least one important achievement of HLF-4 is that it brought the largest and most varied mix of development stakeholders to date to the table.

More than development aid

The new development paradigm and the *modus operandi* are, as we have said, still very much under construction. They are being studied and monitored more intensively than ever, both by the development agencies themselves and by non-governmental development organisations and independent researchers. Many sceptical and critical comments relate to the technicity of PRSPs, budget support and other instruments of development cooperation. Important shortcomings which have been pointed out relate to the selection and involvement of non-state actors (it is claimed that most of the organisations that are being invited to participate or co-opted are urban organisations with limited political and mobilisation capacity), the interactions between donors and recipient countries (the donors are claimed to have retained too much of a say and too much power) and the incapacity of local governments and local non-governmental and community-based organisations to play their new role.

But the new paradigm has also come in for criticism at a more general level. Development agencies, it is argued, no longer see the causes of impoverishment and of enrichment as being linked. Poverty as a form of injustice is situated at the national level and no longer in international relations. A choice has been made in favour of distributive justice and solidarity, in which the poor are supposed to look after one another. Redistributive justice or solidarity, in which rich people and countries make more of an effort, is not on the agenda.

In this same line of thinking, the Millennium Development Goals and their approach are also criticised. The first seven Millennium Development Goals are time-bound targets, but not the eighth. That goal – developing a global partnership for development – relates almost exclusively to commitments and measures that the rich countries are supposed to take and that can change international relations. In order to keep the pressure up, the American Centre for Global Development together with the renowned journal *Foreign Policy* has developed a Commitment to Development Index as a kind of scoreboard or index that indicates how rich countries are helping or hindering development in developing countries in various ways.

Since 2003 the scoreboard has ranked 22 countries, of which South Korea was the last to join the club. All countries belong to the DAC-OECD and are evaluated in seven policy areas that have a clear effect on the developing countries. In addition to aid quality, the score measures how development-friendly a country is in its trade (taking account of trade barriers), its investments in technology (taking account of government support for research and development), its contribution to international security (including participation in peacekeeping and humanitarian operations), its environmental policy (for example consumption of ozone-depleting substances), its migration policy (taking in migrants and foreign students) and its international investment policy (for example risk insurance). Sweden gained the highest score in 2010, mainly due to its efficient foreign aid programme and migration policies. Denmark, the Netherlands and Norway, also generous donors, have performed relatively strongly for years. Next come New Zealand, Ireland and Finland. New Zealand scores particularly highly on trade and security, Ireland on development aid, and Finland finishes first in the environment component, due to its low CO_2 emissions and high gas taxes. The G7 countries, which in view of their economic and political power are potentially the most

significant for the developing countries, score less well. The USA, although a major economy and a big donor, does not score very well because US foreign aid is small as a share of its income and because it 'ties' a large share of its aid to the purchase of US goods and services. Japan trails the pack because of its scanty aid budget, high tariff barriers, low number of migrants and limited participation in peace missions. Nearly all countries score more highly than they did in 2008. Only Denmark, the UK and Switzerland lost some points. Canada, Europe and the USA have lifted quotas on the import of textiles and clothing, and several countries have removed obstacles to investing with pension funds in developing countries.[18]

In the last few years a consensus has in fact grown up round the idea that development cooperation is not the only factor that either makes development possible or stands in the way of it. In particular, the international trade system is regarded as having the potential to be either a lever or an obstacle. The rich countries still charge disproportionate import duties on products from the Third World (agricultural produce, textiles) or impose volume quotas. Moreover, they subsidise their own exports in various ways.

Triple revolution of goals, players and instruments (Severino and Ray, 2009, 2010)

In their influential working papers on the 'The End of ODA', Severino and Ray (2009, 2010) conclude that, due to a triple revolution in the way development challenges are being addressed, traditional ODA measures are no longer appropriate. While in the past, ODA was driven by geo-strategic considerations (cold war period) and 'compassionate ethics' (up to the turn of the century), a new range of global challenges (environment, security, food crisis, financial crisis, ..) have added complex goals to the development assistance agenda. Secondly, in recent decades state monopoly in development assistance (OECD-DAC) has been replaced on the donor side by the interventions of NGOs, private foundations, business, new bilateral donors, and new UN agencies. Similarly, on the recipient's side, new civil society organisations emerged, together with more active local governments, and the inclusion of local business and financial institutions. Thirdly, a range of new financing instruments emerged with different characteristics from traditional development assistance. On the basis of this analysis, the authors argue that traditional ODA is no longer appropriate as a measure for describing the global policy financing landscape that is taking shape. The authors propose a new measure that takes into account the growing complexity, by measuring progress in three main areas: (1) the financing of economic convergence between countries in the North and the South, (2) the fi-

nancing of basic human welfare which improves access to essential services across the world, and (3) financing for global public goods (environmental protection, international health, etc.).

The Uruguay Round of GATT (1986-1994) did little to change this. The attempts to draw up a new agenda for negotiations in Seattle (1999) foundered and demonstrated that the bargaining machinery of the World Trade Organisation (WTO) does not work when the developing countries are structurally marginalised (Lamy, 2002). Many also doubted whether the new round of trade negotiations, the WTO's so-called Development Round which was kicked off in Doha (Qatar) in 2001, would offer many genuine new opportunities to developing countries to benefit from further trade liberalisation. The Doha Development Agenda has since then consisted of negotiations to open up agricultural and industrial markets, and of the General Agreement on Trade and Services (GATS) and the Agreement on Trade-Related Aspects of Intellectual Property Rights (TRIPs).

But international circumstances and power relations have altered at lightning speed in recent years and produced multiple conflicting clusters of interests. In 2001 it seemed as though the global economy was being weakened by a recession and a high level of insecurity due to terrorism. New economies gained greatly in strength, with the BRIC countries (Brazil, Russia, India and China) at their head, giving the non-Western countries more self-confidence. The Doha Round, which was supposed to be completed in 2005, became bogged down in a complex tangle of proposals and trade-offs, but also in psychological warfare between key negotiators. At the 2011 annual conference of the World Economic Forum in Davos (Switzerland) the British Prime Minister David Cameron called for the Doha talks to conclude by the end of the year, saying that "we've been at this Doha round for far too long. It's frankly ridiculous that it has taken 10 years to do this deal".

Aid for Trade

In 2005 there was a growing realisation that the developing countries could not derive any benefit from the outcome of the Doha Development Round. They are not ready for their markets to be opened up as they lack the necessary basic infrastructure and skills. The WTO therefore set up a new working programme in 2005: Aid for Trade.

In 2008, the Swedish Agency for International Development Cooperation (Sida) spent around two per cent or 34 million euro on Aid for Trade programmes, of which 70% went to global and regional programmes. Half of this budget was used to develop an international trade policy and a set of rules that would take account of the interests of the South. The other half of the budget went to trade development, which includes business support, banking, financial services, industry and agriculture.

Above all, Sweden paid for developing countries' participation in regional and multilateral trade negotiations. The rest of the budget was used to improve their trade capacity.

Cooperation means partners

Inevitably, national donors have also been greatly influenced by the international trends in development thinking and practice outlined above. Starting out as a neo-colonial project, development cooperation has gradually evolved into a tool which is used to a significant degree for combating poverty. We would even support the contention that the international framework is increasingly determining the standards of national development policy. At any rate, this is certainly true for those, such as the ministries of development cooperation, who started development cooperation as specialists. National development agencies now have to take account of standards, benchmarks and agreements which have been established at international level. They are increasingly in contact with their counterparts in other countries and with international institutions.

But to reduce national donors to a national version or a branch of an international cooperative alliance of donors for development would be to distort the picture. Earlier, we pointed out that each national system has its own way of working. It has its own subculture, its own controversial issues and its own distinctive national power relations. In addition, we observed, it can be regarded as a national marketplace.

Internationally: among specialists

Studies of development aid constantly revive a polemic between the so-called realists and idealists.[19] The former group stresses that bilateral aid is primarily used to support the donor's own foreign-policy interests. The idealistic school points to donors' humanitarian motives. Schraeder, Hook and Taylor (1998) investigated the aid policy of the USA, Japan, Sweden and France in Africa in the 1980-1989 period. Altruism, it was found, was not a decisive element in aid policy, despite the donor countries' humanitarian rhetoric. What they did find was a clear link between the African states' ideological position and the volume of aid they received. Trade relations were very closely correlated with

aid flows. This was a remarkable observation, particularly for a country such as Sweden which has always prided itself on its untied generosity.

Omoruyi (2001) has adapted the study and considered the motivations behind the aid given by the USA, Japan, Norway and France. He also included the post-Cold War period in his study. He found that poorer African countries had more chance of getting a slice of the aid pie from the USA, Japan and Norway. This was not the case for France.[20] He concluded that a kind of international aid regime has arisen which determines the principles and standards by which donors must abide. Even an idiosyncratic donor such as the USA, he argued, has internalised these principles and standards. However, he added that it was not just France that took its own interests into account. Although in the case of Norway poorer countries were treated preferentially, there was still a positive correlation between the volume of aid that they received and their place on the index of strategic minerals and the value of their imports from Norway.

So what makes up the current aid regime or paradigm? And is it true that the donor countries are increasingly falling into line with this aid regime? Earlier we discussed the Paris Declaration, which was signed in 2005. This refers to the need for ownership, alignment, harmonisation, a results focus and mutual accountability. The donor community has also been singing from the same hymn-sheet for years regarding the preferred destinations for aid. They should be the Least Developed Countries, it is argued. To this can be added the point that virtually everyone in the traditional development community is convinced that it is preferable to opt for projects in countries which are institutionally weak and for programmes in stronger countries. Larger projects and programmes are preferred, because large numbers of small projects overwhelm the recipients and saddle them with countless administrative and other burdens. The recipients, it is also said, need to know where they stand. That means that aid must be predictable and not constantly fluctuating. Untied aid is not just more productive, it is also better than tied aid, which obliges recipient countries to use the aid (often a loan that has to be repaid) for purchases in the donor country (which may be too expensive and not always the most sensible choice). In recent years, there has been a conviction that giving budget support is a better form of aid than project or programme support. With budget support, a direct financial injection is provided into the budget of the government or the NGO with which the donor wishes to work. This is a sign of trust, but also compels the partner to take responsibility. Because it

is not always easy to trust relatively weak governments or institutions, which lack or flout proper rules, have few if any mechanisms for preventing corruption and few if any competent personnel, budget support is reserved for the better pupils in the class. But whether donors give budget support or project or programme support, it must be coupled with efforts to reinforce the partner's governance and management capacity.

The proof of the pudding is in the eating, as the saying goes. In other words, to what extent are we seeing a form of development cooperation which complies with the norms and standards that are being defined internationally? We already know that – apart from a few countries – international donors have not kept their word regarding the quantitative norm of 0.7%. What about the other norms?

David Roodman from the Center for Global Development (2010), which was mentioned earlier, has processed the DAC data and put forward 'quality-adjusted aid' statistics in order to complement the Commitment to Development Index in a qualitative way. For each of the 22 donor countries, he looked at combined expenditure on ODA and evaluated its quality. To do this, he performed a number of fairly complex – but sensible – operations.

First, Roodman cleaned up the official aid figures. After all, when a debt is cancelled which related to a loan for purchasing military equipment, how can one justify regarding this as development aid? In 2003, for example, Congo was declared to be the biggest recipient of development aid because it had supposedly received more than USD 5 billion. Only a fraction of that amount actually reached Congo: around USD 4.5 billion related to very old loans that had nothing to do with development. He also deducted not just the capital that developing countries repay when they have received a loan, but the interest they pay on it too. After all, the donor country is getting this money back, and that reduces the burden of its development efforts.

Donors have undertaken time after time to invest a significant proportion of their aid funds in poorer countries. Moreover, the international donor community has come to the conclusion that programme aid is the more appropriate tool for well-governed countries (such as Chile), while project aid is more suitable for badly run countries (such as DR Congo). Programme aid to badly run countries[21] is thus penalised by Roodman. Of course, such countries may also be poor. He therefore penalises to a lesser extent countries which give project aid to poor but corrupt governments.

The aid community also wants to take better account of recipient countries' absorption capacity. They have to deal with too many different donors at the same time. Each donor regularly sends 'missions' to the recipient country for project identification and monitoring, for checks and evaluations and so on, and each introduces its own rules and procedures. Recipient countries are incapable of processing all of this. Roodman has therefore also penalised countries if they have too many small projects and programmes, since this involves high transaction costs for the recipients.

Finally, Roodman also gives a bonus. Donors score better if they invest a higher proportion of their aid via international institutions. A reward is also given to countries that stimulate charity from private actors by introducing beneficial tax policies.

The following graph gives an overview of the quality efforts of the DAC countries. It gives pause for thought.

Quality Adjusted Aid (bilateral + multilateral; USD millions), 2009

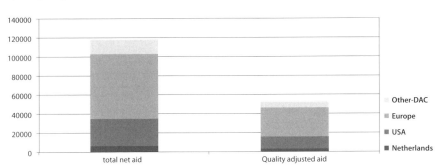

Source: ROODMAN, *An Index of Donor Performance,* 2010.

The graph shows that – if we follow Roodman's reasoning – not even half of total development aid meets the strict criteria that the donors have set themselves. Some countries do better than others, though. More than half of the aid of Canada, Denmark, Finland, Ireland, Italy, the Netherlands and the United Kingdom qualifies for a quality label. This is a positive evolution, compared to Roodman's earlier evaluations (of 2004 and 2005), in which only Ireland and Denmark 'passed' with more than 50%. The USA meets the international norms and standards with 42% of its aid and Japan with a puny 35% of its. All countries have made progress over the past five years according to Roodman's

quality barometer. It is hard to assess, however, how aid quality has changed over the years. Could it not be the case that it is mainly, if not exclusively, the traditional and specialised aid institutions that have drawn inspiration from the new aid paradigm and adapted to it?

There is a fair amount of peer pressure on the national ministries for development cooperation to comply with the Paris Declaration, for example. The frequent interactions between these ministries within the framework of the OECD Development Assistance Committee make it possible for donors to borrow each other's policies, to adopt ideas, working methods and strategies from one another. But other ministries and state agencies which we know to be playing an increasingly important role in development cooperation are often not even aware of this international consensus and repeatedly reinvent the wheel. It is worth noting, incidentally, that the non-governmental development organisations which have been and remain so critical of official development policy have so far failed to take on board a milestone like the Paris Declaration in order to work on the quality of their own activities.

Development cooperation am-bushed

The attack on the USA on 11 September 2001 also had far-reaching implications for international cooperation. President Bush declared in 2002 that development aid was an essential part of the USA's national security strategy and stepped up aid budgets dramatically. The USA embarked on a kind of chequebook diplomacy in which developing countries which cooperated with the 'Coalition of the Willing' in the Iraq War were handsomely rewarded with development money. During the operations in Afghanistan and Iraq, emergency and other aid organisations were and still are subordinate to military primacy. Reference is made to 'embedded development co-operation'. Many NGDOs feared that their work was being increasingly exploited for political ends and were not at all keen on humanitarian-military cooperation. But international organisations also experienced the consequences of the prevailing political agenda. Multilateral relations became more 'bilateralised' than ever: in other words, UN organisations came under pressure to adapt their programmes to national donors' priorities.

New programmes gained more attention within development cooperation: crisis prevention, conflict transformation, even support for security systems (Kivimäki, 2003). Within the Development Assistance Committee, there was discussion about the role of development aid in preventing terrorism. It was suggested that work should be done with groups of problem youngsters so that they could be kept out of the reach of terrorism. Reinforcing the capacity of the private banking sector and the minis-

tries of finance would make it possible to thwart opportunities for corruption and terrorism financing.

In 2005, Bush announced that the USA was opting for transformational diplomacy: the USA's aid should go to democratic and well-governed states, and encourage states to 'behave responsibly in the international system'. According to Carol Lancaster (2008), the former assistant director of USAID, this means that recipient countries should comply with the USA's foreign and security policy. The Bush administration therefore undertook fundamental reform of the USA's development aid. USAID was integrated into the State Department. A Millennium Challenge Corporation was also established to lend support to states which 'govern justly, invest in their people, and encourage economic freedom'. The military were granted 22% of the development budget to train security services, but also to build schools and drill wells. In this way, hearts could be won and trouble prevented.

This 'role expansion' of the military apparatus has aroused concern among development specialists in the USA and elsewhere, especially as 'mission creep' has also been observed in other ministries, while they themselves have to be content with a shrinking budget to perform the real development work.

There were high expectations for change in policy and the implementation of USA official development assistance when president Obama came to office in 2008. Expectations were heightened again during Obama's speech at the millennium top in September 2010. However, while the budget for official development increased during his first years in office (from about 27.4 Billion US$ in 2008 to about 29.7 billion US$ in 2009), the implementation of development assistance remains fragmented, with many foreign aid programmes housed in more than 50 executing agencies besides USAID. The consolidation of the main development agency USAID has not yet materialised and any restructuring of the aid system is been hindered by political opposition forces in congress.

Of course, countries do not make agreements just about development cooperation, but about trade, investments, monetary policy, security, transport and the environment. These negotiations are conducted not by the development cooperation ministers – who are sometimes said to defend the interests of the Third World as opposed to national interests within the cabinet – but by colleagues who are out to safeguard national interests. Despite this, development aid becomes involved at a certain point. One example is the Kyoto Protocol (1997), which was entered into to reduce and impose a ceiling on greenhouse gas emissions. By 2008-2012, the European Union as a whole is supposed to reduce its emissions of greenhouse gases (including co2) to 8% less than their 1990 level. However, Kyoto provides for a number of flexibil-

ity mechanisms. One of these, the Clean Development Mechanism (CDM), offers the possibility of carrying out projects in developing countries and laying claim to a proportion of the reduced emissions of greenhouse gases there, under strict conditions[22]. Naturally, the question is who will finance these projects. In many countries, eyes are being cast at the development cooperation budget. Indeed, at its annual meeting in Paris in April 2004 the OECD Development Committee accepted – under severe pressure from Japan and other countries – the principle that CDM projects could be partially taken into account in ODA.

Recipient countries: donor darlings and donor orphans

So far we have said little about the recipient countries. This is no coincidence. Development cooperation did not arise at the request of the developing countries. It was Belgium, for example, that offered a 'friendship treaty' to the young nation of Congo in 1960, in the form of technical aid coupled with the protection of Belgian economic and political interests in Congo. For a long time, technical cooperation dominated development aid, even when the transition was made to project or programme aid. Western experts 'gave' our development expertise to the 'recipient' countries or partner NGOs. Only in the last

Composition of gross bilateral ODA in 2007 (USD 97 billion)

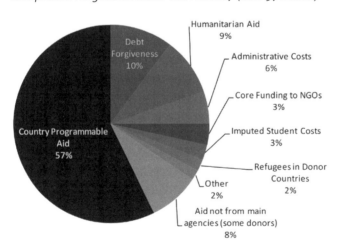

source: OECD-DAC, *DAC Report on Aid Predictability,* 2009

ten years or so have cooperation workers received a new job description. They are now seen instead as 'intermediaries', 'facilitators' or 'colleagues'.

The partners in the recipient countries – governments and local organisations – still have little control over development cooperation. They play little or no role in setting the goals for aid or determining working methods, and they rarely if ever evaluate our efforts. As the table above shows, local governments control only 57% of the official aid they receive to conduct their own policies; also known as 'country programmable aid'. Despite the slight progress that has been made in comparison to 2005 (when only 47% of programmable aid was reported) and despite all the rhetoric about ownership, it is not the local partners but the Western and international actors who shape development cooperation. The local partners are 'receptors' or 'filters' for development cooperation. They have to compete against the donors, who have their own agenda and working methods. They are confronted with the contradictory preoccupations and interests of the numerous donors. Some actors clearly opt for maximum ownership by local partners, but many others are explicitly and exclusively interested in the 'flow-back', the benefits of cooperation for the home country.

Zimbabwe: from donor darling to pariah

Since its independence in 1980, Zimbabwe has been popular with international donors. The call of Zimbabwean President Robert Mugabe for reconciliation, his strong commitment to strengthening the education system and the presence of a vibrant agriculture-based economy contributed to Zimbabwe becoming one of the success stories of Southern Africa. From 2000 onwards, with the government party suffering a setback in a referendum to change the constitution and subsequent parliamentary elections, the situation in Zimbabwe deteriorated rapidly. Political violence, the forced redistribution of white-owned farms, weak governance structures, hyper-inflation and the erosion of social services became the order of the day. In 2008 Zimbabwe had the lowest life expectancy in the world at just 42 years and was ranked 169 out of 169 countries in the Human Development Index. The establishment of a government of national unity in 2009 contributed to some modest economic recovery and a degree of political stability and increased food security but the humanitarian situation remained fragile (www.Globalhumanitarianassistance.org).
While the Zimbabwean government became a pariah among Western donors during that time, with targeted sanctions being imposed on government officials, of-

ficial development assistance and humanitarian aid increased considerably during the period of crisis, as shown in the graph below. However, because of weak governance structures, direct funding to the public sector remained low and funding has predominantly been channelled through multilateral and civil society organisations and NGOs.

Total humanitarian aid as a share of official development assistance (ODA), 1995-2009

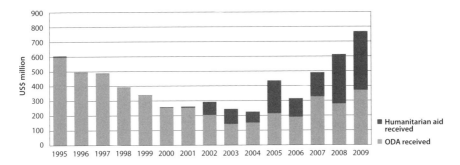

Source: www.globalhumanitarianassistance.org/countryprofile/zimbabwe

A second set of questions needs to be asked in this connection. How do we choose partners in the South? What profile do they have? Do they have the capacity necessary to achieve the goals that the donors have in mind? We can start by taking a look at the destination of aid.

The following table shows us the ten countries that received the most aid in 2008. You would probably have expected the list to consist exclusively of African and Least Developed Countries. In fact, there are just three African and five Least Developed Countries. Iraq, Afghanistan and Sudan are rightly associated with the fight against international terror. But isn't India also a donor? It is indeed, but it still receives much more than it gives. Both parties to the transaction are happy: we give India aid assistance in order to gain a place in the economic miracle that is taking place there, and they are happy to receive as it gives them a bit of extra financial leeway. Does there then follow a long list of countries which also receive a lot? Yes, the list is still a long one, but no, the others do not receive much. The top ten receive just under one third of all the aid distributed by the rich countries.

Top 10 ODA recipients (2008)

	Countries	Development level	Government effectiveness score
1.	Iraq	Low middle-Income country	-1.41
2.	Afghanistan	LDC	-1.55
3.	Ethiopia	LDC	-0.41
4.	Palestinian Adm. Areas	n.a.	n.a.
5.	Vietnam	Other low-income country	-0.16
6.	Sudan	LDC	-1.38
7.	Tanzania	LDC	-0.34
8.	India	Low middle-income country	-0.01
9.	Bangladesh	LDC	-0.89
10.	Turkey	Upper middle-income country	+0.29

Source: OECD, *Development aid at a glance,* 2010; WORLD BANK, *Worldwide Governance Indicators 1996-2009*

In the case of several of the countries we have just seen, it is inconceivable that they are really dependent on Western aid: after all, their economies are performing respectably on their own. In fact, a country is said to be dependent on development aid if that aid represents more than 10% of the economy's own output. The following table lists the hapless world leaders in dependence.

Top 10 aid-dependent countries (in 2008)

	Country	ODA as % GNI	Status	Government effectiveness score
1.	Liberia	54.1	LDC	-1.32
2.	Afghanistan	46.8	LDC	-1.55
3.	Burundi	37.8	LDC	-1.22
4.	Guinea-Bissau	29.6	LDC	-1.10
5.	Malawi	26.9	LDC	-0.58
6.	Mozambique	21.6	LDC	-0.34
7.	Rwanda	21.0	LDC	-0.16
8.	Sierra Leone	19.1	LDC	-1.16
9.	Congo, Dem. Rep.	15.9	LDC	-1.69
10.	Guyana	14.5	Lower middle income country	-0.21

Source: WORLD BANK, *World Development Indicators,* 2010; WORLD BANK, *Worldwide Governance Indicators 1996-2009*

With the exception of Afghanistan and Guyana, all are African and, with one exception, all are Least Developed Countries. Each and every one is a country that we identify with development cooperation. ODA is virtually the only external source of financing for development for these LDCs. As can be seen from the KOF globalisation index among other sources, they are also scarcely involved in the increasingly close interaction between the world's dynamic economies and societies.

Despite this, they together receive less than 10% of the international aid pie.

How do we end up with such lists? Why does the aid not simply go to the poorest countries which need it the most?

Six factors definitely play a role. In the first table, what is striking is the prominent place occupied by countries directly involved in the 'war on terror'. During the last five years, Iraq and Afghanistan have received a great deal of extra support not just from the USA, but from many other donors too. Figures assembled by Stephen Browne (2006), a UN expert, show a clear correlation between military aid and development aid. Countries (such as Colombia, Indonesia, the Philippines, Yemen and Mauritania) which take up arms against terrorists have been rewarded for doing so.

Commercial and other economic interests certainly continue to play a role, too. The Chinese are not alone in promising Congo large amounts of development aid in order to facilitate their commercial relationship with that country: West African oil-producing countries have seen their support from the USA triple (Angola, Gabon, Nigeria) in recent years or even quintuple (Cameroon).

The spending pressure is not a negligible factor. Many developing countries have weak institutions, poor governance and little development capacity. Donors therefore prefer to 'switch' at least a substantial proportion of their aid via somewhat better-run governments or to countries which give donors plenty of space and freedom to get their aid to the population either directly or via local NGOs. The result is favoured countries (donor darlings) where a horde of donors competes for attention and projects, and donor orphans on whom nobody is prepared to spend much.

Donors want to be able to operate conveniently and efficiently. This is why countries where English is spoken receive more aid than others: there are more donors with officials and experts at home who know English than who know French, Spanish or Portuguese. But donors do not just look for countries with which the same language can easily be spoken. There also needs to be com-

mon ground ideologically. Thus Sweden for years opted for countries run by politicians with a social democratic vision.

Having a presence in a country does not just ensure experience and a certain tradition of providing aid in that particular context. It also means that lobbying groups are created (experts, mixed marriages, businesses, NGOs) which want cooperation with that country to continue for years to come, for a variety of reasons. This is most likely to be seen when one considers the aid that is given to former colonies. It can be seen from the following table that all ex-colonial powers still show a clear preference for their former colonies.

The colonial preference (2008-2009)

Donor	Number of colonies in donor's top 10 (2008-2009)	ODA to colonies/total Net ODA (%) (2009)
Portugal	7	38.54%
United Kingdom	7	21.88%
France	5	25.06%
Spain	8	17.62%
Belgium	3	12%
Germany	1	3.2%
Italy	1	1.77%
The Netherlands	2	4.42%

Source: OECD, *Aid Statistics: Donor Aid Charts (2008-2009)* ; OECD-DAC, *ODA Disbursements,* 2009.

So is no consideration given to combating poverty and addressing basic needs? Stephen Jones re-examined this question thoroughly in 2005. He discovered that there was an explicit poverty focus in development cooperation in the case of 3 of the 9 top donors: Sweden, the UK and the Netherlands.

The consequence of all this is that the poorest countries – and hence Africa – are less central to development cooperation than the public imagines. The Least Developed Countries have been promised for years that they will receive 0.15% of the rich countries' wealth. In 2008, less than half of the traditional donor countries kept that promise (being Ireland, Finland, United Kingdom, Luxembourg, Norway, Denmark, Sweden, the Netherlands and Belgium).

It is also possible to conclude from the tables that numerous developing countries lack the real capacity to devise a policy, mobilise and manage government resources and boost growth and development. A score has also been given to every country for the effectiveness of its government. Except for Turkey, this

score was negative in every case. That means that there is work to do, and that it is no easy matter to work in these countries because the government is often more of a hindrance than a help. But it is not just the government that grapples with capacity problems: the same is also true of many local non-governmental organisations and other non-profit-making institutions such as universities. Because taxpayers and private donors in the rich countries also want resources to be used properly, many donors are therefore inclined to stand in for the local institutions or be constantly looking over the shoulders of local ministers or officials. It has now been realised that this does not really help: it is very expensive having everything done or monitored by international personnel, and it means that the local partners never assume responsibility and do not get a chance to learn and grow in their role. So what capacity do governments and other actors in developing countries need?

It is first necessary to look at the institutional capacity of the government or local NGO in question. By this we mean the capacity to play a role in the overall socio-institutional system. This implies that the government or local institution is in a position to define its role; that it is able to develop positive patterns of interaction with other actors who are also active in the field; and that it can mobilise resources (money, competent employees, relationships) which make it possible to fulfil its role.

Moving on from this last point, there is secondly a need for organisational capacity. In other words, the government department or local institution needs to be structured in such a way that it can achieve its goals in a purposeful, efficient and effective manner. The appropriate internal structures and working methods therefore need to be in place.

Finally, only when these institutional and organisational foundations have been laid can there be development capacity. This means that the actor who already has the right institutional and organisational features also has the skills needed to achieve the development goals. To put it another way, the actor needs to have the right talent at its disposal to reach the poor, boost economic growth or develop social services.

Two crucial problems arise here. Firstly, there is a problem of 'sequencing'. The simplest way to achieve a development goal consists of finding an experienced partner institution which already has the requisite institutional, organisational and development capacities. The problem is that such a partner is hardly ever found in countries with a low level of development. This implies that development agencies do not just need to keep in mind their ultimate

development goal: they must also invest in the path that leads towards it. In other words, development cooperation must also contribute to the partners' institutional, organisational and development skills. It also means that a quick fix is not possible. Impatience is thus out of place.

A second problem also arises. Technical assistance, development aid, development cooperation or international cooperation is always an interactive process. The quality of relations between the parties concerned is a variable which to a significant degree determines the outcome. To give an example, the negative chemistry that arose between donor countries' interests and business interests on the one hand and the interests of a political and business elite in the partner countries on the other hand was the cause of the numerous shortcomings identified in development aid in the 1990s. Concrete examples here are the projects that donors financed with grants and concessional loans and which generally came to be regarded as white elephants.

Official bilateral cooperation: fractions and fragmentation

Official bilateral cooperation is actually the hub of international cooperation. It still represents two-thirds of all aid flows. It is on the basis of this bilateral co-operation that relations with recipient governments arise, that a donor country acquires experience in the field and that ideas grow up about possible strategies for dealing with the numerous obstacles and problems encountered on a daily basis in development cooperation. Experience of bilateral cooperation also predisposes a donor country to deal in a certain way with its own NGO sector and determines the amount of resources and the importance it attaches to the multilateral institutions.

Small players and institutional pluralism

However, most bilateral donors are small players. The following graph summarises the efforts of just over 50 donors.

Overseas Development Aid

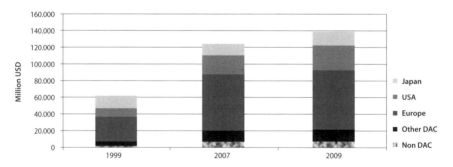

Source: OESO DAC Aggregate Aid Statistics.

As the graph makes clear, Europe is the biggest donor: around 58% of all aid comes from the Old World. The fact that Europe stands out in this way today

97

is not just to do with the growth in the aid portfolio of virtually every European country, but also with the accession of generous and slightly less generous member states (Sweden, Finland, Austria in 1995; Central and Eastern European countries in 2004). But, as we will see, individually the 27 member states contribute relatively limited resources. Only Germany is responsible for more than 10% of global ODA. France and the UK contribute around 8.5%, the Netherlands 5% and Belgium 1.8%. The biggest donor, the USA, provides 20%, while for all its wealth Japan contributes only 7.3%.

However, not only do the donors contribute individual fractions of ODA, but the landscape is also highly fragmented. The traditional donor countries all set up specialist development agencies or ministries in the 1960s and 1970s to carry out and/or coordinate aid actions. There has been constant institutional tinkering, but one or more institutions have always taken a leading role at any given time. In the USA, for example, the United States Agency for International Development took firm control of development policy, and the Overseas Development Administration (ODA) did the same in the UK. USAID quickly became the largest (and most powerful) bilateral aid institution in the world, but since the Bush administration it has faced many other ministries and state agencies which have competed with or overshadowed it. Meanwhile, the successor to the British ODA, the Department for International Development (DfID), became the trendsetter and the leading bilateral donor under the Blair government (Morrissey, 2005). Other very important agencies which appeared on the aid scene and still play a prominent role are the Japan International Cooperation Agency (JICA) and the German Federal Ministry for Economic Cooperation and Development (BMZ).

But in every donor country we can see a growing trend towards institutional pluralism. Other ministries and government departments (such as national banks and parastatal agencies) are also entering the aid sector. The DAC and specialist aid institutions are very concerned about this fragmentation of cooperation, which has already assumed substantial proportions in a number of countries, as the following table makes clear.

Table: Fragmentation of aid

Country	Number of government departments involved	Most important department(s)	% ODA controlled by most important departments in 2009
US	50	USAID	56.66
Sweden	4	Sida	77.53
Germany	15	GIZ	57.67
Canada	9	CIDA	73.59
Belgium	Nearly all ministries	DGD	69.09
France	14	Secr. d'Etat à la Coopération	85.94
Ireland	6	DCD Irish Aid	85
Switzerland	5	SDC and SECO	71.22
The Netherlands	8	Minbuza	99.22

Source: Budget4Change; OECD-DAC, *DAC country peer review reports*

In a number of countries an attempt has been made to gain coherence in the multiplicity of official development initiatives. There are good reasons for this. The ministries of employment, public health, the environment, security, finance, economic affairs, trade and foreign affairs have their own reasons for engaging in development cooperation, but these are not necessarily compatible with, for example, the Millennium Development Goals. They also have their own approaches, and again, these do not automatically coincide with the approach suggested by the Paris Declaration. Things become problematic when the policies of certain ministries are harmful to developing countries or when the opportunity is neglected to make national policy development-friendly in numerous other fields.

Several countries have therefore introduced legislation on international cooperation. So far, this has been done by Austria, Italy, Spain and Belgium. However, the Belgian experience shows that such legislation is insufficient. Nearly ten years after its introduction, an evaluation shows that it has produced a situation where the specialist services (DGD and BTC) feel controlled by the legislation to a great extent, whereas other ministries fail to comply with it at all. Even a number of instruments that have been created since then by DGD (such as the Belgian Investment Company for Developing Countries) do not adhere to the legislation (Fonteneau & Koval, 2008). In order to achieve more effective coherence, Spain therefore compiled a master plan in 2005 in addition to legislation. As well as the development specialists at

the ministry and the NGDOs, all other ministries and the regional and local authorities were consulted. In this way, Spain wants to ensure that development cooperation becomes a key element of foreign policy rather than a subordinate facet of foreign affairs. The legislation and the master plan unlock aid policy, so to speak, and offer a framework and instruments for a proper development policy.

The first country to have launched such a whole of government approach is Sweden. In 2003 the then social democratic government launched a Policy for Global Development which stipulated that all ministries had to contribute to fair and sustainable development. But even in a country with a long tradition of central policy control, the road towards greater coherence is strewn with obstacles. The new government listens to other pressure groups. Each ministry has its own agenda and is rarely prepared to yield to the higher goal of sustainable international development.

In the meantime, various other donor countries have also looked for methods for deploying aid resources in a more uniform, coordinated fashion. In the USA, the position of Director of US Foreign Assistance (DFA) was created in 2005. This person has coordinatory powers over the numerous aid programmes created in government departments and agencies in recent years. The first coordinator introduced a whole series of measures to streamline American aid. As a result, he drew a storm of protest because the different departments felt that everything was being centralised so as to align all aid efforts with the 'war against terror'.

In the Netherlands, finally, a Homogeneous Budget for International Cooperation (HGIS) was created to ensure alignment between the ministries and their international programmes. As a result, the Netherlands has an instrument for ensuring consistency in the use of the more than 6.5 billion euro that the country invested in international cooperation in 2011, including 5 billion in development cooperation. The Dutch ODA budget is established at a certain percentage of the GNP; for 2011 this is 0.8%.

In search of an institutional foundation for development cooperation

As can be seen, the policy field of development cooperation in fact has a completely contradictory relationship with other, conventional policy fields. On the one hand, those within development cooperation realise that they can-

not do the job on their own. They want to act as a lever, ensuring that other ministries (with more power) also help to achieve the goals of development cooperation. Most of them would, for example, argue that debt cancellation is an essential precondition for creating a development-friendly context in Third World countries. This is a task in which a ministry of finance also has a role to play. The ministries of foreign affairs, trade, employment and work, healthcare and agriculture can conduct a policy that either has a positive impact on Third World countries, or has negative consequences for them, and which may even undermine efforts at development cooperation. Some therefore even argue that development cooperation should become a 'horizontal or transversal role', which is not only carried out by a specialist department, but constitutes an integral element of the other government services.

On the other hand, according to many experts the goals and working methods of development cooperation are beyond question. Concessions to economic, trade or diplomatic objectives and interests on the part of the donor country are unwelcome to the development sector. And the department must always ensure that the portfolio and activities are not 'colonised', 'contaminated' or 'exploited' by other departments. Thus the argument is put forward in favour of far-reaching autonomy in determining the goals and policy of development cooperation.

This difficult position has led to a quest in many countries for an ideal political and institutional foundation for development cooperation. Especially during the final decade of the last century, many Western donor countries worked on the policy toolkit of official development cooperation. According to Cox, Healey and Koning (1997), the formal organisational structure of development cooperation in the (European) donor countries differs on three important points.

Firstly, there is the degree of integration or fragmentation of the cooperation apparatus. This has consequences for the coordination and coherence of the range of aid offered. The Netherlands, Switzerland and Ireland, for example, have government agencies which manage virtually all aid instruments and devise policy for them. By contrast, the American and French models are particularly fragmented.

Secondly, there is the degree of autonomy the specialised ministry or agency has in defining its development policy. In most OECD countries, the organisations responsible for development cooperation are formally integrated in the ministry for foreign affairs. This means that the minister responsible for devel-

opment cooperation is continually compelled to find a compromise between his own goals and the specific political and sometimes commercial objectives of the more powerful ministry for foreign affairs. In a number of countries an attempt is made to safeguard the specific character and autonomy of development policy by creating a separate department or by legally determining the goals and policy, governance, management and control mechanisms. It would be interesting to know to what extent this relative autonomy has a positive effect on the choice in favour of combating poverty and the distribution of resources for the benefit of the poorest countries and population groups.

Thirdly, there is the degree of freedom involved in the implementation of an autonomous development policy. This is related to the extent to which the development ministry or agency is subject to interference from the higher political echelons in the execution of its tasks. In recent years, an attempt has been made in various countries to limit such interference by increasingly entrusting the implementation of development programmes to autonomous or semi-autonomous agencies. This is the case with BTC in Belgium, Lux-Development in Luxembourg and the European Commission's EuropeAid, as well numerous executive agencies in the UK (the Commonwealth Development Corporation, the Natural Resources Institute, the British Council). Another solution consists of decentralising the executive role to field offices which gain considerable room for manoeuvre. Sweden's Sida and, until recently, USAID are examples of this.

Decentralisation in order to get closer to the public, or for other reasons?

It has become clear by now that other government departments are writing a significant part of the development cooperation story. That story would still be a straightforward one, if it were only the ministerial department for development cooperation and the other national government departments that were involved. In fact, though, the trend towards localisation means that plenty of other actors are also showing up to take on or even take over part of the official aid commitment.

The 'Structured Dialogue' initiative of the European Commission was launched in March 2010 and aims at the effective inclusion of Europe's local and regional authorities together with civil society organizations in EC development cooperation. The initiative departs from the Accra Agenda for Action

as a leading frame that focuses on the contribution of local and non-state actors to the Paris Declaration strategy.

At present, there is considerable debate in various Western countries about the role that regions, sub-states or provinces can play in development cooperation. In a number of countries, including Germany, Switzerland, France, Canada, Austria, Spain, Italy and Belgium, there is in fact a fairly long tradition of involvement on the part of subnational authorities in development cooperation. Particularly in the last three of these countries this debate is fairly fierce at the moment, and reflects the emotional upheavals concerning the organisation of the state. The sub-states or regions have their own approaches in these three countries, whereas the other countries have or are seeking central control.

The table below indicates the proportion of the aid money that comes from subnational authorities in a number of these countries. In all of them, the budget that these authorities are investing in development cooperation is slowly but surely increasing in absolute terms. More than USD 1.5 billion of ODA currently derives from subnational authorities. However, the rate of growth is no higher than that recorded at federal or national government level.

Table: aid money from subnational authorities

Country	% of ODA
Spain	14 – 16%
Germany	9 – 11%
Belgium	4 – 5%
Italy	2.4 – 3.09%
Austria	0.7 – 2.41%
Canada	0.8 – 0.9%
France	0.7%

Source: Budget4Change; OECD-DAC, *DAC country peer review reports*

Development cooperation by subnational authorities in these countries encompasses a very broad range of activities, but a number of trends can be distinguished (DAC, 2005). For example, they prefer investments in education and healthcare. They frequently collaborate with non-governmental organisations and other private initiatives from the region in question. And their resources are distributed among a large number of countries and a very large number of projects which receive small budgets.

The arguments for sharing out competence

Those in favour of giving greater powers in the area of development cooperation to sub-states or other subnational authorities straddle party lines in most countries.

Some advocates argue that communities and regions can develop much broader and more solid support for this area than the federal government. They are closer to the general public, it is said, and are able to elicit much more support from the public for the problems in the Third World, which are currently regarded as rather remote. This was confirmed by the discovery by Roeland Janssen (2008) that confidence in official development assistance was higher in a number of the countries with a high degree of decentralisation (Germany, Belgium and Austria) than elsewhere. However, he added that this was equally to do with the fact that the subnational governments in these countries also invest a lot of money in development education.

Subnational governments often argue that they can collaborate effectively with other subnational governments in developing countries. The OECD's Development Assistance Committee also takes this position for granted. France even has an explicit national policy of supporting such *coopération décentralisée* and encourages regions and large cities to join with local businesses, schools and civil society in forging links (*jumélage*) with a region or large city in the South.

The arguments for closing ranks

The opponents also have a whole range of arguments, however. They point to the historic steps that the development community has just taken with the Millennium Development Goals and the Paris Declaration. The new aid architecture is predicated on more coordination and harmonisation, not more fragmentation and vying for attention.

Development cooperation, the opponents also argue, is an integrated area. Most projects and programmes include activities that relate to different policy fields at the same time, such as agriculture, healthcare and education. It is undesirable, indeed impossible, to separate these components out and organise programmes in accordance with the division of powers in Spain, Belgium or Germany.

Development cooperation should be based on the needs of the recipient countries, the opponents add. If sub-states get involved, there is a danger that they will be far more focused on what they themselves can or would like to do

than on what is needed in the countries themselves. This is not the way to get good development cooperation. What you end up doing is turning the principle of 'think global, act local' on its head. The result is 'think local, act global'.

Moreover, in the countries in question there is invariably a very uneven commitment to development cooperation. Some regions are not even prepared to act globally. Sub-states which do get involved mainly push the aid money in the direction of their own NGOs, schools, universities and consultants. They resist any move towards coordination at national level.

The opponents also point out that development cooperation is increasingly being coordinated at international level. When European member states come together in Benin to align their programmes with one another, the sub-states are not invited, the reasoning goes. Another example: the World Bank is unlikely to think of inviting German Bavaria or Spanish Andalusia to a donors' meeting about boosting the recovery and economic development of Southern Sudan. In any case, the ODA will still need to be added up by a federal authority that is recognised by the OECD-DAC.

Moreover, the opponents emphasise that the recipient countries are certainly not asking for more involvement by sub-states, as this would mean having to engage in discussions with even more institutions about even smaller sums of money. If every region were to start providing development aid autonomously in each of the aforementioned countries – which is not yet the case – this would add over a hundred donors, each with its own priorities, procedures and rules.

Europe's development cooperation patchwork

By definition, development cooperation is always largely a multilateral affair. We have already seen how the national aid culture and patterns in each donor country have been inspired to a significant degree by what other actors and institutions have said or done. It could be argued that all development cooperation is increasingly taking on collective, multilateral characteristics.

European development cooperation is the nearest supranational level for European donors and belongs to the second pillar of the development cooperation sector. The influence between the levels is asymmetrical in nature: national development cooperation is more influenced by European cooperation than vice versa. As we mentioned earlier, the EU member states together, taking both their national efforts and those of the European Commission into account, are the largest donor group: they provide around 60% of global ODA.

Europe is a major donor not just by volume, but also by working method and content. As we will see, Europe has always been a trendsetter and an important laboratory for innovations in the sector. At meetings on European development policy ideas, practices and experiences are exchanged. New ideas are picked up, trends are sounded out and people gain important information. But the member states are also able to help decide about and shape European development policy.

Also important are the bodies established by the Lomé Agreement and later by the Cotonou Agreement, as these make it possible for the EU member states and the African, Caribbean and Pacific countries (known as the ACP countries) to manage the development programme jointly. The decision-making channels are the ACP-EU Council of Ministers, the ACP-EU Joint Parliamentary Assembly and the European Economic and Social Committee.

In addition, the members of the European Parliament are able to bring up the concerns of their countries or of particular groups for discussion in various commissions, working groups and plenary sessions.

Thus the European development aid system is crucial, but also highly complex.

The complexity is closely related to the political development of Europe itself and the associated history of European development cooperation, and with the awkward complementarity between the development aid of the Commission and the Union on the one hand and of the member states on the other hand.

In order to understand trends in Europe and in European development policy, some academics rely on a liberal, intergovernmental explanatory model. To put it simply, they argue that the European decision-making process is determined by the member states. One good example of this can be found in the late 1950s, when France and (to a lesser degree) Belgium wanted the market position of their colonies and former colonies to be safeguarded in a burgeoning European environment, and therefore ensured that development relations also became a European concern. The intergovernmental deal that was needed became a reality in the first Yaoundé Convention, an association agreement signed in 1963 involving the European Economic Community and 18 African ex-colonies.

As well as the national actors, however, supranational actors such as the European Commission itself also undoubtedly play an important role in European development policy. Thus, as well as offering a platform and managing a common development fund with the member states, the Commission has acquired the status of an additional European actor in development cooperation. According to the neofunctionalists, there is more going on. They refer to the spill-over effect from policy sectors and decisions. The reforms of the Lomé Convention and the development of a Common Foreign and Security Policy (CFSP) have certainly affected each other. The successive Yaoundé, Lomé and Cotonou framework agreements with the group of African, Caribbean and Pacific countries ('ACP-group') have largely determined how the EU deals with Third World countries as a whole.

Another illuminating explanatory model is provided by the paradigm of multilevel governance. This is based on the premise that national authorities have to take account of and are influenced by both supranational institutions and non-state actors. This offers us a better understanding of how, for example, the member states are supposed take account of the guidelines set out by the European Commission for each ACP country in the framework of the Cotonou Agreement when designing their own country strategy papers and indicative programmes. Moreover, the national indicative plans that are drawn up by the Commission in conjunction with local governments are themselves influenced by local and international non-governmental organisations.

Seeking identity and complementarity

These different, fairly complementary explanatory schemes help us understand how a complex triple-layered system of international aid has arisen in Europe. First of all, a broad range of instruments for development cooperation arose which were managed within the Commission and its various directorates. The European Development Fund also continued to develop, as the administrator of the fund for the implementation of the ACP-EU partnership and as an important intergovernmental apparatus. Thirdly, the individual European member states continued to develop their own national development cooperation without seeking coherence and coordination with efforts at the European level.

The basis for European development policy lies in the Treaty of Rome (1957). However, it acquired a legal basis only with the Treaty of the European Union, also called the Maastricht Treaty (1993), and was reinforced by the Treaty of Lisbon (2009). The treaty makes clear the fact that the Union now has the competence to conduct its own development cooperation policy. The Lisbon Treaty has codified the Union's external policy objectives in a way that was not found in the previous Treaties. The objective of poverty reduction and eradication, central to the Union's development cooperation policy, has been recognised as one of the key elements in the Union's external policy objectives. Interestingly, the treaty also stipulates that the development cooperation policy and the humanitarian aid of the Union and those of the members states have to complement and reinforce each other and that coordination efforts will be stepped up.

Since the early 1990s, continuous debates have been conducted regarding the complex European aid mechanism, its role and its impact. In order to bring the multiple objectives and instruments into line with the new international development cooperation agenda (e.g. the MDG, the Paris Declaration and the Accra Agenda for Action) and evolutions in the external relations strategy of the Union (e.g. the creation of the European External Action Service in 2010), policies, action priorities, programmes and instruments were systematically reviewed.

From Yaoundé to Cotonou: from association to agreement

Cooperation between Europe and the developing countries dates back to the infancy of the European construction itself. The Treaty of Rome, which came into force on 1 January 1958, included various articles which were to have a profound impact on relations between the European Economic Community (EEC) and its six member states on the one hand and the associated countries and regions on the other. Member states were permitted to support these countries and regions in their economic, social and cultural development. In Article 132, the associated countries and areas were obliged to apply to all EEC member states the preferential tariffs and special trading arrangements that were applied to the home country. Associated countries and regions would gradually gain freer access to the markets of all member states for all their products. The European Development Fund (EDF) was established for the financing of projects.

But in the early 1960s, many colonies gained their independence. The political and economic ties between the former colonies and the EEC were continued via the first Yaoundé Convention (1963-1969). That association agreement was signed by the six EEC member states and eighteen Associated African States and Madagascar (AASM). The agreement's provisions differed in a number of respects from those of the Treaty of Rome. Trade liberalisation was accelerated and more aid was made available, partly in the form of loans. The EDF received more funds and also started to finance technical aid.

In the late 1960s, international relations underwent fundamental changes. Politically, Africa was very unstable. Export income fell and economic growth stalled. The Group of 77, at that time the most powerful intergovernmental organisation of developing countries, called for a global and structural approach to development problems (the New International Economic Order). The recipe prescribed by the Second Yaoundé Convention (1969-1975) was the same, however: the development of the social and economic infrastructure in former colonies, economic cooperation and reciprocal preferences. The one difference was that more money was earmarked for financial aid.

In 1973, the United Kingdom joined the EEC, and it brought with it a group of twenty independent states in Africa, the Caribbean and the Pacific Region. The same year also saw the signing of the Georgetown Agreement in connection with negotiations for a new treaty. The ACP Group was formally established: the African, Caribbean and Pacific Group of States.[23]

The agreement entered into in Lomé in 1975 between nine European countries and 46 ACP countries no longer referred to an 'association', but instead to a 'unilateral system of preferences with the ACP countries'. The Lomé Convention was constructed around two main principles: preferential status for the ACP countries' export products (no customs duties and a reserved market share) and development aid. For the purposes of reciprocal trade, a distinction was made between ACP products which fell within the scope of the European Common Agricultural Policy and other ACP products. For the former group, preferential arrangements were defined, but the other products could be exported to the EEC countries virtually without restriction. The principle of reciprocity was no longer applied here.

In addition, trade protocols were entered into for sugar, bananas, rum and pork. Thirteen basic products also became eligible for the Stabex Fund, a stabilisation fund to counteract the losses suffered by ACP countries due to price fluctuations.

The first Lomé Convention attached great importance to support, via development aid and soft loans, for the ACP countries' industrial development. For this purpose, the Industrial Development Centre (CDI) was also established to provide industrial information and promote cooperation between industrial sectors in ACP countries and in the EEC.

The Second Lomé Convention (1980-1985) between the nine EEC member states and 56 ACP countries continued along the same lines, but more of an emphasis was placed on the food issue in the ACP countries. The financial package for aid and for the Stabex Fund was expanded. Sysmin, a stabilisation fund to counter price fluctuations in mining, was also established.

The Third Lomé Convention (1985-1990) paid even more attention to the food situation and agricultural problems in the ACP countries, as well as to employment, the protection of private investments, aid effectiveness and the burden of debt. Respect for human rights was referred to in the preamble only. This convention was more of an aid treaty than its predecessor. The focus shifted from project to programme aid and the aid budget was significantly increased.

The last Lomé Convention (1990-1995) again introduced a number of new features. The convention was for a term of ten years. Human rights were incorporated as a fundamental element of the treaty. The environment, gender, the private sector and decentralised development were subjects of particular attention. It was also agreed that the Stabilisation Fund should henceforth consist exclusively of grants.

At the revision of Lomé Convention IV in 1994-1995, a number of interesting changes were made. Respect for human rights, democratic principles and the rule of law were incorporated as essential elements. This meant that infringements could lead to the partial or total suspension of aid (after consultation with the other ACP countries and the 'accused' state). It was the first development agreement to contain such a standard. In addition, in the field of trade cooperation there was a slight expansion of the preferential access for ACP agricultural produce to the European market. Finally, a first form of phased programming was introduced with respect to development financing. This meant that only 70% of the promised aid would be made available on the signing of the National Indicative Programme (NIP). The remaining 30% was allocated only after an evaluation of performance during the first phase.

Strengths and weaknesses of the ACP-EU partnership

The successive Lomé Conventions formed the world's most extensive financial and political framework for North-South cooperation. A number of original features served as a model for many other development agreements.[24]

- Dialogue and partnership on an equal footing
  From the start, equal partnership was given a central role in the working of the Lomé Conventions. The ACP countries were given a key function in the management of the programme, and Europe's role was supportive. A few common institutions were given the task of ensuring permanent dialogue between the partners: the ACP-EU Council of Ministers, the Committee of Ambassadors and the Joint Parliamentary Assembly.
  However, it was clear that the so-called Lomé culture was coming under pressure in the final years. Programming and implementation were increasingly controlled by the EU, and many ACP actors had neither the desire nor the capacity to act as equal partners.

- Contractual and predictable
  In each new convention, the parties gave a contractual undertaking to observe a number of principles and achieve certain goals. The most groundbreaking of these were the human rights clause and the structural adjust-

ment goals. The European countries undertook to grant the ACP countries a combination of aid and trade benefits (on a non-reciprocal basis) for the duration of the convention. Each country was allocated a national budget which it could claim. But this principle gradually came under pressure. Following the introduction of the system of phased programming, certain parts of the budget were allocated only if the recipient country demonstrated respect for the principles of proper management.

- Aid and trade
  The Lomé Conventions made provision for both predictable flows of money and resources and non-reciprocal preferential treatment for a set period. The stabilisation funds (Stabex and Sysmin) were intended to protect the ACP countries against excessive income fluctuations for their main export products (such as cocoa, coffee, peanuts, tea and minerals). On the trade side, the EU also agreed to the import of certain quotas of sugar, pork and veal, bananas and rum.

From the 1990s, the Lomé system came under considerable pressure. Various internal papers exposed the system's weaknesses, the macroeconomic environment and political context altered drastically and, worst of all, results were not forthcoming. The debate in the 1990s largely shaped the new Cotonou approach. We here outline the main points of that debate.

- Fewer common interests
  When the first Lomé Convention was signed, there were still very close historical and psychological links between the relevant European and ACP countries. By the 1990s, the latter were no longer so high on Europe's agenda. In addition, the ACP countries themselves had fewer and fewer interests in common, and as a group they no longer looked exclusively to Europe for the solution to their problems.

- Politicisation of the conventions?
  The first three conventions emphasised economic cooperation. From the late 1980s onwards, we see 'soft' (i.e. political) conditions finding their way into the conventions. Respect for human rights, democratic principles and the rule of law were put forward by Europe as 'essential elements' of the contract with the ACP countries. Infringement of these principles could

lead to the partial or complete cessation of aid. According to many ACP countries, this eroded the principle of equal partnership.

- Trade liberalisation
  With the introduction of the single market in 1992, we had acrimonious debate in Europe about preferential access to the French and British markets for 'ACP bananas'. Europe and the ACP countries had to ensure that their preference systems were compatible with the process of trade liberalisation that was being implemented in Europe and worldwide via the Uruguay Round and the WTO. The pillars on which ACP-EU trade cooperation was founded thus came up for discussion. The preferential treatment enjoyed by the ACP countries was inconsistent with the principle of non-discrimination set out in Article 1 of GATT. That principle was the cornerstone of the international trade system, and meant that any preferential treatment given to one member also applied to the other members. An exception could be made if the preferential treatment was reciprocal and allocated to all developing countries; but the preferential treatment within the framework of Lomé did not meet either of these conditions.

- Complexity and limited impact
  In practice, complex bureaucratic machinery was built up round the conventions and the European Development Fund. New goals, instruments and procedures were being added all the time, generating bureaucratisation and inefficiency. Little if anything was known about the impact of this on the ACP-EU aid regime, but the results in terms of ACP access to the European markets were pitiful. The ACP countries' share of the EU market fell from 6.7% in 1976 to 3% in 1998. The diversification of the ACP countries' production and trade was another goal that was not achieved. By the late 1990s, 60% of total exports from the ACP countries still consisted of just ten products.

The Cotonou Agreement

Under great pressure, the European Commission in 1996 initiated a wide-ranging consultation about the future of ACP-EU cooperation which resulted in a Green Paper. The EU wanted fundamentally to recalibrate its cooperation

efforts. The ACP countries wanted to maintain the unique and privileged relationship that had developed through the Lomé Conventions. The spirit of the EU mandate was adopted, but the ACP countries did succeed in modifying the proposals that were most controversial for them. The new agreement was signed by the EU, the 15 EU member states and the 77 ACP countries in Cotonou (Benin) on 23 June 2000.

The redefined partnership was established for twenty years. However, the agreement includes a clause which makes a five-yearly revision possible. This has led to two revisions, in 2005 and 2010. There is also a financial agreement which determines every five years what funds are made available via the EDF.

The Cotonou Agreement also determines the general goals and principles of cooperation. As the first article shows, the signatories align themselves with the international consensus on international cooperation: '[t]he partnership shall be centred on the objective of reducing and eventually eradicating poverty consistent with the objectives of sustainable development and the gradual integration of the ACP countries into the world economy.'

The fundamental principles underpinning cooperation are as follows:

- equality between the partners and ownership of the development strategy: it is up to the ACP states to determine the development strategy for their economy and society as a sovereign right;
- the central government is the main partner in the agreement, but other actors, such as the private sector and civil society organisations, can also participate;
- reciprocal obligations (such as respect for human rights) will be monitored via dialogue;
- the principles of differentiation and regionalisation are accepted: cooperation agreements can vary to reflect the partner's level of development, needs, performance and long-term strategy. Special attention is also paid to the regional level. Furthermore, a choice is made in favour of special treatment for the Least Developed Countries and consideration for the vulnerability of landlocked and island states.

The agreement is also much more of a political agreement than the Lomé Conventions were. It is agreed that the parties, by means of political dialogue, can discuss any subjects of common interest. It is also accepted that a number of core values form the basis of the partnership. They are called the 'essential elements': respect for human rights, principles of democracy and the rule of law.

Their infringement can lead to aid being suspended. Because ACP countries feared arbitrary and unilateral suspensions, the principle of good governance was included in the agreement as a 'fundamental' rather than an 'essential' element'. Thus the breaching of the principle of good governance, for example due to lack of institutional capacity in the ACP country, cannot in itself lead to the suspension of cooperation; on the other hand, serious cases of corruption, such as bribery, can do so.

The agreement is firmly based on the principles of multilevel governance. Not government, but governance is central: a political and social model of governance is opted for in which the state plays a role, but always in interaction and cooperation with the non-state actors. A role is also assigned to actors at various levels – international, regional, national and local. The European Commission and its delegations in the ACP countries work actively to give civil society a place and a role in their relations with the governments. Some Third-World countries object to this in principle or on political grounds, but the Commission attaches particular importance to this form of cooperation. Even at regional and international level, it supports the organisation and participation of non-state actors. At international level, interactions are made possible via the ACP Civil Society Forum, the ACP Business Forum and the ACP Local Government Platform.

Dialogue, aid and trade remain the three most important pillars of ACP-EU cooperation. The majority of EDF funds consist of grants to finance the development programmes of individual ACP countries. To receive them, however, these countries must first compile a National Indicative Programme and consult civil society. Seven ACP regions have also been defined which can obtain financial and technical support for the implementation of their Regional Indicative Programmes.

Naturally, the Agreement explicitly makes choices regarding areas of focus. Economic development (including more support for structural adjustment), social and human development (e.g. the promotion of social dialogue) and regional integration and cooperation are high on the list of priorities. Gender, the environment and institutional development are regarded as cross-cutting themes which need to be considered in any development initiative.

The private sector is accorded a very special place. Not only can organisations from civil society and the business community help to define the National Indicative Programmes, but they can also implement part of them. Moreover, a new Investment Facility has been created to stimulate investments and rein-

force the capacity of local financial institutions. The European Investment Bank also offers loans for the private sector in the ACP countries. In comparison with previous agreements, much more emphasis is now placed on the needs and performance of the recipient countries in the distribution of resources.

The part of the agreement relating to trade underwent radical revision. Economic Partnership Agreements (EPAs) were proposed. These were intended to create a free-trade area between the European Union and the ACP group which was compatible with WTO rules. Thus non-reciprocal tariff preferences become a thing of the past, with the sole remaining exception of the Least Developed Countries. The negotiations for the EPAs were carried out per region. In this way, six different groups were formed. The EPAs follow five principles. Firstly, they are defined as development instruments. They also serve to promote regional integration so that the regions concerned themselves become levers for social, economic and financial interactions between the relevant countries. Many also believe that regional integration in the developing countries can, by analogy with the European experience, be a powerful tool in conflict prevention. The third principle is that the EPAs must safeguard the so-called *acquis*. In other words, the ACP countries must be able to retain equal access to the European market. In addition, the EPAs must be compatible with the rules of the WTO, and only the Least Developed Countries can claim exceptions.

---

6 Economic Partnership Agreements:

West Africa: the 16 member states of the Economic Commission of West African States (ECOWAS) plus Mauritania;

Central Africa: the 6 member states of the Economic and Monetary Community of Central Africa (CEMAC) plus the Democratic Republic of Congo and Sao Tomé and Principe;

East and South Africa (ESA): here, negotiations proceed separately with the East African Community (EAC) and the East and Southern African Countries (ESA);

Southern Africa: the Southern African Development Community (SADC); with South Africa, however, the EU-South Africa Trade Development and Cooperation Agreement remains in force;

The Caribbean: All Caribbean states (since 2008)

The Pacific: the Pacific islands.

Non-governmental organisations have campaigned vigorously against the EPAs. But members of the European Parliament, academics and much of the political elite in the ACP countries are also highly critical of this exercise in liberalisation. The catastrophic social and political consequences of trade liberalisation in the 1990s are still seared in the collective memory. The criticism is from several different angles.

Firstly, the power relationship between the negotiating partners is asymmetrical. The gross national income of all countries in the Caribbean region, for example, is equivalent to the capital of a medium-sized European bank. Europe, it is claimed, takes a very tough stance in the negotiations. ACP countries fear that if they do not sign the trade agreements, they will receive less development support.

Moreover, the governments of the ACP countries fear that they will be weakened by the transition as a whole. Many countries derive more than 40% of their tax income from import duties. Europe is requiring drastic reductions in these. The effects in social and economic terms are unknown. The ACP countries are therefore asking for benchmarks to be set in the agreements. If these are not achieved, they want to renegotiate the agreements.

Arriving at regional agreements is very difficult, as only 10% of the goods can benefit from protective measures. This creates tensions between the countries in the regions concerned. Every country wants its own dominant sector or infant industry, for example sugar, fishing or the paper industry, to be exempted from liberalisation.

As the text box above illustrates, countries are being obliged (i.e. by Europe) to accept these difficulties and work with countries which are not natural partners. That is not a good basis for stimulating mutual trade and investment and achieving lasting peace.

The European Development Fund

Unlike the other agreements between the EU and developing countries, the Lomé Conventions and the Cotonou Agreement are 'mixed agreements': they have been signed by both the European Commission and each of the EU member states.

The EDF's mixed and intergovernmental character is also apparent from the fact that it is made up of voluntary contributions from the EU member

states and the European Commission's budget. It is financed according to its budgetary requirements. Individual member states' contributions can vary greatly from year to year.

For several years, the European Parliament has been calling for the EDF to be integrated into the general European budget, so that more democratic control can be exercised over it and to ensure greater transparency and greater flexibility of implementation.

The tenth European Development Fund, the purpose of which is to finance the Cotonou Agreement between 2008 and 2013, has an overall budget of 22.7 billion euro. To this can be added the unspent budgets (the so-called RAL or *reste à liquider*) of previous funds. The fact that these amount to several million euro is attributable to bureaucratic sluggishness on both sides, as well as absorption problems on the part of the ACP countries.

This money is put together by the member states. Each has to stump up a certain percentage of the fund. The biggest payers are Germany, France and the United Kingdom. They were requested to contribute 23.36%, 24.30% and 12.69% respectively in 2010.

Other instruments

Europe also has a cooperation relationship with a number of other regions and countries. This never consists exclusively of aid: political dialogue and a trade dimension are always linked with it. In addition, countries, international organisations, actors from the private sector and non-governmental development organisations also rely on one of the many financing windows provided by the Commission.

The European Commission has carried out thorough reform of its instruments for supporting non-member states. A whole series of regional programmes were run during the 2000-2006 period, but these have been reduced to just three for the 2007-2013 period: ENPI, IPA and DCI.

ENPI: The European Neighbourhood and Partnership Instrument has a budget of 11 billion euro for the 2007-2013 period, to stimulate sustainable development along the EU's frontiers and promote neighbouring countries' participation in the EU's internal market. The idea is also that the EU and

neighbouring countries should bring their regulations more closely into line with one another. An important component of ENPI is cross-border cooperation: the EU finances programmes of EU member states and non-member states which have at least one border in common. In this way, they are able to arrive at joint solutions to joint problems.

IPA: The Instrument for Pre-Accession Assistance was created to give aid and support to all candidate member states and potential candidates. The first category includes Croatia, Turkey and Macedonia. The second category consists of Albania, Serbia, Montenegro and Bosnia-Herzegovina. The goal of the IPA is to strengthen democratic institutions, to promote and protect human rights, the rights of minority groups and fundamental liberties, and to stimulate the development of civil society and cross-border cooperation at regional level. For the 2007-2013 period, the IPA has a budget of around 13 billion euro.

The DCI: The Development Cooperation Instrument was created in 2007 to support various types of cooperation between EU member states and non-member states, in the areas of development, economics, finance and science and technology. The achievement of the Millennium Development Goals and hence poverty reduction are central. The DCI has a budget of 17 billion euro. Its target group includes all countries not eligible for support from the IPA and the ENPI.

In addition to the above geographical instruments, the EU also has a number of thematic instruments in the context of its external relations: the Instrument for the Promotion of Democracy and Human Rights, the Instrument for Stability, Humanitarian Aid, Macro-Financial Assistance and an instrument for giving support to 'Non-State Actors and Local Authorities in Development'.

European support for water supply and sanitary facilities

In 2000, the United Nations General Assembly adopted the Millennium Development Goals. In point 7, the international community undertakes to work actively on a sustainable environment. Sustainable access to safe drinking water is an important element of this. The European Commission is also convinced that poverty reduction

and development must be linked with the presence of water and sanitary facilities. It wants to work on several fronts to ensure access to drinking water for all. Among other things, the Commission has therefore set up the European Union Water Initiative. Since 2004 more than 32 million people have gained access to an improved water supply. As a result the poverty level has fallen and people's health has improved considerably. The time that used to be spent looking for and fetching water can now be used for other economic activities. Employment is being created through links with other programmes. Hygienic water facilities have helped to eradicate cholera, thus eliminating epidemic-related costs for both the governments and individual citizens. Thanks to training courses given in connection with the water and sanitary programmes, local people have gained various administrative and technical skills which they can also use for other initiatives and on the employment market. Finally, success has also been recorded at the institutional level, in that the European Commission is encouraging the partner countries to bring their water policies into line with the principles of integrated water resources management.

Europe: a major pioneer?

As of 2010 Europe finally managed to bring more harmony into its aid apparatus with the merger of different Directorates General. EuropeAid is now the single contact point for stakeholders both inside and outside the EU. It is also the single interlocutor for the European External Action Service (the European Union's diplomatic corps) and for all sectoral Directorates General.

A couple of years before the Commission had already made a move to deconcentrate the management of its development cooperation, in application of the subsidiarity principle. Anything that can be decided and managed more effectively on the spot in the country in question should take place there and not in Brussels, that was the argument. The more than 100 Commission delegations in the partner countries have thus gained a great deal of responsibility for cooperation.

None of this is by any means straightforward, given that Directorates-General and Commissioners such as those responsible for Trade, Enlargement, Climate Action and Economic and Financial Affairs regularly handle development-related issues. It will be no surprise that the relationship of EuropeAid with the European External Action Service and with the Humanitarian Aid Department is particularly delicate and often contentious. Moreover, many

member states cling to the idea that Europe's multilateral and development policy should remain the prerogative of the national governments.

'Coherence, coordination and complementarity' are therefore put forward as the magic formula within the reforms of European development cooperation. The question of coherence is definitely the thorniest of these, given that the EU has been criticised on a number of occasions for its ambivalent policy by both Third World countries and by the non-governmental sector. More specifically, the Common Agricultural Policy and the Common Fisheries Policy are alleged to stand in the way of development for Third World countries.

But how can coordination and complementarity be achieved? After all, the expansion process makes these things difficult. Ten new member states from Eastern Europe and the Mediterranean region joined the EU in May 2004, and in January 2007 Bulgaria and Romania also joined. These countries are also expected to contribute to collective European efforts for international development. From being 'competitor recipients' they are supposed to become 'emerging donors'. Several countries have set up a basic infrastructure for development cooperation. Thus most Central European and Baltic member states have set up a development department within the ministry of foreign affairs. Yet Vencato (2007) concludes that these development departments will find it particularly hard to coordinate and steer the numerous fragmented development efforts of the different ministries. Nor is the political agenda that they bring with them to be underestimated. The new member states appear to have more interest in the former Soviet Republics and Central Asia than in the Least Developed Countries. Moreover, they prefer emergency aid initiatives to structural development cooperation.

EU development aid as a whole thus now consists of 27 national donors and the EU itself. Add to this the numerous other ministries and official agencies operating in each country as well as the various Directorates-General within the European Commission, and it becomes apparent that Europe is saddled with a gigantic problem of coordination. It is for this reason that, after a great deal of consultation, in May 2007 the Council adopted a 'Code of conduct on division of labour in development policy'. It was implemented soon afterwards.

The European Code of Conduct

The Code of Conduct stipulates three dimensions in the division of labour:
* *in-country*: how many donors are working in a country, and in which sectors?
* *cross-country*: which countries receive more and which countries receive less?
* *cross-sector*: what are the donors' comparative strengths?

Two main principles run through the whole system:
* leadership and ownership must lie with the partner country
* the volume and predictability of aid must increase

The Code consists in particular of eleven guiding principles:
* every EU donor should concentrate on a maximum of two sectors in any country
* other activities should be redeployed through delegated cooperation or by transferring funds to general budget support.
* there should be a leading donor for each priority sector
* delegated cooperation: donors can ask one another to act on their behalf
* there should be a maximum of three to five active donors in each sector
* these principles should also be applied at regional level
* all member states should compile a list of their priority or concentration countries
* solutions should be sought together for 'orphaned' or 'neglected' developing countries
* each EU donor should analyse its strengths and try to improve these further
* existing programmes should be run in a more coordinated fashion, and new aid instruments should be addressed jointly
* the reforms should be deepened; coordination should take place in the field but also between head offices and field offices.

Europe has not imposed this Code of Conduct on the member states, but believes strongly in the peer pressure it creates. NGOs have viewed this with a great deal of scepticism. The European Commission does not have a mandate to coordinate the whole process. Rather than a sensible division of labour, we may end up with labour-intensive division, the NGOs argue (ECDPM & ActionAid, 2007). To spur on this voluntary process, the Commission has developed an online tool: the EU Donor Atlas. This makes it possible to see which member state is active where and what it does; what gaps there are and what overlaps. The Atlas serves as a strategic tool, providing a picture of developments with regard to complementarity. But whether all of this will be enough to arrive at a single European development policy and whether Europe will make the jump from multilateral framework to bilateral donor remains to be seen.

A choice in favour of Africa?

The pioneering Cotonou Agreement has not prevented the proportion of aid from Europe for Africa from falling over the years. In 1987 and 1988, the EU's net aid expenditure in sub-Saharan Africa still averaged 53% of its total aid budget; it now represents barely 36.8% (2008). The European Commission itself does not seem to be setting a good example. Aid to nearer regions such as the Balkans and the Mediterranean Region in particular received higher priority. In 2008-2009, Turkey, Serbia and Morocco were among the top ten recipients of aid from the Commission, receiving more aid money than all the African countries except for Ethiopia. This suggests that the Commission's aid policy is influenced to a significant degree by its frontier policy and its security policy.

That does not mean that Europe as a whole is no longer an important donor for the African countries. Many European donors have made smaller decreases in their aid to Africa, and several have even recorded striking increases (France and the Netherlands, for example). Adding all European budgets for aid to Africa together, Europe is easily the biggest donor in that continent. If a joint or closely coordinated approach to overall European aid efforts emerged in Africa, Europe would undoubtedly be able to assert its priorities over those of other significant donors such as the World Bank and the USA.

The same goes for sectoral choices. The European countries and the Commission spend far more of their money on education, healthcare, social services and support for national governments and the local civil society than other donors. Moreover, they opt for aid to the Least Developed Countries more than other donors. Some twenty of these countries, including Rwanda and Burundi, receive more than 50% of their total aid from the European countries and the Commission.

Multilateral cooperation: the UN galaxy

What we wrote earlier about the strengths and the dynamic that have shaped European development cooperation is even more applicable to the multilateral institutions of the United Nations. The UN and the conglomerate of its organisations belong to the second pillar of the development cooperation sector but are more than development institutions. Only a few UN organisations, such as the United Nations Development Programme (UNDP), are exclusively concerned with this area. Most UN institutions pay special attention to particular development issues to the extent that they are directly relevant to their mandate and area of competence. Thus the Food and Agriculture Organisation (FAO) was not established to tackle famine in developing countries, but to ensure food security worldwide. When the FAO establishes international food standards in its *Codex Alimentarius*, that has implications for both developed and less developed countries. Again, when the World Health Organisation (WHO) publishes its annual World health statistics report it compiles data from all its 193 member states.

As is the case with the European institutions, the structures, activities and approaches of the UN institutions are more than the result of interactions between countries. Supranational institutions have a dynamic of their own and their own room for manoeuvre. Like the European institutions again, they have become important institutions and nodal points for multilevel governance. Member states and, increasingly, non-state actors (employers' and workers' organisations, businesses, NGOs) take part in the decision-making process in these organisations. That then filters down into national decision-making, legislation and government practice in individual countries. This is why we so often hear our national politicians say that our country needs to do something in connection with the Kyoto Agreement or the negotiations at the WTO.

The UN and development cooperation

Where development cooperation is concerned, however, we need to understand the UN organisations in a different light from the European institutions and programmes. The UN institutions are in the first place consensus-seeking and normative organisations. Recent examples of consensus-building and norm-setting are the Millennium Development Goals and the troubled Doha Development Round of the WTO. Every UN organisation has discussions in progress with its members about dozens or even hundreds of items all the time. Consensus and norms need to be established through dialogue between those who contribute a lot and receive little (directly) and those who contribute little and receive a lot. Thus in this sense the UN is a development actor whenever it can develop a consensus or a norm that is beneficial to the Southern countries. A second mechanism of UN development cooperation is technical assistance. The UN institutions all have countless teams whose task is to help member states with technical tasks. These may relate to irrigation, ICT, meteorological technology, transport, customs management, social legislation and so on. With its technical assistance the UN seeks to fill specific gaps in knowledge or technology. A third mechanism is loans and (to a lesser extent) grants for projects and programmes. Most UN funds and banks that give loans do so on a concessional basis. Many UN organisations are working hard on their fourth pillar: giving policy advice to national governments or institutions.

The UN system

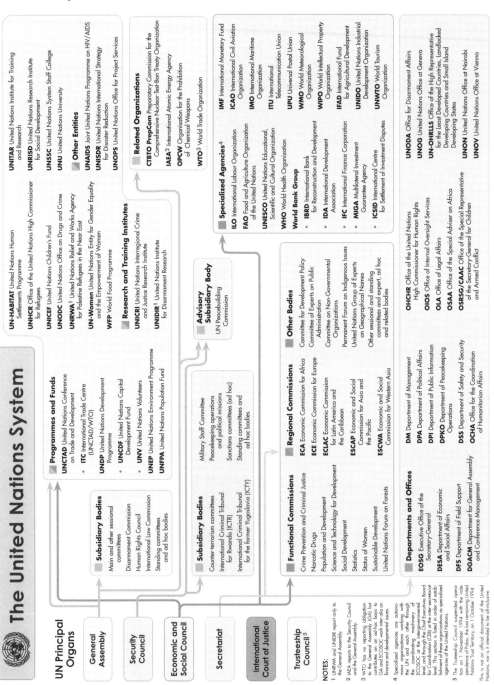

The United Nations System

UN Principal Organs

General Assembly

Subsidiary Bodies
Main and other sessional committees
Disarmament Commission
Human Rights Council
International Law Commission
Standing committees and ad hoc bodies

Security Council

Subsidiary Bodies
Military Staff Committee
Peacekeeping operations and political missions
Sanctions committees (ad hoc)
Standing committees and ad hoc bodies

Economic and Social Council

Functional Commissions
Crime Prevention and Criminal Justice
Narcotic Drugs
Population and Development
Science and Technology for Development
Social Development
Statistics
Status of Women
Sustainable Development
United Nations Forum on Forests

Regional Commissions
ECA Economic Commission for Africa
ECE Economic Commission for Europe
ECLAC Economic Commission for Latin America and the Caribbean
ESCAP Economic and Social Commission for Asia and the Pacific
ESCWA Economic and Social Commission for Western Asia

Other Bodies
Committee for Development Policy
Committee of Experts on Public Administration
Committee on Non-Governmental Organizations
Permanent Forum on Indigenous Issues
United Nations Group of Experts on Geographical Names
Other sessional and standing committees and expert, ad hoc and related bodies

Secretariat

Departments and Offices
EOSG Executive Office of the Secretary-General
DESA Department of Economic and Social Affairs
DFS Department of Field Support
DGACM Department for General Assembly and Conference Management

DM Department of Management
DPA Department of Political Affairs
DPI Department of Public Information
DPKO Department of Peacekeeping Operations
DSS Department of Safety and Security
OCHA Office for the Coordination of Humanitarian Affairs

OHCHR Office of the United Nations High Commissioner for Human Rights
OIOS Office of Internal Oversight Services
OLA Office of Legal Affairs
OSAA Office of the Special Adviser on Africa
OSRSG/CAAC Office of the Special Representative of the Secretary-General for Children and Armed Conflict

UNODA Office for Disarmament Affairs
UNOG United Nations Office at Geneva
UN-OHRLLS Office of the High Representative for the Least Developed Countries, Landlocked Developing Countries and Small Island Developing States
UNON United Nations Office at Nairobi
UNOV United Nations Office at Vienna

International Court of Justice

Trusteeship Council[3]

Programmes and Funds

UNCTAD United Nations Conference on Trade and Development
∘ ITC International Trade Centre (UNCTAD/WTO)
UNDP United Nations Development Programme
∘ UNCDF United Nations Capital Development Fund
∘ UNV United Nations Volunteers
UNEP United Nations Environment Programme
UNFPA United Nations Population Fund

UN-HABITAT United Nations Human Settlements Programme
UNHCR Office of the United Nations High Commissioner for Refugees
UNICEF United Nations Children's Fund
UNODC United Nations Office on Drugs and Crime
UNRWA[1] United Nations Relief and Works Agency for Palestine Refugees in the Near East
UN-Women United Nations Entity for Gender Equality and the Empowerment of Women
WFP World Food Programme

Research and Training Institutes

UNICRI United Nations Interregional Crime and Justice Research Institute
UNIDIR[1] United Nations Institute for Disarmament Research

UNITAR United Nations Institute for Training and Research
UNRISD United Nations Research Institute for Social Development
UNSSC United Nations System Staff College
UNU United Nations University

Other Entities

UNAIDS Joint United Nations Programme on HIV/AIDS
UNISDR United Nations International Strategy for Disaster Reduction
UNOPS United Nations Office for Project Services

Advisory Subsidiary Body

UN Peacebuilding Commission

Related Organizations

CTBTO PrepCom Preparatory Commission for the Comprehensive Nuclear-Test-Ban Treaty Organization
IAEA[2] International Atomic Energy Agency
OPCW Organisation for the Prohibition of Chemical Weapons
WTO[3] World Trade Organization

Specialized Agencies[4]

ILO International Labour Organization
FAO Food and Agriculture Organization of the United Nations
UNESCO United Nations Educational, Scientific and Cultural Organization
WHO World Health Organization
World Bank Group
∘ IBRD International Bank for Reconstruction and Development
∘ IDA International Development Association
∘ IFC International Finance Corporation
∘ MIGA Multilateral Investment Guarantee Agency
∘ ICSID International Centre for Settlement of Investment Disputes

IMF International Monetary Fund
ICAO International Civil Aviation Organization
IMO International Maritime Organization
ITU International Telecommunication Union
UPU Universal Postal Union
WMO World Meteorological Organization
WIPO World Intellectual Property Organization
IFAD International Fund for Agricultural Development
UNIDO United Nations Industrial Development Organization
UNWTO World Tourism Organization

Subsidiary Bodies
Counter-terrorism committees
International Criminal Tribunal for Rwanda (ICTR)
International Criminal Tribunal for the former Yugoslavia (ICTY)

NOTES:

1 UNRWA and UNIDIR report only to the General Assembly.

2 IAEA reports to the Security Council and the General Assembly.

3 WTO has no reporting obligation to the General Assembly (GA) but contributes on an ad-hoc basis to GA and ECOSOC work inter alia on finance and development issues.

4 Specialized agencies are autonomous organizations working with the UN and each other through the coordinating machinery of ECOSOC at the intergovernmental level, and through the Chief Executives Board for Coordination (CEB) at the inter-secretariat level. This section is listed in order of establishment of these organizations as specialized agencies of the United Nations.

5 The Trusteeship Council suspended operation on 1 November 1994 with the independence of Palau, the last remaining United Nations Trust Territory, on 1 October 1994.

This is not an official document of the United Nations, nor is it intended to be all-inclusive.

International institutions adhere to a doctrine of neutrality and technicity. Development is regarded as the addressing of something that is lacking. That which is lacking can be identified in a rational, neutral manner. The proposed functional and technical solutions always serve the general interest. The UN continues to adopt such an approach, because it must always find a consensus between viewpoints which may be diametrically opposed. All themes are therefore depoliticised and neutralised. But this also makes it possible to approach issues which may be highly sensitive, as for example 'good governance' or human rights. By approaching them as technical issues and placing more emphasis on management aspects than on the underlying conflicts and malpractices which lie behind mismanagement, an artificial consensus can be created about the subject, and intervention can be carried out via UN programmes (Boas and Mc Neill, 2003).

There is a considerable amount of rivalry between the different UN institutions, relating to areas of competence, resources and, increasingly, knowledge. Each institution claims to have the best pool of knowledge and competence in its own domain, but also systematically goes outside its field so as to be able to put forward a more holistic or interdisciplinary approach. Child labour is about children (UNICEF) and labour (the ILO); reproductive health (the WHO) is primarily of concern to women (UNIFEM). And who is not concerned with the consequences of globalisation? The World Bank, UNCTAD, the WTO, the ILO…

Thus there is a lot of overlapping and competition within the UN family, as the following box shows. In the healthcare sector in particular, large numbers of international organisations and funds contend for a place, large or small. As a result, over a hundred bilateral and multilateral development institutions are currently active in the field of healthcare (as well as hundreds more NGOs).

Overlapping and competition in the UN family

Healthcare: WHO, UNICEF, World Bank, UNAIDS, Global Fund for Aids, TB and Malaria (GFATM), GAVI...
Education: UNICEF, UNESCO, World Bank, UNFPA, ILO, Education for All/Fast Track Initiative…
Agriculture: FAO, IFAD, WFP, World Bank, ILO...
The environment: UNEP, GEF, Montreal Protocol, Forest Carbon Partnership Facility, World Bank…

Good governance and democratisation: UNDP, World Bank, IMF, ILO...
Civil society: UNDP, World Bank, ILO, FAO...
Emergency aid: OCHA, UNHCR, World Bank, UNICEF, WFP, UNFPA, UNRWA...

This 'mission creep' is not just informed by an internal drive to address every issue, but is also encouraged by national donors, and increasingly by large foundations too. These have their own agendas and for diplomatic, political or strategic reasons may put their resources into a specific international organisation. This will not wish to or will lack the boldness to refuse to implement that agenda along with its own, even if the programme which is proposed and financed does not belong directly to its core business. Obviously, this increasing earmarking of the support given by national donors and foundations to international institutions jeopardises their neutrality. Half of the aid (ODA) given by national donors to international organisations is already said to be earmarked (IDA, 2007). Some international organisations are dependent on donor-financed projects and programmes for more than three-quarters of their funding. Their survival (and growth) on the development cooperation market thus depends on them.

It is generally accepted that the World Bank is best equipped to attract, adapt, integrate and spread ideas and knowledge around a very wide range of themes. The *World Development Reports,* which have been published since 1978, are highly influential. They deal with themes that you would not immediately associate with a bank and that often lie within the scope of a sister organisation. Examples include the World Bank reports on such disparate themes as conflict and security, climate change, service provision, sustainable development, poverty alleviation, healthcare, employment and agriculture.

The only serious intellectual competition comes from the UN Development Programme (UNDP), which has issued the *Human Development Reports* since 1990. In them, support is given to the multidimensional paradigm of human development as an alternative to the narrower neoliberal paradigm of the World Bank.

DAC Gross Multilateral ODA – Three-year annual average (2006-8) disbursements

Institution	Total (USD millions)	Relative share (%)
EU Institutions	12.340	37
WB Group	7.662	23
UN Funds & Programmes	3.152	9
Other UN	2.856	9
Regional Development Banks	2.809	8
The Global Funds	2.272	7
Other Multilateral Agencies	2.336	7
Total Multilateral ODA	33.427	100

Source: OECD, *2010 DAC Report on Multilateral Aid*

Between 2004 and 2008 the UN family received approximately 10% of all ODA. The European Commission, that other great multilateral club, controlled nearly the same amount on its own and total aid to EU institutions accounted for 37% of all multilateral ODA. (DAC, 2010) For years, the World Bank's International Development Association was the largest multilateral donor institution. For the past few years, the European Commission has held that position.

The World Bank: not a cooperative

The World Bank group is the most important 'supplier' of development assistance in the UN family. The group consists of various closely interconnected institutions which emerged from the original International Bank for Reconstruction and Development (IBRD). The term 'World Bank' relates specifically to the IBRD (established in 1945) and the IDA (1960). The group also includes the IFC (1956) and MIGA (1988). The International Monetary Fund (IMF) is often mentioned in the same breath as the World Bank. Unlike the World Bank, however, the IMF is not a true development organisation. Its mission is far more restricted. The Fund only gives loans to member states which do not have enough foreign currency to pay for purchases made in other countries. It is no coincidence that the World Bank and the IMF have become associated with each other. Their philosophy on development never diverges greatly; they are often involved in joint strategies, such as the Structural Adjustment Programmes in the 1980s and 1990s and the Multilateral Debt Relief Initiative launched in 2006. Countries often have to obtain the agreement of their

joint staffs before these organisations will provide support. That goes for the poverty reduction programmes, for example, which really do have to be approved by those in charge of the two organisations. Their staff is often accused of seeking one-size-fits-all solutions for all developing countries and having little or no feeling for the Least Developed Countries. The bank has large offices in every middle-income country, but no representatives at all in Djibouti, Eritrea and Gambia, for example.

All banks and funds of these Bretton Woods institutions (named after the place where they were created in 1944) almost exclusively give loans, coupled with technical advice. Only recently has a grant occasionally been given.

The goal of the International Bank for Reconstruction and Development (IBRD) is to reduce poverty in middle-income countries and creditworthy poor countries. To this end, it provides loans, policy advice and technical assistance to the governments of these countries. It obtains its funds from private and institutional investors in North America, Europe and Asia.

The International Development Association (IDA) gives interest-free loans to the 79 poorest countries. The IDA thus gives 'soft loans': they have a repayment period of 35 to 40 years, with a grace period of 10 years. Only the administrative costs are charged.

The goal of the International Finance Corporation (IFC) is to provide financing for private companies in the South, in order to stimulate the development of the countries concerned. The IFC promotes the introduction of capital from within and outside the country for these companies.

The Multilateral Investment Guarantee Agency (MIGA) encourages foreign investments in developing countries by offering foreign investors guarantees against political risks such as war or civil unrest.

Senior officials at the World Bank like to present their institution as a cooperative, oriented towards resolving social and economic problems and with member countries having a say in decisions. But the World Bank's capital comes from governments, not from private sources. Capitalisation takes the form of a more limited share of paid-in capital and a larger share of guaranteed or callable capital. A country's voting rights depend on the sum of the two. Thus the cooperative principle of equal voting rights does not apply. The World Bank is able to offer cheap loans to poorer countries because it itself has a very high credit rating, and is thus able to borrow cheaply on the market.

Voting weightings in the World Bank group (2010)

	% votes IBRD	% votes IFC	% votes IDA	% votes MIGA
EU (27)	28.46	31.17	30.52	27.55
EU (15)	25.56	28.96	26.30	23.70
United States	16.36	23.59	11.16	14.98
India	2.78	3.38	2.84	2.56
China	2.78	1.02	2.04	2.64
El Salvador	0.02	0.01	0.23	0.17

Source: WORLD BANK, *Board of Directors Voting Powers*, 2010

As the above table shows, Europe, not the United States, is the biggest player in the World Bank group. But here too, we find that Europe has not yet succeeded in speaking with one voice.

The United States' influence on the World Bank (and the IMF) is disproportionate to its voting rights. Research shows that countries which align their voting behaviour within the UN with that of the United States are more likely to receive a loan. Larger loans are earmarked for countries where American banks have a significant stake, and whose regimes are regarded as allies of the USA. Jordan has on several occasions experienced at first hand the fact that the World Bank (and the IMF) is not immune to pressure from this large shareholder. When that country refused to support the USA in the Gulf War of 1990-1991, not only was development aid from the USA discontinued, but the World Bank and the IMF also temporarily stopped paying out their loans. When Jordan later began publicly criticising Saddam Hussein's regime, the taps were turned on again. And just three months after the signing of the historic peace accord with Israel in 1994, the country received approval for a large agricultural loan (Harrigan et al., 2006).

Regional development banks

Like the World Bank, the African, American, Caribbean and Asian development banks give loans from funds which they themselves raise on the international capital market. The members of these banks are both developing countries from the region and donor countries (from inside or outside the region). Although non-regional donor countries come up with most of the capital (paid-up and guaranteed capital), they do not command a majority of

the votes in the regional development banks. However, their votes are weighted according to the amount of subscribed capital.

The African Development Bank group is itself composed of the African Development Bank, the African Development Fund and the Nigeria Trust Fund. It is the only regional bank which originally tried to get off the ground without donor support. Only in 1982 were non-regional partners admitted. Since then, various traditional donor countries have become major underwriters of the African Development Bank, but the new donors have also sought to enter the African continent via the bank. Thus Turkey has become its 25th non-regional member: it sees the bank as a lever which will help involve Turkish businesses in large infrastructure projects on the continent (Özkan, 2008).

The United Nations Development Programme

The United Nations Development Programme (UNDP) was established in 1965 through the merger of a number of existing UN institutions. It was designed to be the hub and driving force of the UN's development efforts. The UNDP has a resident representative in 166 countries and is thus one of the few multilateral organisations with staff in virtually all developing countries. It functions in more or less the same way as a non-profit-making organisation. In formal terms, voting rights within the organisation do not depend on the financial contribution of the member state concerned. Contributions to the UNDP are voluntary. Core resources are spent in accordance with the UNDP's own priorities and programmes. Non-core resources are subject to agreements with the donors. In this way, donors can impart their own emphases and preferences.

The UNDP has become increasingly dependent on a small group of countries (the Scandinavian countries, Canada and the Netherlands). Due to financial problems, it has thoroughly altered its approach by placing less emphasis on technical assistance programmes (which are more expensive) and more on policy advice.

Identifying and forecasting emergency situations

Within the UN, various institutions have a mandate to take action during famines and to prevent them. Despite this, the international community continues to be shocked when yet another acute food shortage arises which affects hundreds of thousands of people. In the period from 1998 to 2007, 287 food disasters were recorded, which af-

fected more than 1 billion people, nearly 400,000 of whom died as a result. The losses caused by such disasters are considerable, and for the same period are estimated at more than USD 30 billion (IFRC, 2008). In 2004 the World Food Programme therefore launched a programme to reinforce the capacity of countries and international humanitarian agencies to identify and forecast emergency situations. Also involved in the Strengthening Emergency Needs Assessment Capacity (SENAC) project are specialists from other UN institutions, the European Commission, bilateral donors, universities, NGOs (such as Oxfam and Care and Save the Children UK) and foundations (such as the Citigroup Foundation and the Gates Foundation).

Thanks to the SENAC project, the WFP now operates needs assessment in a manner which is transparent and technically correct, and it is known whether a crisis will really involve food security problems that will exceed the adjustment capacity of the local population and government. The WFP also determines what kind of aid is needed and in what quantity, who needs it, how it should be provided and for how long.

In this context, the international community is now better informed about the workings of the local food markets in vulnerable countries such as Niger, Haiti and Ethiopia. There is also a better understanding of the effect that food aid has on these markets and the local population: how it can create dependency and migration flows and how other households to which food is not provided react. Alternative aid, for instance in the form of cash, is now also regarded as an important option. WFP's Food Analysis Unit also arranges for the training of national food security agencies: these gather 'pre-crisis information' which is useful for gaining a better understanding of the food security situation and picking up signals of an imminent crisis in good time.

And why then did East Africa face one of its most severe food crises in 2011? Not because WFP did not know that it was about to arrive. It did know. Not because it did not warn decision-makers. It did warn them. But because CNN and the BBC were not around.

The rise of new vertical programmes on the UN market

We mentioned earlier the rise of vertical programmes. These are usually attached to a so-called lead agency within the UN, but bundle together the resources and strengths of various different institutions. They also explicitly seek additional resources from national donors and private companies and foundations. Molenaers and Renard (2007) rightly point out that they have scarcely succeeded in mobilising additional resources. The majority of funds simply do the rounds of the same traditional bilateral and multilateral donors. Most of these programmes work in parallel with the UN's existing bureaucracies,

steer clear of the various coordination mechanisms operated by the donors and recipient countries and take a highly interventionist and action-oriented approach. They go for 'quick results and quick wins'. In many countries, their dynamism enables these programmes to carry governments and other actors with them. The best known example is the Global Fund, which works to combat TB, aids and malaria. In 2010 the Fund, which is a unique collaborative venture involving various UN institutions, bilateral donors, multinational businesses and civil organisations, allocated USD 21.7 billion in 144 countries for 579 grants and disbursed USD 9.3 billion. Since its establishment, more than 150 million people have been tested for HIV, and more than 3 million antiretroviral treatments have been started; 23 million people have been treated for TB; 160 million mosquito nets impregnated with insecticide have been distributed and 142 million people have been treated for malaria. By contrast with the new aid consensus, the Fund's activities are heavily focused on outputs (reaching people in need) and only to a lesser extent on outcomes (having a long-term effect on the lives of the beneficiaries and taking a policy-driven approach to the problem). Ironically, though, the large quantity of resources used to combat these three diseases undermines the capacity of the local health services to deal with other diseases. Local health workers prefer to work for these programmes because they are paid better, because they are more prestigious and because they receive better supervision.

We mentioned the GAVI Alliance earlier. This organisation works to lower the mortality rate in children under the age of five, via access to vaccinations. To do this as efficiently as possible, the GAVI Alliance also focuses on strengthening supply systems. From its foundation in 2000 until 2009, GAVI paid out USD 2.2 billion, contributing to the 4th MDG by preventing 5.4 million deaths.

The Education For All Fast Track Initiative (EFA) was started in 2002 by the World Bank and a number of partners to help low-income countries achieve the Millennium Development Goal for education. By 2015, children everywhere, boys and girls alike, should be able to complete a full course of primary schooling. The EFA Fast Track Initiative is a consultation platform at global and national level. On the financial side, two funds are important: the Catalytic Fund (CF) and the Education Program Development Fund (EPDF). Via these two funds, donors can make contributions to the EFA Fast Track Initiative. In the period from 2003 to 2010, both funds raised no less than USD 1.7 billion.

Education for All not on track

The release of the Millennium Development Goals report (UN, 2010) was a sobering experience for the Education for All movement. Despite some remarkable successes in, for example, Tanzania, where over the period from 1999 to 2008 the enrolment ratio doubled and reached 99.6%, calculations revealed that it would be impossible to achieve universal primary education in the developing world by 2015. In the same period, enrolment in primary education continued to rise, from 83% to 89% in 2008. The number of school age children who remain out of school went down from 106 million to 69 million. However, the report indicates that to achieve the goal by the target date, all children at official entry age for primary schooling would have had to be attending classes by 2009. Unfortunately, in half of the sub-Saharan African countries, about a quarter of the children of enrolment age were not attending school in 2008. In addition, drop-out rates remain high in sub-Saharan Africa.

These figures confirm that progress in reaching both the EFA goals and the MDGs is too slow. What are some of the underlying causes? According to the 2010 Global Monitoring Report, EFA has been seriously underfunded (with annual shortfalls of about 12 billion dollars (Singh, 2011, p.65)), partly due to the prevailing financial crisis. Other scholars (Mundy, 2006) conclude that EFA is faced with a continuation of older educational ODA problems, such as the competition between lead agencies, a gap between international rhetoric and the provision of resources, and no motivation to empower multilateral channels of funding. The last means that the majority of aid flows to education remain bilateral, and therefore more difficult to coordinate. Similarly, scholars provide evidence of the coordination and accountability problems of UNESCO, one of the leading UN agencies in EFA. There are also challenges on the partner country side. For example, coordination challenges between the National EFA Forums and the Regional and Sub regional EFA Forums have resulted in weak National Plans of action. Apart for not reaching the enrolment goals, a growing number of reports have pointed to the problems that arise regarding educational quality due to the drastic growth in the number of pupils in national schooling systems (Lewin, 2007). Finally, evidence is growing that the attention exclusively on basic education has resulted in the underfunding of secondary and tertiary education, "widely acknowledged as essential if poor countries are to achieve sustainable development" (Riddell, 2007).

A vertical programme, the Forest Carbon Partnership Facility (FCPF), has also been set up in order to tackle the deforestation problem. This makes sense, as 80% of carbon above the ground and 40% of underground, soil-bound carbon is found in forests. Deforestation is a significant cause of carbon emissions. The conclusion has been reached that forests are of more value to humans when they are left standing than when they are cut down. The FCPF, a global partnership

which became operational in June 2008, seeks to support this vision, and two mechanisms have been set up for the purpose. Firstly, there is the Readiness Mechanism, which offers support to 37 REDD (Reduce Emissions from Deforestation and forest Degradation) developing countries with a tropical or subtropical climate. These countries are offered a number of positive incentives to limit the carbon emissions caused by deforestation and forest degradation. They are required to devise a national strategy and design a monitoring system. Once this has been achieved, a country can gain financial support from the Carbon Finance Mechanism. Hitherto, 13 countries have submitted their Readiness Preparation Proposals (PR-Ps) and the Carbon Fund will become operational in 2011. 16 major donors have already pledged around USD 345 million to the FCPF.

The Emerging Africa Infrastructure Fund (EAIF) was created in 2002 to give financial support to private businesses which invest in large-scale infrastructure projects in sectors such as telecom, transport, water or energy. Its support is in the form of commercial loans, but the projects which are financed must demonstrably promote economic growth and reduce poverty, stimulate equality and participation and promote social, economic and cultural rights. The EAIF has recently increased its funding capacity to USD 600 million. A number of projects have proved so successful that it has been possible to repay the loans early.

Finally, the Montreal Protocol is a treaty which was drawn up in 1987. To date, some 196 countries have ratified the Protocol, and it is regarded as one of the most successful global environmental treaties. It contains agreements on the drastic reduction of chemicals that can harm the ozone layer, such as chlorofluorocarbons. In 1991, a Fund was started to support developing countries whose annual emissions of ozone-depleting substances are less than 0.3 kg per capita. The countries which are eligible for support are also sometimes referred to as Article 5 countries, referring to the article in the Montreal Protocol which sets out this condition. For the 2009-2011 period, the Multilateral Fund has a budget of USD 490 million at its disposal. Like many funds, the Montreal Protocol is under spending pressure. Half a billion dollars from the previous phase have still not been spent.

'Deliver as one': seeking cooperation on the market

Since the creation of the United Nations, an average of three or four new international institutions or programmes have been established every year. Many in the UN are concerned about the chaos that has resulted from this. The UN

labyrinth is becoming paralysed by overlaps, competition, high transaction costs and coordination problems. Moreover, the 'out-of-system' channels, such as the vertical programmes and the emerging donors, are bringing in new actors, new working methods and a different mentality. At the same time, people are beginning to realise that the opaque structure that the UN has turned into is unable to cope with global problems. It is for this reason that in September 2005 former UN secretary Kofi Annan set up a 'High-Level Panel' to devise proposals to enable the UN to act with greater unity and effectiveness.

The core idea that the panel put forward was that there should be extensive collaboration between the institutions in each country. In order to 'deliver as one', it was suggested that a single UN leader should be appointed in each country, a single programme drawn up, a single budget arranged and, where possible, a single building used. Along with the other proposals to merge a number of agencies and reinforce the UN's strategic coordination capacity, this collaborative exercise would generate annual cost savings of 20%. Certain donors supported the idea immediately and promised additional money for the countries where this happened. The so-called Utstein group, a kind of pressure group consisting of Germany, the Netherlands, Norway and the UK, promoted the idea strongly, seeing it as an essential link in the process of simultaneously reforming the UN and implementing the principles of the Paris Declaration. More than 30 developing countries immediately put their names forward as locations to try out this new approach. It was set up instantly in eight countries. Again, though, there were power struggles. Certain countries, such as Rwanda, adopted the idea eagerly and sought to focus the support they got from the UN agencies on healthcare and education. Certain agencies which were not active in these sectors felt excluded as a result, and saw finance bypassing them. Others preferred not to be housed in the single UN building, but wanted to take up residence in the line ministry formally responsible for healthcare or education. Again, there was a struggle between those who wanted to make it a donor-driven process and those who wanted to make it an owner-driven process.

The whole process has met with considerable resistance from a number of specialised agencies and programmes which place great reliance on their public profile. But large developing countries have also used delaying tactics because they first want a place on the UN Security Council.

The NGDOs: bringing values onto the market

The non-governmental development organisations (NGDOs) sector – the third pillar of development cooperation – has occupied an increasingly centre-stage position in the last few years. The non-governmental organisations that form the organisational core of this new social movement have definitely found their way into the media and become an important source of information on development issues. Governments and UN organisations are earmarking more and more money to subsidise their activities and increasingly engaging in dialogue with the organisations' experts. Other organised social action groups – trade unions, environmental and peace movements – which constitute the driving force behind what is generally known as the 'global justice movement', have forged alliances with the key players in the NGDO sector. Together with other civil organisations, they stand for a value-driven, rights-based form of development which is regarded as superior by the international community. Witness the fact that since 1997, four Nobel Peace Prizes have been awarded to NGDOs or leading figures in the NGO community: the International Campaign to Ban Landmines (1997), Médecins sans Frontières (1999), Wangari Muta Maathai

from the Kenyan Green Belt Movement (2004), Mohammed Yunus from the Bangladeshi Grameen Bank (2006) and Liu Xiaobo of the PEN international (2010). The first is a western donor-NGDO. The Green Belt Movement and Grameen Bank have southern roots. Interestingly Grameen Bank has taken up the traditional role of western NGDOs with its developmental work in different other developing countries. PEN international can join the long list of fourth pillar organisations which we will discuss later.

The NGDO sector explicitly presents itself in many Western countries as a new social movement. Sociological research into the phenomenon even sees it as the historical forerunner and the best structured and organised of the new social movements.

The NGDOs have been an historical forerunner not just of the new social movements, but also of the network movements which have sprung up everywhere since the latest wave of globalisation. While social movements (including the new ones) are characterised by a continuous striving for unity of ideology, praxis and organisation, network movements are characterised by a rather different architecture and approach. Unlike the traditional social movements, such as the trade union movement, they thematise an issue without seeking to achieve a coherent and consistent ideology or vision. Participation is less streamlined, less orchestrated and less permanent than with traditional social movements. Mobilisation is often virtual, and does not take place in a fixed context. As well as organisations specialising in a given field, all kinds of other actors can be involved: research institutes, media groups and so on. In such cases, some researchers have even dropped the term 'social movement', preferring terms such as 'mixed actor coalitions', 'alliances' or simply 'networks' (Develtere & Huybrechts, 2008).

A movement with many faces

In few Western countries is the NGDO sector highly integrated. More commonly, there are dozens or even hundreds of private development organisations which are recognised by their governments as NGDOs. All of them taken together constitute the northern NGDOs (which also include NGDOs from Australia and New Zealand!), a very comprehensive and wide-ranging sector. But the NGDO archipelago has just a few major players and tens of thousands of minor ones. This becomes apparent when one views the following table in perspective.

The five largest NGDOs

NGO	2009 revenue (USD)
World Vision	1, 221,383,000
Catholic Relief Services	781,000,000
Care USA	692,148,000
Plan International	535,000,000
Save the Children International	445,565,000

Source: NGO websites; Charity Navigator

The world's largest NGDO, World Vision, has a budget larger than that of many official donors, including Austria, Finland, Portugal and Greece. The northern NGDOs reported a combined turnover of more than USD 20 billion for 2009. When we consider that the five NGDOs immediately behind these front-rankers, including Oxfam UK, Action Aid and Médecins sans Frontières, have a combined turnover of less than USD 1 billion, it becomes clear just how fragmented the NGDO sector is.

But we need to look beyond the NGDOs, as they are not the only specialist private organisations occupied with the Third World. In most countries there are also country committees or country working groups (such as a Myanmar Committee), working groups (for issues such as female circumcision), coalitions (the Clean Clothes Campaign), foundations and funds, press agencies (such as the IPS-Inter Press Service), cooperative partnerships (such as Oikocredit), think tanks (such as the Center for Global Development), fair trade shops (in most western countries), fair trade cafés (in countries such as Austria, Italy and Belgium) and interactive websites.

The NGDO sector also is very much intertwined with a large number of other civil society organisations for which development cooperation is a subsidiary agenda. In many western countries the trade union movement and the cooperatives are highly active in development cooperation. In the USA the same is also true of the foundations and student organisations.

A sector with many roles

As well as having many faces, the NGDO sector has also taken on many roles. The sector and its actors present themselves as idealistic workers for a good

cause, as zealous entrepreneurs in development projects, as awkward or ugly customers and as troublemakers.

An idealistic, altruistic image is consciously cultivated in order to develop and maintain support for fund-raising. The message is that there is a need that can be alleviated, and the best way to do that is through individuals taking responsibility by contributing to the NGDO in question (financially, through voluntary work, etc.). Volunteering – the giving of time and money of one's own free will – is the existential core of every NGDO. In the English-speaking countries, the terms NGO and 'private voluntary organisation' are interchangeable. The NGDOs seek to give a place to this voluntary participation through campaigns. In recent years, this has been packaged with increasing professionalism. Many NGDOs have become large, professionally run concerns with hundreds of members of staff, marketers, lobbyists, in-house research departments, planners and project implementation managers. They dispense action-inspiring idealism to their militant campaigners, and generosity-inspiring emotionalism and altruism to their donors. As activists and donors constitute overlapping segments in every NGDO, they need to strike an optimal balance between the two spheres.

The non-governmental development organisations have also taken on the role of zealous entrepreneurs in development projects. Their preferred sectors are education and training, healthcare and rural development. The collective message here is that the NGDOs are efficient and effective actors in the development process itself. They have succeeded in gaining active support, not just among a broad swathe of public opinion, but among governments and businesses too. Moreover, in many donor countries, the funds that the NGDOs receive from governments have risen dramatically since the introduction of subsidy systems in the 1970s.

On the basis of OECD figures, we have calculated that NGDOs carry out projects and programmes worth some USD 20 to 25 billion every year. Most of the money is raised from the general public: an estimated USD 17 billion per year. This really is an estimate, as only the figures that the NGDOs report to their governments and that are then reported by the governments to the OECD are known. It is even harder to calculate the contributions in kind made by people via NGDOs. According to Riddell (2008), who performed calculations on the basis of data available in the USA, private donors give USD 1.5 billion of goods (clothes, school equipment, etc.) to the NGDO community every year.

NGDOs in most Western countries also receive government subsidies to finance their projects. The NGDOs' degree of dependence on this varies from country to country and from NGDO to NGDO but can be very high. Interestingly, since the late 1980s donor governments have also discovered NGDOs to be comparatively inexpensive implementers of their own bilateral projects. They ask competent NGDOs to run hospitals, build schools, and even give training to local officials. The extent to which the NGDOs should allow themselves to be used by government as subcontractors and consequently alienated from their own supporters is a subject of heated debate in many donor countries. At what point are they getting too close for comfort? At what point do they become alienated from their own private supporters?

This close inter-relationship with the government agenda does not sit well with the other guise that the NGDO sector likes to assume, namely that of militant, awkward or ugly customer. During the first twenty years of its existence, the sector was a lobbying group which opposed governmental or official development cooperation and insisted on its non-governmental profile. Later, a broader critique of the prevailing international model was formulated, and other societal and economic institutions and actors, multinationals, financial institutions and international monetary institutions, were also challenged with regard to their role in the North-South divide. The NGDOs developed this role professionally, making use of their field experience, research departments and media-supported campaigns. They mobilised and still mobilise public opinion through constantly demanding more responsible political behaviour and policies and by naming and blaming policy-makers who do not follow their suggestions. It is undoubtedly the case that the NGDO sector has considerable influence in many countries with respect to difficult political issues such as the relationship between the UK and the Mugabe regime in Zimbabwe, debt restructuring and the availability of HIV/AIDS drugs. Some critical stakeholders have been arguing for years that the NGDOs should prioritise this kind of advocacy and lobby action in favour of significant changes to the imperfect system over the myriad of concrete projects that offer only short-term relief to the minority of the population in the South.

For about two decades, NGDOs have also been trying to put pressure on economic actors. Multinationals involved in the banana industry, in soft drinks, in the clothing sector, in construction, in dredging, in the financial sector, in the extraction of raw materials, etc. know what we are talking about. NGDOs

know to find their Achilles heel, to expose whatever it is that is bad that they are doing in Southern countries and to picture them as real culprits. By means of activities such as the Clean Clothes Campaign, exposing the bad working conditions in the clothing industry, they have demonstrated that 'purchasing power can be converted into social power'.

Since the NGDO sector's early days NGDOs have also at regular intervals played the role of actual or potential troublemaker. Governments and the business community in both donor and recipient countries are often not at ease with these well-funded and very vocal activists. Cambodia, Bahrain, Sudan and Venezuela are among the countries that have recently tightened their grip on the NGDO community. But it is not just the usual suspects who do so. In many recipient countries non-profit-making workers are monitored, harassed and even jailed, as Devex, a digital network involving over 500,000 development workers, regularly reports. Mandatory, burdensome registration and broad government discretion to restrict, control and shut down NGDOs are common practice in many recipient countries. Organisations in Ethiopia, for example, must notify regulatory authorities within seven days of a general assembly meeting. In Tanzania, an international NGDO must 'refrain from doing any act which is likely to cause misunderstanding' in local civil society.

But NGDOs are not always the ones who make waves. They are also highly effective at riding the crest of the wave and attacking specific aberrations in society and the economy. Examples include successful campaigns in which NGDOs have entered into shifting coalitions with trade unions, consumer organisations, peace activists and the media, for instance in order to impose codes of practice on producers of baby milk powder, to get landmines banned, and to get mega-dam projects postponed or cancelled. Large organisations have magnanimously admitted that they have been forced to yield to NGDO pressure or have had their eyes opened by the NGDOs. Thus the World Bank acknowledges that it revised its structural adjustment approach of the 1990s on the basis of research material and arguments which largely derived from NGDO circles.

Several generations of NGDOs

The NGDO sector is often publicly perceived as an amalgam of different non-governmental initiatives. Some of these emphasise charitable and humanitarian interventions, others structural measures in favour of the Third World, and

others still the need to transfer know-how. This diversity is based on the five periods or trends which have led to the creation of a succession of new non-governmental development initiatives.

The first generation consisted of the colonial pioneers. In the context of community development initiatives in the colonies and mandated territories – mainly supported by the Catholic and Protestant churches – lay volunteers were activated. Volunteers were also involved in structures such as education, administration and healthcare. Specialist organisations such as the Damien Foundation were established for the purpose.

As early as the inter-war period, the basis was laid for the second generation of NGDOs. Both the churches and the labour movement set up NGOs to address the needs of the victims of the war in Europe, and subsequently turned their attention towards the developing countries.

From 1940 to 1960 several trends and movements can be seen emerging within the NGDO community, each of which influences the others.

Firstly, several humanitarian and Christian NG(D)Os were started which sought to provide aid to victims of the Second World War, the Korean War and poverty in Africa. Oxfam (originally the Oxford Committee for Famine Relief) originated out of protests against the British government's refusal to give any help to hundreds of thousands of starving Greeks during the war. Within both the Protestant communities and the Catholic churches in the north, NGDOs were founded which could rely on a very broad and committed body of supporters among religious and laypeople alike. Some of the biggest NGDOs originated in this way: Caritas Internationalis, World Vision (USA), Center for Concern (USA), Christian Aid (UK), CAFOD (UK), Manos Unidas (Spain), Misereor (Germany) and many member organisations of the World Council of Churches.

In addition, NGDOs were established to give further support to the institutions and organisations that had been created during the colonial period. Many of these were of church origin. The task of these NGDOs was to maintain links with the Catholic parishes and Protestant congregations in the developing countries. But they also needed further to expand and finance the network of social services associated with these Christian institutions. Other social movements such as the trade union movement and the cooperative movement also set up their own NGDOs to support their colleagues in the South.

At the same time, there were very widespread calls not just to give money for the poor countries, but actually to work for them, and a number of the

145

largest organisations for volunteers were created, such as UK Voluntary Service Overseas in 1958, the US Peace Corps in 1961 and the Dutch organisation SNV in 1963. These volunteers, who received a modest government salary, were expected to engage in the local culture, live with the people and gradually bring about change and improvement through processes of 'inculturation'.

On the other hand, a pro-Third-World school of thought developed which aimed to carry out a far more radical project. Inspired by the Latin American *dependencia theorists* , proponents of these views argued that there was a clear link between the underdevelopment of Third World countries and speedy development of Western capitalism. Such views emerged at universities and were responsible for numerous new non-governmental initiatives. NGDOs sought to provoke debate about the international system and North-South relations and support the emancipatory initiatives of the working classes in the Third World. These NGDOs had much sympathy for the non-aligned nationalist countries such as Cuba, Chile, Tanzania, Algeria and India.

Midway through the 1980s, debate arose in France about the fundamentals and the implications of the pro-Third-World ideology (Brauman, 1986). Particularly in charity circles, and more specifically in the recently established Médecins sans Frontières/Doctors without borders (1980), a new vision of non-governmental development action was launched. The emphasis was placed on humanitarian law, which legitimises emergency aid interventions even when governments invoke their sovereign right of self-determination. Moreover, this vision led to criticisms of the dysfunctionality of many Third World states. Blame for the development problem was no longer attributed to the international system, as it had been by the 'pro-Third-Worlders', but to actors and institutions in the Third World countries. Development organisations themselves were maintaining inefficient, bureaucratic and even corrupt and oppressive regimes, it was argued.

Southern NGOs becoming NGDOs

So far most NGDOs have come from OECD countries. They specialise in defending the interest of civil society organisations in recipient countries and giving them financial and other support. For some years some domestic civil society organisations that were set up to solve local problems have branched out into other developing

countries. In this way we see the Bengali micro-finance organisations BRAC and Grameen Bank experimenting with micro-finance in Afghanistan or Africa. Indian dairy cooperatives give support to Kenyan dairy cooperatives. "Un techo para mi pais", a local NGO promoting decent housing in Chile has ventured out into 19 Latin American countries. It would be interesting to know if these Southern NGOs that become NGDOs in other developing countries differ from the Northern NGDOs in terms of their vision and approach or the impact of their work.

Not only did the vision of development change profoundly, but preference began to be given to different types of intervention. This generation of organisations stood back from supposedly emancipatory projects, preferring technical interventions for which specific know-how was required. In this sense, they were 'technicians without borders'. Dozens of specialist organisations were created which followed the example of Médecins sans Frontières: there are now 'without borders' organisations of vets, journalists, pilots, lawyers, architects, engineers and teachers. Also, organisations specialising in water supply, sanitary facilities, entrepreneurship, microfinance, rural electrification, the marketing of agricultural produce and environmental conservation opted to provide local communities with new development instruments via an appropriate technical and technological approach without much regard for the flaws in the policy environment in which they operated.

A sector with many different visions and strategies

As our brief historical outline shows, the NGDO sector is a colourful collection of organisations and movements with highly diverse backgrounds and rationales. This partly explains the diversity of analyses, ideologies and visions within the NGDO sector, which certainly cannot be described as subject to an ideological monoculture. Depending on when they were created, NGDOs may focus on making voluntary work possible, on alleviating acute needs, on giving support to 'partners', on bringing about changes in North-South relations and supporting emancipatory projects or on carrying out humanitarian or technical interventions.

In most countries, the national NGDO sector has so far not come up with a consistent common vision or joint strategy. Few countries have strong um-

brella organisations or federations. InterAction, the largest American NGDO coalition, is arguably one well-known exception to this. It has 188 members, which together run three-quarters of all private NGDO funds in the USA. It employs a mere fifty or so professionals, but its 23-strong board of directors includes several of the world's largest NGDOs. The organisation takes a highly critical line on the USA's official development policy, and lobbies effectively using 'evidence-based policy alternatives'. Standards are imposed on its own members in terms of integrity, quality and effectiveness. Each member has to report on these areas every year.

The difficulty for most national NGDO communities is that – unlike the 'old' social movements – they lack fixed democratic and participatory working methods for arriving at a joint, crystallised decision about their vision and developing their own strategies on the basis of that vision. There are no NGDO congresses, colloquia or conferences meeting at regular intervals and following procedures enshrined in statutes to present the organisations' collective vision and joint actions for the discussion and approval of supporters or members.

The following diagram is a schematic attempt to situate the divergent visions on development and strategies within the NGDO sector.

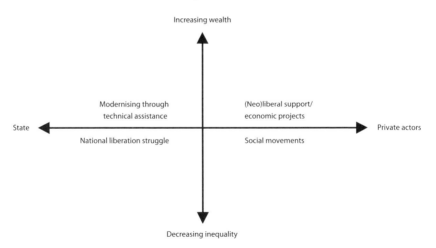

The first, vertical axis reflects the fact that some organisations argue that the Third World problem can only be resolved by wealth creation in the Third World, while others see reducing the inequality between North and South as the solution. The second, horizontal axis indicates the various actors who can

and must play a key role in carrying out the development agenda. There is the government in the Third World, but private actors can be an alternative. The resultant matrix yields four different strategies.

The first strategy, which is advocated by one wing of the NGDO sector, aims to increase the wealth of developing countries by promoting a modernisation process. The state is assigned a central role in this. This strategy was especially popular during the first and second UN Development Decades (1960-1970 and 1970-1980), and coincided with attempts by developing countries to modernise their own production apparatus through a strategy of import-substitution industrialisation (ISI), create their own markets and build up a state-run network of social welfare insitutions. The NGDOs supported these efforts, mainly by sending out technical personnel (health workers, teachers, agricultural experts, irrigation specialists, engineers, etc.) and by providing financial support for the construction of health centres and schools, for the building of roads, for water supply and for the establishment of marketing institutions such as agricultural cooperatives.

The radicalisation of the NGDO sector in the 1960s which was mentioned earlier coincided with a more general paradigm shift in thinking about development and underdevelopment. This was partly influenced by the *dependencia* thinkers, who pointed to the unequal exchange relations between developed and underdeveloped countries and to the dependence relationships between central and peripheral countries. According to this school of thought, radical action was needed to bring national and above all international inequalities to an end. Countries from the Third World needed to detach themselves from the international system and steer an independent course. In many countries, they argued, the national elite acted as a bridgehead, helping maintain the international capitalist system, and this meant that independence could be achieved only by means of a national liberation struggle, followed by a state-led emancipatory strategy.

Many NGDOs therefore opted to give financial and technical support to national liberation movements. In countries with a conservative dictatorship, support went to the opposition, which in some cases had to operate clandestinely. In countries where a liberation movement had succeeded in gaining power, there was cooperation with the local authorities, with social organisations associated with the national unity party and with specific government departments. In this way, a significant element of the NGDO sector became

149

allied to nationalist and populist regimes which were trying out a 'third way'. Well-known examples are the support given to the African socialism of Julius Nyerere (Tanzania), the left-wing experiment of Salvador Allende (Chile), the Sandinista regime (Nicaragua) and Fidel Castro's communist Cuba. The failure of these regimes did not bring this trend within the NGDO community to an end. A contemporary version of the 'third way' is found in the global justice movement, which opposes the neoliberal model and again argues in favour of a more central role for the state in the development process. A growing group of NGDOs offers Third World governments both intellectual and practical support in the defence of their interests in international forums such as the WTO and the World Bank.

The collapse of the one-party states and the subsequent democratisation movement in many Third World countries from the mid-1980s onwards also created political circumstances within which new civil actors could emerge and operate. This 'associative revolution' was to a large extent indebted to support from the Western non-governmental world. In the first phase, certain Western NGDOs initiated non-governmental structures, mainly acting alone. In doing so, they worked as social engineers, deliberately recalibrating the local social and associative fabric.

The NGDOs' difficult task

It is estimated that more than 600 million people in the developing world (Riddell, 2008) come into some form of contact with NGDO projects and programmes. NGDOs explicitly target the poorer sections of the population. A study by Gilles Nancy and Boriana Yontcheva of the IMF (2006) shows that the NGDOs have opted for a poverty alleviation approach on their own initiative, and are not influenced by the strategic considerations of a subsidising party such as the European Commission. Most evaluations suggest that a majority of the NGDO projects succeed in achieving their immediate goals: the school works, the well is used, the bush radio reaches the farmers, the coffee gets onto the international market. But NGDOs do more than that. They also give people self-confidence and bring them into contact with the outside world.
Yet there are also serious challenges to face.

NGDOs often say and think that they work with the poor. But few check whether this is actually the case, and numerous studies have shown that it is particularly difficult – even for groundbreaking projects such as the Grameen Bank – to reach the poorest of the poor (Develtere & Huybrechts, 2005). Those living in extreme poverty

rarely have a fixed dwelling, are hard to reach and are excluded by other poor and not-so-poor people. Communities in poverty and extreme poverty are riven by conflict and intrigue. In their subsistence economy, the risks are high and the margins between success and failure slight. Poor people therefore play it safe or focus on what is convenient to them. '*Nakei kobeta coop!*' ('I'll try to do a deal') is a sentiment expressed every day by millions of Kinois (inhabitants of Kinshasa). People are prepared to take on even things that are physically impossible or morally unthinkable to keep going for another day, writes Donatien Olela (2007). Setting up an '*ONG-bidon*' (false ngo's), '*ONG-de-serviette*' or 'aid-lobbying NGO' is a tried and tested method. For them, development cooperation is a market in which a deal can be struck. In return for payment, savvy intermediaries also known as '*courtiers du développement*' or 'aid-brokers' give advice to these local 'survival NGOs' so that they can use the right words ('gender', 'participation', etc.) and make the right symbolic gestures (produce a leaflet, set up a small savings fund, etc.) to get the foreign development worker to come up with the goods.

But even for the more substantial local NGOs with a respectable track record the development sector is a complex market environment. They are approached by countless northern NGDOs, but also by the World Bank or USAID, with requests to reach the poor together. They may be rewarded handsomely for doing so, but in exchange must ask the impossible of the poor: voluntarily to help build a clinic or school, to take time to devise a poverty plan for the village, to collect money for repairs to the well, even to save the natural environment and solve the local unemployment problem. If the Millennium Development Goals are not achieved will the NGDOs and the poor then be to blame?

At times, fairly interventionist methods have been and still are used which primarily hark back to the associative models from Europe and North America or which are inspired by a limited number of highly successful initiatives (for example the microfinancing system of BRAC and the Grameen Bank in Bangladesh). At times, more participatory methods have been and still are used which take local analyses and civil traditions as their starting-point. For this purpose, special project and programme instruments were developed such as the participatory rural appraisal (PRA) and result-based management. Later, many NGDOs adapted their role somewhat, often presenting themselves as facilitators for and partners to local civil society. Thus we find that the Western NGDOs increasingly tend to provide financial and technical support to local community-based organisations, trade unions of farmers, fishermen or workers, women's groups and movements, cooperative and mutual initiatives. The 'empowerment' of local communities which stand up for their rights is a

crucial element of this approach. NGDOs therefore also attempt to bring these communities out of their isolation, dragging them into the broader decision-making field and bringing them into contact with national governments and international institutions so that the voice of the poor people that they represent can be heard during policy discussions about poverty reduction plans or even the liberalisation of the international markets.

Although Western NGDOs and their local partners set great store by the 'partnership idea' and working on an equal footing, their relationship remains rather ambiguous and asymmetrical. Increasingly, Western NGDOs are professionally organised and have a clear agenda for which they have or seek support from Western private and public sponsors. Southern civil organisations are often fragile structures, which are highly dependent on Western financial and technical support and to a great extent derive their legitimacy from their capacity to channel funds to the district or members in question. Critics also deplore the tendency to address everything via local NGOs, calling it 'NGO-isation'. NGOs take over the role of governments in healthcare, education and many other fields, and through their emphasis on service provision and their focus on financial solutions for every problem, they tend to quash the militant spirit of social movements such as trade union movements, farmers' organisations and other emancipation movements which would have been capable of fighting for structural solutions on their own (Jad, 2007).

The chicken or the duck...

Care USA is one of the biggest NGDOs in the United States and the world. In 2009, this organisation had a budget of almost USD 700 million. Care USA pays particular attention to the situation of women and their opportunities, believing that women have the potential to help their families and communities escape from poverty. Thus women are central to all Care USA projects, whether they relate to education, drinkable water, efforts against HIV/AIDS or addressing the consequences of climate change. A lot of attention has been paid to this last theme in particular in recent years. For example, in 2007 Care USA started a project in Bangladesh. One of the biggest challenges that the local population has to learn to deal with there is the constant threat of flooding due to climate change. Care helps local people, especially women, to adapt their way of life to this threat. Many of the measures that are devised are both simple and effective. Before Care came to the area, many women kept chickens, for example, but whenever the population experienced flooding, these would drown.

This was a severe blow to families that were largely dependent on poultry. Together with its local partners, Care started up a programme to encourage women to buy ducks instead of chickens. The idea caught on, and the resilience of the population increased. Flooding now has less impact on their standard of living.

A final strategy – the most recent one – returns to the idea that the role of development organisations is to increase the target group's income through wealth creation rather than redistribution. According to this school of thought, development agencies, including NGDOs, should primarily be creating opportunities for local private actors. This can be done by setting up or improving local institutions, such as property rights or marketing mechanisms, or by giving support to local entrepreneurs. Many NGDOs have adapted their approach along these lines, and invest in 'income-generating projects'. The supporters of the social movement approach prefer collective action and promote cooperative entrepreneurship or initiatives in the social economy. A second group opts for private entrepreneurship, with some organisations giving support to 'micro-entrepreneurs' (usually one-man or family businesses) and others preferring medium-sized companies.

A movement with a plural support base

The northern non-governmental organisations have a fairly ambiguous relationship with their support base. Yet along with the work they do to improve the standard of living in the Third World, their support base is the most important source of legitimacy for NGDOs. It consists of adherents, constituents and supporters. No NGDOs have members.

'Adherents' agree with the decisions that NGDOs (or a specific NGDO) have made. They have a more or less emotional and ideological connection with the sector as a whole or with a specific NGO. For example, they may also be in favour of increased public support for development cooperation, or share the conviction that education is the most important vector for social development, or accept the idea of a Tobin tax, as proposed by some NGDOs. Adherents can be individuals but also associations or businesses. Increasingly large organisations, such as trade unions, or businesses explicitly support the mission of (some sectors of) the NGDO community. There are few contacts

between the adherents and the NGDOs; NGOs do not even know how many adherents they have. Only surveys can tell them that. Longitudinal research in Belgium, for example, shows that only a minority of people know what the term 'NGDO' stands for; few know what NGDOs really do, in the donor country and in the recipient country. Even so, there is still a great deal of trust in NGDOs: they are popular, yet little understood (Pollet, 2010).

'Constituents' are adherents who do not confine their backing to theoretical advocacy, but also contribute financial, material and human resources that make the projects of the NGDOs or a particular NGDO possible. Again, these constituents can be individuals or associations or businesses. However, this support comes on a voluntary basis and on their own initiative. They provide their support without the NGDO even asking for it. Examples include people who contact an NGDO's local campaign coordinator to help raise funds, who take the initiative of setting up a new fair trade shop in a given location, or who set up an Internet community to do with an NGDO project, for example via Facebook. Enterprises making a link to a particular NGDO on their website are also constituents of the NGDO sector.

Finally, the 'supporters' consist of those adherents and constituents who can be mobilised. When called upon to do so, they are ready to provide extra financial, material and human resources. You can expect them to be the warmest adherents and the most active constituents. NGDOs go to great lengths to extend and activate their support base. They are primarily interested in loyal supporters who can themselves recruit new adherents and constituents. The supporters organise training activities, immersion trips, debate series, petitions and fund-raising campaigns. From this group, volunteers are co-opted to represent the voice of the social base at the NGDOs' board and general assemblies.

The NGDOs expect adherents, constituents and especially supporters to provide financial support for their actions here and in the Third World.

For several years now the US-based Center for Global Prosperity has done groundbreaking work in compiling data that tell us something about the generosity in different countries. They concluded in their 2010 report that American citizens, through voluntary contributions of time and money, gave more than any other DAC donor gave in ODA alone. Total US philanthropy in 2008 totalled USD 37.3 billion and exceeded official US development assistance (26.8 billion). Of the USD 37.3 billion of philanthropy 11.8 billion (32%) went to private and voluntary organisations (mainly NGDOs); this is about USD

38 per American. This does not make the Americans the most generous supporters of NGDOs in the world, as the Swiss donate approximately USD 66 to NGDOs. But it makes them more enthusiastic supporters of NGDOs than the Danish and Dutch (who donate approximately USD 23 per year to NGDOs) or the Spanish (USD 8 to 9).

The sector breaks free from the NGDOs

As specialised organisations, the non-governmental development organisations attempt to channel and shape social support for development cooperation as much as they can. Yet they have only partially succeeded in doing so.

Research shows that a growing group of people give support to people or organisations in the Third World without a northern NGDO being involved. Probably this points to the large number of other channels by which people have direct or indirect contact with people and groups in the Third World. These certainly include the support groups of missionaries and development workers, but also the possibilities for remitting money in favour of international and foreign organisations and the financial adoption of a project or person via specialist websites.

Moreover, we should also mention the increasing number of alternative forms of involvement and participation which have arisen thanks to greater individual mobility and modern information technology. The NGDOs are themselves great promoters of such forms of *engagement distancié* (Ion, 1997), by which individuals are called upon via demonstrations, marches, the Internet and other IT channels to join in and help shape public opinion on a specific issue, in order to bring social and political pressure to bear, often across national borders.

Analysis of the movement for the abolition of child labour, which made its voice heard internationally in the mid-1990s, shows that NGDOs played an important but not exclusive role in it. Trade unions, women's organisations, youth movements and numerous non-organised individuals took part in demonstrations, passed petitions round and engaged in discussion with policymakers at home and in international organisations. Many did so in an international setting. The fact that the ILO Worst Forms of Child Labour Convention of 1999 was ratified by 132 countries in less than three years shows that such a transnational network movement is capable of applying a great deal of political pressure (Develtere & Huybrechts, 2008).

155

This last example shows that NGDOs have not gained a monopoly over representing and shaping public opinion about Third World issues. Increasingly, we are seeing new players who also have a 'Third World-friendly agenda'. In other words, the issue is currently in the process of being mainstreamed – partly thanks to the NGDOs themselves. Important new actors in the field are the media, local authorities, certain segments of the business world, schools, youth and student organisations, trade unions and all kinds of foundations. Many new actors do not just develop a discourse about North-South issues, but actually travel out to the Third World. This generally happens through cooperation with fellow institutions in a Third World country, and is known in some European countries as 'decentralised cooperation'. Such 'twinnings' between local authorities, trade unions and student organisations in North and South do not just mean a multiplication of financial flows from North to South: they also lead to an exponential increase in contacts, relationships and exchanges between individuals, groups and institutions.

As a consequence, the relationship between the non-governmental development sector and the government is also changing. Since the introduction of the subsidy systems in the 1970s, the NGDOs in most countries have had an exclusive relationship with the government. Recognised and registered NGDOs have been regarded as the most important non-state stakeholders on development policy and the only potential recipients of subsidies for project work, awareness-raising campaigns and the posting of cooperation workers. In several countries, such as the USA, the Netherlands and the Scandinavian countries, other social organisations such as foundations, trade unions and cooperatives gained recognition as early as in the 1980s as development actors, but the funds that they obtained (then and now) from the governments were and are only a fraction of what is allocated to the NGDOs.

Is a new social movement becoming a network movement?

The NGDO sector has developed over the last four decades into an important actor in the area of development cooperation and North-South relations. It has thematised the Third World problem as a public and collective challenge, and has succeeded in creating a fairly broad basis of support for the issue and for its own work. However, the outline we have given raises questions about the common denominator within the movement.

In terms of the vision or ideology developed by the sector, there is no coherent discourse to be found. A mosaic of analyses and opinions circulates within the sector. Some of the analyses can be related to the historical roots of many NGDOs. Moreover, it has to be acknowledged that the national and international networks and coalitions in which organisations and individuals from the national NGDO movements operate are also introducing new elements all the time which are adopted without much internal discussion.

With regard to the praxis or involvement of the supporters too, the image that arises is that that of a network. With the exception of a very limited group, the specialised organisations in this new social movement do not have close ties with their activists. Rather, we see a fairly large group of individuals who are broadly sympathetic to the approach taken by the NGDOs, but limit their contribution in terms of time and extent. Individuals circulate freely within the sector. They put together their own menu of participation. Other networks offer them the opportunity to get involved with the NGDOs, yet retain a far greater distance. Examples of this are chequebook activism and Internet militantism, both of which are made possible by financial and digital networks.

Finally, the organisational dimension of the NGDO sector likewise has a network character. The organisational bases are profoundly heterogeneous and multiple. The sector has never generated an organisational model that can be used by all newcomers in the field. Rather, all actors try to develop their own model. As a result, the domain-specific organisations include registered and unregistered non-profit-making organisations, foundations, cooperatives, social entrepreneurs and other types of organisation.

In addition, many other non-specialised organisations are also active in the sector's field of action. We refer here to a whole host of civil and social organisations, businesses, school communities and local authorities which, as mentioned earlier, are also helping to 'make waves' concerning the Third World issue.

That is partly also the case with the international networks with which the NGDO sector has become inextricably linked. In the first place, branches of large international NGO concerns (World Vision, Plan International, Tear Fund International, Save the Children International, Oxfam International) can be seen emerging in both the North and the South. Usually, they are not home-grown, but bring a mission, philosophy, organisational form and working method with them from the USA or the UK. Secondly, we are seeing the tentative integration of national NGDOs in broader international contexts such

as the European NGO Confederation for Relief and Development (Concord) and hundreds of international NGO networks. But in each of these cases, the national branch still has a great deal of freedom to develop its own organisation, set its agenda and seek out a supporters' base.

It seems thus that the third pillar of development cooperation, as much as the first and the second, is becoming increasingly heterogeneous under pressure from local dynamics as well as international ones.

A fourth pillar on the market

In addition to official bilateral development cooperation (the first pillar), the international institutions (the second pillar) and the NGDOs (the third pillar), a fourth pillar is rapidly developing. The mainstreaming and localisation of development cooperation represent an unstoppable sociological process. A succession of new individuals and groups are taking short-term or more institutionalised initiatives which they themselves regard as development aid (Develtere, 2008; Develtere & De Bruyn, 2009).

Such 'decentralised cooperation' can assume many forms. Professional groups set up their 'without Borders' organisations (Architects without Borders, Journalists without Borders, Lawyers without Borders, etc.) or their 'without Holidays' organisations (Doctors without Holidays, Architects without Holidays, etc.). Students and former students get together for joint projects. Businesses or businesspeople venture into their own development projects. Western service clubs network with service clubs in Africa, Asia or Latin America. Schools and colleges network over the Web with schools in developing countries or organise exchanges. Northern youth movements interact with southern youth movements. Feminist organisations mobilise support against women-unfriendly or degrading practices such as female circumcision and *purdah* (the isolation of women). Trade union federations invite unionists from the Third World and work together within multinationals. Sports clubs recruit talent from the South and invest in local clubs in Ghana or Liberia. Environmental NGOs buy up tropical forest in order to protect natural fauna and flora.

The term 'fourth pillar' which is applied to this highly heterogeneous group of initiatives (as well as the term 'private initiatives' used in the Netherlands or the French '*coopération décentralisée*') suggests that this is a kind of left-over category, or at least an alternative form of aid. We can regard it as a fourth institutional group which is positioned alongside the three traditional pillars. A glance at the key players among these new development workers can tell us a great deal about their various characteristics and the consequences of their actions. This is where we will start, but such an institutional analysis is not

enough. We can learn more by also adding generational, domain-specific and methodological dimensions. This will make it clear that there is more going on: development cooperation is being mainstreamed and de-specialised. At lightning speed.

The key players of the fourth pillar

In order to gain recognition from one of the three traditional pillars of development cooperation, one needs the fiat of one's peers. For example, the OECD's Development Assistance Committee determines what counts as 'official aid'. In fact, though, the official development agencies regard only their own work as development aid. They attempt to dismiss the work of their colleagues at the ministry of employment or health as 'not proper' or 'not as good' or 'not as correct' aid. We see a similar situation among international organisations and NGDOs. Some newcomers are admitted to the community; others are viewed askance. However, there are not many means of keeping specific institutions outside the club. All you can do is use gentle compulsion to encourage them to take part in processes such as the UN's 'Deliver as One' which we mentioned earlier, or encourage national governments to give subsidies only to NGDOs and organisations that meet certain criteria.

One of the basic tenets of this book is thus that we are seeing a significant increase in the number of institutions, within governments, the UN and civil society, that are not regarded as belonging to the club of development specialists. Some of them do not even want to belong. They do not want to be development workers: rather, they want to do some good in the South because it 'works for them', as well as working for certain people in the South. Yet this new, fourth pillar has injected considerable dynamism. We will take a look at the big eight: the missions, the trade unions, the farmers' organisations, the health funds, the businesses, the cooperatives, the migrants' communities and, finally, the foundations and philanthropists.

The missions: the fourth pillar avant la lettre
The Catholic Bretons, Basques and Flemings are well-known in many Third World countries for the work of their missionaries. The same goes for Protestant missionaries from the USA or the Scandinavian countries. In all donor countries, the religious have remained pivotal figures in international solidar-

ity. Many have forged temporary or lasting ties with churches, parishes, congregations, projects or communities in Africa, Asia or Latin America. This decentralised cooperation has never been completely contained within the overarching work of congregations or of the relevant NGDOs. Missionaries have always maintained exclusive and direct ties with their families and supporters, independently of the religious congregations and NGDOs to which they belong or with which they work.

However, missionary work has been neither uniform nor static. Many missionaries have made their mark as linguists and ethnographers, painstakingly recording local languages and customs, and have acted as advocates of a respectful encounter between Christianity and the local religion. They have provided insights and a prism for gaining a better understanding of local views of the world. Placide Tempels' description of the Bantu philosophy and Franz Magnis' work on Javanese ethics have contributed fascinating material for discussion between local intellectuals and those who want to come to their country to 'do good'.

Many priests, pastors and nuns have set their role in the framework of a broader theology of emancipation or liberation. Several have become famous for their support for emancipation movements for oppressed nations and for misunderstood linguistic groups, by analogy with the emancipation and language movements in Europe.

After the colonies gained their independence, the North remained an important 'supplier' of missionaries. Many of them became involved in more than just evangelical work, and extended their role by engaging in community development via education, health and agriculture projects. Many missionaries and lay workers were greatly influenced by the catholic bishops' conference at Medellin (1968), the spread of liberation theology which offered a church-based and social response to poverty and oppression and emerging African theologies with their stress on inculturation.

Alternative ideas for the Third World based on a Christian vision have also developed from within the World Council of Churches. The Council represents virtually all Orthodox churches, but also the Protestant reform churches. In 1975 the Oikocredit Ecumenical Development Cooperative Society was established as a result of reflections within the World Council. Its goal was to invest in justice by offering loans to productive businesses run by poor people. Oikocredit is one of the world's largest providers of private financing for microloans; it finances 579 microfinancing institutions in Africa, Asia, Latin America and Eastern Europe.

Over the years, various churches and faith groups have set up structures to support the development work of their missionaries with funds that they themselves have raised from their support base or obtained via the bilateral donors' subsidy programmes.

Some priests, nuns and evangelical preachers have developed their own support groups, which make use of the appealing nature of their work and a network of family and friends to raise additional funds for their projects. In a number of cases, such activities have acquired autonomous status in separate non-profit-making associations, foundations or NGDOs so that the provision of support can continue even after the death of the 'founder'.

Humanitarian *jihad*

Christians are not the only ones with their own mission and the conviction that they have a duty to concern themselves with other people's lot. Since the 1980s we have seen a proliferation of Islamic non-governmental organisations and networks which energetically offer support to poor fellow-Muslims in Central Asia, West Africa and even the Caribbean. Some have ties with the radical Muslim brotherhoods. They are disenchanted with political Islam, which has not succeeded in creating an Islamic society, and they now want to Islamicise society from the bottom up, starting from within the mosques. Ghandour (2002) conducted a sociological study of the humanitarian *jihad*. A number of large Islamic private organisations, such as the International Islamic Relief Organisation and al-Madina al-Munawara Charity, both from Saudi Arabia, and the Islamic Heritage Society from Kuwait, play a leading role in it. Through the religious commandment to engage in *zakat* ('purifying one's possessions'), mosques and associations can raise millions for aid actions of all kinds. In various Islamic countries, there are special *zakat* funds and *zakat* foundations to collect alms from the faithful. It is not uncommon that a Malinese Muslim pilgrim who returns from Mecca can build a new mosque as well as a clinic and school in his village thanks to the generosity of his fellow-pilgrims.

The financial scale of these transfers from the religious world should not be underestimated. Oikocredit, mentioned earlier, relies on 36,000 individual investors and 600 institutions (most of them church-related), to whom 'credit means belief in people who are worth believing in'. Oikocredit has so far reached about 17 billion borrowers, of whom 85% are female, in more than 70 countries. It has a total outstanding capital of USD 430 million and up to 842 running projects.

According to the Index of Global Philanthropy (2010), in 2008 religious organisations in the USA donated USD 8.2 billion of development aid, equivalent to around 30% of the American government's aid budget. A substantial proportion of the funds of these church communities is still handed over to large Christian NGDOs such as World Vision, but the Index refers to a study which demonstrates that a growing proportion is used by congregations to give support to sister churches and associated social and development projects.

The trade unions: a win-win situation for employees

For years, there was great suspicion of trade unions in development cooperation circles. They were definitely not regarded as development actors. In the last fifteen years, there has been a clear shift in this respect. The issue of concern to trade unions in the North and South, namely protecting social rights, began to take its place among the concerns of development actors with the World Summit for Social Development (Copenhagen, 1995). International organisations such as the OECD and the World Bank came to the conclusion that working conditions are important factors in economic and social development (Gallin, 2000; Aidt and Tzannatos, 2002). In certain large development programmes, such as the EU-ACP Cotonou Agreement, the participation of social partners (workers' and employers' organisations) is an essential element of the cooperation model. Many bilateral donors finance the union-related development cooperation activities of their own national trade unions.

The trade union movement has been involved in the South since the colonial period. In most colonies, a trade union was initially set up for the colonials themselves, usually as a section of the union in the home country. When many overseas territories were affected by social unrest in the 1920s, modest steps were taken towards 'native trade unionism'. For example the English opted for 'responsible trade unionism', meaning docile trade unionism. Under the supervision of the white trade unions and the ministry of work, the first steps in trade union development and social dialogue were taken. Technical advice was provided, funds were made available and unionists from the colonies attended training courses with their northern partners.

In most Third World countries, the post-colonial period was one of monolithic trade unionism, in which the union (such as UNTZa in Zaire) was a subordinate and subservient instrument of the single political party (the MPR in Zaire). Despite this, the northern trade unions – in the teeth of much opposition – continued their cooperation with these parapolitical structures. In

quite a number of northern countries, trade unions made the case for greater trade union freedom in the South, and supported clandestine trade unions or particular unionist tendencies operating at the margins of politics (Madounga and Fonteneau, 1998). A great deal of support for the unionist movement in the South came from the Scandinavian countries, the USA (AFL CIO), Germany (DGB), the Netherlands (FNC and CNV), the UK (TUC) and Belgium (ACV and ABVV).

Two important developments have turned the trade unions into important actors in development cooperation in the last couple of decades. Firstly, the democratisation process, which got off the ground in most Third World countries from 1989-1990, has also led to a proliferation of new trade unions. Secondly, the expansion of international trade and the liberalisation of the financial markets – in other words globalisation – have led to increased interest in and concern about social rights.

Trade union development cooperation is based on a number of dimensions. Some forms can be regarded as development cooperation in the strict sense. Others are better labelled as international cooperation, with an important international economic and political significance. Although this is not often associated with development cooperation, we will take a brief look at it, as it constitutes the framework within which the trade unions organise their development cooperation.

One very important lever for trade union development cooperation is the large international umbrella organisation, the International Trade Union Confederation (ITUC), and the eleven global unions which bring together national trade unions from different sectors and occupational groups. The ITUC, the product of a merger between the International Confederation of Free Trade Unions (ICFTU) and the World Confederation of Labour (WCL) in 2006, represents more than 176 million workers in 151 countries and territories.

Modern, international network trade unionism brings national trade unions into constant contact with colleagues in the Third World and the social problems they face. Together, they conduct campaigns such as 'Decent work, Decent life', 'Fair Play at the Olympics' and 'Decisions for life: What working women want'. The ITUC has its own solidarity fund to help trade unions suffering from repression, but most support to trade unions in the Third World is still provided bilaterally.

International framework agreements

Trade unions have instruments other than money and technical advice at their disposal with which to address social and labour problems in the South. International framework agreements are one example. By October 2008, 72 such agreements had been signed by multinational companies and the international trade union movement. As a result, more than 5 million workers are in theory better protected, because their employers have agreed to respect fundamental labour rights in every country where the company operates. However, studies have shown that there is still a long way to go. Workers in developing countries rarely know that their companies have entered into such an agreement; subcontractors often fall outside its scope; it is not easy to process complaints; and monitoring compliance is time-consuming and complex, and not a priority for many multinationals.

The international trade union umbrella organisation has advisory status to the UN's Economic and Social Council and to specialised institutions such as UNESCO and the FAO. In recent years it has also maintained frequent contact with the World Bank, the IMF and the WTO. But the most important lever for the trades unionists' international strategy is the ILO. Every year, trade unions take part in the International Labour Conference. During the conference, which is attended by representatives of each member state's government and employers' and workers' organisations, international conventions and recommendations with regard to trade union freedom and social rights are always on the agenda. The ILO decided a few years ago to promote five 'core labour standards': freedom of association and the right to collective bargaining, the elimination of forced and compulsory labour; the abolition of child labour and the elimination of discrimination in the workplace.

Trade unions and NGDOs

In many countries, mutual interest between trade unions and NGDOs is growing. Until recently, the relationship was much more tense. In a special issue of *Development in Practice* devoted to the subject, Deborah Eade stated that relations between trade unions and NGDOs were for long characterised (and often still are) by ignorance, mistrust, rivalry and at times open hostility (Eade, 2004). There are various reasons for this. Trade unions have a sociological or class basis that is different from that of NGDOs, and this means that they have a different organisational culture. Trade un-

ions are mandated organisations on which members and grassroots activists have a significant impact. NGDOs often have little contact with their grassroots, and as a result are able to speak out more quickly and freely. Trade unions defend a number of general social principles, but do so by standing for private interests, whereas NGDOs usually stand for public interests.

Although the two groups have drawn closer, tensions remain. Thus the international trade union movement believes that it gets few opportunities to participate fully in international development programmes and initiatives, unlike the NGDOs. Examples include the Poverty Reduction Strategies and the EU-ACP Cotonou Agreement. The (international) trade union movement also complains about the fact that, in many programmes and agreements such as the Millennium Development Goals, attention is paid to the health and education sectors (mainly at the insistence of the NGDOs), but employment policy (a trade union demand) is completely ignored.

The farmers' movement: the call of globalisation

Traditional development cooperation actors, especially the NGDOs, are deeply sceptical about the Western farmers' movement. There is a firmly rooted idea that the Western farmers' movement has corporatist instincts which are partly responsible for creating the global crisis on the food market and the lack of food security and sovereignty in developing countries. The NGDOs' strategy has long consisted of exposing and complaining about the dysfunctionalities and perverse effects of the world food market. European and American agricultural policy is lambasted because it does not give farmers from the developing world the opportunity to bring their produce onto their home markets and export it to the Western market at reasonable prices. However, many NGDOs started supporting farmers' unions and organisations in developing countries in the 1990s.

The new respect for the farmers' organisations in the last five to ten years is related to a structural trend. The agricultural agreement which came into effect with the establishment of the WTO in 1995 definitely changed the position of the farmers' unions. Europe shifted its policy from price support to direct subsidies (per hectare, per pig) combined with capped production. Efforts were also made to create a second approach relating to rural policy and integrating aspects of sustainable development. The liberalisation agenda has not yet been completed and is being pursued further in the context of new negotiations within the WTO. The farmers' organisations have become enmeshed in an intricate tangle of conflicts of interest between North and South, between the

USA and Europe, between farmers and the food industry, between national food companies (including farmers' cooperatives) and multinational companies, between the call for good but safe food and the protection of farmers' social status and income, between the trade union movement and the NGDO sector and so on.

The response of the farmers' movement is influenced by a number of strategic choices. Firstly, a choice has been made in favour of cooperation within the International Federation of Agricultural Producers (IFAP), which has evolved from being a lobbying group dominated by Western farmers' organisations into a platform of 112 national farming organisations from 87 countries. The IFAP claims to represent more than 600 million farming families. Within the organisation, a common standpoint is sought on topical themes such as the liberalisation of world trade, the global sugar trade, the poverty alleviation agenda and sustainable development. Like the trade unions, the farmers' unions within IFAP and outside it are trying to become the legitimate mouthpieces on all agriculture-related subjects.

A second option consists of the reorientation of the development cooperation engaged in by farmers' movements. In 2003, AgriCord, a cooperative venture of agri-agencies, was set up. AgriCord is an integral part of the International Federation of Agricultural Producers (IFAP). Seven NGOs linked with the farmers' movements which participate in it have developed a joint programme in support of farmers' organisations in the Third World. This involves capacity development for their organisations, marketing produce from the Third World and developing contracts between producers and processing businesses (Stessens, 2004).

The OVOP movement: One Village One Product

The 'One Village One Product' movement was launched under the charismatic leadership of the then governor of the Oita prefecture in Japan. The movement encourages people to select one product in their rural village or region that will then be promoted nationally and globally. The core ideas of this movement are: think global, act local; self-help and creativity; and human development. The movement has now broken through at the international level and taken root in numerous developing countries; first in Asia, later in Africa and Latin America. With support from the Japanese development agency JICA, tens of thousands of people from developing countries have now attended courses in Oita. Experts with hands-on experience from the OVOP movement give on-the-spot advice to villages in the far-flung corners of the Philip-

pines or Lesotho and look at how 'local treasures' such as dried fish, porcelain, soap and jam can be turned into internationally valued products.

The health funds: ensuring solidarity

The health insurance funds or 'mutuals' are another actor of traditional civil society in many European countries which has increasingly emerged in recent years as a dynamic development actor. In short, they have made a comeback. In the colonial and early postcolonial period, they made attempts also to set up mutual structures in the wake of the emerging trade union movement, but the colonial and post-colonial governments, although they could see the virtue of cooperative formulas, did not believe in the strength of mutual insurance.

In the early 1990s, there was renewed interest in Belgian, French, Spanish and German health insurance fund circles in the situation in developing countries. This was provoked by a number of developments in the health sector in the Third World and by the explicit demand from development actors for support and expertise. In the late 1980s, important international organisations such as the World Bank, the WHO and UNICEF had reformulated their policies with regard to the health sector. They dropped the idea that a welfare state on the Western model was possible. The impoverished developing countries were regarded as incapable of offering free high-quality healthcare to all classes of the population. The Bamako initiative launched by the WHO and UNICEF in 1987 meant among other things that patients had to contribute to healthcare costs themselves via so-called users' fees, that representatives of local communities had to participate in the running of local health centres ('primary healthcare'), and that preference was to be given to generic and basic drugs.

In many cases access to healthcare grew worse. Starting in 1986, the Congolese NGO CDI-Bwamanda successfully experimented with the development of a mutual insurance system that was intended to promote access to its hospital. The Belgian Institute for Tropical Medicine also looked into solidarity-based insurance formulas to make the health services in the Congolese territory of Kasongo financially self-reliant. At the same time, development actors were discovering the unpublicised existence of a wide variety of endogenous communitarian, cooperative and mutual financing mechanisms, which had been set up without foreign support by women's groups, trade unions or health workers in Africa and elsewhere in order to make health care financially accessible (Atim, 1995).

In 1999, the International Labour Office started the global programme Strategies and Tools against Social Exclusion and Poverty (STEP). It is now one of the most important programmes for the promotion of 'microinsurance initiatives in healthcare'.

The American development institute PHR, the German GTZ, the Association Internationale de la Mutualité (AIM) and the French Network for Support to Health Mutuals (RAMUS) have also launched support programmes for emerging solidarity-based insurance initiatives in the health care sector in developing countries. Particularly in West Africa, these development agencies and mutual societies are collaborating in the framework of La Concertation, a network which is stimulating the exchange of information, expertise and experiences about microinsurance systems in healthcare in Africa.

With failing states and health systems and the complete absence of social protection mechanisms in many developing countries, there are particularly high expectations of private but solidarity-based insurance systems. Most observers have noted steady though not spectacular growth in the sector (Churchill, 2006). At present, approximately 78 million poor people are believed to have microinsurance to cover their health care expenses.

Companies: more (than) profit?

The business sector has always had a very ambiguous relationship with development cooperation. On the one hand, it is interested in development cooperation as a market and seeks to appropriate part of its turnover. Official cooperation, the NGDOs and the multilateral actors inevitably turn to the business sector for the supply of goods and services such as medicines, vehicles and logistical support. In doing so, the traditional development cooperation players accept that business is motivated by profit-seeking, not altruism. Moreover, they want the relationship to be conducted under market conditions as far as possible. In essence, this is also the subject of the debate about tied aid.

On the other hand, the business sector also presents itself as a lever, catalyst or even driver of development and development cooperation. By analogy with economic and social development in mature market economies, reference is made to the essential and central role of businesses in initiating and injecting dynamism into the economy in developing countries. Who has better credentials in this area than businesses in the rich countries, which made the whole thing happen? Why should the business sector itself and the government not

dedicate resources ensuring that businesses can achieve development goals? So go the arguments.

The traditional development cooperation actors view this ambivalent position on the part of the business sector with suspicion. Profit and development goals are incompatible, they argue. When it comes down to it, the development objective is subordinate to the profit objective. Some NGDO circles have become so sensitive to the development-impeding role of businesses that they have evolved into non-business organisations.

The business sector has undeniably redefined its position and role in development cooperation. In this connection, a number of causes and trends can be identified.

Repsol: a slick approach

One example of a multinational investing in development cooperation is Repsol, a Spanish gas and oil company. It recognises that it has a responsibility towards developing countries and has therefore set up a number of foundations. For example, there is the Repsol YPF Ecuador Foundation, created to contribute to the country's social development. When it comes to setting up and carrying out programmes, the foundation always enters into partnerships with specialist organisations. For the Professionalization of Young People project, for example, the Repsol YPF Ecuador Foundation worked with the European Union and the Ecuatoriano Populorum Progressio Fund. In 2009, 2% of Repsol's net profit (USD 3.1 million) was invested in social projects, which include community development, social integration, health and education and training.

The business world's image took a severe knock in the mid-1990s when it became clear that quite a lot of development cooperation money was being invested on the basis not of needs in the partner countries, but of the short-term interests of specific companies. This gave rise to a process of 'untying' development cooperation in various donor countries. Strategies for this gradual untying of development aid were devised within the OECD's DAC and in World Bank circles.

It was not only the perverse or even pernicious role of business in development cooperation that was exposed in this period. A fairly broad-based, but mainly media-driven movement also arose which pilloried the role of com-

panies (especially Western and multinational companies) in the developing countries. Campaigns such as the Rugmark Campaign, the Nike Campaign and the Clean Clothes Campaign demonstrated that NGDOs had found the weak spot in big companies' image-building. The new rallying cry became 'Consumer power rules'. NGDOs developed – often along with other actors such as the consumer or trade union movement – a 'corpwatch' practice, as a result of which businesses could continually feel them breathing down their neck.

But, as Simon Heap (2000) notes in his book on the relationship between NGDOs and businesses, not all NGOs have developed an antagonistic relationship with the business sector. Some NGOs have opted for a 'neutral' strategy, for example by looking for routes towards a more positive contribution from businesses via government involvement. Another category prefers 'cooperative' collaboration with business, and attempts to change corporate policy and practices from within. Thus NGDOs may attempt to raise funds within one or more businesses and try to involve those businesses, their managers or their personnel in selecting, carrying out and monitoring the supported projects.

Influenced by the trend towards corporate social responsibility, a number of businesses have not waited to be prompted by the NGDO sector to redefine their position and role with regard to development cooperation. Many companies have set up business foundations to plough part of their profits back into society, among other things by supporting projects or programmes in developing countries. Some do it in a direct way. The business philanthropy option can go even further. Certain businesses have found their way into cause-related marketing or emotional marketing. They adopt public standpoints on controversial themes (the arms trade, sustainable development, etc.) or present themselves as ethical, environmentally friendly or Third World-friendly businesses: the Body Shop is a well-known example. Others launch 'personnel volunteer programmes', in which employees' efforts on behalf of a good cause (often a development project) are rewarded by, for example, funding the ticket for a project visit or paying an employee's salary during a month of voluntary work in Malawi.

Far from innocent!

Not all businesses behave particularly innocently. One example is vulture funds, which we mentioned earlier.

How a vulture fund works is illustrated by Zambia's experience. In 2007, Donegal In-

ternational, a private investment fund based, ironically enough, in the British Virgin Islands, bought an old debt that Zambia owed to Romania. The original debt was for USD 15.5 million. Donegal took it over from Romania for USD 3.3 million, but wanted Zambia to repay the full amount: the original principal, unpaid interest and late payment penalties. Grand total: USD 55 million. Donegal took its claim to a London court. After a great deal of lobbying by international organisations, donors and campaigners, Zambia was required to pay 'just' USD 15 million to Donegal.

In April 2010, the Debt Relief (Developing Countries) Act was passed in the UK, which could be seen as the first vulture funds Act because it impedes such funds from operating in the UK. One of the reasons why this law came into being was the vigorously led 'End the Vulture Culture' – campaign of the Jubilee Debt Campaign organisation.

In the last ten years, most bilateral donor institutions have also developed instruments to encourage the private sector to play a role in development cooperation. Many have set up special agencies to promote private sector involvement in development work. Schulpen and Gibbon (2002) discovered similar strategies on the part of most donors which also raised similar questions. The link between the private sector's goals with regard to development cooperation and the goal of other development cooperation actors (i.e. poverty alleviation) is highly abstract and theoretical. But the incoherence they found was not just confined to the content of the work. The freestanding status of the agencies which are supposed to carry out development work from within the private sector ensures idiosyncratic procedures and working methods which do not always coincide with those of the rest of the development cooperation sector. This makes coordination and harmonisation difficult. The instruments and methods used mean that countries from the middle income group are the main ones to benefit, because they have the best starting positions for private sector investments. Moreover, it tends to be the businesses in those countries which are already relatively effective which are able to attract investment and support. The amounts involved are often fairly large (for the sector). Finally, most programmes opt for a series of standard inputs which are presumed to be relevant in every developing country. The starting-point is not the strengths and weaknesses of the private sector in the chosen poor countries, but the instrument available for use.

The United Nations likewise encourages the business sector to express its responsibility towards the developing world not just by putting part of its profits back into society, but by making its business policies and profit-seeking socially responsible.

For example, the Global Compact initiative of former UN secretary general Kofi Annan seeks to involve businesses in the challenges of globalisation. Hundreds of companies all over the world are now engaging in the initiative on a purely voluntary basis – the engagement does not involve any legally binding measures. Global Compact simply asks businesses to respect and implement certain values in the areas of human rights, labour rights, the environment and tackling corruption. In this way, the private sector can help build a more sustainable and inclusive global economy. In recent years, the idea has also been going round in UN corridors that the 4 billion poor possess a huge amount of 'dead capital' (de Soto, 2001) and that at the bottom of the pyramid are numerous creative entrepreneurs and value-conscious consumers with whom business can profitably be done (Prahalad, 2006). In a recent report, the UNDP (2008) uses numerous case studies to demonstrate that the private sector can work step by step to overcome the many obstacles to doing business with the poor. Private businesses need to collaborate with governments, donors, NGDOs and philanthropists in order to do so. For example, the products and services which are provided need to be adapted to the poor. The government has to be persuaded that poor people need legal ownership of their land and homes before they are able to take risks. For example, poor people cannot get a loan from the bank if they are unable to provide evidence that they have a legally recognised dwelling-place. Moreover, poor people have a good knowledge of the local market and brilliant ideas. Who else but poor people would have imagined that there is a market for camel's milk and derivative products?

The cooperatives: working together

The promotion of cooperative enterprise is taken very seriously both by NGDOs and in many bilateral and multilateral programmes. In 2002, the ILO adopted another new Recommendation on the Promotion of Cooperatives (no. 193) at its annual conference. In it it calls, among other things, for more collaboration on the part of cooperatives from the North with their counterparts from the South. The United Nations has declared 2012 as 'International year of cooperatives', stressing the unique contributions of cooperatives to socio-economic development.

In various countries, the cooperative movement in fact has a long tradition of international cooperation. There are the great pioneering examples from the United States, such as Land O'Lakes and the National Co-operative Business

Association, but in countries such as Sweden, Germany, Italy, Great Britain, Spain, Belgium, Canada and Japan cooperatives have likewise been working for years to build up a cooperative sector in the developing countries. The nature of their contributions has varied hugely, and is largely influenced by the fact that they themselves are businesses, albeit ones with a social and participatory tradition. Thus although the northern cooperatives also give technical assistance to their partners in the South, such assistance tends to lay more stress on business aspects than it does with other actors (such as the government or NGDOs). The Canadian cooperative bank Desjardin, for example, has a worldwide reputation for its support for the development of cooperative banking institutions.

Cooperating Out Of Poverty: COOPAfrica

In the 1970s and 1980s, the cooperatives in Africa were particularly strongly supported. Their governments firmly believed that cooperatives were better adapted to the local culture. Donors – with the World Bank, the European Commission and the Scandinavian countries at their head – helped to devise a policy for this and gave generous loans and technical advice to cooperatives.

Then the structural adjustment programmes came along and turned everything upside down. The cooperatives in Africa, the World Bank concluded, were not genuine cooperatives. They were too much like government enterprises which were inefficient and politicised. So support for cooperatives or anything that smacked of government management was withdrawn.

Surprisingly, it turns out fifteen years later that there is a dynamic cooperative movement in many African countries (Develtere, Wanyama & Pollet, 2008). Was the neglect an unexpected blessing? There are certainly no fewer cooperative enterprises active on the African continent than there were back then, and there may even be more. It is estimated that around 7% of Africans are members of a cooperative. Often, it is the only organisation on which they can count. Many cooperatives are small businesses. Some are giants by African standards. For instance, the cooperative savings funds in Cameroon have more than 45 million euro in their accounts.

In 2007, with support from DFID, the International Labour Organisation launched a Cooperative Facility for Africa, COOPAfrica. COOPAfrica is currently already active in 9 African countries. A supply-oriented strategy is combined with a demand-oriented strategy. Via COOPAfrica, experts from the African and international cooperative movement offer advice on modernising cooperative legislation and reforming the support structures, such as the umbrella organisations for cooperatives. Cooperatives which wish to do so can receive support from a so-called Challenge Fund. For example, using money from the fund, a cooperative savings fund in Tanzania can

receive support from a savings fund in Kenya with developing insurance products and offering them to its members in addition to its existing services. Since its inception in 2008, the Challenge Fund has financed about 70 projects throughout the African continent.

Many cooperative organisations also have a somewhat different approach from that of other actors when it comes to giving financial support. The Dutch Rabobank, a 'triple-A cooperative bank', gives guarantees to financial institutions in developing countries that give loans to farmers and to cooperatives that put their coffee, tea, cocoa, fruit or cotton onto the international market via fair trade circuits. From within the international Rabo group, Rabo International Advisory Services also gives technical advice to cooperatives and rural banks in developing countries.

One feature that is typical of cooperatives is the attention they pay to the legislative and regulatory framework in developing countries. For example, the German agricultural cooperatives are working to make legislation and government action in a number of Latin American countries more business- and cooperative-friendly. The existence of cooperative shops in some countries also offers numerous possibilities. In the UK, as in Italy and Switzerland, the Co-op shops have become significant vendors of fair trade products: 40% of the bananas and 20% of the coffee from the shops are fair trade.

Fair trade: exploitation barometer?

In 2001, a definition of fair trade was adopted by the international fair trade movement: '[f]air trade is a trading partnership, based on dialogue, transparency and respect, that seeks greater equity in international trade. It contributes to sustainable development by offering better trading conditions to, and securing the rights of, marginalized producers and workers, especially in the South.'

There are two main fair trade movements: one in Europe and one in North America. The European Fair Trade Association (EFTA) consists of 11 organisations which import fair trade products into 9 European countries (Austria, Belgium, France, Germany, Italy, the Netherlands, Spain, Switzerland and the United Kingdom). Together, all products that are sold by these organizations generate a retail value of USD 250 million. About 50% of the products are sold via traditional fair trade shops, but supermarkets are also becoming important channels via which fair trade products are finding their way to consumers. A sizeable market share has successfully been achieved with certain

products. Fair trade bananas account for approximately 50% of the Swiss banana market, and 20% of coffee in the UK qualifies for fair trade labelling.

The Fair Trade Federation is a trading association for North American fair trade organisations. Presently, there are approximately 250 Federation members, of which 78% are profit-making and 22% are non-profit-making. The FTF's members have a combined turnover of more than USD 150 million. Compared with the figure for 2006 (USD 60.05 million), this represents a 146% increase.

Research by Anna Milford (2004) has shown that fair trade's positive effect on the living conditions of member cooperatives in the South is not just because a minimum price is guaranteed and part of the profit is also invested in social projects: fair trade destabilises the local cartels that often have power over the farmers, because the latter become much more aware of how the market works and of alternative prices and purchasers. Thus non-members also benefit when the wholesalers are obliged to behave more correctly. For these non-members, fair trade functions as an 'exploitation barometer'.

Migrants' remittances: not foreign money

The relationship between migration, development and development cooperation has attracted considerable interest in recent years. This is not surprising when one realises how strong the links are between emigrants and their country of origin, and how much money these migrant communities send home every year. According to World Bank estimates, in 2010 the developing countries received no less than USD 325 billion from their emigrants, meaning that the amount has almost doubled in five years. Moreover, the Index of Global Remittances (2010) describes remittances as 'providing stability in an economic storm', pointing to the fact that this type of private capital flow – despite or maybe because of the economic recession – has continued to grow. The countries which received the most are, in descending order, India, China, Mexico, and the Philippines. All four are middle-income countries. At first sight, the remittances do not look particularly significant. The USD 55 billion sent home by the 11.4 million Indians all over the world represents just 4% of national GDP. Yet it opens the door to the world. That USD 55 billion is more than three times more than the private foreign direct investment and twenty-five times more than the official development assistance that India receives. Although poor countries receive far less support from their emigrants, this financial injection can be far more significant. Take Tajikistan in Central Asia. The 1 million Tajiks abroad sent USD 2.1 billion home in 2010. That represents

more than one-third of the country's GDP and is seven times more than the official aid it receives.

There is no disputing the fact that the migrant communities still send far more money back to their country of origin than is registered, and that in total they give over three times more 'aid' to their home countries than official development assistance. The data collection system used by the World Bank is mainly based on data from the national banks. These relate almost exclusively to payments made via banks and companies, and this means that transactions conducted via institutions such as Western Union (which are preferred by many migrants because the service they provide is faster and better) are not recorded. But perhaps even more important are the numerous indirect or informal transfers. People send goods or take banknotes or cheques with them on their regular visits to their countries of origin. There are many informal networks which make it possible to get funds via intermediaries and institutions to the family. Reliable data about the volume of these informal transfers do not exist, but studies show that in many countries the informal transactions are far more extensive than the formal ones.

It is almost invariably assumed that migrants and migration have a positive effect on the home country's development chances. However, it is generally accepted in debate that there can also be negative aspects for the home country. It is usually the more dynamic and better-educated members of the workforce who leave. Before their departure, their own society has already invested a great deal in them, and they thus leave behind them a deficit in human capital (the brain drain). 30% of all people with higher education from Ghana and Sierra Leone live abroad. Three-quarters of Africa's emigrants are graduates. A study has shown that there are more African scientists and engineers working in the USA than in the whole of Africa put together (Edgren, 2002). Given that the possibility of migration is so prominent in the collective consciousness, young people prefer training that is suitable for the foreign labour market (footballer, fashion model or programmer) to any that is useful locally (lawyer, accountant or weaver). Moreover, those who return home, the remigrants, have apparently acquired few if any new skills in the host country. Even so, the benefits of migration are believed to outweigh the costs.

The migrant communities maintain preferential ties with their countries, regions and families of origin. In their host country, they come into contact with a 'modern' culture in which entrepreneurship and ideas such as human rights are taken seriously. They expand the networks on which the country

of origin and the home base can rely to attract investments, acquire knowledge and technology and tap sources of finance. As well as an emotional link and strong motivation, they also have a long-term commitment, language skills and transcultural baggage – all key elements for sustainable and effective cooperation. But could it be that migrants bear a certain resemblance to Janus, the Roman god with two faces? For example, Devesh Kapur (2007) warns against turning a blind eye to the 'long-distance nationalism' of many migrant communities and their tendency to finance extremist groups in their country of origin.

Thus there is much discussion in the literature about the pros and cons of remittances. Virtually the only thing that anyone agrees on is that they have a positive effect on the recipient country's balance of payments. But are they not primarily used for private consumption purposes rather than for investment? On the other hand, is that necessarily a problem? After all, increased consumption is a lever for development. But is it not the case that remittances mainly go to well-off families in well-off communities in countries which are not particularly poor?

---

3 for 1 in Mexico

Capital transfers from migrant communities can also have far-reaching political consequences for the home country. Take Mexico: on average, every Mexican receives USD 250 per year from abroad. Most of this is received directly from family in the USA. Its political effect should not be underestimated: this support from abroad makes many Mexicans far less dependent on the political bosses who seek to bribe them for votes.

For a number of years, so-called Mexican Home Town Associations have been springing up rapidly across the USA. There are now over 3,000 such clubs, financing more than one-fifth of infrastructure work in the Mexican towns concerned. The Mexican government is encouraging this formula via the 3-for-1 programme. For every dollar that comes from a Home Town Association, the federal authority as well as state and city authorities each contribute one themselves.

During the last ten years, both remittance-receiving countries and development organisations have been trying to optimise and streamline the phenomenon of migrant solidarity. With varying success, a number of countries are trying to get migrants to use official channels for their transactions. Some countries

are offering their migrants concessional rates of duty on imports of machinery and equipment, or giving business training to returning migrants.

Development actors of the first, second and third pillars have drawn attention to the migrant community, and the same applies in reverse. However, it is far from easy to reconcile the two sectors' cultures, goals and methods. This has been discovered by countries such as the Netherlands and France, which have been experimenting for a number of years with formulas for involving the migrant community in development programmes.

Foundations: the philanthropic revolution

Take a few of the major problems with which Third World countries contend, and you will find that important foundations are working on them. This has been the case for several decades (Scott, 2003). The Green Revolution, which by introducing new cereal variants ensured an enormous increase in agricultural productivity in India in the 1960s and 1970s, was made possible by research financed by the Rockefeller Foundation (US). Research into solutions for parasitical and viral diseases such as hookworm, malaria and yellow fever is largely financed by large foundations such as the Gates Foundation (US), the Nuffield Foundation (UK) and the Wellcome Trust (UK). Foundations such as the Ford Foundation and the Carter Centre (US), the Friedrich Ebert Stiftung and the Konrad Adenauer Stiftung (Germany) run and finance democratisation programmes and lobbying by civil organisations such as NGOs, farmers' organisations and trade unions in the Third World. In 2009, a total of USD 3 billion was granted by the Bill and Melinda Gates Foundation (US), which invested over USD 1 billion in health and food programmes.

Such foundations are almost always set up by a wealthy individual, although they may also be set up by (or in memory of) prominent figures or by private companies. Usually they operate with a starting capital (a gift or bequest), but in many cases they start fund-raising from the general public or the government after a while. The OECD has calculated that at the start of the present century, around USD 3 billion was being invested by foundations from the DAC countries in development aid (Scott, 2003). Most of the money came from the United States. In 2008 US foundations gave over USD 4.3 billion to the developing countries. A recent small-scale survey by the European Foundation Centre has shown that in Europe 40% of the foundations are engaging in international activities.

The number of foundations is also increasing exponentially in the Third World countries themselves. They reflect changing patterns of local philanthropy. In countries like India, Bangladesh, China, Indonesia, South Africa and Kenya, foundations have been established to raise funds among the traditional elite, the burgeoning middle class, local businesses and branches of multinational companies. Celebrities from the South are taking inspiration from North American philanthropy. For instance the Senegalese singer Youssou N'Dour has put his weight behind a microfinance institution in his country. The great NBA star Dikembe Mutambo is trying to give something back to his native Congo via his foundation. He financed a hypermodern hospital in the working-class districts near Ndjili and paid for the participation of a Congolese basketball player in the Atlanta Games.

According to the Index of Global Philanthropy 2008, in 2000 you had to give away at least USD 16.8 million to be among the top 50 donors. By 2008, that figure had risen to USD 38.4 million. In 2008-2009, due to the global economic crisis and recession, private capital flows towards developing countries decreased dramatically from USD 325 billion in 2007 to 121 billion in 2008. However, despite this sharp decline, private giving continues to constitute the bulk of the total economic support from developed to recipient countries. The vast majority of these major philanthropists have set up a foundation for the purpose and are located in the United States. In the USA, philanthropy is an essential dimension of elite behaviour. In a country where there is no welfare state, philanthropy cannot be equated with spontaneous generosity or the need to help. Philanthropy is a social duty associated with the privileged position of the upper class. The desire for prestige or access to certain social circles is also a factor.

In the USA, giving to international causes increased fourfold in the 1990s, making such causes the main philanthropist purpose. However, this phenomenon was not confined to the large foundations. According to Kharas (2007), more than half of this growth has come from smaller foundations and less prosperous households (which give to foundations or NGDOs).

As stated, international philanthropy is also growing in Europe. Theresa Lloyd (2004), who conducted a survey of wealthy Britons (with assets worth between EUR 4 and 85 million), found that most of them had set up a foundation or fund to channel their philanthropic activities, or were working via the Charity Aid Foundation. Around 30% of the donors in the survey were also supporting initiatives outside the UK.

The Aga Khan Foundation

The Aga Khan Foundation (AKF) is one of the many philanthropic institutions from the Ismaili Muslim community. This community is a lesser-known sect within Shiism which has a long tradition of giving and charitable work. The foundation itself is run by the Aga Khan, the Imam of the Ismailis, who also provides most of the foundation's revenue. The foundation and its 3,060 personnel provide more than USD 150 million of financing every year, mainly in Asian and African countries, but also in Europe and North America. The support goes into education, healthcare, rural development and civil society. Via partnerships, the foundation offers intellectual and financial support to other governmental and non-governmental organisations. Sometimes it also starts up its own programmes. In Alai and Chon Alai, the two poorest districts in Kyrgyzstan, the AKF has trained a number of community health promoters and volunteers so that they can organise awareness-raising campaigns. As a result, some 90,000 people in 76 communities are now better able to assess their needs in terms of healthcare, to analyse the underlying causes of diseases and to change their behaviour. Before the AKF started this programme, most women were not aware of any link between exclusive breastfeeding for the first six months and the growth, health, development and survival of their child. Babies were often given bottled milk instead. By 2007, 90% of mothers were aware of this important connection. As a result, the number of children with diarrhoea and diseases caused by infection has fallen, leading to a drastic fall in the mortality rate. But the local health promoters trained by the AKF have not just emphasised the important link between children's survival and suitable nutrition: they have alerted the population of Alai and Chon Alai to the importance of suitable nutrition for everyone, regardless of age. In response, more than 20 villages have decided to create vegetable gardens, with support from the Aga Khan Foundation. It has been possible to address a number of vitamin deficiencies in this way. More than 160 such gardens have already been created.

A new generation of altruists?

A second way of approaching the new trends in development cooperation and the emergence of a fourth and distinctive pillar is to consider change over time. In recent years in particular, the number and diversity of players in development cooperation has been increasing. Unfortunately, few data are available as yet with which to build up an overall picture. In France, 182 networks of '*initiatives de coopération décentralisée*' (Develtere et al., 2007) have been registered, while in the Netherlands 6,400 temporary and not-so-temporary

initiatives have been counted (Bouzoubaa & Brok, 2005). In the USA, there are thought to be more than 2,000 Mexican migrant organisations focusing on the development of their regions of origin, and in France more than 700 '*organisations de solidarité internationale issues des migrations*' (OSIMs) have come together in a forum (De Haas, 2006). In Flanders, our own HIVA survey counted over 1,100 non-temporary, institutionalised initiatives. Larger structures such as trade unions, health funds and foundations were not taken into account. A total of between 25,000 and 60,000 people are thought to be active in these Flemish initiatives. Moreover, the amount that these initiatives collect is equivalent to the funds mobilised by the traditional NGDOs (Develtere & Stessens, 2007).

The emergence of new players is partly connected with or the result of the broader social development of globalisation and increasing contact with other cultures and countries. New communication technologies such as the Internet and increased mobility have opened up access for individuals to other parts of the world. The world has become flat, argues Thomas Friedman (2005). A new global architecture of participation has arisen. The more businesses, organisations, websites and software encourage the people to get involved as consumers and producers, the more successful they become. Moreover, there is growing interest in behaving as a citizen of the world. Labour migration from the South, the development of migrant communities and the associated civil society have led to a transnational development trend, in which a new market for the sale of products and services from the South has been created in the destination countries in addition to money and material resources being sent to the countries of origin. Organisations and institutions are also extending their networks, often to incorporate similar organisations in other countries, and are developing international cooperation and action strategies. For example this has taken place with European, North American and Japanese farmers' movements and trade union federations. Moreover, the local and regional sections of these social movements are developing small-scale solidarity actions with partners in the South. Again, the focus on corporate social responsibility has led businesses to set up international solidarity actions. On the cultural level, theatre companies, authors and musicians from the North are forging ties with the South and exploring cooperation and exchange links. The rise of sustainable tourism and backpack tourism has led not just to a new industry but to more contacts between tourists from the North and people from the South.

Globalisation has also changed the way the South and its people are perceived. Instead of people and their organisations being regarded as passive and in need of aid, they are now seen as equal partners with talents, expertise, experience and knowledge from which lessons can be learnt in the North, or which are seen as attractive. The new players therefore often act out of a genuine interest in the people of a specific region, rather than for ideological reasons or with a view to changing the world.

Even so, changing the world can still be a motive for action. Awareness-raising campaigns and education about the North-South issue and the message that 'changing the world starts with yourself' have inevitably had an impact. The focus on the development issue has become an everyday concern: it is not something that is pushed only during short-term media campaigns by the large NGDOs, as used to be the case. Citizens and organisations have discovered or created their own ways of getting involved in development cooperation on a more permanent basis. The traditional development cooperation organisations offered few forms of action other than donating or raising money. Organisations and citizens have developed their own initiatives and set up their own projects, sometimes on their own, but more often with direct contacts in the South and via the international professional or social networks to which they belong.

The other three pillars arose in order to find a solution to the North-South divide; by contrast, the new generation of fourth-pillar initiatives represent a response to globalisation, a challenge to everyone to be a global citizen, global business or global organisation – one which shows solidarity. It is no longer the world that people want to change, but the lives of the friends that they have got to know and value on the other side of the planet.

Starting from a different field

The new trends in development cooperation can also be considered in the light of the fields from which initiatives are started.

The traditional development cooperation actors have a common jargon, ways of interacting, methodologies, instruments, values and standards. They regard themselves, and are regarded by wider sections of the public, as specialists in development cooperation. After all, most institutions and organisations in the first, second and third pillars were created specifically in order to focus on development cooperation.

The new players' story is different: in numerous cases they were not set up for the purpose of development cooperation or in order to change North-South relations, but already existed in their country as professional experts in their own field, which was not necessarily related to development cooperation. On the basis of their own experiences within their sector or of everyday life, they started to work with people in the South. For example, this may be because they want to share their expertise with colleagues grappling with the same problems. Businesses exchange experiences, municipalities, hospitals and schools establish cooperation links with similar institutions in the South and exchange experiences. The trade unions join forces and together set about improving working conditions in both the North and the South, instead of specifically focusing on the conventional poverty alleviation programmes. In a globalising society, it is preferable if the cobbler does not stick to his last: rather, he should try to collaborate with other shoemakers.

In this way, new needs and possibilities are also being discovered – in the North as well as in the South. The traditional development institutions are not blind to this trend, and are starting to adapt their approach in specific projects accordingly. In this way, they are contributing to the ongoing de-specialisation and mainstreaming of development cooperation. Thus in the Netherlands, Oxfam-NOVIB is supporting migrants' organisations which want to work with microfinance institutions in the South. The Belgian NGDO Worldsolidarity, the Christian Mutual Health Fund of Belgium and the International Labour Organisation have published a manual on microinsurance in healthcare. Together with German, American and French bilateral development organisations, health insurance funds and NGDOs, they are promoting solidarity-based health insurance in Africa.

But bilateral donors are also trying to streamline this trend. The American USAID has set up an Office of Global Development Alliances for the purpose. The multi-stakeholder alliances that it is encouraging in this way are based on the idea of private-public cooperation. By 2010, about 1,000 such alliances had been created by USAID and more than 9 billion in combined private and public resources were generated. The Sustainable Forest Products Global Alliance, for example, seeks to promote sustainable logging practices. USAID gives this alliance basic financing. The World Wildlife Fund manages the Global Forest and Trade Network, a network of more than 360 businesses from more than 30 countries which wish to practise 'responsible forest management'. Metafore –

a programme of the NGO GreenBlue – promotes, together with American businesses, the responsible purchase and use of wood and paper. The forestry department of the ministry of agriculture gives it technical assistance. A private company, Home Depot, contributes funding and its purchasing model.

An alternative way of working

As has already been said, the development cooperation community solemnly believes in a number of principles. One of these is that a fair relationship with partners in the South must be incompatible with acting out of self-interest. The inequality between North and South is so great (both financially and in terms of capacity) that the South can never catch up, it is held, unless it receives absolutely all the benefits of cooperation. In other words, investment in development cooperation must not yield any profit for the donor. You have to operate 'à *fonds perdus*' ('sunk capital'); you literally have to give away without expecting a return.

The new generation of fourth-pillar initiatives seems to prefer other options. This is not surprising, as it starts from its own working, living or travel experience. It want to enrich this by working with people from the South. Thus they seek a win-win situation, and it follows that they do not confine themselves to giving. They invest money, time, experience and so on, and look for a return on investment. Both parties stand to benefit.

Furthermore, the conventional development cooperation actors have, through a process of trial and error, developed a methodology over the decades that is based on a 'planning logic', in which a long-term vision, processes, programmes and ownership are central. The Paris Declaration of March 2005, which has been signed by hundreds of development institutions and recipient countries, is a good summary of the consensus within the conventional development community. It states that development cooperation should be based on the following principles: national ownership, alignment with national priorities and procedures, harmonisation and coordination of development aid, results-oriented working and – finally – mutual accountability. Thus the starting-point is for institutions and people from the South to develop their own long-term strategies and associated programmes which they themselves control. Autonomous and adapted to local ways of working, they address the needs of the target group and build up rights.

By contrast, the new players set out from an 'anthropo-logical' approach, in which faith in the qualities of people with specific talents is central, as is frequent personal interaction with partners from the South. In practice, work therefore focuses on concrete – often short-term – projects, in which people can use their talents optimally. The benefits of cooperation and exchange need not be reaped exclusively by the community or institution in the South: the actor in the North may also benefit if this is possible. A win-win situation is sought – explicitly in some cases.

Panorama perspective or tunnel approach?

In their enthusiasm, many of the new actors have forgotten that development co-operation is a craft – and a particularly difficult one at that. After all, if it were easy, the situation in many developing countries wouldn't be so wretched, would it? Or is the enduring misery in the Third World to be ascribed to incompetence or even a lack of desire to evolve and grow on the part of governments, businesses and institutions themselves in those countries? Granted, many of the problems in the developing countries are related to the shortcomings of the local institutions, including local universities and other education centres. There is often a lack of institutional capacity: of vision and long-term strategy, of impact on the environment, and of eagerness and willingness to learn or to pick the brains of those who have proven that there is a way forward. Organisational capacity is also far from ideal in many cases. Decision-making bodies do not work properly, and human and financial resources are lacking or are not deployed properly. And of course this has implications for the development capacity of the institutions concerned. They are not really an effective lever for local development.

But let's be honest. Don't we happily engage in pointing the finger of blame like this because it is a convenient way of disguising the fact that our voluntary efforts are not always (or perhaps that should be 'are rarely') efficient and effective? To what extent does our cooperation lead to capacity building? To what extent are we helping to reinforce the institutional, organisational and development capacity of our 'partners'?

The tunnel approach with which we very often operate in development cooperation is one of the greatest obstacles here. We start from our own position, our own ambitions, just as we do when we drive into a tunnel. The boot of our car has our own luggage in it: the knowledge we have developed in our own society, the experiences we have accumulated in our part of the world, the things we have read at home, and above all, perhaps, the knowledge that we generated for our own society and economy. We also set out with our own individual driving skills, style and speed (which may include a tendency to 'step on it'!). Once we are in the tunnel, we simply look ahead.

All our energy is put into reaching the light at the end of the tunnel. We don't need to look to the left or right, we reason, as there are only solid walls. Gradually, we start to suffer from narrowed vision and short-sightedness. In the dimly lit tunnel we may even go colour-blind. The drive is monotonous. We think that we are driving, but in really we are being driven.

Yet the reality in the Third World is far more colourful, more chequered, more varied than our tunnel approach allows us to perceive. The reality is a panorama. The road is bumpy, and there are unexpected bends, beautiful views, dangerous precipices, obstacles along the way. A panorama perspective makes development cooperation much more realistic: harder but also more fascinating. You gain a sense of what local people and institutions are really like. You discover that your car (and your luggage) may not be suitable for the terrain. They may not even be desirable – who knows? You realise that there is a long way to go, but you don't know the route in advance (there's no GPS!). You have to start by asking for directions – from those who live and work there. They may also need to hurry to your rescue if your car ends up in a ditch. If that happens, it's best to let them sit behind the wheel.

The new development cooperation of the fourth pillar and that of the specialists: tunnel or panorama? 'You pays your money and you takes your choice…'

The development of a concrete cooperation discourse in which individuals' expertise is used enables the new players to focus on the South without needing to gain command of the specific jargon and working methods of the traditional development cooperation specialists.

Mainstreaming development cooperation

When we consider the recent trends in development cooperation in terms of the aspects described above, we see that there is more going on than just the arrival of new players on the development cooperation stage and the establishment of a fourth pillar. Thanks to the efforts (including awareness-raising campaigns and information provision) of the traditional development cooperation organisations and an increasingly globalised society, interest has arisen among wider sections of the population and a range of institutions and organisations in getting involved with development cooperation, and forms of cooperation with like-minded and similar actors in the South have been promoted which enable citizens and organisations to use their own expertise on a day-to-day basis.

Development cooperation is no longer the exclusive preserve of specialists: it is the business of the whole of society, of everyone. The mainstreaming of development cooperation means that non-specialists can do their bit by donating money and resources to the traditional organisations, but can also roll up their sleeves and design concrete projects.

The mainstreaming of development cooperation raises a number of questions. Firstly, there is discussion about the possible impact of fourth-pillar initiatives. On the one hand, some development specialists (active in the NGDO sector, government and the academic world) argue that most fourth-pillar initiatives have no structural impact on the countries or regions where they are in place, because their projects are small-scale, short-term and insufficiently embedded in the economic or social development policy of the major traditional development actors, disregarding the discourse, tools and methodologies that have been developed and used by the latter over the last few decades. As a result, the door is open to the repetition of mistakes made in the past by the traditional development actors. Others, including the fourth-pillar organisations themselves, argue that their projects do in fact have a positive impact on local people who take part in them. That impact may be small, but it is not to be underestimated. In addition, these initiatives make an important contribution to raising public awareness in the North (particularly among those who are involved in the project), for example about specific problems in the South. So far, however, the proponents of these views have lacked any data to support their position. There is virtually no research into fourth-pillar initiatives, and this means that there is very little reliable information available about their impact.

It's not all about the money!

Although fourth-pillar initiatives have to account for their activities only to a limited extent, more and more attention is being paid in the Netherlands to their quality. The Dutch foundation Wilde Ganzen therefore commissioned a survey to look at the crucial factors affecting the project results of fourth-pillar initiatives, or what are known in the Netherlands as private initiatives. Sara Kinsbergen (2007) studied ten projects in India and came to the conclusion that three factors are of fundamental importance to the success of a project: cooperation between the local partner and the fourth-pillar organisation, the capacity of both the local partner and the private initiative, and the latter's enthusiasm and commitment.

The research shows that mutual trust, openness and respect are particularly important

for obtaining immediate positive results, such as teaching materials being purchased for several classes in a rural Indian town. Good communication is vital, but actually to achieve the project's goal, for example to improve the learning conditions of several dozen children, more is needed. The best results are obtained when the local partner assumes a leading role. After all, the latter has the best cultural and contextual knowledge and will be in a better position to assess whether the project is suitable and will attract the target group. As well as affecting the outcome of the initiative, the allocation of roles also has an impact on its institutional sustainability. If the fourth pillar organisation assumes the leading role, it is far harder for the local partner to take this over when the cooperation comes to an end.

In fact, Kinsbergen found that the local partner's capacity is far more important than that of the Dutch fourth-pillar organisation. The partner's organisational structure is particularly crucial. A broad structure is needed in which responsibility lies with several people. If a narrow organisational structure with a single leader is the foundation of the project, this can be very risky. For example, the leader may become overburdened, in which case the immediate results will suffer. What if the leader decides to leave? That may spell the failure of the project and the end of the organisation. A project's sustainability is influenced not just by the local partner's organisational structure, but by the network to which that partner has access. If the local partner has access to an extensive, well structured network, it will be easier to continue the project after support from the North has been discontinued. The risks in terms of sustainability are thus considerably reduced by a network.

Kinsbergen identified another factor which influences project results: the enthusiasm of the volunteers of the fourth-pillar organisation. This has a positive effect on the direct results, because more funds are raised with which more can be achieved. However, a very enthusiastic fourth-pillar organisation can be counter-productive for a project's ultimate result and sustainability, because enthusiasm means that the fourth-pillar initiative is closely involved in the whole process and tends to put its own stamp on it. As a result, fewer responsibilities are assigned to the local partner.

Closely linked to this is the question whether fourth-pillar organisations communicate the big story behind North-South issues or the harmful consequences of globalisation for the population when they are promoting their activities. Traditional development organisations try to explain the structural causes of North-South problems to the general public, whereas, according to some development specialists, fourth-pillar initiatives focus more on a concrete problem without setting it in a broader context. A concrete story (for example the need for wells) is easier to sell than an intricate analysis of the underlying structural reasons for wells not being constructed by the government in a given area.

Humanitarian aid:
in good shape or going downhill?

The development sector has not been immune to the consequences of the increasingly frequent and complex emergency and crisis situations in the world. For example, there have been the famines in the Horn of Africa in the early 1990s and again in the early 2010s, the genocide in Rwanda in 1994, the war in Central Africa since 1996, collateral damage from the wars in Iraq and Afghanistan, the earthquake in the Iranian city of Bam in 2003 and the Asian tsunami in 2004, the plague of locusts that was responsible for widespread harvest devastation in West Africa in the same year, the war in the Darfur region of Sudan, the hurricanes that ravage the Caribbean and Central America every year, the recurrent flooding in Bangladesh, and the 2010 earthquake in Haiti.

The number of reported disasters has increased dramatically in the last ten years. Between 1994 and 1998, an average of 428 disasters were recorded every year, but between 2003 and 2007 the average was 727 per year. It was countries with poor human development in particular that experienced an increase in the number of disasters. In the last ten years, an average of more than 100,000 people have lost their lives in a disaster every year. The number of other victims is considerably higher, of course (and has likewise been rising recently): people who lose their homes, suffer famine, run out of drinking water, and so on. Between 1998 and 2007 their numbers were estimated by the International Federation of Red Cross and Red Crescent Societies at 280 million per year. Geophysical catastrophes such as floods and hurricanes are occurring more often than they used to, but drought and famine remain the most deadly disasters (IFRC, 2008). In its new World Disasters Report, the IFRC focuses exclusively on urban risks, and the need for 'good urban governance' that has evolved out of the massive and global urbanization trend. (IFRC, 2010) The quality of (housing) infrastructure and disaster preparedness determines to a large extent whether living in a city increases or reduces disaster impacts. The different impacts of the earthquakes in Santiago de Chile (magnitude 8.8) and Port-au-Prince (magnitude 7.0), both in 2010, illustrate this observation: the earthquake in Chile took the lives of a couple of hundred people, while in Haiti no fewer than 200.000 citizens lost their lives.

Naturally, the cost of all these disasters is very high: an average of around USD 100 billion per year. However, this figure should be interpreted with due caution. The financial value ascribed to infrastructure in industrialised countries is many times higher than that in developing countries. We should also bear in mind that, by definition, a disaster lacks any short-term solution. If in 2005 your cornfield was destroyed by locusts, you lost a leg in a landmine explosion, your only cow died in a drought or your hut was plundered by passing militiamen, you are very unlikely to have recovered from this personal disaster in 2010 – even if you have received a lot of aid.

In this context of increasingly common disasters, it is not surprising that emergency and post-conflict aid have increased substantially. In 1996 the DAC donors gave a combined total of approximately USD 2.7 billion in emergency aid, while in 2001 that was estimated at USD 4.2 billion, and in 2009 at USD 8.6 billion. Nor are the DAC donors the only ones to provide resources for humanitarian interventions: multilateral organisations take money from their reserves when disasters occur; new donor countries also put their hands in their pockets; and especially for disasters which receive wide media coverage, the general public will happily give an extra euro, dollar or rupee to the humanitarian NGOs. Worldwide humanitarian assistance was estimated at USD 15.1 billion in 2009; this is 11% less than the year before (USD 16.9 billion) but nonetheless 2.5 billion dollars more than in 2006-2007. Global Humanitarian Assistance, a respected observer of the world of humanitarian aid, arrived at this figure by including 'humanitarian' aid that is not directly classified as such by the DAC, but still represents assistance for those who have been the victims of a disaster. Examples include clearing landmines or taking in light weapons.

Global humanitarian assistance in 2008 (ODA)

Bilateral humanitarian aid from DAC countries	USD 4800 million
multilateral humanitarian aid	USD 6900 million
private contributions to NGOs' emergency aid	USD 3700 million
private contributions to Red Cross and UN	USD 400 million
humanitarian aid from non-DAC countries	USD 1100 million
total	**USD 16.9 billion**

Source: GHA, *Global Humanitarian Assistance Report*, 2010

The inroads made by emergency aid into the available development budget have been growing steadily for years. In 1980, scarcely 1.3% of all ODA was used for interventions in disasters. In 2008, the proportion was nearly 12%. Traditionally, most humanitarian assistance comes from the USA. In 2008, the USA spent nearly 13% of its aid budget on emergency situations. The USD 4.38 billion that it spent was all tied to the purchase of goods and services in the USA. At USD 2 billion or 6 to 7% of its aid budget, the European Commission has also become a very important emergency aid contributor. The individual member states contributed a combined additional total of USD 3.6 billion for emergency aid in 2008.

The above figures show that the general public's generous support for emergency aid funds goes beyond what it pays in national taxes. Disaster appeals motivate many people to give money to NGOs, the Red Cross or UN institutions such as Unicef. A number of very large NGOs have specialised in emergency aid operations, although most opt for an integrated approach consisting of structural development programmes, emergency aid and rehabilitation projects. The largest emergency aid organisations include Caritas Internationalis, Catholic Relief Services, the Red Cross and Red Crescent Movement, Save the Children, Oxfam and Médecins sans Frontières/Doctors without Borders.

What place for emergency aid?

In most donor countries, the twofold trend towards more emergency aid and more 'politicised' emergency aid has proceeded unchecked. Despite its far-reaching implications, this trend has never been the subject of serious public debate.

Until the 1980s, emergency aid was invariably a mere palliative. It served short-term goals (such as food distribution during famines) and was largely arranged in cooperation with the governments in developing countries, which were still regarded as legitimate and sovereign actors. Humanitarian aid was supposedly politically neutral and not partisan. But in less than two decades, a humanitarian system or space has emerged which has assumed completely different dimensions. Because many disasters are directly attributable to mismanagement, a lack of development capacity and corruption in the state, or to civil and inter-state conflicts, humanitarian intervention is regarded as a duty of the international community, as a contribution to the universal application

of the rights of all humans to the basic necessities of life and to freedom of movement, organisation and opinion. No government has the right to stand in the way of these things.

Humanitarian action is increasingly being linked to new political goals and to the political reaction of donors to complex aid situations. For many donors, emergency aid has become an integral part of their strategy for transforming conflict, stemming violence and making liberal development strategies possible (Curtis, 2001). Examples of the politicisation of emergency aid are seen in the international response to recent complex crises in countries such as Afghanistan, Iraq, Serbia, Sierra Leone, the Ivory Coast, Sudan and Central Africa. Thus techniques such as compulsory repatriation are used, and conflict resolution is coupled with humanitarian aid, the blocking of food aid and even the incorporation of emergency aid in military structures and operations. In this way, emergency aid becomes detached from the two other components of cooperation: rehabilitation and structural aid. It becomes an instrument of (global) foreign policy rather than of development policy.

This trend is diametrically opposed to the conclusions of international NGDOs and development institutions about the pitfalls of traditional emergency aid (Lindenberg and Bryant, 2001), and the new approach they have adopted. 'Active humanitarian aid' is the name often given to the new approach. As the table below shows, the new approach proceeds from a long-term strategy (which starts with an early warning and ends with structural aid) which is based on local capacities and is organised in a coordinated fashion. This approach is also not politically neutral, but – unlike the dominant strategy mentioned earlier – it is not an instrument of foreign policy.

A new vision of emergency aid

	Traditional vision	New vision
A disaster	Is regarded as a natural phenomenon or the consequence of a conflict.	Is a natural phenomenon, but its effects have a structural basis. The poorer segments of the population are more than proportionately affected.
The affected population	Is primarily the victim, without any capacity of its own.	Consists of people and groups with their own potential and capacity to understand and solve problems.
What should be done first?	Provide services to the population: transfer resources.	At the same time, together with local government institutions or NGOs, make a diagnosis and set action priorities.
To deliver basic services…	…the state and foreign organisations need to get organised.	… local organisations need to get mobilised to determine needs, arrange services, set up coordination with the state and foreign organisations and establish a monitoring system.
Time frame	Everything is considered in the short term: food aid, clothing, drugs…	Work is done in the short and medium term: emergency work and rehabilitation as an element of structural development ('a continuum of emergency aid, rehabilitation and structural development').
Healthcare	Curative, epidemiological screening, distribution of drinking water. Doctors are experts.	Environmental factors are studied thoroughly (access to drinking water, drainage etc.) in order to keep the health situation under control. The population is involved in the process.
Local organisations	External agencies try to set up organisations which meet their criteria.	Existing organisations are involved.
The economy	External resources are injected to solve a short-term problem.	Local resources are preferred and there is awareness of the disruption to the market caused by emergency aid.
Reconstruction	Involves returning to a state of 'normality' (the *status quo*).	Provides a chance for new structures and new solutions to structural problems.
New disaster?	Wait until a new disaster happens.	Develop early warning systems and use new technologies for them as much as possible.

Needs and promises

The most fundamental principle that the humanitarian aid community seeks to observe is that the humanitarian response to a disaster must be based on needs. Political or diplomatic motives are viewed askance. Cultural or ideological instincts should not play a part, either. Even the presence or absence of resources should not affect willingness to help. This 'humanitarian imperative' is enshrined in the 'Code of Conduct for the International Red Cross and Red Crescent Movement and NGOs in Disaster Relief' of 1994 and in the so-called Sphere Charter of 2004. The Code of Conduct starts from the position that saving lives is the greatest imperative. But emergency aid should also strengthen the capacities of the affected population and reduce their vulnerability. T. Vaux (2006) notes that the code became a popular 'badge' for emergency aid organisations. You could display it on your T-shirt, but nobody was checking whether you actually complied with it. In fact it soon became clear that few took the code very seriously. It was drawn up and signed in the midst of the Rwanda crisis of 1994, in which nearly a million people lost their lives in one of the most barbaric civil wars ever as the international community looked on. Hundreds of organisations travelled out to help, and turned Rwanda and the camps in East Zaire into a chaotic and hypercompetitive environment the like of which had never been seen before. Reading the catalogue of fiascos from that time still brings many emergency aid workers out in a cold sweat. Organisations – some of them huge, others one-man ventures – competed for money, for influence in the camps, for victims, for media attention, for competent local personnel, and so on. Aid resources were traded by opportunistic dealers, or driven off to other areas in army trucks. In the meantime, the war raged on, and to cap it all considerable quantities of aid resources were seized by the ringleaders of the genocide and used in the conflict.

Traumatised by this experience, several large emergency aid organisations and the Red Cross and Red Crescent Movement took another initiative: the Sphere Project. Sphere was supposed to refine the sense of responsibility in the sector, promote good practices, make dialogue and coordination possible, and ensure that sufficient resources were obtained for the disasters that happen so often. According to Vaux, the result of the Sphere Project has been that the emergency aid sector has returned to focusing on a minimalist agenda: saving lives (and not development). Its goal was to exclude unwanted and incompetent Western aid organisations. The unintended effect was that local organisations,

which usually have no disaster experience but considerable experience of the local terrain, were thrown out at the same time.

What neither the code of 1994 nor Sphere could address, of course, is the need to have sufficient resources for all disasters. Within the United Nations, the UN Office for the Coordination of Humanitarian Affairs (OCHA) has the task of mobilising aid for complex emergency situations and natural disasters. For the first category of emergency situation, OCHA works with a so-called Consolidated Appeals Process, and for the second with Flash Appeals. The following table shows at a glance that certain disasters make more of an impression on donor governments and their taxpayers than others.

UN emergency aid appeals 2010

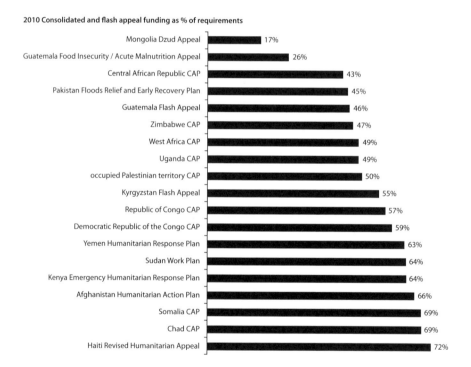

2010 Consolidated and flash appeal funding as % of requirements

Mongolia Dzud Appeal	17%
Guatemala Food Insecurity / Acute Malnutrition Appeal	26%
Central African Republic CAP	43%
Pakistan Floods Relief and Early Recovery Plan	45%
Guatemala Flash Appeal	46%
Zimbabwe CAP	47%
West Africa CAP	49%
Uganda CAP	49%
occupied Palestinian territory CAP	50%
Kyrgyzstan Flash Appeal	55%
Republic of Congo CAP	57%
Democratic Republic of the Congo CAP	59%
Yemen Humanitarian Response Plan	63%
Sudan Work Plan	64%
Kenya Emergency Humanitarian Response Plan	64%
Afghanistan Humanitarian Action Plan	66%
Somalia CAP	69%
Chad CAP	69%
Haiti Revised Humanitarian Appeal	72%

Source: OCHA, *Humanitarean Appeal: Consolidated Appeal Proces*, 2010

To ensure that sufficient resources are on hand to facilitate swift action whenever there is a disaster, the Central Emergency Response Fund (CERF) was established in 2006. The aim of this UN fund is to avoid the need for appeals to

be launched on a case by case basis in emergency aid situations. In 2010, CERF invested USD 139 million in 17 countries. More than 80 governments and plenty of private actors have already given resources to CERF. In 2010, more than USD 423 million was pledged. But even in this submarket of emergency aid it is hard to get the actors to operate in a different way, as is demonstrated by the fact that the fund has so far succeeded in attracting less than 5% of all emergency aid resources.

Lessons from the tsunami

The earthquake on 24 December 2004 in the Indian Ocean and the subsequent tsunami had disastrous consequences in 14 countries in South-East Asia. There was an unprecedented display of solidarity, both in the West and in many developing countries. Huge numbers of humanitarian aid actions were initiated. In total, more than USD 14 billion was raised. This was not just the doing of official and specialist bodies; private individuals also raised money, got on the next flight out there or went to give psychological support as traumatologists. In Aceh, one of the worst-hit regions of Indonesia, more than 300 organisations were present during the first month after the disaster.

In 2005, a Tsunami Evaluation Coalition was set up to scrutinise the provision of humanitarian aid to South-East Asia. The report by Telford and Cosgrave (2006) that this coalition brought out a year later did not hold back in its criticisms of the way humanitarian aid was provided. Even so, a number of positive points were mentioned. For example, unlike in many other humanitarian actions, there was no gap between the rescue work and the reconstruction actions. Several months after the disaster, signs of reconstruction could already be seen. In Sri Lanka, 80% of the wrecked fishing fleet and equipment was very quickly repaired. This was a blessing for the fishermen and the local economy. But despite the creation of a 'high-profile Special Envoy for Tsunami Recovery' (former US President Clinton), coordination was sub-standard. The organisations (both governmental and non-governmental) that were present behaved like deadly rivals in a competition for the money that had been made available by donors and private individuals. Because of this competition, the emphasis was primarily on high-profile projects with quick results, such as building houses and boats. But in some situations projects of this type did not provide a solution, and there was more need for sustainable programmes, in which aspects such as gender or nature restoration were central. There were other issues, too. During the first few days, and in some cases even the first few weeks, after the disaster the rescue operations were mainly initiated by local organisations, often with support from national institutions such as the army. When the international humanitarian community rushed into the disaster area, it ignored the local population and this local self-help. In many cases, local ownership was actually undermined, for example by the non-provision of in-

formation to the local organisations. Rather than being reduced, the vulnerability of local communities was increased by such practices.

The report's overall conclusion was thus negative. The Tsunami Evaluation Coalition argued that the international humanitarian system lacked the necessary qualities and capacities to respond to large-scale disasters. The report suggests four changes that should make an appropriate response possible in the future. The humanitarian aid system needs to be fundamentally reoriented. The emphasis must lie on supporting local communities' rescue and reconstruction priorities rather than simply on donating aid. All international actors concerned must work on their capacity to respond to disasters. The international community must set up a system of accreditation and award certificates to organisations which engage in humanitarian aid provision in a professional manner. Finally, the financing system for humanitarian interventions needs to be more neutral, more flexible, more efficient and more transparent.

Cash-and-carry on the market?

For years, sending aid in kind, in the form of food, blankets, tents or drugs, has been the dominant approach to humanitarian aid provision. Recently, though, this view has been challenged by the idea that in some humanitarian crises financial aid in the form of cash is a more appropriate response, although the advocates of humanitarian aid in cash state very clearly that this is only possible if the local market has the right conditions. Are the products that are needed sold on the local market? How competitive is that market and can it offer a response to a growing demand for certain products? How great is the risk of price increases? The debate between the two viewpoints is also known as the 'in cash or in kind debate'.

Opponents of the idea of giving financial humanitarian aid object for various reasons. They believe that humanitarian aid in this form is more susceptible to corruption. More than goods, money attracts those who do not really need it; thus there is a real chance that financial aid will end up in the pockets of the elite. Moreover, local organisations can do what they like with the cash they have acquired. There is thus a risk that in conflict regions, for example, money will be used not for humanitarian aid, but for buying weapons. Thus this is a problem of fungibility. Opponents are also very concerned about the possibility that the cash will be used for antisocial purposes. For example if men are the traditional money managers, there is the risk that they will use it to

buy alcohol and not to feed their hungry children. Giving humanitarian aid in the form of banknotes also involves a considerable security risk, both to donor personnel and to the recipients. The risks of theft and violent attacks increase.

Those in favour of financial humanitarian aid reject a number of these criticisms. They argue that the corruption and security risks associated with this kind of aid provision are not greater than, but fundamentally different from, those associated with traditional humanitarian aid. After all, cumbersome or valuable goods have to be stored in a secure location. In addition, the dangers that cash involves can be minimised by using banks and other financial institutions. According to the proponents, the risk of antisocial purchases is also less significant than suggested. Evaluation reports show that in the overwhelming majority of cases the money that is provided is used for the basic goods needed, such as food and soap. There is very little evidence of antisocial purchases. The proponents also argue that the security risks mainly relate to the transport of the money, but that this can be addressed by making the transport less noticeable. Money that is transported less visibly may even involve less danger than voluminous consignments of goods. It is also argued that there are a number of inherent advantages associated with this type of humanitarian aid provision. The local population's ownership is respected. It can choose for itself what to spend the money on, and it will therefore meet its needs more effectively. The fact that it itself can make a choice is also empowering. Moreover, this approach has a less disruptive impact on local markets. Yet while goods often have a demoralising effect on local commerce and production, financial humanitarian aid can contribute to inflation. As there is more money in circulation, there is a chance that the prices of the most coveted goods will rise.

Thus both forms of humanitarian assistance have their advantages and their drawbacks. The goods-based approach remains dominant, but a gradual yet noticeable shift has taken place in recent years. After the 2004 tsunami, the governments of Thailand, India, Sri Lanka and Indonesia provided money instead of goods. And in Zambia and Malawi, financial aid is increasingly used as an alternative to food aid.

The unbearable lightness of the support for development cooperation

Policymakers and other players in development cooperation have a big problem. They do not know whether the public supports them in what they do. Yet they need its support: the government and other players operate with tax revenue, and that is best used on things that the public actually supports. During a high-level meeting of the Development Assistance Committee of the OECD (Paris, May 2001) various development cooperation ministers reported that 'their' public opinion had increasingly been falling away in recent years. NGDOs and other development organisations racked their brains about the best way to involve their supporters more, get the public to give more financial support and extend their support base.

The uneasy relationship with the support base

Talking about the support base is like discussing whether a glass is half-full or half-empty. The support base is always there, but it may be large or small, dormant or active, negative or positive... The same is true of support for anything: a new motorway, windmills in a densely populated area, extending working hours, a political party – and so too for an NGDO.

If the players in the development sector take such a keen interest in their support base, they have special reasons for doing so. These are very much related to the sector's characteristics.

Take the government. Policymakers who work on development cooperation seek support for their policy domain in general and their policy choices in particular. They want the views, attitudes and behaviour of the general public or of particular groups that might be interested in the policy to be positive, or at least neutral. But such views and attitudes and such behaviour are not very readily expressed in the case of development cooperation: the political support base is largely latent and not activated. Development cooperation is not a theme that really stirs high feelings in a nation's political and social sphere. It has too little connection with matters of immediate concern to do

so. It relates to what Fowler refers to as long distance obligations (Fowler, 1992), which have little topicality in everyday social and political debate. Moreover, support for development cooperation is not based on people's direct and short-term interests.[25] Such support is less easily appealed to, less clearly defined, less readily mobilised and demonstrated collectively on fewer occasions. The marches, demonstrations or happenings associated with other issues, by which people nail their colours to the mast, are not effective tools for mobilisation here. The support base for development cooperation is thus far more diffuse, fragmented and vague than it is for many other social issues, and this makes it far harder for policymakers in the development sector than it is for their counterparts working on other issues to gain a feel for, an understanding of or a handle on the support base, or to muster public support for what they do.

But there is another factor. The social and political support bases for development cooperation also have few links with each other. Development policy evolves without reference to public opinion and with little input from the majority of the organised support base. By contrast with many other domains, we can speak here of an advocacy void or a democratic deficit. Policy lacks transparency, is developed without much consultation and is rarely subjected to the test of public opinion. The minister for development cooperation can easily act in isolation: he or she can seek out new partner countries, take up new themes and alter budgets, and expect little protest in cabinet, parliament, public opinion or even the sector. Like no other minister, he or she can make substantial changes of course. Unlike fellow-ministers responsible for education, healthcare, the infrastructure or the armed forces, the minister for development cooperation has a (fairly large) budget at his or her disposal which is free from any corresponding long-term spending commitments and is not examined with a fine-tooth comb by all kinds of interest groups.

Other players in the sector, the NGDOs for example, have a similarly ambiguous relationship with their support base. As we have seen, their support base consists of adherents, constituents and supporters. Few, if any, NGDOs have members. The supporters are changing all the time. People are quick to come forward if asked to do so, but equally quick to step back again. Many of those who donate money shop around among the different NGDOs, giving money now to one, now to another. Many wait until there is a campaign and they are explicitly asked for support.

No (more) aid fatigue?

Up to 1991, there was a clear upward trend in the percentage of Europeans who regarded development aid as an important subject; after that, the percentage started to fall. As the following table shows, in public support for development cooperation in Europe this drop was only temporary with the years after 2000 providing higher percentages than before. The table also illustrates that public support varies from country to country.

Percentage of the population regarding development aid as an important issue

	Europe	The Netherlands	Belgium
1983	67%		(n.a.)
1987	75%		(n.a.)
1991	80%	81%	75%
1995	77%	79%	59%
1996	82%	89%	67%
1998	75%	88%	55%
1999			73%
2002	82%	92%	73%
2004	91%	93%	86%
2009	88%	86%	81%
2010	89%	88%	87%

Source: EUROPEAN COMMISISION, *Eurobarometer* no. 36, no. 44.1, no. 50.1, no. 58.2 and no. 62.2; Develtere, 2003; Pollet & Huybrechts, 2007; Pollet, 2010.

What lay behind this decline in interest and support? An OECD study (Smillie et al., 1998) summarises a number of general reasons which help to explain the unfavourable trend in public opinion in the 1990s:
- distaste in a number of European countries for malpractices on the part of the official development agency;
- increasing media coverage which reinforced the impression that aid to the Third World is ineffective;
- increasingly frequent appeals to the public for emergency aid initiatives, which may have affected its willingness to provide long-term aid;
- limited knowledge on the part of the public regarding development co-operation policy and field results.

Since 2000, support for development cooperation has started increasing again virtually everywhere in Europe. Riddell (2007) found a number of studies that demonstrate that support for development aid is likewise increasing in Canada, Japan, Australia and New Zealand. Thus there is no aid fatigue – no longer, at any rate. This is also apparent when the public are asked whether less or more aid should be given.

Support for development aid (2002)

Country	% in support of aid
Austria	68.7
Belgium	75.0
Denmark	92.5
Finland	91.6
France	73.6
Germany	79.3
Greece	93.7
Ireland	84.9
Italy	92.5
Luxembourg	95.4
Netherlands	92.3
Portugal	77.5
Spain	88.1
Sweden	91.9
UK	78.3
USA	54.0

Source: Diven and Constantelos, *Explaining generosity,* 2009

It is clear from the above table that Americans are much less supportive of aid to developing countries than Europeans.

With respect to inter-continental differences, it should be noted that US citizens are found to be much more critical about the foreign aid programmes of their government than Europeans. Diven and Constantelos (2009) have analysed data from the World Values Survey to explain the differences between the general public opinion on both sides of the Atlantic Ocean. Their main conclusions are that the public's attitude towards foreign aid is positively correlated with the amount and quality of information that is provided about (international) aid programmes. In the USA, citizens turn out to be very badly informed, for example about the cost of development cooperation and its

share of the federal budget. So people overestimate the cost of providing aid and their generosity as tax payers.

There are also a number of fundamental ideological differences that contribute to an understanding of the transatlantic gap in public opinion, among which is perceived personal responsibility.

Finally, Diven and Constantelos point to the importance of a healthy level of trust in the national donor government and institutions, but also in the recipient country's institutions. They argue that the United States in particular could gain the confidence of its citizens by stimulating a positive attitude towards foreign aid.

Interestingly, in the USA, where public opinion is highly critical of aid, a growing majority seems to be advocating more aid…provided other countries increase their aid budgets too (Riddell, 2007).

Popular, yet little understood

All the support base surveys show that the public in donor countries knows relatively little about development issues and development cooperation. HIVA research has shown that more than half the people of the Flemish region in Belgium know little or nothing about the situation in the Third World (Pollet & Huybrechts, 2007). It was not just subjective knowledge that turned out to be limited: objective knowledge, measured using a number of quiz questions, was also poor. In particular, few people know which minister(s) are responsible for the development cooperation portfolio. The percentage of people who know that we spend less than 1% of our wealth on official development cooperation was only 28%. In the Netherlands, the level of knowledge about development cooperation is apparently somewhat higher. According to research by Motivaction (2008), 47% of the Dutch have an accurate idea of the budget for development cooperation. A majority of people overestimate the aid budget. This is the case in Europe, but is even more striking in North America. Canadian research has shown that the average citizen thinks that the government gives five times more aid than is really the case. Americans overestimate their generosity by a factor of twenty. The Dutch and Swedes are clearly better informed about development cooperation than many other Europeans. In 2009, 64% of the Dutch and 45% of Swedes had heard of the Millennium Development Goals, whereas the average for Europe as a whole was barely 24%. Few

people know which countries receive the most support. Moreover, there is a huge discrepancy between what the sector actually does (technical assistance, budget support, working with civil society, etc.) and what people think it does (emergency aid, installing water pumps, building schools, etc.) (Pollet, 2010).

Despite the limited subjective and objective knowledge, the level of appreciation for the development work that is done turns out to be quite high. The work of the NGDOs is particularly well regarded. They are seen as best suited to taking on the difficult task of development work and are also considered to be the most effective performers. Most surveys also point to a high level of confidence and appreciation for the work of the UN institutions. People's own national governments are viewed with greater scepticism: they are regarded as less well-suited to the task, and there are doubts about their performance.

Public opinion regards development work as the business of specialists and those with appropriate credentials. Yet there is also a growing belief that businesses, cities and local authorities, trade unions and even individual citizens are fit to tackle development work. HIVA research in Belgium has shown that thinking in favour of these new actors has evolved very rapidly and very positively over the last five years. What is more, although public opinion is still somewhat doubtful about the value of these 'fourth-pillar players' for the South, private opinion about the role of my own business, my football club or the next-door neighbour who is working out in Senegal is thoroughly positive. In the Netherlands, one-third of the working population believes that its own business or organisation should be working with a business or organisation in a developing country.

Something needs to be done: but by whom?

Most public opinion polls about development cooperation show that the vast majority of the population believe that the gap between the rich North and the poor South is unacceptably large. Blame is ascribed both to political leaders in the Third World who keep their own people in poverty, and to Western countries which recklessly deplete the third world's natural resources.

These views are coupled with quite pronounced pessimism. Only a minority think that poverty in Africa will decrease in the years ahead, and believe that the Millennium Development Goals will be achieved.

There is a view among the public that we can take various measures to help

the Third World. Only a few believe that developing countries must solve their own problems without support from the North. Opening up markets to products from the Third World is regarded as having the most development potential, but efforts to promote democratisation in developing countries and the eradication of corruption in Third World governments are also widely backed.

Should taxes be increased to pay for such measures? A number of surveys, in the UK and elsewhere, suggest that there is little support for such an idea, whereas American research has concluded that a majority of Americans would not object to additional taxes if it meant poverty could be eliminated from the world (Riddell, 2007).

Of course, citizens can also take action themselves. In keeping with tradition, many citizens support the national NGDOs or church organisations which are internationally active. However, donation behaviour is hard to measure. Can people remember accurately what and how much they have given over the past year? How do you add up what people have transferred out of their bank accounts to charities, what they have given to volunteers who come round collecting for charity with stickers or pencils and what they have put in the collection at church? Do people distinguish between a good cause in their own country and what they give for Third World projects? Nearly three-quarters of Dutch people in a survey in 2010 told interviewers that they gave money to a development project. Slightly more than half of the Flemish respondents (51.3%) claimed the same thing during surveys in the same year (Pollet, 2010). Virtually all studies conclude that those who give and those who do not are fairly fixed and stable population groups. After the tsunami disaster as well as after the Haiti earthquake, giving to charity assumed unprecedented proportions. But this does not really mean that there was a 'disaster dividend'. The traditional non-givers became equally enthusiastic givers for a while, but then stopped giving money to charity again. Givers and non-givers turn out to refer mainly to their own income to explain why they do not dig deeper into their wallets for the Third World. Naturally, they also believe it is important that the money actually gets there and that their contribution makes a difference.

To a limited extent, citizens can also display solidarity with the Third World in their consumer behaviour. However, fair trade products certainly aren't filling up the shopping trolleys. In surveys in the Netherlands and Flanders, between a quarter and a third of people say that they regularly buy a fair trade product. But the figures from the fair trade circuit suggest that consumers will

pay a supplement in order to give Third World producers a 'fairer' price for their work for only a small fraction of their shopping.

In the United States, recent research revealed that 88% of American consumers describe themselves as 'socially responsible' and 'conscious' shoppers. Despite this positive attitude, an Alter Eco Study of 2008 found that no more than six consumers out of ten could spontaneously name a fair trade organization and only 10% of the respondents declared that they had recently bought a fair trade product. (FTF, 2009)

Finally, involvement in fourth-pillar initiatives has been on the rise in the last few years. This may be an indication of a growing sense of self-responsibility. Limited research data from the Netherlands and Belgium indicate that considerable volunteering energy and financial resources are being devoted to this fourth pillar. In the case of Flanders, this is equal to the time and money that the Flemish already devote to the conventional NGDOs. Perhaps this will provide a shot of adrenaline, which will surge through the ageing veins of the development community and give it a fresh burst of vitality.

Drawing up the balance sheet

Between 1960 and 2010, the DAC countries spent just over USD 3,000 billion on official development aid. Other donors contributed a further USD 150 billion. Aid has represented a very important financial flow for the developing countries for a long time. In real terms, the total ODA provided by the DAC members rose by around 48% between 1970 and 1980 and by a further 32% in the 1980s. From 1993 to 1997 there was a significant drop, and the increase in the total volume of aid resumed only in 1998. With USD 129 billion ODA reached its highest level ever in 2010.

So if desperately few developing countries are able to produce a good economic and social report despite all this aid and generosity, should we conclude that aid is an ineffective tool? Or is such a conclusion unwarranted?

To answer this particularly difficult question, we need to consider at least four other questions. The first relates to the overall balance sheet: is it all that negative, or have development efforts contributed to specific positive results in terms of economic growth and human development? A second question relates to the extent of the input: has there really been a large amount of development cooperation? The next question concerns the recipients: does the aid actually reach the countries most in need of it? Finally, there is the most complicated question of all: how efficiently are the resources used? Are we achieving the right results, the ones that we want, with development cooperation?

Progress, but too little, too slowly and not for everyone

When we consider the situation in most countries in the South, we are entitled to ask what has been achieved in more than forty years of development cooperation.

Simply to conclude that the developing countries have not made any progress would demonstrate a lack of historical perspective. Over the past half-century, the international community has been guilty of much self-deception, put up plenty of smokescreens and made many unwise promises, but in a

number of respects progress has undeniably been made. By 1977, smallpox had been successfully eradicated. In the 1990s, the number of children who died from diarrhoea was halved. That was largely achieved by improving access to drinking water and distributing a simple sugar-salt solution (oral rehydration therapy or ORT); 87% of the world's population now has access to clean drinking water. Moreover, 188 countries are now polio-free: only parts of Afghanistan, India, Nigeria and Pakistan still have the disease. The reduction in the infant mortality rate (IMR) in developing countries from 100 to 72 deaths per thousand resulted in 10,000 fewer under-fives dying each day. Globally, the malnutrition rate has fallen by more than 30%. The rate of schooling has increased by around 75%, resulting in a worldwide enrolment in primary education of 89%. The national consumption and export of high-grade products from developing countries have increased substantially since the early 1990s.

In one sense, we can thus assess the past decades in relative terms in an optimistic light. When the emphasis is on the historical perspective, progress in social development can indeed be observed.

At the same time, there is no getting round a number of significant problems that make any triumphalism misplaced. A 2008 report from the World Bank shows that the developing countries are poorer than we had previously thought (Ravaillon & Chen, 2008). This is because the cost of living in the Third World has for long been underestimated. As a result, the World Bank no longer looks at how many people have to manage on USD 1 per day, but on USD 1.25 per day. Thus 1.4 billion people can be regarded as very poor: that represents 25% of the population of the Third World, but for each individual concerned the poverty rate is 100%! Even so, considerable progress has been made over the last 25 years. According to the new World Bank data, there were still 1.9 billion people living in poverty in 1981. The greatest progress has been recorded in the Far East, especially China. In South Asia, poverty has also fallen, but due to demographic changes there are more poor people there now than there were 25 years ago. In Africa, poverty has not decreased. 50% still live below the poverty threshold there, and that means that there are now 380 million poor Africans: the figure has nearly doubled in 25 years. Moreover, these figures from Ravaillon and Chen refer to the year 2005. In the meantime, the price of cereals and rice has more than doubled, and there has been a worldwide economic recession. The group of those living in hunger, which according to the FAO was already increasing by 4 million people per year, will continue to grow as a result. The depth of the poverty is also becoming more acute. The

average income of the millions of poor Africans is already less than USD 0.60 per day. According to Paul Collier (2007), there are currently around 1 billion people in the poverty trap: he calls them 'the bottom billion'. They live in 58 countries, mostly in Africa, but Haiti, Bolivia, Laos, Cambodia, Yemen, Myanmar, North Korea and the Central Asian countries are also on the list. 73% of these poor people have experienced civil wars; 29% live in countries where there is conflict over natural resources; 30% have no access to the sea but are surrounded by hostile neighbours, and 76% have had weak governments for decades.

From 2000 until the onset of the recession, the low-income countries were recording an average annual growth rate of 6% – more than the high-income countries. But the growth spurt was mainly experienced in the Asian countries. Growth was and still is primarily achieved through increased exports. However, as UNCTAD (2010) explains in a recent report on the Least Developed Countries, this growth dynamic is concentrated in most countries on a few enclaves which have few links with the rest of the economy and which mainly generate poorly-paid jobs.

Even when we use a broader definition of development, the resultant picture is far from rose-tinted. In terms of the human development index (HDI), 21 countries slipped back between 1990 and 2005. Except for Zimbabwe, all countries witnessed an increase in their human development index between 2005 and 2010. The gap between rich and poor countries has increased, and in many places the gap between stronger economic areas (the coast of China, northern Mexico, southern Brazil) and the rest of the country is also growing.

For the new millennium, the international community has made a commitment to take a systematic and concerted approach to development problems. How far off the different goals are we? The following scheme indicates in detail which goals have been achieved by the different regions, for which each region is on track, and for which no progress or stagnation has been recorded.

Millennium Development Goals: 'distance to target'
Source: UNITED NATIONS, *MDG Progress Chart*, 2010

Goals and Targets	Africa		Asia	
	Northern	**Sub-Saharan**	**Eastern**	**South-Eastern**

GOAL 1 | Eradicate extreme poverty and hunger

	Northern	Sub-Saharan	Eastern	South-Eastern
Reduce extreme poverty by half	low poverty	very high poverty	high poverty	high poverty
Productive and decent employment	very large deficit in decent work	very large deficit in decent work	large deficit	very large deficit in decent work
Reduce hunger by half	low hunger	very high hunger	moderate hunger	moderate hunger

GOAL 2 | Achieve universal primary education

	Northern	Sub-Saharan	Eastern	South-Eastern
Universal primary schooling	high enrolment	moderate enrolment	high enrolment	high enrolment

GOAL 3 | Promote gender equality and empower women

	Northern	Sub-Saharan	Eastern	South-Eastern
Equal girls' enrolment in primary school	close to parity	close to parity	parity	parity
Women's share of paid employment	low share	medium share	high share	medium share
Women's equal representation in national parliaments	very low representation	low representation	moderate representation	moderate representation

GOAL 4 | Reduce child mortality

	Northern	Sub-Saharan	Eastern	South-Eastern
Reduce mortality of under-five-year-olds by two thirds	low mortality	very high mortality	low mortality	moderate mortality

| Asia | | Oceania | Latin America & Caribbean | Commonwealth of Independent States | |
Southern	Western			Europe	Asia
very high poverty	low poverty	---	moderate poverty	low poverty	high poverty
very large deficit in decent work	very large deficit in decent work	very large deficit in decent work	moderate deficit in decent work	small deficit in decent work	large deficit
high hunger	moderate hunger	---	moderate hunger	low hunger	moderate hunger
moderate enrolment	moderate enrolment	---	high enrolment	high enrolment	high enrolment
parity	close to parity	almost close to parity	parity	parity	parity
low share	low share	medium share	high share	high share	high share
low representation	very low representation	very low representation	moderate representation	low representation	low representation
high mortality	low mortality	moderate mortality	low mortality	low mortality	moderate mortality

213

Millennium Development Goals: 'distance to target'
Source: UNITED NATIONS, *MDG Progress Chart*, 2010

Goals and Targets	Africa		Asia	
	Northern	**Sub-Saharan**	**Eastern**	**South-Eastern**

GOAL 5 | Improve maternal health

	Northern	Sub-Saharan	Eastern	South-Eastern
Reduce maternal mortality by three quarters*	moderate mortality	very high mortality	low mortality	high mortality
Access to reproductive health	moderate access	low access	high access	moderate access

GOAL 6 | Combat HIV/AIDS, malaria and other diseases

	Northern	Sub-Saharan	Eastern	South-Eastern
Halt and reverse spread of HIV/AIDS	low prevalence	high prevalence	low prevalence	low prevalence
Halt and reverse spread of tuberculosis	low mortality	high mortality	moderate mortality	high mortality

GOAL 7 | Ensure environmental sustainability

	Northern	Sub-Saharan	Eastern	South-Eastern
Reverse loss of forests	low forest cover	medium forest area	medium forest area	high forest cover
Halve proportion without improved drinking water	high coverage	low coverage	moderate coverage	moderate coverage
Halve proportion without sanitation	moderate coverage	very low coverage	low coverage	low coverage
Improve the lives of slum-dwellers	moderate proportion of slum-dwellers	very high proportion of slum-dwellers	moderate proportion of slum-dwellers	high proportion of slum-dwellers

GOAL 8 | Develop a global partnership for development

	Northern	Sub-Saharan	Eastern	South-Eastern
Internet users	high usage	low usage	high usage	moderate usage

| Asia | | Oceania | Latin America & Caribbean | Commonwealth of Independent States | |
Southern	Western			Europe	Asia
high mortality	moderate mortality	high mortality	moderate mortality	low mortality	low mortality
moderate access	moderate access	low access	high access	high access	moderate access
low prevalence	low prevalence	moderate prevalence	moderate prevalence	moderate prevalence	low prevalence
moderate mortality	low mortality	moderate mortality	low mortality	moderate mortality	moderate mortality
medium forest area	low forest cover	high forest cover	high forest cover	high forest cover	low forest cover
moderate coverage	high coverage	low coverage	high coverage	high coverage	moderate coverage
very low coverage	moderate coverage	low coverage	moderate coverage	moderate coverage	high coverage
high proportion of slum-dwellers	moderate proportion of slum-dwellers	moderate proportion of slum-dwellers	moderate proportion of slum-dwellers	---	---
low usage	high usage	low usage	high usage	high usage	moderate usage

Are we really that generous?

We have repeatedly stressed that the volume of aid invested in developing countries since the 1960s is particularly volatile. In the last five to ten years, until the financial and economic crisis of 2008, aid budgets were on the increase again in most rich countries. Numerous countries had solemnly promised to raise their aid budgets. As a result of the UN Financing for Development conference in the Mexican city of Monterrey (2002), the donor countries promised a combined additional amount of USD 16 billion per year. Within the European Union, various national ambitions to raise aid budgets were set out. By 2010, the member states wanted to spend 0.53% of their combined GNI on development aid, 0.17% for the new member states and 0.56% for the EU 15. The European Union aspires by 2015 to increase its general official development aid to 0.7% of GNI.

Promises of more aid

Country	% of GNI by 2010 (Promises)	% of GNI 2010
Sweden	1%	0.97%
Luxembourg	0.9%	1,09%
Netherlands	0.8%	0.81%
Denmark	0.79%	0.9%
Ireland	0.51%	0.53%
Belgium	0.7%	0.64%
France	0.51%	0.5%
Spain	0.56%	0.43%
Finland	0.51%	0.55%
United Kingdom	0.51%	0.56%
Germany	0.51%	0.38%
Austria	0.51%	0.32%
Portugal	0.51%	0.29%
Greece	0.51%	0.17%
Italy	0.51%	0.15%
New member states	0.17%	0.11% *

* This is the average % of the 12 new EU member states
Source: oECD/DAC.

At present, the total aid given by the rich countries is almost USD 130 billion.
Yet we are not that generous.

Fraser (2005) has worked out that we in the rich countries give the average equivalent of one cup of coffee per person per week in development aid – probably less than what we spend on food for our cat or dog. In the last few years, incidentally, we have given considerably less than in the early 1960s; yet we have become three times richer during that period. According to OECD figures, the support that the population of the rich countries gives to NGDOs has increased slightly, from 0.03% of our wealth in the early 1990s to 0.04%. Our collective sense of generosity distorts our perception regarding the capacity of development agencies to achieve real changes in the Third World with the 'ample' resources at their disposal. Many expect NGDOs – most of them with the income of a small or medium-sized enterprise – to be able to solve highly complex and varied problems in countries and regions which lack the basic prerequisites for such an outcome (properly functioning government, existing infrastructure, human capital, economic and social fabric).

We are also forced to conclude that we are not particularly generous because our priorities clearly lie closer to home. According to the UNDP, European countries give around USD 8 per year to every African, yet every European cow costs USD 913 per year in subsidies. Japan gives USD 1.47 to every African, yet every Japanese cow is worth USD 2,700 in subsidies. The war in Iraq cost the USA an estimated USD 720 million per day. America's investment in African development is around USD 15 million per day.

According to the development economist Jeffrey Sachs (2005), an extra USD 124 billion per year is needed to help finance the basic needs of the 1.1 billion people in extreme poverty. That is more than twice the amount that is available to the poor. The current aid volume simply needs to be doubled to achieve this goal. Compare that with what the Western countries spend on agricultural subsidies (around USD 250 billion), marketing (around USD 450 billion) or defence (over USD 600 billion).

It should also be noted that countries often make themselves out to be more generous than they really are. The ODA is calculated with considerable creativity at times. Take debt cancellation. Creditors use a variety of techniques to include the cost of debt alleviation in their budgets and their books. A country such as the USA takes account of the depreciation in the value of the debt, and only includes the discounted value that is cancelled in its calculations; France, Japan and Belgium do not do this.

Who is receiving aid?

The next question is whether the limited amount of aid actually reaches the countries and people most in need of it.

There are international agreements regarding this. The donor community has repeatedly undertaken to devote 0.15% of GNI to aid for the Least Developed Countries (LDCs). In 2001, a promise was also given that aid to the LDCs would be completely untied.

The LDCs, representing approximately 10% of the world's population, not only have a particularly low income (an average of less than USD 765 per capita): their share of international trade is also very slight (0.5%). This makes them more reliant on development aid than other countries. It can be concluded from the table below that although the LDCs do receive more aid per person than fifteen years ago, that aid has less impact on their national economies.

ODA by income category, 1990-2008

Region	ODA per head 1990	ODA per head 2008	% of GDP 1990	% of GDP 2008
All developing countries	9.4	23.7	1	0.7
Least developed countries	19.5	38	7.3	6.7

Source: WORLD BANK, *Data on countries and economies,* 2010.

However, the DAC countries have not yet kept their promises. Rather than 0.15%, a mere 0.09% of collective GNI goes to the Least Developed Countries.

Moreover, as the following diagram makes clear, the 12 other low income countries receive almost as much aid as the 49 Least Developed Countries do. No surprise since the gluttons of aid, Pakistan and Nigeria, belong to the former group.

218

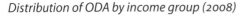

Distribution of ODA by income group (2008)

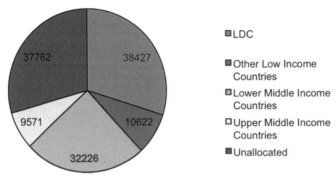

Source: OECD-DAC, *Aid at a glance,* 2010

There is a popular notion that Africa in particular is given generous quantities of development aid. Yet since 1960 Asia has received over USD 40 billion more aid than Africa: it received significantly more support than Africa up to the 1990s. It is true that the aid intensity is greater for Africa than for any other continent: per head of population, Africa has always received more aid, and relative to GNI aid has always represented a more significant contribution there. Yet although several African countries derive a very large proportion of their income from development aid, it is revealing that not a single country has ever received as much support as South Korea (USD 170 per head and 20% of GNI) and Taiwan (USD 190 per head and 40% of GNI) in the 1950s.

The effectiveness and impact of development cooperation

This brings us to the hardest question: can development aid or cooperation contribute anything significant to the development process in Third World countries? This question is particularly difficult to answer, if only because we are discussing an 'unguided missile' which is constantly changing direction.

Defenders of development cooperation are fond of pointing out that aid has been a very significant factor in the spectacular success of a number of countries – Indonesia and South Korea in the 1970s, Bolivia and Ghana in the 1980s, Uganda and Vietnam in the 1990s. International programmes supported the Green Revolution, the measures to combat river blindness and the immunisation campaigns against children's diseases.

A recent example is Mozambique, which thanks to large-scale international support has signed a peace treaty and been able to organise a process of national reconciliation. Initially, 80% of the government budget was provided by donors. Thanks to that support, 2 million refugees were repatriated, 96,000 soldiers from both sides of the conflict were disarmed, elections were organised and social services reconstructed. This is a textbook example of what can be achieved with aid. Since the start of development aid (the Marshall Plan, the World Bank, etc.) as an instrument for getting post-war Europe back on its feet again, we have known that large-scale aid can be particularly effective and provide a substantial boost in post-conflict situations.

The aid sector has always been the subject of fierce controversy. Radical opponents of development aid were found in the early decades in both the so-called dependency school and the liberal school. The former group regarded development aid as an instrument of neocolonial dominance that prevented the Third World countries from developing. The liberal school emphasised that aid blocked economic development because it was in the interest of bureaucracies in both the donor and recipient countries to consolidate their inefficient, often corrupt aid industry and not to create the conditions for sound (i.e. free-market-based) economic development. Peter Bauer, the leading advocate of the liberal school, bluntly stated that the concept of the Third World or the South and the policy of official aid are inseparable. They are two sides of the same coin. For him the Third World is the creation of foreign aid: without foreign aid there is no Third World (Bauer, 1981). Bauer has many successors even today. The Ghanaian economist George Ayittey, for example, has been speaking out for years against the 'vampire states' in Africa, which give their people no development opportunities, yet are kept in power by development aid. The Zambian-American economist Dambisa Moyo stirred up much controversy with her suggestion that the time has come to turn of the aid tap (Moyo, 2010). In her much discussed book "Dead Aid" she sketches the way in which over-reliance on aid has trapped many African countries in a vicious circle of aid dependence, aid-induced corruption, market distortion, and further poverty, leaving them with nothing but the 'need' for more aid.

Both schools argue in favour of 'trade, not aid'. As well as their motivation for scrapping aid, the alternatives they propose differ fundamentally, however. According to the dependence school, a New International Economic Order will solve all the problems; the liberal school believes that the free market will bring the solution.

In the 1990s, a kind of donor fatigue arose in most rich countries. One of the most widely cited causes for the erosion of public support for development aid was lack of clarity about the positive impact of the support that had been given. However, what actually happened in many donor countries was that a set of arguments against aid was built up on the basis of negative cases. 'White elephants' were held to prove that aid was not being spent efficiently, and was also failing to deliver the expected effectiveness and impact. Critics claimed that aid money also distorted local price mechanisms in a way that was harmful to the country's development (rising exchange rates, falling interest rates). Moreover, aid was said to make it possible for recipient governments to engage in unproductive spending, maintain the army and the apparatus of repression and keep local taxes low (including for the rich). And few examples were found of bilateral and multilateral aid projects that had actually succeeded in reaching the poor (Griffin and McKinley, 1996). It has since become clear that all this proves is that there were shortcomings with the aid apparatus. In other words, there were problems with the performance and efficiency of development aid.

Evaluation trends

Within the conventional development cooperation sector, without any fanfare, an evaluation culture has emerged over the last ten to fifteen years. On the website of the DAC Evaluation Resource Center there are now several thousand evaluation reports contributed by around thirty bilateral and multilateral donors. The evaluations show that most development projects succeed in achieving the direct goals which have been set, for example the construction of a clinic. Most donors claim to succeed in more than 75% of their projects. Moreover, the proportion of successful projects is apparently rising. But a critical look at the many evaluations shows that the success rate is particularly high for projects with tangible, clearly delineated objectives, such as the construction of schools, the writing of textbooks or the provision of training. Projects with more complex social objectives such as institutional reinforcement or changes in behaviour with regard to gender are definitely no less relevant – quite the reverse – but are harder to plan, more sensitive to all kinds of internal and external factors, and are often such that success cannot be expressed in hard figures.

In any case, it is often hard to ascribe success (or failure) to the project or programme itself, as numerous other factors are involved over which neither the donor nor the local actors have any control: macro-economic developments, political problems, natural disasters and so on. Moreover, a project usually has control only over the resources it invests, and has to operate via all kinds of existing intermediary structures. Whether the final target groups ultimately change their behaviour, or experience the

221

benefits of a new service, depends on far more than just the project. This is called the 'attribution problem'.

Because development organisations are under great pressure to prove that they are operating efficiently and effectively and have a lasting impact on people's lives, many have set up meticulous monitoring and evaluation mechanisms. The jargon terms for these are 'project cycle management' and 'results-based management', and their best-known component is the logical framework or logframe, so called because a fairly strict link is sought between a project's general goals (for example reducing women's vulnerability), its direct goals (for example giving access to small loans), activities (for example establishing a microfinancing institute, training the women, etc.) and a budget (for example 100,000 euro). There is now a general feeling in the sector that these tools oblige everyone to engage in highly sterile and bureaucratic procedures. They work well for predictable projects with easy-to-grasp outcomes, but cannot cope with social change processes. What is more, if you put in the necessary effort you may gain an understanding of what has changed among the target groups – in our example a reduction in women's vulnerability – but it is usually impossible to work out exactly why this is the case, and what the project's contribution has been. The result is that you learn little from the process. Alternative approaches for planning, monitoring and evaluation are now emerging. One such approach, 'outcome mapping', is illustrated in the next text box.

Outcome Mapping – an alternative approach for planning, monitoring and evaluation

The evaluation unit of the International Development Resource Centre in Canada developed the 'outcome mapping' approach together with its Southern partners because it had encountered four fundamental challenges in assessing and reporting on development impact (Earl & Carden, 2003). Firstly, impact is influenced by many actors and factors besides the activities of one development organisation. Secondly, sustained change is ultimately in the hands of the local actors and out of the control of the development organisation. Thirdly, information about long-term impact is often not helpful to adjust the programme because it takes too long to emerge and it is difficult to link or attribute to one specific programme. Fourthly, an emphasis on demonstrating impact runs the risk of ignoring the development of the learning capacity within development organisations. The following features of the outcome mapping approach can help organisations to address the above mentioned challenges: Outcome mapping helps a programme to track changes in the behaviour, practice or relationships of the people or actors with whom the programme works directly. These actors are called the programme's boundary partners. They are the local change agents that are supported by the programme, who will continue their work, even after the end of the development programme. For example, students' clubs and curriculum

development committees were boundary partners in an environmental education programme in Zimbabwe that implemented outcome mapping.

Regular monitoring cycles are a key feature in outcome mapping. These cycles are characterised by processes of self-assessment and collaborative learning and help programme staff and the programme boundary partners to learn about the programme results, the programme activities that may have contributed to these results and the programme team's own internal performance.

A vibrant global outcome mapping learning community (www.outcomemapping.ca) shows that more and more development organisations are developing an interest in outcome mapping and are starting to implement this alternative planning, monitoring and evaluation methodology.

During the same period, there was growing scientific interest in the subject, and various studies were carried out which tried to examine the relationship between aid and goals in a more sophisticated manner. The persistent theme running through the findings is that under certain conditions aid does have a favourable impact on a country's or a community's economic and social development. Development aid ensures that poor countries which lack sufficient savings of their own to finance investments get the chance to do so anyway. Capital goods and technology are scarce in the poor countries themselves; development aid consists of hard currency with which they can be purchased on the international market. Moreover, aid can ensure that the recipient government, which can count on only limited tax revenue locally, is still able to deliver minimal services.

However, it is increasingly clear that aid does not have a direct impact on economic growth, other than via certain transmission mechanisms: investments, imports, the fiscal regime and public policy (Gomanee, Girma and Morrissey, 2002). It is also assumed that aid has a positive and significant influence on public investments in the recipient countries. But aid is fungible, and enables recipient countries to use their own resources for other purposes. Those 'other' purposes (such as investments in military equipment) are not necessarily compatible with the donor's objectives, which focus on economic growth and human development. Based on his research, Collier (2007) estimates that around 40% of military spending in Africa is unintentionally financed by donors.

Gomanee, Girma and Morrissey (2002) calculated that investments that were financed with aid had the most effect on the economic growth of the African countries studied. They also found that every percentage point increase

223

in the aid:GNP ratio resulted in an increase in growth of 0.3 per cent. Aid can serve as a lifebelt even for the very poorest. According to Collier (2007), aid to the 58 poorest economies, where the poorest 1 billion people are trying to survive, has added around one per cent of growth over the last thirty years. When you bear in mind that growth in these countries was far lower than one per cent, it becomes clear that development aid has prevented these countries from completely collapsing.

Studies commissioned by the World Bank in the second half of the 1990s came to similar conclusions. Financial aid has a positive impact only if the recipient country applies the right policy measures. That result is mainly explained by the tendency of recipient governments with poor policies to use the aid for government spending rather than for growth-promoting investments. In countries with a sound economic policy, foreign aid does not replace private initiative. Instead, aid works as a magnet, attracting private investments. Every dollar of aid brings in nearly two dollars of investment, it is claimed. Aid is primarily efficient and effective if it reinforces local institutions and policies. If the latter receive financial support, coupled with knowledge transfer, they will be in a position to provide better services to the population and the economic actors (Dollar and Pritchett, 1998; Burnside and Dollar, 2000).

Yet much uncertainty remains about the alleged causal and fruitful relationship between aid and good policy. Does aid encourage good policy, or does good policy attract aid? There are plenty of examples to illustrate the point that aid money has not accelerated the required reform and democratisation processes: rather, it has slowed them down.[26] It looks as though in any case donors have a very limited influence on the policies of their partner countries. The local political environment and power relations have a far greater impact on the way in which governments manage state affairs than donors (Devarajan et al., 2000). Donors can often exert pressure to ensure that the government apparatus of the recipient country is adjusted on paper, but they have less control over actual changes. Moreover, psychology plays a role here. Governments and their populations do not like being dictated to by foreign countries. It elicits resistance – even to proposals which may be rational and sensible.

At one time, use was made of so-called ex ante policy conditions: countries were required to promise reforms – no more and no less. And promise they did, time after time, without anything much coming of those promises. When this was realised, donors began to link aid to the recipient governments' performance, a practice also known as ex post or outcome conditionalities. A

modest but clear shift was seen in favour of countries with better policies and against those with worse policies. This then led to a debate about the 'cost of neglect'. Turning off the tap to or reducing cooperation with weak states can mean that they completely disintegrate, their populations are left in the lurch and civil war ensues. The DR Congo and Somalia are telling examples of this. Even the more recent process or governance conditionalities, in which the recipient government is required to enter into dialogue and cooperate with the private sector and civil society (trade unions, local NGOs, churches, etc.), come up against insurmountable problems in such countries. Why should an incumbent president have to soft-soap the de facto opposition and even give them a share of the aid pie? Do the donors want to undermine his position of power?

Aid helps, but it isn't the solution

Numerous studies thus show that aid can help, but that it isn't the solution. Various developing countries have made great socio-economic progress in recent years: Barbados, Botswana, China, Costa Rica, Mauritius, Malaysia, South Korea. Other countries, such as Cuba and Sri Lanka, may not rate so highly with regard to economic growth, yet do better than other countries in their region in terms of human development. Some local NGOs can also boast excellent results in terms of the number of people that they reach, the services they deliver and the levers for development that they offer to their members or clients. Examples of this are the microcredit institutions Grameen Bank and BRAC in Bangladesh, the women's organisation SEWA in India, the farmers' organisation Groupement Naam in Burkina Faso, the Hundee organisation in Ethiopia which promotes seed banks, savings funds and women's participation among the Oromo people, the Movement of Landless Farmers in Brazil and the savings and credit cooperatives in Jamaica.

The following are some of the features that we invariably find in such countries and organisations:

their development strategy had already been defined before much development aid was given;

their policy choices and visions are very clearly formulated, and development aid has to fit in with them;

they lay stress on social justice and redistribution;

they promote institutions and structures (political parties, associations, community based organisations, cooperatives...) which can ensure local ownership;

they encourage local participation within those institutions;

they invest in the long term, and adopt a programme approach rather than a project approach;

225

they are expansive and growth-oriented, and they seek a scale of operations that generates efficiencies;

they involve very poor, less poor and not-so-rich people (target mix);

and: they are all societies or systems with an interest in the ideas and experiences of others. They pick up on external opportunities and integrate externally acquired knowledge in their own processes.

Development cooperation: a stumbling-block?

Studies referred to earlier sought to identify how recipient countries should behave. In recent years, there has also been growing interest in how donors should behave. After all, whether projects and programmes are designed and executed by official or non-governmental, bilateral or multilateral agencies, the institutions concerned always have their own philosophies and their own approaches. Those philosophies and approaches can themselves be the cause of poor performance, and hence a lack of effectiveness and impact for aid (Martens et al., 2002). They can push local governments and populations into erroneous ways of thinking, and encourage attitudes and behaviour that are not conducive to self-reliance. In recent years, fierce debate has broken out. The protagonists are the economists Jeffrey Sachs and William Easterley. Sachs has declared that it is possible to eradicate poverty from the world within a single generation if the will to do so is there along with the right plans and strategies. Above all, he calls on donors to take a more generous and ingenious approach to development aid. Easterley opposes the development planners who seek to adopt a strategic and centralist approach to poverty. He wants to replace them with seekers who understand and accept the mechanisms of the market. According to him, the overconfident and incompetent donor community is itself to blame for underdevelopment and poverty.

When we discuss the role of the aid apparatus itself, we are naturally primarily considering the coherence of the donor countries' development cooperation policy and general policy. What is the point of reinforcing developing countries' export capacity if donors' trade policy maintains import barriers? Or of investing in the demobilisation of combatants and the construction of peace in a country, while simultaneously exporting light weapons to the same region? And how can environmental policy be aligned with development cooperation policy?

As regards the development agencies themselves, one significant criticism is that the bureaucratic structures and mechanisms that they use are themselves dysfunctional, or at least constitute obstacles to development.

Financial donors and cultural nitwits

In his book *State of Denial*, Bob Woodward (2006) refers on several occasions to the cultural short-sightedness of the US army in Iraq. In March 2004, Condoleezza Rice sent Frank Millar, a senior director of the National Security Council, to Iraq. There, he went with a Humvee patrol as it drove through the notorious defiant Shia slum Sadr City. He saw poverty there of the kind that breeds the desire for vengeance. There was no drinkable water, and the sewers were blocked. The people lived amid filth and simply dumped their rubbish and faeces in front of their houses. The American soldiers were being deployed more as engineers than as infantrymen. They were setting up water distribution systems and repairing roads. The money for these ad hoc projects came from the Commander's Emergency Response Program (CERP), a form of official American development aid. Millar concluded that these funds needed to increase and be made available more quickly. They were having a clear impact on the population. He was struck by the Iraqis' response: they seemed friendly, and their attitude was certainly not hostile. Little children would greet the passing soldiers with big smiles and give them the thumbs-up. He noted that it was not their middle finger that they were sticking up, but what he failed to realise was that in Iraq sticking up your thumb is equivalent to the middle-finger gesture in the US!
American soldiers do not have a monopoly over such blunders. Even practised development workers constantly come up against intercultural obstacles in their relations with partners. How long does it take to realise that the friendly Tanzanian with his humble *ninaomba* ('I beseech you') expects just as much compliance from the donor as his Kenyan counterpart – sometimes felt to be aggressive – who instead says *ninataka* ('I want')? Again, many have been happy to give money to rescue Malinese *talibé*, children in Koran schools who have not seen their parents for years, have to live with a *marabout* and scour the streets, begging or picking pockets. But who exactly are they rescuing? Their parents, the *marabout* and the children themselves believe that they are saved, thanks to their religious classes. How do you approach 'development' in a society that attaches more importance to shame than honour? How do you deal with societies without clocks, where people take more time than in donor societies which do have clocks? Bob Elsen (2007) from the Living Stone Centre for Intercultural Entrepreneurship has developed a practical 'coconut model' for this, which is useful for anyone wishing to think about the cultural environment in which he or she wishes to work. Just as with a coconut, you have to penetrate five layers to gain a better understanding of a culture. The outer skin is hard, but instantly visible: the clothes, the etiquette, the language and the rituals. Then comes the pith. Here

one finds the conventions and attitudes that are dominant and stubbornly ingrained in a culture. Next one encounters the shell of the coconut seed – the symbols that every culture has and that are hard for outsiders to grasp. The coconut flesh lies even deeper and is also juicier: it consists of the foundations of a culture with its beliefs, norms and values, attitudes, ways of dealing with emotions or violence. Finally, one comes to the milk, the cultural patterns. Cultures differ fundamentally in the extent to which they are based on community or individualism, on democracy or justice, on status or skill, on rules or flexibility, and so on.

Most development agencies work with fairly standardised set-ups which leave little space for variations. Standardisation is used as a complexity-reducing mechanism that is supposed to ensure that the different actors (the legislative, executive and bureaucracy in both the donor and recipient country) back the institution's multiple goals and that the ways in which tasks are carried out by the various parties concerned (from the head office in the donor country to local personnel 6,700 kilometres away) are compatible. In recent years, innovations have been introduced in the management of the aid apparatus. Particularly worth noting is the decentralisation of the toolkit: part of the apparatus is deconcentrated and a number of powers are delegated. As a result, local departments of the bilateral donors are assigned a more important role and have more room for manoeuvre. Moreover, part of the task is outsourced to private actors such as NGDOs, consultancies or local companies. In some cases, a public-private partnership is sought with such private institutions.

The Samaritan is trapped...and so is the man he has helped

Anyone who has ever been involved in a cooperation project knows how many complex relational elements are involved which are hard to discuss. Earlier we referred to the tendency on the part of both parties (donor and recipient) to fudge the question of the material ownership of the thing that is given, whether it is a well or a computer. There is also the question of how much I should give. Is it sensible to give more than the amount of resources held by the partner himself? Should I give cash so that my partner can decide for himself what to use it for, or resources in kind so that I can be sure that they are used properly? Should I give 'cold money' ('*argent froid*') without conditions, or 'hot money' ('*argent chaud*') that has to be repaid in some way? For how long should I give? Should I state from day one that I intend to cooperate over the long term, or should we get to know each other properly first? Does he have to put all his cards on the table if I prefer to keep some of mine back? Should I dissuade

him, or even forbid him, from also working with other donors on the grounds that they are not following my strategy? Does it make sense to break off cooperation as soon as something goes wrong, or is that the moment to strengthen my resolve and get everything back on track again?

Essential though such questions are, they are rarely the subject of discussion in the sector, and almost never the subject of research. Gibson (2005) has taken a somewhat more in-depth look at one specific issue from the viewpoint of a collective action theory. He speaks of the Samaritan's dilemma. The Samaritan has a psychological need to help, but would of course like the recipient also to make enough of an effort to get out of trouble. The recipient would of course like the donor to continue with his efforts. He is thus likely to promise to make a big effort, but he fails to carry this through in practice. The Samaritan, who wants his intervention to bring about the right results on a long-term basis, is forced to continue with his support...

The recipient might also be described as being in a 'Catch 22' situation. The expression is based on the situation of the insane airman Orr, who in Joseph Heller's satirical novel is unable to tell his superiors that he is crazy because that would demonstrate sanity and he would then have to carry out more bombing raids. The recipient is in a similar no-win situation. If he wishes to ignore stupid or irrelevant advice from the donor, he has to do so covertly, otherwise the aid will stop.

Another common dilemma in the development sector can be described as a 'double bind' situation. The position of aid recipients is less powerful, and dependent. They are stumped by contradictory messages – even those implicit in the whole 'ownership discourse', which sound like 'do what I say, but only because it's your own decision'. And do you think that your partner in the South doesn't know that you consider him to be disorganised, inefficient and lacking in pride in the project when it says on your website that you are cooperating with a dynamic self-help group which is making a big difference in the local area?

But confidence in local governments and institutions – despite the fact that they are called 'partners' – is often still very limited. Many still prefer project aid to the more flexible programme approach, and few dare shift to the budget support that enables the 'partner' to work out and implement his own agenda in accordance with his own pace, habits, procedures and methods. Usually, the preference is for a comfortable tunnel approach in which clear goals are set which are pursued single-mindedly. The desire is to see results as soon as possible, and to be able to show off those results to taxpayers or generous donors. This persists despite the fact that it has been proved that development is a particularly complex process, which above all must empower local institutions to build up their own capacity. A radical proposal to resolve this dilemma has

been put forward by Barder and Birdsall (2006). They suggest that development partners (local governments or local NGOs) should be paid afterwards for the proven realisation of the agreed goals, such as achieving a higher rate of schooling or building additional roads. The local partner can decide for itself how to achieve these objectives. That need not be any concern of the donor, who in any case lacks sufficient understanding of local conditions and cultures.

Conclusion

Few will doubt that development cooperation makes sense. A substantial injection of aid money can benefit a country's development, as was demonstrated in South Korea and Taiwan back in the 1950s and 1960s. It can also be deployed strategically and create islands of success, such as the numerous business and technology schools that have been established with development aid in India and have given the country a strategic position in a number of global market segments such as ICT. Thanks to foreign aid, moreover, millions of people live in more decent conditions, are vaccinated against certain diseases, are able to attend school and can form and freely express their own opinions of their political leaders. Some, such as Sarro whom we met in the Introduction, are quite simply able to survive for decades thanks to aid, and gain new prospects through it.

But as we have seen, the supply of development aid is not determined by the demand side. The people, civil society and the government in developing countries all lack a clearly heard voice. This is a striking finding for at least two reasons. Firstly, studies have been published since the 1970s which demonstrate that participation is the key to the success or failure of an aid project or programme. This means that the demand side should be taken into account. Secondly, donors are proclaiming more loudly than ever before their desire to align supply more closely with demand. They have even shown a willingness to hand over ownership of the development process completely to the developing countries themselves.

How then are we to explain the fact that the aid package that developing countries control themselves and are able to use freely for their own programmes is shrinking all the time? Less than 50% of official aid is now locally programmable aid.

The answer is related to developments within the sector itself. What we have called the development cooperation community has become more and more fragmented in recent years. Ten to fifteen years ago, a few UN institutions, 23 donor countries and several thousand NGDOs played first fiddle. They were the experts, and determined the creed that was professed within

the sector. Now there are more than 260 international institutions, more than 50 donor countries, tens of thousands of NGDOs and hundreds of thousands of fourth-pillar initiatives. While the exact definition of development aid remains uncertain, anyone can describe themselves as a development aid actor.

The development sector has also undergone fundamental change as an arena. In the 1990s, the development cooperation community, which at that time was still relatively restricted in size, was still able to achieve a consensus amid the many, often conflicting, views prevalent about numerous development problems. It came up with the PRSPs, the Millennium Development Goals and the Paris Declaration on aid effectiveness – a common agenda, in other words. But the development specialists who arrived at this consensus have lost a lot of ground. To put it another way, their agenda is not shared by the many new players. These set out from their own approaches and interests. For example some international funds are concerned only with the fate of AIDS or malaria patients all over the world; national physics institutes may simply wish to work with colleagues in developing countries to detect climate change more quickly; as emerging economies, China and India are looking for both raw materials in Africa and political friends who will help defend their interests in the UN; and Western football teams may be interested in untapped sporting talent in Africa or Latin America. PRSP? Millennium Development Goals? Paris Declaration? To the new players it sounds like Esperanto – an in-language which is incomprehensible to those who have not been initiated.

So how have things been going with the development sector as a market in recent years? When all concessional aid flows are counted, you arrive at an estimated USD 170 to 220 billion per year (not including migrants' remittances). That undoubtedly represents an expanding market compared with the 1990s. However, it is also one that is increasingly fragmented. At the same time, we are seeing a proliferation of new channels. The 23 traditional aid countries contribute around USD 130 billion, but we have seen that in addition to the specialist ministries for development cooperation in these donor countries, at least 200 other government services account for a very substantial proportion of official aid (ODA). In the USA, the largest donor, no fewer than 50 non-specialist government services control over half the aid budget. In the seven countries for which we considered the role of subnational governments, more than 100 regional authorities may be responsible for some element of official aid. Most new EU member states organise their aid via non-specialist ministries. The 30 or so new donor countries currently contribute USD 15 billion to

the global development pot, often via multiple channels. Moreover, there are also increasing numbers of channels within the UN. Yet these international institutions, programmes and vertical funds add relatively little in the way of extra resources: we estimate their contribution at around USD 35 billion. The northern non-governmental development organisations have succeeded in raising funds for their development work in all kinds of ways. Of course, only the funds that they raise on the philanthropy market count as an extra contribution. That is estimated to be a global total of USD 25 billion. Finally, of course, there are the emerging altruists: the fourth-pillar initiatives. How much they contribute is hard to work out. The foundations are thought to contribute over USD 10 billion. Migrants transfers are estimated at USD 352 billion – more than all other forms of aid put together.

Thus the development cooperation market consists exclusively of small players. The largest, the European Commission and USAID, have an annual budget fluctuating between USD 12 to 15 billion. With a budget of nearly USD 15 billion, the World Bank's International Development Association is the largest international institution. A specialist such as UNDP has to make do with a programme expenditure of about USD 4 to 5 billion per year. But the amount of money available to most bilateral donors and most UN institutions to get development going in dozens of poor countries and for hundreds of people is less than that of a medium-sized city in the USA or Europe. Most NGDOs and foundations aim to make a difference for hundreds of thousands of people with budgets equal to those of small or medium-sized companies. The fastest expanding submarket is that of the migrants' communities. It has to be said that this is the most fragmented of all, as in most cases it consists of aid from individual migrants remitting sums to their families back home.

Competition on the development cooperation market is fierce. Hundreds of institutions and organisations (and the number is growing all the time) are trying to grab a slice of the pie. The growth of the pie itself is outstripped by the growth in the number of players. As a result, each of them has to prove that it is whiter than white, with the best resources and the best experts. In particular, its supply of aid must look nice and professional, which is why plans, strategies and monitoring systems are devised. The intense competition fuels pressure to achieve a distinctive profile and a need to put one's own organisation in the spotlight. The partner in the Third World also needs to look ideal, and if this is not the case ways are needed of ensuring that the goals are reached even so. Intervention is then the name of the game, regardless of the cost.

The competition takes place in a relatively free market. There are few arbitration and supervisory bodies. The OECD's Development Assistance Committee does not police the sector. All it can do is negotiate agreements, and only between the conventional players at that. Only a few countries have a law on development cooperation. NGDOs are guided to a certain extent by common agendas and codes. With the donor governments, they agree the minimum criteria that apply when an NGDO receives subsidies. And coordination efforts such as the Paris Declaration, the European Code of Conduct and the UN's Deliver as One process are politically motivated and not contractual. Once again, we find that only the conventional development specialists feel concerned by them. To what extent these processes will have effects on the transaction mechanisms between supply and demand, given that they are recent and voluntary initiatives, cannot yet be estimated. The same goes for their impact on the distribution of aid money among public or private actors in the Third World, well-governed states and failing states, English-speaking countries and those with other languages, poor and less poor developing countries.

Recent trends have also introduced some positive elements. More actors on the supply side means more choice on the demand side. In developing countries, governments and local NGOs are often happy to incur the additional transaction costs this involves. They are in a better position to set their own agendas if they are dealing with numerous donors. Because donors want to succeed and quick wins can seldom be gained, they are more likely to be willing to inject substantial resources and cooperate over a longer period of time. This in turn gives local governments and NGOs more long-term prospects and offers the possibility of 'growing in the relationship'. Perhaps the most significant positive development of all is in terms of innovation. The considerable competition and the arrival of new players mean that everyone is looking for new insights and development strategies. The smartest are investing in research and development to accompany these innovations. But the positive consequences of this trend are already making themselves felt. Who within the conventional development cooperation community would have imagined that football could be a means of bringing about peace in fractured communities and at the same time promoting the local economy? Who could have hit upon the idea of international framework agreements, signed between multinationals and trade unions, to improve working conditions in developing countries and to maintain high levels of social protection in mature economies? Who would have dreamed ten years ago of fair trade products in the supermarkets, mutual or

solidarity-based health insurance systems, conserving forests by purchasing them, or 'one village, one product' strategies? Who would have thought that a population register could be an important instrument for a city, and that this is something that cities from the North could help with? The development cooperation community is becoming more and more colourful, the debate in the arena more and more intriguing and the innovations on the market more and more surprising.

What remains to be seen is whether all of this leads to 'good' development cooperation. The development cooperation community urgently needs to work on defining what good development cooperation is. Because anyone who has been involved for any length of time will know only too well that there is an art to giving, and that helping out is a tricky business.

Abbreviations

AASM	Associated African States and Madagascar
ACP	African, Caribbean, Pacific Countries
ADB	Asian Development Bank
AFDB	African Development Bank
AFL-CIO	American Federation of Labor and Congress of Industrial Organizations
AIDCO	Europe Aid Cooperation Office
AIM	International Association of Mutual Benefit Organisations
BIO	Belgian Company for Investment in Developing Countries
BIZ	German Federal Ministry for Economic Cooperation and Development
BTC	Belgian Technical Cooperation
CAFOD	Catholic Agency for Overseas Development
CARICOM	Caribbean Community
CCC	Clean Clothes Campaign
CDB	Caribbean Development Bank
CDF	Comprehensive Development Framework
CDI	Centre for Integrated Development
CDM	Clean Development Mechanism
CEMAC	Economic and Monetary Community of Central Africa
CF	Catalytic Fund
CFSP	Common Foreign and Security Policy
CIDA	Canadian International Development Agency
CIDSE	International Cooperation for Development and Solidarity
CNV	National Federation of Christian Trade Unions in the Netherlands
COOPAFRICA	Cooperative Facility for Africa
CSO	civil society organisation
DAC	Development Assistance Committee
DC	development cooperation
DCECI	Development Cooperation and Economic Cooperation Instrument
DFA	Director of US Foreign Assistance

DFID	UK Department for International Development
DGB	German Trade Union Confederation
DGIS	Dutch Directorate-General for International Cooperation
DGOS	Belgian Directorate-General for Development Cooperation
dg RELEX	European Commission Directorate-General for External Relations
EAC	East African Community
EAIF	Emerging Africa Infrastructure Fund
ECHO	European Community Humanitarian Office
ECOSOC	United Nations Economic and Social Council
ECOWAS	Economic Commission of West African States
EDF	European Development Fund
EEC	European Economic Community
EFA	Education for All
EFTA	European Free Trade Association
EIB	European Investment Bank
ENPI	European Neighbourhood and Partnership Instrument
EPA	Economic Partnership Agreement
EPDF	Education Program Development Fund
EPTA	Expanded Programme of Technical Assistance
ESA	East and South Africa
EU	European Union
FAN	Financial Action Network
FAO	Food and Agricultural Organisation
FCPF	Forest Carbon Partnership Facility
FDI	Foreign Direct Investment
FIDES	French Investment Fund for Economic and Social Development
FNV	Dutch Trade Union Federation
FOCAC	Forum for Chinese-African Cooperation
FTF	Fair Trade Federation
GAERC	General Affairs and External Relations Council
GATS	General Agreement on Trade and Services
GATT	General Agreement on Tariffs and Trade
GDI	Gender Development Index
GEF	Global Environmental Facility

GEM	Gender Empowerment Index
GFATM	Global Fund to Fight AIDS, Tuberculosis and Malaria
GNI	gross national income
GNP	gross national product
GTZ	German Organisation for Technical Cooperation
HDI	Human Development Index
HGIS	Dutch Homogeneous Budget for International Cooperation
HIPC	Heavily Indebted Poor Countries
HPI	Human Poverty Index
IBRD	International Bank for Reconstruction and Development
ICCO	Dutch Interchurch Organisation for Development Cooperation
ICFTU	International Confederation of Free Trade Unions
ICT	information and communications technology
IDA	International Development Association
IDB	Islamic Development Bank
IFAD	International Fund for Agricultural Development
IFAP	International Federation of Agricultural Producers
IFC	International Finance Corporation
IFRC	International Federation of Red Cross and Red Crescent Societies
ILO	International Labour Organisation
IMF	International Monetary Fund
IMR	Infant Mortality Rate
IOM	International Organisation for Migration
IPA	Instrument for Pre-Accession Assistance
ISI	Import-Substitution Industrialisation
ITG	Belgian Institute for Tropical Medicine
ITUC	International Trade Union Confederation
LDC	Least Developed Countries
LUXDEV	Luxembourg Agency for Development Cooperation
MAI	Multilateral Agreement on Investment
MDG	Millennium Development Goals
MDRI	Multilateral Debt Relief Initiative
MEDA	Mediterranean Area

MIDA	Migration for Development in Africa
MIGA	Multilateral Insurance Guarantee Agency
NGO	non-governmental organisation
NIEO	New International Economic Order
NIP	National Indicative Programme
NOVIB	Dutch Organisation for International Development Cooperation
ODA	official development assistance
OECD	Organisation for Economic Co-operation and Development
OOIP	objective-oriented intervention planning
PRA	participatory rural appraisal
PRSP	Poverty Reduction Strategy Paper
RAL	reste à liquider
RAMUS	French Network for Support to Mutual Health Organisations
SADC	Southern African Development Community
SAP	Structural Adjustment Programme
SENAC	Strengthening Emergency Needs Assessment Capacity
SIDA	Swedish International Development Cooperation Agency
STEP	Strategies and Tools against Social Exclusion and Poverty
SWAP	Sector Wide Action Programme (or Sector Wide Approach)
TB	tuberculosis
TRIPS	Trade-Related Aspects of Intellectual Property Rights
TUC	Trade Union Congress
U5MR	Underfive Mortality Rate
UK	United Kingdom
UN	United Nations
UNCTAD	United Nations Conference on Trade and Development
UNDP	United Nations Development Programme
UNEP	United Nations Environment Programme
UNESCO	United Nations Educational, Scientific and Cultural Organisation
UNFPA	United Nations Population Fund

UNHCR	United Nations High Commissioner for Refugees
UNICEF	United Nations Children's Fund
UNIDO	United Nations Industrial Development Organisation
UNIFEM	United Nations Development Fund for Women
UNRWA	United Nations Relief and Works Agency
UNTZA	National Union of Zairean Workers
US(A)	United States (of America)
USAID	United States Agency for International Development
WCL	World Confederation of Labour
WFP	World Food Programme
WHO	World Health Organisation
WTO	World Trade Organisation

Endnotes

1 Until 2005 there was also a second list of 'new developing countries' which had been created out of the break-up of the Soviet Union (known as the 'Eastern European and New Independent States'). These states received official assistance, but not official development assistance. The two lists have since then (rightly) been combined.

2 By 1960, public and private capital flows from the rich countries amounted to 0.83% of their GNI. Around three-quarters of this was official bilateral aid.

3 By far the largest Chinese project was the Tamzam railway, which covers more than 1,750 km and connects the Tanzanian port of Dar-es-Salaam with the Zambian city of Kapiri Mposhi.

4 The only official condition is that the recipient country may not give Taiwan diplomatic recognition.

5 The British talked in terms of 'responsible trade unionism' and 'constructive co-operativism' to make it clear that these social organisations were definitely not supposed to act against vested interests.

6 Originally, the Société Générale also kept itself aloof from Leopold II's colonial project. Only in the early years of the 20th century did the Société Générale develop into an active, pro-colonial enterprise.

7 This refers to the colonies and territories that were run by the colonial countries which had lost the First World War.

8 Even so, real changes were taking place in the South at that time. Indonesia declared its independence in 1945, the League of Arab States was created in the same year, India gained its independence in 1947, the state of Israel was established in 1948 and Mao Zedong rose to power in China in 1949.

9 The proposal to set up another international trade organisation was rejected. However, the General Agreement on Tariffs and Trade (GATT) was created.

10 Named after the then US Secretary of State, George Marshall, who devised the plan.

11 Only USD 13.5 billion was actually used during the five-year Marshall Plan.

12 The European Recovery Plan functioned as a 'countervalue fund'. The money at the USA's disposal could be converted into loans, but 70% was used to purchase goods from the USA: USD 3.5 billion was used to purchase raw materials; USD 3.2 billion for food, cattle fodder and fertiliser; USD 1.9 billion for machines and vehicles and USD 1.6 bil-

lion for fuel. Every country was able to indicate its requirements, and the Organisation for European Economic Co-operation (OEEC) decided who got what. The American suppliers were paid in USD. The European recipients had to make payments in local currency into a countervalue fund for the goods. That money could be used by the recipient countries for investment projects.

13   Quoted in *The Guardian*, 16 February 1996.

14   See e.g. the Structural Adjustment Participatory Review International Network (www.saprin.org).

15   This refers exclusively to members of the so-called Paris Club, an informal club of 19 creditor countries (mainly Western countries, plus the Russian Federation).

16   100% cancellation of all pre-2005 debts with the IMF and the AfDB and all pre-2004 debts with the World Bank.

17   The developing countries' tax income relative to GNP is less than half that of the industrialised countries.

18   Creating such a scoreboard is of course particularly complex. The criticism of the index mainly relates to the methodology used. Questions have been raised about the definition of a 'development-friendly policy' and about the weighting procedure.

19   The realistic school in the study of international relations in fact consists of realists and neorealists. The assumptions that they share are as follows: (1) states are the primary actors in the international system; (2) the state acts as a unit; (3) the international system is anarchical and there is no entity with a monopoly on the legitimate use of violence (although the neorealists accept that a certain structure can be identified in the international system); (4) all states try to maintain or extend their power and interests via the international system. The idealistic or liberal school works on the following assumptions: (1) individuals are the primary international actors; (2) states are pluralistic actors which have internal divisions and have to take account of elections and negotiations between groups; (3) states have multiple interests which they seek to defend/extend via the international system, but they also take account of the interests of others.

20   Omoruyi took the view that the French aid regime was still inspired to a large extent by the *besoin de rayonnement*. France is the most generous donor in sub-Saharan Africa, but its aid is concentrated in its former colonies. There is also a positive correlation between French aid and the value of French goods and services imported by the recipient country.

21   Roodman used the governance variable of Kaufmann and Kraay (2008). This indicator takes account of democracy, political instability, legal security, bureaucracy, effectiveness of government and corruption.

22 Among other things, the emissions must be additional to national efforts (which must constitute the lion's share of reduction efforts), and must contribute to the host country's sustainable development goals.

23 The ACP Group was created due to a number of common interests which were shared by the African, Caribbean and Pacific states (especially with regard to the export of sugar to the European market), but also because the countries from the Caribbean and the Pacific Region wanted to take advantage of the African countries' negotiating strength.

24 See e.g. ECDPM, 2002.

25 In the literature, a movement or support base with these characteristics is termed a 'public interest group', as opposed to a 'private interest group' such as a professional federation. This public interest group is interested in development cooperation as a public good.

26 This is apparent, for example, from the analysis of structural adjustment programmes. Dollar and Svensson (1998, quoted in Martens et al., 2002) found that around a third of all World Bank structural adjustment loans failed to achieve their policy goals, but were issued anyway. This shows that the Bank does not rely purely on altruistic motives with regard to economic development, but also takes account of its own interests. A country also needs to be supported to be able to repay the foregoing loans to the Bank. Other donors and creditors put pressure on the Bank to give financial resources to developing countries so that they can repay their loans to them.

Glossary

ACP countries African, Caribbean and Pacific Countries. The ACP group was established by 46 countries in 1975 under the Georgetown Agreement, within the framework of the first Lomé Convention (1975-1979).

Accra Agenda for Action "AAA" was the result of the 3rd High Level Forum On Aid Effectiveness (September 2008). At the summit development partners and recipient countries recognised that evidence showed that there were three major challenges to accelerate progress on aid effectiveness: (a) country ownership is key; (b) building more and effective partnerships (also involving global funds and civil society); (c) achieving development results – and openly accounting for them – must be at the heart of all development actors do.

Aid activity Aid activities include projects and programmes, cash transfers, deliveries of goods, training courses, research projects, debt relief operations and contributions to non-governmental organisations.

Beijing Consensus This term became popular when Joshua Cooper Ramon published a paper on the subject in 1990. He claimed that the Beijing Consensus is based on three main pillars: innovation and experimentation; the rejection of the idea that an increase in GNP per capita must be central, in favour of the position that sustainability and equality must be an essential component of the development discourse; self-determination.

Budget support Direct contribution to the budget of the government in a developing country.

Clean Clothes Campaign A campaign which strives to improve working conditions in the clothing industry via consumer actions.

Commitment A firm obligation, expressed in writing and backed by the necessary funds, undertaken by an official donor to provide specified assistance to a recipient country or a multilateral organisation.

Competitive bidding Transparent tender system in which the size, precise definition and conditions of the contract are publicised, as are the evaluation criteria which will be applied to every tender, and in which any contractor, supplier or vendor can submit a tender.

Country Programmable Aid This kind of aid can be counted on by the partner country in its planning. The CPA is obtained by subtracting the following types of aid from the gross ODA:

- aid that is unpredictable by nature (humanitarian aid and debt forgiveness and reorganisation),
- aid that entails no cross-border flows (development research in donor country, promotion of development awareness, imputed student costs, refugees in donor country and administrative costs),
- aid that does not form part of co-operation agreements between governments (food aid and aid extended by local governments in donor countries),
- aid that is not country programmable by the donor (core funding to national NGOs and International NGOs),
- or is not susceptible to programming at country level (e.g. contributions to Public Private Partnerships, for some donors aid extended by other agencies than the main aid agency).

Development Assistance Committee The committee of the OECD which deals with development co-operation matters. Currently there are 24 members of the DAC: Australia, Austria, Belgium, Canada, Denmark, Finland, France, Germany, Greece, Italy, Ireland, Japan, Korea, Luxembourg, the Netherlands, New Zealand, Norway, Portugal, Spain, Sweden, Switzerland, the United Kingdom, the United States and the European Commission.

DAC List of Recipients The DAC list of ODA Recipients shows developing countries and territories eligible for receiving Official Development Assistance(ODA). The list is designed for statistical purposes, not as guidance for aid or other preferential treatment. In particular, geographical aid allocations are national policy decisions and responsibilities..

Flow back That part of ODA that flows back to the donor country's economy (through purchases, salaries, and the repayment of loan capital and interest).

Foreign Direct Investment (fdi) consists of share capital, reinvested income and long- and short-term capital leading to a lasting interest in an enterprise that is resident in another economy. The lasting interest implies the existence of a long-term relationship and a significant influence on the management of the enterprise (10% or more of the voting power).

Grant Transfers made in cash, goods or services for which no repayment is required.

Gender Development Index A composite index which adjusts the three basic dimensions of human development (a long and healthy life, knowledge, a decent standard of living) by taking account of inequalities between men and women. In other words when women score lower on these dimensions, the result is a GDI which is lower (than HDI – see Human Development Index).). It is one of the five indicators used by the United Nations Development Programme in its annual Human Development Report.

Gender Empowerment Measure A composite index which measures gender inequality in three basic dimensions of empowerment: economic position, political participation and purchasing power.

GNP per capita The gross national product is the value of all goods and services produced in a given country in one year. The GNP per capita is an indicator which is widely used to compare the difference in prosperity between countries. It is calculated by dividing the GNP by the population figure (mid-year). The GNI also takes account of income from abroad, which the GNP does not. As a measurement instrument, GNP per capita leaves much to be desired. For example, it says nothing about the variations between rich and poor in a country.

Government Effectiveness Score This score is a component of the World Bank's Worldwide Governance Indicator. This measures six dimensions of governance: voice and accountability; political stability and lack of violence and terrorism; government effectiveness; regulatory quality; rule of law; control of corruption. Among other things, the Government Effectiveness Score measures the quality of public services, the quality of the civil service and the degree of its independence from political pressure.

Grameen Bank A microcredit bank established by Mohammed Yunus in Bangladesh. This institution issues small loans to poor people without requiring security. The organisation and its founder were awarded the Nobel Peace Prize in 2006.

Group of 77 This intergovernmental organisation was created in 1964 and originally brought together 77 developing countries. That number has now risen to 130, but the original name has been kept because of its historical importance. Via the Group of 77, the developing countries seek to defend their common economic interests and strengthen their negotiating position.

Human Development Index A composite measure based on three indicators: life expectancy at birth; education, measured by the adult literacy rate and enrolment in primary, secondary and tertiary education; and standard of living, measured using purchasing power parity (see separate entry). The index was developed by the UNDP in 1990. Since then, it has been refined, and the UNDP produces an annual report on the HDI of most UN member states (*Human Development Report*). The HDI focuses on a country's average performance. Countries with an HDI of 0.800 or higher are regarded as having high human development. An HDI between 0.500 and 0.799 indicates medium human development, and below 0.500 low human development.

Human Poverty Index An index that attempts to apply the concept of capabilities (developed by Amartya Sen) and to focus on the most deprived social groups. The HPI is composed of five weighted components:
probability at birth of not surviving to age 40 (times 100);
adult illiteracy rate;
percentage of population without access to health services;
percentage of population without access to drinking water;
percentage of children under five who are underweight for age.

Income groups International institutions classify the developing countries into five groups:
LDCs (Least Developed Countries): this group was first classified by the United Nations in 1971 (see 'Least Developed Countries');
LICs (Low Income Countries): countries other than LDCs with an income per capita of USD 1005 or less;
LMICs (Low Middle Income Countries): countries with an income per capita of between USD 1006 and USD 3975;
UMICs (Upper Middle Income Countries): countries with an income per capita of between USD 3976 and USD 12275;
HICs (High Income Countries): countries with an income per capita of USD 12276 or more.

KOF index of globalization An index that measures three dimensions of globalisation (economic, social and political) via a number of variables (including FDI as a percentage of GNP, outgoing telephone traffic, cable television users, number of embassies in the country and membership of international organisations). On the basis of these three dimensions, a general globalisation index is compiled.

La Concertation A partnership of organisations involved in the promotion of mutual health insurance organisations in Africa.

Least Developed Countries. Countries recognised as such by the UN (the list included no fewer than 48 countries in 2011). A number of criteria are used which indicate structural handicaps. Countries must not have a population of more than 75 million; their GNI per capita must be less than USD 905 (average for last three years); they must be economically vulnerable (for example due to the instability of their agricultural production); and human resources must be weak, measured by reference to food, health and literacy. Since the LDC category was initiated only three countries have graduated to 'developing country' status (Botswana, 1994; Cape Verde, 2007, Maldives, 2011).

Malthusian theory An economic theory which states that a country's population grows according to a geometric progression, unless growth is imperilled by famine, disease or war. By contrast, food production grows according to an arithmetical ratio, and this means it is unable to keep pace with the population increase. As a consequence, food shortages arise, creating all kinds of social problems. However, Malthus was unable to foresee the Green Revolution and logistical improvements.

Max Havelaar A fair trade label created in 1982, which offers consumers the guarantee that farmers in the South receive a fair price for their crops and that agricultural labourers work in decent conditions. In this way, an attempt is made to bring coffee growers from developing countries into direct contact with European importers/coffee-roasters.

Mortality rate Various mortality rate variants are used:
the IMR (infant mortality rate) refers to the number of children who die in the first year of life per 1,000 live births in a given year;
the U5MR (underfive mortality rate) expresses the probability that a newborn child will die before reaching the age of five if subject to the prevailing age-specific mortality rate;
the child mortality rate indicates the probability of a child dying between the ages of one and five if subject to the prevailing age-specific mortality rate;
the adult mortality rate is the probability of dying between the age of 15 and 60, in other words the probability for a 15-year-old of dying before reaching his/her 60th birthday if subject to the prevailing mortality rates between the ages of 15 and 60;
the maternal mortality rate indicates the number of women who die during pregnancy or childbirth, per 100,000 live births.

Multilateral aid Contributions (fixed and voluntary) to multilateral institutions or programmes such as the institutions of the UN.

Official Development Aid Grants or loans to countries and territories on the DAC List of ODA Recipients (developing countries) and to multilateral agencies which are: (a) undertaken by the official sector; (b) with the promotion of economic development and welfare as the main objective; (c) at concessional financial terms (if a loan, having a grant element of at least 25 per cent). In addition to financial flows, technical co-operation is included in aid. Grants, loans and credits for military purposes are excluded. Transfer payments to private individuals (e.g. pensions, reparations or insurance payouts) are in general not counted.

Outcome Mapping (OM) is a methodology for planning, monitoring and evaluating development programmes that are oriented towards social change. OM provides a set of tools and guidelines for gathering information on the changes in behaviour, actions and relationships of those individuals, groups or organisations with whom the initiative is working directly and seeking to influence. OM puts people and learning at the centre of development and accepts unanticipated changes as potential for innovation. Outcome Mapping was developed by the International Development Research Center in Canada (Earl et al, 2003)

Partially untied aid Official Development Assistance for which the associated goods and services must be procured in the donor country or among a restricted group of other countries, which must however include substantially all aid recipient countries.

Participatory Rural Appraisal An overarching term for a number of development approaches and methods in which local knowledge and participation are central. In the first instance, this type of programme was mainly implemented in a rural setting, but PRAs have since been successfully implemented in several different contexts.

Purchasing Power Parity (PPP) An exchange rate that takes account of price differences between countries so that output and income can be compared internationally.

Return on investment An economic term indicating the ratio between an investment and the benefit generated by it.

Rugmark A clean product campaign that specifically focuses on child labour in the carpet industry. Carpets which bear the label have been produced in fair conditions, and in particular not by children.

Sector Wide Approach (SWAp) An approach in which all funding for a sector (such as education) is included in a single policy programme, which is carried out under the leadership of the recipient government and uses its procedures and systems.

Technical cooperation Cooperation encompassing both financial support to inhabitants of recipient countries who receive education or training in their homeland or elsewhere, and the payment of consultants, advisers, teachers and administrative personnel in recipient countries.

Tied aid A common practice from the 1960s onwards, in which aid programmes for recipient countries were linked to a requirement to spend part of the received aid on goods and services from the donor country.

Tobin tax A tax on currency transactions first proposed by the American economist James Tobin in 1972. The purpose of the tax is to cushion against serious shocks on the currency market. In addition, such a tax yields a substantial quantity of money that can be used for development cooperation.

Untied aid Aid where associated goods and services may be purchased by the recipient country in the countries of their choice.

World Council of Churches An important international ecumenical Christian organisation with more than 340 member churches. Virtually all branches of Christianity apart from Roman Catholicism are represented on the council

Bibliography

Addison, T., 'Structural Adjustment'. In C. Kirkpatrick, R. Clarke and C. Polidano, *Handbook on Development Policy and Management*. Edward Elgar, Cheltenham, 2002, 42-50.

Acharya, A., et al. 'Proliferation and fragmentation : Transaction costs and the value of aid', *Journal of Development Studies*, Vol. 42, n°1, (2006), 1-21.

Aidt, T. and Tzannatos, Z., *Unions and Collective Bargaining: Economic Effects in a Global Environment*. World Bank, Washington D.C., 2002.

Al-Yahya K. & N. Fustier, *Saudi Arabia as a Humanitarian donor: high potential, low institutionalization,* GPPI Research Paper n° 14, 2011

Atim, K., *Towards Better Health in Africa. A Comparative Study of Community Financing and Mutual Aid Insurance*. Worldsolidarity, Brussels, 1995.

Balasz, S.I., *Aid Allocation of the Emerging Central and Eastern European Donors,* MPRA Paper n° 30234, München, 2011.

Barder, O. and Birdsall N., *Payments for Progress: a Hands-Off Approach to Foreign Aid*, Center for Global Development, Washington, 2006.

Bauer, P., *Equality, the Third World and Economic Delusion*, Harvard University Press, Harvard, 1981.

Bilsen, J. van, *Kongo 1945-1965, het einde van een kolonie*. Davidsfonds, Leuven, 1993.

Bloom, D., et al., *Higher Education and Economic Development in Africa*, Harvard University, Harvard, 2005.

Boas, M. and McNiell, D., *Multilateral Institutions. A Critical Introduction,* Pluto Press, London, 2003.

Booth, D., *Fighting Poverty in Africa. Are prsp's making a difference?* Overseas Development Institute, London, 2003.

Bouzoubaa, H. and Brok, M., *Particuliere initiatieven op het gebied van ontwikkelingssamenwerking,* Nijmegen, Radbout Universiteit Nijmegen, 2005.

Brauman, R., *Le Tiersmondisme en question*, Olivier Orban, Paris, 1986.

Brautigam, D., *China, Africa and the International Aid Architecture,* Working Papers Series n° 107, African Development Bank, 2010.

Broadman, H., 'China and India go to Africa', *Foreign Affairs*, 87, (2008), 2, 95-109.

Browne, S., *Aid and influence: do donors help or hinder?,* London, Earthscan, 2006.

Burnside, C. and Dollar, D., 'Aid, Politics, and Growth', *American Economic Review*, vol. 90 (4), 2000,

Care USA, *The changing times: A plan for change. CARE USA Annual Report 2007*, 2007.
CCIC, *The Paris Declaration on Aid Effectiveness: Donor Commitments and Civil Society Critiques*, CCIC, 2006, 12 p.
Center for global development, *Commitment to Development Index 2007*, Center for Global Development, Washington, 2008.
Center for global prosperity, *The Index of Global Philanthropy and Remittances 2010*, Washington D.C., Hudson Institute, 2010.
Chenery, H., *Redistribution with growth: policies to improve income distribution in developing countries in the context of economic growth*, London, Oxford University Press, 1974.
Churchill, C., *Protecting the poor: A microinsurance compendium*, Geneva, International Labour Organisation, 2006.
Collier, P., *The Bottom Billion*, Oxford University Press, Oxford, 2007.
Cox, A., Healey, J. and Koning, A., *How European Aid Works. A Comparison of Management Systems and Effectiveness*, Overseas Development Institute, London, 1997.
Curtis, D., *Politics and Humanitarian Aid. Debates, Dilemmas and Dissension*, Overseas Development Institute, London, 2001.

Dac, 'Aid extended by Local and State Governments', *DAC Journal*, 6, (2005), 1-53.
Dac, *2007 Progress Report on Untying ODA to Least Developed Countries*, DAC, 2007, 14 p.
Dac, *2008 Survey on monitoring the Paris Declaration: Effective Aid by 2010? What it will take*, OECD, 2008, 148 p.
De Haas, H., *Engaging Diasporas. How governments and development agencies can support diaspora involvement in the development of origin countries*, International Migration Institute, University of Oxford, 2006.
Devarajan, S., (ed.), *Aid and Reform in Africa: lessons from ten case studies*, World Bank, Washington, 2000.
Develtere, P. , *De Belgische Ontwikkelingssamenwerking*, Leuven, Davidsfonds, 2005.
Develtere, P. (ed.), *Het draagvlak voor duurzame ontwikkeling; wat het is en wat het zou kunnen zijn*, De Boeck, Antwerp, 2003.
Develtere, P. and Huybrechts, A., 'The Impact of Microcredit on the Poor in Bangladesh?', *Alternatives*, 30, (2005), 2, 165-189.
Develtere, P. and Huybrechts, A., 'The Movement for the Abolition of Child Labour as an Example of a Transnational Network Movement', *Work, Organisation, Labour and Globalisation*, Vol. 2, n°1, (2008), 165-179.

Develtere, P., The unbearable lightness of public support for traditional development cooperation, *Europe's World Debating Forum*, Autumn 2008.

Develtere, P. and de Bruyn, T., The emergence of a fourth pillar in development aid, *Development in Practice*, Vol. 19, n° 7, 2009, 912-922.

Develtere, P. and Michel, A., *Bilan d'un demi-siècle de coopération belge,* DGOS, Brussels, 2009.

Develtere, P., Pollet, I. and Wanyama, F., *Cooperating out of Poverty, The renaissance of the African cooperative movement,* ILO/World Bank Institute, Geneva/Washington, 2008.

Develtere, P. and Stessens, J., *De vierde pijler van de ontwikkelingssamenwerking in Vlaanderen: de opmars van de levensverbeteraar,* HIVA, Leuven, 2007, 10 p.

Dijkstra, G.A., *The impact of international Debt Relief,* Routledge, 2008, 138 p.

Diven, P.J., and Constantelos J., *Explaining generosity: a comparison of US and European public opinion on foreign aid*, Journal of Transatlantic Studies, vol. 7, issue 2, 2009, 118-132.

Dollar, D. and Prichett, L., *Assessing Aid: What works, what doesn't and why?* World Bank Policy Research Report, Washington, 1998.

Eade, D., 'Editorial Overview'. *Development in Practice*, vol. 14, (2004), 5-12.

Earl, S. and Carden, F., Learning from Complexity: The International Development Research Centre`s Experience with Outcome Mapping. In *Development and the Learning Organization*, Roper L., Pettit J., and Eade D. (eds.), A Development in Practice Reader. Oxfam GB, 2003.

Easterly, W., *The Elusive Quest for Growth. Economists' Adventures and Misadventures in the Tropics*. MIT Press, Cambridge, 2002.

ECDPM and ActionAid, *Whither EC Aid; the Code of Conduct on Complementarity and Division of Labour*, ECDPM, Maastricht, 2007.

ECDPM, *Cotonou Infokit: History and Evolution of acp-eu Cooperation*. ECDPM, Maastricht, 2001.

ECDPM, *EPA Negotiations: Where do we stand?* 2008. (ECDPM, http://www.acp-eu-trade.org).

Edgren, G., *Capacity Development, Incentives and Brain Drain. Background Discussion Note*. Bureau for Development Policy, United Nations Development Programme, New York, 2002.

Elsen, B., Pollet, I. and Develtere, P., *Compass for Intercultural Partnerships*, Leuven University Press, Leuven, 2007.

Europeaid, *Thematic evaluation of the water and sanitation sector: Synthesis report*, Europeaid, Brussels, 2006.

European Commission, 'Innovative financing at global level', *Commission Staff Working Document,* European Commission, Brussels, 2010.

European Commission, *Special Eurobarometer 62.2: Attitudes towards Development Aid,* 2005. (European Commission, http://ec.europa.eu/public_opinion/archives/ebs/ebs_222_en.pdf).

How do we help?

European Commission, *Special Eurobarometer 352: Europeans, Development aid and the Millennium Development Goals*, 2010. (European Commission, http://ec.europa.eu/public_opinion/archives/ebs/ebs_352_en.pdf).

European Commission, *Special Eurobarometer 318, Development aid in times of economic turmoil,* 2009. (European Commission, http://ec.europa.eu/public_opinion/archives/ebs/ebs_318_en.pdf).

Fair Trade Federation, *Report on Trends in the North American Fair Trade Market,* 2009. (Fair Trade Federation (FTF), http://www.fairtradefederation.org/ht/a/GetDocumentAction/i/9930%20%20%20%20%20)
Fieldhouse, D.K., *The West and the Third World*, Blackwell, Oxford, 1999.
Fonteneau, B. and Koval, S., *Evaluation de la loi du 25 mai 1999 relative à la coopération internationale belge*, UCL and HIVA-K.U.Leuven, Louvain-la-Neuve/Leuven, 2008.
Fowler, A., 'Distant obligations: speculations on NGO funding and the global market', *Review of African Political Economy*, vol. 20, n° 55, 1992, 9-29.
Friedman, T., *The World is Flat: A Brief History of the Twenty-first Century,* Picador, New York, 2005.

Gallin, D., *Trade Unions and ngo's: A Necessary Partnership for Social Development*. unrisd, Geneva, 2000.
Ghandour, A.R., *Jihad humanitaire. Enquête sur les ong islamiques.* Flammarion, Paris, 2002.
Gibson, C., et al., *The Samaritan's Dilemma: the Political Economy of Development Aid*, Oxford University Press, Oxford, 2005.
Gomanee, K., Girma, S. and Morrissey, O., *Aid and Growth in Sub-Saharan Africa: Accounting for Transmission Mechanisms*, Credit Research Paper, University of Nottingham, 2002.
Griffin, K. and McKinley, T., *New Approaches to Development Co-operation*. undp, Office of Development Studies, New York, 1996.

Harrigan, J., El-said, H. and Wang, C., 'The Economic and Political Determinants of IMF and World Bank Lending in the Middle East and North Africa', *World Development*, 34 (2), (2006), 247-270.
Harvey, P., *Cash-based responses in emergencies*, London, Humanitarian Policy Group, Overseas Development Institute, 2007.
Hayes, L. and Pereira, J*., Turning the Tables. Aid and Accountability under the Paris framework: a Civil Society Report*, Eurodad, 2008, 58 p.
Heap, S., *ngo's Engaging with Business: A World of Difference and a Difference to the World.* intrac, Oxford, 2000.

Holvoet, N. and Renard, R., *Breaking with the Past: Belgian Development at the Turn of the Century*. Instituut for Development Policy and Management, Antwerp, 2002.

Huyse, H. and Van Ongevalle, j., *Fullfilling the Expectations? The Experiences with the M&E-part of Outcome Mapping in an Education for Sustainability Project in Zimbabwe*, HIVA, Leuven, 2008.

IDA, *Aid Architecture : an Overview of the Main Trends in Official Development Assistance Flows*, IDA, Washington, 2007.

IDA and IMF, *Heavily Indebted Poor Countries (HIPC) Initiative and Multilateral Debt Relief Initiative (MDRI) – Status of Implementation*, IDA/IMF, Washington, 2010.

IFRC, *World Disasters Report. Focus on HIV and AIDS,* Geneva, IFRC, 2008, 248 p.

IFRC, *World Disasters Report. Focus on Urban Risk,* Geneva, IFRC, 2008, 214 p.

INFORMATION OFFICE OF THE STATE COUNCIL, *China's foreign aid*, White Paper, Beijing, 2011.

Ion, J., *La fin du militantisme?,* Editions de l'Atelier, Paris, 1997.

Jad, I., 'NGOs: between Buzzwords and Social Movements', *Development in Practice*, vol. 17, n° 4-5, (2007), 622-629.

Janssen, R., *Ontwikkelingssamenwerking door subnationale autoriteiten. Een context van multi-level governance*, Katholieke Universiteit Leuven, Leuven, 2008 (Diss.Lic.), 113 p.

Jiang, C.L., 'Les relations de la Chine et l'Afrique: Fondements, Réalités et Perspectives', *Monde Chinois*, 8, (2006).

Jolly, R., 'The History of Development Policy', in C. Kirkpatrick, R. Clarke and C. Polidano, *Handbook on Development Policy and Management*. Edward Elgar, Cheltenham, 2002, 15-21.

Kapur, D., 'The Janus Face of Diasporas', in Merz, B.J., (ed.), *Diasporas and Development*, Harvard University Press, Harvard, 2007, 89-118.

Khagram, S., Riker, J. and Sikkink, K., *Restructuring World Politics. Transnational Social Movements, Networks and Norms*. University of Minnesota Press, Minneapolis, 2002.

Kharas, H., *Development Assistance in the 21st Century,* Wolfensohn Center for Development, 2009, 28 p.

Kharas, H., *Trends and Issues in Development Aid,* Wolfensohn Center for Development, 2007, 26 p.

Kharas, H., *The New Reality of Aid,* Wolfensohn Center for Development, 2007, 16 p. KING K., New Actors – Old Paradigms?, in: *Norrag News 44,* sept. 2010

Kinsbergen, S., *Particuliere initiatieven op het gebied van ontwikkelingssamenwerking: De Risico's van het vak,* Center for International Development Issues Nijmegen, Nijmegen, 2007, 29 p.

Kivimäki, T. (ed.), *Development Co-operation as an Instrument in the Prevention of Terrorism.* Nordic Institute of Asian Studies, Copenhagen, 2003.

Knack, S. and Rahman, A., 'Donor fragmentation and bureaucratic quality in aid recipients', *Journal of Development economics,* 83, (2007), 1, 176-197.

Kragelund, P., Back to Basics? The rejuvenation of non-traditional donors' development cooperation with Africa, *Development and Change*, 42 (2), 2011, 585-607

Lamy, P., *L'Europe en première ligne*, Ed. du Seuil, Paris, 2002.

Lancaster, C., *The Chinese Aid System*, Center for Global Development, Washington, 2007.

Lancaster, C., *George Bush's foreign aid: Transformation or chaos?,* Center for Global Development, Washington D.C., 2008, 125 p.

Lindenberg, M. and Bryant, C., *Going Global: Transforming Relief and Development NGOs*, Kumarian Press, Bloomfield, 2001.

Lloyd, T., *Why rich people give*, Association of Charitable Foundations, London, 2004, 366 p.

Madounga, N. and Fonteneau, G. *Le mouvement syndical en Afrique noire. Contributions pour une histoire.* Solidarité Mondiale, Brussels, 1998.

Mana, K., 'Chine-Afrique : Les enjeux d'une coopération', *Congo-Afrique*, XLVIII, n° 425, 2008, 391-401.

Marijsse, S., 'L'évolution récente des relations économiques belgo-zaïroises. L'achèvement de la décolonisation', in G. de Villers (ed.), *Belgique/Zaïre. Une histoire en quête d'avenir.* L'Harmattan, Paris, 1994.

Marijsse, S. & S. Geenen, *Win-win or unequal exchange? The case of the Sino-Congolese 'cooperation' agreements, Institute of Development Policy and Management,* Antwerp, 2009.

Martens, B., Mummert, U., Murrell, P. and Seabright, P., *The institutional Economics of Foreign Aid*, Cambridge University Press, Cambridge, 2002.

Milford, A., Market failure, coffee cooperatives and sustainable labeling – the case of Chiapas, Mexico, in: Defourny J., Develtere P., Fonteneau B. & M. Nyssens (eds.), *The worldwide making of the social economy*, ACCO, Leuven, 2009, 55-86.

Ministerie van buitenlandse zaken, *Resultaten in ontwikkeling: rapportage 2005-2006,* Ministerie van Buitenlandse Zaken, The Hague, 2007, 132 p.

Molenaers, N. and Renard, R., *Ontwikkelingshulp faalt: Is participatie het redmiddel?,* ACCO, Leuven, 2007.

Morrissey, O., 'British Aid Policy in the 'Short-Blair' Years' in Hoebink, P. and Stokke, O. (eds.), *Perspectives on European Development Co-operation. Policy and performance of individual donor countries and the EU,* Routledge, 2005, 161-183.

Motivaction, *Barometer Internationale Samenwerking 2010,* Motivaction, Amsterdam, 2010.

Moyo, D., *Dead Aid – Why aid is not working and how there is a better way for Africa*, D & M Publications, Vancouver, 2010.

Nancy, G. and Yontcheva, B., *Does NGO Aid Go to the Poor? Empirical Evidence from Europe*, IMF, Washington D.C., 2006, 21 p.

OECD, 'Mozambique', *African Economic Outlook*, 2008. (OECD/AfDB, http://www.oecd.org/dataoecd/13/6/40578303.pdf).

OECD, *Progress Report on implementing the Paris Declaration*, OECD, Paris, 2009.

OECD, *Survey on Monitoring the Paris Declaration: Making Aid more Effective by 2010*, OECD, Paris, 2008.

OECD – DAC, 'Aid Extended by Local and State Governments' *DAC Journal*, 6, (2005), 4.

OECD – DAC, *Aid Statistics*, 2010. (02.2010, OECD, http://www.oecd.org/dac/stats).

OECD – DAC, 'Beyond the DAC. The welcome role of other providers of development co-operation, *OECD-DCD Issues Brief*, 05.2010. (OECD, http://www.oecd.org/58.24.45361474.pdf).

OECD – DAC, *DAC List of ODA Recipients*, Paris, OECD, 2008.

OECD – DAC, *Development Aid at a glance*, OECD, Paris, 2010.

OECD – DAC, *Development Co-operation Report 2010*, Paris, 2010.

OECD – DAC, *Scaling Up: Aid Fragmentation, Aid Allocation and Aid predictability*, OECD, Paris, 2008.

OECD – ODI, *Untying aid: is it working?*, Danish Institute for International Studies, Aarhus, 2009.

Olela, D., 'Le secteur informel et le syndicalisme des resistants. Esquisse d'une autre facette du phénomène au travers la quotidienneté congolaise', *Mouvements et enjeux sociaux*, 38, (2007), 63-81.

Omoruyi, L.O., *Contending Theories on Development Aid. Post-Cold War Evidence from Africa*. Aldershot, Ashgate, 2001.

Orozco, M., 'Transnationalism and Development: Trends and Opportunities in Latin America', in Munzele Maimbo, S. and Ratha, D. (eds.), *Remittances. Development Impact and Future Prospects*, Washington D.C., World Bank, 2005, 307-330.

Özkan, M., *Turkey Discovers Africa: Implications and Prospects*, SETA Foundation for Political, Economic and Social Research, 2008.

Paquot, E., *International Solidarity Organisations and Public Authorities in Europe. Comparative Study on National and European Aid and Consultation Schemes. Summary*, Ministère des Affaires étrangères, Paris, 2001.

261

Pearson, L.B., *Partners in Development. Report of the Commission on International Development*, Pall Mall, London, 1969.

Piret, B., *Aide de la Belgique aux pays sous-développés*. Vie Ouvrière, Brussels, 1972.

Piret, B. and Galand, P., *L'aide de la Belgique aux pays en développement*. Contradictions et Vie Ouvrière, Brussels, 1983.

Pollet, I., *General Barometer of the support for development cooperation. Survey on the support for development cooperation among the Belgian public : synthesis report*. PULSE research platform & HIVA, Leuven, 2010

Pollet, I. and Develtere, P., *Het draagvlak voor ontwikkelingssamenwerking in Vlaanderen. Resultaten van een enquête in 2004*. HIVA, Leuven, 2004.

Pollet, I. and Develtere, P., *Het draagvlak voor ontwikkelingssamenwerking in Vlaanderen. Resultaten van een enquête in 2003*, HIVA, Leuven, 2003.

Pollet, I. and Huybrechts, A., *Het draagvlak voor ontwikkelingssamenwerking in Vlaanderen. Resultaten van een enquête in 2007*, HIVA, Leuven, 2007.

Prahalad, C.K., *The fortune at the bottom of the pyramid. Eradicating poverty through profits*, Pennsylvania, Wharton School Publishing, 2006, 273 p.

Ratha, d., Mohapatra, S., Vijayalakshmi, K.M. and Zhimei Xu, *Revision to remittance trends 2007*, Development Prospects Group, 2008.

Ravaillion, M. and Chen, S., *The developing world is poorer than we thought, but no less successful in the fight against poverty*, Policy Research Working Paper, World Bank, Washington, 2008.

Reisen, H., 'Ownership in the Multilateral Development-Finance Non-System', in OECD (ed.), *Financing Development 2008: Whose Ownership?*, Paris, OECD Development Centre, 2008, 42-61.

Repsol, *All about Repsol*, 01.07.2008. (Repsol YPF, http://www.repsol.com/es_en//default. aspx).

Riddell, R.C., *Does Foreign Aid Really Work ?*, Oxford University Press, Oxford, 2007.

Rist, G., *Le Développement. Histoire d'une croyance occidentale*. Presses de la Fondation Nationale des Sciences Politiques, Paris, 1996.

Roodman, D., *An Index of Donor Performance – Working Paper 67*, Washington D.C., Center for Global Development, 2010.

Sachs, J., *The End of Poverty; How we can make it happen in our lifetime*, Penguin Books, London, 2005.

Sardan, O. de, Devarajan, S., Dollar, D. and Holmgren, T. (eds.), *Aid and Reform in Africa. Lessons from 10 case studies*, The World Bank, Washington, 1997 (2002).

Sautman, B. and Hairong, Y., 'Friends and Interests: China's Distinctive Links with Africa', *African Studies Review,* 50, (2007), 3, 75-114.

Schraeder, P., Hook, S. and Taylor, B., 'Clarifying the Foreign Aid Puzzle. A Comparison of American, Japanese, French and Swedish Aid Flows', *World Politics*, vol. 50 (1998), n° 2, 294-323.

Schulpen, L. and Gibbon, P., 'Private Sector Development. Policies, Practices and Problems', *World Development*, vol. 30 (2002), n° 1, 1-150.

Scott, S. et al., 'Philanthropic Foundations and Development Co-operation', *DAC Journal*, vol. 4 (2003), n° 3, OECD, Paris.

Sharman, T., *The Trade Escape: WTO rules and Alternatives to Free Trade Economic Partnership Agreements,* Action Aid International, 2005, 32 p.

Shaw, T., 'Global/Local: States, Companies and Civil Societies at the End of the Twentieth Century', in Stiles, K., *Global Institutions and Local Empowerment. Competing Theoretical Perspectives.* St. Martin's Press, New York, 2000.

Shomba, S. et al.., *Rapport de l'enquête menée dans le cadre du projet d'appui a la structuration et au developpement des capacités de production agricole des populations rurale defavorisées au nord de la province de l'Equateur en République Démocratique du Congo*, CDS, Kinshasa, 2008, 34 p.

Sotero, P., *Brazil as an Emerging Donor: huge potential and growing pains*, World Bank Institute, washington, 2009.

Soto de, H., *The Mystery of Capital*, Transworld Publishers, London, 2001.

Stessens, J., Gouet, C. and Eeckloo, P., *Efficient Contract Farming through Strong Farmers' Organisations in a Partnership with Agri-Business.* HIVA, Leuven, 2004.

Taupiac, C., 'Humanitarian and Development Procurement. A Vast and Growing Market', *International Trade Forum*, October 2001, 7-12.

Telford, J. and Cosgrave, J., 'The international humanitarian system and the 2004 Indian Ocean earthquake and tsunamis', *Disasters*, 31:1, March 2006, 1-28.

Thorbecke, 'The Evolution of the Development Doctrine and the Role of Foreign Aid 1950-2000', in F. Tarp, *Foreign Aid and Development.* Routledge, London/New York, 2000, 17-47.

UNCTAD, *The Least Developed Countries Report*, UNCTAD, Geneva, 2010.

UNDP, *Annual Statistical Report 2006,* United Nations System, 2007.

UNDP, *Creating value for all: strategies for doing business with the poor,* New York, UNDP, 2008.

UNDP, *Worldwide trends in the Human Development Index 1970-2010,* (http://hdr.undp.org/en/data/trends/).

Vaux, T., Humanitarian trends and dilemmas, *Development in Practice*, Vol. 16, n° 3-4, (2006), 240-254.

Vencato, M.F., *The Development Policy of the CEECs : the EU Political Rationale between the Fight Against Poverty and the Near Abroad*, Leuven, Katholieke Universiteit Leuven, 2007 (Diss. Doc.), 330 p.

Wang, J.-Y., *What Drives China's Growing Role in Africa?*, IMF, 2007, 30 p.

Wertheim, W.F., 'Ontwikkelingshulp als neo-kolonialisme', *De Nieuwe Stem* XXII, n°8, 10, (1967).

Williams, S., *Unfinished Business: Ten Years of Dropping the Debt,* London, Jubilee Debt Campaign, 2008, 41 p.

Williamson, J., *The Washington Consensus and Beyond*. Institute for International Economics, Washington, 2003.

World Bank, *2010 World Development Indicators*, Washington D.C., World Bank, 2007.

World Bank, *Boards of Directors: Voting Powers,* 26.08.2010. (World Bank, www.worldbank.org).

World Bank, *Worldwide Governance Indicators 1996-2009,* 2008. (World Bank, www.info.worldbank.org)

Woodward, B., *State of Denial,* Simon & Schuster, London, 2006